THE AMA HANDBOOK OF PROJECT MANAGEMENT

SECOND EDITION

THE AMA HANDBOOK OF PROJECT MANAGEMENT

SECOND EDITION

Edited By

▶PAUL C. DINSMORE, PMP

▶JEANNETTE CABANIS-BREWIN

AMACOM American Management Association

New York | Atlanta | Brussels | Chicago | Mexico City
San Francisco | Shanghai | Tokyo | Toronto | Washington, D.C.

Special discounts on bulk quantities of AMACOM books are available to corporations, professional associations, and other organizations. For details, contact Special Sales Department, AMACOM, a division of American Management Association, 1601 Broadway, New York, NY 10019.
Tel.: 212-903-8316. Fax: 212-903-8083.
Web site: www. amacombooks.org

Library of Congress Cataloging-in-Publication Data

Dinsmore, Paul C.
The AMA handbook of project management/Paul C. Dinsmore, Jeanette Cabanis-Brewin, 2nd ed.
p. cm.
Includes index.
ISBN 0-8144-7271-0
1. Project management—Handbooks, manuals, etc. I. Cabanis-Brewin, Jeanette. II. Title.

HD69.P75A46 2006
658.4'04—dc22

2005015020

Printing number

10 9 8 7 6 5 4 3 2 1

CONTENTS

FOREWORD

This handbook provides a set of principles and processes for those managers and professionals who want to enhance their understanding of the theory and practice of project management. Like all good handbooks, this is a comprehensive reference source for practical how-to-do-it information. This handbook also can be used in project management training programs, as well as in degree programs in universities.

There is a flood of books currently being published about project management. Unfortunately all too many of these books take existing works and recast them in a slightly different light, resulting in minor contributions to the growing literature. *The AMA Handbook of Project Management* is a refreshing change.

This book starts with the Project Management Institute's body of knowledge *(PMBOK® Guide)* and then goes beyond that through a description of the Project Management profession and its challenges and coverage of organizational issues likely to be encountered in the world of project management, ending with a presentation of industry applications of the project approach.

The material in the book comes from authors who are notable contributors in the project management community, ranging from academics to practitioners who grapple with the challenges of managing or teaching in the project management field.

This is a book that should have a conspicuous place on the bookshelf of anyone who wants to improve their professional practice in the use of project management knowledge and skills.

—DAVID I. CLELAND, PHD

DECEMBER, 2004

PREFACE

When the lunar module Eagle landed in the Sea of Tranquility at 13 hours, 19 minutes, 39.9 seconds Eastern Standard Time on July 20, 1969, the event was hailed as one of history's major milestones. It was also one of the most fascinating and significant spin-offs of the U.S. space program and was the development of flexible yet precise organizational structures, forms, and tools that allowed people to work together to reach challenging goals. Out of that grew the modern concept of project management.

Since the Apollo days, project management, applicable both to individual endeavors and to a series of projects called programs, has been applied to many new fields of activity. With the trend toward accelerated change, the scope of project management has expanded from construction projects and aerospace to encompass organizational change, R&D projects, high-tech product development, banking and finance, nonprofit services, environmental remediation ... in fact, just about every field of human endeavor.

Such change in the scope of project management led to the need for a comprehensive update to 1993's *The AMA Handbook of Project Management.* In its day, the first edition of this handbook was a major contribution to the field, pulling together expert practitioners to share their advice on topics such as designing adequate organizational structures, generating and maintain teamwork, and managing the project life cycle. We have retained many of the original authors, as well as including several chapters that still stand as classics in the field. However, the multitude of changes that have occurred in the project management field since the original publication of this handbook ten years ago meant that, in order to keep pace, the new chapters had to outnumber the old.

We have specifically designed he second edition of this book to complement and supplement the *PMBOK® Guide, Third Edition,* and to provide supporting materials for those preparing to take the certification exam, or working to maintain their certification. Students who are taking introductory courses in project management as part of a degree in another field (engineering, information technology, business administration, manufacturing or production management, construction management, etc.), or who are studying for degrees in the field of project management will also find it invaluable. As a complementary and supplementary text, the handbook does not contain materials already published in the *PMBOK® Guide,* but is designed to help those studying project management to understand and integrate the materials contained in that standard, as well as project management concepts and issues which currently are not included in the *PMBOK® Guide.*

The book targets a broad audience, including not only the traditional project management faithfuls, but also professionals involved in organizational development, research, product development, and other associated fields. The book provides a ready reference for anyone involved in project tasks, including upper management executives, project sponsors, project managers, functional managers, and team members. It addresses those working in any of the major program- and project-oriented industries, such as defense, construction, architecture, engineering, product development, systems development, R&D, education, and community development. Whether you are preparing for advancement in the project management field, through certification or by completing university courses in the field, this handbook will be a valuable reference. For those using the book in a classroom setting, discussion questions provided at the end of each chapter help students and peers initiate fruitful discussions about concepts, problems, and ideas in their chosen field.

ORGANIZATION OF THE HANDBOOK

Section 1
The Project Management Body of Knowledge: Comprehension and Practice

This section is designed specifically to aid the reader in learning the basics of project management, and in preparing for taking the Project Management Professional (PMP) certification exam. Chapters 7 through 15, in fact, correspond to chapters of the *PMBOK® Guide, Third Edition* that are tested on the PMP exam. (Note: The certification exam has recently begun to test an area called "Professional Ethics," but because this subject has not yet been added to the *PMBOK® Guide* at this writing, we cover this topic in Section 2 of the handbook.) This section summarizes the basics of project management. It includes the fundamental disciplines and describes the processes required to insure that projects are brought to successful completion.

The organization of the book will be specifically designed to raise student interest and to lead them to further analysis of the project management field. Those preparing for certification are generally studying the field of project management for the first time. Thus Section One of the book introduces the student to the basic accepted practices and principles of project management, as practiced within the project. Note that the *PMBOK® Guide* does not deal with, and the PMP certification process does not test, concepts of project management that extend beyond the bounds of the individual project. Yet the project manager must survive and thrive within highly competitive business organizations, interacting with other organizations both within their employer's organization and from other organizations that have an interest or stake in the project. It is anticipated that as students work through the materials in the first section of this book, they will be generating questions concerning these other aspects of project management that clearly fall outside the individual project (for example, the individual's career potential, the expected contributions of projects to the organization, the requirements to manage multiple projects simultaneously, leadership concepts that cut across organizational lines, management of the power structures and conflicts that typically surround projects, and the interaction of the projects with other major departments of the organization-such as accounting, finance, and other groups being affected by the results of the project). These broader issues are explored in Sections Two through Five of the handbook.

Section Two
The Profession of Project Management

As the student explores the concepts presented in Section One, the issue of professionalism and the development of project management as a profession will be raised. Section Two covers the field of project management as a rapidly growing "profession" that is being supported and developed by a number of professional organizations, particularly in the United States, Europe, and Australia. This section documents the growth and creation of the profession, identifies the major professional organizations contributing to its development, shows the trends and the status of this new profession with a global perspective, and reviews the impact of this professionalizing process on the practitioner of project management and on the supporting organizations. Ethics, professionalism, and career development are the primary topics covered in this section.

Section Three
Organizational Issues in Project Management

Even a certified professional cannot escape the realities of organizational life, and increasingly, the role of the project manager catapults the individual out of the single-project milieu and into organizational issues: multiple projects, maturity measurement, portfolio selection and management, enterprise systems, organizational culture and structure, and alignment with strategy-these areas have become crucial issues in project management in the decade since the first edition of this book was published. Top professionals and academics with specific expertise in these areas have been sought out to provide tutorials on these topics in Section Three.

Section Four
Issues and Ideas in Project Management Practice

Politics; new methodologies and organizational structures; globally diverse teams: Section Four brings together writers on some of the leading edge topics in project management. One thing that is certain about project management: it isn't going to remain static for another ten years. The chapters in this section provide a glimpse of where the discipline and the organizations in which it is practiced may be heading.

Section Five
Industry Applications of Project Management

With the growth of project management in all industry sectors, this section of the book could be 100 chapters long; it was difficult to limit it to a handful of industries. As professionals, the students will need to understand how the basic accepted concepts of project management must be adapted to the environments found in different industries and professions. Section 5 identifies a number of specific industries, technologies and specialty areas in which project management is widely used and recognized, and examines the unique priorities of the project manager in each of these different venues. The overall thrust of this section is designed to demonstrate that the basic concepts of project management apply universally across these venues, even though the specific concepts and ideas may have different priorities and influences on project management practices in each venue.

About the Contributors

Finally, biographical information on all the contributing authors can be found at the end of the handbook. Some of the authors have provided email addresses or website URLs to encourage the interested student to ask questions, learn more, and engage in the kind of dialogue that spurs this fascinating discipline to growth and change.

—PAUL C. DINSMORE, PMP,
RIO DE JANEIRO, BRAZIL

—JEANNETTE CABANIS-BREWIN,
CULLOWHEE, NORTH CAROLINA, USA

FEBRUARY, 2005

ACKNOWLEDGMENTS

In completing this project, we drew upon the knowledge, comprehension, patience, and diligence of many people. The cornerstones of the project have been Dr. John Adams for his invaluable work in developing the revision plans for the second edition; Crispin Piney for his assistance in evaluating chapters in Section One for correctness; our AMACOM editor, Christina Parisi, and Lisa M. Fisher for expert copyediting assistance. Paul Lombard of the PM College also provided subject matter review for some chapters.

Thanks are also due to our own companies, Dinsmore Associates and Project Management Solutions, for making it possible for us to work on this book, and the families and friends who put up with our schedules over the course of the past year.

Most of all, we want to thank the authors who contributed so much of their time and talent to this project, as well as the contributors to the First Edition, who laid the groundwork for this updated version.

Finally, we'd be remiss if we didn't express our appreciation of the Project Management Institute for its work in developing and maintaining the project management standards that form the basis of the profession.

ABOUT THE EDITORS

PAUL C. DINSMORE, PMP

Paul C. Dinsmore, PMP, is an international speaker and seminar leader on project management. He is the author of ten books, including *Winning in Business with Enterprise Project Management* (AMACOM, 1998), and has written more than one hundred professional papers and articles. Mr. Dinsmore is president of Dinsmore Associates, a training and consulting group focused on project management and team building. Prior to establishing his consulting practice in 1985, he worked for twenty years as a project manager and executive in the construction and engineering industry for Daniel International, Morrison Knudsen International, and Engevix Engineering.

Mr. Dinsmore has performed consulting and training services for major companies including IBM, ENI-Italy, Petrobrás, General Electric, Mercedes Benz, Shell, Control Data, Morrison Knudsen, the World Trade Institute, Westinghouse, Ford, Caterpillar, and Alcoa. His speaking and consulting practice has taken him to Europe, South America, South Africa, Japan, China, and Australia. The range of projects where Mr. Dinsmore has provided consulting services include company reorganization, project start-up, development and implementation of project management systems, and training programs, as well as special advisory functions for the presidents of several organizations. Mr. Dinsmore contributes articles to such professional magazines as *PM Network* and *Chief Project Officer*. He participates actively in the Project Management Institute, which awarded him its Distinguished Contributions Award as well as the prestigious title of Fellow of the Institute. He is also on the Board of Directors of the PMI Educational Institute.

Mr. Dinsmore graduated from Texas Tech University and completed the Advanced Management Program at Harvard Business School. He can be reached at paul.dinsmore@dinsmore.com.br.

JEANNETTE CABANIS-BREWIN

Jeannette Cabanis-Brewin is Editor in Chief of the Center for Business Practices, a knowledge center that captures, organizes, and transfers business practice knowledge to project stakeholders through publications, research, and benchmarking forums. The CBP is the research and publishing division of PM Solutions, a project management consulting and training firm. Ms. Cabanis-Brewin has written on project management and organizational development topics for the CBP publications *People on Projects: The Project Management Best Practices Report, PM Library Update,* and the *Best Practices e-Advisor,* as well as for a wide variety of other business and technology publications, including *Chief Project Officer, Projects@Work,* developer.com, *Primavera* magazine, myplanview.com, and *PM Network.* A former staff writer and editor for the Project Management Institute's Publishing Division, her feature articles for *PM Network* have been republished around the world. She has edited two award-winning project management books, including *The Strategic Project Office* by J. Kent Crawford, winner of PMI's 2002 David I. Cleland Literature Award, and is co-editor with James S. Pennypacker of *What Makes A Good Project Manager?* (CBP, 2003). She is also the coauthor, with J. Kent Crawford, of *Optimizing Human Capital with a Strategic Project Office,* (Auerbach, 2005).

Cabanis-Brewin has a BA in English, Professional Writing Concentration (summa cum laude) from Western Carolina University, and has done graduate work in organizational development (WCU) and nonprofit management (Duke University). She can be reached at jcabanis-brewein@cbponline.com, or though the CBP website at www.cbponline.com.

SUPPORTING EDITOR

Crispin ("Kik") Piney, B.Sc., PMP, after many years managing international IT projects within large corporations, is now a freelance project management consultant and trainer. At present, his main areas of focus are risk management, change management, scope management, and organizational maturity, as well as time and cost control. He has developed advanced training courses on these topics, which he delivers in English and in French to international audiences from various industries. He has also carried out work for PMI on a volunteer basis as Design Cell Leader for the creation the Organizational Project Management Maturity Model (*OPM3*™) as well as participating actively in the teams developing the Third Edition of *A Guide to the Project Management Body of Knowledge* for both the English and the French language versions. He is currently acting as coordination architect for the forthcoming PMI Program and Portfolio Management Standards. He has presented at a number of recent PMI conferences in Europe and the USA and published papers in *PMI Network, PMI Journal* and *PMI Today*—as well as some light-hearted project management verse on the allPM Web site. Mr. Piney is based in Nice, France and can be contacted at Kik@PROject-beneFITS.com.

THE AMA HANDBOOK OF PROJECT MANAGEMENT

SECOND EDITION

CHAPTER 1

What Is Project Management? Project Management Concepts and Methodologies

▶FRANCIS M. WEBSTER, JR., PHD, WESTERN CAROLINA UNIVERSITY, RETIRED

▶JOAN KNUTSON

PROJECTS: THE WORK

Projects are ubiquitous. They are everywhere, and everybody does them. Projects are the driving force for many organizations in most industries. Projects can be looked upon as the change efforts of society, and the pace of change has been increasing. Therefore, effectively and efficiently managing change efforts is the only way organizations can survive and grow in this modern world.

One way to describe projects is by example. Most such descriptions start with such things as the pyramids, the Great Wall of China, and other undertakings of ancient history. These were major construction projects, and indeed, construction is inherently a project-oriented industry. But there are other project-oriented industries: pharmaceuticals, aerospace, and IT all operate on a project basis and all are notable for technological developments that have changed the way we live and work.

But not all projects are of such great magnitude. A community fund-raising or political campaign, the development of a new product, creating an advertising program, and training the sales and support staff to move and service a product effectively are all projects. Indeed, it is possible that most executives spend more of their time planning and monitoring changes in their organizations—i.e., projects—than they do in maintaining the status quo.

All of these descriptions focus on a few key notions. Projects involve change—the creation of something new or different—and they have a beginning and an ending. Indeed, these are the characteristics of a project that are embodied in the definition of *project* as found in *A Guide to the Project Management Body of Knowledge (PMBOK® Guide)* published by the Project Management Institute (PMI): "A temporary endeavor undertaken to create a unique product, service, or result."[1] This definition, while useful to project managers, may not be sufficient for others to distinguish projects from other undertakings. Understanding some of the characteristics of projects and comparing projects to other types of undertakings may give a clearer perspective.

Some Characteristics of Projects

▶***Projects are unique undertakings*** that result in a single unit of output. The installation of an entertainment center by a homeowner with the help of a few friends is a project. The objective is to complete the installation and enjoy the product of the effort. It is a unique undertaking because the homeowner is not likely to repeat this process frequently. It is not unusual, however, for multiple units to be involved in a project at one level of detail or another.

▶***Projects are composed of interdependent activities.*** Projects are made up of activities. Consistent with the definition of a project, an activity has a beginning and an end. Activities are interrelated in one of three possible ways. In some situations, one activity must be completed before another can begin. Generally, these *mandatory* relationships are very difficult to violate, or to do so just does not make sense. The relationship of other activities is not as obvious or as restrictive. These more *discretionary* interdependencies are based on the preferences of the people developing the plan. Some activities are dependent upon some *external* event, such as receiving the materials from the vendor. In any of the three instances, mandatory, discretionary, or external, activities have a relationship one to another.

▶***Projects create a quality deliverable.*** Each project creates its own deliverable(s) which must meet a standard of performance criteria. In other words, each deliverable from every project must be quality assured. If the deliverable does not meet its quantifiable quality criteria, that project cannot be considered complete.

▶***Projects involve multiple resources,*** both human and nonhuman, which require close coordination. Generally there are a variety of resources, each with its own unique technologies, skills, and traits. When focusing on human resources, this leads to an inherent characteristic of projects: conflict. There is conflict amongst resources as to their concepts, approach, theory, techniques, etc. Also there is conflict for resources as to quantity, timing, and specific assignments. Thus, a project manager must be skilled in managing both such conflicts.

▶***Projects are not synonymous with the products of the project.*** For some people, the word *project* refers to the planning and controlling of the effort. For others, project means the unique activities required to create the product of the project. This is not a trivial distinction as both entities have characteristics unique to themselves. The names of some of these characteristics apply to both. For example, the life cycle cost of a product includes the cost of creating it (a project), the cost of operating it (not a project), the cost of major repairs or refurbishing (typically done as projects), and the cost of dismantling (often a project, if done at all). The project cost of creating the product is generally a relatively small proportion of the life cycle cost of the product. Figure 1-1.

▶***Projects are driven by the Triple Constraint.*** The Triple Constraint represents the balance of time, resources (human and otherwise), and technical performance (quality). One of these three constraints is the driving or gating factor of each project. Different projects may be driven by a different constraint depending on the emphasis established by management. Being first in the market often determines long-term market position, thus creating time pressure as the major driver. Most projects require the investment of considerable sums of money and/or labor prior to enjoying of the benefits of the resulting product; thus containing resource expenditures may be the driving factor. A need exists for the resulting product of the project to be of the highest quality; for example, a new system within the healthcare industry.

In summary, projects consist of activities, which have interrelationships amongst one another, produce quality-approved deliverables, and involve multiple resources. Projects are not synonymous with product. During the life cycle of any product, the concept of project management is used while during other times, product or operations management is appropriate. And finally, how projects are managed is determined by which of the variables of the Triple Constraint is more important: time, resources, or quality.

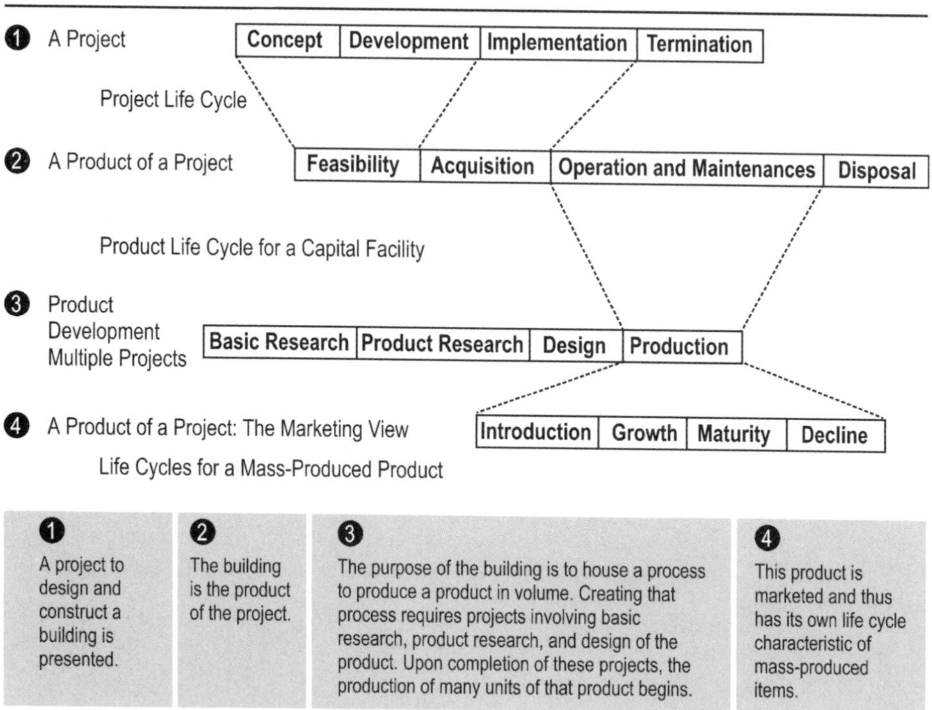

FIGURE 1-1. **COMPARISON OF PROJECT AND PRODUCT LIFE CYCLES**

Development Life Cycles

As one of the characteristics above stated, the "project" is not synonymous with the "product of the project." The work to create the product and the work to manage the project that creates the product are different. However, a Development Life Cycle often integrates work efforts to do both. A Development Life Cycle defines the activities to create the product and designates other activities to plan and control work being performed to create the product. The work efforts related to creating the product might be *Design It, Build It, Quality Assure It,* and *Ship It*; while the activities to manage the project might be *Initiation, Definition, Planning, Execution, Controlling* and *Close-out.*

The activities to create the product are unique to the industry and to the product being created. In other words, the pharmaceutical product life cycle is very different than the software development life cycle. Yet the same project management life cycle could be used to organize and monitor either the pharmaceutical or the software product creation.

Traditional. The design and the use of the integrated product and project life cycles have changed. Traditionally, the product life cycle is decomposed into phases or stages, such as the example above. Each phase is performed, completed, and approved during a Phase Review effort and the next phase begins. This technique is called the Waterfall Development Life Cycle. The project management life cycle works in sync with the product life cycle. Each phase of the product life cycle (for example, the Design phase) would be planned, executed, and controlled before the Build phase begins. In other words, the work efforts to produce the product would be performed serially and only once. The efforts to project-manage the effort would be repeated for each sequential phase of the product life cycle.

Iterative. Recognizing that a phase of the product process might be revisited; for example, during Design something was discovered that necessitated going back and revising the specifications created in the requirements phase. The traditional waterfall can be modified slightly. The modification of the waterfall is called a spiral or an iterative approach.

Relative to the project management efforts, the upcoming phase is planned and managed at a very detailed level while the later phases are planned at a lesser level of detail until more information is gained, which justifies a detailed planning effort. This type of project management effort is referred to as the Rolling Wave, or the phased approach to project management.

Evolving. With time-to-market or time-to-money becoming more important, the above sequential techniques are ineffective. New approaches, such as incremental builds and prototyping, emerge. A prototype (a working model) is produced. The customer "plays" with it, modifying/adding/deleting specifications, until the product is the way that they want it and then the product is officially released to be used by the entire customer community. Incremental build suggests creating a minimally functional product and releasing it. Even before it is in the customer's hands, more features and functions are being added for the next release.

Still not fast enough? Deliverable-driven and timeboxed efforts become the basic premises for these faster (cheaper), better development life cycles. Using the same theory as incremental and interactive, a new "version" of the product must be completed in a specified, but very short period of time. Typical project management schedule charts become extinct or at least modified to accommodate this agile development approach. Short interval scheduling which produces quality-controlled deliverables becomes the mode of the day. Teams become closer and more energetic. Customers start seeing output quicker. Paperwork becomes less important and flexible decision making becomes a necessity. Risks, mistakes, and some wasted time are acceptable. Yet the product is produced faster thus generating revenue and/or containing costs occurs sooner.

In summary, each of the above variations to product/project development life cycles has its place. The trend toward speed will increase. The desire for highest quality products being creating with the minimal cost will influence these techniques as time goes on. Evolution in the area of Development Life Cycles is only for the better of all industries, all disciplines, and ultimately for project management.

PROJECT MANAGEMENT: THE DISCIPLINE

The word discipline has more than one definition, according to Webster's dictionary. The two definitions are: 1) the "rules used to maintain control," and 2) "a branch of learning supported by mental, moral, or physical training." Project management, therefore, is a discipline (definition 2) which requires discipline (definition 1). In other words, project management is a unique branch of learning that deals with the planning, monitoring, and controlling of one-time endeavors.

Some Characteristics of Project Management

▶***Project management is a unique career and profession.*** Its origins can be traced back to efforts such as U.S. Department of Defense major weapons systems development, NASA space missions, and major construction and maintenance efforts, as well as comparable efforts in Europe. The magnitude and complexity of these efforts were the driving force in the search for tools that could aid management in the planning, decision making, and control of the multitude of activities involved in the project and especially those going on simultaneously.

▶***Project management is not just scheduling software.*** There is a misconception that project management is no more than scheduling using PERT (Program Evaluation and Review Technique) or CPM (Critical Path Method) to be found on a piece of software. A more realistic view is that scheduling software is a small part of project management. Software has permitted time scheduling, resource allocation, and cost management to be done much more efficiently and therefore in less time, in more detail, or both. Thus, a project can be planned and executed more precisely, leaving more time to perform the other aspects of project management.

▶***Project management is different than operations and technical management.*** Operations management can be characterized as managing the steady state. As soon as the operation is established, the concern is more with maintaining the operation in a production mode for as long as possible. Technical management tends to focus on the theory, technology, and practice in a technical field concerning itself with questions of policy on strength of materials, safety factors in design, and checking procedures. However, executives tend to be concerned about setting up a new operation (via a project) in order to implement organizational strategy. Project management, then, is the interface between general management, operations management, and technical management, which integrates all aspects of the project and causes the project to happen.

▶***Focus on Integration.*** If there is a single word that characterizes project management, it is integration—to integrate this discipline with other driving factors within every organization. Below is a sampling of those driving factors which influence project management and equally as important, which project management the discipline influences.

Strategic Planning: The Directive. Decisions from the strategic planning process become the directive from which projects are initiated. Project practitioners need to see the connection between the Strategic Plan and the project. Strategic Planning converted into an ongoing Strategic Management Process continues to review strategic objectives and filter down any changes so that the project manager can redirect his/her efforts appropriately.

Resource Allocation: The Critical Success Factor. The project manager must ensure that the allocation of specific resources is adequate but not overcommitted and that the right resources are assigned to the right tasks. This is not a simple procedure because of the number of activities that can be in process simultaneously. Fortunately, project management software provides assistance by identifying overloading or underloading of any one resource or pool of resources. Having identified any problems, human judgment is still required to evaluate and make the final decisions. This essential process both determines the cost of the project (budget) and provides oversight.

Change Management: The Differentiator. Typically change of scope and change of baseline plans come to mind when we say Change Management in the context of project management. However, every project creates significant changes in the culture of the business. Additional focus needs to be paid to planning and managing cultural change generated by projects.

Quality: Win/Win or Lose/Lose. A Quality initiative begins at the same time as the project management discipline. Quality management in the form of Six Sigma and other approaches combines project management techniques with the quality improvement techniques in order to ensure verifiable success.

Mentorship: Transfer from One Generation to the Next. Every person who leaves a company/agency or a division/department takes with him/her the "history," the "networking," and the "knowledge" of past projects. Cultures survive by passing knowledge from the elders to the young. To keep the information needed to perpetuate the project management culture in house, proactive mentorship programs are established to orchestrate the passing of "culture" onto new project practitioners.

Metrics and Close-out: Inspect What You Expect. Originally, metrics were the data collected after a project was completed to be used to plan for the next project(s). As project management has evolved, we've learned that we can't wait until the end of a project to set thresholds and collect the data. Management wants measurement metrics throughout in the project that can be managed using Executive Scorecards or Dashboards. Control procedures need to in place before the project proceeds so that the records can be complete from the beginning. If not, valuable effort can be consumed in retracing the records after the fact, and control can be lost before the project really gets started. Furthermore, legal tests of prudence, common in the utility industry, are better dealt with when accurate and complete records of the project are available.

Productivity: Doing More with Less. The drive to do more with less money and fewer resources, to do it faster, and to produce the highest quality deliverable will never go away. In order to accomplish this mandate, the biggest bang for the buck comes from increasing productivity. Project practitioners use new and creative techniques (automated and non-automated) to facilitate greater productivity.

Maturity Tracking: Managing the Evolution of the PM Discipline. With increased visibility, project management is being asked to account for what it has contributed lately and more importantly for what it plans to contribute tomorrow. In order to answer these questions, a reasonable maturity growth plan specifically designed for the project management discipline is constructed, which evaluates today's environment to ensure planned rather than chaotic growth.

Teams: Even More Distant. Remote or distant teams face the challenge of geography and diversity. Project management needs to address variables such as multi-functional, multi-cultural, multi-generational, multi-gender, and multi-personality project environment

Risk: The Defeating Factor. Risks are the holes in the dike. Too much vulnerability in the dike can make it crumble. If risks are isolated and the potential holes they present are plugged up, the dike will remain sound and solid. The sub-discipline of Risk Management is a major area of focus; one emerging approach is to use the techniques for controlling negative risks (threats) to capture positive risks (opportunities).

Competencies: Today and Tomorrow. Initially, project practitioners focus on their subject matter expertise, such as financial analysis, telecommunications design, or marketing creativity. Those who became involved in projects transition to competencies, such as scheduling, status reporting, and risk management. The next movement is to add general business awareness skills/competencies; such as financial knowledge, facilitation, leadership, problem solving/decision making, and creating/innovation. Each of you must ask what's next in your world.

Behind these integrations exists a superstructure in the form of processes, procedures, and/or methodologies.

PROJECT MANAGEMENT PROCESS: THE SUPERSTRUCTURE

The definition of a project is a temporary endeavor undertaken to create a unique product/service. This work is accomplished by instituting a project management process. As with any other discipline, a process or a methodology is created so that consistent rules and standards are employed. Consistent processes provide a common lexicon of terms, a regimented business system, and a frame of reference from which everyone can work. Below are the key processes within a project management discipline.

▶***Integration Management*** has been described earlier in this chapter.

▶***Scope Management*** ensures "that the project includes all the work required, and only the work required, to complete the project successfully." Project scope includes the features and functions that characterize the product, service, or event, and includes the work that must be done to deliver it with its specified features and functions. Scoping a project is putting boundaries around the work to be done as well as the specifications of the product to be produced. When defining scope, it is wise to articulate not only what is included within the scope but also what is excluded.

▶***Time Management*** is "the processes required to ensure timely completion of the project." The management of time is crucial to the successful completion of a project. The function of time management is divided into six processes: definition, sequencing, resource estimating, duration estimating, schedule development, and schedule control. Definition and sequencing include depicting what is intended to be done and in what order or sequence. Estimating is the determination of the duration required to perform each activity or of the availability and capacity of the resources to carry out the activity. Scheduling portrays the duration on a calendar, recognizing both time and resource constraints. The final deliverable from the scheduling process is the estimated time target to complete the entire project. Schedule control includes a recognition of what has happened and taking action to ensure that the project will be completed on time and within budget.

▶ ***Cost Management*** processes maintain financial control of projects: "planning, estimating, budgeting, and controlling costs so that the project can be completed within the approved budget." Cost estimating is the process of assembling and predicting costs of a project. The cost budgeting process involves establishing budgets, standards, and a monitoring system by which the cost of the project can be measured and managed. Cost control entails gathering, accumulating, analyzing, monitoring, reporting, and managing the costs on an ongoing basis. Cost applications include special cost techniques, such as data bases, to aid in estimating and product life cycle costing, plus topics that affect cost management, such as computer applications and value analysis.

▶ ***Quality Management*** determines the "quality policies, objectives, and responsibilities so that the project will satisfy the needs for which it was undertaken." Quality management implements makes use of quality planning, quality assurance, quality control, and quality improvement techniques and tools. If the requirements for the product of the project are consistent with the real, or perceived, needs of the customer, then the customer is likely to be satisfied with the product of the project. The product either conforms to these requirements or it does not. If the product going to the customer has no defects, he or she can perform his or her task in the most efficient manner—and do the right thing right the first time.

▶ ***Human Resource Management*** comprises all the "processes that organize and manage the project team." It's all about making the most effective use of people, from sponsors, customers, and partners, to individual contributors. Human resource planning and the formation, development, and management of the project team are all part of Human Resources Management. The project manager is responsible for developing the project team and building it into a cohesive group to complete the project. Two major types of tasks are recognized: administrative and behavioral. The behavioral aspects deal with the project team members, their interaction as a team, and their contacts with individuals outside the project itself. Included in these are communicating, motivating, team building, and conflict management. Administrative tasks include employee relations, compensation, and evaluation, as well as government regulations and evaluation. Much of the administrative activity of the project manager is directed by organizations and agencies outside the project.

▶ ***Communications Management*** includes all the activities that ensure "timely and appropriate generation, collection, dissemination, storage, and ultimate disposition of project information." These include Communications Planning, Information Distribution, Performance Reporting, and Managing Stakeholders. Successful project managers are constantly building consensus or confidence at critical junctures in a project by practicing active communications skills. The project manager must communicate to upper management, to the project team, and to other stakeholders. The communications process is not always easy because the project manager may find that barriers exist to communication, such as lack of clear communications channels and problems in a global team environment. The project manager has the responsibility of knowing what kind of messages to send, knowing whom to send the messages, and translating the messages into a language that all can understand.

▶***Risk Management*** includes "risk management planning, identification, analysis, responses, monitoring, and control." Risk management is the formal process whereby risk factors are systematically identified, assessed, and provided for. The term risk management tends to be misleading because it implies control of events. Risk management must be seen as preparation for possible events in advance, rather than simply reacting to them as they happen.

▶***Procurement Management*** covers all we do to "purchase or acquire the products, services, or results needed from outside the project team to perform the work." Planning for purchases or acquisitions, contracting, requesting seller responses, source selection, and contract administration (including closure) are all part of Procurement Management. Inherent in the process of managing a project is the procurement of a wide variety of resources. In most instances, this requires the negotiation of a formal, written contract. In a global business environment, it is essential to understand varying social, political, legal, and financial implications in this process.

In summary, the superstructure that supports the project management discipline relies on professional and practical Scope, Time, Cost, Quality, Human Resources, Communications, Risk, and Procurement Management—all coordinated through the practice of Integration Management. Each of these processes and their subordinated processes create the methodology by which projects are performed in a logical and consistent manner. The level of detail and the amount of rigor is defined by the culture as well as by the magnitude and complexity of the project itself.

CONCLUSION

Projects fill an essential need in society. Indeed, projects are the major mode in which change is accomplished. It is the mode in which corporate strategy is implemented, business change is addressed, productive teams and their necessary competencies are dealt with, quality of deliverables, and tracking pre-established metrics for management's decision making, as well as closing out a project and creating lessons learned are performed.

This discipline changes over time but the basic business premise never changes: Accomplish the right thing right the first time within justifiable time, resources, and budget. Projects are the means for responding to, if not proactively anticipating, the environment and opportunities of the future.

DISCUSSION QUESTIONS

❶ Regarding the eleven driving factors discussed in the section titled "Focus on Integration," what is the maturity level of your organization [High, Medium, Low]? If the maturity level is Low, is that acceptable within your evolution of project management or should something be done to change that?

❷ Regarding the six descriptors of projects found in the section titled "Some Characteristics of Projects," what is the awareness level of the key players within your organization's project management community [High, Medium or Low]? If the awareness is Low, what will you do to move that score up to Medium or even High?

❸ Regarding the key processes found in the "Project Management Process: The Superstructure," to what degree [High, Medium, Low] are these processes being employed? If Low, what action needs to be taken to increase competency and adherence to that process?

Though unscientific, this analysis should suggest to readers which of the chapters in this handbook might offer information about the challenges presently facing them.

REFERENCES

[1] This definition, and all others in this chapter, are derived from the premier standards document of the profession, the Project Management Institute's *A Guide to the Project Management Body of Knowledge, Third Edition.* (Newtown Square, Penn.: PMI, 2004).

SECTION ONE

THE PROJECT MANAGEMENT BODY OF KNOWLEDGE: COMPREHENSION AND PRACTICE

SECTION ONE

Section One: Introduction

PROJECT MANAGEMENT KNOWLEDGE ... PLUS

Serious students and practitioners of project management are already familiar with the *PMBOK® Guide*—the professional standard published by the Project Management Institute. This document provides the foundation for the study and practice of our discipline. Like most standards, it is both very detailed and very high-level. That is to say, each knowledge area and process group described in the *PMBOK® Guide* is described in as much detail as possible when creating a document that must, by definition, apply to all projects in all fields of endeavor. For the new project manager—or the project manager faced with a specific problem in need of a specific solution—such standards often seem frustratingly academic: far removed from the daily grind of getting the work done.

But the *Guide,* while of tremendous value in describing the parameters of the field, was never intended as a step-by-step manual for running a project. Instead, it functions more as an ideal or pure vision of project management. Meanwhile, between the vision and the reality—as poet T.S.Eliot wrote—falls the Shadow.

The chapters that follow are designed to help you take the fundamentals of project management one step further into the sunlight. Respected expert practitioners have supplied chapters on the processes and knowledge areas that, rather than reiterating what you can read in the *PMBOK® Guide,* will help you to apply the standards and principles of the profession. Many of these authors were themselves involved in the 2004 revision of the *PMBOK® Guide.* In addition, supplemental readings related to many of the knowledge areas have been provided. Some of these readings are classics from the first edition of this handbook, while others were specially created to bring the reader up to date on issues and applications related to that knowledge area.

Because this section of the handbook is envisioned as a companion to the *PMBOK® Guide,* we've maintained the language of the standard, describing for example, the "inputs" to and "outputs" of the various processes, even though these terms are seldom used in practice. You probably don't think of assembling your team members as an "input" to the planning process, but perhaps thinking of it that way helps to clarify the importance of this process step. Likewise, outputs are more commonly referred to as "deliverables"—the documents and results that we complete and pass along to keep the project rolling or finish it up.

Chapter 1 provides an overview of the project management profession, and Chapter 2 provides an overview of the bodies of knowledge about it that have been amassed by various professional societies worldwide. In Chapters 3-6, you'll find discussions of the various processes that make up project management: initiating, planning, and controlling in particular receive a full chapter of coverage.

Chapters 8-15 cover the nine knowledge areas accepted as being the basis of project management, while Chapter 16 discusses how to prepare for the PMI certification exam.

Following many of the numbered chapters in Section One, supplemental readings on that knowledge area are indicated by a chapter identified by a letter. For example, Chapter 10 covers the knowledge area of Project Cost Management; Chapter 10-A provides supplemental reading on Earned Value Management.

CHAPTER 2

Bodies of Knowledge and Competency Standards in Project Management

▶ALAN M. STRETTON,
UNIVERSITY OF TECHNOLOGY, SYDNEY

The original version of this chapter, published in the first edition of this handbook, was written when the only knowledge standard for project management was the 1987 *Project Management Body of Knowledge (PMBOK®)*[1] developed by the Project Management Institute (PMI), headquartered in the USA. Subsequent to the publication of the first edition, the *PMBOK®* was completely rewritten and renamed *A Guide to the Project Management Body of Knowledge (PMBOK® Guide)* in 1996, with revised editions published in 2000 and 2004, but with the basic 1996 structure unchanged.[2]

In the meantime, other bodies of knowledge of project management have been developed around the world, notably in the United Kingdom, Europe and Japan. These are all markedly different from the *PMBOK® Guide,* but are the de facto project management knowledge standards in their respective geographic domains. Thus, the current situation is that there is no single universally accepted body of knowledge of project management.

This situation has stimulated numerous efforts to try and define which topics should be included in a global body of knowledge of project management, and how they might be structured. The most notable of these was called the OLCI, initiated in 1998. Results from this initiative will be discussed below.

Another development is the adoption in some countries of performance-based competency standards rather than knowledge standards as a basis for assessing and credentialing project managers. Another global effort, this time for the development of a framework of Global Performance Based Standards for Project Management Personnel was initiated in 2000. Progress and prospects are discussed below. First, we'll examine the origins and natures of key bodies of knowledge and competency standards for project management, and possible future developments.

WHY A BODY OF KNOWLEDGE FOR PROJECT MANAGEMENT?

Knowledge standards or guides, which typically take the form of bodies of knowledge, focus primarily on what project management practitioners need to know to perform effectively.

The most compelling argument for having a body of knowledge for project management is to help overcome the "reinventing the wheel" problem. A good body of knowledge should help practitioners do their job better, by both direct referencing and by use in more formal educational processes.

Koontz and O'Donnell express the need as follows: "In managing, as in any other field, unless practitioners are to learn by trial and error (and it has been said that managers' errors are their subordinates' trials), there is no other place they can turn for meaningful guidance than the accumulated knowledge underlying their practice..."[3]

Beginning in 1981, the Project Management Institute (PMI) took formal steps to accumulate and codify relevant knowledge by initiating the development of what became their *Project Management Body of Knowledge (PMBOK®)*. The perceived need to do so arose from the PMI's long-term commitment to the professionalization of project management. As they stated at the time, "...there are five attributes of a professional body... :

1. An identifiable and independent project management body of knowledge (*PMBOK®* standards).
2. Supporting educational programs by an accredited institution (Accreditation).
3. A qualifying process (Certification).
4. A code of conduct (Ethics).
5. An institute representing members with a desire to serve..."[4]

The initial overambition of trying to codify an entire body of knowledge—surely a dynamic and changeable thing—was tempered in 1996 by the change in title to *A Guide to...*and the statement that the *PMBOK® Guide* was in fact, "a subset of the...Body of Knowledge that is generally accepted as good practice." That is to say that the *PMBOK® Guide* is designed to define a recommended subset rather than describing the entire field.

In summary, PMI sees their subset of the body of knowledge, as set forth in the *PMBOK® Guide,* as a basis for professionalization of project management. The *PMBOK® Guide* is used to support education programs, and for accrediting programs for degree-granting educational institutions. A test on knowledge of the *PMBOK® Guide* is part of the qualifying process for its Project Management Professional (PMP) certification. The United Kingdom, European, and Japanese bodies of knowledge were developed for somewhat different purposes in each case, although all share a purpose to provide a basis for assessment and certification of project management practitioners.

We now look at some of the principal bodies of knowledge of project management in more detail.

PMI's *PMBOK® Guide*

PMI has produced the oldest and most widely used of the bodies of knowledge of project management. It has been modified substantially over the years. In the words of an editor of the *Project Management Journal:* "It was never intended that the body of knowledge could remain static. Indeed, if we have a dynamic and growing profession, then we must also have a dynamic and growing body of knowledge."[5]

The precursor of the *PMBOK®* was PMI's ESA (Ethics, Standards, and Accreditation) report of 1983,[5] which nominated six primary components, namely the management of scope, cost, time, quality, human resources, and communications.

The 1987 *PMBOK®* was an entirely new document, and the first separately published body of knowledge of project management. It added contract/procurement management and risk management to the previous six primary components.

The 1996 *PMBOK® Guide* was a completely rewritten document, which added project integration management to the existing eight primary components. The nine components were then renamed Project Management Knowledge Areas, with a separate chapter for each. Each knowledge area has a number of component processes, each of which is further discussed in terms of inputs, tools and techniques, and outputs. There are some thirty-nine component processes in all.

Integration Management
- Project Charter Development
- Project Scope Statement Development
- Project Plan Development
- Project Plan Execution
- Monitoring and Controlling of Project Work
- Overall Change Control
- Project Closure

Scope Management
- Scope Planning
- Scope Definition
- Work Breakdown Structure Development
- Scope Verification
- Scope Change Control

Time Management
- Activity Definition
- Activity Sequencing
- Activity Resource Estimating
- Activity Duration Estimating
- Schedule Development
- Schedule Control

Cost Management
- Cost Estimating
- Cost Budgeting
- Cost Control

Quality Management
- Quality Planning
- Quality Assurance
- Quality Control

Human Resources Management
- Human Resource Planning
- Staff Acquisition
- Team Development
- Team Management

Communications Management
- Communications Planning
- Information Distribution
- Performance Reporting
- Stakeholder Management

Risk Management
- Risk Management Planning
- Risk Identification
- Risk Assessment
- Risk Analysis-Quantitative and Qualitative
- Risk Response Planning
- Risk Monitoring and Control

Procurement Management
- Planning for Purchases and Acquisitions
- Contract Planning
- Requesting Seller Responses (RFPs)
- Source Selection
- Contract Administration
- Contract Close-out

–Based on information in Chapter 1 of A Guide to the Project Management Body of Knowledge, Third Edition, *(PMI, 2004).*

TABLE 2-1. **THE PROJECT MANAGEMENT PROCESSES, LISTED BY KNOWLEDGE AREA**

The knowledge areas and their component processes in the 2004 *PMBOK® Guide, Third Edition,* are listed in Table 2-1. As you can see, there are now forty-four component processes identified in this model.

Discussion of the nine knowledge areas and component processes are preceded by three chapters on the Project Management Framework, comprising an introductory and overview chapter, and chapters on the project management context and project management processes.

Whereas the *PMBOK® Guide* (1996) aimed to identify and describe *generally accepted* knowledge and practices—i.e., those that are applicable to most projects most of the time, and about which there is widespread consensus about their value and usefulness—a major conceptual change for the Third Edition is that they have replaced the criterion "generally accepted" from the previous editions "to identify that subset of the Project Management Body of Knowledge that is *generally recognized as good practice*" (author's italics), and they go on to explain that "'good practice' means that there is general agreement that the correct application of these skills, tools, and techniques can enhance the chances of success over a wide range of different projects. Good practice does not mean that the knowledge described should always be applied uniformly on all projects; the project management team is responsible for determining what is appropriate for any given project."[7]

While acknowledging that "much of the knowledge needed to manage projects is unique or nearly unique to project management," the 2000 *PMBOK® Guide* went on to note that it does overlap other management disciplines, and that general management skills provide much of the foundation for building project management skills:

> "On any given project, skill in any number of general management areas may be required . . . These skills are well documented in the general management literature and their application is fundamentally the same on a project. . . .There are also general management skills that are relevant only on certain projects or in certain application areas. For example, team member safety is critical on virtually all construction projects and of little concern on most software development projects."[8]

In the *PMBOK® Guide, Third Edition,* this paragraph was replaced by a table defining "general management" as the "planning, organizing, staffing, executing, and controlling the operations of an ongoing enterprise," and listing the categories of such skills that might be of use to the project manager, including financial management and accounting; sales and marketing; contracts and commercial law; manufacturing and distribution; logistics and supply chain management; strategic planning, tactical planning, and operational planning; organizational behavior and development; personnel administration and associated topics; and information technology, among others.

This section of the *PMBOK® Guide* goes on to briefly discuss the key general management skills of leading, communicating, negotiating, problem solving, and influencing the organization, followed by a short discussion of socioeconomic influences.

In summary, the various versions of the *PMBOK® Guide* have focused on (project) management skills that are applicable to most projects most of the time, and have not included in the knowledge areas those general management skills that may be required only on some projects and/or only on some occasions.

The Association of Project Management Body of Knowledge (*APMBoK®*)

Morris[9] [11] notes that when the United Kingdom's APM launched its certification program in the early 1990s, they did it because they felt that PMI's *PMBOK®* did not

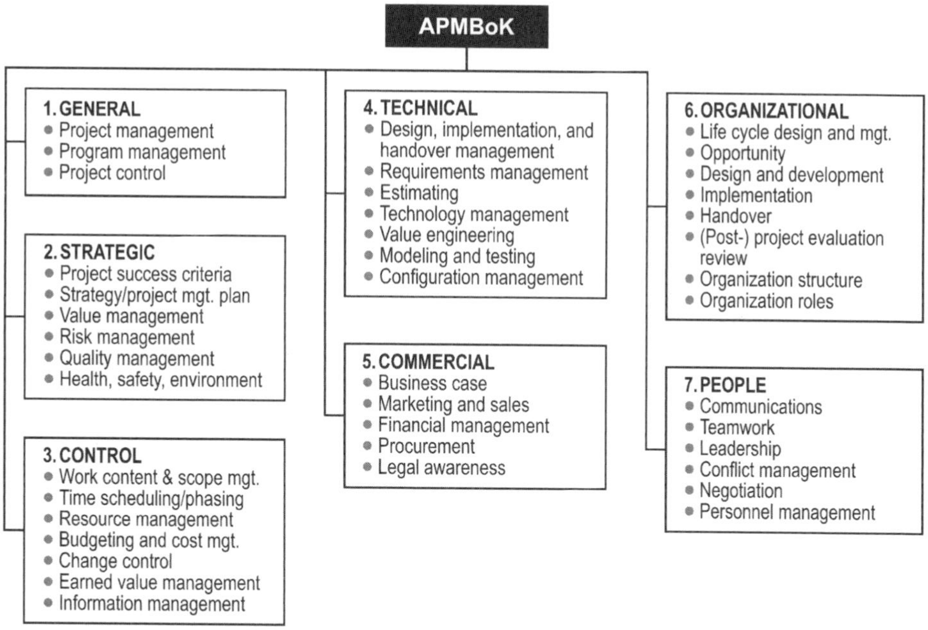

FIGURE 2-1. **THE ASSOCIATION OF PROJECT MANAGEMENT BODY OF KNOWLEDGE**

adequately reflect the knowledge base that project management professionals need. It therefore developed its own body of knowledge, which differs markedly from PMI's.[10]

The fourth edition (2000) of *APMBoK®* was organized into seven main headings, with a total of forty-two component items, which can be represented as shown in Figure 2-1. There are brief discussions of all headings and topics, and references given for each topic.

Morris discusses the reasons why APM did not use the *PMBOK®* model. In essence, he says that the different models reflect different views of the project management discipline. He notes that while the PMI model is focused on the generic processes required to accomplish a project "on time, in budget, and to scope," APM's reflects a wider view of the discipline, "addressing both the context of project and the technological, commercial, and general management issues, which it believes are important to successfully accomplishing projects."

Morris goes on to say:

> ". . . all the research evidence . . . shows that in order to deliver successful projects, managing scope, time, cost, resources, quality, risk, procurement, and so forth . . . alone are not enough. Just as important—sometimes more important—are issues of technology and design management, environment and external issues, people matters, business and commercial issues, and so on. Further, the research shows that defining the project is absolutely central to achieving project success. The job of managing the project begins early in the project, at the time the project definition is beginning to be explored and developed, not just after the scope, schedule, budget, and other factors have been defined . . . APM looked for a structure that gave more recognition to these matters."[11]

One of the key differences between the PMI and APM approaches is that, in its own words, the *PMBOK® Guide's* Knowledge Areas include only knowledge and practices that "are applicable to most projects most of the time," while contextual issues and the like are discussed separately in its Framework section. On the other hand, the *APMBoK®* includes knowledge and practices that may apply to *some* projects and/or *part* of the time, which is a much more inclusive approach. This is demonstrated by the fact that the *PMBOK® Guide* specifically excludes safety (as noted above), while the *APMBoK®* specifically includes safety.

European Bodies of Knowledge

Following the publication and translation of the first editions of the *APMBoK®* in 1992 and 1993, several European countries, including Austria, France, Germany, Switzerland, and the Netherlands, developed their own bodies of knowledge.

The International Project Management Association (IPMA), a federation of national project management associations, mainly European, developed an *IPMA Competence Baseline (ICB)*[12] in the late 1990s. In spite of its name, it is essentially a knowledge baseline, with the primary purpose of providing a reference basis for its member associations to develop their own *National Competence Baselines (NCBs)*. The majority of members have since developed their own baselines, which provide a basis for certification of their project managers.

Another purpose of the *ICB* was to "harmonize" the then-existing European bodies of knowledge, particularly those of the UK, France, Germany, and Switzerland.

The *ICB* comprises some twenty-eight core elements which are not grouped under sub-headings, but are presented in what has become known as "The Sunflower" structure — twenty-eight "petals" radiating out from a central core. There are also fourteen additional elements of project management knowledge and experience, making a total of forty-two elements. The twenty-eight core elements are required to be included in each member's *NCB*.

Japan's *P2M*

In mid-1999, Japan's Engineering Advancement Association (ENAA) received a commission from the Ministry of Economy, Trade, and Industry to establish a new Japanese-type project management knowledge system and a qualification system. ENAA established a committee for the introduction, development, and research on project management, which produced *A Guidebook of Project & Program Management for Enterprise Innovation*—officially abbreviated to *P2M*—in 2001, with English revisions in 2002 and 2004.[13]

The task of issuing, maintaining and upgrading *P2M* is being undertaken by the Project Management Professionals Certification Center (PMCC) of Japan, which is also implementing a certification system for project professionals in Japan, based on *P2M*. PMCC is a not-for-profit organization, whose primary purpose is to promote the effective use of project and program management throughout Japanese industry. *P2M* and its associated certification system are its key instruments for fulfilling this purpose.

The rationale for developing *P2M* and the certification system was a perceived need for Japanese enterprises to develop more innovative approaches to developing their businesses, particularly in the context of the increasingly competitive global business environment, and also a perceived need to provide improved public services. The key concept in addressing this need is "value creation." The recommended means of achieving "value creation" is through developing an enterprise mission, then strategies to accomplish this mission, followed by planned programs to implement these strategies, and then specific projects to achieve each of the programs. The focus of *P2M* is on how to facilitate the effective planning, management, and implementation of such programs and projects.

The original Japanese document comprises around 420 pages, so it is a large and very detailed document.

Alone among the main bodies of knowledge, *P2M* not only covers the management of single projects, but also has a major section specifically on program management.

On the project management side, *P2M* has chapters on the following project management segments or domains:

- Project Strategy Management
- Project Finance Management
- Project Systems Management
- Project Organization Management
- Project Objectives Management
- Project Resources Management
- Risk Management
- Project Information Technology Management
- Project Relations Management
- Project Value Management
- Project Communications Management.

TOWARDS A GLOBAL BODY OF KNOWLEDGE?

The current situation is that there is no one globally accepted body of knowledge of project management. Each main professional association has a vested interest in maintaining its own body of knowledge, as each case has involved such a big investment in, and commitment to, subsequent certification processes. It is therefore difficult to envisage any situation that might prompt professional associations to voluntarily cooperate to develop a global body of knowledge to which they would commit themselves.

Nonetheless, there have been many Global Forums since the mid-1990s, often in association with major project management conferences, which indicates a wide recognition that a globally recognized body of knowledge would be highly desirable.

One particular initiative was the coming together of a small group of internationally recognized experts to initiate workshops, beginning in 1998, to work towards a global body of project management knowledge. This group, known as OLCI (Operational Level Coordination Initiative) has recognized that one single document cannot realistically capture the entire body of project management knowledge, particularly emerging practices such as in managing "soft" projects (e.g., some organizational change projects), cutting edge research work, unpublished materials, and implicit as well as explicit knowledge and practice. Rather, there has emerged a shared recognition that the various guides and standards represent different and enriching views of selected aspects of the same overall body of knowledge.[14]

COMPETENCY STANDARDS

Competency has been defined as "the ability to perform the activities within an occupation or function to the standard expected in employment."[15] There are two primary approaches to inferring competency: *attribute based,* and *performance based.*

The attribute-based approach involves definition of a series of personal attributes (e.g., a set of skills, knowledge, and attitudes) that are believed to underlie competence, and then testing whether those attributes are present at an appropriate level in the individual. The attribute-based approach appears to be the basis for PMI's *Project Manager Competency Development Framework* (PMCDF),[16] although this is intended for use in professional development for project managers rather than in selection or performance evaluation.

The performance-based approach is to observe the performance of individuals in the actual workplace, from which underlying competence can be inferred. This has been the approach adopted by the Australian Institute of Project Management (AIPM) as a basis for its certification/registration program.

Australian National Competency Standards for Project Management *(ANCSPM)*

Several factors combined to lead AIPM to develop competency standards, including a recognition that the possession of knowledge about a subject does not necessarily mean competence in applying that knowledge in practice. The Australian Government was also very influential, through its Department of Employment, Education, and Training, which very actively promoted the development of national competency standards for the professions.

The format of Australian Competency Standards emphasises performance-oriented recognition of competence in the workplace, and includes the following main components:

▶ *Units of competency*: the significant major functions of the profession.

▶ *Elements of competency*: the building blocks of each unit of competency.

▶ *Performance criteria*: the type of performance in the workplace that would constitute adequate evidence of personal competence.

▶ *Range indicators*: describe more precisely the circumstances in which the performance criteria would be applied.

The *ANCSPM* units of competency align with the nine knowledge areas of the *PMBOK® Guide*. The elements of competency are expressed in action words, such as determine, guide, conduct, implement, assess outcomes, and the like. There are generally three elements of competency for each unit, but occasionally more. There are typically two to four performance criteria for each element of competency. *ANCSPM* also has substantial supporting material, which includes "a broad knowledge and understanding of . . . [various relevant topics]" and checklists of "substantiating evidence."[17]

Other Competency Standards

South Africa is developing its own performance-based competency standards. Standards have been completed for a National Certificate in Project Management—NQF Level 4 (SAQA), and work on Levels 3 and 5 is proceeding.[18]

In the UK, the Occupational Standards Council for Engineering produced standards for Project Controls (1996) and for Project Management (1997). These were reviewed in

2001, and the revised standards endorsed by the regulatory authorities in 2002. These are now the responsibility of the Engineering Construction Industry Training Board.[19]

The above standards are formally recognized and provide the basis for award of qualifications within their respective national qualifications frameworks.

Towards Global Performance-Based Competency Standards?

As noted earlier, a global effort for the development of a framework of Global Performance-Based Standards for Project Management Personnel (GPBSPMP) was initiated in 2000. The work of an international group, with representatives from most major international project management associations, has been facilitated from the outset by Dr. L.H. Crawford of the University of Technology, Sydney. The philosophy of this endeavor is to be maximally inclusive, so that emerging standards will incorporate input from virtually all project management knowledge and competency standards developed to date.

When these standards are produced, they will have the potential to be adopted as truly global, because each project management institute/association should be able to see a direct correspondence between its standards and the Global Performance Based Standards. One can only hope that this venture will be successfully completed, and its potential for global adoption realised, for the benefit of all in the project management field.

ACKNOWLEDGEMENT

The author gratefully acknowledges the ready assistance of his UTS colleague Dr. Lynn Crawford, who was particularly helpful in clarifying certain facts and interpretations; and of Crispin Piney, who reviewed the chapter to check the accuracy of my statements about the Third Edition of the *PMBOK® Guide*.

DISCUSSION QUESTIONS

❶ In your own career, what aspects of general management are equally important to project management skills and knowledge? Should project management perhaps be considered a "general management" skill?

❷ Are there aspects of the European and Australian models that you find applicable to your work? Should they be included in the PMI standard, in your view?

❸ Discuss the difference between attribute-based and performance-based competency models. If your competency were required to be measured, which would you prefer to be gauged by?

REFERENCES

[1] Project Management Institute, *Project Management Body of Knowledge* (Drexel Hill, Penn.:PMI 1987).

[2] Project Management Institute, *A Guide to the Project Management Body of Knowledge, PMBOK® Guide,* 2000 Edition, PMI, 2000; and *A Guide to the Project Management Body of Knowledge, Third Edition,* Project Management Institute, PMI, 2004.

[3] Harold Koontz and Cyril O'Donnell, *Essentials of Management* (New Delhi, India: Tata McGraw-Hill 1978)

[4] PMI (1987), p.3.

[5] Project Management Body of Knowledge: Special Summer Issue," *Project Management Journal* 17, No.3 (1986) p.15.

[6] "Ethics, Standards, Accreditation: Special Report," *Project Management Quarterly. PMI: Newtown Square, PA*. August, 1983.

[7] Project Management Institute, *A Guide to the Project Management Body of Knowledge, Third Edition.* PMI: Newtown Square, PA. (2004).

[8] PMI 2004, ibid.

[9] Peter W.G. Morris, "Updating the Project Management Bodies of Knowledge." *Project Management Journal* (September 2001).

[10] Association for Project Management, *Project Management Body of Knowledge (4th Edition)* (Peterborough, UK: APM, Edited by Miles Dixon, 2000).

[11] Morris, ibid.

[12] International Project Management Association, *ICB: IPMA Competence Baseline* (Zurich: IPMA, C. Caupin, H. Knopfel, P.W.G. Morris, E. Motzel, and O. Pannenbacker, 1998).

[13] Engineering Advancement Association of Japan, P2M: A *Guidebook of Project and Program Management for Enterprise Innovation: Interim Translation* (Japan: ENAA 2002).

[14] L.H. Crawford, *Global Body of Project Management Knowledge and Standards.* In P.W.G. Morris & J.K. Pinto (Editors), The Wiley Guide to Managing Projects, Chapter 46. (Hoboken, NJ; John Wiley & Sons, 2004).

[15] L. Heywood, A Gonczi and P. Hager, *A Guide to Development of Competency Standards for Professions: Research Paper 7* (Australia: National Office of Overseas Skills Recognition, Australian Government Publishing Service, April 1992).

[16] Project Management Institute, *Project Manager Competency Development Framework* (Newtown Square, Penn.: PMI 2002).

[17] Australian Institute of Project Management (Sponsor), *National Competency Standards for Project Management* (Sydney, Australia: AIPM 1996).

[18] South African Qualifications Authority, Notice of Publication of Unit Standards-Based Qualifications for Public Comment: National Certificate in Project Management—NQF Level 4. (South Africa: Government Gazette Vol. 437, No. 22846, 21st November 2001).

[19] Engineering Construction Industry Training Board, *National Occupation Standards for Project Management* (Kings Langley, UK; ECITB, 2002).

CHAPTER 3

Project Management Process Groups: Project Management Knowledge in Action

▶GEREE STREUN, PMP, CSQE, ADVANCED NEUROMODULATION SYSTEMS, INC.

One often hears the project management profession's standard, *A Guide to the Project Management Body of Knowledge (PMBOK® Guide),* described as consisting of nine knowledge areas. What's left out of this description is the equally important segment of the standard that describes the processes used by the project manager in order to apply that knowledge appropriately. These processes can be effectively arranged in logical groups for ease of consistent application. These process groups—Initiating, Planning, Executing, Monitoring and Controlling, and Closing—describe how a project manager integrates activities across the various knowledge areas as a project moves through its life cycle. So, while the knowledge areas of the standard describe what a project manager needs to know, the process groups describe what project managers must do—and in roughly what order.[1]

Historically, the definition of the processes that make up projects and project management was a tremendous milestone in the development of project management as a profession. Understanding the processes as described in the *PMBOK® Guide* is a first step in mastering project management. However, as the practice of this profession matures, our understanding of its processes also matures and evolves. This is reflected in the additions and changes made to successive editions of the standard over the years.

In the *PMBOK® Guide, 2000 Edition,* processes were divided into two classifications that were essentially only virtual groupings of the project management knowledge areas; these were classified as the Core and Facilitating Processes.[2] This was an attempt to provide an emphasis to guide the project manager through the application of the knowledge areas in order to implement the appropriate ones on his/her project. However, a clear differentiation between the Core and Facilitating processes was not provided. The project manager also needed information about when and how to use the processes in those classifications. Subsequently many inexperienced project managers used the differentiation to focus on the Core processes while only addressing the Facilitating processes if time permitted; after all, they reasoned, they are "merely" facilitating processes, not core processes.

Therefore a key change was made in 2004 in the *PMBOK® Guide, Third Edition*: the artificial focus classifications of Core and Facilitating processes were removed in order to provide an equal emphasis on all of the processes within the knowledge areas in the *PMBOK® Guide*.[3] To understand this, it is important to know that a process is a set of activities performed to achieve defined objectives. All processes are all equally important for every project; there are no unimportant project management processes. A project manager uses knowledge and skills to evaluate every project management processes and to tailor each one as needed for each project. This tailoring is required since there has never been a "one size fits all" project management approach. Every company and organization faces different constraints and requirements on every project, therefore tailoring must be performed to ensure the competing demands of scope, time and cost, and quality are addressed to fulfill those demands. These demands may require a stronger focus on quality and time, while attempting to minimize cost—an interesting project management challenge.

The odds of a project being successful are much higher if a defined approach is used when planning and executing a project. This approach must cover all processes needed to adapt product specifications, produce a plan, and manage all the activities planned to develop the required product. The project manager will have an approach defined for the project's specific constraints after the tailoring effort is completed.

PROJECT MANAGEMENT PROCESS GROUPS

The Project Management Process Groups are a logical way to categorize and implement the knowledge areas. The *PMBOK® Guide, Third Edition,* requires every process group for every project, however the tailoring and rigor applied to implementing each process group are based on the complexity and risk for the specific project.[3] The project manager uses the Process Groups to address the interactions and required tradeoffs among specified project requirements to achieve the project's final product objective. These Process Groups may appear to be defined as a strict linear model. However, a skilled project manager knows that project artifacts, like the business cases, preliminary plans, or scope statements, are rarely final in their first drafts. Therefore, in most projects the project manager must iterate through the various processes as many times as needed to define the requirements or to refine the project management plan which is used to produce a product to meet the requirements.

The project manager will iteratively apply the processes within the process groups to every project as shown in Figure 3-1. It illustrates how the output of one process group provides one or more inputs for another process groups, or even how an output may be the key deliverable for the overall project.

These Process Groups are tightly coupled since they are linked by their inputs and outputs. This coupling makes it clear the project manager must ensure that each process is aligned with the other processes for a successful project. The Process Groups and their interactions are very specific to the application of the project management knowledge areas to managing a project. A project manager skilled in applying these knowledge areas never confuses the process group interactions with the phases in a product life cycle and is able to apply the interactions in the Process Groups to drive a project life cycle to its successful completion.

At one time or another, every project manager has been involved with a project that was started without appropriate analysis and preparation then ended up costing the company a significant amount. A case in point, a high-level customer manager may mention an idea to someone in a development company and that idea hits a spark. They take the idea and launch into production. When the finished product is completed, there is surprise all around. The customer doesn't remember any request for this product and the production company cannot sell it to anyone else. Now what issues are apparent in this scenario?

- It is not clear whether the idea expressed a valid need.
- It is not clear whether there were real or imagined requirements.
- It is not clear if there was an analysis of a return on investment.
- It is not clear whether there was a delivery date.
- It is not clear whether needed resources were pulled from other projects or if there was an impact to other schedules.
- It is not clear that a market need was established prior to development.

The Initiating Process Group is required to answer these types of questions and to formally begin project activities.[4] The project manager uses the initiating processes to

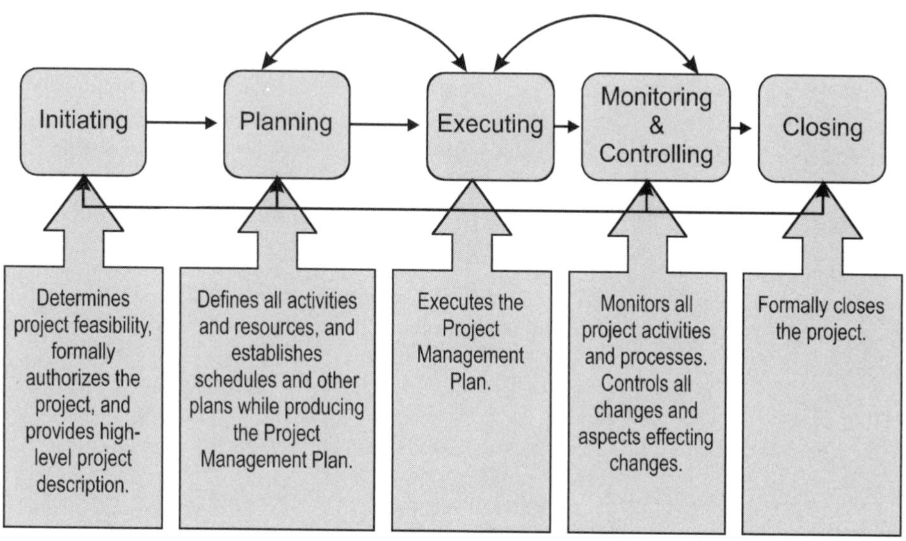

FIGURE 3-1. **PROJECT MANAGEMENT PROCESS GROUPS' INTERACTIONS**

start the project by addressing any issues or risks and project specifics. The project manager must iterate through the needed initiation activities to identify the service or product requiring the project's effort. The organization must take a critical look at the feasibility for creating the product or service as the requirements become more refined. After the appropriate analysis, a Project Charter is produced that addresses at a minimum the following information:

▶It provides formal authorization for the project.

▶It provides a high-level description of the product or service that will be created.

▶It defines the initial project requirements, constraints, and assumptions. The constraints and assumptions typically provide the initial set of negotiating points for the project plan.

▶It designates the project manager and defines the project manager's authority level.

▶It specifies any hard delivery dates if those dates required by the contract.

▶It provides an initial view of stakeholder expectations.

▶It must also provide an indication of the project budget.

The project manager works with the customer to get information to develop the initial scope statement. Typically content detail varies depending on the product's complexity and/or the application area. This document provides a very high-level project definition and should define project the boundaries and project success criteria. It should also address project characteristics, constraints, and assumptions.

The documents developed during this series of processes are provided as input to the planning effort. Unfortunately, some project managers learn a hard lesson about the importance of a defined project plan. A project requires a plan or it will never accomplish what is required by the due date. The plan is used to keep the project on track—a project manager knows where the project is in relation to the plan and can also determine the next steps. The lesson learned is that attempting to run a project without a plan is like trying to travel using a map, but with no current location and without an indication of a direction to take. Therefore, a map is useless to reach a target since there is no starting point or direction to the target. Additional confusion is introduced when some project managers confuse the Gantt chart, which is defined by commercial tools' as a "project plan" with an actual project management plan as defined in the *PMBOK® Guide, Third Edition.*[5] The project management plan provides needed information about:

▶Which knowledge area processes are needed and how each was tailored for this particular project, especially how rigorously each of those processes will be implemented on the project

▶How the project team will be built from the resources across the organization or will be brought in via contract, hired as full-time employees, or outsourced

▶Which quality standards will be applied to the project and the degree of quality control that will be needed for the project to be successful

▶How risks will be identified and mitigated

▶Which method will be used for communicating with all of the stakeholders to facilitate the timing of their participation to facilitate addressing open issues and pending decisions

▶Which configuration management requirements will be implemented and how they will be performed on this project

▶A list of schedule activities, including major deliverables and their associated milestone dates

▶The budget for the project based on the projected costs

▶How the project management plan will be executed to accomplish the project objectives, including the required project phases, any reviews, and the documented results from those phases or reviews.

Planning activities are the central activities the project manager continues throughout the project. They are iteratively revisited at multiple points within the project. Every aspect of the project is impacted by the project management plan or impacts the plan. It provides input to the executing processes, to the monitoring and controlling processes, and to the closing processes. If a problem occurs, the planning activities can even provide input back to the initiating activities, which can cause a project to be re-scoped and have a new delivery date authorized. The project manager integrates and iterates the executing processes until the work planned in the project management plan has produced the required deliverables. The project manager uses the project management plan and manages the project resources to actually perform the work planned in the project management plan to produce the project deliverables. During execution, the project manager will also develop and manage the project team and facilitate quality assurance. The project manager also ensures that approved change requests are implemented by the project team. This effort ensures that the product and project artifacts are modified per the approved changes. The project manager communicates status information so the stakeholders will know the project status, the started or finished activities, or the late activities. Key outputs from executing the project management plan are the deliverables for the next phase and even the final deliverables to the customer.

The project manager uses monitoring and controlling processes to observe all aspects of the project. These processes help the project manager actively learn whether or not there are potential problems so corrective action can be started before a crisis results. Monitoring project execution is important, since a majority of the project's resources are expended during this phase. Monitoring includes collecting data, assessing the data, measuring performance, and assessing measurements. This information is used to show trends and is communicated to show performance against the project management plan.

Configuration management is an essential aspect of establishing project control. Therefore, configuration management is required across the entire organization, including procedures that ensure that versions are controlled and only approved changes are implemented. The project implements aspects of change control necessary to continuously manage changes to project deliverables. Some organizations implement a Change Control Board to formally address change approval issues to ensure the project baseline is maintained by only allowing approved changes into the documentation or product.

The project manager must integrate his monitoring and controlling activities to provide feedback to the executing process. Some information will be feedback to the planning process; however, if there is a high-impact change to the project scope or overall plan, then there will also be input to the initiating processes.

The closing processes require the project manager to develop all procedures required to formally close a project or a phase.[6] This group of processes covers the transfer of the completed product to the final customer and project information, to the appropriate organization within the company. The procedure will also cover the closure and transfer of an aborted project and any reasons the project was terminated prior to completion.

The process groups described above represent the standard processes defined by the *PMBOK® Guide, Third Edition,* required for every project.[7] These processes indicate when and where to integrate the many knowledge areas to produce a useful Project Management Plan. Those processes, when executed, will produce the result defined by the project's scope. Chapters 7 through 15, and their supplementary readings, describe specific details for applying each knowledge area.

DISCUSSION QUESTIONS

❶ During which project management process are risk and stakeholders' ability to influence outcomes the highest at the beginning of the process?

❷ You are a project manager for a major copier company. You're heading up a project to develop a new line of copiers. You're ready to write the scope statement. What should it contain?

❸ You are a project manager working on gathering requirements and establishing estimates for the projects. Which process group are you in? How does knowing this clarify the steps you need to take to perform your assigned tasks?

REFERENCES

[1] Project Management Institute, *A Guide to the Project Management Body of Knowledge, Third Edition,* Project Management Institute, 2004: p. 37.

[2] Project Management Institute, *A Guide to the Project Management Body of Knowledge, PMBOK® Guide, 2000 Edition,* Project Management Institute, 2000: p. 29.

[3] Project Management Institute, *A Guide to the Project Management Body of Knowledge, Third Edition,* Project Management Institute, 2004: p. 37.

[4] PMI, ibid.

[5] PMI, ibid.

[6] PMI, ibid.

[7] PMI, ibid.

CHAPTER 4

Initiation Strategies for Managing Major Projects

▶PETER W. G. MORRIS, INDECO, LTD.

The initiation of a project largely determines how successful it will be. The crucial point about the model presented below is that all the items must be considered from the outset if the chances of success are to be optimized. The project must be seen as a whole, and it must further be managed as a whole. While our focus here is on large, broad, community-based projects, the same principles apply, on a lesser scale, to other projects.

The strategic model for managing projects discussed in this chapter is shown in Figure 4-1. Its logic is essentially as follows:

▶The project is in danger of encountering serious problems if its *objectives,* general *strategy*, and *technology* are inadequately considered or poorly developed, or if its *design* is not firmly managed in line with its strategic plans.

▶The project's *definition* both affects and is affected by changes in *external factors* (such as politics, community views, and economic and geophysical conditions), the availability of *financing,* and the *project duration;* therefore, this interaction must be managed actively. (Many of these interactions operate through the forecasted performance of the product that the project delivers once completed.)

▶The project's definition; its interaction with these external, financial, and other matters; and its implementation are harder to manage and possibly damagingly prejudiced if the *attitudes* of the parties essential to its success are not positive and supportive.

Realization of the project as it is defined, developed, built, and tested involves:

▶Deciding the appropriate project-matrix-functional orientation and balancing the involvement of the owner, as operator, and the project implementation specialists.

▶Having contracts that reflect the owner's aims and that appropriately reflect the risks involved and the ability of the parties to bear these risks.

▶Establishing checks and balances between the enthusiasm and drive of the project staff and the proper conservatism of its sponsors.

▶Developing team attitudes, with emphasis put on active communication and productive conflict.

▶Having the right tools for project planning, control, and reporting.

Let us examine these points in more detail.

PROJECT DEFINITION

The project should be defined comprehensively from its earliest days in terms of its purpose, ownership, technology, cost, duration and phasing, financing, marketing and sales, organization, energy and raw materials supply, and transportation. If it is not defined properly "in the round" like this from the outset, key issues essential to its viability could be missed or given inadequate attention, resulting in a poor or even disastrous project later.

Objectives

The extent to which the project's objectives are not clear, are complex, do not mesh with longer-term strategies, are not communicated clearly, or are not agreed upon compromises the chances of its success. The Apollo program, which placed the first man on the moon, was technically extremely difficult, but its chances of success were helped by the clarity of its objective.

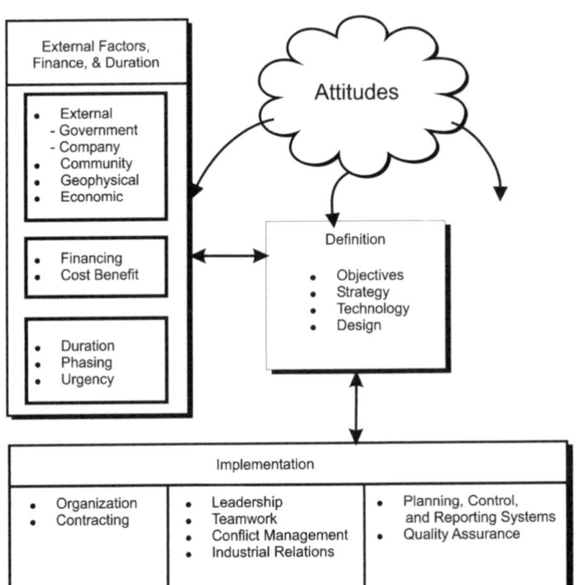

FIGURE 4-1. **STRATEGIC MODEL FOR MANAGING PROJECTS**

It is interesting to compare the Apollo program with a later US plan for a permanent, manned space station orbiting the earth. The space station objective was superficially clear—in former President Ronald Reagan's words, "to develop a permanently manned space station and to do it within a decade." But the objective is in fact far from clear. What, for example, does *develop* really mean? Just design and construct? Surely not. And what is the station's real mission—and hence, what is the project's proper development strategy? Earth observation? A waystation to planetary observation? Experimental purposes? A combination of these? The space station example illustrates that project, or program, objectives should match with viable long-term strategies, otherwise there will be confusion, uncertainty, changes, cost increases, and delays—as there indeed have been.

Strategy

Strategies for the attainment of the project objectives should similarly be developed in as comprehensive a manner as possible, right from the outset. This means that at the prefeasibility and feasibility stages, for example, industrial relations, contracting, communications, organization, and systems issues should all be considered, even if not elaborated upon, as well as the technical, financial, schedule, and planning issues.

Some of the most valuable work on the need for comprehensive planning has come from the areas of R&D and new product development. Valuable work has also been done with regard to development aid projects. The insights of Cassens, Moris, and Paul encapsulate almost everything anyone of good sense would expect regarding what it takes to produce successful development projects.[2] The writings of Cooper, Manfield, and others on new product development similarly relate product implementation performance to environmental and market success.[3]

Technology and Design

The development of the design criteria and the technical elements of the project should be handled with the utmost care. The design standards selected affect both the difficulty of construction and the operating characteristics of the plant. Maintainability and reliability should be critical factors in determining the project's operating characteristics. Many studies have shown that technical problems have a huge impact on the likelihood of project overrun[4]: Thorough risk analysis is therefore essential. The rate of technological change in all relevant systems and subsystems should be examined; technology must be tested before being designed into production (as opposed to prototype) projects; and design changes should be kept to a minimum.

No design is ever complete; technology is always progressing. A central challenge in the effective management of projects is thus the conflict between meeting the schedule against the desire to get the technical base that fits better. The orderly progressing of the project's sequence of review stages—the level of detail becoming progressively tighter, with strict control of technical interfaces and of proposed changes (through configuration management)—is now a core element of modern project management.

Projects as different as weapons systems, process plants, and information systems now generally employ project development methodologies that emphasize careful, discrete upgradings of technology; thorough review of cost, schedule, and performance implications; and rigorous control of subsequent proposed changes.

A major issue in project specification is how great a technological reach should be aimed for without incurring undue risks of cost overruns, schedule slippages, or inadequate technical performance. This was once the most difficult issue to get right on projects. More recently, practice has improved (though there have still been some spectacular disasters), partly because our basic technologies are not progressing into new domains at the rate they were before, but also partly because of the greater caution, care over risk assessment, use of prototypes, etc., which are now more common project practices. It is barely conceivable that we should embark on a brand new nuclear power reactor (AGR) or aerospace project (Concorde) today with the bravura that we did twenty to thirty years ago.

In setting up projects, then, care should be taken to appraise technological risk, prove new technologies, and validate the project design before freezing the design and moving into implementation.

EXTERNAL FACTORS, FINANCE, AND DURATION

Many external factors affect a project's chances of success. Particularly important are the project's political context, its relationship with the local community, the general economic environment, its location, and the geophysical conditions in which it is set.

Political, Environmental, and Economic Factors

Project personnel have often had difficulty recognizing and dealing with the project's impact on the physical and community environment and, in consequence, managing the political processes that regulate the conditions under which projects are executed. Most projects raise political issues of some sort and hence require political support: moral, regulatory, and sometimes even financial. National transportation projects, R&D programs, and many energy projects, for example, operate only under the dictate of the politician. The civil nuclear power business, Third World development projects, and even build-own-operate projects require political guidance, guarantees, and encouragement.

Do non-major projects also need to be conscious of the political dimension? Absolutely. Even small projects live under regulatory and economic conditions directly influenced by politicians; within the organization, too, project managers must secure political support for their projects.

Therefore, these political issues must be considered at the outset of the project. The people and procedures that are to work on the project must be attuned to the political issues and ready to manage them. To be successful, project managers must manage upward and outward, as well as downward and inward. The project manager should court the politicians, helping allies by providing them with the information they need to champion his or her program. Adversaries should be co-opted, not ignored. (The environmental impact assessment process, which will be described shortly, shows how substantive dialogue can help reduce potential opposition.)

Although environmentalism has been seriously impacting project implementation since the 1960s, most project personnel ignored it as a serious force at least until 1987-1988, when a number of world leaders, the World Bank, and others began to acknowledge its validity. Now, at last, most project staff members realize that they must find a way of involving the community positively in the development of their project. Ignoring the community and leaving everything to planning hearings is often to leave it too late. A "consent strategy" should be devised and implemented.[4] Dialogue must begin early in the project's development.

In a different sense, getting the support of the local community is particularly important in those projects where the community is, so to speak, the user—as, for example, in development projects and information technology. The local community may also be the potential consumer or purchaser for the project. Doing a market survey to see how viable the project economics are is thus an essential part of the project's management.

Changes in economic circumstances affect both the cost of the project's inputs and the economic viability of its outputs. The big difference today compared to thirty years ago is that then we assumed conditions would not vary too much in the future. Now we are much more cautious. As with technology, then, so with economics, we should be more cautious in appraising and managing our projects today.

In the area of cost-benefit discounting and other appraisal techniques, practice has moved forward considerably over the last few years. Externalities and longer-term social factors are now recognized as important variables that can dramatically affect the attractiveness of a project. Old project appraisal techniques have been replaced with a broader set of economic and financial tools in the community context with the use of environmental impact assessment procedures.

Initially resisted by many in the project community, the great value of environmental impact assessment (EIA) is that it (1) allows consultation and dialogue between developers, the community, regulators, and others; and (2) forces time to be spent at the front end in examining options and ensuring that the project appears viable. Through these two benefits, the likelihood of community opposition and of unforeseen external shocks arising is diminished. Further, in forcing project developers to spend time planning at the front end, the EIA process emphasizes precisely the project stage that traditionally has been rushed, despite the obvious dangers. We all know that time spent in the project's early stages is time well spent—and furthermore, that it is cost-effective time well spent—yet all too frequently this stage is rushed.

Finance

During the 1980s there was a decisive shift from public sector funding to the private sector, under the belief that projects built under private sector funding inevitably demonstrate better financial discipline. This is true where projects are built and financed by a well-managed private sector company. But private financing alone does not necessarily lead to better projects (as the record of Third World lending shows: weak project appraisals, loan pushing, cost and schedule overruns, white elephants, etc.). What is required is funding realism. The best way to get this is by getting all parties to accept some risk and to undertake a thorough risk assessment. Full risk analysis of the type done for limited recourse project financing, for example, invariably leads to better setup projects and should therefore be built into the project specification process. The use of this form of funding in methods such as build-own-operate projects has had the healthy consequence of making all parties concentrate on the continuing economic health of the project by tying their actions together more tightly to that goal.

The raising of the finance required for the English Channel Tunnel is a classic illustration of how all the elements shown in Figure 4-1 interact, in this case around the question of finance. To raise the necessary billions of pounds required that certain technical work be done, planning approvals be obtained, contracts be signed, political uncertainties be removed, etc. Since the project was raising most of its funding externally, there was a significant amount of bootstrapping required: The tasks could be accomplished only if some money was already raised, and so on. Actions had to be taken by a certain time or the money would run out. Furthermore, a key parameter of the project's viability was the likelihood of its slippage during construction. A slippage of three to six months meant not just increased financing charges, but the lost revenue of a summer season of tourist traffic. The English Channel Tunnel thus demonstrates also the significance of managing a project's schedule and of how its timing interrelates with its other dimensions.

Duration

Determining the overall timing of the enterprise is crucial to calculating its risks and the dynamics of its implementation and management. How much time one has available for each of the basic stages of the project, together with the amount and difficulty of the work to be accomplished in those phases, influences the nature of the task to be managed.

In specifying the project, therefore, the project manager spends considerable effort ensuring that the right proportions of time are spent within the overall duration. Milestone scheduling of the project at the earliest stage is crucial. It is particularly important that none of the development stages of the project be rushed or glossed over—a fault that has caused many project catastrophes in the past. A degree of urgency should be built into the project, but too much may create instability.

It is best to avoid specifying that implementation begin before technology development and testing is complete. This is the "concurrency" situation. Concurrency of course is sometimes employed deliberately to get a project completed under exceptionally urgent conditions, but it often brings problems in redesign and reworking. If faced with this, analyze the risk rigorously, work breakdown element by work breakdown element, and milestone phase by milestone phase.

The concurrency situation should be distinguished from a similar-sounding but different "fast build" practice. (This is sometimes also known as "fast track," but others equate fast track with concurrency. The terminology is imprecise and hence there is confusion—and danger—in this area.) Fast build is now being used to distinguish a different form of design and construction overlap: that where the concept, or scheme, design is completed but then the work packages are priced, scheduled, and built sequentially within the overall design parameters, with strict change (configuration) control being exercised throughout. With this fast build situation, the design is secure and the risks are much less.

The lessons learned on dealing with the challenge of managing urgent projects include:

▶Do not miss any of the stages of the project.

▶Use known technology and/or design replication as far as possible; avoid unnecessary innovation.

▶Test technology before committing to production (prototyping). Avoid concurrency unless prepared to take the risk of failing and of having to pay for the cost of rework.

▶Avoid making technical or design changes once implementation has begun. Choose design parameters broad enough to permit development and detailing without subsequent change (fast build). Exert strict change control/configuration management.

▶Order long-lead items early.

▶Prefabricate and/or build in as predictable an environment as possible and get the

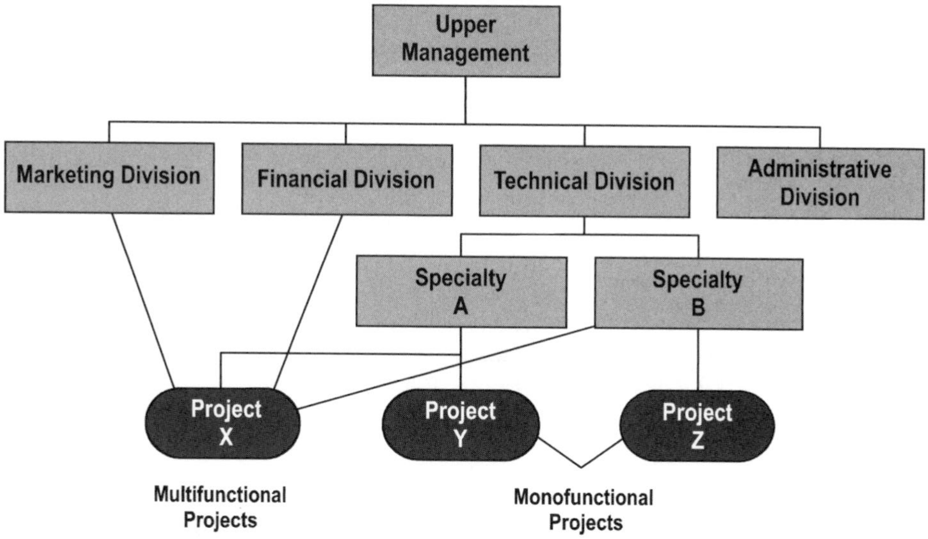

Advantages	Inconveniences
Technical competency	
• Development and maintenance of technical competency in specialized fields • Synergy among specialists	• Filtered perception; lack of an overall view • Difficulty in integrating several specialties: possible conflicts among specialists • Difficulty in creating motivation for the project • Lack of openness to the environment • Risk of neglecting the aspects not related to the specialty
Objectives	
• Concentration on the objectives of the function • Pursuing long-term development objectives • Easy reconciliation of internal objectives	• Conflict of priorities with other functional activities • Difficulty in making effective compromises between the variables quality-time-cost • Nobody is exclusively responsible for project objectives • Subordination of the managerial to the technical
Permanence and stability	
• Horizontal relations are clear • Clear definitions of roles and responsibilities • Efficiency improved by standardization • Stability in interpersonal relations • Well-defined career paths • The possibility for organizational learning	• Difficulty in adapting; resistance to change • Difficulties in the internal circulation of information • Slow decision making
Control	
• Easier control of quality and performance • Flexibility and economy in the use of labor	• The time variable is less well controlled • Limited liaisons with the outside • Lack of visibility for the client • Limited development of management capabilities among the personnel

FIGURE 4-2. **CHARACTERISTICS OF THE FUNCTIONAL STRUCTURE**

The functional structure is a widespread organizational form. It is characterized by a hierarchical, "chain-of command" power structure and specialization into functional "silos." Adapted from Brian Hobbs and Pierre Menard, Organizational Choices for Project Management, AMA Handbook of Project Management, First Edition, *AMACOM 1993: pp 85 and 88.*

ADVANTAGES	INCONVENIENCES
Clear identification of overall project responsibility	Duplication of effort and resources
Good systems integration	Limited development and accumulation of know-how
More direct contact among different disciplines	Employment instability
Clear communications channels with client and other outside stakeholders	
Clear priorities	
Effective trade-offs among cost, schedule, and quality	May tend to sacrifice technical quality for the more visible variables of schedule and cost
Client-oriented	
Results-oriented	

FIGURE 4-3. **CHARACTERISTICS OF THE FULLY PROJECTIZED STRUCTURE**

The fully projectized structure makes projects independent from the rest of the organization, gives the project manager full authority over resources, and facilitates the development of multidisciplinary technical teams. Adapted from Brian Hobbs and Pierre Menard, Organizational Choices for Project Management, AMA Handbook of Project Management, First Edition, *AMACOM 1993: p 90.*

organizational factors set to support optimum productivity. Put in additional management effort to ensure the proper integration at the right time of the things that must be done to make the project a success: teamwork, schedule, conscious decision-making, etc.

Each of these areas, then—external factors, finance, and duration—is both affected by and affects the viability of project definition.

ATTITUDES

Implementation can be effective only if the proper attitudes exist on the project. Unless there is a commitment toward making the project a success, unless the motivation of everyone working on the project is high, and unless attitudes are supportive and positive, the chances of success are substantially diminished.

Commitment and support at the top are particularly important; without it the project is severely jeopardized. But while commitment is important, it must be commitment to *viable* ends. Great leaders can become great dictators; therefore, if sane, sensible projects are to be initiated, they must not be insulated from criticism. Critique the project at its specification stage, therefore, and ensure that it continues to receive objective, frank reviews as it develops.

IMPLEMENTATION

Project management has in the past been concerned primarily with the process of implementation. This implies that developing the definition of the project is somehow not the concern of the project's manager. This could not be further from the truth.

The key conceptual point is not only that the specification process must be actively managed, but that the specification process must consider all those factors that might

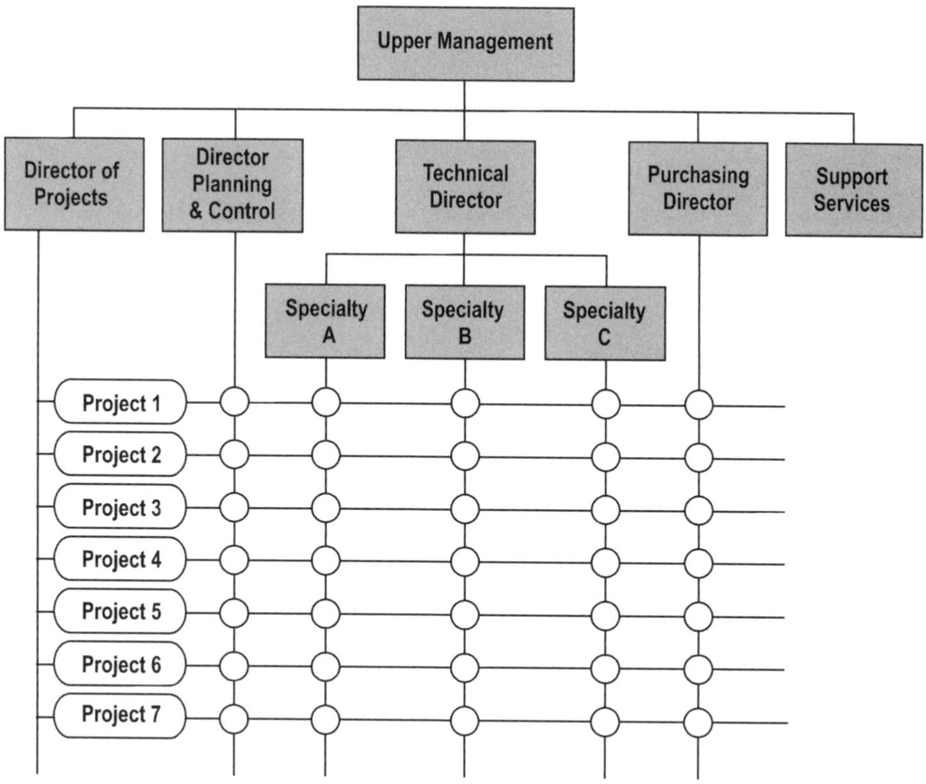

FIGURE 4-4. **THE MATRIX STRUCTURE**

The matrix structure seeks to combine the advantages of the functional and the projectized organization, while avoiding their disadvantages. Project and functional components are administratively independent, but interdependent in the execution of projects. Adapted from Brian Hobbs and Pierre Menard, Organizational Choices for Project Management, AMA Handbook of Project Management, First Edition, *AMACOM 1993: p 91.*

prejudice its success—not just technical matters and economics, but also ecological, political, and community factors and implementation issues.

Organization

Two key organizational issues in projects are deciding the relevant project-matrix-functional orientation and the extent of owner involvement. Both of these must be considered from the earliest stages of project specification.

A fully "projectized" orientation is expensive in resource terms. Many projects start and finish with a functional orientation but "swing" to a matrix during implementation.[5] Note too that implementing a matrix takes time and that effort must be put into developing the appropriate organizational climate. Assistance from the area of organization behavior therefore should be considered when designing and building a matrix organization. (Indeed, this is also true for other forms of project organization.) Figures 4-2 through 4-4 display the characteristics of each of these types of project organizations.

The crucial issues with regard to the extent of owner involvement are the extent that the owner (1) does not have the resources, or (2) does not have the skills, outlook, or experience, but (3) has legal or moral responsibility for assuring implementation of satisfactory standards. The first constraint is the most common. In building and civil engineering, for example, because of the nature of the demand, the owner rarely, if ever, has sufficient resources in-house to accomplish the project. Outside resources—principally designers, contractors, and suppliers—have to be contracted in. The owner focuses more on running the business.

Yet some degree of owner involvement is generally necessary. For if no project management expertise is maintained in-house, then active, directive decision-making of the kind that projects generally require is not available. On the other hand, if operators who are not really in the implementation business get too heavily involved in it, then there is a danger that the owner's staff may tinker with and refine design and construction decisions at the expense of effective project implementation. The solution to this dilemma is not easy to determine. There is no standard answer. What is right will be right for a given mix of project characteristics, organizations, and personalities.

The key point, ultimately, is for owner-operators to concentrate on predetermined milestone review points—the markers in the project's development at which one wants the project to have satisfactorily reached a certain stage—and to schedule these properly and review the project comprehensively as it passes across each of them. Milestone scheduling by owners is in fact now much more accepted as appropriate rather than the more detailed scheduling of the past.

Contract Strategy

The degree of owner involvement is related to the contractual strategy being developed. It is now generally recognized that the type of contract—essentially either cost reimbursable or incentive (including fixed price)—should relate to the degree of risk the contractor is expected to bear. If the project scope is not yet clear, it is better not to use an incentive or fixed-price-type contract: The contract can be converted to this form later. Contracts should be motivational: Top management support and positive attitudes should be encouraged.

The parties to a contract should put as much effort as possible, as early as possible, into identifying their joint objectives. While competitive bidding is healthy and to be encouraged, adequate time and information must be provided in order to make the bid as effective as possible. Spend time, too, ensuring that the bases upon which the bid is to be evaluated are the best: Price alone is often inadequate.

People Issues

Projects demand extraordinary effort from those working on them, often for a comparatively modest financial reward—and with the ultimate prospect of working oneself out of a job! Frequently, significant institutional resistance must be overcome in order for the many factors here being listed to be done right. This puts enormous demands on the personal qualities of all those working on the project, from senior management to the professional team(s) to the workforce.

The roles of project manager, leader, champion, and sponsor should be distinguished. Each is needed throughout the project, but the initial stages particularly require the latter three. Beware of unchecked champions and leaders, of the hype and over-optimism that too often surround projects in their early stages. The sponsor must be responsible for providing the objective check on the feasibility of the project. (For more on these roles, see Chapter 13A on stakeholder management.)

We should recognize the importance of teamworking, of handling positively the conflicts that inevitably arise, and of good communications. Consideration should be given to formal start-up sessions at the beginning of a team's work (mixing planning with team building). The composition of the team should be looked at from a social angle as well as from the technical: People play social roles on teams and these must vary as the project evolves.

All projects involve conflict: Cost, schedule, and technical performance are in conflict. However, conflict can be used positively as a source of creativity. Conflict is managed in this way on the best projects. On some projects it is ignored or brushed over; at best, a creative tension is then lost; at worst, it becomes destructive.

Every effort should be made to plan for improved productivity and industrial relations. The last twenty years have seen considerable improvements in industrial relations, though much remains to be done. Productivity improvements still represent an area of major management attention. Total quality management (TQM), with its emphasis on determining real needs and of improving performance "continuously," has perhaps been one of the most potent concepts in this regard.[6]

Planning and Control

Plans should be prepared by those technically responsible for them and integrated by the planning and control group. Planning initially should be at a broad systems level with detail being provided only where essential and in general on a rolling wave basis. Similarly for cost: Estimates should be prepared by work breakdown element, detail being provided as appropriate. Cost should be related to finance and be assembled into forecast out-turn cost, related both to the forecast actual construction price and to the actual product sales price.

Implementation of systems and procedures should be planned carefully so that all those working on the project understand them properly. Start-up meetings should develop the systems procedures in outline and begin substantive planning while simultaneously building the project team.

STRATEGIC ISSUES FOR ENTERPRISES WORKING ON PROJECTS

The model presented in Figure 4-1 is of course a high-level one; it is bound to be since its essence is its comprehensiveness. Note, therefore, that as one gets into any particular subsystem, the level of detail increases. The two subsystems where models have more commonly been developed in detail are financing and implementation; that is, the areas traditionally discussed as project management.

For the management of projects, then, a strategic model can be said to exist. But what are the chances of anyone ever implementing it? The key is in changing perceptions; and the keys to effecting that are management and education.

The difficulty with project management is that it can encompass such a broad scope of services in different situations. The project manager for an equipment supply contractor on a power station, say, has a more narrowly defined task than the utility's overall project manager. The project manager for the specification, procurement, and installation of a major telecommunications system has a much broader scope than the project manager of a software development program. Yet all involve the elements of Figure 4-1 in some way.

The two strategic questions for enterprises working in project-related industries are to determine:

1. The level and scope of services that one's clients and customers need and are able to buy.
2. Whether one has the organizational capability to supply this level and scope of services.

There is little doubt that the most powerful set of ideas relevant to the first question—the level of services—is that of total quality. The TQM concept forces one to analyze what services one's clients want. (And there may be several different sets of clients in the production chain ranging from one's boss or bosses to, most obviously, the people who are using the services, whether as customers or as colleagues.) This approach to analyzing the effectiveness of one's services is directly relevant to determining not just the extent to which the factors identified in Figure 4-1 are needed, but also the extent to which they need to be organized and delivered in an integrated fashion.

As long ago as 1959, the *Harvard Business Review* identified integration as the key project management function.[7] The question is, however, what needs to be integrated? By fundamentally addressing the client's real needs and the extent to which these are being satisfactorily met, a project manager may see, for example, that on this project the supply of finance, or the ability to provide better value for money, or to build faster, or to provide greater technical reliability, are issues that need better integration within the scope of project services to be provided.

As the level and scope of services become clearer, the second key strategic question arises: that of the organization's ability to deliver. Here, the principal difficulty is that our educational institutions are so far producing people with either a severely limited number of the vision or the ability to manage such a broad array of issues as those outlined in Figure 4-1. For projects to be managed successfully, a wide range of factors may need integrating. Few people have any training across such a broad array, particularly in a project context. Yet there are signs that times are changing, and it is surely very much in the interests of all who work in project-related industries to support such change. The inclusion of Integration Management as a knowledge area in PMI's body of knowledge—an addition that was made since the first edition of this Handbook was published—is one sign of the trend towards greater emphasis on the integrative function of the project manager.

The second evidence of an increasing maturity of project management formation is the growing number of advanced project management educational programs, particularly at the postgraduate level. Postgraduate education is important because a considerable level of technical, organizational, and business integration is being required at senior levels on most of the more advanced projects and programs. Without a well-rounded educational background, as well as real frontline practical experience, there must be some doubt as to our ability to furnish managers capable of meeting the project management demands being made by today's projects.

CONCLUSION

A fundamental task facing any senior manager on a major program or project is to work out how the various factors identified in Figure 4-1 should best be allocated and integrated on his or her project. For managers and educators, a major challenge facing the project management profession is to ensure that we have people with the intellectual breadth and the experience to tackle issues of the diversity and subtlety of those so often posed by today's projects. Every encouragement should be given to the professional societies and the schools and other organizations around the world to develop an appropriate, well-rounded professional formation for the management of projects.

DISCUSSION QUESTIONS

❶ What external factors typically influence the successful implementation of large projects? How do they vary from project to project?

❷ In what way do attitudes affect the project management process? Which stakeholder attitudes are particularly important?

❸ What are the two most important strategic issues for projects? Why is scope such an important issue?

REFERENCES

[1] A. O. Hirschman. *Development Projects Observed.* Washington, D.C.: Brookings Institution, 1967.

[2] R. Cassens, and Associates. *Does Aid Work?* Oxford, England: Clarendon Press, 1986; J. Moris. *Managing Induced Rural Development.* Bloomington, Ind.: International Development Institute, 1981; S. Paul. *Managing Development Programs: The Lessons of Success.* Boulder, Colo.: Westview Press, 1982.

[3] N. R. Baker, S. G. Green, and A. S. Bean. "Why R&D Projects Succeed or Fail." *Research Management* (November-December 1986), pp. 29-34; R. Balachandra and J.A. Raelin. "When to Kill That R&D Project." *Research Management* (July-August 1984), pp. 30-33; R. G. Cooper. "New Product Success in Industrial Firms." *Industrial Marketing Management* 11 (1982), pp. 215-223; A. Gerstenfeld. "A Study of Successful Projects, Unsuccessful Projects and Projects in Progress in West Germany." *IEEE Transactions on Engineering Management* (August 1976), pp. 116-123; E. Manfield, and S. Wagner. "Organizational and Strategic Factors Associated With Probabilities of Success and Industrial R&D." *Journal of Business* 48, No. 2 (April 1975); R. Whipp, and P. Clark. *Innovation and the Auto Industry,* London, England: Francis, 1986. See also F.P. Brooks. *The Mythical Man-Month.* Reading, Mass.: Addison-Wesley, 1982; T.E. Harvey. "Concurrency Today in Acquisition Management." *Defense Systems Management Review* 3, No. 1 (Winter 1980), pp. 14-18; O. P. Karhbanda, and E.A. Stalworthy. *How to Learn From Project Disasters.* London, England: Gower, 1983; *Learning From Experience: A Report on the Arrangements for Managing Major Projects in the Procurement Executive.* London, England: Ministry of Defense, 1987; E.W. Merrow. *Understanding the Outcomes of Mega Projects: Quantitive Analysis of Very Large Civilian Projects.* Santa Monica, Calif.: Rand Corporation, March 1988.

[4] B. Bowonder. "Project Siting and Environmental Impact Assessment in Developing Countries." *Project Appraisal* 2, No. 1 (March 1987), pp. 1-72; N. Lichfield. "Environmental Impact Assessment in Project Appraisal in Britain." *Project Appraisal* 3, No. 3 (September 1988), pp. 125-180; J. Stringer. *Planning and Inquiry Process.* MPA Technical Paper No. 6, Templeton College, Oxford, September 1988.

[5] P. W. G. Morris. "Managing Project Interfaces—Key Points for Project Success." In D.I. Cleveland and W.R. King, eds., *Project Management Handbook.* New York: Van Nostrand Reinhold, 1988; C.E. Reis de Carvalho, and P.W.G. Morris. "Project Matrix Organizations, or How to Do the Matrix Swing." 1979 *Proceedings of the Project Management Institute,* Los Angeles. Drexel Hill, Penn.: 1979.

[6] W. E. Deming. *Out of Crisis.* Cambridge, Mass.: MIT Press 1989; M. Imai. *Kaizen.* New York: Kaizan Institute/Random House, 1986; J. M. Juran, and F. M. Gryna. *Juran's Quality Control Handbook.* New York: McGraw-Hill, 1988.

[7] P. O. Gaddis. "The Project Manager." *Harvard Business Review* (May-June 1959), pp. 89-97.

[8] "Project Managers and Their Teams: Selection, Education, Careers." *Proceedings of the 14th International Experts Seminar,* INTERNET, March 15-17, 1990, Zurich, Switzerland. See particularly the papers by R. Archibald and A. Harpham; E. Gabriel; and R. Pharro and P. W. G. Morris.

CHAPTER 5

Comprehensive Planning for Complex Projects

▶DAVID L. PELLS,
IWORLD PROJECTS & SYSTEMS, INC.

Preparation of a project management plan is a simple, straightforward approach designed to promote and ensure comprehensive project planning. The PM plan is a combination of two plans that are often prepared separately: the traditional management plan, which describes operational management systems and approaches, and the project plan, which includes the work breakdown structure (WBS), logic, schedules, and cost estimates. Thus, they are more comprehensive than either management plans or project plans. They reflect an awareness that the people, the system, and the detailed planning are all critical to project success.

This chapter outlines PM plan contents, including traditional issues such as work breakdown structures, critical path networks, Gantt charts, and earned value. It introduces ideas such as planning for organizational development, health and safety planning, and risk planning. Most importantly, it provides a framework for comprehensive project planning.

ELEMENTS OF A PROJECT MANAGEMENT PLAN

The project management plan typically contains seventeen items, which are discussed below along with descriptive information and suggestions on how to address the topics during the planning process and what to include in the project management plan. The seventeen items are as follows:

1. Introduction/overview
2. Mission and objectives
3. Work scope

4. Planning basis
5. Work breakdown structure
6. Organization development plan
7. Resource plan
8. Procurement and logistics plan
9. Logic and schedules
10. Cost estimates, budgets, and financial management
11. Risk analysis and contingency plan
12. Quality and productivity plan
13. Environmental, safety, and health protection plan
14. Security plan
15. Project planning, control, and administration plan
16. Documentation and configuration management plan
17. Appendix.

Introduction/Overview

The PM plan introduction/overview includes an introduction both to the specific project and to the PM plan document itself. Some background information may be included to set the stage or provide perspective on the information that follows, such as how the project was initiated, who the customer or sponsor is, how the project is funded, or other factors that are important to those who read the plan. Introductions are always short, allowing the reader to move into the PM plan quickly. Additional external or historical information can be referenced or included in the Appendix.

External factors, such as general or specific economic trends, constraints, or opportunities; political or governmental conditions; population demographics; or internal organizational factors, should be discussed.

Mission and Objectives

The purpose or mission of the project is stated in one or two paragraphs, followed by a set of concrete objectives. The mission statement is all-encompassing, establishing why the project exists. Mission statements can be general or specific. They also reference the customer if the project is being performed under contract or for a third party.

Project objectives are outlined as specific goals to be accomplished and to which status they can be applied. For instance, objectives for a small construction project might include a good location; a modern energy-efficient economic design; a fully furnished facility; a complete set of project documents; compliance with all laws, codes, and requirements; a standard profit margin; and a completion date.

Planning becomes straightforward when objectives are defined for key areas. Objectives can be established for every aspect of the project, including scope of work, organization, management, systems, environment, safety, and overall completion of the project (i.e., final cost and schedule dates). Established objectives in the following areas facilitate detailed planning, systems development, and work performance:

- ▶Technical objectives
- ▶Schedule objectives
- ▶Cost objectives

▶Organizational/personnel-related objectives

▶Quality objectives

▶Environmental safety and health objectives

▶Contracting/procurement objectives

▶Management system objectives.

Well-defined objectives enhance the reliability of subsequent planning. Once objectives are stated in concise terms, they allow for the development of the project scope of work and the work breakdown structure.

Work Scope

The work scope section of the PM plan demonstrates how well the project is understood. It includes narrative descriptions of all elements of the project's scope of work. It clearly identifies the products or services to be provided to the customer. The statement of work contains enough information to allow development of the WBS, schedules, and cost estimates, as well as assignment of responsibilities.

This section can address the project phases and include special plans associated with those phases, such as the R&D plan, engineering/design plans, construction plan, manufacturing plan, facility start-up plan, or transition plan. It may also describe the systems management activities, including systems engineering and integration, to ensure project life cycle perspective. In other words, it shows that the activities necessary to ensure that the design and final products meet customer requirements are all planned and managed properly and can be integrated and operated as intended, and that start up, transition, operation, and completion activities are also planned and managed properly.

To simplify preparation, the work scope can be prepared in outline form, which can then be used to develop the WBS. Often the WBS and work scope are prepared in parallel, with the resultant narrative description of the work called a WBS dictionary.

Planning Basis

The planning basis section provides for the documentation of key approaches, assumptions, requirements, and other factors considered during preparation of the PM plan. The following topics are addressed in this section:

▶Project deliverables/end products

▶Requirements

▶Constraints

▶Approaches/strategies

▶Key assumptions

▶Specifically excluded scope.

Project Deliverables/End Products

A list of all products, documents, and services to be delivered to the customer over the life of the project is required.

Requirements

Requirements are specifications or instructions that must be followed during project performance. They may include technical requirements, facilities requirements, data requirements, management requirements, or special instructions. Technical requirements may include codes, standards, laws, engineering or design specifications, models, or examples for mandatory or recommended compliance on the project. When there are mandatory requirements, such as laws, these must be identified and listed, or project performers run the risk of noncompliance and legal prosecution.

Facilities requirements include an initial assessment of types, amount, and quality of facilities needed for the project, along with related utilities, furniture, and equipment. This provides initial bases for estimating quantities and costs associated with those resources. Overlooking facilities issues during project planning leads to schedule slippages, cost overruns, unhappy project participants, and untold headaches for the project managers. For small projects, facility requirements may not be a big issue; for larger projects, they can be critical.

Functional and operational requirements (F&DRs) spell out what the system, facility, or product being produced is intended to do. F&DRs provide the basis for the engineering, design, and planning of the system, facility, or product. Where F&DRs exist, listing or identifying them greatly simplifies and facilitates the design process. Mandatory data requirements, management directives, or special instructions are also identified and documented during the planning process. Special instructions may include directions from the customer or upper management or may be spelled out in contract documents.

Constraints

Constraints may include known technical limitations, financial ceilings, or schedule "drop dead" dates. Technical constraints may be related to state-of-the-art capabilities, interface requirements with other systems, or user-related issues (e.g., software that must run on certain types of personal computers). Financial and schedule constraints can be introduced by the customer and lead time associated with procured hardware or funding/budgetary limits.

Approaches/Strategies

The approach or strategies to be utilized can have a major impact on subsequent planning. For instance, if all project work is to be performed within the parent (host) organization with minimum subcontract support, that approach impacts planning of resources and organizational issues. If work is to be "fast-tracked" by overlapping design and construction activities, or by performing more work in parallel, then that approach can be described. Communication of strategies to project participants can be done effectively by devoting several paragraphs to that topic in this section of the PM plan.

Key Assumptions

Every project is planned under some degree of uncertainty. Therefore, assumptions are required to estimate work scope, schedule durations, resource requirements, and cost estimates. Assumptions are also required when defining the management strategies, systems, and procedures to be utilized.

Major assumptions are to be documented because they can have a significant impact on planning and estimating. This is true on all projects, regardless of size. Large projects, which involve numerous participants and major complexities, generally depend on more key assumptions during project planning than smaller projects. The major reason for documenting key assumptions is to provide the project manager with a basis for revising plans when the assumptions are changed (i.e., when a customer changes his or her mind).

Specifically Excluded Scope

This subject may be needed to limit the scope of work. It highlights specific and relatively obvious issues, such as documentation, training, or follow-on support, which customers often assume but which cost money and have not been included in the project plan. Clarification of these scoping questions saves headaches later, in some cases even avoiding litigation.

Work Breakdown Structure

The WBS is a product-oriented hierarchy of the scope of work embodied in a numbering structure that provides a system for organizing the scope in a logical manner. The WBS is prepared in conjunction with the scope of work, and it should be developed to the level of detail where responsibility for work performance is assigned. Responsibility for each element of a WBS is then established.

The most popular portrayal of a project WBS is in graphic form, similar to an organization chart. This WBS chart displays project elements and tasks in levels and boxes, representing smaller parts of the project. The WBS is a mandatory requirement for the PM plan.

The WBS facilitates the following:

- Understanding of the work
- Planning of all work
- Identifying end products and deliverables
- Defining work in successively greater detail
- Relating end items to objectives
- Assigning responsibility for all work
- Estimating costs and schedules
- Planning and allocating resources
- Integration of scope, schedule, and cost
- Monitoring cost, schedule, and technical performance
- Summarizing information for management and reporting
- Providing traceability to lower levels of detail
- Controlling changes.

The WBS provides a common, ordered framework for summarizing information and for quantitative and narrative reporting to customers and management.

Organization Development Plan

This section of the PM plan addresses organization structure, responsibilities, authorities, interfaces, and personnel development. For every project, how the people involved are organized, assigned responsibilities, and directed needs to be defined and communicated to the participants. In addition, interfaces among participants both inside and outside the project team require planning. Equally important, training and team-building plans need to be established to promote quality and productivity on project work.

Organization Structure

While not all participants may be involved during early project planning, key positions and participating organizations are identifiable fairly early. A preliminary organization structure in graphic form can be prepared and included in the PM plan. Where possible, names, titles, and phone numbers are included on the chart, to promote understanding and communication. Organization charts are dated but not finalized until resource allocation plans are prepared, based on detailed work planning and cost estimates.

Responsibilities

Specific responsibilities of individual project participants are defined as clearly as possible, to promote communication and teamwork and to avoid confusion. For large projects, responsibilities of positions or participating organizations are defined.

Authorities

Much has been written about the "authority versus responsibility" issues in project management, especially in matrix organizations. Project managers or other project participants are "responsible" for project accomplishment without "authority" over the resources being employed. For all projects, it is helpful to recognize these issues and document procedures for resolving conflicts as necessary. Where multiple companies or organizations are integrated into a project organization, contract relationships are referenced or defined, as appropriate. Procedures for resolving problems related to work direction may also need to be established.

Interfaces

On projects involving technical activity, it is common for personnel from the customer's organization to talk directly with technical staff in the project organization. However, when multiple project participants are interfacing with outside entities—either customer representatives, the general public, the press, or others—it is easy for conflicting information to be transmitted. These interfaces can generally be identified and controlled, normally via procedures or established protocols. Clearly defining interfaces highlights where communication is needed and which areas may cause potential communication problems.

Personnel Development

Skills and techniques related to teamwork and effective communication can be critical to a project's success. Many of those skills and techniques, however, may be new or difficult for new project participants. This section of the PM plan outlines the types of training and team-building activities planned for the project. Establishing a plan points out that the project leaders are aware of these issues and plan to improve communication, teamwork, and productivity on the project. In addition, other types of training are necessary on projects, especially if the project utilizes new technologies, equipment, systems, or approaches.

Resource Plan

The resources needed to accomplish the project—personnel, supplies, materials, facilities, utilities, and information/expertise—are identified in this section of the PM plan. The availability of those resources also needs to be determined, including expertise needed for the project that is not available within the organization and may need to be found via hiring, contract, or partnership. Materials required may be available only on the other side of the world, requiring additional planning, time, and expense to secure.

The primary resource planning issues are identification and qualification of the resources required; availability of those resources; quantification, or amount, of the resources required; and timing, or "allocation," of the resources.

Identification and availability of resources are addressed in this section of the PM plan. Quantities and timing of those resources are established during the cost-estimating process and finalized after schedules have been defined. Pricing of resources is how cost estimates are established and becomes the basis for project budgets. However, preliminary estimates of resources required and projected dates needed are included in the PM plan, then finalized when cost estimates and schedules are established. Because of inflation, cost of capital, and other factors, accurate pricing of resources cannot occur until resources have been scheduled, so this process is also fundamental to the cost-estimating process. Resource allocation is also normally included in the cost estimate section of the PM plan, in the form of a time-phased cost estimate.

Procurement and Logistics Plan

Advance planning of the contracting and procurement activities is particularly critical on large projects. Logistics issues related to major equipment, supplies, or materials need to be planned in advance to ensure manufacturing, transportation, and storage by cost-efficient, safe, and timely means. This section of the PM plan includes subcontracting plans, procurement plans, and logistics plans.

Subcontracting Plans

Subcontracting activity has a direct effect on project costs, schedules, and overall success, so it normally receives attention early in the planning process. It may be directly related to the original structure of the project organization if, for instance, joint ventures or other partnering arrangements are established to perform a project. A primary contracting organization may have overall project management and planning responsibilities, but one or more other subcontractors will perform portions of the project. In those cases, the subcontracting arrangements are planned early, or project work can be delayed.

An early planning activity is identifying major subcontracts needed to accomplish project work. This section of the PM plan also includes identification of subcontracting laws, regulations, and requirements to be complied with; identification and description of the major subcontracts anticipated for the project; timing of those subcontracts; potential problems or issues associated with the contracts; and approaches and expertise to be employed during the contracting process.

Procurement Plans

The procurement of equipment, materials, and supplies requires planning to reduce the risk of impacting project schedules and to ensure efficient and cost-effective acquisition. On large projects or projects involving R&D or manufacturing of new systems, key equipment or parts may themselves need to be developed and specially manufactured. In cases involving long lead-time items, procurement planning occurs long before the items are needed on the project, in order to initiate the design and procurement processes for those items. If equipment or parts are not available when needed, the project schedule slips and costs rise.

Logistics Plans

Especially for construction projects, logistics planning is critical. The timing, transportation, delivery, storage, and usage of project materials, supplies, parts, or equipment must be planned, coordinated, and managed for the project to be successful. Unavailability or damage during shipment, storage, or handling causes major problems at the job site. These same issues apply to any projects involving large quantities of procured materials or equipment—and one could argue that they also apply to large professional-skills outsourcing contracts.

This section of the PM plan includes plans related to the physical aspects of procurement: when items will be delivered by vendors; transportation and handling during shipment; warehousing, storage, kiting, and handling at the job site, including inspection, testing, and acceptance procedures; and distribution to project participants as needed for completion of project tasks. Systems and expertise needed to track, manage, and report status on procured items are identified, along with the schedule and approach for establishing those systems and functions. Responsibilities and procedures are identified and defined.

Logic and Schedules

All project work must be scheduled. Schedules include milestone lists, summary schedules, and detailed schedules. This section of the PM plan includes those schedules and the logic and network plans necessary to develop them.

Networks and Logic

Network planning is applied during early planning processes, so that activity relationships are identified, understood, and factored into the schedule. In their simplest form, network plans are simple flow diagrams displaying the order in which activities are to be performed, which activities cannot be started or completed before other activities are started or completed, and what activities must be completed before the overall project is complete. Logical network plans are important for project planning, but they are complex, detailed, and cumbersome for displaying schedule information. While networks are necessary, they may be referenced in the PM plan or attached later. The PM plan, however, should describe the logic applied and establish networks as the basis for the schedules.

Summary Schedules

The summary schedule corresponds to the upper levels of the WBS and identifies key milestones. Additional levels of schedules are developed as required and are compatible with each other, the management summary schedule, and the WBS. Schedules provide information for measuring physical accomplishment of work, as well as identifying potential delays.

Schedules normally include lists of tasks and activities, dates when those tasks are to be performed, durations of those tasks, and other information related to the timing of project activities. Milestone schedules are simple lists of top-level events (i.e., the completion of the key tasks or activities) with planned dates. These same lists are used for reporting schedule progress by adding a column for completion date information.

Milestone schedules, networks, bar charts, and activity listings are included in the PM plan. Detailed schedules may be provided in the Appendix. They are maintained current over the life of the project to reflect current working plans. Schedules also normally identify critical activities so they can receive special attention.

Cost Estimates, Budgets, and Financial Management

Every PM plan includes a cost estimate, a budget, or both. The cost estimate is normally in table format and includes a summary of costs for each major task or element of the project. Financial management includes systems and procedures for establishing budgets, for reporting financial information, for controlling costs, and for managing cash flow.

Cost Estimates

The most straightforward method of estimating costs is to use the WBS and schedule. Each element of the WBS or each activity in the schedule or network can have a cost associated with it. Therefore, the approach is to go down the list of activities or WBS elements and estimate the cost for each one. Costs are estimated by identifying the resources needed for each activity, in what quantities, and at what price. The pricing of the resources depends on the timing, so normally a cost estimate is not finalized until the project activities have been scheduled.

Budgets

Budgets are cost estimates that have been approved by management and formally established for cost control. Actual costs are compared to budgets as the project is completed, to identify variances and potential problems and to provide information on what the costs will be. The budgeting process includes extensive reviews and revisions of the cost estimates, to arrive at the final budget figures.

Financial Management

The requirements, systems, procedures, and responsibilities for project financial planning, management, and control are addressed in this section. Financial control includes cash flow management as well as conventional cost control (standard cost accounting, cost performance reporting, and cost productivity assessment).

Cash flow management involves traditional income and expenditure reporting and analysis. On most projects, funding and funds management are critical, representing the timing at which resources can be scheduled and work accomplished. Cash flow planning and reporting procedures and responsibilities are established in the PM plan, ensuring that funds are available as needed on the project.

Risk Analysis and Contingency Plan

Projects need to be assessed to identify areas containing high degrees of risk—for instance, those activities associated with new research, technical developments, or other tasks that have never been done before. Risk may also be associated with the external environment, such as economic conditions, political uncertainties, weather, geography, public opinion, or labor-related factors. This section of the PM plan provides an opportunity to consider project risks and to develop contingency plans. Topics suggested for this section are risk identification, risk analysis, risk minimization plans, and contingency plans and reserves.

Risk Identification

The WBS is used to identify risks associated with specific elements of the project. Each WBS element is assessed for risk. Risk is higher when new or unproven technologies are required. Greater uncertainty is also expected when all aspects of a task or project element are not yet planned in detail. Finally, risk is generally higher during the early stages of a project or task than when nearing completion.

Risk Analysis

Risk analysis includes a detailed discussion of the risk, including both internal and external factors. An impact table is prepared with factors assigned based on technology status, planning status, and design/project status. Finally, the potential cost and schedule impact is assessed. The impact table includes a worst-case cost estimate for each of the project elements included.

Risk Minimization Plans

Once the risks to the project have been identified and assessed, strategies are needed to minimize them: technology development, modeling, demonstrations, peer reviews, replanning, changes in project logic, reorganization of project participants, contractual changes, etc. The idea is to adapt a proactive, planning-based approach to risk assessment and to minimize project risks through specific actions.

Contingency Plans and Reserves

Changes in technical performance or schedules require a reevaluation of contingency reserves. Risk analysis can be performed in conjunction with cost estimating when estimates of contingency reserves are calculated. Cost estimates may be inaccurate for various reasons, such as engineering errors or oversights, schedule changes, cost or rate changes, external factors, construction or implementation problems, or estimating errors. The amount of reserves depends on the funds available, overall riskiness of the project, and the management approach.

Quality and Productivity Plan

Project management planning itself is a productivity improvement process. This section of the PM plan is where total quality management planning, quality management systems planning, quality assurance/quality control planning, technical performance measurement, and productivity improvement are discussed.

Total Quality Management Planning

The steps to be taken for implementing Total quality management (TQM) on a project are described in this section. TQM in a project environment requires clear policy statements, attention by senior company management, the commitment of the project manager, and the involvement of all project participants. Training programs and major improvements in procedures, systems, and approaches may be involved.

Quality Management Systems Planning

While quality may be defined in terms of technical performance of end products, value to the customer is now regarded as a key measure. Technical quality and customer satisfaction are increased by establishing systems and procedures for ensuring high performance. That means well-defined project requirements or specifications, systems for comparing progress to specifications, and effective feedback mechanisms. This part of the PM plan contains or refers to quality management systems or procedures to be utilized on the project.

Quality Assurance/Quality Control

Quality assurance (QA) is a process of establishing performance standards, measuring and evaluating performance to those standards, reporting performance, and taking action when performance deviates from standards. Quality control (QC) includes those aspects of QA related to monitoring, inspecting, testing, or gathering performance information, as well as actions needed to ensure that standards are met. QA and QC both require discipline and systematic approaches to defining and measuring technical performance. For large projects, formal systems and procedures are necessary, and these can be described or listed in this section of the PM plan.

Technical Performance Measurement

Technical performance measurement is the evaluation of performance against standards, criteria, or requirements established for a project. A procedure is established to evaluate each element of the WBS for technical performance status and for taking corrective action. Evaluation can be by a design committee, chief engineer, QA organization, or group of technical experts. The plan for technical performance management is included or referenced in the PM plan.

Productivity Improvement

Productivity improvement, or reductions in the time and costs to accomplish project objectives, also calls for planning and monitoring. Plans, schedules, and cost estimates can be evaluated for process improvements and efficiencies and performance improvements. Cost-saving methodologies, such as value engineering, can be applied to designs and technical plans. Cost estimates can be subjected to "sensitivity analysis," which identifies areas of the project where the most probable savings can occur. Company procedures, systems, or processes can be reassessed for improvements regarding paperwork, staffing, or time. New products, methodologies, or technologies might increase productivity. Employees also may be encouraged to identify productivity improvements, cost savings, or time-saving processes. This section of the PM plan identifies which of those strategies are used on the project.

Environmental, Safety, and Health (ES&H) Protection Plan

This section identifies all the environmental compliance laws, regulations, and requirements that must be satisfied on the project, and how they will be complied with. It describes the steps to be taken by the project team to protect the environment, the public, and project participants, including safety and health protection plan, ES&H management/information systems, and emergency preparedness.

Safety and Health Protection Plan

The PM plan contains the project safety plan. Each element of the WBS is assessed for safety issues, including potential hazards, opportunities for accidents, and government regulatory requirements. The systems, procedures, and steps to be employed to ensure a safe workplace are also described.

ES&H Management/Information Systems

The systems and procedures to be used for managing and reporting information related to environmental, safety, and health (ES&H) activities on the project are identified and described. Responsibilities and interfaces with outside organizations, often key to compliance with ES&H regulations, are also documented. A matrix chart is used for projects where multiple regulations, systems, and organizations are involved.

Emergency Preparedness Plan

Emergency preparedness involves addressing such issues as fires, tornadoes, floods, power outages, sabotage, terrorism, and the loss of key personnel. Preliminary planning identifies the people who will take charge in each type of emergency. Public services such as fire stations, ambulances, hospitals, police, and evacuation means are identified.

Security Plan

Every project involves security issues that need to be dealt with, including physical security, property protection, and information security.

Physical Security

Plans for providing physical security (gates and fences, guards, electronic access systems or surveillance devices, badges, or contracted security services)—including requirements, responsibilities, tasks and activities, timetables, and procedures—are described or referenced in the PM plan.

Property Protection

Property protection against loss, theft, or damage is needed whenever a project involves acquisition or use of materials or equipment, including hardware, software, vehicles, tools, or other devices. Property protection may also require detailed property management information systems, procurement tracking systems, training, and experienced personnel.

Information Security

For some projects, information security may be the most important security issue facing the project manager. As a project proceeds, key information is generated, including technical information (i.e., design specifications, vendor data, engineering data), cost and schedule information, contract-related information, correspondence, plans, and progress information. This section of the PM plan contains the plans for insuring against loss or damage of key project information. An information security manager for the project may be needed to control access to information; to coordinate passwords, codes, and file names; to ensure backup systems and databases; and to ensure proper usage of procedures and protocols.

Project Planning, Control, and Administration Plan

This section describes the management approaches and systems to be used for managing the project. The PM plan represents the major plan for the project, yet it may be one of many plans prepared—especially if the project is large, complex, and involves many different organizations. If more than one management plan is prepared for the project, they are identified and described here. On large projects a hierarchy of management plans is common, with each participating organization preparing a management plan for its portion of the project. A table should be prepared identifying all the plans to be prepared and their relationship to one other.

Detailed Work Package Plans

Work packages are the lowest level of project work assigned to individuals who then plan and manage detailed project activity. Project activity at the lowest levels of the WBS is planned in work packages, which describe in detail the work scope, schedules, and costs associated with the work. Work package plans are summarized and consolidated to support the information contained in the PM plan. The work package planning process to be used, the assignment of responsibilities, the formats to be used, and the planning procedure can be described in this section of the PM plan.

Project Control

Project control involves procedures, processes, and methods used to determine project status, assess performance, report progress, and implement changes. In addition, on large projects there may also be the need for a formal work authorization process, which documents task agreements prior to the start of work.

Work Authorization

Work authorizations are documents that describe work to be performed, have cost estimates (or budgets) and scheduled performance dates identified, and are negotiated and agreed to by a "requesting" organization and a "performing" organization. Work authorizations are common in large companies doing business with the U.S. government. The work authorization forms and procedures to be used on a project are described in this section of the PM plan.

Cost and Schedule Performance Measurement

The methods and procedures to be used to assess schedule status and how much work has been accomplished over the life of the project are described in this section of the PM plan. For instance, the process and responsibilities for assessing the completion status of each activity in the project schedule are outlined here, as well as any methods to be used for measuring quantities of work completed. Systems and procedures for cost collection, accounting, and reporting are outlined in this section as well. The procedures, systems, and responsibilities for administering and controlling changes to a project's work scope, schedule, and budgets (or cost estimates) are also described in this section of the PM plan. Formal change control systems are required to ensure that plans, baselines, design, and documentation are not revised without appropriate reviews and approvals.

Project Administration

This section of the PM plan describes the reports, meetings, and record-keeping processes associated with project management and administration. The types of management reports are identified and described here. Formats, procedures, and responsibilities are outlined and defined for major reports. A list of reports to be prepared, with distribution and responsibilities identified, can be included in this section or in the Appendix. Reports for both internal and external distribution should be included. Major management meetings to be conducted are identified, including review meetings with customers or management, status meetings, change control meetings, and special meetings to transmit key information. In addition, the system, procedures, and responsibilities for administrative records management on the project. This may be addressed in the document control section of the PM plan, or it can be included here with reference to the overall project systems.

This section may also contain an overview of procedures and responsibilities associated with administering key contracts on the project. Performance measurement and reporting by contractors is described, contract requirements identified, and subcontract management activities identified, including site visits, meetings, and technical reviews.

Documentation and Configuration Management Plan

Documents include plans, administrative documents and records, technical data, engineering and construction documents, procedures and systems-related documents, reports, and correspondence. This section of the PM plan identifies the documents to be prepared on a project and establishes the administrative approach, systems, and procedures to be used to manage that documentation.

For each major element of the WBS, a list of documents or type of paperwork for each participating functional organization is developed. That list includes documents related to management and administration; technical specifications and requirements; R&D, design, and engineering; manufacturing; construction; start-up; and operation or production. The list also includes contracts, compliance documents, and documents prepared by entities external to the project.

Responsibilities for dealing with the documents are identified, from initial preparation of the documents through changes, reviews and approvals, and a distribution list. In addition, document storage and control is addressed. A document responsibility matrix is a simple, straightforward method for communicating the plan for document control. The responsibility matrix lists the documents, then identifies responsibilities for document preparation, revisions, approvals, distribution, and storage.

Document storage is a huge issue for large projects, no less now than when it entailed buildings full of file cabinets. Document storage issues include document identification, version control, data security, and so on.

A document numbering system can be based on the WBS, the project organizational structure, the date, or any other logical order. The numbering system is then used to organize and store project documents and to find the documents over the life of the project.

Security against fire, damage, or theft is also addressed and described in the PM plan, as are backup files for automated data storage systems. Access requirements and plans are also described, including a list of those who will need access, what kind of access (i.e., online, complete, extracts, etc.) frequency, and how that access will be monitored.

The procedures for project document control are identified and described in the PM plan.

Configuration Management

Configuration management can be defined as the process of identifying and documenting the functional and physical characteristics of products, facilities, or systems; of controlling changes to those items and associated documents; and of reporting status of the items or changes to those who need to know. (Note: The term "configuration management" has had other precise connotations on IT projects. When communicating between project management and IT personnel, be cautious in your use of terms to avoid misunderstanding.) The objective is to keep project technical documentation consistent with the project systems, products, hardware, or facilities involved. Where a comprehensive document control system has been implemented, configuration management can be an expansion of the processes for the technical documents and systems.

Configuration management plans include configuration management requirements, configuration identification, configuration control, and configuration status reporting.

On projects for government agencies, configuration management requirements may include compliance with detailed laws, regulations, or contract clauses. This is especially true in such industries as nuclear power, military/weapons systems and procurement, space-related contracting, transportation, and other areas potentially involving environmental, health, or safety issues concerning the general public.

The technical systems, components, facilities, and products that comprise the project and associated technical documents are identified in the PM plan. Technical baseline documents consist of the documents associated with research, design, engineering, fabrication, installation, construction, start up, and operation of each of the technical systems/components of the technical baseline.

Configuration control involves the procedures for administering and controlling changes to the technical baseline and associated documents. Configuration control parallels the more general document control process but places more emphasis on controlling changes to the design and technical configuration of the systems themselves. The configuration control section identifies how changes to the technical baseline are made and fixes the associated responsibilities and procedures for keeping technical documents current. Procedures and responsibilities are identified in a matrix format along with necessary narrative explanations.

A method is established for communicating configuration changes and status information to those who need that information. In general, a procedure with distribution lists for specific documents or system will suffice, provided that responsibilities are assigned for distribution of technical information and documentation.

APPENDIX

The Appendix provides a place to put supporting information, allowing the body of the

PM plan to be kept concise and at more summary levels. In some cases, where a section of the PM plan is prepared as a separate document (for instance, when required by law), it can be included in the Appendix and referenced in the PM plan.

DISCUSSION QUESTIONS

❶ The Project Management Plan combines two plans sometimes prepared separately. What are the advantages for joining those plans?

❷ What are the drawbacks of joining the two types of plans?

❸ What differences are there in the logic of the Project Management Plan as compared to the *PMBOK® Guide?* Why do you think the plan outline differs?

RECOMMENDED READING

Bellows, Jerry L., and Stephen L. Osborn. "Development of the Project Management Plan." 1980 *Engineering Foundation Conference,* August 10-15, 1980 (Henniker, N. H.: AACE, 1981).

Cleland, David I., and William R. King, eds. *Project Management Handbook, Second Edition,* New York: Van Nostrand Reinhold, 1988.

Cori, Kent. "Project Work Plan Development." 1980 *Proceedings of the Project Management Institute.* Drexel Hill, Penn.: PMI, 1989.

Dinsmore, Paul C. "Planning Project Management: Sizing up The Barriers." 1984, *Proceedings of the Project Management Institute.* Drexel Hill, Penn.: PMI.

DOE Order 4700.1. *Project Management System.* Washington, D.C.: U.S. Department of Energy, March 6, 1987.

Humphreys, Kenneth K., ed. *Project and Cost Engineers Handbook, Second Edition,* New York: American Association of Cost Engineers/Marcel Dekker, 1984.

Kerridge, Authur E., and Charles H. Vervalin, eds. *Engineering and Construction Project Management.* Houston: Gulf Publishing, 1986.

Kerzner, Harold. *Project Management: A Systems Approach to Planning, Scheduling and Controlling, Third Edition,* New York: Van Nostrand Reinhold, 1989.

Lock, Dennis, ed. *Project Management Handbook.* London, England: Gower, 1987.

Pells, David L. "Project Management Standards at the Idaho National Engineering Laboratory." *Proceedings of the Northwest Regional Symposium,* jointly sponsored by the American Association of Cost Engineers and the Project Management Institute, April 22, 1988, Vancouver, Canada. Drexel Hill, Penn.: PMI.

CHAPTER 6

Controlling Costs and Schedule: Systems That Really Work

▶RALPH D. ELLIS, JR.,
UNIVERSITY OF FLORIDA (RET.)

In the design and implementation of a project cost control system, the individual characteristics of the organization performing the project and of the project itself must be considered. However, the following criteria should be considered regardless of the specific situation:

▶ *Validity.* The information reported must accurately reflect actual versus estimated costs.

▶ *Timeliness.* The cost data must be reported soon enough so that managerial action can be taken if a problem arises.

▶ *Cost-effectiveness.* Collection and reporting of cost data must be done in a way that does not hinder project progress.[1]

Cost control systems can work if they are set up with these criteria in mind. This chapter covers how to design and implement an effective project cost control system. The examples given are drawn from the construction industry, yet these same principles are applicable to other types of projects.

DEVELOPING A PROJECT COST CONTROL SYSTEM

Establishing a Project Cost Control Baseline

The project cost control baseline is developed from the project cost estimate.[2] Initially, during the conceptual phase, the cost estimate exists only as a preliminary or order of magnitude estimate;[3] as the engineering design progresses, more precise estimates of cost can be developed. A detailed cost estimate, based upon work quantities determined from completed project drawings and specifications, provides the most precise estimate of cost. It is this detailed cost estimate that forms the basis of the project cost control baseline.

However, the detailed cost estimate often cannot be directly used as a control budget. Usually some transformation is required. For example, for bidding or negotiating purposes, the estimate may originally have been organized in a form convenient for the project owner. The project contractor may find it advantageous to reorganize the estimate into a form that matches his or her cost control preferences. Also, the level of detail provided by the estimate may not be appropriate for the control budget.

Several factors should be considered when deciding upon the appropriate level of detail for the cost control budget:

▶How many individual cost elements can the office and field personnel be expected to break actual project costs into for reporting purposes?

▶How many individual cost elements can the project management team effectively review and monitor?

▶How can Pareto's Law be taken into account—that 80 percent of the total project cost is probably represented by only 20 percent of the cost items?

The answers to these questions and the selection of an appropriate level of detail depends upon the characteristics of the project and upon the management resources allocated to manage the project. If, for instance, a cost engineer is assigned to assist the project manager in supervising the collection and reporting of cost control information,

Detailed Cost Estimate

Cost Code Number	Item	Material	Labor	Total
03	Concrete			
03100	Concrete Formwork	71920	125602	197522
03200	Concrete Reinforcement	208105	83100	291205
03310	Cast in Place Concrete	391400	42700	434100
03350	Concrete Finish	0	18900	18900
04	Masonry			
04210	Brick Masonry	4200	3510	7710
04220	Concrete Unit Masonry	2810	3640	6450
04420	Cut Stone	400	720	1120

→

Cost Control Budget

Cost Code Number	Item	Material	Labor	Total
03100	Concrete Formwork	71920	125602	197522
03200	Concrete Reinforcement	208105	83100	291205
03310	Cast in Place Concrete	391400	42700	434100
03350	Concrete Finish	0	18900	18900
04000	Masonry	7410	7870	15280

FIGURE 6-1. **TRANSFER OF PROJECT COST ESTIMATE INFORMATION TO THE COST CONTROL BUDGET**

greater detail may be practical. Generally, it is desirable to maintain more detail on cost items that represent a more significant portion of the project cost.

Consider a project in which structural concrete represents a large percentage of the total project cost. In this case the structural concrete costs should be broken down into a number of cost subaccounts categorized by work operation, such as formwork, reinforcing, and concrete placement. Further subclassification by structural component, such as foundation, slabs, columns, and beams, may also be appropriate. On the other hand, if only a relatively small percentage of the total project cost involves masonry, then all of the masonry cost items in the estimate might be transferred to the project cost control budget as a single summary. Figure 6-1 provides an illustration of how the project cost estimate information might be transferred to the cost control budget.

Establishing a standard organizational listing and coding of all cost items is a prerequisite to the preparation of both the detailed cost estimate and the cost control budget. The standard organization listing consists of a comprehensive list of all conceivable cost items. In the construction industry, such a list might be prepared using the Masterformat published by the Construction Specifications Institute (CSI).[4] The CSI Masterformat provides an extensive classification and coding of cost items relevant to the construction industry and is widely used by manufacturers, architects, contractors, and other professionals.

The standard cost code system should be tailored to the organization's needs. Some cost items found in the CSI standard can be deleted if not within the scope of work performed. Other cost categories can be expanded to provide additional detail in critical areas.

The level of detail resulting from the cost coding system can be adjusted by means of a system of account hierarchy. The highest category is represented as a major account. Each major account is subdivided into subaccounts and subsubaccounts. Cost data can be summarized and collected at any level within the account hierarchy. The CSI contains sixteen major cost accounts. Figure 6-2 provides an example of how the account hierarchy system can be used.

Just as the standard cost code is tailored to the general operation of the organization, the project cost control budget is tailored to satisfy the cost control needs of the specific project. Cost control account categories and levels of detail are matched to the particular characteristics of the project. Then the cost figures are transferred from the cost estimate to the appropriate account in the cost control budget.

A well-designed and accurately prepared cost control budget is an essential requirement for a successful project cost control system. The cost control budget becomes a cost baseline used as a benchmark for monitoring actual cost and progress during the entire project. The cost control budget is also an important ingredient for practically all of the project management activities.

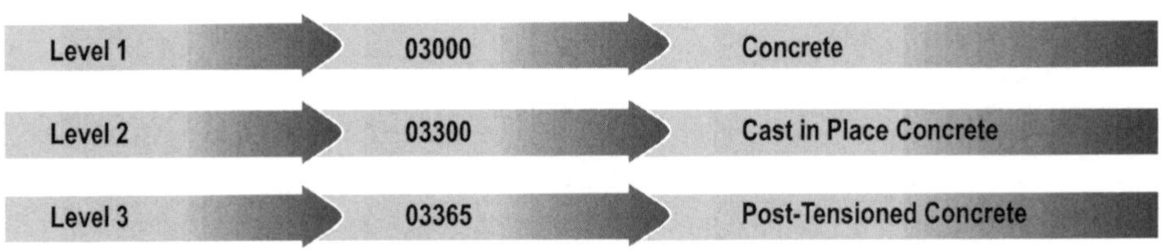

FIGURE 6-2. **EXAMPLE OF COST CODE HIERARCHY**

Collecting Actual Cost Data

The collection of project cost data falls within the scope of activities normally conducted by the organization's accounting system.[5] Project costs are collected, classified, and recorded as a routine accounting function. Individual project costs, when collected at the organizational level and compared with overall income, are a basic component in determining profitability of the enterprise.

Although job cost accounting is a fundamental part of most accounting systems, the job cost accounting format used frequently does not satisfy the requirements of project cost control. Classification and level of detail used in the accounting system may not match with the cost control budget developed for the project. For example, we may wish to examine the labor and material costs associated with a certain category of work tasks such as formwork for cast-in-place concrete. However, the job cost accounting system may provide only a summary of all concrete costs.

Obviously, the greatest efficiency is obtained when the accounting system can directly provide the information required by the cost control system. A great deal of progress has been made in this area, particularly with the use of computerized cost accounting systems. Increased flexibility in the assignment of cost account codes and the production of specialized reports have significantly improved recent computerized accounting packages.

However, as a practical matter, some of the detailed cost breakdown data required by the cost control system may have to be generated separately from the general accounting system. This involves reviewing source documents such as supplier's invoices, purchase orders, and labor time sheets at the project level. The cost data required for cost control purposes can be extracted and recorded in the cost control records.

Regardless of how the actual cost data are collected, they must be organized in accord with the project cost control budget. Comparisons of actual to budget costs can be made only when both categories of costs are classified, summarized, and presented in identical formats. We do not want to compare apples with oranges.

Determining Earned Value

Earned value is the portion of the budgeted cost that has been earned as a result of the work performed to date. Cost values originally assigned to the various items in the cost control budget represent total costs. However, as work on the project progresses, we must periodically compare actual costs with budget costs. In order to make this comparison, the amount of earned value of the total budget must be determined.

Several methods are available for measuring project progress. Each method has different features and provides a somewhat different measure of progress. Sound managerial judgment must be applied no matter which method is used. Progress estimates require honest and realistic assessment of the work accomplished versus the work remaining.

Some of the more common methods of determining earned value are as follows:

▶ *Units completed.* This method involves measuring the number of work units that have been accomplished and comparing the number of completed units with the total number of units in the project.[6] No subtasks are considered, and partially completed units are generally not credited. For example, suppose that 420 linear feet (LF) of 4-inch diameter steel pipe has been installed. If the total project requires 2,100 LF of pipe, then the percentage of completion is 20 percent (420 LF divided by 2,100 LF).

▶*Incremental milestones.* When the work task involves a sequential series of subtasks, the percentage of completion may be estimated by assigning a proportionate percentage to each of the subtasks.[7] For example, the installation of a major item of equipment might be broken down as follows:

- Construct foundation pad 10 percent
- Set equipment on foundation 60 percent
- Connect mechanical piping 75 percent
- Connect electrical 90 percent
- Performance testing and start up 100 percent.

Percentage of completion is estimated by determining which of the milestones have been reached. The accuracy of this procedure depends upon a fair allocation of percentage to the subtask in relation to costs.

▶*Cost to complete.* When properly applied, this method can provide the most accurate representation of project cost status.[8] The cost to complete the remaining work for a given task is first estimated. This detailed cost estimate utilizes both the original cost estimate and any historical cost data acquired so far on the project. The idea is to develop the best possible estimate of the cost required to complete the task. The percentage of completion is calculated as follows:

$$\text{Percentage of Completion} = \frac{\text{Actual Cost to Date}}{\text{Actual Cost to Date} + \text{Estimate Total Cost}}$$

For example, if the actual cost to date for structural steel erection is $18,500 and the estimated cost to complete the task is $6,500, the percentage of completion is calculated as follows:

$$\text{Percentage of Completion} = \frac{18{,}500}{18{,}500 + 6{,}500}$$

$$\text{Percentage of Completion} = 74 \text{ percent}$$

With each of the methods used to estimate the percentage of completion, earned value is calculated as the percentage of completion times the original budget cost for the task.

Reporting and Evaluating Cost Control Information

Cost control status reports can be custom-tailored to suit the preferences of individual managers and to accommodate specific project differences. However, in general, cost status reports should provide an item-by-item comparison of actual cost to earned value.[9] Estimated cost to complete and projected total cost can also be shown. Variations from the cost budget can be presented as a percentage or as an actual value, and categorical

Project: New River Office Complex								Period Ending: 09/30/92	
Item	Cost Code Number	Total Budget Amount	Percentage Complete	Earned Value	Actual Cost	Percentage Variance	Variance Cost	Estimated Cost to Complete	Projected Total Cost
General Requirements	1000	$ 48,523	55.2%	$ 26,785	$ 22,478	16.1%	$ 4,307	$ 40,721	$ 63,199
Site Work	2000	478,925	98.1	469,825	458,799	2.3	11,026	467,685	926,484
Concrete	3000	798,147	74.6	595,418	762,396	-28.0	(166,978)	1,021,979	1,784,375
Masonry	4000	589,991	26.2	154,578	156,887	-1.5	(2,309)	598,805	755,692
Metals	5000	387,240	58.0	224,599	206,251	8.2	18,348	355,605	561,856
Carpentry	6000	142,364	12.0	17,084	16,841	1.4	243	140,342	157,183
Moisture Protection	7000	98,755	0.0						
Doors and Windows	8000	124,721	0.0						
Finishes	9000	211,766	0.0						
Specialties	10000	45,889	0.0						
Equipment	11000	267,451	0.0						
Furnishings	12000	89,010	0.0						
Special Construction	13000	15,600	0.0						
Conveying Systems	14000	82,710	0.0						
Mechanical	15000	1,752,335	12.5	219,042	219,042	0.0	0	1,752,336	1,971,378
Electrical	16000	987,143	18.9	186,570	186,570	0.0	0	987,143	1,173,713
Total Project		$ 6,120,570	33.2%	$ 1,893,901	$ 2,029,264	-7.1%	($ 135,363)	$ 5,364,616	$ 7,393,880

FIGURE 6-3. **MONTHLY COST CONTROL STATUS REPORT**

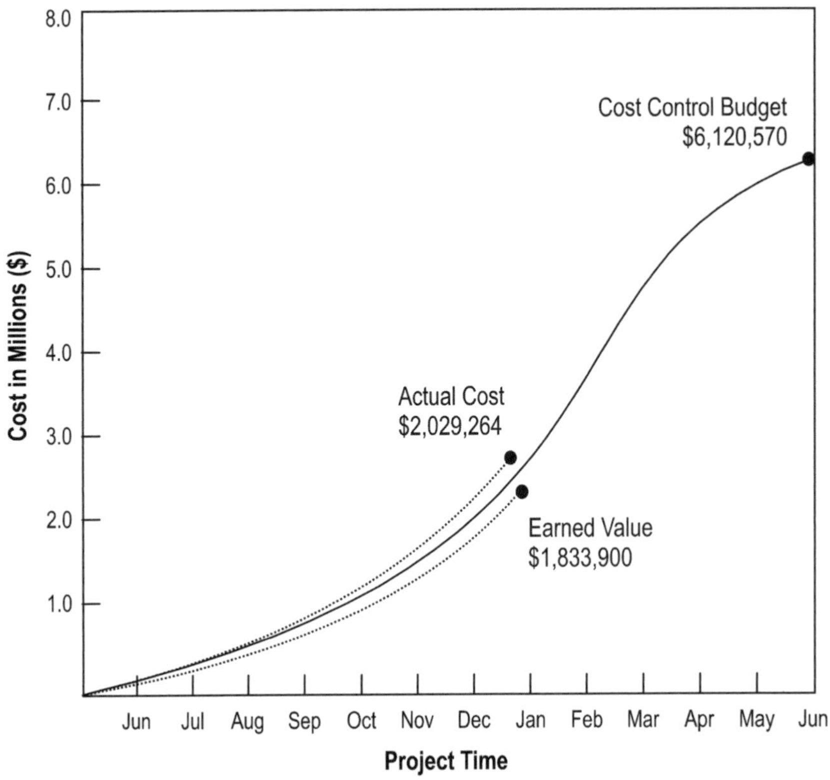

FIGURE 6-4. **COST-SCHEDULE GRAPH**

breakdowns of the cost status can also be shown. It is often useful to separate material, labor, equipment, and subcontract costs.

Figure 6-3 is an example of a monthly cost control status report. The figures listed as "Total Budget Amount" represent the originally estimated costs for each of the cost account categories. Actual costs to date are compared with earned values, and variances are listed. Estimated costs to complete are also given. The projected total cost has been calculated by adding the actual cost to the estimated cost to complete. This report could have been expanded to provide a separate listing of material, labor, equipment, and subcontract costs. The amount of detail can be structured to meet the requirements of the project manager. Managers will be particularly interested in the variance between actual cost and earned value, and the resulting total cost projection. Accuracy and timeliness are equally important in reporting cost control status. If the information is to be of any value to the project manager, it must be provided soon enough to allow for corrective action. Monthly cost control reports should be provided as soon as possible after the end of the month. The time lag between the cutoff of the cost period and production of the report should be as small as possible.

Material suppliers and subcontractors are normally paid monthly; therefore, a monthly cost report seems appropriate for summarizing these costs. However, labor costs are typically paid on a shorter interval, such as weekly. Labor costs are also likely to be more variable and consequently are normally the subject of greater management

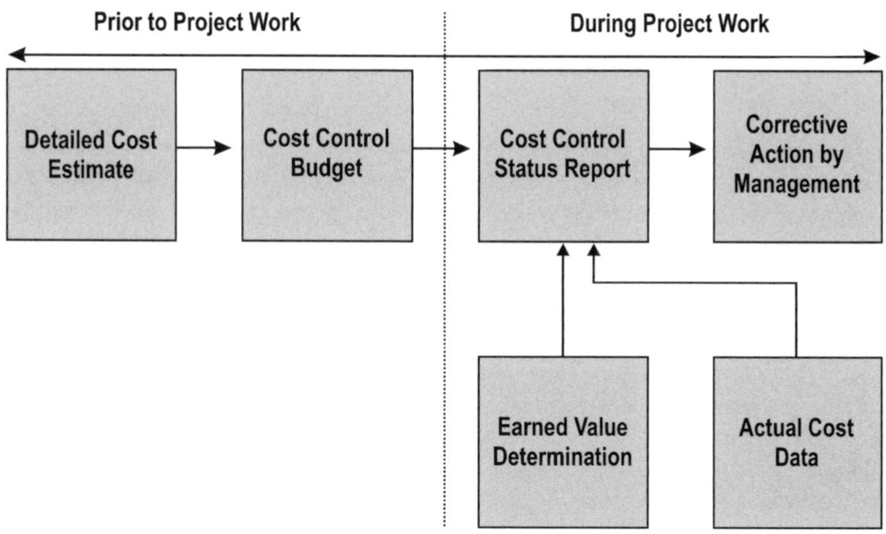

FIGURE 6-5. **ELEMENTS OF A COST CONTROL SYSTEM**

attention. It may be appropriate to generate weekly status reports of labor costs.

Graphical representations of the cost-schedule data are often useful in providing a quick visualization of cost control status. One of the most common is a cost-schedule graph in which actual and budget costs are plotted against performance time. Figure 6-4 is an example of a cost-schedule graph. This example provides a graphical representation of the data included in the cost control status report given in Figure 6-3. In this example, the project is approximately one week behind schedule in time, and total actual costs have exceeded the cost budget by 7.1 percent.

Taking Corrective Action

One of the primary functions of the cost control system is to identify problem areas to the manager early enough so that corrective action can be taken. Although we would not expect actual costs and earned values to be identical, a significant variance indicates a problem. Determining the source of the problem requires an investigation by the project manager. There are many possible causes, such as an estimating mistake, a change in material prices, a change in labor wage rates, or a change in work productivity. The cost control system cannot identify the cause of the problem, but tells the manager where to look for the cause. Additionally, the cost control system furnishes feedback to the manager, showing the effect of any corrective action.

Achieving Project Success by Controlling Costs

Project success depends to a great extent upon management's ability to control cost. Although there may be other important project goals, cost remains a universal measure of success. Projects with substantial cost overruns are rarely considered successful.

Maintaining cost control requires a well-designed and implemented project cost control system. A sound project cost control system performs four basic functions:

1. Establishes baseline cost.
2. Collects actual cost data.
3. Reports and evaluates (including earned value).
4. Takes corrective action.

The level of cost detail and the format of the report documents should be matched to the requirements of the specific project and the management team. Figure 6-5 provides an illustration of the elements involved in a project cost control system and their interrelationship.

Establishing an adequate project cost control system requires an investment. Project managers must take the time before starting project work to develop the structure of the cost control system. They must decide upon cost classification and the appropriate level of cost detail to be monitored. They need to work out actual cost collection procedures.

How will the cost control system interface with the organization's accounting system? Reporting frequencies, procedures, and formats must be determined. Administration of the cost control system also requires the allocation of staff time. However, if management is willing to commit the necessary systems, it is possible to have a project cost control system that really works. Operating without effective cost control is gambling in the dark.

DISCUSSION QUESTIONS

❶ What are the four basic functions of a project cost control system, and how are they interrelated?

❷ What are three common methods for determining earned value on a project? What are the relative advantages of each?

❸ How much cost control is enough? What factors should be taken into account when deciding on the right level of cost control?

REFERENCES

[1] D. Bain. *The Productivity Prescription.* New York: McGraw-Hill, 1982, p. 62.

[2] Construction Industry Institute. *Project Control for Construction.* Austin, TX: CII, 1989, p. 6.

[3] R. L. Peurifoy, and G. D. Oberlender. *Estimating Construction Costs.* New York: McGraw-Hill, 1989, p. 422.

[4] Construction Specifications Institute, *Masterformat.* Washington, D.C.: CSI, 1989.

[5] K. Collier. *Fundamentals of Construction Estimating and Cost Accounting With Computer Applications.* Englewood Cliffs, N.J.: Prentice-Hall, 1987, p. 44.

[6] Construction Industry Institute, p. 14.

[7] Ibid.

[8] Fails Management Institute, *Financial Management for Contractors.* New York: McGraw-Hill, 1981, p. 4.

[9] Powers, S. E., and B. H. Brown. *Walker's Practical Accounting and Cost Keeping for Contractors.* Chicago: Frank R. Walker, 1982, p. 116.

CHAPTER 7

Project Management Integration In Practice

▶GEREE STREUN, PMP, CSQE, ADVANCED NEUROMODULATION SYSTEMS, INC.

Integration was added to the project management body of knowledge as a ninth knowledge area with the 2000 edition of the *PMBOK® Guide*. This addition validated the experiences many project managers had throughout their careers. It underscored the important project management role of coordinating and creating linkages between the various kinds of knowledge, activities, and processes—the role of actually having to integrate all project processes to have an effective project meet its objective.

THE EVOLUTION OF THE INTEGRATION KNOWLEDGE AREA

The 2000 edition of the *PMBOK® Guide* attempted to define the project management processes necessary to integrate the project management activities needed on a project. The three processes described in that document included: a process that speaks about developing a plan, another about executing the project activities in the plan, and the last about coordinating changes across the project.[1] In describing integration as a knowledge area, PMI attempted to provide a foundation to ensure that project management activities are properly integrated and coordinated. However, the description of integration fell short of what a project manager actually needed to effectively manage a project. For example, no mention was made about the critical processes required to initiate all project management processes, to monitor the published plan, or to integrate the closing activities across all project phases.

In 2004, the *PMBOK® Guide* was expanded to provide more detail on the planning, executing, and controlling processes, plus more emphasis on two areas that had not been adequately addressed in any previous editions—the processes around project initiation and project closure.[2] Since a project has small chance of succeeding if either initiating or closing is done incorrectly, additional information about these two areas was provided in the update. The project manager now has specific processes to provide guidance for the initial activities needed to both develop the project charter and a preliminary project scope statement. The project manager can now find guidance for performing the integrative processes needed to produce a comprehensive project management plan, rather than nine individual documents that were implied in the prior release. There is also a clear emphasis on what must be done during project execution. While monitoring and controlling are given the emphasis they deserve for any size project, the integration activities needed to effectively close a project are also defined.

Project managers have learned through trial and error that project management is really an integrated series of processes and activities. These processes are iteratively applied by skilled project managers to effectively lead a project to its completion. On any given day the project manager—while planning and managing a project—must make decisions about needed resources, anticipate problems, and plan their resolution. Trade-offs made between conflicting objectives and the needed alternatives are also detailed within those groups. If the project processes have been properly integrated, the project manager will be tuned to all aspects of the project effort.

The need for integration among the project processes is evident wherever interfaces must be established for the processes to interact.[3] This integration need is evident in a situation such as when a project is assigned a specific delivery date without any regard for the overall product scope. The project manager must identify any risks resulting from this approach and communicate that information to the stakeholders. The stakeholders and the project manager use that information to negotiate a decision on whether the schedule should be extended or to reduce the overall product scope to meet the original schedule. The project manager usually performs many activities concurrently during initiation, including the following:

▶Members of the project team are assigned to initial activities to analyze the scope and attempt to understand the requirements, as well as any assumptions, constraints, and potential risks.

▶The project manager, working with appropriate stakeholders, establishes an initial schedule.

▶Another major effort a project manager performs is setting initial customer expectations. If done effectively, subsequent efforts are facilitated when a consensus decision among the stakeholders must be negotiated on a difficult request. A fine-grained application of this is communicating risk mitigations, including any risks that can't be avoided or resolved.

Companies typically perform a feasibility study after the company is stimulated and becomes aware of a perceived opportunity. The organization uses various methods to make a decision to start a project, while attempting to establish value returned against the projected costs. The company may consider a project for various reasons, such as:

▶The high cost of fuel requires a more efficient and clean energy source. Analysis would be done to determine is there is a real market demand before the project is considered.

▶A company does a business process analysis on its billing and receiving system and finds several areas that are costing the company a great deal of money; therefore a new project is established to improve that system.

▶A company wants to enter the worldwide market and finds they are required to adhere to a new more restrictive standard to even enter the market in Europe or Asia.

▶A start-up wants to build a new ultra-small implantable medical device to aid patient mobility. A project can be started to research this idea and the impact of adding a high-tech manufacturing facility.

The analysis process must also support picking alternative ways of executing the project to meet defined constraints, such as doing the project offshore or purchasing a turn-key system. The result is a Project Charter document and answers at a minimum the following questions[4]:

▶What is the relationship among what is being created and stimuli that causes the need?

▶What are the projected budget limits that will ensure a profit?

▶Who is the project manager and what is the authority level given for this project?

▶What is the initial milestone schedule and will it impact the cost?

▶What are the first cut assumptions and constraints identified for the project?

During the upfront effort the project manager produces a preliminary scope document that defines the project and its expected result.[5] This document addresses the project's characteristics and boundaries and its resulting products. Document content will vary depending upon the application area and project complexity; i.e., is the project building a terminal extension at an international airport, or is it building an online billing system for a pet supply company? The differences in product complexity and the required coordination efforts are very clear to see in this example. A skilled project manager must be able to identify the nuances in the scope of his/her project and respond appropriately to cover the project objectives; the product requirements; any acceptance criteria; assumptions, constraints, and risks; and any contract specifics, such as a non-negotiable delivery date.

The key tool a project manager uses to manage the project is the project management plan. However, the project manager must first perform all activities required to define, prepare, and integrate the activities in the project management plan. If is it an integrated cohesive plan, it will define all information about how the project will be executed, controlled, and closed. The required contents for a project management plan are fairly standard. It should essentially define what, who, the process, and when (with cost).[6]

▶***The what***—the project objective and deliverables.

▶***The who***—the personnel and resources required on the project.

▶***The process***—the project life cycle that will be incorporated into the plan. A diagram can be included to indicate needed process interactions.

▶***The when/cost***—the scheduled due date for each deliverable, including all major milestones.

▶The project's ***production and delivery locations.***

▶Last but not least, any ***communication requirements.*** What is needed to build the stakeholders' support and keep them involved?

The project application area directly affects project execution more than any other project process. Deliverables are produced through the project team's effort as directed by the project manager. Also, during execution the team is acquired and trained if needed. Goods and tools may also be obtained so they can be used during project execution. The project manager manages the team, as the approved changes to the product are received and implemented. While managing all of this, the project manager also manages any technical and organizational interfaces required between the project and the rest of the organization. Documents produced during the project effort are also updated.

Monitoring the project requires the project manager to collect, measure, and analyze information, and to assess measurements to determine trends. Those trends are analyzed and project performance may be modified to reverse those trends. The project manager compares status data to the project management plan to determine whether the project will meet its planned objectives on the specified dates. The project manager also keeps detailed information on any identified risks to ensure the mitigation plans are implemented quickly enough to minimize negative impact to the project.

Change control is a fundamental integration concept, as it touches all project processes. Changes to the project documents and other deliverables are controlled by continually assessing any factors that cause changes and by controlling attempts at adhoc changes. The project manager controls factors around change control by identifying and approving only those changes that need to occur. The project manager does that by ensuring that any changes are completely documented and approved prior to allowing a baseline update.

An automated configuration management system supporting version control is an effective and efficient way to manage changes to project artifacts. An automated system typically supports a high level of security and controls baseline changes. A change control board is typically implemented in many companies to support and enforce integrated change control at the highest level in the company. A corporate configuration policy defines the change control board's responsibilities and the needed interaction with all projects.

How does the project manager know when to start the efforts needed to close a project? A skilled project manager knows that every project process must be properly performed, since each is needed to successfully lead to project completion. The project manager uses the closing processes to establish the integrated procedures to close and transfer a project's deliverables. Administrative and contractual activities must be defined and completed to officially close out a project or a project phase. When the project is closed, documentation and project data must be transferred to the corporate knowledgebase for future reference. The finished product must also be formally accepted by the customer as one of the last closing activities.

These closing procedures also establish the activities required if the project has to be cancelled before it successfully achieves its objectives. If a project is cancelled, there may be penalties or legal ramifications for the company, so project records and data are transferred to the appropriate authorities in the company to resolve those issues.

CONCLUSION

In practice, of course, there is no clear definition of how to integrate project processes, activities, and knowledge. The project manager's role is made both challenging—and rewarding—by the skill gained while attempting to manage the project to facilitate and monitor efforts for success. In fact, a case can be made that integration is the capstone skill for excellent project managers—the skill that, more than any other, reflects the project management role.

It is also clear that the various activities that the project manager performs are not individual one-time events. Rather, they are overlapping integrated processes which occur at varying levels throughout the project. The project manager must be proficient in the knowledge areas; however the project manager's experience really shows when he/she can skillfully integrate those knowledge areas to effectively deliver the project's desired results.

DISCUSSION QUESTIONS

❶ Effective project integration requires emphasis on what?

❷ When is historical information useful during the project?

❸ What does integration mean in project management?

REFERENCES

[1] Project Management Institute (PMI), *A Guide to the Project Management Body of Knowledge, PMBOK® Guide, 2000 Edition,* Project Management Institute, 2000: p. 41.

[2] PMI, *A Guide to the Project Management Body of Knowledge, Third Edition,* Project Management Institute, 2004: p. 77.

[3] An American National Standard, IEEE Standard for Developing Software Life Cycle Processes, ANSI/IEEE Std. 1074-1991, published by Institute of Electrical & Electronics Engineers, Inc., 1992.

[4] PMI 2004, ibid.

[5] PMI 2004, ibid.

[6] An American National Standard, IEEE Standard for Software Project Management Plans, ANSI/IEEE Std. 1058.1-1987 (reaffirmed 1993), published by Institute of Electrical & Electronics Engineers, Inc., 1988.

CHAPTER 8

Project Scope Management In Practice

▶RENEE MEPYANS-ROBINSON
NASHVILLE STATE COMMUNITY COLLEGE

From company to company, although methodology and life cycle may vary, the most critical success factor of any project is comprehensive scope management. The project team formulates the processes, policies, methodology and life cycle to ensure that the work requirements meet the customer expectations. The project definition and scope control must be examined continuously throughout all phases of the project to minimize risks to the outputs.

The project manager is responsible for initiating the planning of the project. With upper management approval, the team can begin to conduct planning sessions to create a statement of work that outlines the customer requirements. The project manager, with the team's input, will analyze documentation and discuss the use of system tools, resources, schedules and budgetary costs to develop the scope management output.

One example of planning for an e-business online education tool involved upper management approval, buy-in from vendors, outsourcing some work elements, sound organization structure, staff support of business activities, change control process and customer input during the implementation phase of the project.

The scope management plan can be developed as an informal or formal document and have as many details to effectively describe the nature of the work to be completed. The document will be used to guide the team throughout all phases of the life cycle. The project manager may decide how the team will define the scope, develop the details of the scope statement, in what format the Work Breakdown Schedule will be designed and finalized, and the mechanism to verify and control the project scope. The document should be designed to focus on the delivery of only the work required and how to achieve the best results of the outcome the product or service.

THE VALUE OF SCOPE MANAGEMENT OUTPUTS

The scope management outputs are extremely important to the overall management of the project and contribute to how the project will be organized. With diligent planning, the project team will see the value of this planning process and outputs of the Scope Management plan. The team will execute and perform Scope Planning, Scope Definition, Create a Work Breakdown Schedule, Scope Verification, and Control. If the project manager eliminates any or part of these areas, the project could be comprised. The project team needs to ensure that each area is addressed and given appropriate attention for project success.

Scope Management Plan

The first output of scope planning is the scope management plan. The project manager should prepare the following:

▶A detailed process to determine the project scope, which is based upon the customers' expectations and team's input taken from similar projects.

▶The development of a Work Breakdown Structure (WBS) and identification of project deliverables.

▶A formalized scope verification process.

▶A written process to control project scope that is agreed upon by the principal stakeholders.

Some other elements of a scope management plan, particularly applicable to working on software development projects, would be to involve all departments, formalize all team rules and guidelines, keep teams small, enforce accountability, focus on long-term objectives during the implementation phases, and maintain a low profile on some aspects of the project. All of these processes and ideas need to be captured in a document or repository so the team can review and verify the work as it progresses. The technical document will be needed for the customer so it is a good process to begin documenting in the planning phase of the project. It will save the team time, eliminate duplication of work and ensure the product is clearly explained for the end-user.

Scope Definition

The second output of planning entails Scope Definition, which is the descriptive detail of the project goal. If the project extends beyond its identified scope, the increased risk is greater for failure. Once the project scope has clear and concise objectives, the team can identify the project assumptions and constraints that are outside the scope. Other documents the project team or specialist creates will aid in supporting the content, such as investment analysis portfolio, budget, software product plans, and market analysis and systems manuals.

What is the value of developing a sound project scope statement? If it is developed properly, everyone will clearly understand all the details of the project, the deliverables, and the boundaries. The product description helps to explain the details for completing the objective. There may be budgetary restrictions and definite limitations that prohibit the advancement of the product. The team has to be sensitive of the customer's constraints and assumptions, so as not to expand the product any further than guidelines and standards dictate, otherwise the deliverables and time/cost schedule may not be achieved. The entire project organization can impact the outcome if decision-making and actions are not followed according to the project plan. The team should begin to identify risks and issues that could cause any delays of the project. The project manager should seek approval during any changes and subsequent phases. Any scope deviations must be communicated immediately to all stakeholders, including the customer.

Work Breakdown Structure

The third output of planning is the development of the WBS, which outlines tasks to be carried out to meet the project objectives. To understand and distribute tasks to team members, the project manager conducts a session to find out what activities need to be accomplished under what phase. When this has been determined and the team has assigned the activities to the lowest level of work (also known as work packages), the project manager can begin to evaluate costs, assign resources, and create a time schedule to those activities. The WBS dictionary describes the component elements, list of associated activities, milestones, the start and end dates, resources required, technical references, and statement of work. Other pertinent documents include bill of materials and risk breakdown structure.

Scope Approval

Once the scope is developed, the elements are thoroughly discussed and agreed on by the project team, stakeholders, sponsor, and the customer. The definition is then signed off formally, and any changes are communicated through the project manager unless an advisory committee has been established to lead this effort. With the acceptance and signed approval of the scope, the scope management plan is the formal document that defines the processes outlined in the project plan. The project manager is responsible to ensure that this process is complete and monitored throughout all phases of the project. If any changes occurr, all information is documented and then communicated to all members of the project team. The customer is to be kept informed of these or any changes during any parts of the life cycle of the project; otherwise, scope creep will occur and put the project in jeopardy through increased risks and unnecessary costs to the project.

Scope Control

The last output of Scope Management is that of Scope Control. The project manager should have implemented a process to ensure the project's goal and objectives will be monitored throughout the project. The project manager must be made aware of any discrepancies of project activities or potential risks promptly that deviate from the baseline or work breakdown schedule, in order to minimize any delays to the schedule which can ultimately cause project failure. The scope management section of the project plan is a formalized document that captures the processes for handling the scope changes. It is the project manager's responsibility to provide guidance for any corrective action and means of communications to all team members involved at any level of the project. If any changes occur, the customer should be immediately informed to make future decisions about the project outcome. With adequate scope control mechanisms executed, the teams progress and performance can be measured. This will resolve any potential issues to the schedule and decrease resource conflicts.

Scope Verification

This process is carried out whenever one or more deliverables are ready to be handed over. It consists of obtaining the stakeholders' formal acceptance of the work completed.

IDENTIFYING THE DIFFERENCE BETWEEN PRODUCT AND PROJECT SCOPE

Project Scope includes all the work to deliver a project's product or service with the specified features and functions. The result could be a single product or have several components. The project will have a start and end date and possess unique characteristics or attributes that produce specific results during the life cycle.

For example, depending on the complexity or high degree of technical aspects of the project, it could be divided into phases for cost or tasks reasons. The innovation of a major system project, issues with contributing organizations, and/or economic risks are other reasons to separate areas into more manageable "chunks" for the team to complete successfully and on time.

Product Scope is the features, functions, and characteristics to be included in a product. The scope will be measured against the set product requirements and is managed throughout the life cycle.

HOW TO DEVELOP A SOUND SCOPE STATEMENT

The guidelines for a good scope statement are that it should be written in a clear, concise, non-technical language targeted for all audiences, in particular, upper management and the customer. The stakeholder and upper management must first understand the nature of the project or product and then be able to conceptualize the end product or service. They will not need to know all the specific activities surrounding the development phases, but are mainly interested in the cost-savings and the market share to match the corporate strategic vision and goal. If the executives can understand the value of the project, the funding and support will be contributed throughout the project. The open communications during all phases is essential for the success of the project and possible subsequent iterations phases.

The customer is more receptive to understand the current project status to make decision points in the planning stage. The customer needs to be able to analyze and research other options if the project is being delayed or if the market dictates other needs. Some corporations are very competitive and the timing and launch of a product is the critical contribution to its success factor.

The project team should obtain all of the customer's requirements and consider these guidelines when planning and creating a comprehensive scope statement:

▶Why are we initiating this project? The project justification statement will help to formalize any doubts of moving forward with the project or product.

▶What is the actual project or product that is being developed? A brief summary statement to explain the specifications.

▶How and what activities will be completed? State what the deliverables or milestones are in the intended project.

▶Quantifiable criteria for project success are documented and the objectives of the project specified.

▶Identify the assumptions and constraints that will not be included in the project requirements.

The steps of writing an effective scope statement should include a project name, date, the project manager's name, project justification, product description, deliverable/milestones, objectives, assumptions, constraints, any issues or risks, who wrote the statement and the date t was written, and the approval with a date. In addition, the project manager should include documents outlining risk analysis, feasibility studies, and financial cost-benefit methods.

A Well-Written Scope Statement: Some Positive Outcomes

The project team, stakeholders, and customer will have fewer questions if the scope statement has addressed all the important aspects of the project objectives. The customer requirements are covered within the Statement of Work and deliverables are projected. The well thought out plan will provide the project manager the guidelines to manage the project and customer expectations. The sound work breakdown schedule, proposed project budget and allocated resources provide the team with parameters to implement a quality product.

Within this scope statement, there are six indicators that can impact the outcome and success of the project. They are:

1. Integration of processes
2. Type of environment or culture
3. Upper management buy-in or support
4. Training and education available
5. Formalized methodology or project management office
6. Dedicated knowledgeable resources

Other factors to consider in selecting good competent team members to perform the work activities are:

1. Develop project plans and time schedule
2. Write documentation standards
3. Determine budget requirements
4. Write an excellent Scope Statement of Work
5. Create an environment to encourage team relationships
6. Motivate individuals to complete activities

The outcome will produce outstanding project results and a clear project approach to define business and technology issues. The content has definite inclusions and exclusions and set objectives. By using these techniques the project planning and control of the scope will be accomplished.

Does your Scope Management Plan meet customer expectations?

The project management team must identify the stakeholders early in the planning phase to determine the project requirements and verify the control of the activities. By conducting thorough scope planning sessions, the project manager will have a well-developed Scope Statement and Scope Management plan that meets the customer approval

1.	Vision	Image of a product
2.	Mission	Develop a strategy
3.	Objective	Long-term goal measured by qualitative and quantitative criteria
4.	Goal	Dedicated milestone
5.	Strategy	Action plan to obtain goal
6.	Organizational Structure	Alignment of resources
7.	Roles	Person responsible to perform activities
8.	Systems	Tools and techniques to achieve goal

FIGURE 8-1. **ELEMENTS OF PROJECT SCOPE**

and project expectations. Figure 8-1 shows a process chart that can help aid in the development of a project and can be used during the planning stage with the team to produce a successful project or product.

QUESTIONS FOR REFLECTION

Has the project manager reviewed the scope statement with the team, stakeholders, and customer? Have you prepared a well thought out definition of the scope of work and does it fit with the budget and time schedule? Prior to moving to the next phase, have the stakeholders, both internal and external in the process, accepted the scope management plan and scope statement? Do you have the necessary sign-off approvals from the management, stakeholders and customer? Do you feel you have spent adequate time in the planning session? Has the team gathered sufficient project requirements and completed enough research to fully understand the components of the project? If other departments are involved in the project, have they been a part of the planning process and do these cross-functional resources have prior approval to perform the work? Are the control measures in place to ensure scope creep does not occur? Does the project manager understand which areas may have flexibility in the schedule? Does the customer understand the project requirements? Does the customer have any budget, time restraints or quality issues for the product?

DISCUSSION QUESTIONS

❶ At the first milestone, the customer complains that the deliverable is incomplete. How would you address this?

❷ What is the role of scope management in improving customer satisfaction?

❸ For a project with which you are familiar, analyze the scope statement. Was it complete and accurate? What issues arose that might have been prevented by better scope management?

CHAPTER 9

Time Management in Practice

▶VALIS HOUSTON, PMP,
ACACIA PM CONSULTING

"Plan the work, work the plan." This simple phrase can be your guide through many difficult times in a project management career. The Time Management Knowledge Area should be applied with the support of a project scheduling tool. Of course, it can be done with 3x5 cards to gather information and then organized in a spreadsheet. However, the spreadsheet will only communicate the proposed plan. Once the project starts and the dynamics of a project ensue—dates slip, unplanned scope is added, resources are suddenly unavailable—managing from the spreadsheet will probably become quite frustrating. The plan will no longer be a tool to provide project tracking and oversight. At that point, you will have lost control of your project.

ACTIVITY DEFINITION

For any project manager just coming on board a project, the critical first steps are to learn about the people involved—both stakeholders and the project team—and to understand the issues that currently exist and exactly what the project is expected to deliver. These steps are forerunners to Activity Definition.

For the steps described in the PMI standard under the heading Activity Definition, you must have a clear understanding of the activities that are outlined in the WBS. This will become important as you identify the inter-dependencies among activities, as well as the type of resources that should be assigned to each of the activities. Start from the beginning, not the end, and resist the temptation to focus too heavily on dates. Although later it will be necessary to come back and look at how the "realistic" plan fits into the needs of the business, at this stage it is important to find out what your people believe are the necessary tasks required for project completion. This can also help to provide the ammunition that you need to fight for a date based on the effort involved.

Such activity definition can be done relatively easily in a project scheduling tool such as MS Project; using this tool will make it easier to accomplish the remaining tasks of Time Management. However, this task can also be done with Post-It notes or 3x5 cards. Give a descriptive title to the task and a brief definition, along with notes gleaned from the team. Detailed notes will be helpful, as you will come back to these notes throughout the project. There is a "notes" section for each task within MS Project to capture this information, or use the back of the 3x5 card.

At this point it is not imperative to have the entire team available; the focus is not on creating dependencies. The leads for each area (in an IT project these might be the Requirements Lead, Development Lead, Test Lead, Lead Architect, etc.) can provide enough input to develop the activities. Essentially, this initial meeting answers the question: What specific actions need to happen to deliver the product defined in the scope statement?

Keep milestones in mind, both external milestones to clients or upper management, along with internal milestones for the team.

Be cautious about identifying tasks that are too broad in scope; for example, "develop website" or "create design document." Dig into the details; push to understand what must be done and how it ties into other activities. If you know something needs to happen, but neither you nor your team lead can put your finger on it, create "placeholders." Keep these "to be determined" placeholders in the plan until you have fully fleshed these out. As you continue to refine the plan (and even after the plan is finished) you may expect to come across activities that were "forgotten" or "unknown" at this early stage of the project. Expect the plan to change.

ACTIVITY SEQUENCING

After developing an understanding of what needs to be done to make your project a success, the next step is understanding the dependencies between the activities. A network diagram (which can be created in a scheduling tool such as MS Project) visually displays how the work in a project comes together. Your project's network diagram will help to flush out the relationships between tasks within a team and dependencies of work between teams. As you focus on the workflow, look for areas where work can be done in parallel. If you don't have a project scheduling tool or are uncomfortable using it at this point, the 3x5 cards and/or Post-It notes that you used in Activity Definition can be placed on a wall or white board to facilitate team discussion.

Focus first on those tasks within a particular team of the project; i.e., developers, testers, etc. Questions such as "what happens after task X?" and "what do you need to get started with Task Y?" move the discussion along. Push for a healthy discussion on what is needed for each of the activities to get started. Are Activities X and Y needed for Z to start? Are there dependencies from outside this immediate team or even from outside the project that are required? For example, do the testers require access to test data that is created by another part of the company? Balance the push for details with the risk of documenting too much detail. One helpful guideline is to base the amount of detail on the complexity and length of the project. High complexity with a large variety of unknowns equates to the need to gather more detail. On a small project of a few months' duration, you can capture tasks of as little as a half-day duration if they are critical ones, but going into greater detail than that isn't recommended. Remember that this will become your plan, and the tracking and oversight of the project will be your responsibility and become administrative overhead for your project team to report out on. Don't make the plan overly burdensome to yourself and your project team.

Ask if tasks can start sooner, as opposed to a "Finish to Start" relationship, although this can be a tricky area. Performing tasks in parallel could potentially result in over-allocation of resources and/or cause more re-work than necessary if a problem occurs with the first task. Nonetheless, if the project is strapped for time or if, during the course of the project you find the project falling behind, knowing what tasks can be started before its predecessor is complete can be a problem-solving strategy that you may have to call upon. Identify these tasks, even if you elect not to perform them in parallel initially.

Beware of overlapping dependencies—tasks that have a Start-to-Start or Finish-to-Finish dependency. These can prove to be a choke-point in the timeline if resources are waiting for work to be completed; they can also be a cause for communication break-down between team members. You probably will not be able to avoid such activities, as they are inherent to all projects, but be sure to add a note that it can be a risk area and needs to be watched carefully.

To determine the sequence of events, bring in a few experts/leads from each sub-team to discuss the dependencies, paying special attention to what is being completed when. Again, as this will become your plan, do not be ashamed if everyone else in the room seems to understand and you don't. Keep asking until the sequence of events is clear. Start tying together activities that come out of these discussions. As you did within teams, push to understand if one team's activities can be started before another team'activity is complete. Is it possible, for example, to overlap Development and Integration Testing? Can completed modules be delivered to the Integration Test environment so that Integration testing can get started? Or is there something that precludes this from happening? Again, use the questions "what happens next?" and "what do you need to get started?"

If there is disagreement among the subteam leads, document any dissenting opinions. If the majority of the team can agree and any additional risks are documented, that should suffice. If not, as the project manager, the decision is yours to make. Investigate the issue further, but don't let issues during planning linger. Again, if necessary create placeholders in the plan for these unknowns and continue to push forward. Remember, the plan will change, so strive for the 80 percent solution.

ACTIVITY RESOURCE ESTIMATING

Activity Resource Estimating was added to Time Management in the 2004 revision of the standard, and with good reason. You cannot create a plan without taking into consideration the most important aspect: the people.

For each defined activity, the project manager will need to understand the type(s) and quantity of each skill set required. Typically Activity Resource Estimating concerns primarily human resources—the project team—but it could also refer to equipment resources. For example, if your project is producing a film, how many of a certain type of camera will be needed? Will they only be available during the mornings because another film will use those same cameras in the afternoon? Along the same line of thinking, you need to know if you will be able to fill all the necessary activities with a name from your project team. If your Team Lead needs more time to ascertain resource availability, assign a generic, yet descriptive resource to the task: "Sr. Java Developer" or "Jr. Tester" should suffice until the Team Lead can provide an exact name. Be sure to highlight this activity, as you will need to come back to it to assign a specific resource. If after reviewing the team's capacity the resource to fill that slot is not available, this is a red flag that you may have more on your hands than the project team can handle. Raise this issue early and try to obtain the necessary skill set from within your organization or, if feasible, from outside the company.

At times, it becomes necessary to assign a resource without fully knowing the details behind an activity. Do not let this be a reason to NOT assign a resource. Someone must be responsible for every activity. Push accountability down to the lowest level possible; ensure that these decisions are not done in a vacuum, but—at a minimum—with the support of the Team Lead for those resources.

Be sure to document any resource constraints that will impact effort, such as a shared resource who only has 60 percent of her time available for your project, or a resource who has 100 percent on your project but does not work on Fridays. Be sure to also capture holidays, vacations, and administrative time that will need to be allowed for during the course of the project. (This can be done in MS Project under the "Change Working Time" dialog box. Individual resource constraints can be applied as well as modifying the base calendar from an 8-hour day to a 7-hour day. If you are not using a scheduling tool this exercise can also be captured in a spreadsheet.)

There are three pieces of information needed to develop a schedule: The actual activities; resource estimating (knowing who will be working on those activities), and finally, the duration of the activities. Do not take Resource Estimating lightly, as not digging in and understanding the constraints and availability of your resources can have serious repercussions on the timeline that may not become known until it is too late.

ACTIVITY DURATION ESTIMATING

At this point, it begins to become apparent how all this planning results in a timeline. For each activity the scheduler needs to understand how much effort is required. Be careful to separate "duration" from "effort." For example, an activity with an effort of 10 days will take 12.5 days (duration) if the assigned resource can only give 80% of his time to your project. If the same 10-day activity has two full-time resources assigned, on the other hand, it is possible for it to be completed faster, with a duration of five days. This is why the Resource Estimating task is so important.

Activity Duration Estimating is not a one-time task. Plan to perform this exercise iteratively, at key points in the project—what the *PMBOK® Guide* refers to as "Progressive Elaboration." This simply means that as we learn more about "what" we are building (Requirements) and "how" we are building it (Design), we are able to refine these estimates and further define a timeline that is more accurate and more attainable.

Early on, the project manager will be asked to let upper management know when the project will deliver results. Progressive Elaboration will allow you to provide a more precise date on when the project will actually be delivered, but not until the project is sufficiently well along. This is the dilemma that faces many projects: committing to a date without having enough information about scope and resources. Although you will likely be told that these dates are just for planning purposes and the team won't be held to them, this is seldom the case. What can help is to instead provide a range of dates, and commit to providing better estimates as further information makes itself available, along the lines of +/- 200% after Inception phase (Deliverable = Scope document),

+/- 75% after Requirements (Deliverable = Requirements document), +/- 25% after Design (Deliverable = Design document), and so on.

There are quite a few estimating tools and techniques available, ranging from parametric estimating and Wide-band Delphi to 3-point estimating (Most likely, Optimistic, Pessimistic). Each company uses techniques that reflect the experiences (positive or negative) that they have had with these tools on past projects, and also reflect the maturity of the company's project management processes. Regardless of the technique utilized, having historical information on past projects will help determine if the inputs and outputs of this tool or technique make sense. It is important that you only lean on project information that is truly similar to your project.

Bottom-up estimating, paired with one of the techniques mentioned above or commonly used at your company, is the recommended approach as it focuses on the low-level details that can only come from your project team. The Time Management chapter of *The PMBOK® Guide* states: "When a schedule activity cannot be estimated with a reasonable degree of confidence, the work within the schedule activity is decomposed into more detail." Stress to the project team that these tasks will be worked by them and they will be held accountable for these estimates. Push for as much information as is appropriate at that particular phase of the project. If you have finished Design Reviews and the Development Lead is not able to provide estimates to a number of activities, then you need to go back to Design.

MS Project allows for the creation of columns in Gantt view in which you can assign "Duration" and "Effort." If using a spreadsheet, you can also update it similarly.

Be sure to keep all the documentation used in this process. As you progress through the project and refine the estimates, this documentation will help remind the team why they made certain decisions. This will help to further refine your estimates with the new knowledge that has been gained. It will also help to build your company's historical database or, if one does not exist, become the first project to go into a historical database.

SCHEDULE DEVELOPMENT

You have defined all the activities and documented all the predecessors and successors, a Resource Calendar is in hand, and you have allocated the proper duration for each activity. Now you are ready to create the schedule.

Remember that the schedule is meant to be updated and refined throughout the project. This first iteration will become the baseline. Unless something major in the project causes you to re-scope and change the baseline, this baseline will become the "square and level" by which progress is tracked.

When creating the schedule, start with external and internal milestones. All activities should support these milestones. Then apply your activities being sure to properly create Summary Level Tasks. Summary Level groupings are best done by subteam, even if it does not flow chronologically. As shown in Figure 9-1, Test Planning is being done during the Design phase, but it is still grouped under the Test Summary Task. This will make it easier for your subteams to quickly find activities related to them and for management to follow interrelated activities.

It is also a good idea to group milestones together and at the top of the schedule. This will provide easy access when you have to give an executive overview of your plan.

Now comes the step in which you apply the time constraints you documented during Activity Sequencing. "Start no earlier than" or "Start as soon as possible" will help to

ID	❶	Task Name	Duration	Baseline Start	Start	Baseline Finish	Finish
1		**My 1st Project**	**99 days**	**NA**	**Tue 12/14/04**	**NA**	**Fri 4/29/05**
2		**Milestones**	**78 days**	**NA**	**Tue 1/11/05**	**NA**	**Fri 4/29/05**
3		Baseline Req. Doc	0 days	NA	Tue 1/11/05	NA	Tue 1/11/05
4		Baseline Design Doc	0 days	NA	Fri 1/28/05	NA	Fri 1/28/05
5		Complete Dev. Item #1	0 days	NA	Wed 3/2/05	NA	Wed 3/2/05
6		Complete Dev. Item #2	0 days	NA	Fri 3/18/05	NA	Fri 3/18/05
7		Complete Dev. Item #3	0 days	NA	Wed 2/23/05	NA	Wed 2/23/05
8		Complete System Test	0 days	NA	Fri 4/29/05	NA	Fri 4/29/05
9							
10		**Requirements**	**21 days**	**NA**	**Tue 12/14/04**	**NA**	**Tue 1/11/05**
15							
16		**Design**	**13 days**	**NA**	**Wed 1/12/05**	**NA**	**Fri 1/28/05**
17		Create Design Doc	10 days	NA	Wed 1/12/05	NA	Tue 1/25/05
18		Walkthrough Design Doc	3 days	NA	Wed 1/26/05	NA	Fri 1/28/05
19		Baseline Design Doc	0 days	NA	Fri 1/28/05	NA	Fri 1/28/05
20							
21		**Development**	**35 days**	**NA**	**Mon 1/31/'05**	**NA**	**Fri 3/18/05**
22		**Development Item #**	**23 days**	**NA**	**Mon 1/31/05**	**NA**	**Wed 3/2/05**
23		Code	15 days	NA	Mon1/31/05	NA	Fri 2/18/05
24		Unit Test	8 days	NA	Mon 2/21/05	NA	Wed 3/2/05
25		**Development Item #**	**12 days**	**NA**	**Thu 3/3/05**	**NA**	**Fri 3/18/05**
26		Code	8 days	NA	Thu 3/3/05	NA	Mon 3/14/05
27		Unit Test	4 days	NA	Tue 3/15/05	NA	Fri 3/18/05
28		**Development Item #**	**18 days**	**NA**	**Mon 1/31/05**	**NA**	**Wed 2/23/05**
29		Code	12 days	NA	Mon 1/31/05	NA	Tue 2/15/05
30		Unit Test	6 days	NA	Wed 2/16/05	NA	Wed 2/23/05
31							
32		**Test**	**78 days**	**NA**	**Wed 1/12/05**	**NA**	**Fri 4/29/05**
33	▤	System Test Planning	25 days	NA	Wed 1/12/05	NA	Tue 2/15/05
34		System Test	30 days	NA	Mon 3/21/05	NA	Fri 4/29/05

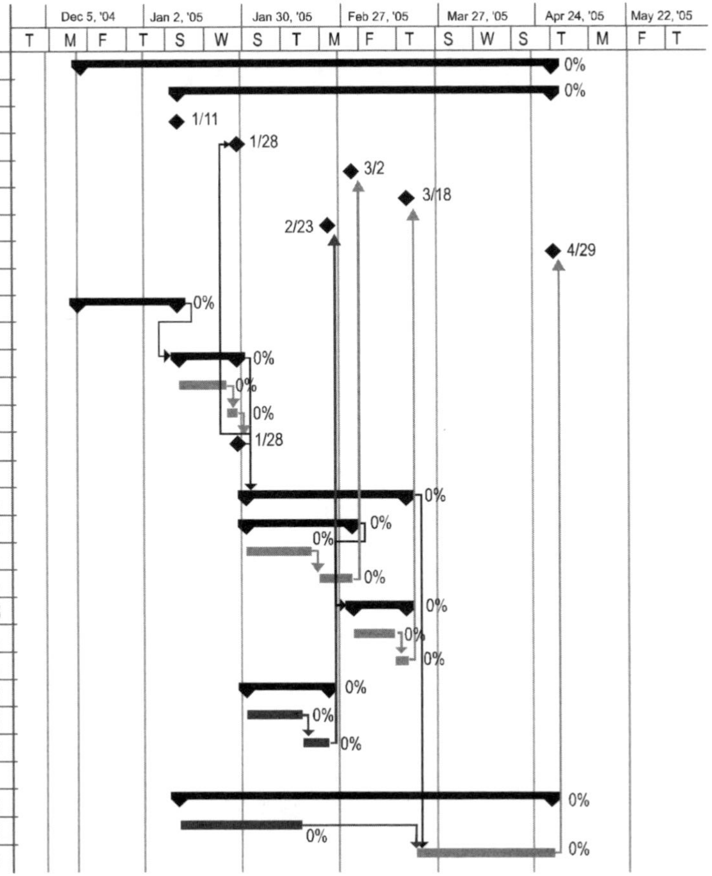

FIGURE 9-1. **EXAMPLE SCHEDULE**

create a dynamic plan that will change as a reflection of tasks completing earlier or later than scheduled. This is where the spreadsheet loses its appeal and project management software becomes a necessity. Keep in mind to apply any Lead and Lag times that you discovered during Activity Sequencing.

There are a number of Schedule Development techniques available. Critical Path is probably the most widely used and is the underlying technique behind MS Project. Also gaining in prominence has been Dr. Eli Goldratt's Critical Chain method (see Chapter 28 for a fuller discussion of Critical Chain). Be sure that the technique you choose is supported by your project management software.

Don't forget to apply the Resource Calendar with its holidays, vacations, shifts, and so on. It is possible for key resources to become over-allocated; for example, Joe Developer is assigned to four 8-hour activities on the same day, resulting in a 32-hour day. Resource Leveling is moving these activities to provide a "best-fit" to keep resources from being over-allocated or to execute activities when key resources are only available at certain times. Be aware that Resource Leveling, although necessary, could result in extending the schedule.

What about replanning? Often you will be asked to expedite the schedule, while keeping the scope intact. Techniques such as Crashing (tradeoffs between cost and schedule in order to determine how to obtain the greatest amount of compression for the least incremental cost) and Fast Tracking (normally sequential tasks done in parallel) are high-risk techniques that, in an effort to deliver faster, can increase cost, increase the probability of rework, and increase the threat of missing the earlier date. When these requests come down, try to work on them with as little interruption to the project team as possible. It always seems that these requests come at the worst time, when taking team members off current work to look at a potential replan of the schedule will assuredly result in missing deadlines on the current work. Instead, pull as few Team Leads as possible to look at replanning. If you are comfortable and have enough knowledge of the project, you can perform this exercise yourself. Have a seasoned project manager review the result to catch any errors in the replan. Try to encapsulate the project team away from these interruptions and keep them working towards the baselined schedule until it is ultimately decided that a replan is necessary.

Congratulations: You now have a project schedule. Review it once more with the team to get buy-in on the Schedule baseline, as this is foundation for Project Tracking and Oversight.

SCHEDULE CONTROL

With a baseline schedule in hand, you are far from finished. You will have to keep it current in order to track progress, to facilitate the inevitable Change Requests, and to assist in providing project status.

In the hands of a mature organization with the proper organizational structure in place, Earned Value is a valuable asset. Even if your organization does not utilize Earned Value, take the time to understand its concepts and try to apply them, even if in a piecemeal fashion. For example, if the cost accounting structure is not in place, you can still graph out the number of Planned Test Cases over time vs. Actual Completed Test Cases. Acknowledging that this is not true Earned Value because Cost is not factored in and you won't be able to extrapolate CPI or SPI, these types of simple graphs can be used to support your intuition about how things are going, and to visually communicate to the team and stakeholders the progress of the team, in this case, that

Testing is ahead of or behind schedule. (See Chapters 10 and 10A for more on Earned Value Management.)

Probably the hardest aspect of Schedule Control is gathering actual progress from the team. Gathering progress is not the problem, it's the subjective sense that "we are at 90%" for over half the duration of the task that can be frustrating, not only to management who hears each week that "we are still at 90%," but also to the developer struggling to complete the task. Be wary of this trap. This is a sign that further decomposition of the task might be necessary to gain better insight into what has been completed and what work still remains.

Receive the Progress Reporting template from management or create one that is judged satisfactory to management and make sure your team is aware of the activities that are being reported to management. At a minimum, key deliverables and critical path items should be represented on your Status report. Be sure to include Start and Finish dates and whether that task is ahead or behind schedule.

If using MS Project, the Tracking Gantt view is recommended. This will show the baseline vs. current task start/finish dates. It will also provide percentage completes for both the Activity and the Summary Task level. This view can quickly show which areas of the project are falling behind and by how much. Continue to ask questions to get a better feel on how much of the activity has been completed and how much is left. Along with asking percentage complete, also ask if the activity will be completed by the baselined end date.

Schedule Control is one of the most important roles in the project. While controlling, continue to be alert for areas in the plan that require refinement. Be on the lookout for schedule slips and take immediate corrective action. Track against the baseline and be prepared for Change Requests.

Continue to research and try out the various techniques and tools described in this Chapter. You are not limited to only one, and only one might not be the best fit for your project. And lastly, remember that you must diligently "plan the work" as this will become the measure of your success and then, just as aggressively, "work the plan" to ensure the project's success.

DISCUSSION QUESTIONS

❶ When have you experienced the impact of poor Activity Resource Estimating on project outcomes? Discuss how the problems might have been prevented using the technique described in this chapter.

❷ Practice identifying Activities using a project you are involved in or familiar with. What issues impact your ability to define the activities in a project?

❸ How would you handle a persistent request from executives for a specific deployment date for your project, prior to having requirements completed?

REFERENCES

[1] Project Management Institute, *A Guide to the Project Management Body of Knowledge, Third Edition,* PMI: Newtown Square, PA.

CHAPTER 10

Project Cost Management in Practice

▶MUHAMED ABDOMEROVIC, PMP,
FKI LOGISTEX

To complete a project within budgeted cost, we must understand how to effectively estimate, allocate, and manage project cost factors. Cost management is normally preceded by activities to define and assign resources to scheduled project activities. This process is known as *resource estimating.*

RESOURCE ESTIMATING

A resource can be people, money, supplies equipment, material, space—anything that is required to accomplish the project work activities. *Resource requirements* are identified by analyzing each activity, and determining the types and quantity of each resource necessary to complete that work. The sum of the resources identified for a given activity can be further specified as the total quantity for that activity. Activities can also be combined to define resource requirements for specified segments of the project, such as life cycle phases or discrete milestones or deliverables.

As we have said, project resource requirements are equal to the sum of the resource requirements of all the scheduled activities. Therefore, before finalizing the resource requirements estimate, it is important to consider the impact of the schedule and availability. In most cases, project estimators assume that resources will be available when required. This may not be the case and it may be necessary to make adjustments to the resource loading in order to arrive at a practical solution. There are many heuristic approaches used to load resources; two of the more popular approaches are considered below:

1. Assume that all project activities start and complete at their early dates. This alternative is a front loaded or *early resource aggregation,* which uses resources as soon as the logic of activities allows.
2. Assume that all project activities start and complete at their late dates. This alternative is a back loaded or *late resource aggregation,* which delays use of resources as much as the float of activities allows.

Since resources are usually limited, rarely flexible, and never unlimited, a performing organization has to achieve project duration within a level of *available resources.* In this procedure, an activity is moved within end limits until it comes into a position where resources are available to schedule the activity. When an activity has resources and schedule dates assigned, it decreases the level of available resources. This procedure continues until the project team finds the best way to perform project activities with available resources, while meeting the project completion date. In practice, we should start by establishing some plans and then simulate different alternatives until we come to an acceptable project schedule. If no alternative can come close to the histogram of available resources, then the project completion date must be delayed.

When project objectives are not flexible regarding the project dates and have to be achieved under a *time-limited schedule,* we approach the problem of resource allocation by:

▶Allocating available resources to critical activities and then determining schedule dates for those activities

▶Allocating resources to other activities, which are not on the critical path, and determining schedule dates for those activities.

When project objectives have no flexibility regarding resource availability and have to be achieved under a resource-limited schedule, then we approach the problem of resource allocation by:

▶Understanding when and under what conditions the project completion date, or completion of certain milestones, can be overrun

▶Finding out if and under what conditions some resources can be overrun.

Once all resources are loaded, scheduled, and obligated, we can proceed to accomplish the remaining activities in cost management.

COST ESTIMATING

Project managers and project stakeholders need accurate information to help them to lead their projects to a successful result. A key foundational control concept is the target estimate because on all projects, the estimate should serve as a guide to shape management actions. Developing detailed, consistent, and reliable cost estimates is the foundation of successful cost management.

From the conceptual project phase (when everything is in an undefined condition) to the completion phase (when all contracts must be signed off and all bills paid), it is always a challenge to estimate contractors' indirect cost and value of their work. Therefore, it is important to prepare, as soon as possible, a preliminary cost estimate structured by bid packages. Aside from that, a resource requirements chart of key resources for each bid package will help avoid qualitative interpretation during the bidding process. The quality of the cost estimate determines later ability to manage contracts included in the project. In general, reliability of cost estimates plays out as follows:

▶Those who can make cost estimating reliable and fast will be able to participate successfully in many bidding events.

▶If the cost estimate becomes more reliable, we can expect a bigger positive difference between the contractor's bid price and the client's allowed price for a particular job.

▶If, in addition to permanent improvement of cost estimate reliability, we want to keep the same level of revenue, we must perform more projects.

▶A positive difference between the contractor's bid price and the client's allowed price for a particular job will be bigger even when all participants in the bidding process increase the reliability of their estimate.

The cost estimating process correlates with the engineering process and evolves over time as well. Therefore, the cost estimate is developed in a certain sequence as knowledge about a project is obtained. An accurate cost estimate is one that falls within an acceptable 5% to 10% range. However, the difference between cost estimate when compared to actual cost can be substantial in the early project phases, usually ranging above 100%. This difference decreases in later project phases; after contracts have been awarded, it should be in the 5% to 10% range. The following sequence illustrates cost estimating stages:

▶The *Order of Magnitude* stage is based on rough technical requirements and related materials and services for the project. It usually estimates total project cost by using the actual cost of similar projects. In this stage, estimators often use the analogous estimating approach to determine their result.

▶The *Conceptual* stage is normally based on more information, such as a preliminary design, feasibility studies, defined specifications for major equipment, and long-lead items. It usually estimates total project cost by estimating quantifiable and scalable parameters for project deliverables and suggesting the alternative with the best balance between cost, duration, and performance for deliverables and project. In this stage, it is normal that 20% of the work (typically the most difficult pieces or the most comprehensively specified) represents approximately 80% of total cost estimate. In this estimating stage, the parametric modeling technique is normally used.

▶The *Preliminary* stage is based on procurement documents, including detail design and specifications for structured components of the project. It usually estimates total project cost by estimating budgets against which invitations for bids can be made. In this estimating stage the bottom-up estimating technique (discussed later)is frequently used.

▶The *Definitive* stage is based on development submittals and cost estimates from selected contractors, and suppliers of materials and equipment. It usually estimates total project cost by estimating structured budget against which contracts can be signed. This stage must include specific contractual conditions that are oriented towards different contractors and regulate their cost estimating submittals. In this estimating stage the client typically asks the bidders to apply the bottom-up estimating technique.

▶The *Control* stage is based on bid, quotation, or proposal from those contractors and suppliers of materials and equipment that have been awarded the contract. In addition to awarded contracts and other external agreements, this cost estimating stage must include detailed estimates for all internal commitments, risks, money costs, overhead, profit, and management reserve. Also, this stage must have a system for collection and cost estimation of change orders.

There is no other decision-making process wrapped in so many unknowns, and at the same time so important, as cost estimating. This process, which has a short duration for completion coupled with an unlimited period during which it can be challenged and criticized, can be divided into three subsystems:

1. Developing and maintaining cost estimating databases or using commercial databases.
2. Identifying the description of the work and specifying quantity and price of work to complete the project. This process could be simplified by using templates developed from previous projects.
3. Calculating and defining the bidding price.

The subsystem of developing and maintaining cost estimating databases, or using commercial databases, relates to all projects within an organization. This is central to an organized and efficient way of cost estimating. Use of cost estimating databases improves the quality of decisions, because both those who prepare cost estimates and those who make the decisions about price often use the same elements for their judgment. This can eliminate most of subjective opinions. The most important data of the subsystems are:

- ▶Description of work to be performed
- ▶Unit of measure for the work
- ▶Classification code of the work
- ▶Quantities of each resource used to perform unit of measure of the work
- ▶Unit price for each resource used to perform the work.

The subsystem of developing a description of work and specifying quantity and price of that work in relation to a specific project enables detailed and reliable work descriptions of individual activities by using a cost estimating database. When all work has been identified in the database, then estimating professionals use project documentation to calculate quantity and price for each line item that describes the work of an activity. This estimating technique is known as activity-based costing or bottom-up cost estimating. If this approach is not feasible, we can apply analogous estimating or parametric modeling techniques. In each case, the cost estimate must be detailed enough that each line item can be assigned by a single work breakdown structure code or specific work breakdown structure components (activities, work packages, or deliverables) and one or more cost accounts for each component. Otherwise, a line item has to be broken down into more components. Figure 10-1 shows an example of work breakdown structure and associated cost elements.

The subsystem of calculating and defining bidding price includes expert judgment, which allows fine-tuning of calculated prices. Such a package contains prices, estimating documentation, assumptions made, and range of possible results of cost, including market conditions, all indirect cost, money costs, overhead, and profit. This material, which

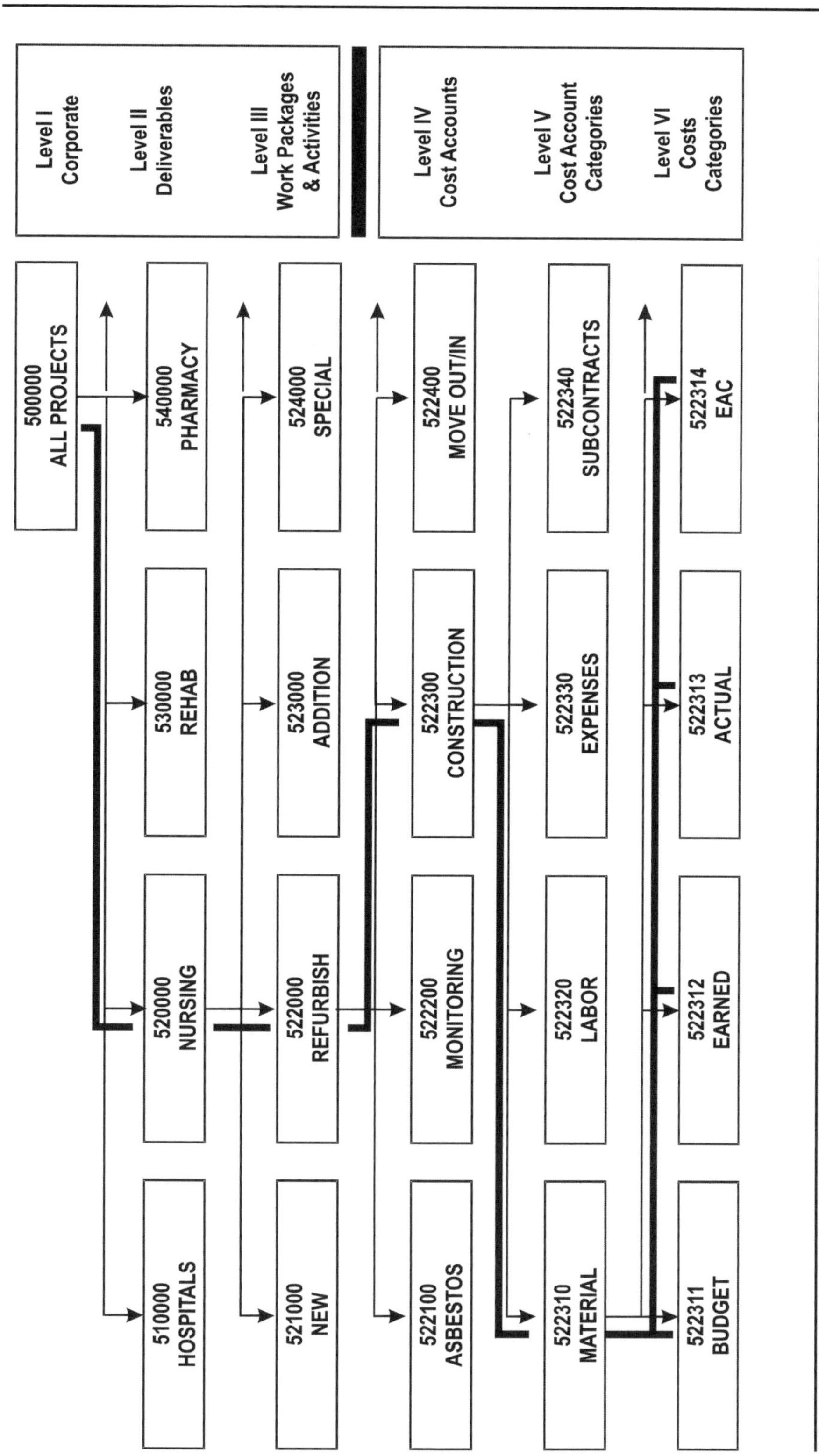

FIGURE 10-1. **AN EXAMPLE OF WORK BREAKDOWN STRUCTURE AND ASSOCIATED COST ELEMENTS**

contains total cost of all resources, except management reserve, is sent to management for the final definition of bidding price. When the project is awarded to the performing company, then the same line items used for bidding purposes will become a part of the database for project progress tracking and the payment application process.

COST BUDGETING

Cost budgeting is the process of aggregating the cost of individual activities to produce a time-phased project cost estimate. A time-phased presentation of a project cost estimate shows total cost at each period during project development and establishes a structure of spending for each particular period. When accepted, this structure will become a guideline for project financial plan and policy, which must be aligned with other projects within the organization.

Time-phased cost estimate is a synonym for *Planned Value (PV), Budget (B), Original Budget (OB), Target Budget (TB), Baseline Cost (BC), Schedule Value,* or *Budgeted Cost of Work Scheduled (BCWS)* and represents the value of the work that should have been accomplished by a specific date. For example, if activity costs are distributed linearly, then planned value by a specific date for an activity is the product of the total planned value and the percent complete of activity duration that the plan should be on the specific date, or:

***Planned Value (PV)* (by specific date) = (OD-RD)/OD) * *Planned Value (PV)* (total)**

(*OD* is Original Duration; *RD* is Remaining Duration. Planned value here is an initial planned value, which has been set as the target budget rather than the current planned value. More detail about this is given in the Cost Control section of this chapter.)

It is important to note that the sum of all of the planned values, or the sum of all the budgeted work for the project, is known as Budget at Completion (BAC). Budget at completion does not change with the ebb and flow of the project; it remains constant unless there is an approved change that formally modifies the baseline. In developing a project cost budgeting system and establishing the BAC, it is necessary to consider all direct and indirect costs.

Direct cost belongs to a specific project task or activity, and will be tracked exclusively to that work product or service. Direct costs are the sum of all resources necessary to accomplish this activity.

Indirect cost belongs to a group of activities because the cost factor is not trackable or exclusive to one task activity. Indirect costs are defined through the cost of all resources necessary to accomplish the group or hammock activity, which encompasses two or more task activities. The keys for specification of indirect cost might be:

- Time oriented, when cost cannot be defined periodically, but its value is shown over a defined period of time; e.g., contingency, overhead, and profit.

- Proportionally oriented, when cost is in direct proportion to some other direct cost; e.g., freight cost to equipment deliveries cost.

Also, regardless of activity type, it is necessary that the following points are defined for each activity:

- Cost amount, or resource quantity and unit price for each resource.

▶Relative start point for activation of cost or resources for the activity. In most cases this start point is between activity start and finish. There are cases when the start point for cost or resources can be outside the activity they are related to; e.g., advance payment for an activity that has to be made one week before the activity can start.

▶A relative end point for activation of cost or resources for the activity. In most cases this end point is between activity start and finish. There are cases when the end for cost or resources can be outside the activity they are related to, such as a retainage payment that is collected for an activity that has to be held for one month after the activity has been finished.

▶A distribution pattern for cost amount or resource quantity over the duration of an activity. This can be specified as a certain cumulative function for total quantity for an activity or as a discrete quantity for each time unit of activity duration.

▶Cost accounts, which show where there is a responsibility for cost amount, or resource quantity for each resource. Each cost account should have cost account categories, which show labor, material, expenses and subcontracts for that account. Cost accounts are used to show resources or cost specifications and establish a budget for different project structures; e.g., work breakdown structure components. Each component within the structures can have many cost accounts, and each cost account can appear in many components.

Cost budgeting is a simulation process that has to be performed until we get satisfactory results across the project scope structure and project organizational structure. As a result of this approach, we come to an initial and fully integrated plan of project cost and schedule. This brings up the question of how detailed a project cost plan should be. The general consensus among practitioners is that this job should be performed as follows:

▶If budget cost has been assigned to each detailed project activity, we can get a precise project plan of project cost and schedule. As this process requires skills across several knowledge areas it, is recommended for experienced users.

▶For projects that have developed a detailed scope structure, it is acceptable to assign resources or cost to a hammock activity, which spans the work package(s) (from start to finish). In that case, cost budgeting is greatly simplified. However, this alternative does not include the planned cost for individual activities; therefore, grouping activities can hide a reason for cost deviation within a work package. Even if we apply this simplified procedure, it is necessary to make a detailed assessment of all work packages that show a negative cost trend.

If we apply a system for cost budgeting based on project management knowledge, then we must develop a procedure that maintains integrity of project cost and schedule. We must assure that:

▶The work breakdown structure is a backbone for other project structures, such as cost estimating structure, organizational structure, and contracting structure.

▶Each activity that has a cost must have one or more cost accounts, which show the responsibility for the cost; e.g., engineering, fabrication, installation, etc.

▶Each cost account should contain one or more cost categories (labor, material, expenses, subcontracts).

▶The first alternative for cost estimating uses the parameters of normal work conditions.

▶The total cost estimate for a project must be distributed to project activities.

▶Costs from particular cost accounts can be summarized only in a single element of the particular project structure; e.g., work breakdown structure.

▶Each project activity must have other codes, which define activity location and summarization of activity information within different project structures; e.g., organizational breakdown structure. Figure 10-2 shows the OBS Code as an interface between key project structures.

▶An activity that has assigned resources or cost cannot be modified or deleted from the plan until the resources and cost differences are transferred to other activities within the project.

▶Specified work and budget cannot be transferred to other activities independently from one another.

▶The budget for work breakdown structure components that are in progress or have not started yet cannot be changed without approved change orders.

Once the project budget has been prepared, it provides the basis for subsequent control of costs.

COST CONTROL

Once we have a project cost plan, our emphasis moves from planning processes to controlling processes. Methodologies for cost control or controlling changes to project budget differ from company to company. Most methodologies include features that help react to changes, find out causes of variances, and act to improve a project trend. They fit within one of following systems:

▶The *standard cost control system* has, for each line item from the plan, two cost categories: planned (or standard) cost and actual cost. Having two cost categories for each line item, we can make a comparison between planned and actual cost and then determine variance. Comparing actual cost to planned cost shows the cost variance on a given date. This variance between planned and actual cost is caused by either:

- Resources used to accomplish the work have been paid more than was planned.
- Resources used to accomplish the work have been consumed in more quantity than was planned.

Therefore, cost analysis based on a standard cost-control system has been focused on two elements: resources and cost of resources. Now we can formulate equations, which calculate planned cost, actual cost and variance for any line item and at any level of the project structure that aggregates a set of line items. By this system:

Planned cost = Planned Quantity * Planned unit price

Actual cost = Actual Quantity * Actual unit price

Total variance = Planned cost – Actual cost

Standard cost control works well for serial production, which creates a large number of the same products. Schedule and cost for a production program are based on a procedure that develops standard activities for one finished unit of a production program or one time unit of a production program.

▶The *project cost control system* assumes that each activity or group of activities become the time and cost controlling center. The system starts with an analysis of work results, i.e., outcomes of the activities performed to accomplish the project. Regarding cost control we should collect: an estimate of percent completed of activity duration, remaining duration to complete each activity, any change orders or pending change orders that impact activity time and cost, and new cost estimate for activity and actual cost for activity.

Although there are many aspects of project cost control, we are concerned, at the start, with value of progress for activities. This value represents the percentage of planned costs allocated to the work that was actually accomplished. The value of the work performed is a synonym for *Total Completed and Stored To Date, Budgeted Cost of Work Performed (BCWP),* or *Earned Value (EV).* If we can measure the quantity of work accomplished, then the Earned Value is calculated as the product of the resource percent complete and the current Planned Value for the resource. If we cannot measure the quantity of work accomplished then Earned Value is calculated as a product of the Planned Value and percent complete of the activity duration, or:

***Earned Value (EV)* (by specific date) = (OD-RD)/OD) * *Planned Value (PV)* (total)**

OD is Original Duration, *RD* is Remaining Duration. As we can see, earned value is calculated with the same equation as planned value, however, planned value here is a current planned value rather than target budget, which has been used to calculate planned value. Consequently, earned value will be different from planned value if current planned value or current schedule dates are different from target budget or target schedule dates. If target budget has not been set, then earned value is equal to planned value at any point of time.

Although this simplified procedure does not measure the quantity of work accomplished or resource consumption for this work, it gives instant results that are usually sufficient and reliable enough for decision makers. (See Chapter 10A for a full discussion of Earned Value Management.)

Collection of Actual Cost (AC) for work elements is an important project function. It is a synonym for *Actual Cost of Work Performed (ACWP)* and represents costs actually incurred for work planned and accomplished during a specific period, usually to the data date. This is the most complicated job in controlling because of difficulties in:

▶Obtaining actual cost related to labor hours spent, material consumed, expenses, and subcontracts of accomplished work element

▶Allocating actual cost of resources exactly at places where they have been planned

▶Bringing together a structure for developing planned value and a structure for accumulating actual cost. As these structures are usually different, a base for analysis of actual cost could be inconsistent.

If we face such a situation, we should look for a procedure that can operate quickly and with enough precision to be used as a routine. The collection of actual cost could be simplified if we assume that most of actual costs have been generated where they have been earned. Therefore, by use of some global calculation we can distribute actual cost proportionally to each earned value amount. This will enable performance measurement

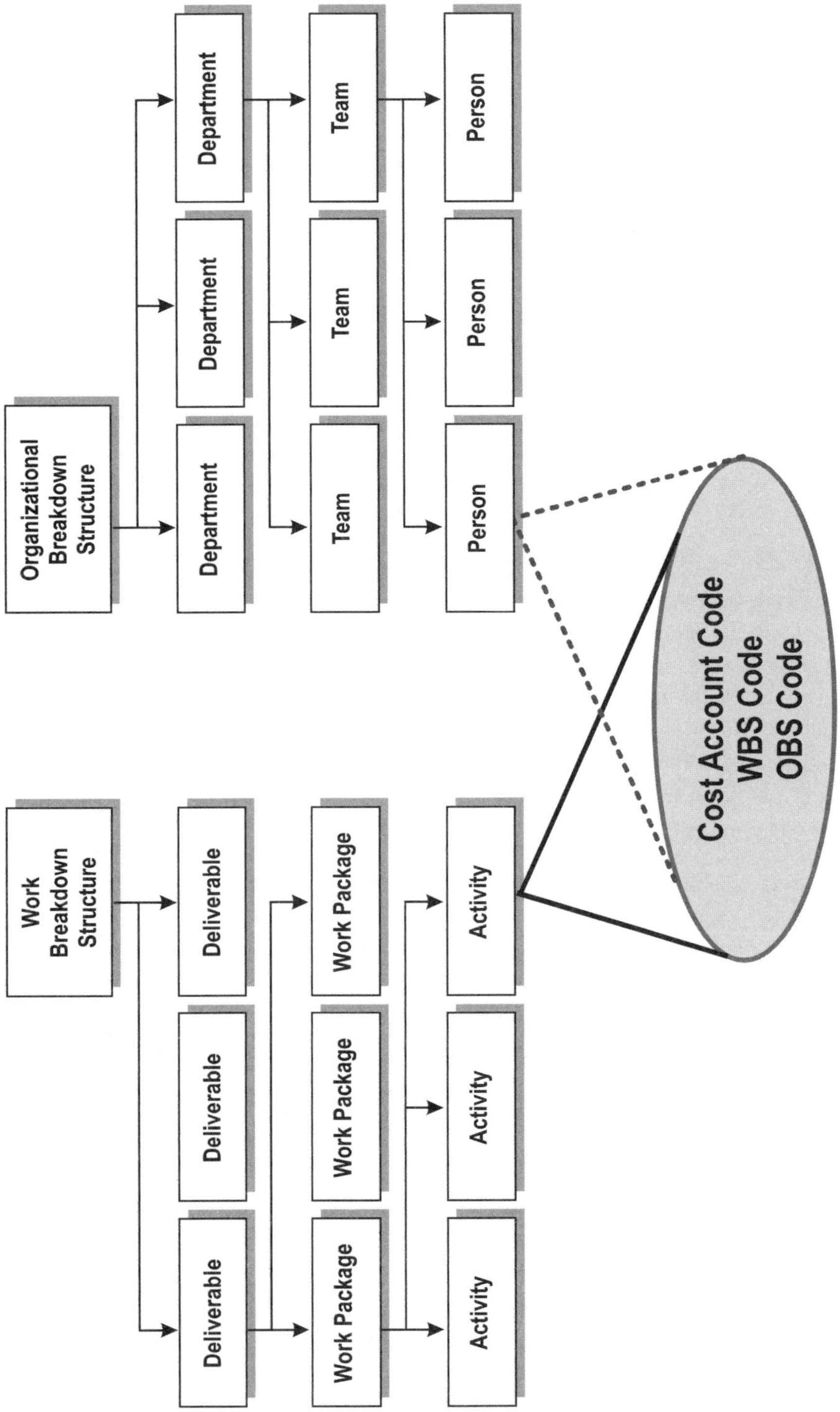

FIGURE 10-2. **OBS CODE AS AN INTERFACE BETWEEN KEY PROJECT STRUCTURES**

at some higher management level. However, from time to time, it is necessary to make a detailed distribution of actual costs to work elements where they have been spent. This will help to get a clear picture of current work elements and also to store the structure of cost amount for use in a future project.

While earned value and actual cost specifics are relevant to task activities and associated direct cost, it should be noted that indirect planned costs are assigned to hammock activities; therefore, they are usually earned as percent of time progress on activities within the group, and their actual costs are usually set equal to earned value.

If, for unpredictable reasons, a change is made to the project work, it is necessary to estimate the cost for that change. This base equation relates actual cost and cost to complete an activity, and forecasts most likely total activity cost:

***Estimate at Completion (EAC) = Actual Cost (AC) + Estimate to Complete (ETC),* where:**

***EAC* is an estimate of total cost that will be used to complete an activity.**

***ETC* is an estimate of the remaining cost to complete an activity.**

This equations works well if assessment of an activity has justified a need to make new ETC for remaining work.

However, in most cases this is not necessary and ETC is calculated from existing data, usually as remaining budget to complete the activity, where:

ETC = Planned Value (PV)* (total, current) – *Earned Value (EV)

This equation works well if assessment of an activity shows that current performance is unique and cannot be used to predict future ETC and EAC.

The concepts we have applied to a singular task can also be applied to the project as a whole. If the organization consistently develops a record of past project performance, then a Cost Performance Index (CPI) can be used to predict future Estimate to Complete (ETC) and Estimate at Completion (EAC). (Note: CPI is defined later in this chapter.) In this situation:

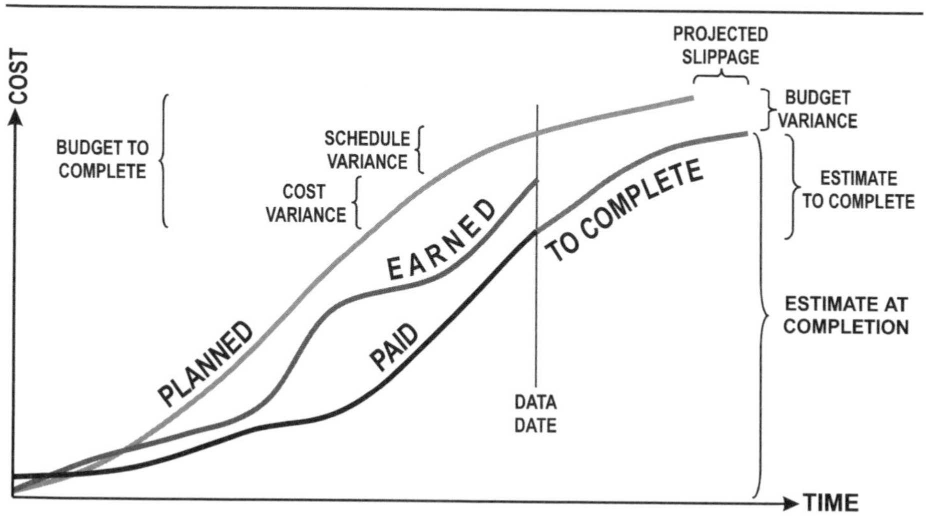

FIGURE 10-3. **THE KEY COST CONTROL CATEGORIES**

	Completion Date	Budget (B)	Estimate at Completion (EAC)	Budget Variance (B-EAC)	Planned To Date (PV)	Earned To Date (EV)	Paid To Date (AC)	Estimate to Complete (EAC-AC)	Cost Variance (EV-AC)	Schedule Variance (EV-PV)
United States	12-Nov-99	109,706,749	109,026,178	680,571	105,395,104	101,448,447	97,299,529	11,726,649	4,148,918	-3,946,657
Alabama	11-Aug-99	12,497,403	11,851,323	646,080	11,678,789	11,188,686	10,995,203	856,120	193,483	-490,103
Mobile	11-Aug-99	7,291,807	7,758,938	-467,131	7,216,807	6,651,704	7,137,940	620,998	-486,236	-565,103
Montgomery	02-Apr-99-A	5,205,596	4,092,385	1,113,211	4,461,982	4,536,982	3,857,263	235,122	679,719	75,000
Florida	13-Oct-99	17,244,697	14,882,200	2,362,497	15,633,683	15,161,686	13,505,345	1,376,855	1,656,341	-471,997
Jacksonville	26-Mar-99-A	5,261,374	4,323,386	937,988	4,648,754	4,723,754	4,061,053	262,333	662,701	75,000
Winter Springs	19-Mar-99-A	5,181,107	4,480,754	700,353	4,635,271	4,710,271	4,292,227	188,527	418,044	75,000
Apopka	13-Oct-99	6,802,216	6,078,060	724,156	6,349,658	5,727,661	5,152,065	925,995	575,596	-621,997
Indiana	27-Nov-98-A	6,795,214	6,901,794	-106,580	6,624,396	6,697,288	6,679,771	222,023	17,517	72,892
Evansville	27-Nov-98-A	6,795,214	6,901,794	-106,580	6,624,396	6,697,288	6,679,771	222,023	17,517	72,892
Kentucky	29-Sep-99	18,429,503	18,146,350	283,153	17,875,646	16,990,433	15,384,654	2,761,696	1,605,779	-885,213
Elizabethtown	17-Jul-98-A	4,592,949	4,454,201	138,748	4,501,073	4,576,073	4,422,283	31,918	153,790	75,000
Crestview Hills	29-Apr-99-A	6,775,868	6,976,676	-200,808	6,672,844	6,752,844	6,759,932	216,744	-7,088	80,000
Louisville	29-Sep-99	7,060,686	6,715,473	345,213	6,701,729	5,661,516	4,202,439	2,513,034	1,459,077	-1,040,213
Maine	02-Oct-98-A	6,124,859	6,248,334	-123,475	6,049,699	6,124,699	6,143,410	104,924	-18,711	75,000
Kennenbunk	02-Oct-98-A	6,124,859	6,248,334	-123,475	6,049,699	6,124,699	6,143,410	104,924	-18,711	75,000
Texas	17-Nov-99	41,483,056	42,536,679	-1,053,623	40,480,874	38,153,638	36,239,736	6,296,943	1,913,902	-2,327,236
Carrollton	25-Mar-99-A	7,169,998	7,195,790	-25,792	6,892,776	6,967,776	6,974,783	221,007	-7,007	75,000
Richardson	28-Jul-99	8,346,824	8,451,711	-104,887	8,714,751	7,950,351	7,118,482	1,333,219	831,859	-224,400
Grapevine	22-Jun-99-A	8,125,416	8,317,792	-192,376	7,900,383	7,975,383	7,259,197	1,058,595	716,186	75,000
Houston	12-Nov-99	8,429,519	8,182,990	246,529	8,257,512	6,617,605	5,810,866	2,372,124	806,739	-1,639,907
Sugar Land	28-Jul-99	5,686,687	6,009,835	-323,148	5,611,687	4,923,758	4,925,308	1,084,527	-1,550	-687,929
Kingwood	30-Mar-99-A	3,724,612	4,378,561	-653,949	3,643,765	3,718,765	4,151,090	227,471	-432,325	75,000
Virginia	12-Aug-98-A	7,132,017	8,459,498	-1,327,481	7,052,017	7,132,017	8,351,410	108,088	-1,219,393	80,000
Virginia Beach	12-Aug-98-A	7,132,017	8,459,498	-1,327,481	7,052,017	7,132,017	8,351,410	108,088	-1,219,393	80,000

FIGURE 10-4. **AN EXAMPLE OF A PROJECT PERFORMANCE REPORT**

EAC = BAC/Cost Performance Index (CPI)
ETC=EAC – ACWP

There are also forecasting techniques, which add the cost of changes directly. Cost of changes can be added to Estimate to Complete (ETC), where:

ETC = Planned Value (PV)* (remaining, current) + current *Change Orders (CO)
ETC = Planned Value (PV) – Earned Value (EV)* + current *Change Orders (CO)

The cost of changes can be added to Estimate at Completion (EAC) or to PV, where:

EAC = Planned Value (PV)* + current *Change Orders (CO)

When we have figured Planned Value (PV), Earned Value (EV), Actual Cost (AC), and Estimate to Complete (ETC), which are the essence of project cost control, we can know:

▶Project status, or the value and meaning of project cost categories and indexes as of the data date

▶Project progress or accomplishments as of the data date

▶Project forecast, or what is projected to happen regarding project progress and result based upon results up to this data date.

Variances and Indexes Used in Cost Management

Based on derived cost categories, we can calculate different variances and indexes to get more comprehensive picture of project development. The variances and indexes have the following meaning:

Budget Variance (BV) shows the difference between Estimate at Completion (EAC) and Budget at Completion (BAC).

Budget Variance (BV) = Estimate At Completion (EAC) – BAC

In real-life projects, Estimate at Completion (EAC) can be used as a projection of the impact of Change Orders (CO). Budget Variance (BV) will show the magnitude of these changes with respect to the target plan. When changes are eventually approved, the baseline will be updated, and the BAC will increase or decrease accordingly.

Cost Variance (CV), shows the difference between Actual Cost (AC) and Earned Value (EV), or how much paid differs from earned. If variance is negative, then payment should be stopped until a detailed assessment of project cost has been done.

Cost Variance (CV) = Earned Value (EV) – Actual Cost (AC)

Schedule Variance (SV), shows the difference between Planned Value (PV) (target) and Earned Value (EV), or how much planned value differs from earned value. We should not use Schedule Variance (SV) to discuss a specific schedule position, but if it is negative, we may want to speed up work. However, a negative Schedule Variance (SV) does not necessarily mean that project completion has been delayed, because negative Schedule Variance (SV) could arise from a delay in activities with positive float. Similarly, a positive Schedule Variance (SV) does not mean that the project completion will be earlier, because a positive Schedule Variance (SV) could result from the acceleration of activities with positive float.

Schedule Variance (SV) = Earned Value (EV) – Planned Value (PV) **(target)**

Figure 10-3 shows the key cost control categories and cost variances.

Besides the cost categories described above, the reader should understand the meaning of cost indexes, which are derived from the cost categories.

Cost Performance Index (CPI), known as cost efficiency indicator, shows Earned Value (EV) against Actual Cost (AC), or the dollar value achieved for each dollar paid. It is favorable if the result is greater than 1.

Cost Performance Index (CPI) = Earned Value (EV) / Actual Cost (AC)

Schedule Performance Index (SPI), known as schedule efficiency indicator, shows Earned Value (EV) against Planned Value (PV), or how much progress (value) accomplished against progress planned. It is favorable if the result is greater than 1.

Schedule Performance Index (SPI) = Earned Value (EV)/Planned Value (PV)

The way in which the cost indexes vary can indicate the need for more extensive use of project management system knowledge in order to determine the adequacy of project progress.

CONCLUSION

Project Cost Management is one area of project management that has the potential to create great discord among project teams, project managers, sponsors, and clients. Or, if it is well done, the reverse is also true: Good cost management can be the foundation of a harmonious relationship among all stakeholders to a project. In addition, well-founded cost management provides a basis for realistic planning and controls of project objectives. When performing the cost management processes described in this chapter, the project manager and team should always be aware that they are laying the knowledge-based groundwork for project success.

DISCUSSION QUESTIONS

❶ If project procurement documents have been approved, what estimating technique should be applied? What percentage of accuracy would be acceptable for a cost estimate at this point of time?

❷ Schedule Variance shows the difference between Planned Value and Earned Value. If the difference is negative, does it mean that project completion date has been delayed? Can we use schedule variance to discuss the project schedule?

❸ For projects with which you are familiar, how did the use—or lack of—the estimating procedures and Earned Value analysis described in this chapter affect project performance? What would you do differently, and why?

FURTHER READING

Abdomerovic, Muhamed. *Brainstorming The PMBOK® Guide*. Louisville, Kentucky, USA: Project Management Publications, 2004.

Abdomerovic, Muhamed. *Contract Payments and Earned Value.* The Measurable News, Summer 2004.
Archibald, Russell D. *Managing High—Technology Programs & Projects.* New York, NY, USA: John Wiley & Sons, Inc., 2003.
Ayers, Chesley. *Specifications for Architecture, Engineering and Construction*. New York, NY, USA: McGraw-Hill Book Company, 1984.
Brown, Lewis J., and Leslie R. Howard. *Principles and Practice of Management Accountancy*. London, UK: McDonald and Evans, 1969.
Fleming, Quentin W. *Cost / Schedule Control Systems Criteria, The Management Guide to C/SCSC.* Chicago, Illinois, USA: Probus Publishing Company, 1988.
Fleming, Quentin W., and Quentin J. Fleming. *Subcontract Planning and Organization*. Chicago, Illinois, USA: Probus Publishing Company, 1993.
Fleming, Quentin W., and Joel M. Koppelman. *Earned Value Project Management.* Newton Square, Pennsylvania USA: Project Management Institute, 2000.
Lipke, Walter. "Connecting Earned Value to the Schedule." *The Measureable News,* Winter 2004.
Project Management Institute (PMI). PMP Role Delineation Study. Newton Square, Pennsylvania, USA: Project Management Institute, 2004.
Wideman, Max R. *A Framework for Project and Program Management Integration.* Newton Square, Pennsylvania, USA: Project Management Institute, 1991.

CHAPTER 10A

Studies in Cost Management: Earned Value—An Integrated Project Management Approach

▶LEE R. LAMBERT, PMP,
LAMBERT AND ASSOCIATES

Earned Value Management (EVM), often referred to simply as earned value, is a productive technique for the management of cost and schedule, which is required on many U.S. government contracts. In recent years, EVM has shown itself to be equally valuable when applied to other complex projects, whether in private, commercial, or government environments.

In the world of EVM, the role of the Control Account Manager (CAM) is pivotal in the process. The project manager and all of the other traditional project management contributors are active participants and have significant responsibilities that can't be underestimated. However, because of the critical role of the CAM, this material is targeted at helping the CAM plan and manage assigned tasks.

The EVM process is essentially the same at all levels of the project or organization. Individual components of the EVM approach addresses work authorization through status reporting. Descriptions of cost accounts, authorized work packages, and planned work packages are emphasized because of their significance in the EVM approach in general and, specifically, because of the role they play in helping the CAM to be successful at the difficult job of balancing the many project management requirements and tasks.

PROCESS OVERVIEW

The first EVM concept (then known as Cost Schedule Control

- AC – Actual cost = ACWP
- ACWP – Actual cost of work performed = AC
- AWP – Authorized work package*
- BAC – Budget at completion
- BCWP – Budgeted cost of work performed = EV
- BCWS – Budgeted cost of work scheduled = PV
- CA – Cost account
- CAA – Cost account authorization*
- CAM – Cost account manager
- CAP – Cost account package*
- CBB – Contract budget base
- CD – Contract directive*
- CFSR – Contract funds status report
- CPR – Cost performance report
- C/SCSC– Cost/schedule control system criteria
- C/SSR – Cost/schedule status report
- CWBS – Contract work breakdown structure
- EAC – Estimate at completion
- ETC – Estimate to complete
- EV – Earned value = BCWP
- FM – Functional manager*
- FTC – Forecast to complete
- LOE – Level of effort
- LRE – Latest revised estimate
- MPMS – Master phasing milestone schedule
- MR – Management reserve
- PCR – Package change record
- PM – Project manager
- PMB – Performance measurement baseline
- PV – Planned value = BCWS
- PWP – Planned work package*
- RAM – Responsibility assignment matrix
- SOW – Statement of work
- UB – Undistributed budget
- VAR – Variance analysis report
- WBS – Work breakdown structure
- WBSM – WBS manager*
- WPM – Work package manager

*These abbreviations are not common. Also note that organizations may use their own terminology.

FIGURE 10A-1. **ABBREVIATIONS AND TERMS**

System Criteria) was introduced in the 1960s, when the Department of Defense Instruction 7000.2-Performance Measurement of Selected Acquisitions exploded on the management scene. The criteria included in the instruction defined standards of acceptability for defense contractor management project control systems. The original thirty-five criteria were grouped into five general categories—organization, planning and budgeting, accounting, analysis, and revisions—and were viewed by many, government and contractor personnel alike, as a very positive step toward helping to solve management problems, while achieving some much needed consistency in the general project management methods used throughout the Department of Defense and, eventually, most major U.S. government agencies.

Today many highly respected organizations in the world, are working within the boundaries of the criteria. Hundreds have received validation or certification by the U.S. government. These organizations represented thousands of government and private projects and programs. Thousands of other contractors have been using the basic principles of EVM without any formal requirements to do so. These organizations have clearly found the concepts and techniques useful on all work, not just that being done for the U.S. government.

It should be noted that not everyone agrees that EVM is the best project management approach. However, in this author's experience, these same critics subtly adapt various components of the EVM concept on their projects and find them extremely valuable and productive management tools. After all, it is hard to argue with the sound business management concepts upon which EVM is based.

Numerous abbreviations and terms are employed in a description of EVM; these are explained in Figure 10A-1.

CRITICAL DATA ELEMENTS OF EVM

There are three critical data elements involved in EVM: Planned Value (PV), Actual Cost (AC), and Earned Value (EV).

Planned Value

The PV is the amount of resources, usually stated in terms of dollars, that are expected to be consumed to accomplish a specific piece of work scope. The PV is more commonly known as the spend plan or cost estimate and has long been employed in the world of project management. In EVM applications, the emphasis is placed on achieving the closest possible correlation between the scope of work to be completed (work content) and the amount of resources actually required to deliver that scope.

Actual Cost

The AC is the amount of resources, usually stated in terms of dollars, that were expended in a specified time period to accomplish a specific scope of work. The AC is more commonly known as the actual incurred cost or simply actuals, and it has also been employed in the world of project management since its beginning. In EVMC/SCSC applications, the emphasis is placed on expending and recording resource expenditures with a direct correlation to the scope of work that has been planned to be completed at the same point in time.

Earned Value

The EV is a measure of the amount of work accomplished, stated in terms of all or a portion of the budget assigned to that specific scope of work. The work accomplishment status, as determined by those responsible for completion of the work, is converted to dollar form and becomes the focal point of all status and analysis activities that follow. The EV is the only non-traditional data element required when utilizing EVM management techniques. The EV, when compared with the PV and AC, provides the foundation for comprehensive management evaluations, projections, and (if necessary) corrective action planning and implementation.

What's in it for the User?

In-the-trenches experience has resulted in two separate observations on utilizing EVM: good news and bad news. Let's take the good news first. The EVM approach:

▶Provides information that enables managers and contributors to take a more active role in defining and justifying a "piece of the project pie."

▶Alerts you to potential problems in time to be proactive instead of reactive.

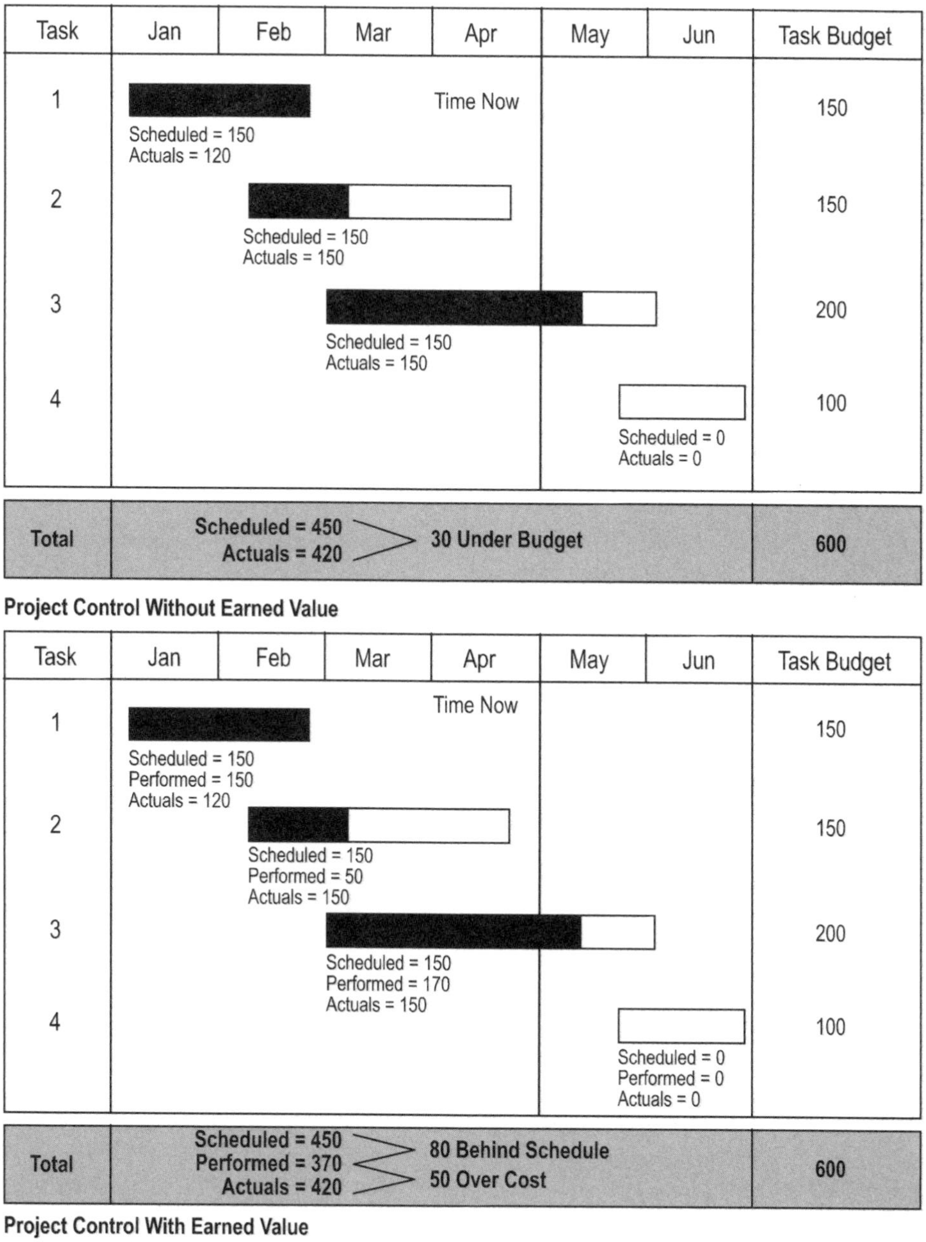

FIGURE 10A-2. **BENEFITS OF USING EVM**

▶Allows you to demonstrate clearly your timely accomplishments.

▶Provides the basis for significant improvement in internal and external communications.

▶Provides a powerful marketing tool for future projects and programs that require high management content.

▶Provides the basis for consistent, effective management system-based training and education.

▶Provides a more definitive indication of the cost and schedule impact of project problems.

▶Allows tremendous flexibility in its application.

On the downside, EVM also most likely:

▶Results in the customer asking for more detail.

▶Results in greater time spent organizing and analyzing data by someone in the organization, although this is becoming less and less of an issue with today's automated project management support capabilities.

▶Requires more structure and discipline than usual.

▶Costs money and organizational resources to develop and implement.

Experience clearly shows the net result to be significantly in favor of utilizing the EVM approach. Figure 10A-2 shows the benefits in graphic form. Without earned value, the example shows an "under budget" situation. Using EVM, the real status of the project is revealed, showing a project behind schedule and over budget. But even with EVM, the management user must remember at all times that using EVM will not:

▶Solve technical problems.

▶Solve funding problems, although it might help.

▶Make decisions for you, although it will help.

▶In any way "manage" your program, project, or work package.

EVM will, however, provide sound, timely information—the most useful commodity for today's managers faced with making extremely difficult decisions.

PROCESS DESCRIPTION

EVM can be successful only if the user recognizes the need for a hierarchical relationship between all the units of work to be performed on a project. This hierarchical relationship is established via the work breakdown structure (WBS). Work is done at the lowest levels of the WBS (work packages); therefore, these critical elements have particular significance when it comes to achieving the most beneficial results from using EVM.

The EVM process involves numerous specific tasks and efforts, which are described in detail below.

Control Account

The control account (CA) is the focus for defining, planning, monitoring, and controlling because it represents all the work associated with a single WBS element, and it is usually the responsibility of a single organizational unit. EVM converges at the control account level, which includes budgets, schedules, work assignments, cost collection, progress assessment, problem identification, and corrective actions.

Day-to-day management is accomplished at the CA level. Most management actions taken at higher levels are on an "exception" basis in reaction to significant problems identified in the CA.

The level selected for establishment of a CA must be carefully considered to ensure that work is properly defined in manageable units (work packages) with responsibilities clearly delineated.

Authorized Work Package

An authorized work package (AWP) is a detailed task that is identified by the control account manager for accomplishing work within a CA. An AWP has the following characteristics:

▶It represents units of work at the levels where the work is performed (lowest level of the WBS).

▶It is clearly distinct from all other work packages and is usually performed by a single organizational element.

▶It has scheduled start and completion dates (with interim milestones, if applicable), which represent physical accomplishment.

▶It has a budget or assigned PV usually expressed in terms of dollars and/or labor hours.

▶Its duration is relatively short unless the AWP is subdivided by discrete value milestones that permit objective measurement of work performed over long periods of time.

▶Its schedule is integrated with all other schedules.

Planning Work Package

If an entire control account cannot be subdivided into detailed AWPs, far-term effort is identified in larger planned work packages (PWPs) for budgeting and scheduling purposes. The budget for a PWP is identified specifically according to the work for which it is intended. The budget is also time-phased and has controls, which prevent its use in performance of other work. Eventually, all work in PWPs is planned to the appropriate level of detail for authorized work packages.

Work Authorization

All project work, regardless of origin, should be described and authorized through the work authorization process, an integral part of EVM. The EVM relates not only to work authorization, but also to planning, scheduling, budgeting, and other elements of project control, which reflect the flow of work through the functional organizations.

Although the control account manager is most concerned with the work authorization process at the authorized work package and control account levels, the total process is presented to provide the CAM with a sense of specific responsibilities within the total system. The authorization flow is traced from customer authorization through contractual change authorization using the following five steps:

1. Authorization for contracted work consists of two parts: the basic contract, and the contractual scope changes.

2. Work authorization for contracted work is provided as follows: The organization's general manager, in coordination with the finance director, provides authorization to the project manager to start work via a contract directive (CD). This directive approves total project scope of work and funding

3. WBS planning target authorization is as follows:

- The WBS manager prepares the WBS planning target authorization.
- The project manager approves the WBS target goal for expansion to the functional control account.
- The WBS target is later replaced by the completed WBS-package budget rollup of CAs.

4. The procedure for control account planning target authorization is as follows: The control account manager prepares a target control account goal for expansion to work packages. The CA target is later replaced by CA-package budget rollup of all planned work packages.

5. Change control is processed as follows: The CAM submits or signs a modified work package form to the EVM information department. These modified work package forms show any internal replanning or customer contractual baseline change that:

- Alters work by addition/deletion, causing CA budget adjustments.
- Causes adjustment of work or budget between CAs.
- The processing department completes a package change record (PCR) for audit trail of baseline revisions (baseline maintenance).
- The project manager or delegated WBS manager approves the add/delete transactions to the management reserve/contingency account controlled by management if the budget adjustment is outside the single cost account. (*Note*: Parties to the original budget agreements must approve revisions.)
- The CA budget cannot be changed by such actions as cost overruns or under runs; changes that affect program schedules or milestones because of work acceleration or work slippage; or retroactive adjustments.

Planning and Scheduling

This description of planning and scheduling from the project level down gives the CAM an overall view of specific responsibilities. Eight factors are involved.

1. Planning and scheduling must be performed in a formal, complete, and consistent way. The customer-provided project master schedule and related subordinate schedules through the control account/work package levels provide a logical sequence from summary to detailed work packages. The EVM logic network schedule works as the tool to make certain that work package schedules are compatible with contract milestones, since the networks are derived from the work package database.

2. Network logic must be established for all interfaces within the framework of the contract work breakdown structure (CWBS).

3. The responsibility assignment matrix (RAM) is an output of WBS planning. It extends to specific levels in support of internal and customer reports. The RAM merges the WBS with the organization structure to display the intersection of the WBS with the control account-responsible organizations.

4. When work plans are detailed, the lower-level work packages are interfaced and scheduled. These work packages are usually identified as either:

- *Discrete effort:* Effort that can be scheduled in relation to clearly definable start and completion dates, and which contains objective indicator milestones against which performance can be realistically measured
- *Level of effort (LOE):* Support effort that is not easily measured in terms of discrete accomplishment; it is characterized by a uniform rate of activity over a specific period of time.

Where possible, work packages should be categorized in terms of discrete effort. LOE should be minimized—typically not more than ten percent.

5. The general characteristics of schedules are as follows:

- Schedules should be coordinated (with all other performing organizations) by the EVM manager.
- Commitment to lower-level schedules provides the basis for the project schedule baselines.
- All work package schedules are directly identifiable as related to CA packages and WBS elements.
- After a baseline has been established, schedule dates must remain under strict revision control, changing only with the appropriate EVM manager's approval.

6. Two categories of project schedules are used.

- Project level schedules are master phasing/milestone schedules, program schedules, or WBS intermediate schedules.
- Detailed schedules are either control account schedules or work package schedules.

  Control account schedules: (1) have milestones applicable to responsible organizations; (2) are developed by the organizations to extend interfaces to lower work package items; (3) are at the level at which status is normally determined and reported monthly to the project CA level for updating of higher-level schedule status and performance measurement; (4) have planned and authorized packages that correlate to the CA, WBS, and scope of work (SOW) and which is reported to the customer; and (5) document the schedule baseline for the project.

  Work package schedules: (1) provide milestones and activities required to identify specific measurable work packages; (2) supply the framework for establishing and time-phasing detailed budgets, various status reports, and summaries of cost and schedule performance; (3) are the level at which work package status is normally discussed and provide input for performance measurement; (4) are the responsibility of a single performing organization; (5) provide a schedule baseline against which each measurable work package must be identified; and (6) require formal authorization for changes after work has started and normally provide three months' detail visibility.

7. Regarding schedule change control, the control account managers can commit their organization to a revised schedule only after formal approval by at least the WBS manager.

8. Work package schedule statusing involves the following:

- Objective indicators or milestones are used to identify measurable intermediate events.
- Milestone schedule status and EV calculations are normally performed monthly.

Budgeting

In accord with the scope of work negotiated by the organization with the customer, the budgets for elements of work are allocated to the control account manager through the EVM process. These budgets are tied to the work package plans, which have been approved in the baseline. The following top-down outline, with five factors, gives the CAM an overview of the EVM budgeting process.

1. Project-to-function budgeting involves budget allocations and budget adjustments. Budget allocations involve the following:

- The project manager releases the WBS targets to the WBS managers, who negotiate control account targets with the control account managers. The CAMs then provide work package time-phased planning.
- When all project effort is time-phased, the EVM information is produced and output reports are provided for the project manager's review. When the performance measurement baseline (PMB) is established, the project manager authorizes WBS packages, which are summarized from the control accounts.
- The WBS manager authorizes the control account packages, which are summed from work package planning. The time-phased work package budgets are the basis for calculating the EV each month.

Regarding budget adjustments, the performance measurement baseline can be changed with the project manager's approval when either of the following occurs:

- Changes in SOW (additions or deletions) cause adjustments to budgets.
- Formal rebaselining results in a revised total allocation of budget.

2. PMB budgets may not be replanned for changes in schedule (neither acceleration nor slips) or cost overruns or underruns.

3. Management Reserves (MRs) are budgets set aside to cover unforeseen requirements (unknown/unknowns). The package change record is used to authorize add/delete transactions to these budgets.

4. Undistributed Budgets (UBs) are budgets set aside to cover identified, but not yet detailed or assigned SOW. As these scopes of work are incorporated into the detail planning, a PCR is used to authorize and add to the performance measurement baseline.

5. Regarding detailed planning, the planned work package is a portion of the budget (the PV) within a CA that is identified to the CA, but is not yet defined into detailed AWPs.

Cost Accumulation

Cost accumulation provides the CAM with a working knowledge of the accounting methods used in EVM. There are six things involved in cost accumulation accounting (for actual costs).

1. Timekeeping/cost collection for labor costs uses a labor distribution/accumulation system. The system shows monthly expenditure data based on labor charges against all active internal work packages.

2. Three factors are involved in non-labor costs.

- Material cost collection accounting shows monthly expenditure databased on purchase order/subcontract expenditure.
- The cost collection system for subcontract/integrated contractor costs uses reports received from the external source for monthly expenditures.
- Regarding the funds control system (commitments):
  —The funds control system records the total value of purchase orders/subcontracts issued, but not totally funded.
  —The cumulative dollar value of outstanding orders is reduced as procurements are funded.

3. Regarding the accounting charge number system:

- The accounting system typically uses two address numbers for charges to work packages: (1) the work package number, which consists of WBS-department-CA-work package; and (2) the combined account number, which consists of a single character ledger, three-digit major account, and five-digit subaccount number.
- Work package charge numbers are authorized by the control account manager's release of an AWP.

4. Regarding account charge number composition, an example of an internal charge number is 181-008-1-01. External charge numbers are alphabetized work package numbers. An example is 186-005-2-AB.

5. Regarding direct costs:

- All internal labor is charged to AWP charge numbers.
- Other direct costs are typically identified as: (1) Purchase services and other; (2) travel and subsistence; (3) computer, and (4) other allocated costs.

6. Indirect costs are elements defined by the organization.

- Indirect costs are charged to allocation pools and distributed to internal work packages. They may also be charged as actuals to work packages.
- Controllable labor overhead functions may be budgeted to separate work packages for monthly analysis of applied costs.

Note that actual cost categories and accounting system address numbers vary by organization. Extra care must be taken to integrate EVM requirements with other critical management information processes within the specific organization.

Performance Measurement

Performance measurement for the control account manager consists of evaluating work package status, with EV determined at the work package level. Comparison of planned value (PV) versus earned value (EV) is made to obtain schedule variance. Comparison of EV to actual cost (AC) is made to obtain cost variance. Performance measurement provides a basis for management decisions by the organization and the customer. Six factors must be considered in performance measurement.

1. Performance measurement provides:

- Work progress status.
- Relationship of planned cost and schedule to actual accomplishment.

0/100	Take all credit for performing work when the work package is complete.
50/50	Take credit for performing one-half of the work at the start of the work package; take credit for performing the remaining one-half when the work package is complete.
Discrete Value Milestones	Divide work into separate, measurable activities and take credit for performing each activity during the time period it is completed.
Equivalent Units	If there are numerous similar items to complete, assume each is worth an equivalent portion of the total work package value; take credit for performance according to the number of items completed during the period.
Percentage Complete	Associate estimated percentages of work package to be completed with specific time periods; take credit for performance if physical inspection indicates percentages have been achieved.
Modified Milestone/ Percentage Complete	Combines the discrete value milestone and percent complete techniques by allowing some "subjective estimate" of work accomplishment and credit for the associated earned value during reporting periods where no discrete milestone is scheduled to be completed. The subjective earning of value for nonmilestone work is usually limited to one reporting period or up to 80 percent of the value of the next scheduled discrete milestone. No additional value can be earned until the scheduled discrete milestone is completed.
Level of Effort	Based on a planned amount of support effort, assign value per period; take credit for performance based on passage of time.
Apportioned Effort	Milestones are developed as a percentage of a controlling discrete work package; take credit for performance upon completion of a related discrete milestone.

FIGURE 10A-3. **ALTERNATE METHODS OF ESTABLISHING PV AND CALCULATING EV**

- Valid, timely, auditable data.
- The basis for estimate at completion (EAC), or latest revised estimates (LRE) summaries developed by the lowest practical WBS and organizational level.

2. Regarding cost and schedule performance measurement:

- The elements required to measure project progress and status are: (1) work package schedule/work accomplished status; (2) the PV or planned expenditure; (3) the EV or earned value; and (4) the AC or recorded (or accrued) cost.
- The sum of AWP and PWP budget values (PV) should equal the control account budget value.
- Development of budgets provides these capabilities: (1) the capability to plan and control cost; (2) the capability to identify incurred costs for actual accomplishments and work in progress; and (3) the control account/work package EV measurement levels.

3. Performance measurement recognizes the importance of project budgets.

- Measurable work and related event status form the basis for determining progress status for EV quantification.
- EV measurements at summary WBS levels result from accumulating EV upward through the control account from work package levels.

- Within each control account, the inclusion of LOE is kept to a minimum to prevent distortion of the total EV.
- There are three basic "claiming techniques" used for measuring work package performance: (1) Short work packages are less than three months long. Their earned value (EV) equals PV up to an 80 percent limit of the budget at completion until the work package is completed. (2) Long work packages exceed three months and use objective indicator milestones. The earned value (EV) equals PV up to the month-end prior to the first incomplete objective indicator. (3) Level of effort: Planned value (PV) is earned through passage of time.
- The measurement method to be used is identified by the type of work package. Note that EV must always be earned the same way the PV was planned. (See Figure 10A-3 for alternate methods of establishing PV and calculating EV.)

4. To develop and prepare a forecast to complete (FTC), the control account manager must consider and analyze:

- Cumulative actuals/commitments
- The remaining CA budget
- Labor sheets and grade/levels
- Schedule status
- Previous quarterly FTC
- EV to date
- Cost improvements
- Historical data
- Future actions
- Approved changes

5. The CAM reports the FTC to the EVM information processing organization each quarter.

6. The information processing organization makes the entries and summarization of the information to the reporting level appropriate for the project manager's review.

Variance Analysis

If performance measurement gives results in schedule or cost variances in excess of pre-established thresholds, comprehensive analyses must be made to determine the root cause of the variance. The CAM is mainly concerned with variances that exceed thresholds established for the project. Analyses of these variances provide information needed to identify and resolve problems or take advantage of opportunities. Three factors are involved in variance analysis.

1. *Preparation*

- The cost-oriented variance analyses include a review of current, cumulative, and at-completion cost data. In-house performance reports are used by the CAM to examine cost and schedule dollar plan vs. actual differences from the cost account plan.
- The calendar-schedule analyses include a review of any (scheduling subsystem) milestones that cause more than one-month criticality to the contract milestones.
- Variances are identified to the CA level during this stage of the review.

PV (BCWS)	EV (BCWP)	AC (ACWP)	Condition of Project
$100	$100	$100	On schedule – On budget
$200	$200	$100	On schedule – Underrun
$100	$100	$200	On schedule – Overrun
$100	$200	$200	Ahead of schedule – On budget
$100	$200	$100	Ahead of schedule – Underrun
$100	$200	$300	Ahead of schedule – Overrun
$200	$100	$100	Behind schedule – On budget
$300	$200	$100	Behind schedule – Underrun
$200	$100	$300	Behind schedule – Overrun

FIGURE 10A-4. **COMPARISONS OF PLANNED VALUE, EARNED VALUE, AND ACTUAL COST**

- Both cost variance and schedule variance are developed for the current period and cumulative as well as at-completion status.
- Determination is made whether a variance is cost-oriented, schedule-oriented, or both.
- Formal variance analysis reports are developed on significant CA variances.

2. *Presentation*

Variance analyses should be prepared when one or more of the following exceed the thresholds established by the project manager: (1) schedule variance (EV to PV); (2) cost variance (EV to AC); or (3) at-completion variance (budget at completion to latest revised estimate, or LRE).

3. *Operation*
   - Internal analysis reports document variances that exceed thresholds: schedule problem analysis reports for "time-based" linear schedule, or control account variance analysis reports for dollar variances.
   - Explanations are submitted to the customer when contractual thresholds are exceeded.
   - Emphasis should be placed upon corrective action for resolution of variant conditions.
   - Corrective action should be assigned to specific individuals (control account managers) and closely tracked for effectiveness and completion.
   - Internal project variance analyses and corrective action should be formally reviewed in regularly scheduled management meetings.
   - Informal reviews of cost and schedule variance analysis data may occur daily, weekly, or monthly, depending on the nature and severity of the variance.

Figure 10A-4 presents some sample comparisons of PV, EV, and AC.

Reporting

There are two basic report categories: customer and in-house. Customer performance reports are contractually established with fixed content and timing. In-house reports support internal projects with the data that relate to lower organizational and WBS levels.

The CAM is mainly concerned with these lower-level reports.

1. *Customer reporting*
   - A customer requires summary-level reporting, typically on a monthly basis.
   - The customer examines the detailed data for areas that may indicate a significant variance.
   - The cost performance report (CPR) is the vehicle used to accumulate and report cost and schedule performance data.
2. *In-house reporting*
   - Internal management practices emphasize assignment of responsibility for internal reports to an individual CAM.
   - Reporting formats reflect past and current performance and the forecast level of future performance.
   - Performance review meetings are held: (1) monthly for cost and schedule; and (2) as needed for review of problem areas.
   - The CAM emphasizes cumulative to-date and to-go cost, schedule, and equivalent personpower on the CA work packages.
   - It is primarily at the work package level that review of performance (EV), actuals (AC), and budget (PV) is coupled with objective judgment to determine the FTC.
   - The CAM is responsible for the accuracy and completeness of the estimates.

Internal Audit/Verification and Review

The control account manager is the most significant contributor to the successful operation of a EVM process and to successful completion of any subsequent internal audits or customer reviews. Day-to-day management of the project takes place at the control account level. If each CA is not managed competently, project performance suffers regardless of the sophistication of the higher-level management system. The organization and the customer should place special emphasis on CAM performance during operational demonstration reviews.

The EV approach to project management may be the most comprehensive and effective method of developing plans and providing decision-making information ever conceived. But to achieve maximum potential benefit, the extensive use of an automated support program becomes inevitable. Software especially developed to support EVM applications is currently available for nearly every computer hardware configuration.

When considering which computer hardware/software combination will best satisfy your needs, carefully evaluate your specific project application; i.e., size of projects, frequency of reporting, ease of modification, potential for expansion, and graphic output requirements. This computer hardware/software decision could be the difference between success and failure in an EVM application, so don't rush it! Make your selection only after a thorough investigation and evaluation. Don't let anyone sell you something you don't need or want.

DISCUSSION QUESTIONS

❶ If you are using EVM data to project the "future state" of a project, at what stage of the project would this data become useful in the decision making process?

❷ How important is the duration of a work package in successfully utilizing the Earned Value approach? Are there any alternatives?

❸ During the status/reporting stage (50% complete) you note that one of the key Cost Accounts on the project has an SPI of .83. What does this mean *and* what would you propose doing about it?

REFERENCES

Defense Contract Management Command (DCMC), Earned Value Management Implementation Guide; www.ntsc.navy.mil/Resources/Library/Acqguide/evmig.doc.

Earned Value Management Standard, Project Management Institute*, 2004; www.pmi.org.

Industry Standard Guidelines for Earned Value Management Systems; www.ntsc.navy.mil/Resources/Library/Acqguide/evms_gde.doc.

Project Management, The CommonSense Approach. Using Earned Value to Balance the Triple Constraint, Lee R. Lambert, PMP/Erin Lambert, MBA 2000 Lambert Consulting Group, Inc.

CHAPTER 11

Project Quality Management In Practice

▶GEREE STREUN, PMP, CSQE,
ADVANCED NEUROMODULATION SYSTEMS, INC.

What do we mean by "quality management" on projects? Often, discussions of quality become confused when it isn't clear whether we are referring to the quality of the process—the process of documenting and executing the project—or to the quality of the finished product. The Project Quality Management processes described in *A Guide to the Project Management Body of Knowledge, Third Edition* address that confusion by including all the activities that determine quality standards, objectives, and responsibilities so that the project will satisfy the quality requirements and produce a product that meets quality standards. The Quality Management processes implement the quality management system through the procedures and processes of quality planning, quality assurance, and quality control. Quality Management facilitates continuous process improvement activities conducted throughout the project effort.

The quality management approach described in the *PMBOK® Guide, Third Edition* is compatible with the other quality approaches.[1] Quality processes should be used on all types of projects. The quality approach when building a house is different from that used when developing software for an embedded medical device. In either case if quality requirements are not met, there could be a negative impact to both the customer and the company building the product. For instance, building a house without the proper architectural diagrams or building inspections can cause costly rework after the customer takes possession of the dwelling, which would leave the developer liable for damages. In the case of an embedded medical device, a patient may be harmed, thus leaving the developing company open for prosecution by the FDA and the legal system.

Quality has many different perspectives as meanings have evolved from different industries, organizations, and application areas. The ISO definition for quality is "the totality of characteristics of an entity that bear on its ability to satisfy stated and implied needs."[2] Additionally, quality can mean:

▶Relative quality—the product or service compared to other products or services

▶Fitness for use—the product or service is able to be used

▶Fitness for purpose—the product or service will meet its intended purpose

▶Meets requirements—the product or service in relation to the customer's requirements

▶Quality is inherent—quality cannot be tested in. The process must support designing in quality, not attempting to test it in at the end of the process.

Quality management processes, when properly implemented on a project, drive the project to advance a company's market position:

▶A high performing quality organization has process improvement initiatives that result in:

- Improving all processes in an organization
- Lowering correction costs
- Stopping recall costs
- Recognizing the impact of implementing quality improvement objectives
- Building a historical repository of lessons learned for future improvement.

▶Use the quality process to build in quality throughout the development process. This costs less than trying to test in quality during the verification phase, and costs much less than a product recall. Long term costs can even include the loss of current and future customers.

▶Know your customer's expectations—what do they really want or need to satisfy their requirements. Keep in mind sometimes they will provide information that is more appropriately a proposed solution, an effective quality effort will strive to elicit the real need.

QUALITY'S TIE TO PROJECT MANAGEMENT

The focus for providing quality services or products has evolved over the years from something that is nice to have to a hard demand by customers for quality products. The customers are becoming more educated in their rights and are holding the producers to a higher standard. Global competition has also brought a stronger emphasis on quality. A company's position in the global market improves when a company increases quality by meeting worldwide customers' requirements. The return on investment comes to the company when the quality equation is appropriately applied—the value of the outcome is greater than the sum of the inputs, thereby reducing overall costs. Quality efforts typically increase overall profitability by making sure the quality costs are less than the cost of delivering substandard product.

A project is defined as a series of processes by the Project Management Process Groups and it is important to continually improve project processes as the project management plan is executed.[3] A skilled project manager recognizes that projects must involve a continuous improvement effort to be successful. The project manager develops the project management plan anticipating problems and developing solutions to achieve the required outcome. This guarantees that activities documented in the project management plan are executed to meet the organization and customer's quality requirements.

When planning a project and meeting the project's quality requirements, the project manager must be skilled enough to consider multiple quality aspects:

- The interactions between all project processes provide a focus on quality aspects. The project manager must ensure the upfront analysis is thorough enough to identify any bottlenecks that will negatively impact process interactions during the project effort.

- The degrees of influence resulting from the conflicting project demands. For instance, will the resources needed on the project be overloaded and not readily available?

- The communication needs to maintain a project's appropriate quality focus. The project manager should define what communication media will be used and the communication frequency required to track quality issues to resolution.

Shortcuts taken during initial project processes will lead to negative impact in both project and product quality and drive up the overall cost to the producing organization. For instance, the project initiation activities could be waived, or the project manager is assigned late in the project, or the project manager is never granted the proper authority to do the job. Another key shortcoming that hits a project is that product specifications are typically incomplete so it is very difficult to plan the complete effort and request needed resources.

Cost of quality is a concept that is often overlooked when planning the quality effort in a project. The term is used to reflect the total price of all efforts to achieve quality in a product or service. The calculations must also take into account the impact from delivering a "bad" product and any retrofit that may result. Key project decisions that impact the cost of quality come from either striving for "zero" defects—how much it will cost the project to achieve this high level of quality, versus achieving "good enough" quality—which may result in costly product recall or warranty claims. A project is temporary; however, the product may have a life of 20 years or more, which means investments in defect prevention should be compared against the life of the product to determine the possibility of an appropriate return on the quality investment. If the customer is dissatisfied as a result of an injury or by financial loss, the risk to future business is immense and total quality cost is potentially beyond measure for a company with unrealized future sales and negative market growth.

Quality planning requires the project manager to have the ability to anticipate situations and plan activities that resolve those situations. Including planned quality activities in the project management plan is critical, because any project activity that is not planned typically will not be done. Therefore it is essential to anticipate quality activities to achieve the defined quality criteria and build them into the plan very early in the process.

The quality management plan is a subset of the overall project management plan and addresses quality assurance and quality control, as components of the continuous process improvement effort within any project.[4] It also includes activities to facilitate improving the overall process by planning activities for analyzing the processes to identify all non-value add activities and then removing them or modifying them.

Quality assurance is a series of umbrella activities for continuous process improvement. Project quality assurance activities are an essential aspect of building in quality

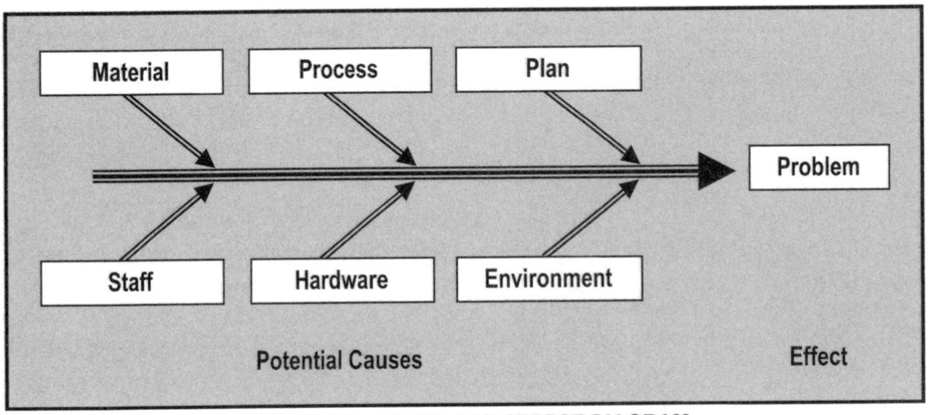

FIGURE 11-1. **CAUSE AND EFFECT DIAGRAM**

rather than trying to test in quality at the end of the development life cycle. Quality assurance continually improves the process reducing waste, allowing processes to operate at increased levels of efficiency.

Quality audits of project activities ensure the project complies with project policies, processes and procedures. Correcting the noted deficiencies results in reduced quality costs and increases the likelihood of the customer accepting the product. Quality audits also confirm that implemented change requests, corrective actions, defect repairs, and preventative actions are correct. Process assessment is very similar to quality audits, but identifies inefficiencies in the process. Root cause analysis is a follow-on activity to both audits and assessments, which analyzes the identified problem, then determines one or more underlying causes, and lastly addresses that problem at an organizational level to prevent future occurrences.

A quality control department performs the monitoring and control required to ensure the project processes and the product comply with relevant quality standards. The project manager must have some knowledge of quality control techniques and tools, such as: [5]

▶*A cause and effect diagram* (Ishikawa diagrams or fishbone diagram), which is a tool used to show how various factors are linked to identified problems or adverse effects. Figure 11-1 is an example of a cause and effect diagram.

▶*Control charts,* which are used to show if a process is stable or has performance that can be predicted. Effectively used control charts illustrate how a process behaves over time. By monitoring and graphing a process's output over time, the chart will show if a process is within acceptable limits over that timeframe. Control charts can be used to monitor plan variances or other outputs to determine if the project management process is in control. Any process found to be outside the defined limits should be targeted for adjustment. Figure 11-2 shows such a control chart.

▶*Pareto charts,* which are histograms representing a distribution that is ordered by occurrence frequency. Each column represents a problem's attributes. The column's height represents the attribute weight or frequency. The distribution shape and width help identify the cause of problems in a process. The rank ordering guides corrective action, which is performed first on occurrences causing the most number of defects.

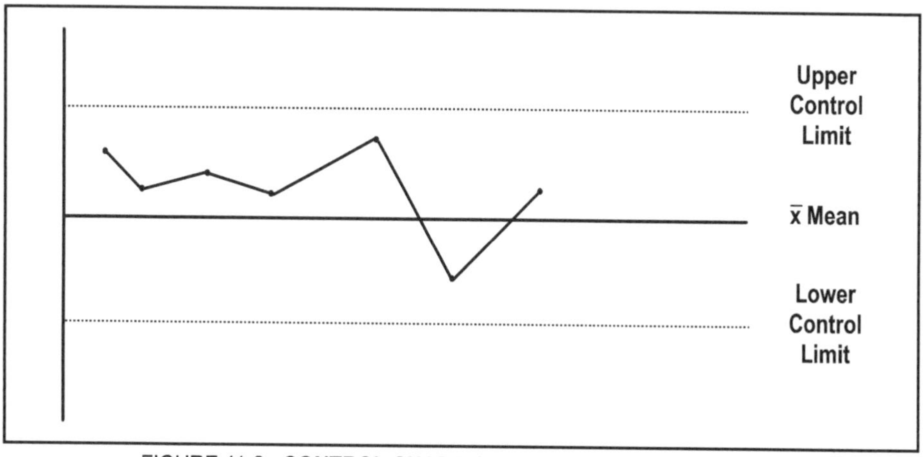

FIGURE 11-2. **CONTROL CHART OF PROCESS PERFORMANCE**

Pareto diagrams are based on Pareto's Law, often called the 80/20 principle, which means a low number of causes or issues (approximately 20%) produce the majority of the problems.

▶*Statistical sampling,* which is actually selecting a limited (80%) part of the population to test. Appropriate application statistical sampling often reduces receiving defective parts or output variation.

▶*Inspections,* which examine a project's artifacts to determine conformance to standards and validate defect repairs. The results of an inspection include measurements and can be generated at any level in the process. Inspections are also used to ensure that processes are being followed as documented.

Quality improvement recommendations and audit findings are used to evolve the project process, the project management plan, and other project deliverables. The quality measurements are fed back to the project management processes to reevaluate and analyze project processes. Planned quality activities ensure a high degree of project and product success, which ensures a high return on investment for the effort invested by the production organization.

DISCUSSION QUESTIONS

❶ What is the purpose of a quality audit?

❷ Discuss how schedule variances can impact the overall schedule, giving examples from projects you are familiar with.

❸ Can you think of examples where Pareto diagrams and the Pareto theory would be useful in improving the quality of a product? In improving the quality of a process?

REFERENCES

[1] Project Management Institute, *A Guide to the Project Management Body of Knowledge, Third Edition,* PMI, 2004: p. 179.

[2] *ISO 9000 Quality Management, Standards Compendium, Fifth Edition;* ISO 8402:1994, Quality management and quality assurance—Vocabulary, published by International Organization for Standardization, 1994.

[3] PMI, ibid.

[4] PMI, ibid.

[5] Schulmeyer, G. Gordon & McManus, James I., *Handbook of Software Quality Assurance, Second Edition,* published by International Thomson Computer Press: 1996.

CHAPTER 11A

Studies in Project Quality Management: Achieving Business Excellence Using Baldrige, Business Process Management, Six Sigma, and Project Management

▶ALAN MENDELSSOHN, OFFICE MAX

▶MICHAEL HOWELL,
BEARING POINT GLOBAL SOLUTIONS

In the challenging global economy of today, many businesses are struggling just to stay alive. Even those that are surviving are finding it more difficult to achieve sustained profitability. No matter what the type of business, no matter what product or service is provided, an organization exists to serve its customers in an efficient and effective way. And when done right, the business will be more profitable.

So what is the secret to success? There is none. What it takes to be successful, what is referred to as "business excellence," is nothing more than good, common sense business management, coupled with strong leadership, discipline, and a lot of hard work. Over the years, however, organizations have honed their skills to be able to better implement those things necessary to serve customers.

In the last thirty years, there have been many buzzwords used to describe different approaches to achieving business excellence. Some of the more familiar names include Quality Improvement, Total Quality Control, Quality Management, TQM, Reengineering, ISO 9000, Six Sigma, Business Process Management, Digital Six Sigma, Baldrige, Lean, and even the more generic term Continuous Improvement. And there are many other names

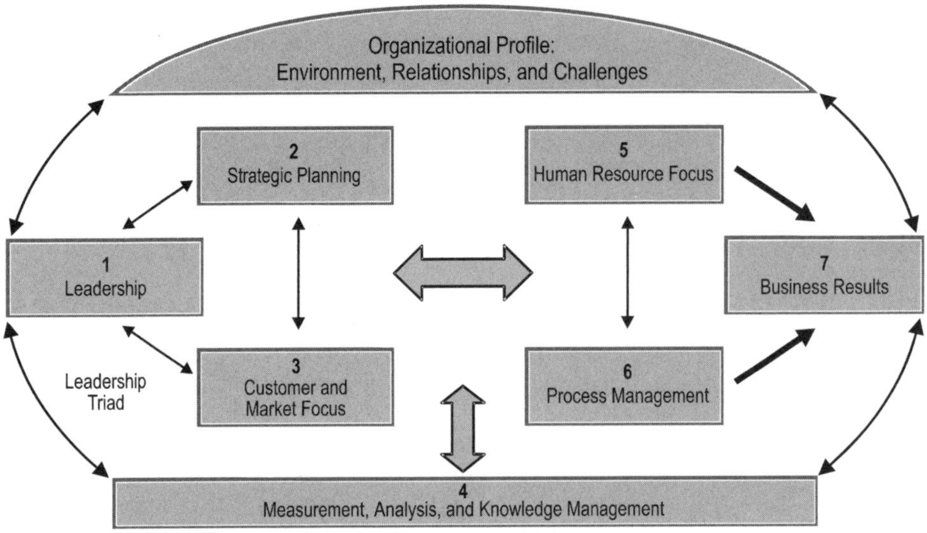

FIGURE 11A-1. **BALDRIGE CRITERIA FOR PERFORMANCE EXCELLENCE FRAMEWORK: A SYSTEMS PERSPECTIVE**

unique to particular organizations or to consultants that are promoting their proprietary approach. When one steps back and looks at all these approaches, there are some common elements that are the keys to success, no matter what they are called.

This article will address three approaches from the above list: Baldrige, Business Process Management, and Six Sigma. Each brings a specific focus that overlaps and complements the other two to achieve business excellence. Whether called by these names or some other names, all three are needed. Project Management, while not in the above list, becomes an enabler to help implement the different methodologies.

Business excellence can now be defined as a holistic, customer focused, process-based systems approach to successfully achieve the goals of the organization. The Malcolm Baldrige National Quality Award's Criteria for Performance Excellence provides the framework for this systems approach—what an organization must do to be successful. Embedded throughout the Criteria is a proactive, integrated, process framework that uses data to make decisions. And to continually improve all the organization's processes and keep them current with changing customer and market requirements, a process improvement approach, like Six Sigma, is needed. The concepts and tools of project management are used to help implement many of the changes that are necessary to make these process improvements.

USING BALDRIGE AS A FRAMEWORK

The Malcolm Baldrige National Quality Award was established in 1987 to recognize organizations that have demonstrated excellence against a set of criteria representing best practices of role model companies. As these practices have advanced, so have the Criteria.[1] The Criteria provide a framework to evaluate how an organization delivers value to its customers and stakeholders and how successful it has been in accomplishing this. Whether the Criteria are used for internal self-evaluation or for assessment as part of a state or national award process, the goal should be the same: accelerate the organization forward in its journey towards business excellence. Those who focus solely on the award miss its real purpose. The most important output of an award is the feedback an organization receives identifying its strengths and its opportunities for improvement. Properly addressing the latter is what makes an organization better.

Criteria for Performance Excellence

The seven Baldrige Categories that are the heart of the Criteria provide the framework for an organization's approach to achieving business excellence. How they connect and integrate is shown in Figure 11A-1.[2] The Organizational Profile at the top of figure sets the context for the way an organization operates.

The organization's Leadership (Category 1) use Strategic Planning (Category 2) processes to set and deploy strategies to support the Customer and Market Focus (Category 3). These Categories set the organizational direction. Using the workforce addressed in the Human Resource Focus (Category 5) to accomplish the work, Process Management (Category 6) approaches are implemented to achieve the desired Business Results (Category 7). The Categories are linked as shown. "All actions point toward Business Results—a composite of customer, product and service, financial, and internal operational performance results, including human resource, governance, and social responsibility results."[3]

> "Measurement, Analysis, and Knowledge Management (Category 4) are critical to the effective management of your organization and to a fact-based, knowledge-driven system for improving performance and competitiveness."[4]

The Seven Baldrige Categories

1. *The Leadership Category* examines: how senior leaders establish the organization's values and set directions and performance expectations; the organization's governance and how it addresses its public and community responsibilities; and how senior leaders review organizational and leadership performance and use the review findings as a basis for improvement.

2. *The Strategic Planning Category* examines how the organization develops its strategic objectives, action plans, and goals and deploys these throughout the organization.

> "The special role of strategic planning is to align work processes with your organization's strategic directions, thereby ensuring that improvement and learning reinforce organizational priorities."[5]

3. *The Customer and Market Focus Category* examines how the organization listens to the Voice of the Customer. It addresses how customer and market requirements and expectations are determined and how relationships are built with customers. The latter includes the key factors that lead to customer acquisition, satisfaction, loyalty, and retention.

4. *The Measurement, Analysis, and Knowledge Management Category* examines: how performance data and information are selected, gathered, analyzed, and improved; how the quality and availability of needed data and information are ensured; and how organizational knowledge is managed.

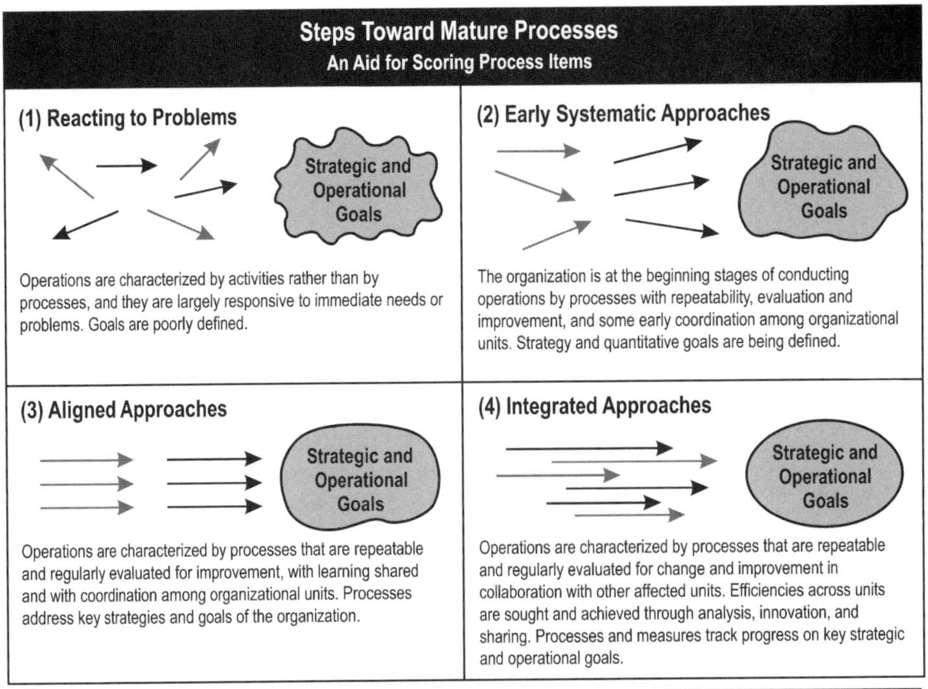

FIGURE 11A-2. **STEPS TOWARD MATURE PROCESSES**

5. *The Human Resource Focus Category* "addresses key human resource practices—those directed toward creating and maintaining a high-performance workplace and toward developing employees to enable them and your organization to adapt to change."[6]

6. *"The Process Management Category* examines the key aspects of your organization's process management, including key product, service, and business processes for creating customer and organizational value and key support processes. This Category encompasses all key processes and all work units."[7] It addresses how the organization identifies and manages its key processes and how it improves them so they are efficient and effective and stay current with changing business needs and directions.

7. *The Business Results Category* examines the organization's performance in key business areas. It measures the organization's progress towards achieving its overall strategy through implementing its approaches defined in Categories 1-6.

Evaluation Using the Criteria

With the Baldrige Criteria providing the framework for business excellence, it is important for an organization to evaluate its progress in the improvement journey. Whether doing an internal self-evaluation or as part of an external assessment, the extent to which the organization has matured in its process implementation will impact the results achieved. Figure 11A-2[8] illustrates the Steps toward Mature Processes.

Progress is evaluated from two perspectives: process and results—the former are addressed in Categories 1-6; the latter in Category 7.

Evaluating processes examines the approaches used, the extent of deployment of these approaches within the entire organization, how these approaches have been improved, and how aligned and integrated the approaches are to support organizational-wide goals.

For results, the current level of performance, trends, and comparisons are evaluated to assess the extent results address key customer, market, process, and action plan requirements.

BUSINESS PROCESS MANAGEMENT AS A FOUNDATION

Everyone has both personal and business processes they are engaged in daily. When what you do is performed over and over again on a frequent enough basis, it is worth paying attention to. An example is driving to work every day. If the process is executed consistently, then the results can be predicted. Business process management is no different. It's all about managing business processes to get the desired results, to consistently and efficiently meet or exceed customer requirements—and in so doing, enabling an organization to be successful and grow. Within the Baldrige Criteria framework, business process management (BPM) becomes the foundation to move an organization forward in its continuous improvement and business excellence journey.

Organizations that have not yet implemented BPM often find themselves working feverishly on everything at once. Typically, the organization will have a lot of projects started, often using disciplined project management techniques, and set financial expectations. The projects, however, are working in a rapidly changing environment. The more cross-functional the process, the greater the chance for miscues and many of the projects or improvement efforts are uncoordinated, perhaps even redundant, with real savings hard to quantify. Often, work priorities shift due to the next crisis management issue, or even from what an executive may have simply said. In many cases, a structured approach from which to select projects does not exist.

Business process management provides a structured approach in an environment where little structure existed before. BPM focuses an organization's resources on the top priority projects and on work that is aligned to the organization's vision, mission, strategies, and goals.

Overcoming the perception that business process management takes too long or perhaps, where a quality system is regarded as just a theoretical exercise, requires a disciplined and structured implementation. Above all else, leadership engagement is a must. Of course, marketing a few successes helps to gain buy-in from those that are sitting on the fence.

What does business process management (BPM) do for you? BPM provides a structured method to manage processes, documents and stores key work processes for easy accessibility and reuse, leverages and builds on knowledge management, captures process dependencies, uses objective process measures, and closes gap between customer needs and process performance.

Why would an organization want to implement BPM? It would allow an organization to control core business processes enabling control of the process outcome. BPM focuses and aligns an organization on top-priorities, creates a common process language, and accelerates organizational learning.

BPM implementation can be broken down into the following key steps:

- ▶Identify top-priority, critical processes.
- ▶Validate customer requirements.
- ▶Model the process.
- ▶Develop process measures.
- ▶Monitor the process.
- ▶Stability—consistent performance.
- ▶Capability—meeting customer needs.
- ▶Flexibility—for new requirements.
- ▶Manage and improve the process.
- ▶Identify critical processes.

A process is a series of repetitive and systematic actions or operations that add value and are necessary in order to produce and deliver a product or service. From a simplistic perspective, a process starts with an input from a supplier, work is performed, value is added, and the product or service is delivered to a customer. A business process is much more complex, typically cross-functional in nature with multiple process levels. An activity at one level becomes a process at the next lower level. And at each level, someone owns the process. Depending on the organization's process maturity, each level process owner may be accountable for the results. The concept of process ownership is important to achieving business excellence.

Top priority or critical processes are those processes that are typically operational in nature and are core to delivering a product or service to external customers. A problem with a top-priority or critical process directly results in not meeting customer requirements or expectations.

Eventually, all critical processes need to be addressed. Which one to look at first can be determined by (1) evaluating the criticality of each process to satisfying customers and achieving organizational goals and (2) evaluating which processes are not performing as expected. The determination of your top-priority processes is extremely important. Typical corporate prioritization is by what is "most broke" or receiving the most top-level scrutiny. Having a structured, disciplined approach to managing core business processes results in incremental continuous improvement and a "pipeline" of projects to work on next.

Validate Customer Requirements

A customer of a process is the person who receives the product or services from the output of the process. Depending on the level of the process and where the process fits into the overall order-to-delivery of the organization, the needs of both external customers and internal customers have to be met. In most organizations, there are always key stakeholder needs that are important and must be addressed.

In many organizations, a number of employees do not have direct interaction with the external customer. They may deal with other functional areas, management, or "next-process" customers. This would be an example of an internal customer. Because all processes should be linked into an integrated system, employees should understand the end-to-end system view and be able to link their efforts to the external customer.

A requirement represents a need or want that the customer expects to have satisfied. Customer requirements are usually translated into specifications an organization operationally understands using various techniques. It is necessary to review the customer requirements frequently with customers to be sure they are specific, measurable, have not changed, and can be provided in a satisfactory format and time frame. This may involve negotiation with the customer if the above criteria cannot be met. The requirement becomes valid only after agreement is reached that (1) the need can be satisfied, and (2) the party responsible for the process agrees to satisfy it. The same criteria apply in validating requirements for both internal and external customers.

In some organizations, other key stakeholder requirements may be as important as customer requirements. For example, in a health care environment, the needs of physicians, families, and insurance companies can play a significant role in how a hospital serves its primary customers—patients. In education, requirements of parents and other stakeholder (e.g., businesses and institutions of higher learning) could impact the way a school teaches its primary customers—students.

An organization also must carefully consider its suppliers and partners. To provide products and services that meet customer expectations and requirements consistently, everyone must understand the end-to-end system and where they fit in the bigger picture. It is important to assess how well the individual pieces are contributing to delivering products and services overall.

Model the Processes

Documentation of the work processes makes them visible. All the steps necessary to achieve the final product need to be shown. A process should be described on simple terms, at a level of detail represented by 4-8 activities. The process for the manager should be at a level of detail reflecting those activities that he or she will personally follow. Each activity block might represent a lower-level process that must also be controlled.

In describing a process, in addition to the flow of activities and their triggering events, it is important to consider the various components that are necessary to make the different steps of the process work. These include people, systems, information and data, materials, tools and equipment, documentation, and environmental factors. Not all components apply to every process or process step. If a process is not performing properly to meet customer requirements, the activities may be correct but one or more of the components of the process could be the problem area.

When looking at any particular process, there are a number of different versions that can be considered. These versions can represent the process as defined in a procedures manual, the process as management thinks it works, the way the process is actually performed—the "as-is" process, the "ideal" process (as-is, but cleaner), or the "future state" process. The most important version to model and measure first is the "as-is" process. Since the output of a process is a direct result of what happens in the process, it is necessary to understand what is currently being done, including what is not working properly, before looking at any future state process.

In the past, processes have been documented using flowcharts. Flowcharts usually show activities, have a single symbol to represent a decision, and may identify the responsible person or function for a group of activities. This, however, is not enough. What happens to complex decisions; how are they represented? What about some of the other components of a process that are absolutely necessary if a process is to work properly?

Modeling a process has a number of benefits not available in flowcharting. In addition to providing visual descriptions of processes, modeling addresses more complex decisions and process components; links to IT systems, people, and other resources; uses an enterprise-wide database with a common language; permits simulation of "what if" scenarios; and can link to measures that are part of a balanced scorecard.

Develop Process Measures

Measuring a process is important to determine if it is meeting customer requirements and to understand how the process is performing.

A results indicator measures whether a process is satisfying the customer's valid requirement, based on those things that are important to the customer—not what is convenient to measure. If the process team uses a different set of indicators from the customer, its interpretation of success may also be different from the customer's.

A process indicator is used to show whether a work process is stabilized and to forewarn of problems that could impact final results. This is the "Voice of the Process" speaking to us. It represents the process owner's view. Located upstream in the process, it alarms for unwanted outcomes.

If the indicators show that the targets are being met but the data show that the process is not stable, then the process owner has been favored by luck. When a process is unstable, anything can happen, and it often does. Response to this instability is usually called firefighting.

If the data show that a process is stable but the indicators show that the targets are not being met, then the process is not capable of achieving the desired results. It must be changed in some way. The Six Sigma problem-solving process is used to eliminate root causes and identify improvements to the process. Process stability is required before addressing capability issues.

Process control requires an understanding of the relationship between the process indicators and the results indicator. For example, if the forecasted date for turnover of new equipment to the customer is the result indicator being monitored, it is also important to follow the schedule for completion of each of the key activities in procuring that equipment. If the engineering activity is running late, this has a direct impact on the turnover date, unless action is taken to correct the situation. By monitoring this process indicator, the process owner can predict whether the customer's required turnover date can be met or can take appropriate action to improve the situation before it is too late. If the process is not controlled upstream of the outcome, the impact is felt downstream, but not by the people who cause the problem. Correcting those things in the engineering process that cause delays may also prevent the same factors from affecting future engineering activities.

Monitor the Process

Once the process has been defined and measures established, the process owner needs to:

▶Confirm the process model with all stakeholders.

▶Start measuring the results and process indicators.

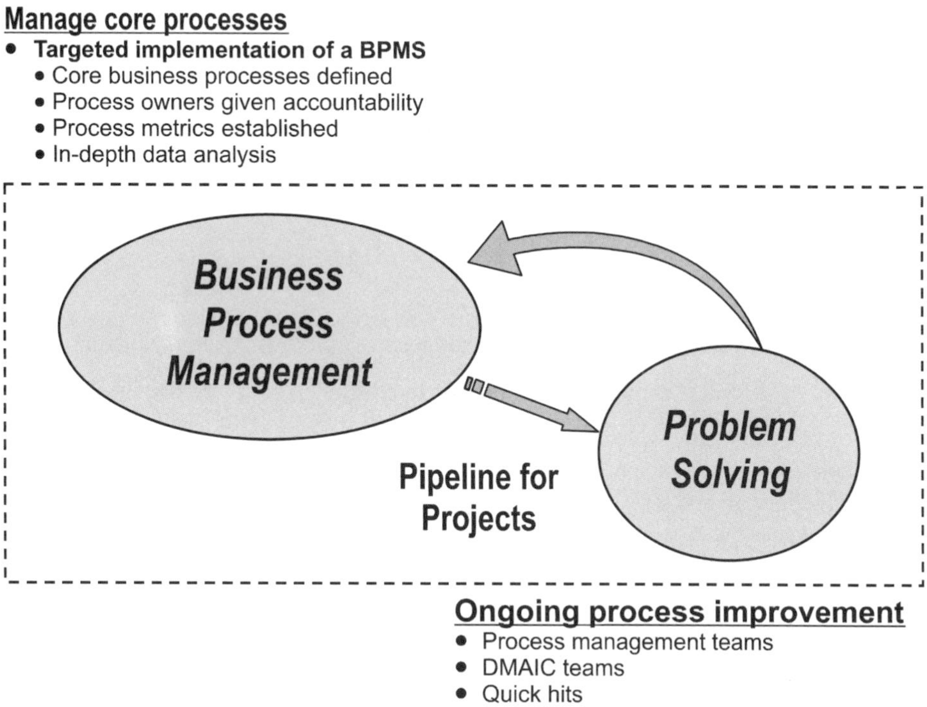

FIGURE 11A-3. **CONTINUOUS PROCESS IMPROVEMENT**

▶Establish targets and thresholds.

▶Manage and improve the process based on the analysis data from the measures.

Managing a process is an ongoing effort. The process owner has to continually confirm that the process is meeting customer requirements, even in a changing market environment, and is doing it efficiently so as not to waste the organization's resources. When it is not, improvements in the process are required. A process improvement approach, like Six Sigma, provides the roadmap and tools to make the needed improvement.

SIX SIGMA FOR IMPROVEMENT

How does Six Sigma play a role with BPM? It all depends on how Six Sigma is positioned and viewed within an organization. As part of achieving business excellence, Six Sigma is viewed here from a problem-solving, project-by-project perspective. The benefits in integrating BPM with the Six Sigma problem solving and design methodology are operational in nature: faster and cheaper. This includes root cause elimination with statistical rigor and hard dollar improvements. The integration of BPM and Six Sigma provides a continuous improvement loop that generates a 'pipeline' for problem solving projects (Figure 11A-3) from core business process measurement and then improves the processes for continued operations and monitoring.

In using a statistical approach, however, it is necessary to weigh the depth and breadth of the use of statistics within the organization. The seven basic continuous improvement tools[9] are often more than sufficient for an organization to start with. As the organization becomes more proficient with the tools themselves, introduction of more advanced statistical methodologies is appropriate. Six Sigma problem solving is a structured, five-step approach built around the DMAIC process. The question answered in each step is shown below.

▶ *Define*—What is the problem?

▶ *Measure*—How big is the problem?

▶ *Analyze*—What is causing the problem?

▶ *Improve*—What can be done to eliminate/reduce the root cause of the problem?

▶ *Control*—How will the process be monitored to ensure the gains are sustained?

From a BPM system approach, Six Sigma is an enabler to a company's continuous improvement journey. The continuous improvement impact, if balanced correctly, can be felt in both the short and the long term. Using Design for Six Sigma methods and tools in the Improve phase will help achieve sustainable, long-term results. Change management now plays a critical role in implementing solutions and leadership must be engaged for the approach to work. Political issues and obstacles need to be addressed early. Developing, establishing, and improving processes can provide breakthrough results and increased capacity, or can address changing customer requirements that will enable an organization to achieve a desired future state. Further discussion of Six Sigma is offered in Chapter 30.

BPM, SIX SIGMA, AND PROJECT MANAGEMENT

So how does project management fit into the discussion Business Process Management (BPM) and Six Sigma?

Implementing the Baldrige Criteria, business process management, or Six Sigma problem solving requires specific skill sets from black belts or quality professionals involved in these efforts. Typical training for these individuals includes project management skills.

Project management skills are important because continuous improvement efforts are often project-based and cross-functional in nature. The project leads are held accountable for completing projects on time and within budget (if applicable), and to deliver improvements based on customer or business requirements. This usually requires managing multiple activities at once, addressing change management issues, and meeting rigorous "tollgate" timelines. In addition, black belts or other quality professionals are routinely assigned multiple projects at any given time. Utilizing project management discipline, such as understanding a project's critical path and the key tasks to be completed, improves the probability of success for the projects themselves.

BPM and Six Sigma are dependent on the project leads possessing the skills to successfully manage the lifecycle of projects. Delivering results are absolutely critical to a program launch in order to gain credibility to the quality system initiative. Project management discipline enables project leads to successfully complete the projects, and therefore, demonstrate the much needed credibility or value to the business leaders.

CONCLUSION

We've defined business excellence as "a holistic, customer-focused, process-based, systems approach to successfully achieve the goals of the organization." The Malcolm Baldrige National Quality Award's Criteria for Performance Excellence provided the framework for this systems approach with business process management (BPM) serving as the foundation to move an organization forward in its continuous improvement and business excellence journey. Six Sigma and project management were discussed as necessary tools to help in this journey.

The important thing to remember is that business excellence is a continuous journey. If an organization does not keep current with changing customer and market needs, someone else will. Profitability and success are challenged and even survival can become an issue. Only by a commitment to provide better, more responsive, innovative, and efficient products and services can an organization continually achieve business excellence.

DISCUSSION QUESTIONS

❶ Although we make the assertion business process management (BPM) the foundation for business excellence, many organizations want to jump into other approaches and tools to reach the end state without first building this foundation. What holds an organization back and what barriers have to be overcome to be able to create this business process foundation?

❷ There appears to be a trend where the traditional boundaries of project management, quality (such as Six Sigma), and other management disciplines are starting to blur as these disciplines merge in their directions. How will this trend shape the approach to achieving business excellence in the future?

❸ With new emerging technologies such as process modeling, workflow, and process automation, there is an increased ability for organizations to receive information for real time measures, process execution, and task management. What kind of impact will this have on achieving business excellence in the future?

REFERENCES

[1] Criteria for Performance Excellence. Gaithersburg, Md: Baldrige National Quality Program, National Institute of Standards and Technology, US Dept of Commerce; 2004. Summarized with permission.

[2] *Ibid*, p. 5.

[3] *Ibid*, p. 5.

[4] *Ibid*, p. 5.

[5] *Ibid*, p. 40.

[6] *Ibid*, p. 47.

[7] *Ibid*, p. 24.

[8] *Ibid*, p. 58.

[9] The seven basic tools are as follows: Checklist, Pareto Diagram, Histogram, Run Chart, Scatter Diagram, Control Chart, and Cause-and-Effect Diagram. Some authors will include the Flowchart instead of either a Checksheet or Run Chart.

CHAPTER 12

Human Resource Management In Practice

▶LEE TOWE, PMP, INNOVATORS, INC.

The *PMBOK® Guide, Third Edition,* view of human resources focuses on the people who carry out activities to complete the project; in other words, the human resources—also known as the project team. Project Human Resource Management consists of four processes that organize and manage the project team. Stakeholders who are not project team members are addressed in other sections of the standard.[1]

Compared to earlier editions of the standard, the 2004 edition added a monitor and control process called "Manage Project Team." All areas of project management involve tracking plans against results, and human resource management is no exception. While the phrase "manage project team" may be somewhat vague, the alternative working name "monitor project team" gave the undesired impression of too much oversight. The four processes are:

1. *Human Resource Planning*—a name change from Organizational Planning to clarify the fact that the process is the first step in Project Human Resource Management.

2. *Acquire Project Team.*

3. *Develop Project Team.*

4. *Manage Project Team*—a new monitoring and control process that emphasizes comparisons of original plans with how team performance.

The number of techniques used to manage project teams reflect common usage, including networking, virtual teams, ground rules, observation and conversation, project performance appraisals, conflict management, and issue logs.

How Human Resource Management Processes Integrate with Other Areas

Breaking project management practices into discrete knowledge areas is a helpful way to understand the important aspects of project management, but also separates actions that should integrate smoothly among those knowledge areas. Here are a few examples of ways that human resource management interacts with other project management areas:

▶Identification of required team members starts with an overall assessment of the resources that will be needed to complete the project. These are first identified in the Time Management chapter of the Guide under Activity Resource Requirements.

▶While general project responsibilities may be shown in project organizational charts or position descriptions, many team member responsibilities are listed as activity assignments in the schedule. More responsibilities may be listed in other portions of the project management plan, such as people assigned to deal with risk (risk responses), quality (quality assurance and control activities that may not be specified on the schedule), or communication (communication responsibilities.)

▶The process of acquiring team members may require hiring people from outside the organization. This would involve the processes described in the chapter on Procurement Management.

PROJECT HUMAN RESOURCE MANAGEMENT PROCESSES

Human Resource Planning

Human resource planning identifies roles and responsibilities that will be required to complete the project. The identification of reporting relationships among those roles is often captured in the form of organization chart of some sort for the project. Finally, a plan for how and when the people will come and go from the project takes shape. The staffing management plan documents all of the human resource planning information.

▶*Inputs.* The three primary inputs for identifying roles and responsibilities are an understanding of the environment in which the project will exist, information from lessons learned in similar situations that may be helpful, and the activities that need to be performed in order to complete the project.

Understanding the environment surrounding the project is vital when planning the best way to staff the project. Which organizations and departments will be involved and affected? How will technical disciplines communicate with one another? What history, including successes and conflicts, do the people likely to be involved with the project share? What relationships and influences already exist? What kind of physical or geographic separations can be expected? These are termed Enterprise Environmental Factors.

"Organizational process assets" is the term given to templates and checklists that have carried over from previous projects. Organizations with mature project management environments create templates based on lessons learned. Templates may include past project organization charts or position descriptions. Organizations may also have built lists of items for consideration, such as team ground rules to consider,

	Acquire content	Manage copyrights and permissions	Create and beta-test site	Approve or identify changes	Proof text	Resolve technical issues
Content Editor	*x*			*x*		
Project Administrator		*x*			*x*	
Webmaster			*x*			*x*

FIGURE 12-1. **RESPONSIBILITY ASSIGNMENT MATRIX: WEBSITE PROJECT**

compliance issues, or training courses that are available. Checklists help reduce the need to reinvent the wheel at the beginning of every project.

The third area of information needed for the human resource management plan is the list of activity resource requirements that emerge as the project deliverables are broken into work packages and then into activities required to create the deliverables. In other words, what needs to be done?

▶*Outputs.* As a result of doing the human resource planning, three outputs are developed: Roles and responsibilities needed to complete the project; a description of how those roles relate, often in the form of an organizational chart for the project; and a plan for acquiring, training, rewarding, and otherwise managing the team.

The work that a project team member is expected to perform is referred to as a set of responsibilities. A communication shortcut that clusters commonly understood responsibilities together for one person is called a role. When a role such as quality control engineer is defined, many responsibilities are associated with that role without listing them all individually. The use of roles saves time. However, one must be sure to clarify boundaries for roles as necessary. For example, if project roles include a quality control engineer as well as a test developer, communication to clarify where one role stops and the next one starts will be necessary. Who will actually carry out quality control tests? Who determines how measurements will be taken? How many tests or samples will be adequate?

Project team members are held accountable for their responsibilities. In order for team members to carry out their tasks, they should be given levels of authority that match their levels of responsibility. Authority is the right to make decisions, apply resources, and sign approvals on behalf of an organization. When authority exceeds accountability, abuse could occur. When accountability exceeds authority, frustration, low morale, minimum productivity, and turnover are likely outcomes.

▶*Tools and Techniques.* Techniques used to define and document human resource responsibilities are organization charts, position descriptions, networking, and organizational theory. Organization charts are usually a set of boxes arranged as a hierarchy. They can be simple or detailed. The organization chart for a small conference could be as simple as naming the project manager and the five people responsible for marketing, registration, speakers, food, and exhibits.

Another way to document responsibilities, which could be considered a type of organization chart, is with a matrix. Sometimes called a responsibility assignment matrix (RAM), the chart lists people on one axis and activities or work packages along the other matrix. The advantages of this format are that by looking across one row, one can get an idea of the total responsibilities that one person has, and by looking down a column, one can confirm that exactly one person is responsible for each activity listed. A matrix of this nature may be generated through the report function of a project scheduling software program.

For large projects or cases where clarity is crucial, position descriptions can list detailed responsibilities for some or all project roles. These may be developed jointly by the people holding the positions and the project manager and may be based on templates from previous projects.

Networking is the practice of developing relationships with other people. It may be helpful at many times in a project, but is listed here as a way to understand how to most successfully staff a project team. A person who lacks practical knowledge of an organizational environment can easily miss identification of roles, responsibilities, and reporting relationships that would be helpful in completing the project.

Acquire Team

As the roles and responsibilities are identified, the people needed to carry them out must be acquired. This step is categorized as an execution process because it is primarily concerned with executing the plans developed in human resource planning.

▶*Inputs.* Not surprisingly, the starting point for this process includes the three outputs of the previous planning process: roles and responsibilities, project organization chart(s), and the staffing management plan. Organizational hiring policies and assistance from the organization's human resource department are other inputs to consider and are collectively known as Organizational Process Assets.

The fifth and most important input is a description of the people who are available to work on the project. This information is listed as part of the Enterprise Environmental Factors. (In earlier editions of the *PMBOK® Guide,* it was called the staffing pool description.) The description may include such things as a person's availability, ability, experience, interests, and how much it would cost to have the person work on the project.

▶*Outputs.* As one would expect, warm-bodied team members are the end result of acquiring the project team. The output is called project staff assignments in order to state the output as a document for the sake of consistency. Part of the documentation for the assignments can include a team directory.

In addition to the project staff assignments, resource availability for the team members is listed as a separate output. Resource availability, e.g., when Joe is not on vacation or when Deb is not dedicated to another project) is necessary in order to develop a sound schedule and is listed as an input to Activity Resource Estimating.

As specific people are brought on board, staffing management plan updates may be necessary. This may be due to the fact that roles may need to be modified to accommodate the actual people that can work on the project.

▶*Tools and Techniques.* The four techniques associated with acquiring the project team are based on three ways people may end up on a team, plus a fourth concept—virtual teams. The first way that team members may be acquired is through pre-assignment.

This means that a person was slated to be on a project at inception. A good analogy of this process takes place in the movie industry. Sometimes scripts are written and then a casting director fills the roles. Other times writers have a particular person in mind as the movie is written. Similarly, some projects are based on the skills of a particular individual.

When team members are drawn from the same organization as the person doing the recruiting, negotiation may be required. And when the project must pull from outside the organization, the technique is referred to as acquisition, a form of procurement.

Listing virtual teams as a technique for acquiring project team members may seem odd at first, but the concept is probably used most often as a way of including team members who may not be able to participate in any other way. Virtual team members are typically located far enough from other team members, making face-to-face meetings not practical during most or all of the project. While distance would be the most common reason for the creation of a virtual team, other reasons may include home offices, different work shifts, and mobility handicaps. The growing use of electronic communication has made virtual teams an increasing trend.

Develop Team

Team development includes two important components: Developing individual abilities and increasing the ability of people to work together as a group.

▶*Inputs.* As a starting point, the project staff assignments provide the list of people who are one the team. The staffing management plan lists training plans and other information pertinent to carrying out team development. Resource availability is the third input and identifies the times that people are available to participate in development activities.

▶*Outputs.* While the primary goal is better performance, the output listed in the Guide is called team performance assessment. The assessment is a verifiable product that can be listed as an output. This does not mean to suggest that a formal, written assessment is required. Ongoing evaluation of a team's effectiveness is simply a way to determine how much additional development work is needed and in what ways it needs to be modified.

▶*Tools and Techniques.* Six straightforward ways to develop a project team's effectiveness are listed. General management skills such as empathy, creativity, and group facilitation are useful when working with team members. Training and team-building activities are common team development approaches. The use of ground rules helps a team minimize problems and work together better as a group.

Co-location is the practice of placing some or all of the project team members together for part of all of the project. Even teams that will operate primarily as virtual teams can benefit from a meeting early in the project where people come together to meet one another and clarify expectations. And finally, recognition and rewards can be utilized to encourage desirable behavior and results.

Manage Team

Managing the project team involves monitoring performance, giving feedback, resolving issues, and coordinating changes. It is a monitoring and control process.

▶*Inputs.* All control processes compare things that have been planned with things that are actually taking place. So the inputs of a controlling process can usually be broken into three categories: 1) what was planned, 2) what is happening, and 3) other information that will explain how the control process is to be performed.

The control inputs that document what the human resources have planned to accomplish are the roles and responsibilities, the project organizational charts (both outputs of Human Resource Planning), and project staff assignments (an output of Acquire Project Team). The staffing management plan contains a mix of information. Some of the information describes plans that can be used as control points, such as compliance, safety, and training needs. The staffing management plan may also instruct the project management team on how to conduct the control activities.

The control inputs that document what the human resources are actually doing include the team performance assessment (an output of Develop Project Team), work performance information (an output of Direct and Manage Project Execution), and performance reports (an output of Performance Reporting). The team performance assessment and work performance information both focus on individual abilities and how well the team is functioning as a group. The performance reports provide information regarding budget, schedule, and scope performance that will guide decisions related to managing the team.

Organizational process assets are listed as an input that contains neither plans nor performance information. The organizational assets include items such as web sites, annual recognition dinners, and newsletters that can be utilized when managing the team.

▶*Outputs.* When actual team performance is compared with the original plans, there are several possible outputs. Requested changes can be made to the change control body in order to receive approval for staffing changes. Recommended corrective actions could include additional training or disciplinary actions. Recommended preventive actions could include cross-training or further role clarification.

Another output that results from managing the team is an update to the organization's process assets. Information that falls into this category includes input given to the appropriate supervisors in the organization concerning the performance of team members. Lessons learned as a part of the control process are also forwarded to the people who collect this information, such as a centralized project management office.

As project changes take place, the project management plan may need to be updated. The plan may need to be changed to reflect changing team member roles, awards to be made, or the addition of a new off-site team session.

▶*Tools and Techniques.* The four techniques listed for managing the project team are observation and conversation, project performance appraisals, conflict management, and an issue log.

One of the simple ways that project managers have of comparing what has been planned with what is actually taking place is by observing people and conversing with them. Another technique for managing team members is with a project performance appraisal. The project manager or someone else with supervisory responsibilities needs to provide feedback to team members in order to encourage positive performance and to uncover questions and concerns. The degree to which this is a structured event depends on variables such as the project's length and complexity and how much feedback occurs during the normal course of the project.

Conflict management techniques will allow differences of opinion to be raised, but minimize a loss of teamwork caused by negative feelings and actions among team members. Solid project management practices like communication planning, team building, and role clarification do a lot to reduce conflict before it arises. Ground rules can be established that include a process for addressing conflict among team members.

An issue log is the fourth technique for managing the project team. When issues are raised, a log will track the issue and list who is responsible for taking action and a target date for closure. Logs vary from meeting minutes in that they are usually cumulative throughout the length of the project and will continue to list an issue until it is closed.

ISSUES NOT EMPHASIZED IN THE *GUIDE:* CONFLICT MANAGEMENT

Conflict management is an area of emphasis on the PMP Examination, and rightly so. Research has indicated that the most intense conflict is between project managers and functional departments. The same study determined that the major sources of conflict are, in descending order of frequency:

1. Schedules
2. Project priorities
3. Manpower resources
4. Technical opinions
5. Administrative procedures
6. Cost objectives
7. Personalities.[2]

There are five principal strategies for managing conflict. The first is by far the best in most circumstances:

1. Problem solving: Confront and collaborate to resolve the issue (Win/Win)
2. Compromise: Bargain to get some satisfaction for both parties (Lose/Lose)
3. Smoothing: Discount differences to achieve harmony (Lose/Lose)
4. Withdrawal: Avoid, deny, or postpone issues (Lose/Lose)
5. Forcing: Impose one's viewpoint (Win/Lose)

Note that compromise is considered lose/lose because both parties are assumed to give in to some degree and not arrive at an optimum solution. Withdrawal may be okay in the short run if a cooling off period is needed. Forcing may seem like a poor approach, but the person who forces a solution (possibly as a result of being in a position of authority) "wins," resulting in a win-lose outcome. The long-term effects of persistent forcing, however, can be detrimental not merely to the work relationship, but to business outcomes.[3]

Additionally, here are three motivational theories that can help the project manager better understand how to lead and inspire the team.[4]

▶*McGregor's Theory X—Theory Y.* McGregor believed one could classify managers into two categories: Theory X and Theory Y. Theory X managers are of the belief that workers are basically lazy and dislike work. They need to be watched and prodded at all times. Theory Y managers believe that workers want to do well and will do so in the right environment. They need to be supported and allowed freedom to do their work. Needless to say, the kind of person who functions well in the project team environment is more likely to respond to a "Theory Y" manager.

▶*Maslow's Hierarchy of Needs.* Maslow created a pyramid of five levels of needs. He believed that a person could not be motivated by higher levels of rewards until lower level needs had been met. The foundation and first level is physiological needs: water, food, and even oxygen. The second level is a feeling of safety and security: stability and protection. The third level includes social or affiliation needs: feeling like one is accepted by friends and part of a group. The fourth level is esteem: respect by others as well as self-respect and confidence. The top, fifth level is self-actualization: the feeling of and continuous desire for fulfilling one's potential. This theory may seem of limited practicality at first glance. Yet there are many situations in the workplace where people are expected to perform and achieve at a very high level while their confidence or physical well-being is undermined, and it's good for a project manager, who is accountable for the results of a team's work, to be aware of how damaging this situation can be. For example, in a workplace of cubicles where some team members are constantly made uncomfortable by a co-worker's angry phone conversations, the sense of safety is eroded, and a project manager familiar with Maslow's work will be aware that this can impact the team's output.

▶*Herzberg's Hygiene/Motivation Theory.* Herzberg believed that things people may consider motivational could be broken into two categories: Hygiene and Motivation. Hygiene factors include working conditions, salary, status, and security. Without these basic requirements, a person will certainly be dissatisfied with her work. Yet higher levels of these things—a safer workplace, a better salary—cannot be assumed to provide feelings of motivation. Instead, often people feel that these improvements are simply the way things should have been all along. True motivation factors include achievement, recognition, growth, and advancement opportunities. Both areas must be addressed in order to minimize the dissatisfaction and maximize the motivation.

DISCUSSION QUESTIONS

❶ Identify the Enterprise Environmental Factors involved in a project you are familiar with. What impacts might they have on your management of a project staff?

❷ You need to decide whether a team should be co-located or if they can operate virtually. What factors should play into your decision?

❸ The project team just completed a status review meeting at which Abigail tried to prevent conflict by responding that problems the testers were experiencing weren't really so bad and could probably be resolved during the following week. She was surprised when the tester who was present seemed to explode the second time she used that approach. He didn't think she fully appreciated the magnitude of the problem. What conflict management technique was she trying to use? And what would have been a better approach? Apply this approach to a team conflict you are familiar with. Could you have positively affected the outcome by handling it differently?

REFERENCES

[1] Project Management Institute. (2004) *A Guide to the Project Management Body of Knowledge, Third Edition,* PMI: Newtown Sq., PA.

[2] John Adams, et al. (1997), *Principles of Project Management,* PMI: Newtown Sq., PA.

[3] Vijay K. Verma, *Human Resource Skills for the Project Manager,* PMI, 1996.

[4] Verma, ibid.

CHAPTER 12A

Studies in Project Human Resource Management: Interpersonal Skills

▶PAUL C. DINSMORE, PMP,
DINSMORE ASSOCIATES

Teamwork means people cooperating to meet common goals. That includes all types of people doing work that calls for joint effort and exchange of information, ideas, and opinions. In teamwork, productivity is increased through synergy: the magic that appears when team members generate new ways for getting things done and that special spirit for making them happen.

Lessons can be drawn from nature regarding collective effort for get things done: bees and ants perform amazing tasks as they work in chaotic unison to achieve their community goals; lions and other predators often hunt jointly to increase the sometimes poor odds against their speedy and nimble prey; and whales parade around in circles to corral schools of fish, who in turn try to elude their marine predators by flashing back and forth in darting schools. In the case of these creatures, working together is about survival. They have learned to do it over the ages and these practices are imbedded in their DNA.

While human beings have evolved over the ages as well and have developed ways of working together, both in times of war and in peace, because of the incredible complexity of the human creature, survival-based teamwork is not as inherent as in the case of nonhuman creatures. This means that the capability of working together for teams of humans has to be developed in each new situation and must adapt to the galloping changes that mankind insists on developing. One of those changes involves the relationship of time and place of team members.

In times past, teamwork was generally developed in settings where workers shared a common workplace and time frame. In other words, people worked at the same place, during the same hours. While that situation still exists, increasingly teams are at least partially virtual, meaning that some members may never see other important colleagues of the team. Such is the case in outsourced development of IT projects, or design and construction of aircraft and ships, both of which may be scattered about the globe. This requires ways of dealing with team communications in non-traditional ways.

For instance, traditional meetings may no longer take place. Virtual meetings will increasingly use broad bandwidth for capturing video, audio, and text. And the meeting contents will be digitally tagged so the information can be accessed promptly. Even face-to-face meetings can be recorded digitally for future reference. Virtual teams, of course face some special issues that must be dealt with: the project team must be trained and ready to use the technology; trust and rapport must be established among many stakeholders, who are often widely spread geographically; and the technology chosen must meet the project needs and be sufficiently user friendly to be appealing to team members.

Yet, in spite of rampant change and technological advances, the fundamental aim of teamwork remains largely the same: getting people to work together effectively to meet common goals.

BENEFITS AND PITFALLS OF TEAMING

Teamwork offers a number of concrete benefits:

▶*Teamwork enhances success.* Teamwork helps your group excel at what it's doing and boosts its chances of "winning."

▶*Teamwork promotes creativity.* The team approach stimulates innovation and encourages people to try new approaches to problems.

▶*Teamwork builds synergy.* The mathematical absurdity "2 + 2 = 5" becomes possible.

▶*Teamwork promotes trade-offs and solves problems.* Teamwork creates a problem-solving atmosphere that facilitates decisions about schedule, cost, and performance.

▶*Teamwork is fun.* Working together for a common cause creates group spirit, lightens up the atmosphere, and reduces tensions and conflicts.

▶*Teamwork helps large organizations as well as small groups.* The team concept can be used to involve an entire company culture as well as to stimulate a small department.

▶*Teamwork responds to the challenge of change.* Teams thrive on opportunities to improve performance and show how they can adapt and adjust in order to win.

There are also pitfalls to watch out for:

▶*There can be negative synergy.* When the team doesn't get its act together, then synergy becomes negative and the equation becomes "2 + 2 = 3."

▶*There can be excessive independence.* Ill-guided or poorly built teams wander off course and start doing their own thing as opposed to meeting overall goals.

▶*Time is needed to build and maintain the team.* If company culture is not team-oriented, a lot of time and effort is needed to create the team spirit.

▶*Decision-making may be slow.* Getting a group to make a decision on a consensus basis is a time-consuming task.

Why is teamwork increasingly important? One reason is that change—economic, societal, cultural, environmental, technological, political, and international—continues to take place at an accelerating rate. And change has a dramatic impact not only on individuals but also on organizations. Task forces, departmental teams, cross-functional teams, and project teams are replacing the cumbersome hierarchical organizational structure of the past in many organizations. Teamwork enables organizations to be nimbler, more flexible, and better able to respond swiftly and creatively to the challenge of today's competitive business environment.

Several factors have speeded this trend toward team approaches to business planning and operations:

▶The success of the Japanese management style, which stresses employee involvement in all phases of the work

▶The rejection by newer generations of autocratic leadership

▶Rapid changes in technology that create a need for quick group responses

▶Emphasis on corporate quality, which requires team effort on an organizational scale.

Team building encompasses the actions necessary to create the spirit of teamwork. Research by Tuckman and Jensen[1] indicates that the team-building process is a natural sequence that can be divided into five stages:

1. Forming
2. Storming
3. Norming
4. Performing
5. Adjourning.

A detailed description of the team-building process follows.

FIVE CLASSIC TEAM-BUILDING STAGES

Stage 1: Forming

In this stage, the manager and the group focus more on tasks than on teamwork. They organize the team's structure, set goals, clarify values, and develop an overall vision of the team's purpose. The manager's role is to direct these efforts and to encourage group members to reach consensus and achieve a feeling of commitment.

Stage 2: Storming

This stage is less structured than the first stage. The manager broadens the focus to include both accomplishing tasks and building relationships. As the social need for belonging becomes important to group members, the emphasis is on interpersonal interactions: active listening, assertiveness, conflict management, flexibility, creativity, and kaleidoscopic thinking. The group completes tasks with a sense of understanding, clarification, and belonging. The manager relies not only on actual authority but also on leadership skills, such as encouragement and recognition.

Stage 3: Norming

In this stage, the team-building process is more relationship-based than task-oriented. Since recognition and esteem are important for group members, the manager relies on communication, feedback, affirmation, playfulness, humor, entrepreneurship, and networking to motivate the team. Group members achieve a feeling of involvement and support.

Stage 4: Performing

At this point, the team is operating very much on its own. Management style is neither task- nor relationship-oriented, since the team members are motivated by achievement and self-actualization. The manager's role in this phase is to serve as mentor/coach and to take a long-range view of future needs. Team members focus on decision-making and problem solving, relying on information and expertise to achieve their goals.

Stage 5: Adjourning

Management concern in this wrap-up stage is low-task and high-relationship. The manager focuses on evaluation, reviewing, and closure. Team members continue to be motivated by a feeling of achievement and self-actualization.

THE TEN RULES OF TEAM BUILDING

The five team-building stages show how teams evolve over time. That process can be accelerated by applying the following ten principles of team building. Each principle helps create the spirit that gets people to work together cooperatively to meet goals:

1. *Identify what drives your team.* What is the driving force that makes teamwork necessary? Is it an external force like the market? Is it internal, like organizational demands? Is it the needs of the group itself? Is the leader the only driver? Or is it perhaps a combination of these factors?

2. *Get your own act together.* Are you a bright and shining example of teamwork? Could you shine even brighter? Polish your interpersonal skills and show your teamwork talents on a daily basis.

3. *Understand the game.* All teams play games. Do you know the game and how much you can bend the rules? Each game of business is different and rules need to be rethought.

4. *Evaluate the competition.* First, know who the real market competition is. Then size it up so that your team can become competitive with a larger outside opponent.

5. *Pick your players and adjust your team.* Choose qualified players who know the basics, and teach them the skills that they don't have. Also, make sure the team players are in the right spots.

6. *Identify and develop inner group leaders.* Team builders learn to identify inner group leadership early on. If you want to develop the full capacity of your team, then delegating, mentoring, and coaching must become part of your daily habit.

Ten Rules	Five Phases				
	Form	Storm	Norm	Perform	Adjourn
1. Identify what drives your team	0				
2. Get your own act together	0	0	0		
3. Understand the game	0	0	0		
4. Evaluate the competition	0				
5. Pick your players and adjust your team	0	0	0	0	
6. Identify and develop inner group leaders		0	0	0	
7. Get the team in shape	0	0	0		
8. Motivate the players			0	0	
9. Develop plans	0		0		
10. Control, evaluate, and improve			0		0

FIGURE 12A-1. **TEAM-BUILDING RULES AND THE FIVE PHASES OF TEAM BUILDING**

7. *Get the team in shape.* It takes practice and training to get athletic teams in shape. The same is true for other teams. Start with training in the fundamentals of teamwork—things like active listening, communicating, and negotiating—and see that they are practiced on a daily basis.

8. *Motivate the players.* The only way to get people to do things effectively is to give them what they want. The secret is to discover what individuals really want and, as you deal with them, to relate to those desires—whether they be recognition, challenge, a chance to belong, the possibility to lead, the opportunity to learn, or other motivators.

9. *Develop plans.* In teamwork, the process of planning is more important than the plan. Team members must become so involved in the planning process that they can say with conviction, "This is our plan."

10. *Control, evaluate, and improve.* Knowing the status of things at any given time is important for teams to be successful. Sometimes that's a tough task. To make sure you maintain the right spirit, involve your team members in creating your control instrument.

The ten rules outlined apply throughout the five team-building phases. Greater emphasis, however, is appropriate during certain periods. Figure 12A-1 shows the phases in which the rules tend to be most applicable.

PLANNING FOR AND IMPLEMENTING TEAMWORK

Get People Involved

The key to successful team planning is involvement: Get people involved at the outset of your team-building effort to win their personal commitment to your plan. One simple technique for involvement includes a questionnaire in which team members are asked to assess the need for team building. A sample questionnaire is shown in Table 12A-1. In the test, team members rate the degree to which certain team-related problems appear. If

Instructions: Indicate the degree to which the problems below exist in your work unit.

		Low			High		Score
1.	Quality of communication among group members	1	2	3	4	5	_____
2.	Clarity of goals, or degree of "buying into" goals	1	2	3	4	5	_____
3.	Degree of conflict among group members and/or third parties	1	2	3	4	5	_____
4.	Productivity of meetings	1	2	3	4	5	_____
5.	Degree of motivation; level of morale	1	2	3	4	5	_____
6.	Level of trust among group members and/or with boss	1	2	3	4	5	_____
7.	Quality of decision-making process and follow-through on decisions made	1	2	3	4	5	_____
8.	Individuals' concern for team responsibility as opposed to own personal interests	1	2	3	4	5	_____
9.	Quality of listening abilities on part of team members	1	2	3	4	5	_____
10.	Cooperativeness among group members	1	2	3	4	5	_____
11.	Level of creativity and innovation	1	2	3	4	5	_____
12.	Group productivity	1	2	3	4	5	_____
13.	Degree that team perceptions coincide with those of upper management and vice versa	1	2	3	4	5	_____
14.	Clarity of role relationships	1	2	3	4	5	_____
15.	Tendency to be more solution- than problem-oriented	1	2	3	4	5	_____
	TOTAL						_____

Test Result: Add up your scores. If the score is over 60, then your work unit is in good shape with respect to teamwork. If you scored between 46 and 60 points, there is some concern, but only for those items with lower scores. A score of 30 to 45 indicates that the subject needs attention and that a team-building program should be under way. A score of between 15 and 30 points means that improving teamwork should be the absolute top priority for your group.

TABLE 12A-1. **TEAM MEMBERS' QUESTIONNAIRE**

the team is newly formed, the questionnaire should be answered from the perspective of anticipated problems. Then test results are tabulated and group discussion follows in search of a consensus on how to obtain team development. This consensus approach generates synergy when the team carries out the planned activities. In addition, potential differences are dealt with in the planning stage before resources are fully committed.

Group planning approaches are used in programs such as quality circles, total quality management, and participative management, as well as project management. The management skills required to make these group planning efforts effective include interpersonal communications, meeting management, listening, negotiation, situational management, and managerial psychology.

The right planning process produces a quality plan to which the parties involved are committed. Some methods that enhance the planning process are discussed below.

▶*Creativity sessions.* Techniques for boosting creativity include brainstorming, brain-writing, random working, checklists, and word associations.

▶*Consensus planning.* A plan reached through group discussion tends to yield a program that is well thought through, with a high probability of being implemented.

▶*Decision-making models.* Formal models for making decisions can be used as a basis for planning. Some common techniques are decision trees, problem analysis, decision analysis, implementation studies, and risk analysis.

You should build a team like you were putting together a puzzle. It involves:

▶Individuals (like the separate puzzle pieces)

▶One-on-one contacts (like pairing up matching pieces)

▶Small groups (like the subsets of the puzzle)

▶Large groups (like the overall picture that the whole puzzle represents).

This means that in team building, just as in putting together a puzzle, you need to view the whole range of team factors, from the characteristics and talents of the individual team members to the overall picture: the team's immediate goals and long-term objectives and how the team fits into the larger organizational scene. Some of the concrete steps that transform groups into teams are discussed below.

Set a Good Example

Here the focus is individual. As team leaders concern themselves with developing their own skills and knowledge bases, then the other pieces of the puzzle begin to gravitate and fall into place. All team leaders communicate their management philosophies to some extent by setting both overt and subliminal examples.

The manager who trusts subordinates and delegates authority to key project members can expect others to emulate that style. Likewise, an open give-and-take approach fosters similar behavior in the team and in others associated with the project under way. Through the team leader's own actions, team members' best behavior is called to the forefront.

Coach Team Members

Coaching requires some schooling in the "different-strokes-for-different-folks" philosophy, which assumes that people with different temperaments react differently to a standardized "shotgun" approach. Thus, each individual needs to be singled out for a special shot of custom-tailored attention in order for coaching to be effective.

A coaching session can be as simple as a chat with a subordinate who made a mistake about why something happened and what can be done to keep it from recurring. It can be a formal interview by the manager, who goes into the session with a tailor-made approach. Or it can be a formal appraisal session using classic management tools, such as job descriptions and performance standards.

Train Team Members

Training may involve small groups or the overall group or may incorporate all the stakeholders involved in the team's efforts. Informal training sessions can be conducted in various forms, such as lectures, roundtable discussions, and seminars.

Lectures are a one-dimensional form of training. They put large amounts of information into short time frames. Lectures given by experts can bring top-quality information to the team members. When the speaker is well known, the lecture stimulates special interest.

Roundtable discussions are open-forum debates on pertinent subjects. They give participants a chance to air their views and present their opinions and ideas frankly. The goal may be to establish a consensus or to provide a basis for planning in-depth training programs.

Seminars or workshops combine the informational content of the lecture with opportunities for participation offered by the roundtable. In seminars or workshops, information is dispensed in smaller doses, interspersed with group discussions and debates. Seminars are established around a longer time frame than lectures or roundtable discussions. Two- to three-day seminars are the most popular, but one-day events are acceptable, and five-day seminars are right for more in-depth coverage.

Set Up a Formal Team-Building Program

Of the approaches aimed at heightening team synergy, a formal team-building program is apt to bring the best results because:

- The longer program duration provides greater opportunity for retention of concepts as they are reworked throughout the program.
- On-the-job application of the concepts provides timely feedback while the course goes on.
- In-depth treatment can be given to subjects.
- Enough time is available to build a consensus among participants.
- Effective interpersonal relations are developed.

The Key to Successful Teamwork

Since effective teams are all highly interactive, teamwork depends heavily on the interpersonal skills of the members. In a team setting, this personal interaction takes on a special importance because the number of relationships among members is sharply increased. Sometimes, this creates a traffic problem. Just as vehicle traffic flows more smoothly when drivers have developed their abilities, observe protocol, and behave courteously, the same is true in team situations where members have learned how to work together skillfully and cooperatively.

What are some of the skills that each team "driver" needs to operate effectively in a team situation? They include listening, applying techniques to deal with interpersonal conflict, negotiating, and influencing.

Listening

Communication, no matter how clear and concise, is wasted unless someone is listening actively to the communicator's message. When team members know how to listen actively, overall effectiveness is boosted. Here is the attitude that represents good listening:

> "I am interested in what you are saying and I want to understand, although I may not agree with everything you say. You are important as a person, and I respect

you and what you have to say. I'm sure your message is worth listening to, so I am giving you my full attention."

Other listening pointers include:

▶Maintaining eye contact;

▶Not interrupting;

▶Keeping a relaxed posture.

Good listening also requires the listener to focus on both the communicator's content and feelings and then to extract the essential message being conveyed.

Dealing with Interpersonal Conflict

Interpersonal conflict can occur whenever two or more people get together. It's an inevitable part of team dynamics. There are five basic techniques for dealing with interpersonal conflict:

1. Withdrawing (pulling out, retreating, or giving up)
2. Smoothing (appeasing just to keep the peace)
3. Bargaining (negotiating to reach agreement over conflicting interests)
4. Collaborating (objective problem solving based on trust)
5. Forcing (using power to resolve the conflict)

Application of these techniques depends on the situation. Effective team members recognize that conflict is inevitable and rationally apply appropriate conflict resolution modes in each given situation. Here are some of the applications:

▶Use *withdrawing* when you can't win, when the stakes are low, to gain time, to preserve neutrality or reputation, or when you win by delay.

▶Use *smoothing* to reach an overarching goal, to create an obligation for a trade-off at a later date, to maintain harmony, to create good will, or when any solution will do.

▶Use *bargaining* (also called conflict negotiation) when both parties need to be winners, when others are as strong as you, to maintain your relationship with your opponent, when you are not sure you are right, or when you get nothing if you don't make a deal.

▶Use *collaborating* when you both get at least what you want and maybe more, to create a common power base, when knowledge or skills are complementary, when there is enough time, or where there is trust.

▶Use *forcing* when a "do or die" situation exists, when important principles are at stake, when you are stronger (never start a battle you can't win), to gain status or demonstrate power, or when the relationship is unimportant.

Negotiating

Team members are likely to find themselves dealing with both third-party and in-house situations that call for major negotiation skills. The type of negotiation that tends to be effective in team settings is called principled negotiation. This is negotiation in which it is assumed that the players are problem solvers and that the objective is to reach a wise outcome efficiently and amicably.

Principled negotiation also assumes that the people will be separated from the problem, that premature position-taking will be avoided, that alternative solutions will be explored, and that the rules of the negotiation will be objective and fair. This means focusing on interests rather than on positions and implies fully exploring mutual and divergent interests before trying to converge on some bottom line. The tenet *invent options for mutual gain*—calling for a creative search for alternatives—is also fundamental to principled negotiation.

Influencing

In team situations, individual authority lags well behind the authority of the group. Therefore, effective teams depend on the ability of members to influence one another for the good of the common cause. Influence management includes the following principles:

▶*Play up the benefit.* Identify the benefit of your proposal for the other party (items such as more challenge, prestige, or visibility, or the chance for promotion or transfer). Then emphasize that benefit in conversations so that the message is communicated.

▶*Steer clear of Machiavelli.* Avoid manipulation. Concentrate on influencing with sincerity and integrity.

▶*Go beyond "I think I can."* Successful influence managers don't waste time questioning whether things can be done. Their efforts are aimed at how the task will be performed and what needs to be done to make it happen.

▶*Put an umbrella over your moves.* Effective influencing hinges on strategic planning, to give direction and consistency to all influencing efforts.

▶*Tune in to what others say.* Successful influence managers learn to identify others' expectations and perceive how given actions contribute toward fulfilling those expectations.

▶*Size up your plans for congruency.* Make sure there is a fit between proposed actions, testing your plans for consistency, coherence, and conformity.

▶*Remember: "Different strokes for different folks."* Be sure to adapt your approach to fit each person's individual characteristics. Size up your targets and adjust your presentation to individual needs.

▶*Watch your language!* Be careful with what you say and how you say it. Screen out pessimism and other forms of negativity, putting positive conviction into what you say to increase the impact of your message.

When team members are schooled in these basics, teamwork is likely to come about rapidly. Synergy is generated as people work together to meet common goals.

DISCUSSION QUESTIONS:

❶ In the classic team building model (forming, storming, norming, performing, adjourning), what factors typically can upset the sequence outlined? How can these be overcome?

❷ Classify the ten rules of team building in two categories: "Must do" and "Highly desirable to do." Discuss with colleagues.

❸ Of the five conflict resolution techniques, which is most commonly used on most projects? Which in your opinion is the most effective? Are there circumstances where you have used a less-desirable method with a good outcome?

REFERENCES

[1] B. W. Tuckman, and M. A. Jensen. "Study of Small Group Development Revisited." *Group and Organizational Studies* (1977).

FURTHER READING

Blake, Robert R., Jane S. Mouton, and Robert L. Allen. Spectacular Teamwork. New York: John Wiley & Sons, 1987.

Bonabeau, Eric, and Christopher Meyer. "Swarm Intelligence: A Whole New Way to Think About Business." *Harvard Business Review,* May 2001: 107–114.

Bucholz, Steve, and Thomas Roth. *Creating the High Performance Team*. New York: John Wiley & Sons, 1987.

Dinsmore, Paul C. *Human Factors in Project Management,* Revised Edition. New York: AMACOM, 1990.

Dyer, William G. *Team Building: Issues and Alternatives.* Reading, Mass.: Addison-Wesley, 1987.

Foti, Ross. "The Virtual Handshake." *PM Network,* March 2004: 28–32.

Hastings, Colin, Peter Bixby, and Rani Chaudhry-Lawton. *The Superteam Solution.* London, England: Gower, 1986.

Heany, Donald F. *Cutthroat Teammates*. Homewood, Ill.: Dow Jones-Irwin, 1989.

Larson, Carl E., and Frank M. J. LaFasto. *Teamwork.* Newbury Park, Calif.: Sage, 1989.

CHAPTER 12B

Studies in Project Human Resource Management: Leadership

▶HANS J. THAMHAIN, PHD, PMP
BENTLEY COLLEGE

More than any other organizational form, effective project management requires an understanding of motivational forces and leadership. The ability to build project teams, motivate people, and create organizational structures conducive to innovative and effective work requires sophisticated interpersonal and organizational skills.

There is no single magic formula for successful project management. However, most senior managers agree that effective management of multidisciplinary activities requires an understanding of the interaction of organizational and behavioral elements in order to build an environment conducive to the team's motivational needs and subsequently lead effectively the complex integration of a project through its multifunctional phases.

MOTIVATIONAL FORCES IN PROJECT TEAM MANAGEMENT

Understanding people is important for the effective team management of today's challenging projects. The breed of managers that succeeds within these often unstructured work environments faces many challenges. Internally, they must be able to deal effectively with a variety of interfaces and support personnel over whom they often have little or no control. Externally, managers have to cope with constant and rapid change regarding technology, markets, regulations, and socioeconomic factors. Moreover, traditional methods of authority-based direction, performance measures, and control are virtually impractical in such contemporary environments.

Sixteen specific professional needs of project team personnel are listed below. Research studies show that the fulfillment of these professional needs can drive project personnel to higher performance; conversely, the inability to fulfill these needs may become a barrier to teamwork and high project performance. The rationale for this important correlation is found in the complex interaction of organizational and behavioral elements. Effective team management involves three primary issues: (1) people skills, (2) organizational structure, and (3) management style. All three issues are influenced by the specific task to be performed and the surrounding environment. That is, the degree of satisfaction of any of the needs is a function of (1) having the right mix of people with appropriate skills and traits, (2) organizing the people and resources according to the tasks to be performed, and (3) adopting the right leadership style.[1] The sixteen specific professional needs of team personnel are as follows:

1. *Interesting and challenging work.* Interesting and challenging work satisfies various professional esteem needs. It is oriented toward intrinsic motivation of the individual and helps to integrate personal goals with the objectives of the organization.

2. *Professionally stimulating work environment.* This leads to professional involvement, creativity, and interdisciplinary support. It also fosters team building and is conducive to effective communication, conflict resolution, and commitment toward organizational goals. The quality of this work environment is defined through its organizational structure, facilities, and management style.

3. *Professional growth.* Professional growth is measured by promotional opportunities, salary advances, the learning of new skills and techniques, and professional recognition. A particular challenge exists for management in limited-growth or zero-growth businesses to compensate for the lack of promotional opportunities by offering more intrinsic professional growth in terms of job satisfaction.

4. *Overall leadership.* This involves dealing effectively with individual contributors, managers, and support personnel within a specific functional discipline as well as across organizational lines. It involves technical expertise, information-processing skills, effective communications, and decision-making skills. Taken together, leadership means satisfying the need for clear direction and unified guidance toward established objectives.

5. *Tangible records.* These include salary increases, bonuses, and incentives, as well as promotions, recognition, better offices, and educational opportunities. Although extrinsic, these financial rewards are necessary to sustain strong long-term efforts and motivation. Furthermore, they validate more intrinsic rewards such as recognition and praise and reassure people that higher goals are attainable.

6. *Technical expertise.* Personnel need to have all necessary interdisciplinary skills and expertise available within the project team to perform the required tasks. Technical expertise includes understanding the technicalities of the work, the technology and underlying concepts, theories and principles, design methods and techniques, and functioning and interrelationship of the various components that make up the total system.

7. *Assisting in problem solving.* Assisting in problem solving, such as facilitating solutions to technical, administrative, and personal problems, is a very important need. If not satisfied, it often leads to frustration, conflict, and poor quality work.

Influence Base	Organizationally Derived Components	Individually Derived Components
Authority	Position, Title Office Size Charter Budget, Resources Project Size, Importance	Respect Trust Credibility Performance Image Integrity
Reward Power	Salary, Bonuses Hire, Promote Work, Security Training, Development Resource Allocation	Recognition, Visibility Accomplishments Autonomy, Flexibility Stimulating Environment Professional Growth
Punishment	Salary, Bonuses Fire, Demote Work, Security Resource Limitations	Reprimand Team Pressure Tight Supervision Work Pressure Isolation
Expert Power	Top Management Support	Competence Knowledge Information Sound Decisions Top Management Respect Access to Experts
Referent Power		Friendship Charisma Empathy

TABLE 12B-1. **THE PROJECT MANAGER'S BASES OF INFLUENCE**

8. *Clearly defined objectives.* Goals, objectives, and outcomes of an effort must be clearly communicated to all affected personnel. Conflict can develop over ambiguities or missing information.

9. *Management control.* Management control is important for effective team performance. Managers must understand the interaction of organizational and behavior variables in order to exert the direction, leadership, and control required to steer the project effort toward established organizational goals without stifling innovation and creativity.

10. *Job security.* This is one of the very fundamental needs that must be satisfied before people consider higher-order growth needs.

11. *Senior management support.* Senior management support should be provided in four major areas: (1) financial resources, (2) effective operating charter, (3) cooperation from support departments, and (4) provision of necessary facilities and equipment. It is particularly crucial to larger, more complex undertakings.

12. *Good interpersonal relations.* These are required for effective teamwork since they foster a stimulating work environment with low conflict, high productivity, and involved, motivated personnel.

13. *Proper planning.* Proper planning is absolutely essential for the successful management of multidisciplinary activities. It requires communications and information-processing skills to define the actual resource requirements and administrative support necessary. It also requires the ability to negotiate resources and commitment from key personnel in various support groups across organizational lines.

14. *Clear role definition.* This helps to minimize role conflict and power struggles among team members and/or supporting organizations. Clear charters, plans, and good management direction are some of the powerful tools used to facilitate clear role definitions.

15. *Open communications.* This satisfies the need for a free flow of information both horizontally and vertically. It keeps personnel informed and functions as a pervasive integrator of the overall project effort.

16. *Minimizing changes.* Although project managers have to live with constant change, their team members often see change as an unnecessary condition that impedes their creativity and productivity. Advanced planning and proper communications can help to minimize changes and lessen their negative impact.

THE POWER SPECTRUM IN PROJECT MANAGEMENT

Project managers must often cross functional lines to get the required support. This is especially true for managers who operate within a matrix structure. Almost invariably, the manager must build multidisciplinary teams into cohesive work groups and successfully deal with a variety of interfaces, such as functional departments, staff groups, other support groups, clients, and senior management. This is a work environment where managerial power is shared by many individuals. In the traditional organization, position power is provided largely in the form of legitimate authority, reward, and punishment. These organizationally derived bases of influence are shown in Table 12B-1. In contrast, project managers have to build most of their power bases on their own. They have to earn their power and influence from other sources. Trust, respect, credibility, and the image of a facilitator of a professionally stimulating work environment are the makings of this power and influence. These individually derived bases of influence are also shown in Table 12B-1.

In today's environment, most project management is largely characterized by:

- Authority patterns that are defined only in part by formal organization chart plans
- Authority that is largely perceived by the members of the organization based on earned credibility, expertise, and perceived priorities
- Dual accountability of most personnel, especially in project-oriented environments
- Power that is shared between resource managers and project/task managers
- Individual autonomy and participation that is greater than in traditional organizations
- Weak superior-subordinate relationships in favor of stronger peer relationships
- Subtle shifts of personnel loyalties from functional to project lines

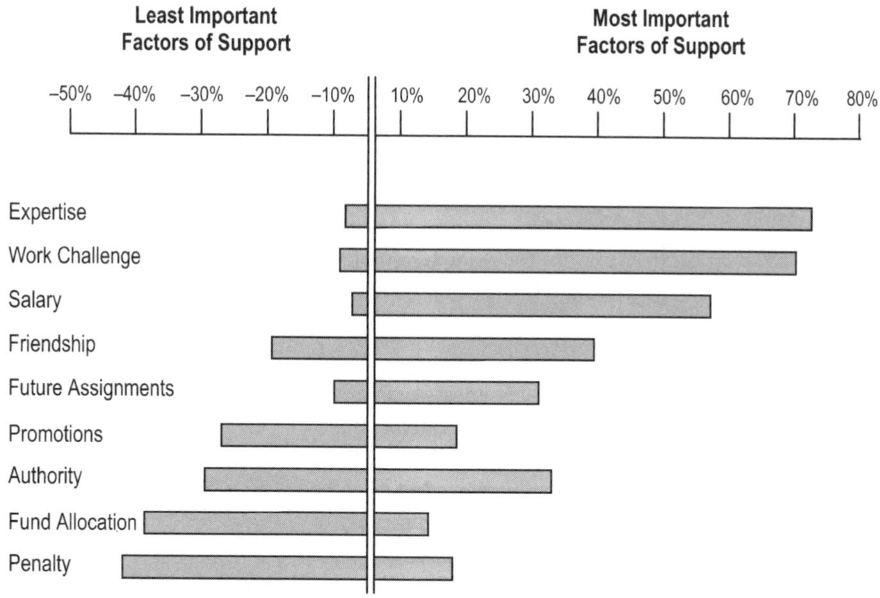

TABLE 12B-2. **THE PROJECT MANAGER'S POWER SPECTRUM**

▶Project performance that depends on teamwork

▶Group decision making that tends to favor the strongest organizations

▶Reward and punishment power along both vertical and horizontal lines in a highly dynamic pattern

▶Influences to reward and punish that come from many organizations and individuals

▶Multi-project involvement of support personnel and sharing of resources among many activities.

Position power is a necessary prerequisite for effective project/team leadership. Like many other components of the management system, leadership style has also undergone changes over time. With increasing task complexity, increasing dynamics of the organizational environment, and the evolution of organizational systems such as the matrix, a more adaptive and skill-oriented management style has evolved. This style complements the organizationally derived power bases—such as authority, reward, and punishment—with bases developed by the individual manager. Examples of these individually derived components of influence are technical and managerial expertise, friendship, work challenge, promotional ability, fund allocations, charisma, personal favors, project goal indemnification, recognition, and visibility. This so-called Style II management evolved particularly with the matrix. Effective project management combines both the organizationally derived and individually derived styles of influence.

Various research studies by Gemmill, Thamhain, and Wilemon provide an insight into the power spectrum available to project managers.[2] Project personnel were asked to rank nine influence bases; Table 12B-2 shows the results. Technical and managerial expertise, work challenge, and influence over salary were the most important influences that project leaders seem to have, while penalty factors, fund allocations, and authority appeared least important in gaining support from project team members.

LEADERSHIP STYLE EFFECTIVENESS

For more than ten years, the author has investigated influence bases with regard to project management effectiveness.[3] Through those formal studies it is measurably and consistently found that managers who are perceived by their personnel as (1) emphasizing work challenge and expertise, but (2) deemphasizing authority, penalty, and salary, foster a climate of good communications, high involvement, and strong support to the tasks at hand. Ultimately, this style results in high performance ratings by upper management.

The relationship of managerial influence, style, and effectiveness has been statistically measured.[4] One of the most interesting findings is the importance of work challenge as an influence method. Work challenge appears to integrate the personal goals and needs of personnel with organizational goals. That is, work challenge is primarily oriented toward extrinsic rewards with less regard to the personnel's progressional needs. Therefore, enriching the assignments of team personnel in a professionally challenging way may indeed have a beneficial effect on overall performance. In addition, the assignment of challenging work is a variable over which project managers may have a great deal of control. Even if the total task structure is fixed, the method by which work is assigned and distributed is discretionary in most cases.

RECOMMENDATIONS FOR EFFECTIVE PROJECT TEAM MANAGEMENT

The project leader must foster an environment where team members are professionally satisfied, are involved, and have mutual trust. The more effective the project leader is in stimulating the drivers and minimizing the barriers shown in Figure 12B-1, the more effective the manager can be in developing team membership and the higher the quality of information contributed by team members, including their willingness and candor in sharing ideas and approaches. By contrast, when a team member does not feel part of the team and does not trust others, information is not shared willingly or openly. One project leader emphasized the point: "There's nothing worse than being on a team where no one trusts anyone else. Such situations lead to gamesmanship and a lot of watching what you say because you don't want your own words to bounce back in your own face."

Furthermore, the greater the team spirit and trust and the quality of information exchange among team members, the more likely the team will be able to develop effective decision-making processes, make individual and group commitment, focus on problem solving, and develop self-forcing, self-correcting project controls. As summarized in Figure 12B-2, these are the characteristics of an effective and productive project team. A number of specific recommendations are listed below for project leaders and managers responsible for the integration of multidisciplinary tasks to help in their complex efforts of building high-performing project teams.

▶*Recognize barriers.* Project managers must understand the various barriers to team development and build a work environment conducive to the team's motivational needs. Specifically, management should try to watch out for the following barriers: (1) unclear objectives, (2) insufficient resources and unclear findings, (3) role conflict and power struggle, (4) uninvolved and unsupportive management, (5) poor job security, and (6) shifting goals and priorities.

▶*Define clear project objectives.* The project objectives and their importance to the organization should be clear to all personnel involved with the project. Senior management can help develop a "priority image" and communicate the basic project parameters and management guidelines.

▶*Assure management commitment.* A project manager must continually update and involve management to refuel its interests in and commitments to the new project. Breaking the project into smaller phases and being able to produce short-range results are important to this refueling process.

▶*Build a favorable image.* Building a favorable image for the project in terms of high priority, interesting work, importance to the organization, high visibility, and potential for professional rewards is crucial to the ability to attract and hold high-quality people. It is also a pervasive process that fosters a climate of active participation at all levels; it helps to unify the new project team and minimize dysfunctional conflict.

▶*Manage and lead.* Leadership positions should be carefully defined and staffed at the beginning of a new program. Key project personnel selection is the joint responsibility of the project manager and functional management. The credibility of the project leader among team members with senior management and with the program sponsor is crucial to the leader's ability to manage multidisciplinary activities effectively across functional lines. One-on-one interviews are recommended for explaining the scope and project requirement, as well as the management philosophy, organizational structure, and rewards.

▶*Plan and define your project.* Effective planning early in the project life cycle has a favorable impact on the work environment and team effectiveness. This is especially so because project managers have to integrate various tasks across many functional lines. Proper planning, however, means more than just generating the required pieces of paper. It requires the participation of the entire project team, including support departments, subcontractors, and management. These planning activities—which can be performed in a special project phase such as requirements analysis, product feasibility assessment, or product/project definition—usually have a number of side benefits besides generating a comprehensive road map for the upcoming program.

▶*Create involvement.* One of the side benefits of proper planning is the involvement of personnel at all organizational levels. Project managers should drive such an involvement, at least with their key personnel, especially during the project definition phases. This involvement leads to a better understanding of the task requirements, stimulates interest, helps unify the team, and ultimately leads to commitment to the project plan regarding technical performance, timing, and budgets.

▶*Assure proper project staffing.* All project assignments should be negotiated individually with each prospective team member. Each task leader should be responsible for staffing his or her own task team. Where dual-reporting relationships are involved, staffing should be conducted jointly by the two managers. The assignment interview should include a clear discussion of the specific tasks, outcome, timing, responsibilities, reporting relation, potential rewards, and importance of the project to the company. Task assignments should be made only if the candidate's ability is a reasonable match to the position requirements and the candidate shows a healthy degree of interest in the project.

▶*Define team structure.* Management must define the basic team structure and operating concepts early during the project formation phase. The project plan, task matrix, project charter, and policy are the principal tools. It is the responsibility of the project manager to communicate the organizational design and to assure that all parties understand the overall and interdisciplinary project objectives. Clear and frequent communication with senior management and the new project sponsor is critically important. Status review meetings can be used for feedback.

▶*Conduct team-building sessions.* The project manager should conduct team-building sessions throughout the project life cycle. An especially intense effort might be needed during the team formation stage. The team should be brought together periodically in a relaxed atmosphere to discuss such questions as: (1) How are we operating as a team? (2) What is our strength? (3) Where can we improve? (4) What steps are needed to initiate the desired change? (5) What problems and issues are we likely to face in the future? (6) Which of these can be avoided by taking appropriate action now? (7) How can we "danger-proof" the team?

▶*Develop your team continuously.* Project leaders should watch for problems with changes in performance, and such problems should be dealt with quickly. Internal or external organization development specialists can help diagnose team problems and assist the team in dealing with the identified problems. These specialists also can bring fresh ideas and perspectives to difficult and sometimes emotionally complex situations.

▶*Develop team commitment.* Project managers should determine whether team members lack commitment early in the life of the project and attempt to change possible negative views toward the project. Since insecurity often is a major reason for lacking commitment, managers should try to determine why insecurity exists, and then work on reducing the team members' fears. Conflict with other team members may be another reason for lack of commitment. If there are project professionals whose interests lie elsewhere, the project leader should examine ways to satisfy part of those members' interests by bringing personal and project goals into perspective.

▶*Assure senior management support.* It is critically important for senior management to provide the proper environment for the project team to function effectively. The project leader needs to tell management at the outset of the program what resources are needed. The project manager's relationship with senior management and ability to develop senior management support are critically affected by his or her credibility and visibility and the priority image of the project.

▶*Focus on problem avoidance.* Project leaders should focus their efforts on problem avoidance. That is, the project leader, through experience, should recognize potential problems and conflicts before their onset and deal with them before they become big and their resolutions consume a large amount of time and effort.

▶*Show your personal drive and desire.* Finally, project managers can influence the climate of their work environment by their own actions. Concern for project team members and ability to create personal enthusiasm for the project itself can foster a climate high in motivation, work involvement, open communication, and resulting project performance.

A FINAL NOTE

In summary, effective team management is a critical determinant of project success. Building the group of project personnel into a cohesive, unified task team is one of the prime responsibilities of the program leader. Team building involves a whole spectrum of management skills to identify, commit, and integrate the various personnel from different functional organizations. Team building is a shared responsibility between the functional managers and the project manager, who often reports to a different organization with a different superior.

To be effective, the project manager must provide an atmosphere conducive to teamwork. Four major considerations are involved in the integration of people from many disciplines into an effective team: (1) creating a professionally stimulating work environment, (2) ensuring good program leadership, (3) providing qualified personnel, and (4) providing a technically and organizationally stable environment. The project leader must foster an environment where team members are professionally satisfied, involved, and have mutual trust. The more effectively project leaders develop team membership, have a higher quality of information exchanged, and have a greater candor of team members. It is this professionally stimulating involvement that also has a pervasive effect on the team's ability to cope with change and conflict and leads to innovative performance. By contrast, when a member does not feel part of the team and does not trust others, information is not shared willingly or openly.

Furthermore, the greater the team spirit, trust, and quality of information exchange among team members, the more likely the team is able to develop effective decision-making processes, make individual and group commitments, focus on problem solving, and develop self-enforcing, self-correcting project controls. These are the characteristics of an effective and productive project team.

To be successful, project leaders must develop their team management skills. They must have the ability to unify multifunctional teams and lead them toward integrated results. They must understand the interaction of organizational and behavioral elements in order to build an environment that satisfies the team's motivational needs. Active participation, minimal interpersonal conflict, and effective communication are some of the major factors that determine the quality of the organization's environment.

Furthermore, project managers must provide a high degree of leadership in unstructured environments. They must develop credibility with peer groups, team members, senior management, and customers. Above all, the project manager must be a social architect who understands the organization and its culture, value system, environment, and technology. These are the prerequisites for moving project-oriented organizations toward long-range productivity and growth.

DISCUSSION QUESTIONS

❶ Discuss the issues of self-direction and empowerment. Where is it necessary and where is it risky? What are the managerial limitations and challenges of empowerment?

❷ How can managers and team leaders "earn" their authority, especially when crossing functional lines and dealing with organizations over which they have no formal authority?

❸ List and discuss the characteristics of effective project teams. How could you measure team effectiveness? How could you measure the qualities (characteristics) of an effective team? How can you develop these qualities?

REFERENCES

[1] H. Barkema, J. Baum and E. Mannix, "Management Challenges in a New Time," *Academy of Management Journal, Vol.* 45, No. 5 (2002), pp. 916-930; K. English, "The Changing Landscape of Leadership," *Research Technology Management,* Vol. 45, No. 4 (Jul/Aug 2004), p. 9; C. Feld, "Getting it Right," *Harvard Business Review,* Vol. 82, No. 2 (February 2004), pp.72-79; A. Parker, "What Creates Energy in Organizations?" *MIT Sloan Management Review,* Vol. 44, No. 4 (Summer 2003), pp. 51-60; R. Rodriguez, M. Green, and M. Ree, "Leading Generation X: Do the Old Rules Apply?" *Journal of Leadership and Organizational Studies,* Vol. 9, No. 4 (Spring 2003).), p.67.

[2] G. Gemmill and D. Wilemon, "The Hidden Side of Leadership in Technical Team Management," Research Technology Management, Vol. 37, No. 6 (Nov/Dec 1994), pp. 25-33; H. Thamhain and D. Wilemon, "Building Effective Teams for Complex Project Environments," *Technology Management,* Vol. 5, No. 2 (May 1999), pp. 203-212; H. Thamhain, "Leading Technology Teams," *Project Management Journal,* Vol.35, No. 4 (December 2004), pp. 35-47.

[3] I. Kruglianskas and H. Thamhain , "Managing Technology-Based Projects in Multinational Environments," *IEEE Transactions on Engineering Management,* Vol. 47, No. 1 (February 2000), pp 55-64: H. Thamhain, "Working with Project Teams," Chapter 18 in *Project Management: Strategic Design and Implementation,* Cleland and Ireland, eds., (New York: McGraw-Hill, 2002); H. Thamhain, "Managing Innovative R&D Teams," *R&D Management,* Vol. 33, No. 3 (June 2003), pp. 297-312; H. Thamhain, "Managing Product Development Project Teams," Chapter 9, pp.127-143; *PDMA Handbook of New Product Development,* Kenneth Khan, Editor (New York: Wiley & Sons., 2005).

[4] H. Thamhain, *Management of Technology,* Chapter 5 (New York: Wiley & Sons, 2005); H. Thamhain and D. Wilemon, "Leadership, Conflict, and Project Management Effectiveness," Executive Bookshelf on Generating Technological Innovations, *Sloan Management Review* (Fall 1987), pp 68-87; H. Thamhain, "Linkages of Project Environment to Performance: Lessons for Team Leadership," *International Journal of Project Management,* Vol. 22, No. 7 (October 2004), pp. 90-102.

CHAPTER 13

Project Communications Management in Practice

▶RENEE MEPYANS-ROBINSON
NASHVILLE STATE COMMUNITY COLLEGE

Delivering a sound communication management plan to all team members, sponsors, and stakeholders (including the customer) is one key to a successful project. The distribution of project information is critical to ensure all information is communicated in a timely fashion throughout all phases of the project.

The project manager is responsible for sharing important dates, setting up meetings to discuss issues, and identifying risks early in the planning phase in order to eliminate problems that can occur in the implementation phase. All team members are to inform and provide status of the project developments, which could impact the outcome of the product or service. The coordination and communications will have a direct impact on whether the project meets the customer expectations, budget, and delivery date.

The Communication Management Plan is based upon five fundamental questions being answered in the planning sessions of the project:

1. Who will make decisions on issues?
2. Who will develop an action list of tasks and who will be responsible for the tasks?
3. When will these tasks be completed and reported?
4. How will other pertinent information be distributed?
5. To whom will the information be delivered?

The implementation of the project plan and strict enforcement is necessary for the success of the project. The project manager should have the team's buy-in before proceeding with the plan. The development of plans, policies, standards and procedures, objectives, goals, strategies, organizational structure, charts, emails, conference calls, and small group meetings all make up the components of this plan.

THE VALUE OF COMMUNICATION MANAGEMENT OUTPUTS

The dedicated team should outline the primary objectives of the communication plan and agree on how the project will be distributed, the timeframe of the delivery, the mechanism and frequency to inform team members, customers, stakeholders and sponsors, and perhaps anyone who has a vested interest in the product or service. During the planning phase, the project manager is required to outline a detailed strategic plan that covers all component areas.

The Communication Management Plan

The output of these planning sessions will produce the Communication Management Plan. The document should contain crucial information on the following:

- How, when, and where to archive project documentation
- The process of project reporting, such as status reports, technical data, project minutes, and presentations
- How to distribute schedules, timesheets, and risks/logs throughout the project
- When and where status reports will be announced or sent to team members, stakeholders, and customers.

The project manager should update the Communication Management Plan on an as-needed basis and when changes develop or tasks are complete.

Information Distribution: The Project Management Plan and Organizational Process Assets

The output for Information Distribution is the Project Management Plan (PM Plan) and Organization Process Assets. The relevant sections in the PM Plan describes the approach chosen for securing and storing project records on a database or company's repository through emails, formal letters, and status reports.

Information exchange can be accomplished through symbols, signs, behavior, verbal communications, physical touch, or visible movements as well as documented in written form. A good communicator has the ability to convey a message without any misunderstandings and with clarity. Poor communications may contribute to misunderstandings over scope changes, delivery dates, incorrect customer requirements, and failure to articulate the corporate vision within the project's goals. It's important to remember that, unless your message was understood clearly, *communication* hasn't taken place—no matter how much you said or wrote on the subject!

Why is the distribution of information so important to the overall success of the project? The customers, team members, and all stakeholders need to be kept apprised of the most recent project developments and the schedule to minimize future risks that can impact the delivery date. The inability to communicate critical details could cause project failure.

Performance Reports

Because the entire corporate structure can be impacted by one project, it is essential the project manager document all project actions. The team can learn about previous projects and gain new knowledge that can assist the project manager and executives to direct the project's outcome. To ensure the project management team has sufficient current data to make decisions from market trends or competitor's products can help provide the effective delivery of the project without jeopardizing the quality of the project, increasing costs, or delaying any schedules. The project manager has to implement the best process for distribution of information by researching past projects' lessons-learned documents and previous project records similar to this project, understanding project reports, reviewing presentations, and obtaining feedback from stakeholders.

Manage Stakeholders: Resolve Issues, Update Management Plan, and Process Assets

The value of performance reporting is continually mentioned throughout the project and program and will be communicated in the scope document, schedule, and budget report, and quality assurance testing documents. Forecasting and estimating are key areas in this process. The performance reports may provide additional information on scope changes and any project management plan updates, and make recommendations or corrective actions within the project. The project manager is responsible for documenting any issues or concerns to ensure this is communicated among all stakeholders. Using the triple constraint as a guide will help the project manager manage customer expectations throughout the life cycle of the project to closure.

IDENTIFY COMMUNICATION METHODS

The Sender-Receiver Model is one way of thinking about communication that is commonly used in corporations. The sender can transmit an idea or decide how to convey this message by voice, symbols, verbally, or non-verbally. One critical element is the level or tone of noises that can impact the message that is being delivered. The receiver obtains the message and then begins to process this information and interpret the idea. The filter aspect of the message corresponds to potential distortions based upon the receiver's culture, background, experience, and position within the company.

Here are five fundamental questions that the project manager should consider when sending messages:

1. Who are you communicating with?
2. What actually needs to be communicated?
3. What method is being used?
4. How does this communication impact or change the project?
5. When does the message need to be received or responded to?

There are a few barriers that arise within the Sender-Receiver Method that the project manager should be aware of. For example, due to personal or cultural biases, the receiver may hear only what he or she wants to hear. The same message can be perceived differently; therefore, the receiver should evaluate the source (Sender) before communicating back with a response. The tone or selection of words can mean different things to different people. Pay attention to those non-verbal cues that are hidden in the message or directive. Is the receiver or sender emotional about the message?

Ideally, a "feedback loop" can be established between sender and receiver so that the content of a message is iteratively clarified until both parties are sure they are really communicating—that is, the sender is getting the intended point across, and the receiver understands what is meant and responds appropriately.

How does the project manager ensure the message intent is being transmitted fully? Here are some techniques to apply:

▶Provide a forum to ensure the communications are being delivered

▶Try sending message in a different type of format.

▶Make sure the message is delivered in a clear and concise manner without any noise interruptions and cannot be misinterpreted.

▶Establish good communications early in the planning phase—this is a benchmark for future correspondence.

▶Select an appropriate time to communicate.

▶Always reinforce major points.

▶Implement a common language—no technical jargon or shortcuts.

▶Communicate in person using eye contact and listening skills.

▶Make sure the listener takes a moment before responding to reflect on what is being said and the impact of the message.

▶Be honest, direct, and make "I" statements.

▶Decode each message.

▶Respect each other's opinions.

▶Match verbal or non-verbal body language and expressions.

Many project managers value two-way communication because it provides an atmosphere for productive brainstorming meetings and builds trust among team members, which is critical in the planning phase of the project.

The project manager who recognizes the value of this method talks individually with team members to find out each team member's communication preferences. By paying attention to this upfront, the project manager can minimize conflicts during the course of the project. When communication is smooth and productive, it provides opportunities to stimulate creative thinking and problem solving, and reduces or eliminates the possibility of operating in a crisis mode.

Demonstrate Communication Methods

Communication channels are important in creating an atmosphere for successful implementation. Exchange information with all stakeholders and customers about all the aspects of the project (status reports, procedures, risks, and issues) and share feedback from other departments. Sharing information empowers people to learn and feel part of the team effort. Networking informally strengthens relationships and connects members with a common bond.

The project manager needs to determine how to communicate internally as well as externally to have effective communications in a cross-functional or project-driven department. Most project communications are internal, performed either formally by status reporting or presentations to stakeholders at various phases of the project, or informally via email. How much external communication needs to be done depends on where the PMO resides in the corporate organizational structure. In a project-driven organization, the project manager may spend little time communicating status and results and 75% of his or her time working with the customer, consultants, and outside agencies.

Influencing Factors That Have an Impact on How Communications are Received.

All messages are filtered through the receiving individual's personal perceptions, which can at time present a barrier, and in all cases affects how the message is interpreted. Environment, culture, language, educational background, and experience all affect how communication is perceived and processed. Sometimes team members with strong or appealing personalities will draw others to their point of view or perception of the problem or issue. The way information is presented contributes to how team members review or execute the data and thus potentially affects the outcome of the problem or issue.

Individuals' attitudes, emotions, and built-in prejudices about the project will be reflected in how motivated they are to perform and complete activities. It's important to deliver project information in a variety of formats and give plenty of chances for people to ask questions and clarify issues; if the information is distorted either by the project manager's delivery style, or by a team member's "filters," there could be ambiguity or incorrect assumptions made about the data.

When presenting project information, the presenter needs to organize thoughts and topics so the target audience can clearly understand them. A common mistake of project managers is giving unclear instructions or activity assignments, which causes the team member to leave the meeting to perform work going in the wrong direction. A good technique is for the project manager to reiterate the main points of the message, and have the team member recap his or her understanding of the issues or action items. A follow-up email outlining these action items with a scheduled due date is also a good practice.

The project manager will need to talk with team members and find out what method they feel comfortable with in communicating these action items. Each team member should respond back both individually and as a team. It is good to have established multiple communication mediums and processes. Determine what the most effective method is for each team member, and for the team as a whole. The interface between team members is very important to the success of the project.

Is verbal or non-verbal communication more effective? We normally think of verbal communication as taking place in person, delivering presentations or reporting an activity. What happens if there is silence from team members? Are team members quiet for a reason or is it a cultural attitude, such as respect for the presenter? Pay attention to the tone of your message. In non-verbal communications—a category in which the majority of communication falls—the message may not be interpreted correctly. Touching, personal space, and privacy are all aspects of non-verbal cues that can be culturally charged.

How to Organize and Conduct Productive Meetings

We have all attended meetings where we questioned why we were there. The project manager needs to decide if the meeting is needed. Are there any immediate problems or issues that require resolution? What are the consequences if the meeting is not held?

The project manager also must conduct effective meetings. The project manager should decide what type of meeting to conduct and who should be included, such as upper management, individuals, the entire team, remote team members, and the customer.

Tips for Meeting Organization

▶Limit discussion to specific topics.

▶Encourage all members to participate or contribute on topics.

▶Identify and recap action items.

▶Always reinforce goals, deliverables, and expected outcomes.

▶Instill control mechanisms and rules for meetings.

▶Document the meeting by recording minutes. When topics being discussed are sensitive, there are computer-based meeting technologies by which participants can make anonymous contributions to the discussion that you may want to consider.

▶Determine your target audience. Is the language (including technical terminology or jargon) appropriate for the meeting members? Eliminate any language barriers so everyone can exchange information. Engage an interpreter if necessary on a multicultural team.

▶Appoint or hire a facilitator to minimize conflicts and direct the flow and timing of the meeting. It is impossible for the same person to both facilitate and record a meeting; likewise the manager in charge of outcomes should not try to facilitate.

Techniques for Conducting Successful Meetings

1. Start the meeting at the scheduled time.
2. Conduct the meeting with an agenda.
3. Involve team members to report project status.
4. Ask the team for feedback on discussion points.
5. Assign action items.
6. Allow the team to have buy-in on issues and solutions.
7. Determine the next steps or next meeting time.
8. End on time.

Here are some considerations to think about for the various target audiences of project meetings:

▶***Senior Management Meetings***. What does senior management want to know and hear about this phase of the project? Most executives are involved in many meetings; their time is limited so the meeting content needs to be brief, concise, and light on jargon or technology terminology, and presented on a high-project level. They will have some basic questions, but it an excellent learning tool for them to understand more details of the project. Also, team members want to hear the executive's perspective of what they think about the project and any new direction for the product or corporation. How does this product fit with the company's strategic mission and goals?

▶***Individual Meetings***. The project manager should take time to talk with every member privately about the progress and current status of the project. This is a great way to get to know each team member and discover what his or her motivation and contribution will be toward the project. The individual now has the opportunity to discuss any personal issues or problems or any time constraints for completing the work.

▶***Team Meetings***. Team meetings promote and provide the chance for team members to begin establishing relationships and cooperative methods to work on issues, risks, and activities. The project manager can inform the entire team of any project developments and then discuss concerns about the project. They can discuss solutions to problems, any changes, and corrective action for the next phase. It also encourages participation between the team members regardless of attitudes, philosophy, and status within the company. It brings commitment and accountability. Teamwork is essential for successful projects by sharing ideas, instilling integrity and respect for one another, and building synergy and creativity amongst their peers. Team members begin to trust each other and openly share potential risks and project status.

▶***Remote Team Meetings***. Distributed team members must conduct business mostly through emails, fax, conference calls, and video conferencing when available. They need to be assured that the other team members hear their issues and consider their solutions. Cooperation may be more difficult in this situation, but buy-in is very important for these team members. They must work harder to build relationships and trust, and the project manager also has a responsibility to make sure that all team members are included in communications, whether remote or on-site.

▶***Customer Meetings***. The project manager should schedule periodic meetings with the customer either individually or with the team. It can be done informally or formally by written or verbal communications to discuss the status of the project or to discuss any concerns. A formal presentation with some graphics adds a nice touch and the customer appreciates being kept informed with current updates of the project.

What is the Project Manager's Responsibility in Preparing the Project Meetings?

1. Set the agenda or compile status reports.
2. Assign who will make decisions on approving tasks, equipment, and assigning resources.
3. State the objective and goals for the meeting.
4. Assign deliverables on a weekly or monthly basis.
5. Report on the project expectations from the management's viewpoint.
6. Inform team members on deadlines.

IDENTIFY COMMON COMMUNICATION ISSUES

The team needs clear direction from upper management to ensure that the deliverables will be met. This will save time, reduce costs, and make sure the schedule milestones are being met. The project manager needs to keep an open-door policy for team members to talk about the project. Time management is critical for team members, especially the project manager. Document time logs or use dashboards for reporting time against the project. Prioritize workload that correlates to the project scope. To make improvements in this area, record how much time is spent on the phone or email. Schedule time with team members instead of conducting impromptu meetings. If there are continual misunderstandings from team members, pay attention to how the emails are written or how verbal requests are given. Provide clear instructions of expectations and require more written documentation. If someone is not performing an adequate job, hand that task off to other team members. There could be organizational changes that cause decisions to be made and delays in the project, due to lack of resources or qualified resources to perform the activities. There may be different levels of management with hidden agendas or egos involved that cause restrictions to the original scope of the project. Or perhaps the customer has not provided clear requirements or has changed their direction. Suddenly there may be conflict between team members causing a risk to the project.

Why are Some Project Managers Not Effective in their Role as Communicators?

At times a project manager is too critical and micromanages to a level not acceptable to the team. Team meetings become ineffective. Or perhaps the project manager does not communicate bad news from the customer or upper management. Even though this project manager may think he or she is shielding the project team, the outcome is likely to be more painful than simply communicating negative information as it arises. Has the project manager provided good status reporting and distributed techniques, project plans, budgets, and templates to team members? Project managers must confront facts or present full documentation of project issues, risks, and status. Is the project manager intimidated by upper management? Does the project manager work well with the customer and keep customers informed of the status? Does the project manager immediately communicate any problems to the correct team members or management?

How to Effectively Manage Communications Throughout the Project

The project manager clearly needs to understand or detect any problems early in the process or identify in the planning phases. The project manager needs to have good listening skills, as it is important not to filter any bad or good news out. He or she needs to listen to facts—make the project plan, the requirements, the scope statement, and the budget the foundation of all communications. Communicate the nature of the project to all team members and stakeholders and allow for a question and answer session.

The project manager should be knowledgeable and capable of executing planning phases of the project while organizing, directing, motivating, and controlling. The communication management plan is the source document and tool to generate synergy amongst the team members and produce project results.

Effective communications can be the deciding factor of a successful project to meet the project's deadline and budget requirements, and to deliver a quality product to satisfy customer and stakeholder expectations.

DISCUSSION QUESTIONS

❶ Have you had experiences where diversity of backgrounds on a team has caused communication problems? How have these been dealt with? How should they have been dealt with?

❷ What would be the differences in a communication plan for a virtual or distributed team vs. a co-located team?

❸ What communication methods would you use to deliver bad news to the project team? How might the way bad news is communicated affect the team's response to a challenging situation?

FURTHER READING

Booher, Diana. *Communicate with Confidence.* McGraw-Hill, 1994.
Silberman, Mel. *101 Ways to Make Meetings Active: Surefire Ideas to Engage Your Group.* Jossey-Bass, 1999.
VicKer, Lauren and Ron Hein. *The Fast Forward MBA in Business Communication,* Jossey-Bass, 1999.

CHAPTER 13A

Studies in Communications Management: Achieving Project Success Through Team Building and Stakeholder Management

▶JOHN TUMAN, JR., MANAGEMENT TECHNOLOGIES GROUP, INC.

A project is a success if all the work goes as planned. This assumes the project has a well-developed plan and that there are no surprises. In a successful project, objectives are well defined, work is accomplished as scheduled, and resources are used efficiently. Furthermore, the client is pleased with the final results. Most important, the whole job is done without mishap, controversy, or lawsuit. In addition, management acknowledges a fine job and rewards everyone handsomely.

Projects seldom work out this way. One reason is that project objectives have different meanings for different people. Work tasks run into roadblocks, get delayed, and consume resources. Critics attack the project, unexpected problems develop, and people get discouraged and quit. Project success means handling all the unexpected problems and getting the job done to project stakeholders' satisfaction. Project teams increasingly address a complex mix of issues, problems, and aspirations. These include not only the goals and ambitions of project participants, but also of outside parties. To be successful, project teams must understand who determines success, what their motivations are, and what the costs involved are.

WHO DETERMINES PROJECT SUCCESS?

In every undertaking there are parties with a vested interest in the activities and results of the project. The motivations of the

Project Stakeholders	Stakeholders Include	Stakeholders' Criteria for Project Success	Stakeholders' Impact on Project Success
Project Champions	• Entrepreneurs • Developers • Investors • Visionaries • Clients/Customers • Politicians • Community Leaders	• Good return on investment • Services and products available at minimum expenditure • End result as envisioned • Rewarding experience • Enhanced reputation	• Very high • Normally the project cannot exist without project champions
Project Participants	• Project Manager • Project Team • Engineers • Constructors • Vendors • Suppliers • Regulatory Agencies at all Levels • Legal, etc.	• Complete project on time and within budget • Meet all objectives • Satisfy other stakeholders' goals and desires	• Very high • Project participants can make or break the project
Community Participants	• Community Members • Special Interest Groups • Religious Leaders • Political Groups • Social and Ethnic Groups • Environmentalists	• Benefit the community • Minimize impact on community • Satisfy special interest • Stop, delay, change the project • Profit from project	• High • May require extra efforts and resources to satisfy demands, concerns, objectives
Parasitic Participants	• Opportunists • Activists • Causes • Information Media: Radio, TV, Newspapers, Magazines, etc.	• Opportunity for self-fulfillment/ aggrandizement • Opportunity to promote own views, ideas, or philosophy • Opportunity for profit or gain	• Low to high • Impact could be significant if other stakeholders can be influenced

TABLE 13A-1. **FOUR GROUPS OF PROJECT STAKEHOLDERS**

project sponsors and those who do the work are obvious. Individuals affected by the project are concerned. Still, others are motivated by political, social, environmental, and economic interests. These parties are called *stakeholders:* individuals with some kind of stake, claim, share, or interest in the activities and results of the project.

The role of the stakeholders and the influence they have is not always understood by project managers. This can be a serious problem for several reasons. First, the project manager has to build a project team that has the skill to address all stakeholder requirements and concerns. Second, the team must develop strategies for dealing with different levels of stakeholder power. Finally, resources must be obtained to deal with stakeholder issues that are beyond normal project demands. Project managers must study the different stakeholders to understand how they can influence project success.

Project stakeholders can be categorized into four main groups, as shown in Table 13A-1. These include: (1) project champions, (2) project participants, (3) community participants, and (4) parasitic participants. The potential role and influence of each group is discussed in the sections that follow.

Project Champions

Project champions are those who have some reason to bring a project into being. These stakeholders include the developers, investors, and entrepreneurs motivated by profit. The group also includes the visionaries who are trying to create something for the future or for the benefit of others. Also included is the client or customer with a specific need, politicians, community leaders, and others who want to satisfy the needs of their constituents. The role of the project champion is significant; in most cases the project cannot exist without them. Furthermore, the judgments, evaluations, and perceptions of these stakeholders probably have the greatest effect in confirming project success. The project champions must be fully satisfied, or the project is not a success. Obviously, the composition of the project champions as well as their needs and perceptions can vary widely. In some cases, the individual goals and objectives of those within this group are in conflict with each other.

Project Participants

This group of stakeholders includes organizations and individuals who are responsible for planning and executing the project. Typically, this includes the project manager and project team, engineers, constructors, vendors, suppliers, craftspeople, and regulatory agencies at the local, state, and national levels. The involvement of the project participants is again fairly obvious. Success from their viewpoint means accomplishing the project goals and receiving appropriate recognition.

Community Participants

These stakeholders include groups or individuals who are directly affected by the project. Community participants create the environment that surrounds the project. The group can materialize because of environmental, social, political, economic, health, or safety concerns. These stakeholders can be a few households concerned about increased traffic from a new facility or a religious group opposed to a new technology. They can have a profound impact on a project. For example, antinuclear groups have stopped the construction of nuclear power plants, environmentalists have halted highway construction programs, and religious groups have challenged genetic research projects.

Parasitic Participants

This group of stakeholders presents an interesting and important challenge to project managers. Parasitic participants consist of organizations and individuals who do not have a direct

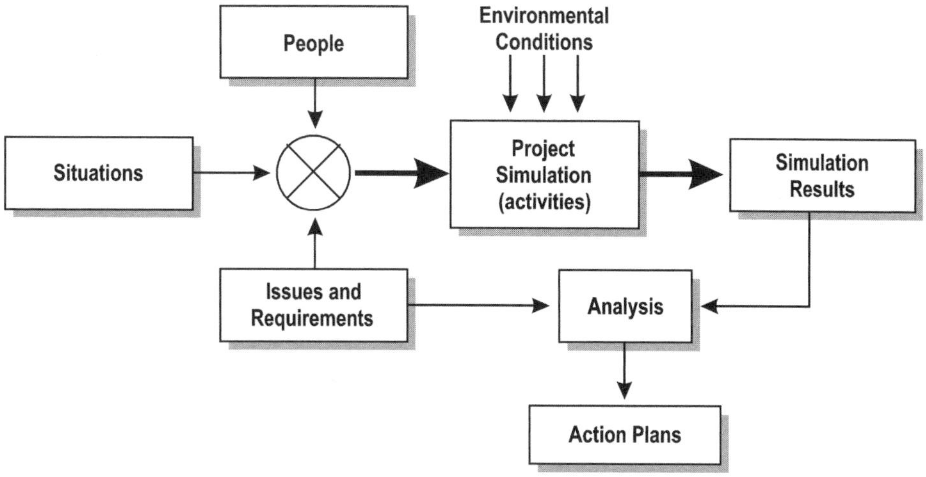

Elements of the Project Management Success Model	
People	The designated project participants. Identify the key decision makers and contributors to the planning, organizing, and controlling of the project activities and resources.
Situations	The specific problems defined within the context of the conditions, wants, and limitations that the actual project is expected to experience.
Issues and Requirements	The specific concerns, problems, and requirements that the project will face. This includes cost, schedule, and technical issues of the project as well as organization, staffing, communications, legal, political, cultural, and social issues.
Environmental Conditions	The outside influences that impact the project. They may include physical conditions (i.e., geographic, climate, etc.), political, legal, social/cultural, economic, infrastructure, etc.
Project Simulation	Special exercises and problems in which the project participants interact to deal with specific issues and requirements for given situations and conditions.
Simulation Results	Data on how the project participants interacted with each other; their reactions to problem situations and environmental conditions and the actual decisions and solutions formulated to address specific problems.
Analysis and Action Plans	An evaluation of the simulation results against the issues and requirements of the project, to determine if the project team can effectively carry out their responsibilities. The specific actions relative to people, procedures, plans, systems, and resources to be taken.

TABLE 13A-2. **PROJECT MANAGEMENT SUCCESS MODEL**

stake in the project. In this group we find the opportunists, the activists, and others who are looking for a focal point for their energies, internal drives, and desires to promote their personal philosophies and views. By definition, this group is distinct and different from those whose members have legitimate concerns about the impact of a project on their community

Project Stakeholders	Power Factors and Weights			Success Goal Factors and Weights			
	Impact Resources (0.35)	Impact Success (0.65)	Weighted Score (x-Axis)	Difficulty 0.5	Risk/ Unknowns 0.35	Conflict 0.15	Weighted Score (y-Axis)
Project Champions							
Developers	3	4	2.60	5	4	2	4.20
Client/Customers	2	4	3.30	3	4	2	3.20
Politicians	1	5	3.60	3	1	3	2.30
Community Leaders	4	5	4.65	5	1	4	3.45
Visionaries	1	3	2.30	2	1	2	1.65
Project Participants							
Project Management	5	2	3.05	3	3	3	3.00
Vendors	1	2	1.65	3	4	1	3.05
Regulators	1	2	1.65	4	5	5	4.50
Constructors	4	1	2.05	2	2	1	1.85
Community Participants							
Special Interest Groups	2	2	2.00	5	1	5	3.60
Environmentalists	3	2	2.35	4	1	5	3.10
Parasitic Participants							
Media	4	5	4.65	4	5	1	3.90
Activists	4	3	3.35	5	5	5	5.00

TABLE 13A-3. **TECHNIQUE FOR IDENTIFYING AND RANKING SUCCESS GOALS OF STAKEHOLDERS**

or way of life. The distinction is that the primary motivation of the parasitic participant is one of self-aggrandizement. The project provides the parasitic participants with an opportunity for activity, visibility, and self-fulfillment, and a platform to promote their philosophy or ideas.

This group also covers the information media: radio, TV, newspapers, magazines, etc. The information media use the interest, attention, concerns, or controversy that can surround a project as a vehicle to sell their products. If projects can be made to appear controversial, sensational, dangerous, exciting, or risky, they become more newsworthy. Usually, the information media have no direct stake in the project, yet their influence on the project can be devastating.

Success Modeling

Can we model success? Experience and common sense teach us that some project teams

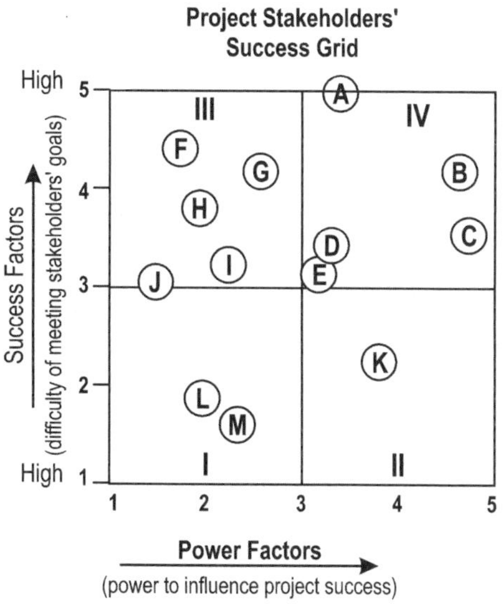

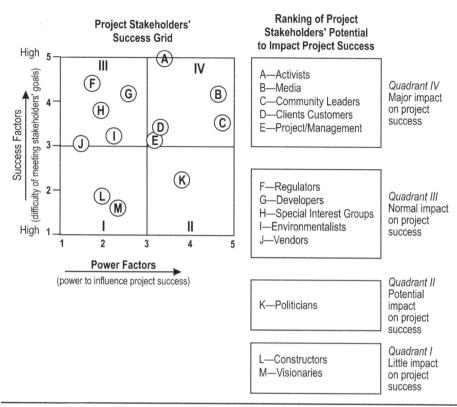

Ranking of Project Stakeholders' Potential to Impact Project Success

A—Activists B—Media C—Community Leaders D—Clients Customers E—Project/Management	*Quadrant IV* Major impact on project success
F—Regulators G—Developers H—Special Interest Groups I—Environmentalists J—Vendors	*Quadrant III* Normal impact on project success
K—Politicians	*Quadrant II* Potential impact on project success
L—Constructors M—Visionaries	*Quadrant I* Little impact on project success

TABLE 13A-4. **STAKEHOLDER SUCCESS GRID**

function better than others. Most of the time we do not see what the team actually does; however, we do see and judge the final results. To learn from others, we need to look at the specific actions that make them different, better, or unique. Ideally, we want to capture this experience in a way that helps to guide our thinking and spark our creativity.

Success modeling provides a tool and a methodology that disciplines project managers to define consciously and deliberately the criteria for success of the project. In addition, success modeling provides a framework for team building, strategy development, and actual planning and control of project success.

Models can be used to represent a project (see Table 13A-2). Furthermore, we can simulate the project environment to test the soundness of the project models. Thus, it is possible to test different assumptions about project plans and organizational approaches before actually starting the project. The goal of modeling and simulation is to determine if the project team, plans, procedures, and systems are correct before committing resources to the project.

We can use modeling techniques to build a team for a specific undertaking within a specific environment. Furthermore, these techniques can help to create a cultural framework for team success. Creating a success model involves a number of specific steps that are discussed in the following sections.

Establish Project Success Goals

Defining the project success goals sets the baseline for measuring project success. The success goals must include the stakeholders' needs and desires as well as the cost, schedule, and technical objectives of the project. We can get information about the stakeholders by talking to them and opening lines of communication—i.e., advertising, surveys, public meetings, information hot lines, etc. Also, the relationships among stakeholder goals must be established. Are there conflicting goals? Are any of the goals mutually supportive? Do these goals have a positive or negative impact on the project?

A stakeholder study is called for in the conceptual phase. For a straightforward project, the stakeholders' goals may be simple and easy to understand. They may even be compatible with the project team's goals. However, for a complex or controversial project, there is usually a bewildering array of stakeholders' concerns and interests. The project team must sort out the different concerns and interests and determine which stakeholders have the leverage to hinder project success.

Table 13A-3 presents a technique for identifying and ranking project stakeholders. This technique produces numerical values to establish the power of the stakeholders and the degree of difficulty of their goal. In evaluating project stakeholders' success goals, we look at the characteristics of the goals (difficulty, conflict with other goals, etc.) and the power that each stakeholder has (to impact project resources, success, and so on). Then, a simple 1 to 5 scale is used to rate each factor. Each rating is multiplied by that factor's weight to obtain the weighted scale. The scales and weights used should reflect management's requirements. For example, a finer scale would be used for a project that has many factors to consider.

The final weighted scores are then used to develop a stakeholder success grid, as shown in Table 13A-4. The success grid shows the relationship between the difficulty of the stakeholders' goals and their power to influence project success. The information from the success grid is ranked by quadrant. In the example shown in Table 13A-4, stakeholders not directly involved in the project—activist groups, the media, and community leaders—have a major impact on project success.

From these analyses, the project team members can develop plans and processes to focus their energy and resources where they will do the most good.

Identify the Success Process

Management processes are required to accomplish project work effectively and efficiently. Project work involves planning, organizing, and directing resources and people to address stakeholder issues and project cost, schedule, and technical objectives. Often, stakeholders focus on the qualitative aspects of the project. Their concerns include health, safety, reliability, quality, and environmental issues. Nevertheless, the team must implement a process to manage all the project's requirements and activities in a systematic manner. For simplicity, we can break down the project's responsibilities into two types of activities: hard and soft.

Hard activities relate to the business of planning and controlling work scope, task, resources, practices, and standards. Hard activities also encompass the basic management functions of communicating, information processing, and decision making. Soft activities relate to behavioral modifications and opinion shaping. These include training, team building, community relations, advertising, and promotion. Later in this chapter we will discuss ways of dealing with soft project activities.

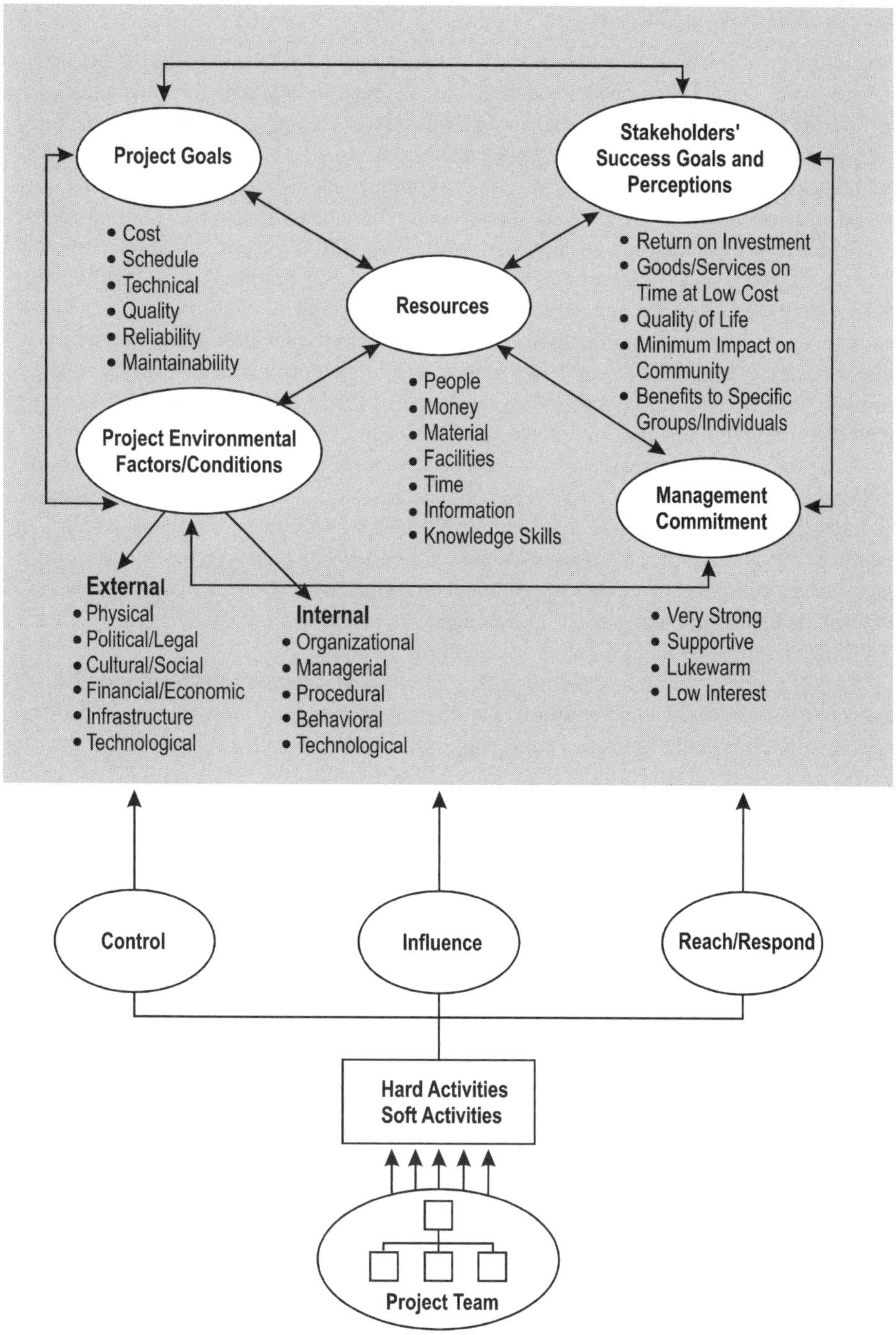

TABLE 13A-5. **PROJECT SUCCESS MAPPING**

Map the Success Characteristics

Successful project teams develop a culture and a management style that fits the project environment. These teams understand the political, legal, social, and economic situation, as well as the infrastructure and physical conditions. Project teams must analyze their project environment as a military leader evaluates the terrain before a battle. The team must thoroughly evaluate the demands of its project environment and ask the question, "What must we do and how must we act to be successful under these conditions or in these situations?"

Project success mapping, as shown in Table 13A-5, first looks at the five components that are vital to project success: (1) the resources available; (2) the difficulty of the project itself; (3) the demands and perceptions of the stakeholders; (4) the conditions and problems presented by the project environment; and (5) the level of management and sponsor commitment. The second step is to determine the project team's ability to (1) control, (2) influence, and (3) react/respond to all of the requirements and problems presented by the five main components for project success.

The project team controls, influences, or reacts/responds to needs and situations by engaging in both hard and soft activities. In hard activities, the team controls, influences, or reacts/responds to project requirements by managing resources, applying practices or standards, or doing more or less work (scope of work). The team can also control, influence, or react/respond to project requirements through soft activities. That is, the team can seek to shape opinions and attitudes and modify behaviors through training, team building, advertising, promotion, and community relations.

Project success mapping thus provides a simple way for the project team to identify the activities, demands, and conditions that they must manage. From this analysis, the team can determine the kinds of people they want on the team.

Develop a Project Success Scenario

Project teams must decide at the outset how they will deal with stakeholders, handle problems, and respond to emergencies or unexpected events. Team members can describe in brief vignettes how to operate in different situations to ensure success. Project success scenarios help the team members establish the values, standards, norms, and management style that are best for their project environment.

Define the Project Team's Modus Operandi

Success scenarios provide a way for project teams to develop ideas about their culture and philosophy of operation. However, the team must formalize its thinking and define a specific management style and way of doing business. The team should develop a modus operandi that describes its philosophy, values, vision, and mission. This document is broader in scope than the typical project management manual. The modus operandi is the charter that guides the development of the project team and its policies, procedures, and systems throughout the life of the project.

In summary, the success model is designed to reduce the real-life cost of on-the-job learning. By forcing the team to examine the project environment and the stakeholders' demands, we hope to avoid many project pitfalls. However, a success model is a dynamic instrument, and it should be refined as the project evolves. Thus, the project team can build a knowledge base of ideas, plans, decisions, and results and continually improve the model for future undertakings.

DISCUSSION QUESTIONS

❶ For a project with which you are familiar, develop a list of all stakeholders. Consider external stakeholders as well as internal.

❷ Are there stakeholders on your list that perhaps were not included in the planning for the actual project? How did this impact project outcomes? What could have been done differently?

❸ Do you agree with the author's characterization of the media and issue-oriented activist groups as "parasitic"? If not, what might be a more constructive framing of these stakeholder relationships?

FURTHER READING

Cohen, Judith L., and John R. Adams. "Learning From Project Managers: Lessons in Managing Uncertainty." 1984 *Proceedings of the Project Management Institute,* Philadelphia. Drexel Hill, Penn.: PMI.

Fitzgerald, J. W. H. "Because Wisdom Cannot Be Told." *Program Manager* (September-October 1985).

Gadeken, Owen C. "Why Engineers and Scientists Often Fail as Managers." *Program Manager* (January-February 1986).

Grove, Andrew S. "How to Make Confrontation Work for You." *Fortune* (July 1984).

Hadedorn, Homer J., and Arthur D. Little. "Profiling Corporate Culture." *Today's Office* (October 1984).

Marutollo, Frank. "Taking Issue With Theory 'Y.'" *Program Manager* (July-August 1984).

Mitchell, Eddie. "Creating High-Performing Programs by Modeling, Assessing, and Implementing Excellence." *Program Manager* (March–April 1986).

Muntz, Peter, and Robert Chasnoff. "The Cultural Awareness Hierarchy: A Model for Promoting Understanding." *Training and Development Journal* (October 1983).

Owens, Stephen D. "Leadership Theory and the Project Environment: Which Approach is Applicable?" 1983 *Proceedings of the Project Management Institute,* Houston. Drexel Hill, Penn.: PMI.

Shearon, Ella Mae. "Conflict Management and Team Building for Productive Projects." 1983 *Proceedings of the Project Management Institute,* Houston. Drexel Hill, Penn.: PMI.

Shell, Richard L., Ray H. Souder, and Nicholas Damachi. "Using Behavioral and Influence Factors to Motivate the Technical Work." *IE* (August 1983).

Tuman, John, Jr. "Improving Productivity in the Project Management Environment Using Advanced Technology and the Behavioral Sciences." 1983 *Proceedings of the Project Management Institute,* Houston. Drexel Hill, Penn.: PMI.

Whitney, Diana K., and Linda S. Ackerman. "The Fusion Team: A Model of Organic and Shared Leadership." *Journal of the Bay Area OD Network* 3, No. 2 (December 1983).

Wilemon, David L. "Learning in High Technology Project Teams." 1983 *Proceedings of the Project Management Institute,* Houston. Drexel Hill, Penn.: PMI.

Wilemon, David L., and Hans J. Thamhain. "A Model for Developing High Performance Project Teams." 1983 *Proceedings of the Project Management Institute,* Houston. Drexel Hill, Penn.: PMI.

CHAPTER 14

Risk Management in Practice

▶DAVID HILLSON, PHD, PMP, FAPM, FIRM,
RISK DOCTOR & PARTNERS

The word "risk" is a common and widely used part of our daily vocabulary, relating to personal circumstances (health, pensions, insurance, investments etc), society (terrorism, economic performance, food safety etc.), and business (corporate governance, strategy, business continuity etc.). One area where risk management has found particular prominence is in the management of projects, perhaps because of the risky nature of projects themselves. All projects to some extent are characterized by the following:

- ▶Uniqueness
- ▶Complexity
- ▶Change
- ▶Assumptions
- ▶Constraints
- ▶Dependencies
- ▶People.

Each of these factors introduces significant risk into every project, requiring a structured and proactive approach to the management of risk if the project is to succeed.

Many see risk management as a key contributor to the success of both projects and businesses. This arises from the clear link between risk and objectives, embodied in the definition of the word. For example, *A Guide to the Project Management Body of Knowledge, Third Edition* states: "Project risk is an uncertain event or condition that, if it occurs, has a positive or negative effect on at least one project objective."[1] Other international standards and guidelines use similar definitions, always linking risk with objectives.

This is why risk management is so important, and not just another project management technique. Risk management aims to identify those uncertainties with the potential to harm the project, assess them so they are understood, and develop and implement actions to stop them occurring or minimize their impact on achievement of objectives. It also has the goal of identifying, assessing, and responding to uncertainties that could help achieve objectives. Because it focuses attention on the uncertainties that matter, either negatively or positively, risk management is a Critical Success Factor for project (and business) success. Where risk management is ineffective, a project can only succeed, if the project team is lucky. Effective risk management optimizes the chances of success, even in the face of bad luck.

Fortunately risk management is not difficult. The process, tools and techniques outlined in the *PMBOK® Guide* and similar guides offer a straightforward way of implementing an effective approach to managing risk on projects.

DEFINITION OF RISK

Before describing the risk management process, it is obviously important to understand what it is we are trying to manage. The definition of "risk" quoted above clearly includes two distinct types of uncertainty: those that if they occur will have a negative effect on a project objective, and those that would have a positive effect. In other words, *risk includes both threat and opportunity*. At first sight this causes some hesitation for people new to the concept: "Surely everyone knows that risk is bad! Risk is the same as threat, but isn't opportunity something different?"

In adopting this inclusive definition of risk, the Project Management Institute is not unusual, but is completely consistent with the current trend in international best-practice risk management. Many other leading standards and guidelines from project management organizations worldwide take a similar position.[2]

Taking this position has significant implications for all aspects of risk management, including thinking, language, and process.[3] That's why, as the body of knowledge documents have evolved, they have come to include a wider definition of risk. For example, in the *PMBOK® Guide, Third Edition,* both threat and opportunity are treated equitably, and the objectives of risk management are stated as "to increase the probability and impact of positive events, and decrease the probability and impact of events adverse to the project."[4] The aim is to use the same risk process to handle both threats and opportunities alongside each other, giving double benefits from a single investment.

PROCESS SUMMARY

Risk management is not rocket science, and the risk process simply represents structured common sense. The steps in the process follow a natural way of thinking about the uncertain future, by asking and attempting to answer the following questions:

- ▶What are we trying to achieve? (Planning)
- ▶What uncertainties could affect us, for better or worse? (Identification)
- ▶Which are the most important uncertainties to address? (Analysis)

▶What could we do to tackle these uncertainties, and what will we do? (Response planning)

▶Let's do it—and how do things change as a result? (Monitoring and control)

These questions are reflected in the risk management process outlined in the *PMBOK® Guide:*

▶Risk management planning—deciding how to approach, plan, and execute the risk management activities for a project.

▶Risk identification—determining which risks might affect the project.

▶Qualitative risk analysis—prioritizing risks for subsequent further analysis or action.

▶Quantitative risk analysis—numerically analyzing the effect on overall project objectives of identified risks.

▶Risk response planning—developing options and actions to enhance opportunities and to reduce threats to project objectives.

▶Risk monitoring and control—tracking identified risks, monitoring residual risks, identifying new risks, executing risk response plans, and evaluating effectiveness.

Various tools and techniques can be used to assist with each step, and they can be implemented at differing levels of detail on different projects. Successful risk management, however, only requires structured thinking and action, following a common-sense process in the face of uncertainty.

Risk Management Planning

The first step of the risk management process is *not* risk identification. Because risk is defined in terms of objectives, it is necessary first to define those objectives that are at risk, i.e., the scope of the risk process. The *PMBOK® Guide* describes this as "the process of deciding how to approach and conduct the risk management activities for a project."

This statement indicates that risk management is not "one-size-fits-all." It is necessary to scale the risk process to meet the risk challenge of each particular project. Projects that are risky or strategically important will require a more robust approach to risk management than those that are more simple or routine. Scaleable aspects include: methodology, tools and techniques, organization and staffing, reporting requirements, and the update and review cycle.

A number of other factors need to be decided before embarking on the risk management process. These include:

▶Setting the thresholds of how much risk is acceptable for the project by identifying the risk tolerances of key stakeholders, resolving any differences, and communicating the conclusions to the project team.

▶Defining terms for qualitative analysis of probability and impact on the project, related to specific project objectives. Where terms such as "high," "medium," and "low" are used, their meanings must be agreed upon in order to provide a consistent framework for assessment of identified risks.

▶Definition of potential sources of risk to the project. This may be presented as a hierarchical Risk Breakdown Structure (RBS), perhaps drawing on an industry standard or an organization template. An example RBS is given in Figure 14-1.

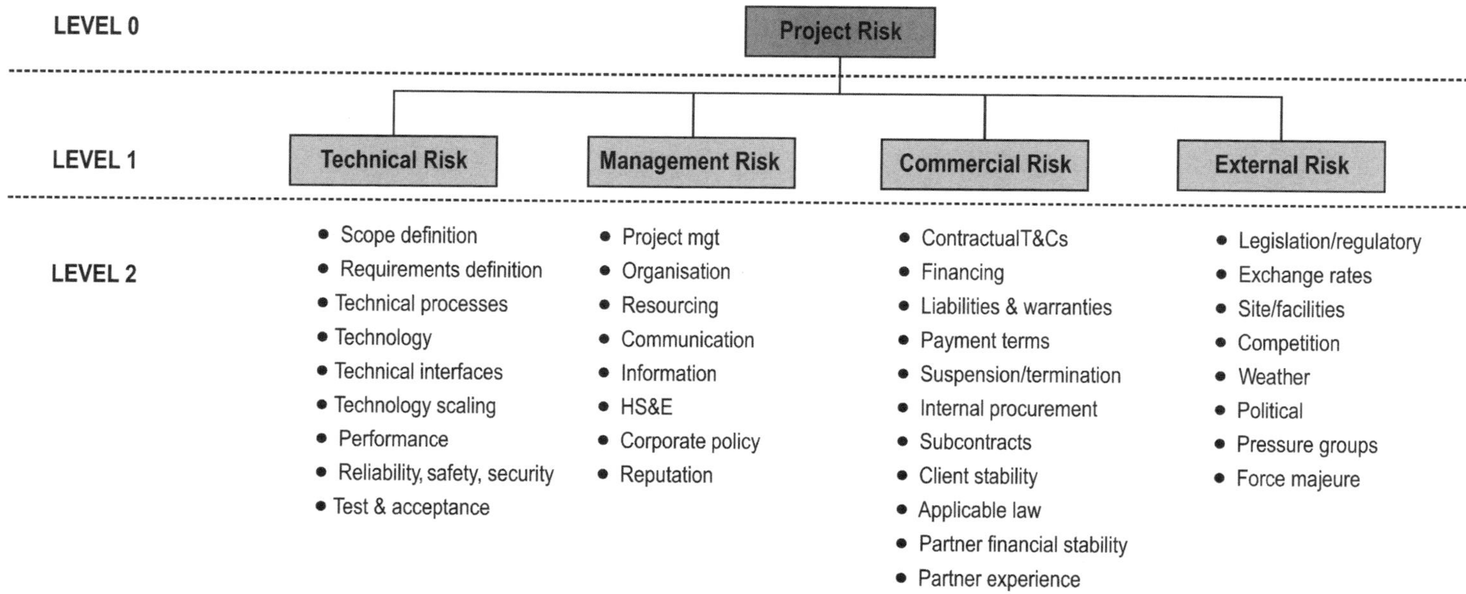
LEVEL 0
Project Risk
LEVEL 1
Technical Risk
Management Risk
Commercial Risk
External Risk
LEVEL 2
Scope definition
Requirements definition
Technical processes
Technology
Technical interfaces
Technology scaling
Performance
Reliability, safety, security
Test & acceptance
Project mgt
Organisation
Resourcing
Communication
Information
HS&E
Corporate policy
Reputation
ContractualT&Cs
Financing
Liabilities & warranties
Payment terms
Suspension/termination
Internal procurement
Subcontracts
Client stability
Applicable law
Partner financial stability
Partner experience
Legislation/regulatory
Exchange rates
Site/facilities
Competition
Weather
Political
Pressure groups
Force majeure

FIGURE 14-1. **EXAMPLE RISK BREAKDOWN STRUCTURE (RBS)**

The decisions made during this step of the process are documented in a Risk Management Plan, which forms an integral part of the Project Management Plan. The Risk Management Plan should be reviewed during the project and updated where necessary if the risk process is modified.

Risk Identification

Because it is not possible to manage a risk that has not first been identified, some view this initial step as the most important in the risk process. There are many good techniques available for risk identification, the most common of which include:

▶Use of brainstorming in a workshop setting, perhaps structured into a SWOT Analysis to identify organizational strengths/weaknesses and project opportunities/threats

▶Checklists or prompt lists to capture learning from previous risk assessments

▶Detailed analysis of project assumptions and constraints to expose those that are most risky

▶Interviews with key project stakeholders to gain their perspective on possible risks facing the project

▶Review of completed similar projects to identify common risks and effective responses.

For each of these techniques, it is important to involve the right people with the necessary perspective and experience to identify risks facing the project. It is also helpful to use a combination of risk identification techniques rather than relying on just one approach—for example perhaps using a creative group technique, such as brainstorming, together with a checklist based on past similar projects. The project manager should select appropriate techniques based on the risk challenge faced by the project, as defined in the Risk Management Plan.

It is also a good idea to consider immediate "candidate" responses during the risk identification phase. Sometimes an appropriate response becomes clear as soon as the risk is identified, and in such cases it might be advisable to tackle the risk immediately if possible, as long as the proposed response is cost-effective and feasible.

Whichever technique is used, it is important to remember that the aim of risk identification is to identify risks. While this may sound self-evident, in fact this step in the risk management process often exposes things that are not risks, including problems, issues, or complaints. The most common mistake is to identify causes of risks or the effects of risks, and to confuse these with risks.[5]

▶*Causes* are definite events or sets of circumstances which exist in the project or its environment, and which give rise to uncertainty. Examples include the requirement to implement the project in a developing country, the need to use an unproven new technology, the lack of skilled personnel, or the fact that the organization has never done a similar project before. Causes themselves are not uncertain because they are facts or requirements, so they are not the main focus of the risk management process. However, tackling a cause can avoid or mitigate a threat or allow an opportunity to be exploited.

▶*Risks* are uncertainties that, if they occur, would affect the project objectives either negatively (threats) or positively (opportunities). Examples include the possibility that planned productivity targets might not be met, interest or exchange rates might fluctuate

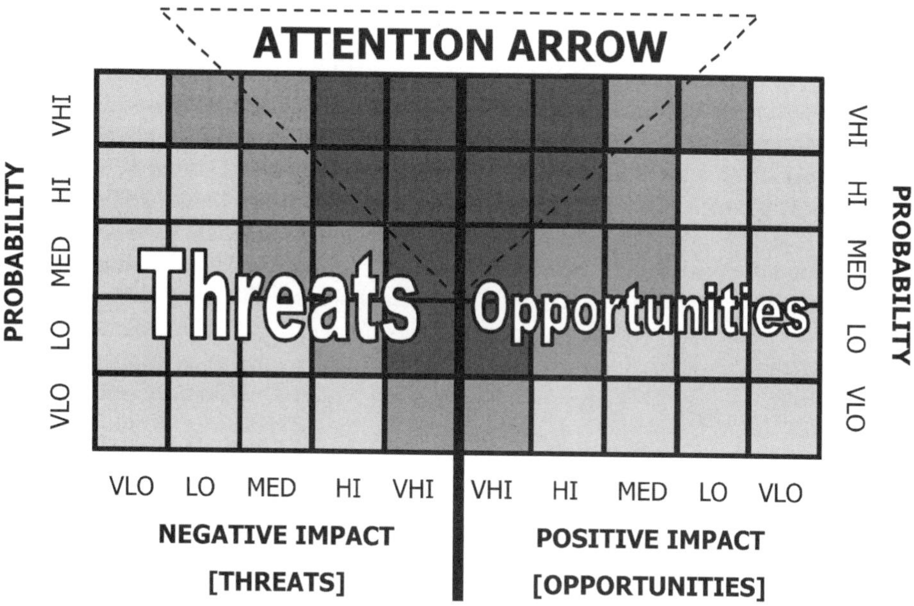

FIGURE 14-2. **"MIRROR" PROBABILITY-IMPACT MATRIX FOR THREATS AND OPPORTUNITIES**

significantly, the chance that client expectations may be misunderstood, or whether a contractor might deliver earlier than planned. These uncertainties should be managed proactively through the risk management process.

▶*Effects* are unplanned variations from project objectives, either positive or negative, which would arise as a result of risks occurring. Examples include being early for a milestone, exceeding the authorized budget, or failing to meet contractually agreed performance targets. Effects are contingent events, unplanned potential future variations that will not occur unless risks happen. As effects do not yet exist, and indeed they may never exist, they cannot be managed directly through the risk management process.

Including causes or effects in the list of identified risks can obscure genuine risks, which may not then receive the appropriate degree of attention they deserve. One way to clearly separate risks from their causes and effects is to use *risk meta-language* (a formal description with required elements) to provide a three-part structured "risk statement" as follows: "As a result of <*definite cause*>, <*uncertain event*> may occur, which would lead to <*effect on objective(s)*>." Examples include the following:

▶"*As a result of using novel hardware* (a definite requirement), *unexpected system integration errors may occur* (an uncertain risk), *which would lead to overspend on the project* (an effect on the budget objective)."

▶"*Because our organization has never done a project like this before* (fact = cause), *we might misunderstand the customer's requirement* (uncertainty = risk), a*nd our solution would not meet the performance criteria* (contingent possibility = effect on objective)."

▶ *"We have to outsource production* (cause)*; we may be able to learn new practices from our selected partner* (risk)*, leading to increased productivity and profitability* (effect)*."*

The use of risk meta-language should ensure that risk identification actually identifies risks, distinct from causes or effects. Without this discipline, risk identification can produce a mixed list containing risks and non-risks, leading to confusion and distraction later in the risk process.

Finally, the risk identification step of the risk process is where the Risk Register is launched, to document identified risks and their characteristics. Where software tools are used to support the risk process, these usually offer a Risk Register format, though some organizations develop their own. The Risk Register is updated following each of the subsequent steps in the risk process, to capture and communicate risk information and allow appropriate analysis and action to be undertaken.

Qualitative Risk Analysis

Risk identification usually produces a long list of risks, perhaps categorized in various ways. However, it is not usually possible to address all risks with the same degree of attention, due to limitations of time and resources. And not all risks deserve the same level of attention. It is therefore necessary to be able to prioritize risks for further attention, in order to identify the worst threats and best opportunities, which is the purpose of the qualitative risk analysis phase.

The definition of risk we are working from indicates that risk has two dimensions: uncertainty, and its potential effect on objectives. The term "probability" is used to describe the uncertainty dimension, and "impact" describes effect on objectives. For qualitative analysis, these two dimensions are assessed using labels such as "high, medium, low," where these have been previously defined in the Risk Management Plan. The probability of each risk occurring is assessed, as well as its potential impact if it were to occur. Impact is assessed against each project objective, usually including time and cost, and possibly others such as performance, quality, regulatory compliance etc. For threats, impacts are negative (lost time, extra cost, etc.), but opportunities have positive impacts (saved time or cost, etc.).

The two-dimensional assessment is used to plot each risk onto a Probability-Impact Matrix, with high/medium/low priority zones. A recent innovation is to use a double "mirror" matrix, to allow threats and opportunities to be prioritized separately, and creating a central zone of focus, as shown in Figure 14-2. This zone contains the worst threats (with high probability so they are likely to happen unless managed, and high impact so they would be very bad for the project) and the best opportunities (where high probability means easy to capture, and high impact means very good).

Another important output from qualitative analysis is to understand the pattern of risk on the project, and whether there are common causes of risk or hot-spots of exposure. This can be assessed by mapping risks into the Risk Breakdown Structure (RBS) to determine whether any particular causes give rise to large numbers of risks, and by mapping risks into the Work Breakdown Structure (WBS) to identify areas of the project potentially affected by many risks.

Quantitative Risk Analysis

On most projects, risks do not happen one at a time. Instead they interact in groups, with some risks causing others to be more likely and some risks making others impossible. Quantitative risk analysis considers risks individually, and allows development of a good understanding of each one. It is however sometimes necessary to analyze the combined effect of risks on project outcomes, particularly in terms of how they might affect overall time and cost. Addressing this requires use of a quantitative model, and various techniques are available, including sensitivity analysis, decision trees, and Monte Carlo simulation.

Monte Carlo is the most popular quantitative risk analysis technique because it uses simple statistics, it takes project plans as its starting point, and there are many good software tools to support it. Decision trees, though, are particularly useful for analyzing key strategic decisions or major option points.

One key aspect of quantitative risk analysis models that is often overlooked is that it is essential to include both threats and opportunities. If only threats are considered, then the analysis is only modeling potential downside, and the result will always be pessimistic. Since the risk process aims to tackle both threats and opportunities, both must be included in any analysis of the effect of risk on the project. Indeed some vital elements of the risk model, such as three-point estimates, cannot be properly determined without considering both upside (to produce the minimum/optimistic/best-case estimate) as well as downside (for maximum/pessimistic/worst-case).

When developing Monte Carlo risk models, it is easy to use available software tools to create simple models that do not reflect the complexities of the risks facing the project. In particular, simply taking single values of duration or cost in a project plan or cost estimate and replacing them with three-point estimates is not sufficient to model risk quantitatively. Other modeling techniques should be used to reflect reality, including the following:

▶Different input data distributions, not just the typical three-point estimate (for example, the modified triangular, uniform, spike/discrete, or various curves)

▶Use of stochastic branches to model alternative logic (these can also be used to model key risks)

▶Correlation (also called dependency) between various elements of the model, to reduce statistical variability.

It is important to recognize that additional investment is required in order to implement quantitative risk analysis, including purchase of software tools, associated training, and the time and effort required to generate input data, run the model, and interpret the outputs. As a result, in many cases the use of quantitative techniques may not always be justified. Often enough, information can be obtained from quantitative analysis to allow effective management of risks, and quantitative analysis techniques can be seen as optional. Quantitative analysis is most useful when projects are particularly complex or risky, or when quantitative decisions must be made, for example, concerning bid price, contingency, milestones, delivery dates, etc.

Three potential shortfalls should be mentioned when considering the use of quantitative risk analysis techniques. The first is the importance of data quality, to avoid the GIGO (garbage in-garbage out) situation, and attention must be paid to ensuring good quality inputs to the model. Secondly, it is always necessary to interpret outputs from risk models, and quantitative analysis will not tell the project manager what decision to make. Finally it is essential to be prepared to use the results of risk modeling, and to take decisions based on the analysis. We should beware of "analysis paralysis," because quantitative risk analysis is merely a means to an end, and must lead to action.

Risk Response Planning

Having identified and analyzed risks, it is essential that something be done in response. As a result, many believe that the risk response planning phase is the most important in the risk process, since this is where the project team get a chance to make a difference to the risk exposure facing the project.

When introducing tools and techniques for risk response planning, the *PMBOK® Guide* uses an important word, stating the following: "Several risk response *strategies* are available," [italics mine]. It is important to adopt a *strategic* approach to developing risk responses, in order to focus attention on what is being attempted. Too often, project teams resort to a "scatter-gun" approach, trying a wide range of different responses to a given risk, some of which may be counterproductive. It is better first to select an appropriate strategy for a particular risk, and then to design action to implement that strategy, producing a more focused "rifle-shot" aimed at managing the risk effectively.

A recent development in the evolution of PMI's standard is to introduce strategies for addressing opportunities along with threat-focused strategies. The opportunity strategies match the common threat strategies, creating three pairs of proactive response strategies, and a final last-resort strategy:

▶***Avoid/Exploit:*** For threats, the aim of avoidance is to eliminate the risk to the project, making the threat impossible or irrelevant. To exploit an opportunity means to make it definitely happen, ensuring that the project gains the additional benefits.

▶***Transfer/Share:*** These strategies require involving another person or party in managing the risk. For threats, the pain is transferred, together with the responsibility for managing the potential downside. In a similar way the potential gain from an upside risk can be shared, in return for the other party taking responsibility for managing the opportunity.

▶***Mitigate/Enhance:*** Mitigation of a threat aims to reduce its probability and/or impact, while enhancing an opportunity seeks to increase it.

▶***Accept:*** For residual threats and opportunities where proactive action is not possible or not cost-effective, acceptance is the last resort, taking the risk either without special action or with contingency.

Having chosen a strategy, the project team should then develop specific actions to put the strategy into practice. It is at this point where most risk management processes fail. Whichever response strategy is selected, it is vital to go from options to actions, otherwise nothing changes. However many project teams identify and assess risks, develop response plans and write a risk report, and then "file and forget." Actions are not implemented and the risk exposure remains the same.

The key to making sure risk responses are implemented is not to allow risk responses to be seen as "extra work" to be done when project tasks are complete. Risk responses are genuine project tasks, i.e., work to be done in order for the project to succeed. They should therefore be treated like any other project task. Each risk response should be fully defined, with a duration, budget, resource requirement, owner, completion criteria, etc. A new task should then be added to the project plan for each agreed risk response, and these should be completed, reviewed, and reported on like all other project tasks.

Risk Monitoring and Control

The purpose of this final phase of the risk process is to ensure that the planned responses are achieving what was expected, and to develop new responses where necessary. It is also important to determine whether new risks have arisen on the project, and to assess the overall effectiveness of the risk management process. These aims are best achieved through a risk review meeting, though it is possible on smaller projects to review risk as part of a regular project progress meeting.

This step also involves producing risk reports at various levels and for different stakeholders. It is important to communicate the results of the risk process, since the aim is to actively manage the risks, and this is likely to require action by stakeholders outside the immediate project team. Risk reports should form a basis for action, and include clear conclusions ("What we have found") and recommendations ("What should be done").

Risk management is a cyclic iterative process, and should never be done just once on a project. Risk exposure changes daily, as a result of external events as well as from the actions (and inactions) of the project team and others elsewhere in the organization. In order to optimize the chances of meeting the project's objectives, it is essential that the project team have a current view of the risks facing the project, including both threats and opportunities. For risk management, standing still is going backward.

OTHER ISSUES

The risk process outlined in standards and guidelines such as the *PMBOK® Guide* is well accepted and forms a good basis on which to build effective management of project risk. However a number of other issues must be considered if risk management is to be fully effective. It is beyond the scope of this chapter to present these in detail, but they deserve at least a mention.

First and foremost is the fact that all risk management is done by people. This introduces the human factor into the picture, requiring proactive management like any other aspect of the risk process. The risk attitudes of both individuals and groups exercise a major influence over the risk process, which must be recognized and managed. The situation is complicated by the action of subconscious perceptual factors and heuristics that affect the risk attitudes adopted by people.[6]

Secondly, organizational culture has a significant influence over the effectiveness of the risk management process. Where senior management do not recognize the existence of risk, or see risk identification as a sign of weakness, or view resources allocated to contingency or risk responses as wasted, risk management will be an uphill struggle. Conversely, the organization that knows how to take risk intelligently will reap the undoubted benefits from minimizing threats and capturing opportunities.

Linked to this is the need for internal sponsorship of the risk process. A risk champion within an organization can promote buy-in for its use at all levels, encouraging project teams and senior management to recognize risk and manage it proactively, sharing best practice and developing corporate experience. This is one of the accepted success factors for risk management and should not be neglected.

The need for an efficient infrastructure to support the risk process must also be recognized. Software tools, training, templates, specialized resources, etc. all have a part to play in making risk management effective. The organization must be prepared to invest in risk infrastructure, and ensure that it is well integrated with project management and other parts of the business.

The aim of paying attention to these factors in addition to the risk process is to develop risk-maturity within an organization and its people. This represents a position where all the necessary pieces are in place to allow risk to be managed proactively and effectively, with a supportive culture, efficient processes, experienced people, and consistent application. When these elements are present together with the tools and techniques described above, risk need not be feared on any project. Instead it should be welcomed as an opportunity to address the uncertainties inherent in all projects, optimizing the chances of achieving project objectives and delivering successful projects.

Risk management is an essential contributor to project and business success, because it focuses attention on achievement of objectives. By defining project risk as "an uncertain event or condition that, if it occurs, has a positive or negative effect on at least one project objective," risk management offers a means of tackling those risks with the potential to harm the project (threats) as well as those that could help (opportunities). Concentrating on proactive management of these two aspects maximizes the chance that the project will succeed.

Not only is risk management essential, but also it is not difficult. A simple structured process exists to identify, analyze, and respond to risks, and this can be applied to any project whether it is simple or complex, innovative or routine. The benefits of adopting a structured approach to managing risk are obvious: more successful projects, fewer surprises, less waste, improved team motivation, enhanced professionalism and reputation, increased efficiency and effectiveness, and so on. With these benefits available from adopting such a simple process, risk management deserves its place as one of the most important elements of project management.

DISCUSSION QUESTIONS

❶ Define project risk, and explain the relationship between uncertainty, risk, threat, and opportunity.

❷ What are the differences between a cause, a risk, and an effect? Use risk meta-language to describe a situation on a project you are familiar with. Does this help you distinguish between them?

❸ Name the basic risk response strategies for threats and opportunities, and give an example of each.

REFERENCES

[1] Project Management Institute, *A Guide to the Project Management Body of Knowledge, Third Edition,* Project Management Institute, 2004: p. 238.

[2] IEC 62198:2001 "Project risk management—Application guidelines"; ISO/IEC Guide 73:2002 "Risk management vocabulary—Guidelines for use in standards"; Association for Project Management. 2004 "Project Risk Analysis & Management (PRAM) Guide" (second edition). APM Publishing, High Wycombe, Bucks UK: Australian/New Zealand Standard AS/NZS 4360:2004 "Risk management." Standards Australia, Homebush NSW 2140, Australia, and Standards New Zealand, Wellington 6001, New Zealand.; British Standard BS6079-3:2000 "Project Management—Part 3: Guide to the management of business-related project risk." British Standards Institute, London, UK; BS IEC 62198:2001 "Project risk management—Application guidelines,"

British Standards Institute, London, UK; and BSI PD ISO/IEC Guide 73:2002 "Risk management—Vocabulary—Guidelines for use in standards." British Standards Institute, London, UK.

[3] Hillson D. A. 2003. "Effective opportunity management for projects: Exploiting positive risk." Published by Marcel Dekker, New York, USA, 2003.

[4] PMI, ibid.

[5] Hillson, D. A. "Project Risks—Identifying Causes, Risks and Effects." *PM Network, 14:* 2000: 48–51.

[6] Hillson D. A., & Murray-Webster R. "Understanding and Managing Risk Attitude Using Applied Emotional Literacy." Published by Gower, Aldershot, UK. ISBN 0-566-08627-1 (forthcoming).

FURTHER READING

Chapman, C. B., and S. C Ward. *Project Risk Management: Processes, Techniques and Insights* (second edition). Chichester, UK: J Wiley, 2003.

Cooper, D. F., S. Grey, G. Raymond, and P. Walker. *Project Risk Management Guidelines: Managing Risk in Large Projects and Complex Procurements.* Chichester, UK: J Wiley, 2004.

Grey, S. *Practical Risk Assessment for Project Management.* Chichester, UK: J Wiley, 1995.

Schuyler, J. *Risk and Decision Analysis in Projects* (second edition). Newtown Square, PA: Project Management Institute, 2001.

Vose, D. *Risk Analysis—A Quantitative Guide, Second Edition.* Chichester UK: J Wiley, 2000.

Williams, T. M. *Modelling Complex Projects.* Chichester, UK: J Wiley, 2002.

CHAPTER 15

Project Procurement Management In Practice

▶JUDITH A. EDWARDS, PHD, PMP,
DIEBOLD, INC.

Procurement practice is one of those things that organizations and teams acknowledge is important up to a point—the point of actually *performing* the practice. The rationale for not implementing the procurement practice is that it costs too much or takes too long. However, many failed procurement outcomes have root cause in avoiding key elements in the process. The risk of not performing the process is seldom assessed when waivers or deviations occur. Yet many organizations owe their successful outcomes to project procurement management best practice.

Procurements should be a "project" and managed as such, even for small efforts. In this chapter, we will outline roles and responsibilities for a procurement project team and offer best practices, lessons learned, and methods of increasing opportunities for success derived from actual procurement experiences.

PROCUREMENT PROCESS AND PROJECT

A variety of process standards and guides are available to organizations, including IEEE Std 1062 from the software standards collection,[1] Software Engineering Institute (SEI),[2] and other sources.[3] The overall process in those sources is very similar to that found in *A Guide to the Project Management Body of Knowledge, Third Edition*.[4] Although the first two references indicate software procurement standards, those process descriptions are essentially the same as any general procurement.

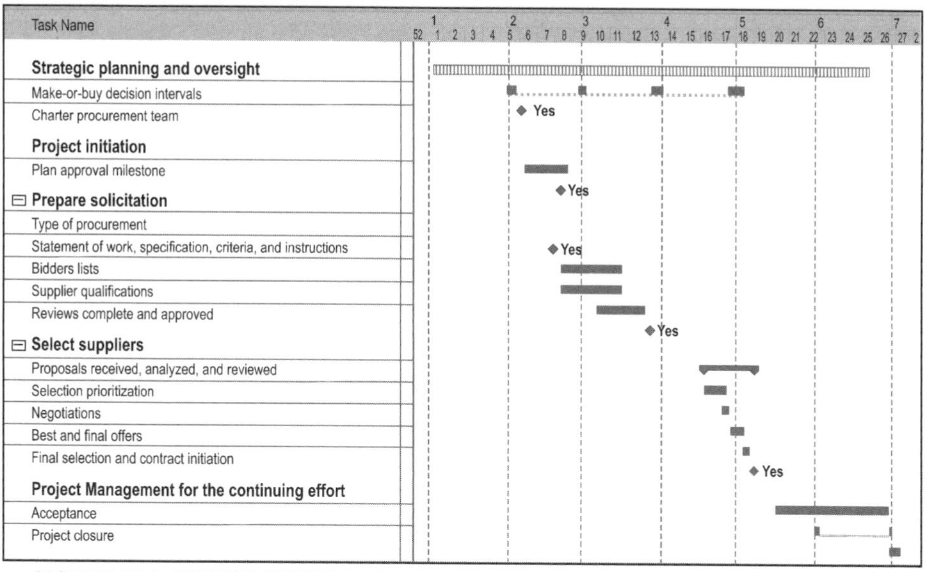

FIGURE 15-1. **PROCUREMENT PROJECT MANAGEMENT ACTIVITIES AND DURATION**

This process evolved to solve many problems and issues with procurements in meeting the desired business objectives. Standard procurement processes were developed to:

▶Overcome or reduce instances of contract fraud abuses

▶Reduce risk

▶Describe the needed goods and services

▶Monitore and control costs and performance

▶Determine criteria for selection and acceptance.

Procurement efforts satisfy the definition of "project" as they seem to be unique with varying complexity and timeframes. Usually, the procurement is embedded in a larger project effort. Each effort should have a project manager in the role to assure the processes are completed and the team functions toward the desired objectives. This should be the case regardless of short duration for simple tasks or commodity purchases, or long-term for significant outsourcing or new product development.

Figure 15-1 shows typical timelines for a moderate scoped procurement effort where the timescale represents periods after initiating the effort from the strategic planning. After the make-or-buy decision point, other strategic milestone reviews may indicate "go" or "no go" based upon the information obtained during the various project phases or processes.

In the schedule representation for procurement effort, the project actually starts with initiation and planning to cover the preparation of solicitation documents, qualifying sellers (if necessary), and performing the selection. The execution of the project includes the monitoring and control of the seller while the seller executes the project. Co-development may be involved by the buyer organization. Acceptance of deliverables may occur

Phase	Initiating	Solicitation	Selection	Management/ Executing	Monitoring & Controlling	Closing
Role	**Typical responsibility per phase**					
Project manager	Receives the charter; integrates directions into project planning; reviews past lessons learned	Procurement planning; prepares statement of work; approves specifications; submits solicitation documents	Co-lead: technical selection tasks	Project interface to stakeholders	Monitors project; communicates status	Completes archival for the project; creates lessons learned
Buyer*	Review planning	Reviewer	Co-lead: business tasks	Business and finance interface	Monitors seller performance and payment milestones	Completes procurement records and files
Legal	Participates	Creates contract terms & conditions; defines end-item data rights	Reviews; handles negotiations	Reviews	Issues reviews; change management	Contract closure
Technical specialist or lead	Review planning	Prepares technical specifications	Supports technical issues and reviews	Reviews and supports acceptance	Technical status of the effort	Supports archival efforts
Business unit manager	Strategic plan	Make-or-buy decisions	Reviews and approvals	Receives performance status	May require scope changes	Business deployment
Steering committee	Oversight	Oversight	Oversight	Oversight	Oversight	Oversight

***Notes:**
- Typically the buyer role is from the procurement or purchasing organization.
- Outsourcing roles adds risk to be managed in addition to procurement risks.
- Other oversight may be needed to assure accountability of all participants to guard against fraud or mismanagement.

TABLE 15-1. **RESPONSIBILITY ASSIGNMENT MATRIX (RAM)**

at varying points depending on the contract agreements. The final closure includes the closure of the effort as well as the contract. The project effort depends on a variety of knowledge worker experiences that are outlined in the roles/ responsibility description below.

ROLES/ RESPONSIBILITIES

Typically, no one person will have the entire set of skills for completing the entire set of tasks for legal, technical skills, business, purchasing, and project management. Therefore, forming a team with members from various disciplines will be beneficial to provide checks and balances in the procurement project processes. The further justification for the procurement becoming a project lies in this variety of teaming relationships, set of stakeholders, and unique business needs situations. This coordination of the procurement will need an assigned project manager who understands the business and technical needs.

In Table 15-1, the Responsibility Assignment Matrix (RAM) shows the complexity of activities and roles involved for a typical, medium-sized organization. Note that in the RAM, the following situations may occur for the project:

▶One person may hold more than one role.

▶Some roles may be outsourced.

▶Role tasks may be delegated.

▶Other stakeholders will be involved as procurement situations and issues arise during the executing or monitoring and control phases.

The project RAM should be updated as changes occur during phase transitions. Some phases will require more experienced knowledge workers who are tasked to integrate and deploy the procured items.

Contention in roles and responsibilities will be reduced when organization processes and procedures address how the team is formed, functional requirements for the roles, and the processes to be performed. The organization standard practices should also include:

▶Managing the acceptable sellers

▶Qualifying new, potential sellers

▶Defining the selection process

▶Deriving the criteria based on type of purchase

▶Controlling scope changes

▶Reporting for oversight, defined for the project, approvals, and processes.

SELECTION OF THE PROCUREMENT PROJECT MANAGEMENT TEAM

As you initiate the project, thought must be given to the make-up and training for the team members. The following list contains some of the factors in the selection:

▶Members who interface with the seller should be "peers" to gain the confidence and set the working relations.

▶Task leads will need project management as well as negotiating skills.

▶Responsibility and methods for accepting the product or services need to be clearly defined; for example, defined in a joint RAM for the seller and the buying organization.

▶The size of the team will be dictated by the business and technology factors, and the complexity and risk for procurement

▶Stakeholders involvement need to be identified in the project planning.

▶Other stakeholders' considerations may be needed for procurement project. They may include: project management office, line management, managers with dependencies on the procurement outcome, quality organization, business units, other services, and manufacturing.

Lessons learned and best practices organized by project management area or phase	
Project management area or phase	Lesson learned or best practices
Process	• Risks increase by avoiding steps in the process. The standard process evolved to avoid risks or correct a failure or issue. • Incomplete steps in procurement may add costs and time later. • For a trained knowledge worker, the effort to follow the process is not excessive. • Organizational tools and standard templates aid the preparation of the solicitation documents and reinforce training on procurement processes.
Contract types	• Large organizations with supply chain management will require interface processes based on purchase type, seller category, qualifications, and information automation access. • Cost control begins with the specifications and seller qualification processes. • Ownership rights for end-deliverables must be clearly specified. • Commercial-off-the-shelf purchases are often called COTS. If these are inappropriate or not planned, then the purchase might better be called COSTS.
Initiating	• The team should review lessons learned on earlier procurement efforts during initial planning phases. • Risks should be identified and managed.
Seller selection	• Time spent in qualifying sellers often means better working relationships and less risk. • It is not practical to expect the seller's systems to duplicate the buying organization. Where common processes or infrastructure is important, then define the needed capability in the work statements. • The low-cost bidder may be the highest risk. • Reference checking is a good way to learn others' experiences in dealing with candidate sellers.
Planning	• Procurement needs to be managed to assure the products meet the specifications and work statements. • Plans need to address risk management.
Risk management	• Payment milestones assure the buyer is getting specified deliverables while reducing risks. The payment criteria should be defined in the work statements. • Risks must be managed regardless of the seller size and experience.
Training	• Often procurement processes are so rarely exercised that refresher training is necessary to assure compliance to the organization practices.
Project management	• Detailed specifications and work statements reduce the potential future claims for scope changes. • Outsourcing should be a project supported by a project manager and a plan. • Recurring, commodity purchases may still need technical acceptance and change management.

TABLE 15-2. **LESSONS LEARNED AND BEST PRACTICES ORGANIZED BY PROJECT MANAGEMENT AREA OR PHASE**

Lessons learned and best practices organized by project management area or phase	
Project management area or phase	Lesson learned or best practices
	• Interfaces to the seller must be controlled by the buyer and project manager to prevent unauthorized scope changes. • Project manager for the procurement project should be a peer of the seller's team so as to effectively manage the effort. • Problems occur if the seller becomes the primary project management interface to the end customer.
Business management strategy	• "Buy" objectives may have little to do with in house capability. The technical team needs to understand the roles and relationships and strategy. • "Should cost" needs to be determined for the life cycle and total cost of ownership, not just the cost of the delivered items or services. • Outsourcing does not necessarily save staff, time, or costs. The organization objective should support strategic business needs. • Outsourcing should not be a "me too" decision. • It is unlikely that a procurement will succeed without a project team.
Roles and responsibilities	• Technical team needs to perform the acceptance and validation of the delivered items that are defined in the planning. • Often companies assume that the purchasing organization is responsible for the entire process. The development organization then fails to understand their role in the upfront planning. This results in key elements of the process being missed.
Executing	• Regardless of past experiences with a seller, procurements are not risk free. • Sellers may need additional support since they may not understand the domain where their products or services will be used. • It is good for the seller to "hear and see" the voice of end customer to understand their needs and to assure that the outcome will be successful.
Change management	• If the specification needs to be changed to eliminate unneeded features or tasks or to assure success of project, then is must be done. Obtaining the wrong system will be most likely lead to sunk costs or major rework.
Seller risks	• Dealing with financially troubled organizations is a major risk to seller cash flow. • Incurring added seller efforts for micro management by large organizations will increase claims and non productive work.
Closing	• Canceling projects can be very costly. • Not canceling projects can also be very costly. • Terms and conditions of the contract should clearly define the termination process and the payment methods involved.

TABLE 15-2. CONTINUED

As the team is formed, the next section provides some experiences, lessons learned, and best practices from a variety of procurements.

PROCUREMENT LESSONS LEARNED AND BEST PRACTICES

Drawing from experience in a variety of procurement projects including long duration, expensive efforts to relatively simple commodity purchases for both defense, and commercial projects, Table 15-2 organizes lessons learned and best practices by knowledge area or project management phase. These suggestions based on experience in the field do not repeat but amplify recommendations or practices described in the *PMBOK® Guide*.

Some table items were adopted from a major support software procurement for a defense project.[5] The software project procurement practices are not different from procurement process in general. The next section suggests methods for obtaining successful outcomes.

INCREASING OPPORTUNITIES FOR SUCCESS

Procurement involves risks. Some techniques have been shown to be success enablers. Here are some recommended methods for "getting it right the first time":

▶Hold early "bidders" conference to obtain feedback on the statement of work and specifications. These can be held by teleconference. It is essential that all potential sellers hear the same message. Seller comments need to be managed for non-disclosure of competition sensitive information. From the feedback, hold a follow-up conference to show the updated documents. This also helps the sellers to determine their response strategy.

▶Obtain a "should cost" during the make-or-buy decision period to gage the seller responses more accurately. Underbids by significant amounts will need believable justification for how the effort can be managed to cost without defaulting.

▶Do not rush through the procurement process steps only to find that the best opportunities for seller selection were missed or the specifications are incomplete, requiring new bids.

▶Competitive bidding is considered a risk reduction method that avoids locked-in solutions or favoritism. If the procurement process is performed well, then the procurement effort should yield the best outcome for the buyer.

▶Determine how to impose on the seller reasonable quality standards for the end product or service. The end result cannot be better than the weakest quality component.

▶Form integrated product development teams as part of the project team and stakeholders.

▶Assure that the team is adequately trained on procurement processes. Provide refresher training for those with immediate need.

▶Update organization practices with lessons learned and best practices.

▶Define the responsibility and accountability for the team. Retain visibility into the project procurement practices and results. Audit the project for adherence to the practice and the project work statement and specifications.

▶Reduce risks by using the two-person (or more) rule to assure oversight and that evaluations are fair.

▶Require justifications for sole-source purchases to avoid buying in haste and repenting later. Cost/benefit analysis should be part of each decision process step.

▶Exercise strict change control on both sides of the buyer/seller relationship.

Thoroughly understanding the procurement process and practicing project management tenets aids efficiencies for the organization in getting products and services to market. Next, let's examine some considerations in applying lessons learned to several different sizes, or classes, of procurements.

SCENARIOS BASED ON "CLASS" OF PROCUREMENT

Three scenarios summarize procurement considerations based upon size or "class" of procurement. The guidance is given to increase the probability of successful outcomes, avoid defaults, and reduce sunk costs.

Scenario 1. Existing Items From Catalogs or Commercial-Off-the-Shelf

In buying existing items, some requirements specification or criteria need to be defined for their selection. Often much time and money is wasted when the purchased item becomes "shelf ware" because the desired capability was never defined. The definition needs to be more than either someone saw a demonstration or the competition uses it. The goal is to satisfy a business need.

The purchased items should be evaluated against the requirements. When deficiencies are found, an estimate is needed to determine the total cost to integrate the items into the end product. Often a slightly more expensive item would save integration and troubleshooting efforts.

Experience or training is also needed to assess purchased items' quality. Volume purchase requires higher levels of specification for reducing rework or recalls. The selection of an existing item will be dependent on the degree of risk the organization wants to assume. The result may end up with throwaway items and unnecessary costs for efforts. Key to the approach is investing in upfront feasibility or prototyping.

Scenario 2. Minimum Modifications to Existing Seller Items

An existing item may not completely meet the business needs unless it is modified. The procurement strategy may be to hire a seller to update their product to meet the specification.

Here, the solicitation documents need to clearly describe the responsibilities between the buyer and seller for the integrated solution and its support. If both organizations work on the item, then the responsibility is not clear, nor can it easily be determined how to maintain the item. Defined separation of responsibility and efforts is a good management approach. It is also important to focus domain knowledge on areas of expertise. The seller may be an expert in their technology but not in the business application where their products will be deployed. The buyer can provide the needed interface for the domain.

Strict management of product development interfaces aids in isolating difficulties and solutions. Decomposition allows better estimating of costs and integration efforts. Managing to clearly defined interfaces simplifies the tasks. It is difficult to have total system knowledge of complex systems. By partitioning the effort along defined decomposition and interfaces, the buyer/seller teams only need to know their functionality and the interface requirements. The next scenario considers allocating the entire component to the seller for development.

Scenario 3. Major New Development

In this instance, the buyer is procuring totally new technology or unique solutions. The size of the effort may be small, but very critical as for some autonomous or embedded systems. The buying organization may be dealing with what Moore called *Crossing the Chasm*[6] to plan and manage the delivered items from feasibility or research developments through integration to a stable environment. Specification practices may need to go through a variety of stages for preliminary to final versions. For risk reduction, "go/no go" decision can be made based on performance at each stage. At some point, the buyer can even require a proposal for the subsequent stage. If performance is poor or objective not met, then the effort can be re-competed.

In this scenario, the procurement goal is typically to transform a unique feature or capability into a stable product. A high degree of new technology or special implementations incurs more risk. The procurement strategy should involve a phased approach to prove various incremental deliveries. In a phased approach, stage the effort of development from minimum required functionality in pre-production to several increased capability solutions. Key parts of the procurement project involve planning, risk management, monitoring and control, integrated change management, quality control acceptance, and communications.

The three scenarios cover aspects of project procurement management. The following summary section reviews the basic processes covered in this chapter and is supported by exercises at the end.

CONCLUSION

The project procurement process knowledge area has had significance to business and industry over the years. Since trends indicate that outsourcing and other procurements will continue in the future, project managers should master the project procurement processes. A project effort usually begins after the make-or-buy decision from the strategic business planning. At several checkpoints, the decision can be made to go forward with the procurement to the next phase. The project procurement process steps are listed as follows:

1. Plan the purchase and acquisition.
2. Plan the contracting.
3. Request seller responses.
4. Select sellers.
5. Perform contract administration.
6. Perform contract closure.

Supporting project processes include: the overall project planning, monitoring and control, stakeholder communications, and integrated change management.

The effort should be established as a two-phase project to cover (1) the activities through seller selection and (2) managing the sellers through project and contract closure.

Important aspects of this knowledge area's processes include:

- ▶Documentation, including plans, work statements, specifications, and acceptance criteria
- ▶Project management performed at both the buyer and seller
- ▶Skills training covering procurement processes, negotiations, assessment of capabilities, and performance

▶Defined roles and responsibilities defined throughout the procurement project.

"Classes" of procurement may range from commodities, to commercial-off-the-shelf (COTS), to minor modifications to existing products, to special services, to unique/customized developments. Different controls and risk management are needed for each class.

DISCUSSION QUESTIONS

❶ You are planning to buy new technology (choose an area) for a product or service. Use reference materials and the Internet to determine a beginning supplier list to answer the following:

▶What should go into the make-or-buy analysis?

▶What are your seller selection criteria?

▶Using cost benefit analysis, what are the pros and cons of sole source procurement versus competitive selection?

❷ Create a risk register for the following classes of procurement:

▶Very small effort, new seller.

▶Very large effort, major company as seller.

▶Company with financial difficulties or history of downsizing.

❸ In performing due diligence at the candidate sellers, what are the questions or areas that you would want to ask before entering into a business relationship? What project methods would be used to monitor and control the seller's effort?

REFERENCES

[1] IEEE Standard 1062 *Recommended Practice for Software Acquisition*. New York: Institute of Electrical and Electronics Engineering, Inc.

[2] Chrissis, M.B., M. Konrad, and S. Shrum. *CMMI Guidelines for process Integration and Product Improvement*. Boston: Addison Wesley, 2003.

[3] Mitulski, F.A. *Managing Your Vendor*. New Jersey: Prentice-Hall ECS Professional, 1993.

[4] Project Management Institute. *A Guide to the Project Management Body of Knowledge, Third Edition*. PMI: Newtown Sqare, PA, 2004.

[5] Edwards, J.A., and B.L. Mowday. "How to buy a compiler." WADAS: Washington Ada Symposium 1984 (March 1984) – 1994 (July 1994), New York: Association for Computing Machinery (ACM), Symposium, March 1984 – 1994.

[6] Moore, G.A. *Crossing the Chasm*. New York: Harper Business; Revised edition, 2002.

CHAPTER 15A

Studies in Procurement Management: Managing to Avoid Claims

▶IRVING M. FOGEL, P.ENG
FOGEL & ASSOCIATES, INC.

Design professionals are spending more of their time and money—and their insurance carriers' money—defending themselves against claims being made by owners, contractors, casual passersby, and third-party users, such as passengers in elevators and tenant employees. Usually, the design professional's exposure to losing when defending against these claims results from something other than technical failure. It results instead from the failure to manage properly. The design professionals fail to manage or administer their efforts properly during the predesign and design process, they fail to manage and administer their work properly during the bidding process, they fail to manage and administer their responsibilities properly during the construction phase, and/or they fail to manage and administer properly the postconstruction or closeout phase of the project.

Design professionals think of themselves as professionals skilled in the application of aesthetic, functional, and scientific principles to achieve pleasing and practical results. They often lose sight of the fact that in the process, they must manage contracts in order to try to avoid claims and to be prepared to defend themselves if and when claims are made against them. A claim or lawsuit resulting from the failure to manage or administer properly is no less grievous than one resulting from a design error. The design professionals must never forget that they are also contract managers—managers of contracts with clients, consultants, and others. The management and administration of the contracts is no less important than the management and administration of and performance of the design and, where they act as construction administrators, the management and administration of the construction process to ensure the successful completion of the project.

The design professionals' contracts usually define the phases of a project as the study and report phase, the preliminary design phase, the bidding or negotiating phase, and the construction phase. For administrative and management purposes, there is also a preprofessional service contract phase.

THE PHASES OF PROJECT CONTRACTING

The Preprofessional Service Contract Phase

Although no services are being performed as yet, the foundation for many disputes is often laid during the preprofessional service contract phase of the project because of poor communication and the lack of proper documentation. The contract usually includes language outlining and limiting the scope of services and responsibilities. It also contains provisions for the arbitration of claims and disputes that arise from differences in the interpretation of the language. We must try to eliminate the need for activating the provisions on dispute resolution.

In order to avoid the costs that result from arguing over what is meant by the contract, the professionals must try to communicate as clearly as possible during the negotiation phase what they intend to do and what they intend not to do. In addition to communicating, they must also document their understanding of their scope of services document with the same care that they devote to their design calculations. Too often, people honestly believe they hear what they would like to hear, when in truth something else is promised. The contract can't cover everything, and professionals have certain responsibilities that are never covered or eliminated by contract.

The Study and Design Phases

Again, during the study and design phases, "consultation with the owner" is a major consideration. To avoid disputes, we must consult, communicate, and document.

Agreements with consultants must detail, *in writing*, the duties and responsibilities of the parties. The work performed by consultants must be reviewed for conformance with the agreements. Lines of communication must be established so that all concerned are kept informed of changes and/or other facts that may affect their work.

During these phases, as a result of the development of the design, factors affecting the cost of the project must be communicated to the owners to allow them the privilege of determining, in advance, if and how their money will be spent. Letting the owners decide in advance whether they want to pay for something and properly documenting the decisions or agreements reached can help prevent the often-heard argument, "If I would've known, I wouldn't have gone ahead with it or I would've done something different."

Design professionals regularly rely on representations made by others who are "supposed" to know. The design professional has a responsibility to document the representations and at least check whether the oral representations made are in conformance with the published literature. Many disputes result from the acceptance of oral representations that are contrary to the literature published by the organization being represented.

The professionals responsible to the client for the total package have the responsibility for coordinating their work and that of all consultants. This responsibility must be diligently managed and administered. "My consultant made a mistake" *may* be a valid defense. You don't, however, want to get to the point where you have to defend yourself. The cost of a defense and vindication may ultimately be greater than paying without defending.

Standard specifications are truly standard. They are, however, neither all-inclusive nor valid for all projects. They must be checked and conformed to the particular project for which they are intended, and the drawings and specifications must be conformed to eliminate conflicts.

The design professional usually has the responsibility to advise the client of any changes in the original cost estimate for the project. A procedure must be established to track the estimated cost of construction as it relates to the originally established construction budget. This tracking process can also help determine conformance with the original concept: overdesign or, possibly, underdesign. In either case or in neither case, the relationship between the current estimated cost of construction and the preliminary estimate will be known.

The Bidding or Negotiating Phase

Many design professionals believe they can relax once the bid package is complete and that there really isn't much to do until construction starts. This is not true. They have many responsibilities during this phase of the project, most of which are basically managerial or administrative.

There are differences between contracts that are let by competitive bidding and those awarded as a result of negotiation. It is not true, however, that the services during the bidding phase of a publicly bid contract that nominally will be awarded to the lowest responsible responsive bidder are strictly of a pro-forma nature. At a later date, many things can either come back to haunt or protect us: conducting prebid meetings, conducting prebid site conferences, answering questions, provisionally approving substitutions, and recording what is done and what is said by the proper issuance of addenda, or the lack thereof.

The design professionals are usually required to assist the owner in evaluating bids or proposals. When analyzing a bid, the professionals must verify that all the conditions are met and that all the documents required to be submitted have been submitted. Before certifying that a contractor is "capable" or "competent," you as the professional must verify that the contractor is, in fact, whatever it is you are certifying, and you must document what you did to satisfy yourself. When you certify that a bid is "reasonable," you may be taking on a lot more responsibility than you wish. Remember that a bid is based on an estimate, and an estimate, by definition, is an estimate. There is at least one instance where in support of the validity of his "excess" costs or damages, one of the contractor's major arguments was based on the fact that the engineer had "verified" the estimate as valid and all-inclusive.

The Construction Phase

The professional's responsibilities during the construction phase of a project are more subject to interpretation than his or her duties and responsibilities during any other phase of the project. This is truly the phase during which the perceived responsibilities may be greater than the actual. Also, paraphrasing an attorney discussing the subject, "if you have the right, you have the duty." (Note that "construction," depending on the industry or application area, may also be characterized as implementation or performance—the same principles apply.)

During this phase of the project, in addition to the responsibility for coordinating with his or her own consultants and client, the design professional may have the responsibility of dealing with the constructor. There may be additional managerial and administrative responsibilities relating to other consultants, to inspecting organizations, and to testing laboratories that have been contracted with directly by the client.

In addition to the engineering competence required to judge technical compliance with the contract, to review shop drawings, to review schedules, and to review proposals for substitutions and/or modifications, the design professional may have both technical and administrative responsibilities relating to the contractors' applications for payment and change orders. In addition, depending on contract and/or perception, the design professional may have many other rights, responsibilities, and duties that require management.

The Closeout Phase

Although contracts do not usually identify a closeout phase, per se, it's a distinct phase requiring its own management. Before certifying completion—by whatever title—in addition to the "punch list" efforts that may be required, the professional must assure that all the administrative aspects of finalizing the contract are met. This includes but is not limited to filing certificates with governmental agencies; issuing certificates to the contractor or contractors; verifying "as-builts"; ensuring that all the operating manuals and warranties that are called for are in fact received; and documenting that all the contractual responsibilities have been complied with.

CLAIMS PREVENTION

Most management failures result from errors of omission and not errors of commission. One of the simplest and yet most efficient ways to minimize the probability of missing something is to prepare a checklist for each project, no matter how small. The checklist can be based on a generic list used by the engineer for all projects, but the list must be modified to include the requirements of that specific project.

Because most claims arise as a result of errors of omission on the part of the professional, a good place to start is to follow through on each of the following action items:

▶Check drawings or plans for proper coordination between technical specialties.

▶Check to see that the information in the drawings or plans conforms to the written word of the specifications/requirements.

▶Read the boilerplate language to see that it conforms, specifically and uniquely, to the project under consideration.

▶Enter into written agreement with consultants detailing exactly what their responsibilities are.

▶Review the work performed by consultants for conformance with agreements.

▶Check the finalized program against the estimate or budget to determine the current validity.

▶Communicate properly with consultants so that a change wrought by one that affects the work of another is properly accounted for.

▶Include owners in the communications process to permit them the privilege of determining, in advance, how their money will be spent.

▶Establish a reasonable time frame for review.

▶Establish reasonable durations for implementation.

▶Specify scheduling using one of the many available network scheduling techniques.

▶Review the specifications to determine whether items specified are still available (or, for that matter, whether they have been available for the past "X" number of years).

▶Check whether the information given by a sales representative or sales engineer is valid or in conformance with the specifications sheet prepared by the very company he or she represents.

▶Check the bids, quotations, or proposals for conformance with the contract documents.

▶Review the insurance requirements of the contract documents to assure compliance.

▶Review the schedule carefully, and react in a proper and timely manner.

▶Establish and adhere to an orderly system of controlling or keeping track of the documentation.

▶Retain the backup information or supporting data for the approval, modification, or rejection or payment requests.

▶React in a timely manner to requests for clarification or interpretation of the project documents.

▶Monitor the progress of the project and report objectively to the owner as required.

▶Take responsibility for discrepancies and/or omissions in the project documents.

▶Issue clarifications and instructions in a timely fashion.

Reacting to a Claim

If confronted with a claim, management reaction must be prompt and positive. Attorneys and insurance carriers must be notified and assisted, without reservation, in mounting a defense. Delay in mobilizing both information and resources for contesting the claim results in weakening the defendant's position, even in relationship to unfounded claims.

DISCUSSION QUESTIONS

❶ For a project you are familiar with, describe how the contracts and other project documentation contributed to smooth closure of the project. What could have been done better or differently?

❷ The author discusses this subject from a design/engineering perspective. How do his guidelines relate to other types of projects in other industries?

CHAPTER 16

Preparing for the Project Management Professional Certification Exam

▶THEODORE BOCUZZI,
PMP, TRB CONSULTING

The Project Management Institute's project management certification program is ISO 9001-certified in Quality Management Systems. The highest certification credential awarded under this program is the Project Management Professional (PMP), which has become the credential of choice for many industries and corporations that provide project management services. Although it is not the only project management-related certification, the PMP is highly regarded throughout the world. Many organizations have begun to require it for individual advancement or for employment. Although the PMP is not a license or registration and does not provide legal authority to practice project management, as do certifications that are legally required and competency-based (such as the Australian certification program), it does advance project management competency of the individual and of the organizations for which they perform projects.

As this book goes to press, the information in this chapter is the most up-to-date available. However, we fully expect the profession and the certification process to undergo many changes, and the specific details of the exam and other certification requirements to change. Even the body of knowledge, as testified to by the fact that the *PMBOK® Guide* is now in its third revised edition,[1] changes over time. Project management profession as a profession is relatively young. Like other professions, its standards and certifications are evolving over time and in response to business and social pressures. The parallel can be drawn to the evolution of other professional certifications: the CPA provides one example.

In the early days of that profession, accountants managed the financial records of businesses, but didn't always treat accounting events consistently. As the accounting profession recognized the inconsistencies of accounting techniques they worked to form a series of generally accepted practices. Changing economic times (notably, the 1929 crash) and increased criticism added impetus to the development of uniform standards and a certification program to enhance credibility and professionalism. Early versions of the CPA examination were not as comprehensive or as difficult as the versions given out today; 20 years ago, it was not necessary to have a degree to be eligible to take the exam. So, we can expect the PMP itself to evolve and go though a series of changes to reflect the changing standards and requirements of the project management profession. In the event that project management is truly recognized as a profession, with all the serious accountability issues that this designation raises (malpractice and licensing for example), those changes will become even more significant.[2]

To achieve PMP certification, there are three sets of requirements that must be met, in education, experience, and ethical behavior. One must meet the educational and experiential requirements required, agree to follow the Project Management Professional Code of Conduct, and pass the PMP certification examination. Passing the exam is a mark of official and public recognition of an individual's ability to meet specified standards in field of project management. To get complete details about the certification process and the most current information available about the certification exam, as well as any upcoming or possible changes, the reader should visit Project Management Institute's website or request the *Certification Handbook* from PMI.[3]

THE CERTIFICATION PROCESS: AN OVERVIEW

To be eligible for certification, candidates must agree to abide by PMI's Professional Code of Conduct, complete a specified number of hours of formal project management training (35 hours at this writing), and meet the educational and experiential requirements that are described in detail in the *Certification Handbook*. Preparing the application packet is a project in itself. The documentation required includes the examination application, experience verification forms, project management education forms, the application fee schedule, other demographic information, and the PMI Professional Code of Conduct. Signing the application indicates that you accept the responsibilities outlined in the "PMP Certificant and Candidate Agreement and Release," including abiding by the Code of Conduct, which states that as a PMP you will always act with integrity and professionalism, contribute to the project management knowledge base, enhance individual competence, balance stakeholder interests, and respect personal, ethnic and cultural differences.[4]

▶*Documented training.* Candidates must provide documentation for the required number of hours of formal project management training in any of the nine knowledge areas: scope, time, cost, quality, human resources, communications, risk, procurement, and integration management. To fulfill this requirement, candidates must have successfully completed courses offered through a university or college academic or continuing education program, or any course or program offered by training companies, consultants, PMI component organizations, distance-learning companies, or employer-company sponsored programs. (Note: PMI Chapter meetings cannot be included as part of this requirement.) The courses must be complete at the time of application.

Project	Dates	Length (Months)	Hours
Project A	02/01/2000—09/31/2000	8	1,000
Project B	06/01/2001—10/31/2001	5	500
Project C	02/01/2002—08/31/2002	8	1,000
Project D	06/01/2002—11/31/2002	6	750
Project E	04/01/2003—09/31/2003	6	750
Project F	08/01/2003—05/31/2004	10	1,200
Total	02/01/2000—06/31/2004	**43**	**5,200**
Less Overlap 1 (D–C)	06/01/2002—08/31/2002	3	
Less Overlap 2 (F–E)	08/01/2003—09/31/2003	2	
Qualifying Months/Hours		**38**	**5,200**

TABLE 16-1. **CALCULATING HOURS OF PROJECT EXPERIENCE**

▶*Documented experience.* The certification requirements acknowledge that not all project managers are formed in the classroom by offering options that allow credit for practical experience. Educational and experiential requirements are divided in two categories:

1. Candidates with a Baccalaureate or equivalent degree should be able to demonstrate a minimum of 4,500 hours of project management experience within the five process groups. The candidate must show a minimum of 36 non-overlapping months of project management experience within a six year period prior to the application date.

2. Candidates with a High School Diploma or equivalent credential must demonstrate a minimum of 7,500 hours of project management experience within the five process groups. The candidate must show a minimum of 60 non-overlapping months of project management experience within an eight year period prior to the application date.

Table 16-1 shows how to calculate hours of experience in the case of projects with overlapping months.

This candidate has 43 months of project management experience within a 53-month time frame. However, within these 43 months, two projects overlap a total of five months. The five overlapping months are subtracted from the 43 months of total project experience demonstrated, allowing the candidate to indicate 38 months of project management experience. Candidates are not required to subtract the overlapping hours; the total hours worked on all projects is counted.

The Project Management Experience Verification Form included in the application is used to summarize your role, the deliverables you managed, and the hours you spent on the project. Deliverables that you managed are reported by process groups. For example, you might report your activities on a project as follows (note that these deliverables are described in very general terms for the purpose of this example; on an actual application form, you would want to be more specific and detailed in your descriptions):

Project	Initiating Process	Planning Process	Executing Process	Monitoring & Controlling Process	Closing Process	Total Hours
Project A	0	525	300	150	25	1,000
Project B	0	300	150	50	0	500
Project C	100	400	300	150	50	1,000
Project D	0	425	200	100	25	750
Project E	0	475	175	50	50	750
Project F	200	450	300	150	100	1,200
Total	**300**	**2,575**	**1,425**	**650**	**250**	**5,200**

TABLE 16-2. **SORTING PROJECT EXPERIENCE INTO PROCESS GROUPS**

Initiating Process

▶Project charter development

▶Feasibility study

▶Business case development

▶Preliminary project scope statement development

Planning Process

▶Scope planning

▶Scope definition

▶Create WBS

▶Schedule development

▶Cost estimating

▶Risk identification.

Executing Process

▶Direct and manage project execution

▶Perform quality assurance

▶Information distribution

▶Create work packages.

1. You have a $100,000 project, which is 60% complete. The earned value (EV) is $58,000; the actual cost (AC) is $62,000. What is the cost variance?

☐ A) -$4,000 ☐ B) -$2,000 ☐ C) $4,000 ☐ D) $2,000

2. The decision process for project continuation or termination should not consider which of the following?

☐ A) Sunk costs ☐ B) Time to complete ☐ C) Direct labor costs ☐ D) Indirect costs

3. Your $100,000 project requires 5 tasks to complete:

- Task 1 starts today and has an estimated duration of 2 days.
- Task 2 cannot start until Task 1 is completed and has an estimated duration of 6 days.
- Task 3 cannot start until Task 1 is completed, but must be completed before Task 4 starts, and has an estimated duration of 4 days.
- Task 4 cannot start until Task 2 is completed and has an estimated duration of 8 days.
- Task 5 cannot start until Task 4 is completed and has an estimated duration of 1 day.

What is the Critical Path?

☐ A) 15 days ☐ B) 17 days ☐ C) 19 days ☐ D) 21 days

Answers: 1 (A), 2 (A), 3 (B)

Adapted from Ward, LeRoy J., PMP Practice Test and Study Guide. *Arlington, Virginia, USA: ESI International, 2004.*

TABLE 16-3. **SAMPLE EXAM QUESTIONS**

Monitoring and Controlling Process

▶Monitor and control project work

▶Manage project team

▶Performance reporting

▶Integrated change control

▶Scope control

▶Schedule control

▶Cost control.

Closing Process

▶Close project

▶Contract closure.

Candidates report only the hours that they actually worked on the project. The hours are listed by the amount of time spent in any one or more of the five process groups. Table 16-2 shows how to summarize qualifying hours into process groups.

You are not required to report a minimum amount of hours in any of the five process groups for an individual project; however, candidates must show experience in all five process groups when the hours are totaled.

The PMI Certification Department selects at random a percentage of applications for audit prior to granting eligibility. If selected, the candidates may be asked to submit verification of the projects documented on the Experience Verification Forms (for example, a signed letter from a supervisor or manager); copies of degrees or transcripts may also be required.

Once you have passed the application hurdle, PMI will issue you a letter confirming your eligibility to take the exam. Now, the real work begins.

PREPARING FOR THE EXAM

The process of preparing to take the exam differs widely from individual to individual. It's important to have a good understanding of your own study habits, strengths and weaknesses. Some candidates attend a specialized course, of which there are many available. Some prefer to study on their own, using some of the many materials on the market. Candidates can choose from books, sample exams, flash cards, online sites, and training courses. Many PMI Chapters have study classes or networks where members meet to help one another study.

Differences in age, social relationships, family position, maturity, patience, and interests require different training approaches. People also have differing learning speeds and styles based on their cognitive styles. The typical student attention span for standup lecture is seven to ten minutes. Thus, effective training delivery must vary between lecture, hands-on, textbook, video, CD, computer and other media to keep your attention. Distance learning has great a potential application for teaching the theory behind project management and acquiring the basic concepts and language. One benefit of computer-based training via CD-ROM or the Internet is timely delivery, which may in fact be more important than depth of content. However, classroom training will never go away, because the classroom is where students get to apply concepts and get feedback on an immediate basis from teachers and from fellow students, so that performance and understanding are validated.[5]

Regardless of how you choose to prepare, the first step is to understand the nature of the examination itself.

What's on the test?

The PMP certification examination tests the applicant's knowledge and understanding of project management skills, tools, and techniques with a battery of multiple-choice questions (200 questions at this writing) randomly selected from a large database. The examination questions are derived from the *Project Management Professional Role Delineation Study,*[6] which describes, in statements, the specific tasks Project Managers perform during the planning and execution of a project, why each task is performed, and how each task should be completed. Identified with each task statement are the associated skills, tools, and techniques required to complete the task. Examination questions developed from these task statements assess the candidate's knowledge and ability to apply the proper project management skill, tool, or technique. The candidate must correctly answer at least 81percent of the questions in order to pass. (Unanswered questions are scored as wrong answers.)

The questions are organized into six domains. PMI determined the relative importance of each domain to the practice of project management and applied a weight to each domain; the domains weighted most heavily are covered by the highest percentages of questions on the exam. The domains (and the percentage of questions relating to them) are, at this writing:

1. *Initiating* (11.57%): Tests knowledge of how to determine project goals, deliverables, process outputs, and resource requirements; how to document the project constraints and assumptions; how to define the project strategy and budget; how to identify the project performance criteria; and how to produce formal documentation.

2. *Planning* (22.71%): Tests knowledge of how to refine the project strategy, how to create the Work Breakdown Structure (WBS), how to develop the resource management plan, how to refine the time and cost estimates, how to establish project controls, how to develop the project plan, and how to obtain project plan approval.

3. *Executing* (27.50%): Tests knowledge of how to commit and implement project resources, how to manage and communicate project progress, and how to implement quality assurance procedures.

4. *Monitoring and Controlling* (21.03%): Tests knowledge of how to measure project performance, how to refine project control limits, how to manage project changes and take corrective action, how to evaluate the effectiveness of correction action, how to ensure project plan compliance, how to reassess project control plans, how to respond to risk event triggers, and how to monitor project activity.

5. *Closing* (8.57%): Tests knowledge of how to obtain acceptance of project deliverables, how to document lessons learned, how to facilitate project closure, how to preserve product records and tools, and how to release resources.

6. *Professional and Social Responsibility* (8.62%): Tests knowledge of how to ensure integrity, how to contribute to the knowledge base, how to apply professional knowledge, how to balance stakeholder interests, and how to respect differences.

What's Not on the Exam

As comprehensive as the exam strives to be in testing the candidate's knowledge of project management processes and methods, there is much in the daily life of the project manager that is not on the exam. It does not test for leadership or interpersonal communication skills, for example, which are critical to being a successful project manager. Being certified is a good thing, but it is by no means enough. Simply winning the PMP designation does not guarantee success. A good project manager has general management skills and industry knowledge in addition to project management knowledge. Just as with any certification or degree, you still must turn theory into practice. Any credential is only worth the paper it is written on if you cannot apply what you have learned.

Getting started

In order to organize your study time, it is first necessary to perform a gap analysis of your existing project management knowledge. One strategy is to take the "Basic Knowledge Assessment"—an online test containing 100 multiple-choice questions similar to the questions on the exam, which is provided by PMI for a fee. (BKA Request Forms are available for download on the PMI website.) Test results are be sent to candidates via e-mail.

Other, paper-based sample tests are also available on the market. In any case, the certification process starts with an assessment of the gaps in skills and knowledge. Having identified areas needing more attention, the candidate should undertake a study of the most current edition of the *PMBOK® Guide*. This is the foundation document used to both create and prepare for the exam; however, it is not the sole reference. Candidates should read widely on the topic of project management. PMI maintains a list of suggested materials for PMP exam preparation on their bookstore website; many of them, like this *Handbook*, are designed to help candidates deepen their knowledge of both the body of knowledge and its applications. Ideally, the background gained from studying the standards document will be deepened through a more detailed study of suggested readings and other methods, such as participation in professional symposia, training, online learning, and networking with fellow project managers to discuss professional problems and share best practices. (Note: Older materials may reference earlier editions of the standard; check and compare release dates to be sure you are working with up-to-date materials.) For a sample of some test questions, see Table 16-3.

Preparing for the exam takes time and dedication. The amount of time you will need to spend in study depends on your current knowledge base. Some "fast-track" courses claim to prepare you for the exam in five days or less. However, it is more reasonable to expect that it may take from 100 to as many as 400 hours to properly prepare for the exam. One expert suggests that, even if you plan to take a "fast-track" course, you spend hundreds of hours studying *before* taking the course.[7] Historically, approximately 70% of candidates pass the certification exam the first time; one of the top reasons candidates fail is the lack of proper preparation. It is recommended that the candidate prepare for the exam prior to submitting an application. This enables you to take all the time you need to properly prepare without the stress of meeting the eligibility deadline.

Study tips

Studying should begin by knowledge area. A step-by-step approach to preparation might include the following milestones:

- Perform gap analysis to determine the areas in which your knowledge is lacking.
- Learn the purpose of each knowledge area. (See Appendix F in the *PMBOK® Guide* for a useful summary.)
- Learn the definitions of key terms in each knowledge area, referencing the Glossary in the *PMBOK® Guide.*
- Memorize the names of process groups.
- Learn the process steps within each knowledge area.
- Learn the Inputs, Tools and Techniques, and Outputs to each of the 44 process steps.
- Learn formulas, particularly earned value calculations.
- Learn which of the 44 process steps is required in each of the five process groups.
- Learn how to apply these processes to projects, as many of the questions on the certification exam are situational. This is where the individual's own professional experience on projects comes into play.[8]

To make the process easier on your personal time, keep your study materials handy wherever you go. If you are waiting in the airport or a doctor's office, spend the time studying. Take practice exams and analyze your results, comparing attempts to see where you've improved and where you still have work to do. Keep the scores as a motivator to do better.

Don't try to memorize definitions first. Concentrate your efforts first on the high-level ordered lists: the five process groups, the nine knowledge areas, and the 44 component processes.

Be on the lookout for how the processes flow, how the output of one process becomes the input of another. Make note of their exceptions, for example, where change requests are an input or where they are an output.

Note the differences between the processes in each knowledge area. Know the tools and techniques, especially where they involve further analysis—for risk management in particular.[9]

Some candidates for the PMP are put off by the aspects of preparation that appear to be simply rote memorization. However, the value of the PMP is largely due to the understanding that comes from sharing a common terminology, the importance of which cannot be overstressed. The experience of studying for the exam in itself is valuable because of this—even if you never take or pass the test.

This is one reason why "fast-track" programs have earned some criticism. As one project management writer notes:

> "They encourage cramming, not the development of long-term knowledge and comprehension. When we were in high school, our learning choices often reflected one of two avenues: learn the fundamentals of the principles being taught and, through a relatively deep understanding, be able to apply them to different situations and problems; or cram at the last minute, relying on short-term memory and triggers to recall the essentials, never to be recollected or used again. We face the same choice preparing for our PMP."[10]

Therefore, try to plan an exam preparation approach that prepares you, not just for taking the exam, but for your life as a project manager after the exam.

TAKING THE EXAM

The computer-based exam is administered at locations across the globe, on dates scheduled by PMI; generally, the candidate is able to schedule a time and place that are convenient to his or her schedule. Candidates are allotted four hours to complete the exam. Prior to starting the exam, the candidate should record any relevant reference information, including formulas, on scratch paper, because 240 minutes to answer 200 questions makes time of the essence. If you can quickly answer questions from the recorded information, it gives you extra time to spend on the more difficult questions.

As with any test, read each question thoroughly to be sure you understand what the question is asking. Carefully review each of the four multiple-choice options, eliminating options that are obviously incorrect, and select the answer. Avoid spending too much time on difficult questions; flag those questions for review afterwards. One important strategy is to remember that the questions are based on the concepts presented in the *PMBOK® Guide*. If an answer to a question conflicts between the *PMBOK® Guide* and your professional experience, the answer from the *PMBOK® Guide* is the correct one in the context of the exam. If you are unable to answer, it is better to guess at an answer than leave the question unanswered.

Candidates learn whether they have passed or failed immediately after completing the exam, when their results are displayed on the screen. The exam administrator provides a report that will indicate how many questions were answered correctly within each process domain, and each candidate receives an official summary of the exam results from PMI within 14 business days. These reports will be most useful to those who do not pass the exam, forming the basis for their study plan for the next attempt.

Those who pass the exam may begin using their PMP designation immediately. Candidates who do not pass the PMP certification exam may to retake the exam up to three attempts within one year.

KEEPING CERTIFICATION CURRENT

Project management is an ever-changing field, so certification isn't forever. PMP certification is granted for three years and must be maintained by fulfilling the Continuing Certification Requirements (CCR). All PMPs are required to achieve a minimum of 60 Professional Development Units (PDUs) during a three-year CCR cycle. One PDU is earned for each hour the PMP participates in a classroom, workshop, or conference on a project management topic. A PDU may also be earned for activities that advance the profession of project management. There are five categories where PDUs may be earned:

1. Completing formal academic training.
2. Performing professional activities or completing self-directed learning activities. Credit for a published article, for example, falls under this category.
3. Attending classes offered by PMI Registered Education Providers.
4. Attending classes offered by other education providers.
5. Volunteering services to professional or community organizations.

PMPs may report their PDUs or view their CCR transcript online. It's recommended that you keep all documentation of PDUs for at least 18 months after the end of the three-year CCR cycle for which they were submitted, just in case you are randomly selected for a CCR audit. Those who earn greater than 60 PDUs during one 3-year CCR cycle may transfer up to a maximum of 20 hours to their next 3-year CCR cycle. Those who fail to submit their required 60 PDUs by the end of their 3-year CCR cycle will have their certification suspended; if the required PDUs aren't submitted within six months after the completion of their 3-year CCR cycle, certification is revoked and the ex-PMP must begin the application process over and retake the exam.

Becoming a PMP will place you in a prestigious group of project managers. It will demonstrate to current and potential future employers that you possess the skills necessary to lead projects to successful completion. Having the PMP credential after your name will gain you the confidence, respect, and recognition that you desire from your peers. It indicates that you know how to apply proven project management processes and methodologies that will bring projects to a successful completion, regardless of the industry. In addition, your pursuit of PMP certification makes your career choice and direction clear to a potential employer: it says that you are serious about project management. A certification provides proof of your commitment, willingness to learn, and desire to succeed—a proactive approach by someone willing to take charge.

DISCUSSION QUESTIONS

❶ Taking into account your work schedule, personal commitments and learning styles, and using the information on the process and study tips in this chapter, make up a schedule for yourself for the project of earning the PMP.

❷ Considering your past experience and study, which areas of the test do you expect will prove most challenging to you? Be honest! Use the results of your self-assessment to compile a set of study resources.

❸ Do a little dreaming: How will your professional life change once you have earned your certification? In what ways will it be more rewarding? More challenging?

ACKNOWLEDGEMENT

The author gratefully acknowledges the contribution of content for this chapter by Muhamed Abdomerovic, PMP.

REFERENCES

[1] Project Management Institute (PMI), *A Guide to the Project Management Body of Knowledge, Third Edition.* Newtown Square, PA: PMI, 2004.

[2] *Mark E. Mullaly, PMP.* The 'P' In PMP: Are We Really A Profession? Gantthead.com. Accessed December 1, 2004.

[3] Project Management Institute (PMI). *PMP Certification Handbook.* Available at: http://www.pmi.org. On the PMI website, see also Project Management Institute (PMI). *Project Management Professional (PMP) Examination Details and the CCR Program Handbook.*

[4] Project Management Institute (PMI). *Code of Professional Conduct.* Available at: http://www.pmi.org.

[5] Dennis Smith, Making Training Pay: A Trainer's Perspective, *Best Practices Report*, Aug. 2002.

[6] *Project Management Professional Role* Delineation *Study* (PMI, 2001).

[7] Peter Nathan, Gerald Everett Jones. *PMP Certification For Dummies, Wiley,* 2003.

[8] Table 3-45 of the *PMBOK® Guide, Third Edition,* maps the 44 project management processes into the five Project Management Process Groups and the nine Project Management Knowledge Areas.

[9] Nathan and Jones, ibid.

[10] Mark E. Mullaly, PMP. "Training for PM Certification: The Good the Bad and the Highly Questionable," www.gantthead.com; posted on October 16, 2002; accessed Jan, 19, 2005. See also "Project Management in Practice" by Mark Mullaly; and "Studying for PMI Certification: Follow This Project Manager on the Path to Certification by Donna Boyette," both accessed at www.gantthead.com Jan. 29, 2005.

FURTHER READING

Cleland, David I., and Harold Kerzner. *A Project Management Dictionary of Terms*. New York, NY, USA: Van Nostrand Reinhold Company, 1985.

Ward, LeRoy J., ed. *Project Management Terms, A Working Glossary.* Arlington, Virginia, USA: ESI

International, 1997.

Project Management Institute (PMI). *Q & As for the PMBOK® Guide.* Newton Square, Pennsylvania, USA: Project Management Institute, 2004.

SECTION TWO

THE PROFESSION OF PROJECT MANAGEMENT

Section Two: Introduction

THE PROFESSION OF PROJECT MANAGEMENT

Project management has evolved from the "accidental profession" of years ago—when no one actually planned to become a project manager, but just happened into the position—to a profession based on formalized bodies of knowledge, such as PMI's *PMBOK® Guide* and those developed by other professional organizations, such as the International Project Management Association (Europe) and the Association of Project Managers (U.K.), among others.

Where once project management was merely an add-on to the role of a civil engineer or systems engineer, today it is more commonly identified as a career choice in and of itself. The rapid growth of the discipline's primary professional organization—the Project Management Institute—from under 15,000 members when the first edition of this handbook was published in 1993, to well over 150,000 members as this book goes to press, and growing at a rate of over 5,000 new members per month, gives us a good indication of the rapid "mainstreaming" of the project manager role.

Since formal certification programs appeared in the 1990s, more emphasis has been given to seeing project management as a profession-something that has a defined body of knowledge based on specific principles-and subject to qualifications and knowledge testing based on a formal process. There is an evolving trend towards developing professional certification that is not only knowledge-based but also competency-based, thus taking into consideration experience records and other formal professional qualifications.

Many companies require certification for advancement, or recognize certification as part of the advancement path in careers. In formal bidding processes for professional services related to projects, client organizations often call for certified project professionals.

The trend towards formal qualification continues to gallop along as professional associations develop more sophisticated certification programs, companies require qualified professionals within their own ranks, and the practitioners of project management strive to sharpen and enhance their craft. Only one organization was offering project management certification in 1993, the Project Management Institute—and only in the English language. Today, there are at least four significant organizations offering certification in the world: the Project Management Institute (PMI) is the clear leader in this field with over 100,000 certified project managers worldwide as of January 2005, while the Project Management Association (PMA) in England has over 9,000 certified project managers; the International Project Management Association (IPMA), representing over 24 mostly European countries, reports over 5,000 certified project managers; and the Australian Institute of Project Management reports an additional 1,000 certified project managers.

In 1993, we could identify approximately five North American degree programs in project management. Just ten years later, there were more than 33 degree programs in the United States and Canada alone.

Professionalism is a personal commitment, but it must be supported by institutions, including professional societies, educational institutions, and the organizations that employ project managers. It also requires a great deal from the individual. The more seriously an occupation is taken as it moves into the category of the professions, the more serious are the implications of unprofessional or unethical behavior on the part of the practitioner.

In this section of the handbook, we focus on the career of project management: What are the ethical issues facing project managers? Thomas Mendel, a visiting professor of management at a number of Canadian universities, explores this topic and provides thought-provoking ethical cases for your consideration. Is project management in fact a profession? If not, what must we do to ensure that it becomes one? Professors Janice Thomas and Bill Zwerman of the University of Athabasca address these issues. What competencies are required of the project manager, and how are these developed? What does the new project manager have to look forward to in the course of his or her career? J. Kent Crawford and Jeannette Cabanis-Brewin discuss project management competencies and career paths.

CHAPTER 17

Project Management Ethics: Responsibility, Values, and Ethics in Project Environments

▶THOMAS MENGEL, PHD, PMP
UNIVERSITY OF NEW BRUNSWICK

The construction of a new dam and power generator increases the service and viability of a regional supplier of electrical power, it decreases the emissions of greenhouse gas through a reduced need for power generated by fossil fuel, and it generates local employment and revenues not easily available otherwise. However, it also disrupts the scenic environment and changes the habitats for humans and other beings in a rural river valley and it will most likely be followed by other projects to come.

Good or bad? Right or wrong? In trying to meet requirements, project management includes decision making based on choices and criteria. Ethics will be used as one basis for the decisions to be made.

TERMS AND CONCEPTS OF ETHICS AND ETHICAL DECISION MAKING

Values, Morals, and Ethics

Values are the major motif of our actions and endeavors (e.g., preserving our environment, making profit). They provide us with orientation and serve as a basis for responsible decisions.[1]

In order to make daily choices about good or bad behavior easier, societies and groups tend to develop principles and rules that guide our conduct. These morals are codified convictions and expectations as to what is considered good behavior (e.g., shop locally).

Finally, ethics are the systematic combination of values and morals to enable rational and values-based judgments and decisions about what ought to be done. Ethics include criteria and processes allowing to arrive at or to assess personal decisions or behavior in terms of good or bad and right or wrong (e.g., religious ethics, corporate codes of conduct).

Systems of Ethical Decision Making

Ethical decision making tends to be easy in the case of one option serving one value. Facing several options serving one value or conflicting choices (e.g., the introductory dam project), we need to enter a decision making process based on ethical considerations helping us to sort out the ethical dilemma and arrive at an ethically sound decision.[2]

Results-based systems focus on the "good" end. They are interested in good results, neglecting how they came about. In a rather simplistic economic environment, for example, a cost-benefit-analysis will lead to a decision in favor of the greatest gain. In more complex situations, however, it becomes difficult to weigh the level of gain of a majority against the level of pain for a minority. A more elaborate approach by Rawls[3] is built on the concepts of fairness and cooperation. Trying to eliminate personal preferences by pretending that the actors were under a "veil of ignorance" hiding their personal situation and status, Rawls argues that not knowing who exactly will benefit from any given decision will most likely produce just decisions.

Rules-based systems focus on "right" conduct. Behavior is considered "right" if based on "right" principles, independent of its results. Good will and universal applicability of the principles of actions provide the major criteria for evaluating decisions. However, this approach does not easily help to decide in the case of conflicting principles.

ETHICAL CONSIDERATIONS IN PROJECT MANAGEMENT

Ethical hotspots

Ethics deals with right actions and good results. Project Management strives for meeting project requirements through project activities. Hence, every aspect of project management involves ethical considerations and may produce an ethical dilemma. However, "ethical hotspots"[4] in project management are areas of interest to the public and issues that touch on basic, generally accepted values (human rights, preservation of our environment, financial honesty, etc.).

Benefits of Managing Ethics in Project Environments

Enron, Arthur Andersen, WorldCom, and other companies have brought ethical questions to the forefront of business and project environments. Thus managing ethics is expected to lessen the liability and maintain the professional integrity of executives and project managers. Furthermore, managing ethics has proven to provide companies with financial advantages and improved public image.[5] However, beyond tactical considerations, ethical reasoning per se and values-oriented leadership[6] become part of a comprehensive organizational and project strategy in trying to "maintain a moral course in turbulent times…[and to] support employee growth and meaning."[7]

Existing Approaches to Managing Ethics in Project Management

While many project teams implement codes of conduct for their projects, ethical reasoning begins to emerge in some particular project management areas. The Centre for Computing and Social Responsibility at De Montfort University (UK) is striving to make implicit ethical considerations explicit for software project management.[8] Some dominant ethical principles (honor, honesty, bias, adequacy, due care, fairness, social cost, action) are used within the project management process to produce a "Software Development Impact Statement." First, stakeholders and ethical issues are identified (generic). Then, this process is applied to the work breakdown structure (specific), ensuring the consideration of ethical aspects in all project activities. Approaches like these may be the cornerstone of managing ethics comprehensively in project environments.

Ethical Standards in Business and Project Management

International Standards of Business Ethics

In trying to increase awareness and appreciation of cultural differences, various standards of global business ethics have been published.[9] The secretary-general of the United Nations, Kofi Annan, has started the latest and most comprehensive initiative in January 1999. In challenging business and other leaders to support and implement core values within their corporate and public practices and policies, and to support his vision of "a more sustainable and inclusive global economy,"[10] Annan has initiated the United Nations Global Compact and put forward nine principles regarding human rights, labor, and the environment. On its first Leader's Summit on June 24, 2004 in New York, the principles have been enhanced by a tenth against corruption. "Today, hundreds of companies from all regions of the world, international labour, and civil society organizations are engaged in the Global Compact."[11]

Project Management Institute Standards of Ethics

The Project Management Institute (PMI), "the world's leading not-for-profit professional association for project management,"[12] takes professional responsibility and ethical conduct of its members and certified Project Management Professionals (PMP) seriously. Thus, the institute has presented respective statements and codes at various levels.

While the 2000 edition of the *PMBOK® Guide* only briefly touched on ethical norms that may "affect the way that people and organizations interact" and on "social-economic, environmental sustainability,"[13] the edition of 2004 put more emphasis on the professional responsibility the project management team has to its stakeholders and refers to the respective codes PMI members and Project Management Professionals (PMP) certified by the PMI need to adhere to. Furthermore, it suggests considering the social, economic, political, and physical impact of projects beyond the existence of the project organization. Finally, it points out the need for project teams to consider and understand their environment, including ethical issues.

Every member of PMI receives the "Member Code of Ethics." The Code requires members to "conduct their work in an ethical manner in order to earn and maintain the confidence of team members, colleagues, employees, employers, customers/clients, the public, and the global community."[14] It explicitly declares the personal commitment of each member to maintain integrity, accept responsibility, seek enhancement of professional capabilities, practice with fairness and honesty, and encourage others to act ethically and professionally.

Additionally, a PMP "agree[s] to support and adhere to the responsibilities described in the PMP Code of Professional Conduct."[15] The responsibilities to the profession include truthful information regarding the certification program and the individual's qualifications, experiences and services, cooperation regarding ethics violations, disclosure of possible conflict of interest, compliance with regional or national laws, regulations and ethical standards, and respect towards intellectual property. Furthermore, the responsibilities to customers and the public include providing truthful statements concerning costs, services and expected results, maintaining and satisfying the scope and objectives of services, confidentiality, ensuring a conflict of interest, not influencing or interfering professional judgments, and refraining from bribery.

MANAGING ETHICS IN PROJECT ENVIRONMENTS

Ethical Considerations for the Project Life Cycle and Organization

Phases[16] in projects are supposed to reduce complexity, increase transparency, and allow for controlled transitions and reviewed handoffs. *Reviews* are meant to detect problems and suggest solutions. Reviews may even be used to stop projects that no longer seem to be feasible within the given constraints. It is the responsibility of project managers and team members to honestly and truthfully report any problems regarding phase deliverables and to care for a thorough review of the phase they are about to close. Although rushing could be tempting and may even be supported by time constraints put forward by stakeholders, giving in without clearly discussing the impact and associated risk is irresponsible and unprofessional conduct.

Communication with and management of project stakeholders is at the heart of successful project management. Furthermore, identifying stakeholders, determining their requirements, and managing their influence involve ethical considerations including varying levels of responsibility. Project managers need to comprehensively determine the impact of any decision to be made. Expectations of funding or otherwise powerful authorities need to be balanced with conflicting requirements of other stakeholders. In order to comprehensively manage stakeholder expectations and conflicting issues, objectives and values need to be carefully addressed and openly discussed. The focus needs to be on customer satisfaction without disregarding others.

Furthermore, project needs have to be balanced with *organizational influences:* systems, cultures, and structures need to be considered. While team and project cultures may be innovative and leading the change, the possible difference to organizational culture and hierarchy has to be "managed" in loyalty to superiors and to the organization as a whole.[17]

Ethical "Hotspots" in the Project Management Processes and Knowledge Areas

The project manager is responsible for tailoring project management processes according to the needs of the project and the organization. Since tradeoffs are inevitable, the ethical implications of all decisions need to be assessed.

While defining the project during the *initiating processes,* the project team needs to understand the values, concerns, and expectations of stakeholders and analyze the possible impact of the project. That may help the project manager to create buy in and evaluate the existence of a strong and broad enough basis for the project to move forward.

The focus of ethical considerations in the *planning processes* is defining the detailed objectives and preparing the best course of action. Translating the general impact analysis of the project on various stakeholders into the detailed project activities and deliverables documented in the work breakdown structure is a helpful approach to base planning decisions on ethical reasoning. Furthermore, all planning processes need to be conducted and communicated honestly and thoroughly both internally and externally.

Executing, monitoring, and controlling processes implement the plans with the ethical focus again being on communicating timely and truthfully with all stakeholders and on continuing to manage their expectations in balance with changes in and around the project environment. In spite of daily pressures and necessary control measures, not loosing sight of stakeholders as human beings having values, objectives, and feelings rather than mere resources or obstacles of project improvement becomes the major ethical challenge of execution and control. Customer satisfaction and team development are the main criteria for measuring project progress and success. Both depend on correct, comprehensive, and careful information and feedback in a timely manner.

Finally, the *closing processes* need to formalize acceptance, evaluate stakeholder satisfaction, and bring the project to an orderly end. Including evaluations of the impact analysis and stakeholder management processes in final lessons learned and post implementation reviews will further improve the processes of ethical decision making and conduct.

Guidelines for Managing Ethics in Project Environments

Some ethical principles for project management have emerged in our earlier discussions. A clear vision—including values—needs to be part of project leadership and should be aligned with policy, practice, and communication to become effective. Project managers need to be "obsessed"[18] with basic values like fairness, honesty, due care, and integrity. They need to feel comfortable communicating intensely with a variety of internal and external stakeholders and taking their perspectives seriously. Ethical decision making requires commitment to solving problems collaboratively based on shared values. However, accountability calls for personal rather than collective responsibility in a professional context. The human, social, and environmental cost and impact of decisions and actions need to be analyzed, considered and balanced with other project and stakeholder requirements in a local and global perspective. The initial results of that process and later changes need to be documented in both a product- or service-oriented Project Deliverables Impact Statement (ProDIS) and a process-oriented Project Management Impact Statement (ProMIS).

Specific project management guidelines on ethical decision making can help implementing the ethical principles:

▶Include ethical dimensions in all decision-making procedures.

▶Use checklists and samples for the ProDIS and ProMIS.

▶Make ethics decisions in groups and make them public (use of "veil of ignorance" approach[19]).

▶Define a joint process and mutually agreeable criteria for ethical decision making.

▶Apply both ethical principles and evaluation of the possible results and impact.

▶Continually evaluate and improve the procedures of ethical decision making.

Finally, although corporate project management policies and procedures for managing ethics are no prerequisite for managing ethics in individual projects, they will substantially help in doing so. However, top-down commitment is paramount. If senior executives do not live up to the core values of the corporation and fail to communicate both their shortcomings and their continuous strive for ethical growth, all further efforts in ethical programs will be perceived as dummy activities merely aiming at deceiving the public. Thus, on top of the possible development of codes of ethics or conduct, ethics management needs to be implemented as a comprehensive and corporate-wide process using cross-functional teams.

Furthermore, ethics management needs to be integrated in other management practices in order to become effective. Ethicists and ethics committees may then be functions supporting the ethics management process by designing and implementing procedures to develop the Impact Statements (ProDIS and ProMIS) and to resolve ethical dilemmas based on vivid corporate values and principles. Both leaders and managers as well as special ethics functions need to hold and support regular challenging meetings confronting values statements with practical conduct and procedures and thus updating and improving both.

All involved in that process need to be educated and trained in ethics management and ethical reasoning and decision making.

Last but certainly not least leaders and managers need to install a corporate culture that values forgiveness and continuous effort for improvement. The survival of such a culture will depend on the valued perception of ethical integrity and moral courage even in the light of their occasional negative impact on the bottom line. Most probably this culture can best be implemented and nurtured by leaders serving[20] both their various stakeholders and a joint mission based on shared values.

Sample Exercises

Exercise 1: You are a passionate non-smoker concerned about public health and a member of an anti-smoking organization. As PMP, you are being offered an assignment as the responsible project manager for an external client in the tobacco industry. Your job would be to design and implement a sales initiative aimed at an increased market share of that client.

a. I accept. My boss has told me that increasing the market share of one company in a saturated market will most probably not increase smoking. In addition, if I don't accept, somebody else will.

b. I accept. My involvement with the anti-smoking organization is "my business" and not publicly known.

c. I decline and insist on my company rejecting the assignment due to its general unethical background.

d. I decline and indicate my private involvement to my boss and state my concern that I cannot serve both the external client and my anti-smoking organization.

Answer: d. Your affiliation definitely creates a conflict of interest that according to the PMP Code of Professional Conduct needs to be indicated to your superior.

Exercise 2: As a project manager in a foreign country, you are in charge of contracting various suppliers. During the solicitation process one of the applicants for a contract offers your team free and preferred on-site housing.

a. I politely but firmly reject that offer. Accepting gifts by suppliers is perceived to be unethical on global as well as on professional standards.

b. I accept. In the culture of that particular country, this is not considered unethical but rather a common and friendly gesture among business partners.

c. I decline. Acceptance would create a dependency that will make objective negotiations regarding costs, time, and quality of the work performed more difficult.

d. I accept. That offer does not provide me with a personal advantage because I will be staying in a first-class hotel when I am on-site. Instead, it improves the situation of my team.

Answer: a. Accepting a gift from a supplier is explicitly mentioned as being unethical by professional standards and standards of global business ethics.

Exercise 3: You are a project manager bidding for a project management contract. The contracting agency approaches you with the request to reduce the estimated costs by 30% based on the same deliverables and constraints.

a. I recalculate the bid by considering cheaper material and labor for items that have not explicitly been mentioned in the bid.

b. After seriously reconsidering, I will truthfully present all the details and indicate that delivering the expected level of quality in the given timeframe has its price.

c. Cost projections at this stage are rough estimates only. So reducing the bid by 30% now to get the contract and recovering the missing amount "elsewhere" during the run of the project is a rather "normal" way of managing projects on a contract basis.

d. I know that competitors have underestimated the actual costs to get the contract. Thus I need to do the same in order not to disadvantage my company.

Answer: b. Professional codes of conduct require the project manager to always truthfully present all information to the best of his or her knowledge.

A comprehensive model of project management ethics and of managing ethics in a project environment needs an integrative approach including both an ethical analysis of the process as well as of the impact of project decisions. Existing approaches of business ethics and of project management-related codes of conduct and ethical guidelines serve as a first basis for ethical decision making in project environments based on professional responsibility and conduct. Managing ethics in project environments needs to inspire an appropriate project culture and include the mechanisms that assure and improve ethical decision making, actions, and results.

Corporate leadership based on the model of servant- and values-oriented leadership will certainly support managing ethics in project environments. However, professionals in project management are challenged to implement project management ethics even in an unfavorable corporate or organizational environment. They may succeed if they passionately lead and manage projects by comprehensively serving both the project mission and requirements as well as the expectations of their stakeholders and by orienting towards mutually acceptable values throughout the various project phases and processes.

DISCUSSION QUESTIONS

❶ How would you define "integrity"?

❷ What are the key elements of the PMP Code of Professional Conduct? Do you feel they cover all the issues that may arise in practice? If not, what issues are missing from the Code?

REFERENCES

[1] Frankl, Victor E. *Man's Search for Meaning*. New York: Simon & Schuster, 1985; Mengel, Thomas *From Responsibility to Values-Oriented Leadership—6 Theses on Meaning and Values in Personal Life and Work Environments.* International Network on Personal Meaning. Positive Living E-Zine, August 11, 2004. Available: http://www.meaning.ca/articles04/mengel-responsibility.htm.

[2] Hartman, Laura P. ed. *Perspectives in business ethics*. New York: McGraw-Hill, 2002: 6-10; Singer, Peter ed. *A Companion to Ethics.* Malden: Blackwell Publishers, 1999: 205–218, 230–248.

[3] Rawls, John. *A Theory of Justice.* Cambridge: Harvard University Press, 1971.

[4] Rogerson, Simon, and Donald Gotterbarn "The Ethics of Software Project Management," in: Collste, G. (editor), *Ethics and information technology*. Delhi: New Academic Publishers, 1998: 137–154.

[5] Paine, Lynn S. *Value Shift. Why Companies Must Merge Social and Financial Imperatives to Achieve Superior Performance.* New York: McGraw-Hill, 2003; Barnett, Rebecca *How Business Ethics Failed Corporate America (And What We Must Do Next).* In: ProjectMagazine. 3/7 (2002). Available:

http://www.projectmagazine.com/v3i7/ethicsv3i7.html.

[6] Mengel, Thomas. *Values-oriented Leadership: Designing Personal and Corporate Future.* Colloquium within the Graduate Program in Counselling Psychology. Trinity Western University. November 1, 2003. Available: http://www.twu.ca/cpsy/colloquia_past.asp; Mengel, Thomas, Dale Christenson, Janice Thomas, and Coral Trisko *In Search for Meaning—Project Management Perspectives on Change, Crisis and Loss.* Symposium and Presentation at the Third International Conference on Personal Meaning, Vancouver, July 2004.

[7] McNamara, Carter *Complete Guide to Ethics Management: An Ethics Toolkit for Managers,* 1999. Available: http://www.managementhelp.org/ethics/ethxgde.htm.

[8] Rogerson, Simon, and Donald Gotterbarn "The Ethics of Software Project Management," in: Collste, G. (editor), *Ethics and Information Technology*. Delhi: New Academic Publishers, 1998: 137–154.

[9] Hartman, Laura P. ed. *Perspectives in Business Ethics*. New York: McGraw-Hill, 2002: 730–746.

[10] *The Global Compact* at http://www.unglobalcompact.org/Portal/Default.asp.

[11] Ibid; on August 1, 2004, there were already more than 1,700 participants listed.

[12] Project Management Institute. *Building Professionalism in Project Management.* Newtown Square, PA: Project Management Institute, 2002.

[13] Project Management Institute. *A Guide to the Project Management Body of Knowledge.* Newtown Square, PA: Project Management Institute, 2000: 27. For the new edition see: Project Management Institute. *A Guide to the Project Management Body of Knowledge, Third Edtion.* Newtown Square, PA: Project Management Institute, 2004.

[14] Project Management Institute. *Member Identification Card and Member Code of Ethics.* Newtown Square, PA: Project Management Institute, 2000.

[15] Project Management Institute. *Project Management Professional Code of Professional Conduct.* Newtown Square, PA: Project Management Institute, 2000. Available at: http://www.pmi.org/prod/groups/public/documents/info/pdc_pmpcodeofconduct.pdf.

[16] PMI 2004, ibid. Pages 19-24.

[17] Ibid. pp. 27–32.

[18] McNamara, Carter. *Complete Guide to Ethics Management: An Ethics Toolkit for Managers,* 1999. Available at: http://www.managementhelp.org/ethics/ethxgde.htm.

[19] Rawls, John *A Theory of Justice.* Cambridge: Harvard University Press, 1971; See section 1 in this chapter.

[20] Greenleaf, Robert. K. *Servant Leadership: A Journey into the Nature of Legitimate Power and Greatness.* Mahwah, NJ: Paulist Press, 1977.

CHAPTER 18

Professionalization of Project Management: What Does It Mean for Practice?

▶BILL ZWERMAN, SOCIOLOGY DEPARTMENT, UNIVERSITY OF CALGARY

▶JANICE THOMAS, PHD, CENTER FOR INNOVATIVE MANAGEMENT, ATHABASCA UNIVERSITY

As we move into the 21st century, work has become more knowledge-oriented and information workers in various occupations have recognized the similarity of their work to the traditional "professions" of the 20th century. Many of these occupations, led by teaching, nursing, and social work and including financial planners, surveyors, and many others, have embarked on professionalization initiatives seeking the recognition and privileges traditionally associated with medicine, law, accounting, engineering, and a very few other occupations.

In the last decade of the 20th century, project managers launched a similar professionalization mission. The Project Management Institute (PMI) stated that its mission is "to further the professionalization of project management" with the explicit intent of developing a new profession. Today many project managers view project management as a "profession." Over 65 percent of PMI's membership explicitly recognize project management as a profession.[1]

There is no question that these individuals conduct themselves in a professional manner when carrying out their responsibilities. Yet, there is equally no doubt that project management has not today attained the status of a traditional profes-

Exclusive control—esoteric and systematic BOK	Members have a monopoly on understanding and applying the BOK
Autonomy of practice	Members control the standards of society
Norm of altruism	Members act in best interest of client
Authority over clients	Professionals control the client/practitioner relationship
Distinctive occupational culture	Occupation is set apart by a distinctive set of norms, values, and symbols
Recognition	Usually legal requirement for specific training and preparation prior to practice

FIGURE 18-1. **TRAITS OF A PROFESSION**

sion as defined in sociological terms where a profession is recognized as a special kind of occupation with a particular set of characteristics that carry with them a set of privileges and responsibilities. Professions are recognized by law in the western world and there are very few accepted in most western jurisdictions.[2]

DEFINITION OF A PROFESSION

Professions have been studied in sociology for over 75 years when it was recognized that there existed a class of occupation that was typically accorded a higher degree of privilege and rewards than other occupations. Original studies of the professions focused on identifying the unique characteristics that distinguished professions from non-professions. This "trait approach" to professionalization typically identified the set of characteristics outlined in Figure 18-1 as fundamental to a profession.[3, 4]

These studies also identified the need to drive out malpractice and protect the public as a driving force in the legal recognition of the profession. The occupations of law, medicine, and lately engineering and accounting, typically formed the basis of study for research on the traditional professions.

According to trait theory, nursing, teaching, and social work (among others) are classified as "semi-professions" as they possess only some of the traits or have only partially developed some of the traits required by an occupation to be considered fully professional. Project management clearly fits into the "semi-profession" category[5] as explained below.

Professionalization, or the path to professional status, requires consideration of both what a profession looks like (the traits) and the process by which these characteristics are attained. Figure 18-2 identifies the key activities usually associated with professionalization.

Abbott[6] suggested that professions begin with the recognition by people that they are doing something that is not covered by other professions and the formation of a professional association. Forming a professional association defines a "competence territory" that members claim as their exclusive area of competent practice. The professionalization activity and its claims to professional status must be placed in historical, economic,

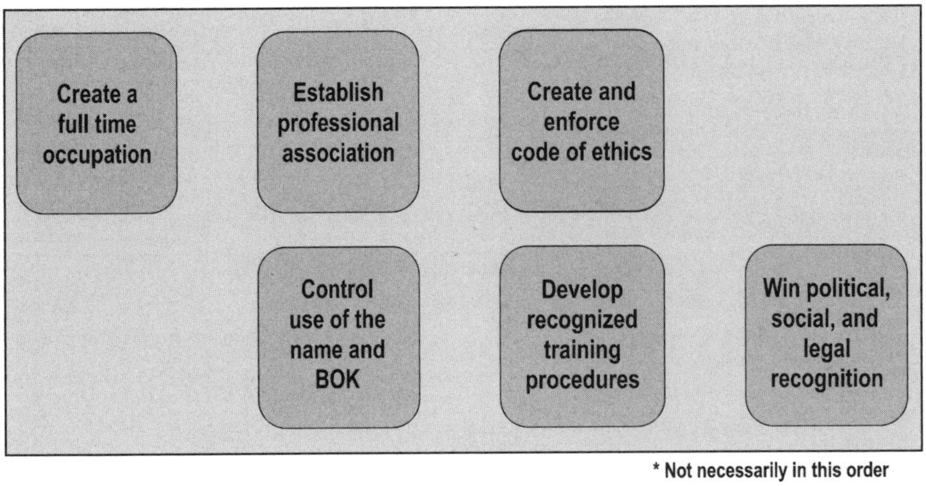

FIGURE 18-2. **THE PROCESS OF PROFESSIONALIZATION**

political, and social context and seen as being fundamentally shaped by these conditions, rather than assuming that claims to professional status are objective, inevitable, and timeless. Claims to professional status (for example, "autonomy" or "esoteric knowledge") are perceived as strategies in exerting occupational control and autonomy vis-à-vis other groups, including bureaucratic managers.[7]

Understanding professionalization as a struggle between occupations to exert control and gain autonomy can provide superior insights into the historical struggle of occupations such as nursing, teaching, social work, and project management to achieve professional status. Indeed, some have pointed out that even the firmly established professions (such as medicine and law) are increasingly subject to broad social change questioning their traditional status, especially in the age of cutbacks.[8,9] Thus, we turn to an examination of the status of project management in attaining the characteristics of a profession and then the requirements of professionalization through the processes and exercise of power with particular emphasis on what project management can learn from the struggles of other "semi-professions" and the actions of the various professional associations world wide to advance this initiative.

Status of Project Management

Figure 18-3 summarizes project management's status in terms of developing the characteristics of a profession.

Clearly, project management has not yet achieved most of the characteristics of a traditional profession. Next we will look at the activities various project management bodies and practitioners have embarked on to achieve these characteristics.

THE PATH TO PROFESSIONALIZATION

The path to professionalization is composed of several lines of activity as introduced in Figure 18-3. Each of these activities is introduced below with reference to the actions of other emerging professions, and to the implications for project management in accomplishing this goal.

Exclusive control—esoteric and systematic BOK	No—BOKs are beginning to be recognized but still highly contested
Autonomy of practice	No—members *contribute* to the standards of practice
Norm of altruism	Not usually—societal impact of failed projects not recognized
Authority over clients	Not usually—project managers tend to work within corporations
Distinctive occupational culture	Possibly—certain aspects exist
Recognition	Not yet—PM not legally recognized as a profession in any jurisdiction

FIGURE 18-3. **THE STATUS OF PROJECT MANAGEMENT**

Full-Time Occupation

Being recognized as a full-time occupation rather than a skill or technical tool required of a variety of occupations can be seen as the first step towards formal recognition of the "worth" of an occupation as separate from the other potential occupations within which this skill is practiced. An occupation has truly arrived in most western jurisdictions when governments begin to collect occupational statistics. Until recently the only statistics available on the number of project managers worldwide came as estimates provided by PMI—no occupational statistics were available. Without being a recognized occupation, project management could never attain profession status and would always be seen as an attribute perhaps of some other profession (like architecture). Recently, we are told the US government recognized project management as an occupation and will begin collecting occupational statistics (though this has not been confirmed at press time). Thus, it appears that project management has been recognized as an occupation.

Monopoly Over Use of the Name

However, while the occupation has been recognized, there is still no clear definition of what a project manager is. In order to reach profession status, the term "project manager" must be captured and controlled. As long as anyone can use that designation without regard to training or certification, it will be impossible to create an occupation that can lay claim to "professional" status. To date it appears that anyone will be able to self-report as a member of the project management occupation without reference to qualifications.

All analyses of "professionalization" processes include this criterion; but it should not be viewed in absolute terms. All claims to professionalization include a negotiated statement regarding what the practitioners include in their claims and what they leave out. Doctors don't claim control or competency over everything in the domain of work in health. Teachers don't claim the exclusive right to practice in all learning situations.

Gaining control over the name will require defining which project management activities are to be the sole jurisdiction of professional project managers. What "projects" will "professional" project managers assume as theirs? and what will be left to anyone else who wants them? Where does the casual practitioner fit into the world of projects and where does the "professional" project manager enter? Not all projects are equal and not all projects require a professional. Currently, some of this activity is happening in individual organizations, as they create career ladders for project managers and define what qualifications are required for the use of the term within their organizational activities, and within some national jurisdictions in terms of competency rankings.

However, the protection of that designation or "name" will be ongoing, continuing part of the struggle between occupations, and between occupations and employers, to achieve control over the work. Through this ongoing process, the limits of the practice will be negotiated through time. Nurses do a number of things today that they did not do twenty years ago: witness the arrival of the Nurse Practitioner. This will require lobbying activities to win the right to that name and continuing efforts to police the use of the name. Conducted in a piecemeal fashion within various organizations and professional associations, this is likely to be a messy process.

Control Over the Body of Knowledge

The claim to "professional status" ultimately rests on the ability of the practitioners to lay claim to more or less exclusive command of an esoteric body of knowledge which they declare to be essential to good practice. The inability to make this claim convincingly is, perhaps, the primary factor responsible for the failure of teachers and social workers to achieve full recognition as "professionals." Nurses, on the other hand, suffer not from the lack of a "hard scientific" body of knowledge, but rather from the fact that another group of professionals, physicians and surgeons, has laid claim to controlling that body of knowledge. Project management fits somewhere between these extremes.

The emergence of project management BOKs is a significant step in the right direction, but the development of a full-blown body of knowledge for project management will require a great deal of elaboration. In particular, professional bodies will have to be able to argue convincingly that the methods, ideas, and tools embedded in the project management BOKs and mastered by the professional project managers improves their ability to deliver projects and add value to clients. This is not a claim that can be substantiated by solid research evidence at this point in time—primarily because serious research on project management issues is still relatively rare.

Indeed, while the creation and maintenance of project management BOKs is a step in the right direction, so far there is no exclusive body of knowledge that holds the position of Generally Accepted Accounting Principles or recognized medical diagnostic tests in the world of project management doctrines. Project management guidelines are promulgated by other project management professional associations worldwide as well as those crafted by individual gurus and large companies. Without agreement on what this body of knowledge is and who is in charge of developing and maintaining it, professionalization will be difficult to achieve.

Education

Upgrading knowledge and developing recognized and ever more comprehensive educational programs has been a key aspect of professionalization in every case of a modern occupation striving to upgrade to "professional" status. The major established professions and the three semi-professions of particular interest to project management—teaching, social work, and nursing[10]—all lay claim to their own faculty/college within the university higher-education system. Accounting is the only profession that resides in someone else's home (business or management faculty/colleges); the others all have their own deans. To date, project management has no clear home within the university setting. It is found in one of several locations, including business, engineering, or planning, and many universities provide no academic project management education, focusing only on providing project management training and professional certification preparation. Most training in project management still resides within corporate training, consulting, and professional organizations—entirely outside higher education. Development of a recognized academic discipline will be crucial to the professionalization project. While there will always be a demand for a wide array of educational offerings, the emergence of the academic discipline will entail negotiations between professional associations and academics.

Role of the Professional Associations

Professional associations in traditional professions are the center of control for the practitioners; they represent the interests of the practitioners to the outside world and enforces standards within the profession. A strong association mediates between public and private authorities on behalf of practitioners and directly influences the power and influence that accrues to that profession.

Today there are a variety of local and global professional associations alternately vying for recognition and authority in the project management world, and cooperating to improve project management's chances of becoming a 21st-century profession (See Crawford 2004a and b for more comprehensive discussions of these developments[11,12]). These and other important association initiatives are introduced below:

International Project Management Association (IPMA)

IPMA began as a community of practice for managers of international projects in 1965 but has evolved into a federation of approximately 30 national project management associations representing 20,000 members primarily in Europe, Asia, and Africa (see IPMA Website). The IPMA has developed its own standards and certification program, which is comprised of a central framework and quality assurance process plus national programs developed by association members. This association competes on a global basis with the programs of the Project Management Institute. However, recently the two organizations have been trying to find common ground for working together.

Project Management Institute

PMI began as the national project management association for the United States of America in 1969. Until the 1990s, this was a relatively small professional association. However, the 1990s witnessed exponential membership growth. By the late 1990s, PMI recognized that its membership of over 100,000 was becoming international in nature. While PMI's headquarters continues to be in Philadelphia, PA, and the organization continues to be subject to the laws of that state, in 2003 the first of three planned regional service centers was opened in Europe.

PMI's large membership and global mandate suggests that it is the "leading non-profit professional association in the area of project management" (http://www.pmi.org). However, it is still largely American in membership, nature, and approach (Crawford, 2004).

In addition to certification and registered education programs, PMI has instituted university accreditation programs. To date all of these programs are voluntary in nature. PMI has also initiated government lobbying both in North America and in emerging markets like China in recent years.

Regional Project Management Associations

There are almost 300 regional PMI chapters, national members of IPMA, or other national associations in the world today. A few are notable due to their size or activity in developing bodies of knowledge, standards, or certification programs. The Association for Project Management (APM) of the UK has a membership of 13,000 and has been actively involved in defining the project management body of knowledge over the years. The Australian Institute of Project Management (AIPM) began in 1976 and operates independently of both PMI and IPMA. It has been a leader in encouraging the development of national project management associations in the Asia Pacific region. AIPM has also worked closely with the Australian government to develop national competency standards. Project Management South Africa is another independent professional association that has worked closely with their government to define performance-based competency standards. The Japan Project Management Forum is based on corporate rather than individual membership and has been actively involved in capability enhancement, the promotion of project management, and the development of a Japanese project management body of knowledge. The Project Management Research Committee of China has also been active in publishing the China National Competence Baseline.

Global Efforts

In addition, there have been efforts underway for the last decade to define a global approach to project management integrating the efforts of the independent associations and perhaps setting the foundations for a future global profession.

Certification/Licensing and Control

To attain professional status, professional associations must be given legal responsibility for designating who is qualified to practice. This may be very complicated, with a number of certification and licensing alternatives such as those found in medicine, or much simpler, as in the more generic licensing of teachers. If there is no effective certification and/or licensing scheme, then it will be impossible for practitioners to lay claim to any sort of special status or privileges. Certification is the key to control of the name and to control of admission to practice. In project management today, there are a number of largely voluntary certification approaches in project management ranging from knowledge-based assessment to competency standards based on practice.

In North America (and increasingly globally), PMI has a largely knowledge-based approach based on acquiring five years of project experience and then passing a test assessing knowledge of the concepts and terms included in their body of knowledge. Aggressive global growth over the last decade has given the Project Management Professional (PMP) designation widespread recognition and many organizations are using it as an entrance requirement when hiring project managers. In this way, the PMP certification is beginning to control entry into the practice of project management in many jurisdictions.

Other professional associations (for example, IPMA or AIPM) have more comprehensive certification processes that assess levels of project management knowledge and performance starting at the team member level and progressing up to project or program directors. All of these certification processes are largely voluntary, but in some countries (such as Africa or Australia), government involvement in certification has come close to providing legal recognition for certification.

AREAS OF CHALLENGE OR CONCERN

To date, no government has recognized the imperative to protect the public from the malpractice of individuals calling themselves project managers, even in the face of billion-dollar overruns on public projects. It is unlikely that governments will independently pursue actions to create a project management profession. In most jurisdictions, there is some question as to whether or not they even understand that there is a developed occupation of project management, despite the fact that individual organizations and associations establish standards and define programs for hiring and advancing project managers. It is also unlikely that private corporations will request or require the formation of a profession, as protecting their short-term interests is not likely to encompass creating this situation. Some may support the initiative, but many will resist in order to protect their autonomy and rights over the management of work.

For project management to become a "profession," it requires the concerted effort of its practitioners and professional associations in pursuing this objective. Keys to achieving this status are as follows:

- Developing a defensible definition of project management, which can be used to gain protection of the occupational name
- Developing a well-defined and complex body of knowledge, which can be claimed by the profession and unequivocally asserted to create value
- Elaborating significant independent academic educational programs with an associated set of research programs
- Creating and enforcing a code of ethics for all practitioners using the title Project Manager.
- Winning political, social, and legal recognition of the value of regulating project management for the good of society.

The most significant challenge facing the professionalization effort is gaining recognition and acceptance of the changes required of both professional associations and practitioners. Under a profession model, professional associations refocus from supporting the advancement and growth of practice in general to defining, regulating, and representing the collective "rights" of professional project managers. Practitioners at the same time need to decide whether they see project management as a profession that should be self-regulating and to which they are willing to submit their practice for judgment, or whether they would rather see it continue as an occupation subject to the whims of the market or even a tool kit of use in many occupations. These differences are significant in scope and have serious implications for development of either the occupation or profession.

IMPLICATIONS FOR PRACTITIONERS

Regardless of the potential for project management to achieve "professional" status, the promulgation of written standards, and the acceptance of these standards by important jurisdictions and organizations, has serious implications for the way a craft is practiced. Today courts and other organizations can take these standards into account in defining negligent or competent practice. Some feel that it is only a matter of time before project managers are held legally accountable for the outcomes of projects. The Auditor General's Office of Canada and many other organizations are attempting to use the ANSI standard *PMBOK® Guide* as a measure of project manager competence.

Clearly the professionalization effort has already created some serious implications for practitioners. Several of these are discussed below.

Bureaucratization of Practice

Practice standards and official guidelines in professional practice require that either practitioners follow the guidelines appropriately or justify why the particular context of activity required some other approach. Members of traditional professions maintain copious case notes and journals to enable them to reconstruct their professional reasoning if necessary. Professionals must be able to show that they followed established practice guidelines or justify why they did not. Many project managers operating in fast-paced environments may see this as unnecessary and time consuming when there is no clear evidence that the guidelines provide better results than other approaches.

In many ways, this bureacratization of project management has led to complaints of increased "overhead costs" of project management at exactly the time practitioners are striving to streamline practice in order to increase the value added. Tradeoffs between following guidelines and getting things done in a timely fashion are already replete in project management discussions. Further professionalization without clear identification of when and where these guidelines need to be applied and when they can be shortcutted will exacerbate these conflicts. Interesting paradoxes are sure to arise.

Value of Certification

The value of certification is a hotly contested issue in project management. Many argue that the knowledge-based certifications that exist today simply show that you have some background knowledge and can pass an examination, not that you can successfully manage projects. Again there is no clear evidence that certification increases the success of project managers on any clearly definable criteria.

In fact, certification and licensing are not designed to eliminate poor performance or to guarantee a very high standard in all cases. It has more to do with providing an adequate screening mechanism and controlling the entry of individuals into the profession. The value of licensing doctors came from eliminating thousands of quacks and incompetents and raising the general standard. As a consumer or patient, it is still up to you to find a "good" physician. The potential values arising through certification/licensing (professionalization) of project management are:

- Raising the general level of practice
- Increasing the status of the practitioners

▶Increasing the rewards for practicing project managers

▶Screening out most of the individuals who should not be claiming that they are competent to practice.

However, most of these benefits come from setting the entrance criteria significantly high that not anyone who takes a course and studies can pass the exam. Failure rates on these "bar exams" are usually kept to a significant level. As the value of holding the certification rises, individual practitioners can expect the educational bar to be raised on attaining certification.

Benefits and Costs of Professionalization

The benefits of professionalization accrue to the majority of practitioners in terms of providing guidelines of practice, increased status, and recognition, but superstars often fail to see any benefit. Michael Jordan doesn't need the players' union, but most of the NBA players benefit from it. All professional project managers would benefit from increased status, pay, and authority in the project environment. However, many of the most successful practitioners likely already enjoy these benefits and are likely to oppose any constraints imposed on them. Those for whom managing projects has become an intuitive process of doing what is necessary will chafe against the need to document their decision processes. Expert project managers will be required to certify and abide by the laws of the professional association if they intend to continue practicing.

Professionalization also creates a legal liability to be assumed by practitioners. Costs of insurance and personal liability can be quite high, as evidenced by malpractice costs in medicine. The liability assumed by an uncertified, unlicensed worker is considerably less than that assumed by a registered, licensed member of a profession. The seal of the profession carries with it a personal liability associated with "bad" practice. A failed project managed by an ordinary employee does not carry the same possibility for the assumption of personal liability. In projects that go terribly wrong, these costs could be substantial.

Costs to projects and organizations also rise as requiring professional project management practice. These costs are usually seen in two particular areas. The first is in the cost of acquiring the services of a professional. The second is in the loss of control over organizational practices. Using a professional project manager requires recognizing the judgment of the project manager in many areas that were traditionally the responsibility of the organization's management alone. Internal project management standards can only be applied as long as they adhere to the standards promulgated by the profession. Where there is a discrepancy, a professional project manager must go with the professional standard. Both of these can increase the costs of projects.

Costs to individual practitioners include the necessity to maintain current understanding of the body of knowledge and to continually update and upgrade skills. It will no longer be enough to master a body of knowledge and apply it as well as possible. It will now be necessary to ensure that your practice lives up to the evolving standards set by an outside body. Maintaining professional status becomes a cost and necessity of carrying out your professional practice. Certification will no longer be voluntary and membership costs will usually rise to cover the increased costs of policing and developing the profession. Some form of insurance against malpractice is also likely to become a necessity.

Professionalization is often seen as a noble goal for emerging knowledge occupations. The activities of project management associations throughout the world reflect the growing efforts to attain this goal by achieving professional recognition. However, there remains much to be done to develop the characteristics and recognition of a traditional profession. Obtaining the status of a full profession will require significant effort from the members of an occupation to work together to achieve recognition. Gaining control over the characteristics of a profession requires both heavy initial investment and ongoing efforts directed at maintaining this status. Recognizing the benefits and costs of this type of initiative are a solid first step to developing the necessary commitment of practitioners to this lofty goal.

CONCLUSION

This chapter endeavors to provide practitioners with the background to clearly understand the issues involved in professionalization. From this foundation it is possible for individual practitioners to make informed choices about the activities they undertake to ensure their practice fits within this model and the implications of doing so. The process of initiating project managers into these practices will make a difference in how project management is understood and practiced in organizations.

DISCUSSION QUESTIONS

❶ If project management were formally recognized as a profession, how would it make a difference you in your practice of project management?

❷ What aspects of professionalization do you think would improve project management practice? Hamper it?

❸ How can you contribute to the development of a project management profession?

REFERENCES

[1] Project Management Institute. *Project Management Factbook.* Newtown Square, PA: Project Management Institute, 1999.

[2] Italy is a noted exception where many occupations, if not most, are recognized as professions with a legal mandate enforcing privileges and responsibilities of membership.

[3] Roach Anleu, Sharyn L. The Professionalisation of Social Work? A Case Study of Three Organizational Settings. *Sociology* 26 (1992): 23–43.

[4] Hugman, Richard. Organization and Professionalism: The Social Work Agenda in the 1990s. *British Journal of Social Work* 21 (1991): 199–216.

[5] Zwerman, B., and Thomas, J. "Potential Barriers on the Road to Professionalization," *PM Network*, Vol. 15 (2001): 50–62.

[6] Abbott, Andrew. *The System of Professions*. Chicago: University of Chicago Press, 1988.

[7] Aldridge, Meryl. Dragged to Market: Being a Profession in the Postmodern World. *British Journal of Social Work,* 26 (1996): 177–194.

[8] Hugman, Richard. Professionalization in Social Work: The Challenge of Diversity. *International Social Work* 39 (1996): 131–147.

[9] Labaree, David F. Power, Knowledge, and the Rationalization of Teaching: A Genealogy of the Movement to Professionalize Teaching, 62 (1992): 123–154.

[9] Zwerman, B., Thomas, J., Haydt, S., and Williams, T. Professionalization of Project Management: Exploring the Past to Map the Future. Newtown Square, PA: Project Management Institute.

[10] Crawford, L.H. Global Body of Project Management Knowledge and Standards. In P. W. G. Morris, and J.K. Pinto (Editors), *The Wiley Guide to Managing Projects* (Vol. Chapter 46). Hoboken, NJ: John Wiley and Sons, 2004a.

[11] Crawford, L.H. Professional Associations and Global Initiatives. In P. W. G. Morris, and J.K. Pinto (Editors), *The Wiley Guide to Managing Projects* (Vol. Chapter 56). Hoboken, NJ: John Wiley and Sons, 2004b.

CHAPTER 19

Competency and Careers In Project Management

▶J. KENT CRAWFORD, PMP,
PROJECT MANAGEMENT SOLUTIONS, INC.

▶JEANNETTE CABANIS-BREWIN,
CENTER FOR BUSINESS PRACTICES

Research into the causes of project failures has identified a primary cause of troubled or unsuccessful projects: the lack of qualified project managers.[1] At one time, this lack was primarily due to the fact that real, trained project managers were, in fact, quite rare. Project management was "the accidental profession," not one that people chose and trained for. Today, with the proliferation of degree programs, training courses, and a growing professional body, this is less true. The problem facing projects now is an organizational one. In many organizations, employees have very little incentive to assume the position of project manager, largely due to a disconnect surrounding what the role entails. Organizations have historically assumed that technical capabilities of individuals could be translated into project management expertise. Because of this, professionals who have worked for years to earn the title of senior engineer or technical specialist have been unwilling to exchange their current jobs for the role of project manager. The role is added to their regular job description, instead of being viewed as a legitimate function to be valued by the organization, and which requires a special set of skills. Therefore, many organizations still haven't connected the value of the project manager to the success of the organization.

A second, related reason is that poor role definition—for all the roles in a project, but especially for the project manager—

places even qualified personnel into situations where they are doomed to failure by requiring them to do too much and be expert in everything.

Clearly it's time for organizations to become more systematic in the way they deal with the human resource challenges posed by the project environment. To explore a framework for the division of labor on projects that we think works both for the people and for the project outcomes, let's start by examining the historical role of the project manager.

WHAT DOES A PROJECT MANAGER DO?

The project manager's challenge is to combine two discrete areas of competence:

▶ *The art of project management*—Effective communications, trust, values, integrity, honesty, sociability, leadership, staff development, flexibility, decision making, perspective, sound business judgment, negotiations, customer relations, problem solving, managing change, managing expectations, training, mentoring, and consulting.

▶ *The science of project management*—Plans, WBS, Gantt charts, standards, CPM/precedence diagrams, controls variance analysis, metrics, methods, earned value, s-curves, risk management, status reporting, resource estimating, and leveling.

Because of the nature of the enterprises that were early adopters of project management (military, utility, construction industries), the profession "grew up" in an environment with a strong cost accounting view and developed a focus on project planning and controls—an emphasis on the science. This is the kind of project management that we think of as being "traditional" or "classic" project management. However, it simply represents an early evolutionary stage in the life of the discipline.

Since then, we have seen the emergence of countless trends. Project management is being used in nearly all industries, and across all functions within those industries. Organizations have flattened out, matrixed organizations have taken root, and new information technology has allowed people to communicate more effectively and reduce cycle-times across all business processes. As a result, management began pushing more projects onto an increasingly complex organization. The role of project manager is now very demanding and requires an ever-expanding arsenal of skills, especially "soft" or interpersonal skills.

What makes a good project manager?

The debate about project manager skills and competencies is well into its third decade. Thus we have lists compiled by a dozen or so organizations, academics, and consultancies expressing views on "the good project manager." What project manager skills, competencies, and characteristics do these lists agree on?

Technical or Industry Expertise

A baseline of technical or industry knowledge is what gets a project manager candidate in the door. Commonly, a project manager has an undergraduate degree in some technical specialty—and while that can mean engineering or computer science, with the broadening of the project management field, it can also mean a degree in marketing or one of the helping professions (health care, social work, education, law). Industry knowledge gained from work in a particular field, such as construction, information technology, or health care, is added to that baseline. Into this category also fall the technical aspects of project management: facility with project management software tools, for example.

Interpersonal and General Management Skills

But the bulk of the skills required—the skills upon which the role seems to succeed or fail—are those that are variously termed "Organization and People Competencies" (Assoc. for Project Management, U.K.), "Personal Competencies" (PMI), or "High Performance Work Practices" (*Academy of Management Journal,* 1995). PMI's list of project manager roles reads like a soft-skills wish list: Decision maker, coach, communication channel, encourager, facilitator, and behavior model.[2] This last item was explored in research by Dr. Frank Toney of the University of Phoenix. In his book *The Superior Project Manager,* he states that "honesty" trumps education, experience, and even intelligence as a desirable quality in project managers.[3]

Thus, the "new project management" is characterized by a more holistic view of the project that goes beyond planning and controls to encompass business issues, human resource issues, organizational strategy portfolios, and marketing. The new project management places its focus on leadership and communication rather than a narrow set of technical tools, and advocates the use of the project management office in order to change corporate culture in a more project-oriented direction.

As a result, the role of the project manager has expanded in both directions: becoming more business- and leadership-oriented on one hand, while growing in technical complexity on the other. This puts both project managers and the organizations they serve in a bind. The title "project manager" often falls to an individual who carries a "kitchen-sink" job description that ranges from strategic and business responsibilities to paperwork to writing code: the "monster job."

The solution to this problem is being worked out in many best-practice companies where the implementation of enterprise-level project management offices allows the development of specialized project roles and career paths. Best-practice companies define specific competencies for these roles, and provide "a fork in the road" that allows individuals who are gifted strongly either on the art side of the ledger—as program and project managers and mentors—to flourish, while allowing those whose skill lies in the science of project management to specialize in roles that provide efficiency in planning and controlling projects.

The Fork in the Road.

Because the project leader has been found to be one of the most (if not the single most) critical factors to project success, much effort has been devoted to understanding what project managers can/should do to enhance the chances of project success. Leadership, communication, and networking skills top the list. In spite of the importance of leadership characteristics for project managers, researchers and practitioners have observed that project managers in many organizations are seen by senior management as implementers only.[4]

Confusion of roles and responsibilities would be averted if these two very different roles—leader and implementer—were not both referred to as "project managers." Organizations can avoid this problem by determining beforehand who has the best mix of traits and skills to be a superior project manager, or the potential to become one, and by creating career paths for both technically-oriented project managers and leadership-oriented project managers so that senior management can fully appreciate the breadth of the roles necessary to the effective management of projects. Technical project managers tend to focus more on process while business project managers are more concerned with business results. Ideally, a balance between the two is required, determined by the project type, organization culture, and systems.[5]

And there are other roles that can be broken out of the "monster" job description, further streamlining the leadership work of the project manager. Many tasks that have long been part of the project management landscape feature elements of administrative work, for example.[6] In addition, project managers must be "grown" in the organization through a series of roles that develop the individual in positions of increasing responsibility: a career path.

IDENTIFYING AND ASSESSING COMPETENCY

One of the first things an organization must do is inventory the skills required for effective project management at all levels. After a skills inventory is developed, the key attributes of those skills must be determined and a profile developed. This is also the first step in developing competency requirements. Christopher Sauer, in his study of successful project-based organizations, points out that organizational capability is built from the ground up: by making it possible for the people who do projects to do their best.[7] Focusing on building project manager competencies to the "best" level means first identifying what needs to be improved. To do this requires a competency assessment program.

Dimensions of Individual Competence

Competence may be described in different ways, but there are four dimensions that seem to be universally acknowledged:

Knowledge

For project managers, the "body of knowledge" contains more than simply specific knowledge about how to plan and control projects—the knowledge outlined in the *PMBOK® Guide*. There's also knowledge in their chosen discipline (engineering, marketing, information systems, etc.); knowledge of other disciplines that come into play in the industry in which they work, such as regulatory law or technology advancements; and knowledge of the business side (finance, personnel, strategic planning). Knowledge in all these areas can be built up through reading, classroom training, research on the Internet, and the kind of informal knowledge transfer that takes place constantly in the workplace and in professional associations.

Skills

For a project manager, skills may fall into any of three areas: their area of subject matter expertise (engineering, marketing, information systems); project management skills related to planning and controlling; or human skills (influencing, negotiating, communicating, facilitating, mentoring, coaching). The technical skills become less and less important as the project manager's responsibility for the managerial skills grows; this is one reason why excellent technologists have often failed as project managers. As roles become more abstract—one of the hallmarks of knowledge work—the difficulty of defining the competencies necessary becomes complex. Skill at using a scheduling tool is easy to quantify; skill in strategic thinking, innovation, or teambuilding is much harder.

Personal Characteristics

On the intangible, but extremely important, side of the ledger, are things like energy and drive, enthusiasm, professional integrity, morale, determination, and commitment. In recent years, a number of project management writers have focused on these traits as being perhaps the most important for project managers, outweighing technical knowledge and skills. To focus on a few of these:

▶***Honesty.*** Project managers are role models for the entire project team. They must conduct themselves honestly and ethically in order to instill a sense of confidence, pride, loyalty, and trust throughout their project team. An honest and trustworthy project organization leads to greater efficiency, fewer risks, decreased costs, and improved profitability.

▶***Ambition.*** Ambition is an important factor in business goal achievement. Project managers must be careful that their ambition doesn't make them ruthless or selfish. They must use their determination to accomplish goals for the organization, as a whole, rather than for their own personal gain. However, achievement orientation, as defined in the ground-breaking work on motivation by David McClelland, comprises a focus on excellence, results orientation, innovation and initiative, and a bias toward action, and is very desirable in project managers.[8]

▶***Confidence.*** Leaders who are confident in their decisions are most likely to succeed. The most confident project managers believe that they have full control of their actions and decisions, versus the belief that outcomes are due to luck, fate, or chance. Superior project managers are confident in their decisions, proactive rather than reactive, and assume ownership for their actions and any consequences.

Experience

When knowledge can be applied to practice, and skills polished, experience is gained. Experience also increases knowledge and skill. Experience can be gained in the workplace, or as a result of volunteer activities.

The first step toward competency-based management is to understand the patterns that are repeated by the most effective employees in their knowledge, skills, and behaviors—in other words, competencies that enable them to be high performers. This "architecture" of effectiveness for a given position is a *competency model.*[9] A competency model comprises a list of differentiating competencies for a role or job family, the definition of each competency, and the descriptors or behavioral indicators describing how the competency is displayed by high performers. There are two types of competency models:

▶*Descriptive competency models* define the knowledge, skills, and behaviors known to differentiate high performance from average performance in the current environment or recent past. Descriptive models can have high validity because they are built from actual data about the difference between average and star performers.

▶*Prescriptive models* lean toward describing competencies that will be important in the future. They are helpful in dynamic environments or to help drive a major change in culture or capabilities.

The best competency models combine features from each category.

Models for Project Management

Within the last decade, research attention has been focused on identifying competencies for project managers. The seminal work in this field was done by the Australian Institute of Project Management (AIPM), whose National Competency Standard for Project

Management was adopted by the Australian Government as part of that country's national qualification system. In England, the Association for Project Management (APM) created competency standards for project controls specialists and project managers. The publication of US-based PMI's competency standard in 2002[10], after five years of developmental work, established another framework for thinking about the components of competence in a project management context. The existence of project manager competency models streamlines the adoption of competency-based management for project-oriented companies. Although all these assessment frameworks are quite different, they do have certain themes in common.

From our point of view, a project manager competency assessment should determine who has the best mix of traits and skills to be a superior project manager, or the potential to become one.

Once competencies are defined, it is time to conduct an assessment of the identified project management populations. The assessment process should be clearly focused on building strengths, not on eliminating staff; mitigating fear of assessments through open communication is critical.

Let's look at one model in detail: The Project Manager Competency Assessment Program (PMCAP) co-developed by PM College and Caliper International, a human resources assessment firm.[11]

Like other competency assessment systems, the PMCAP has three components: a multi-level knowledge test, a personality and cognitive assessment, and a multi-rater survey reviewing the current workplace performance of project managers. These three instruments address three aspects of competence: Knowledge of project management concepts, terminology, and theories; behavior and performance in the workplace; and personal traits indicative of the individual's project manager potential. Thus it is both descriptive and prescriptive.

▶***Knowledge.*** The Knowledge Assessment Tool tests the candidate's working knowledge of the language, concepts, and practices of the profession with questions based on the Project Management Institute's *PMBOK® Guide,* the ISO-approved industry standard.[12] On an individual basis, the candidate can see how they scored on each knowledge area, how they compared to the highest score, their percentile ranking, and how many areas they passed. For the organization, an aggregate table provides insight into the areas that need improvement for their entire population. This information is used to begin developing a targeted education and training program designed to meet those needs.

▶***Behavioral Assessment.*** A second area of assessment is in behaviors exhibited in the workplace. This requires the use of a multi-rater tool (sometimes called a 360-degree tool), which allows the acquisition of feedback on the project managers' behavior from a variety of sources—typically peers, subordinates, supervisors, and/or clients, but always someone who has first-hand knowledge of the candidate's behavior in the workplace. For example, it might examine the creation of a stakeholder communication plan, the development and distribution of a team charter, or the execution of a risk management plan. Individuals rate themselves on their competency in several key performance indicators. The independent assessors then rate the individuals on those same criteria. Ratings are compared. A multi-rater assessment provides holistic view of the individual's project manager behaviors and serves as a gauge for determining which behaviors demonstrate areas for potential growth.

▶***Potential.*** The potential to perform the project manager role is evaluated through a series of questions that test the ability to solve problems, handle stress, be flexible, negotiate, deal with corporate politics, manage personal time, and manage conflict. The candidate's score is compared to high performers (project managers who show the highest level of competency). The results of this assessment indicate an individual's potential to survive and thrive in the role of a project manager.

Project Manager Competencies

According to research conducted by PM College in conjunction with Caliper, 70% of the competencies of a project manager overlap with the competencies of a typical mid-level functional manager. These competencies can be summarized as:

▶***Leadership.*** This is usually characterized by a sense of ownership and sense of mission, a long-term perspective, assertiveness, and a managerial orientation. Leaders focus on developing people, creatively challenging the system, and inspiring others to act.

▶***Communication.*** This includes written and oral communication, as well as listening skills, and competent use of all available communication tools. Understanding communication differences, and not letting them become a barrier to project success, is key in order to clearly delegate responsibilities and instructions to the project team. Project managers also must serve as the liaison between the project team and executive team. Skilled project managers know when to speak, when to listen, and how to resolve issues and conflicts in a calm and professional manner. A related skill, *negotiation,* is a daily feature of the project manager's life. Among the issues that must be negotiated with clients, executives, contractors, functional managers and team members are scope, changes, contracts, assignments, resources, personnel issues, and conflict resolution.

▶***Problem Solving Skills.*** These include proactive information gathering/strategic inquiry (this goes hand in hand with the "bias for action"—project managers actively seek out information that might impact the project instead of waiting for it to surface, and apply that information in creative ways); systematic/systemic thinking—project managers must be able to both focus on the details of a problem and see it in the context of the larger organizational or business issues.

▶***Self-Assessment/Mastery.*** Best practices project managers are able to consider their actions in a variety of situations and critically evaluate their own performance. This introspective ability enables the great project managers to adjust for mistakes, adapt for differences in team personalities, and remold their approaches to maximize team output.[13]

▶***Influencing ability.*** This is the ability to influence others' decisions and opinions through reason and persuasion, the strategic and political awareness and the relationship development skills that are the basis for influence, and the ability to get things done in an organizational context.[14]

Gap analysis is the next step after assessment of competency. The knowledge gaps are determined by examining the differences between the demonstrated level of knowledge and the level of knowledge that is required. The behavioral gaps are identified by examining the differences between the self-rating of the project manager candidate and the rater's score. The gaps in both knowledge and behavior, based on the size of the gap, are targeted as developmental opportunities. The results of this integrated assessment are used to create professional development plans for project manager candidates.

While an individual assessment is being conducted, the organization should be determining what roles they will need to ensure an improved level of project performance. Possible roles include team leaders, multiple levels of project managers, program managers, project portfolio managers, project executives, project office directors, and chief project officers. With each of these roles, the organization will need to create effective job/role descriptions that define performance/competency expectations, experiential requirements, and prerequisites of whatever technical skills are required.[15,16,17]

As project managers expand into new industries, additional areas of competency will emerge. The project manager's role is evolving away from technical, tool-based project management (especially in knowledge-based organizations such as R&D), and towards a broader "art" of leadership. But that doesn't mean the science can be left behind. Equally as important are the competencies that many companies are successfully sorting into a new "starring role": the Project Planner.

The Emergence of the Project Planner Role

A project planner supports the project manager by taking over critical, detail-oriented, time-intensive tasks, such as the ones discussed above. As a result, the project manager is free to focus on more strategic project goals and objectives. Earlier in this chapter, we discussed the core tasks of the *leader*. It's worthwhile noting that the core tasks of the *manager* have been identified as:

- Planning the work
- Organizing the work
- Implementing the plan
- Controlling results.

These tasks align with the role of planner. Together, the project manager and planner/controller resolve the leader/manager dilemma by supplying both aspects of these roles in collaboration.

What Makes a Good Project Planner?

In order to efficiently handle the responsibilities outlined above, the successful project controller/planner must possess technical expertise in project management software and related spreadsheet and/or database (financial, resource) tools, as well as business process expertise in cost budgeting and estimating, risk analysis, critical path diagramming and analysis, resource forecasting, and change control. In contrast to the project manager candidate, the ideal project planner has the following personal and professional characteristics:

- Logical thinker and problem solver
- Organized and detail-focused
- Numbers-oriented
- Able to interpret complicated and interconnected data

▶Communication skills, especially as they apply to project information

▶PM software expertise

▶Application software expertise (accounting, procurement, etc.).

Just as with project managers of varying experience and skill, you'll find a hierarchy in the project planning and controls arena. A serious project controls person will have a breadth of experience that encompasses many of what we have termed "specialty areas," like change (configuration) control, risk management (from the perspective of quantifying risks with the tools), issues management, action item tracking, multi-project reporting, executive reporting, scheduling integration, organizational resource management, multi-project resource analysis, forecasting, leveling, multi-project what-if analysis, management of the organizational (enterprise) resource library, schedule estimating, cost estimating, etc. And, just as with project managers, the organization will benefit from establishing a career path from the specialist team member level to a sophisticated divisional project controls position.

One insurance executive characterized the roles relationships in this way:

> "We like to think of the project manager as the CEO of the project, and the project planner as the CFO. Like the CEO and CFO, both the project manager and project planner carry out crucial duties, and both need to possess significant, albeit different, skill sets and experiences in order to bring the projects in on time, within budget, and at agreed quality levels."[18]

Project Team Members: Specialty Roles in Project Management

The team member position is where the actual day-to-day work of the project planning, estimating, statusing, and analysis is done. Within this level, more definitive project management roles—depending on the organization—can include: Project Controllers, Project Analysts, Schedulers, Business Analysts, Estimators, and Systems Analysts. In addition, there are some new, evolving specialty roles, such as:

▶***Knowledge Management Coordinator***. Sometimes formerly known as the "librarian," this role has grown to include the maintenance of project records, standards, methods, and lessons learned which must be stored in a project database/repository. In a large organization, the maintenance of such a repository can develop into a full-time job. Once envisioned as a clerical task, the SPO librarian is now evolving into a sophisticated knowledge-management function and will become a be a fruitful source of benefits and value to the entire organization for historical data, successful practices, and effective templates, with knowledge that was previously lost with changes in and transitions of personnel.

▶***Methodologist.*** Best practice or process experts, they provide training, project oversight, quality assurance, and methodology development.

▶***Resource Manager.*** In organizations with significant project activity, the responsibility for resource management may become a full-time job. One major insurance company titles this role the "Project Manager Role Steward." Individual project managers, rather than having to "beg, borrow, and steal" resources wherever they can find them, turn to the resource manager for assistance. The RM prioritizes resource requests, manages the "fit" of resource skills to project requirements, manages and balances scarce technical resources, forecasts and aids in planning for acquisition of resource shortfalls, and secures assignment of key resources to projects according to the project's relative rank on the organization's prioritized project list.

▶***Organizational Development Analyst.*** Another project human-resource management role that has been identified in some organizations, the ODA "floats" among projects identifying the human issues that often derail projects before they become a problem and working to resolve them. ODAs are a liaison between projects and the HR department.[19]

Table 19-1 outlines these positions and how one may be promoted to a higher division.

Competence-Building Activities

▶***Case Studies.*** One way to approximate the real-world application of professional skills is to create cases that highlight complex situations that demand skillful performance. Reading and studying such cases, the learner sees how to exercise judgment in applying any particular guideline or rule of thumb. As an organizational learning activity, project personnel can practice their problem-solving skills, either online or at lunch-hour learning sessions, by reviewing cases based on an actual organizational story or event.

▶***Mentoring and Coaching.*** Mentoring is a perfect match for project management development. For project managers, mentoring—whether we called it that or not—has always played an important role in professional development. As members of "the accidental profession," project managers more often than not learned how to manage projects by managing projects and by observing other project managers in action. And mentoring still remains "the most effective way to bring new project managers up to speed quickly."[20]

Frank Toney, Ph.D., of the Executive Initiative Institute, identifies mentoring as both a skill the project managers should master for success, and as one of the few reliable routes to competence in the project-based workplace. Lynn Crawford, of the University of Technology at Sydney (Australia), a leading project management thinker who was instrumental in developing Australia's government-mandated competency measurement system for project managers, recommends mentoring and other social learning modes (such as communities of practice), as important learning tools for project management.[21]

Just as artificial-intelligence researchers interview seasoned professionals to create an expert system, the best project managers can be interviewed to elicit how they have solved difficult problems in the past.[22,23]

Beyond mentoring, professional coaching combines self-focused personal value measurements, personality-type testing, and style-preference identification with feedback on personal and professional behaviors from a broad group of people. The professional coach is most likely educated in a behavioral field, such as psychology, and combines education and training with years of experience working with other clients to provide extremely valuable insight. Their counsel will help leverage strengths and eliminate behaviors that might derail success.[24]

▶***Personal Development Plans.*** Professional growth is also personal growth—a commitment to self-improvement. People who continuously seek feedback, work on their listening skills, polish communication skills, build relationships, and demonstrate control of their personal lives will rise above their peers. Yet many individuals passively accept (or grumble about) whatever growth programs are on offer by the organization.

Instead, individuals should be encouraged to construct a personal development plan. The essence of this plan is to know yourself and the environment, build a road map to

Position	Organizational Level
Leadership Track	
Chief Project Officer	Enterprise
Strategic Project Office Director	Enterprise
Project Office Director	Divisional/Departmental
Portfolio Manager	Enterprise
Manager of Enterprise Project Managers	Enterprise
Manager, Project Managers	Divisional/Departmental
Global Program Manager	Enterprise
Enterprise Program Manager II	Enterprise
Enterprise Program Manager I	Enterprise
Enterprise Project Manager II	Enterprise
Enterprise Project Manger I	Enterprise
Program/Project Mentor I, II	Enterprise or Divisional
Program Manager II	Divisional
Program Manager I	Divisional
Project Manager III	Divisional
Project Manager II	Divisional
Project Manager I	Divisional
Technical Track	
Chief Project Officer	Enterprise
Strategic Project Office Director	Enterprise
Project Office Director	Divisional
Manager of Enterprise Project Support	Enterprise
Manager, Project Support	Divisional/Departmental
Enterprise Project Controller	Enterprise
Project Controller I	Divisional
Project Planner II	Divisional
Project Planner I	Divisional/Departmental
Project Estimator II	Divisional
Project Estimator I	Divisional/Departmental
Project Scheduler II	Divisional
Project Scheduler I	Divisional/Departmental
Specialty Positions	
Systems Analyst	Any level
Knowledge Management Coordinator	Any level
Methodologist	Any level
Technical Advisor	Any level
Budget Analyst	Any level
Business Analyst	Any level
Issues Management Coordinator	Any level
Change Control Coordinator	Any level
Risk Management Coordinator	Any level
Organizational Development Specialist	Any level

TABLE 19-1. **PROGRAM/PROJECT MANAGER CAREER GROWTH POTENTIAL**

Project Controller:
A Project Controller brings knowledge of and experience with implementing and using project controls to the team. Professionals in this category are hands-on experts in using project management software to plan and schedule tasks, manage interdependencies, roll-up and/or integrate plans and schedules, report status, and produce suggestions on how to make control process improvements.
Project Team Leader:
A professional, the Project Team Leader has a proven track record in effectively applying the project management principles to project performance, attainment of the triple constraint and high team performance/motivation. The Project Team Leader has led medium project initiatives (generally 6 months in duration with up to 10 core team members.
Project Manager:
An experienced manager capable of successfully directing the planning, development and implementation of medium-large projects according to cost, schedule and scope requirements. The Project Manager participates in project initiation activities, including plan and budget preparation; leads the project management team in successfully executing the project as planned and budgeted throughout the project life cycle; and oversees the project closure activities including the collection of lessons learned.
Program Manager:
A recognized leader and manager well versed in the principles of project management, strategic and tactical planning, coordinating and integrating multiple large and complex projects into a comprehensive program. The Program Manager is capable of working with the client in defining their business drivers and defining how the program and project objectives meet the benefit triggers for business success.
Senior Project Manager:
A recognized leader and manager capable of successfully directing the planning, development and implementation of large and complex projects according to cost, schedule and scope requirements. The Senior Project Manager participates in all phases of the project (from concept to closure) and often has worked in a global environment or setting.
Mentor:
A project management professional with extensive project and program experience capable of working with project managers and project teams to help them put the processes, skills and support structure in place to effectively establish and manage projects. Typically, mentors provide consulting services to program managers, project managers, program/project teams and corporate managers. The Project Management Mentor is well versed in leading and managing program/project team members from diverse backgrounds, and within global and virtual settings. In program/project crisis the mentor can be called in to fill-in for an extended period of time for the senior project manager or program manager.

TABLE 19-2. **EXAMPLE CAREER PATH FOR A PROJECT MANAGER**

adapt and grow, and take personal ownership for change. Constructing a personal development plan requires openness to feedback, maturity to change behaviors, and willingness to practice new techniques.

Personal growth comes through self-evaluation and appraisal against personal standards, role models, group norms, peer behavior, and corporate or team culture. Input to the plan comes from both personal evaluation and relational sources, including supervisors, peers, clients, mentors, and friends. Reading is another critical resource for gaining new insights. Experiential education—conferences, seminars, and the like—is another important source for personal growth.[25]

Level I	Level II	Level III
Project Coordinator A professional educated and trained in project management principles and knowledge areas (scope, schedule, cost, quality, risk, human resources, communications, and procurement). Project Coordinators have particular knowledge in the area's triple constraint: schedule, budget and scope/quality development, and monitoring. Project Coordinators are also involved with reviewing project deliverables and technical documentation.	**Planner I** A professional educated and trained in project management principles and knowledge areas (scope, schedule, cost, quality, risk, human resources, communications, and procurement). Project Planner I has a strong knowledge base in defining and tracking the project's triple constraint: schedule, budget and scope/quality development, and monitoring. Project Planner I has often led small project initiatives (generally less than a month in duration with 1-2 people). Project Planner I has often become involved with creating and reviewing project deliverables and technical documentation, and is capable of leading facilitation sessions for group reviews and project charter definitions.	**Planner II** A professional educated and trained in the project management principles and knowledge areas (scope, schedule, cost, quality, risk, human resources, communications, and procurement). Project Planner II has a proven track record in effectively applying the project management principles both to the project's triple constraint: schedule, budget and scope/ quality development, and monitoring, and to managing risks, quality, communications, and resourcing. Project Planner II has led small-medium project initiatives (generally 1-3 months in duration with 3-6 people). Project Planner II often leads the creation of and facilitates the review of project deliverables and technical documentation.

TABLE 19-3. **PROJECT COORDINATOR AND PROJECT PLANNER ROLES AND RESPONSIBILITIES**

Organizational Issues

Often in our discussion of competence, we focus narrowly on the personal traits and abilities of individuals. But even capable individuals still cannot work miracles within dysfunctional teams and organizations. That's why culture change, not merely individual competence assessments, is required. "Organizational pathology," says David Frame, is behavior rooted in an organizational culture that works against the best interest of the organization and its members. Organizations that punish the bearers of bad news are an example. Organizations that insist on applying outworn solutions to new problems similarly stifle personal competence in their members. The result? A "a profoundly unhappy workforce."[26]

To develop the organization's project management capability, says Christopher Sauer, it is desirable both to institutionalize the development of individual capabilities and to create learning that extends beyond the individual project manager's skills and experience. He recommends the project office, as "a focal point in the organization," where an environment conducive to the development and practice of project management capabilities can flourish.[27]

PROJECT MANAGEMENT CAREER PATHS

One thing that companies can do to support competence is to nurture the people who are

In excellent mentoring, questions that the project manager might ask of the mentor include:	Is there a better way to ______________________ ? What should I watch out for if I ______________________ ? Is this a good way to ______________________ ? How do others ______________________ ?
Excellent mentors often reply with explanatory answers or with questions that help the project manager see the situation more clearly, such as:	Have you considered ______________________ ? Do you know how to ______________________ ? What are your choices ______________________ ? What do you think will happen if you ______________________ ? What have you done in the past ______________________ ?

Adapted from Diana Mekelburg, Excellent PM Mentoring, *People on Projects, June 2001. Used by permission of the publisher.*

TABLE 19-4. **EXCELLENT MENTORING QUESTIONS**

responsible—to ensure that project managers have a clear and desirable career path that includes training, promotion criteria, recognition of achievement, and the opportunity to progress to the highest possible levels in the organization.[28] Developing a career structure is essential to the development of an organization's project management capability. The career path structure serves three purposes:

1. It allows the organization to match a project manager's level of competence/experience to the difficulty and importance of a project.

2. It assures project managers that the investments they make in developing their professional skills will be rewarded.

3. It provides an incentive for people to stay with the company, because they can see a clear promotion path.[29]

Tables 19-2, 19-3, and 19-4 show examples of career path structures for project management, on both the leadership ("art") and technical sides ("science").

The objectives of any career development program should be to improve skills, assess an employee's readiness for advancement, define professional skill areas, create an equitable salary structure, create a positive and open environment for career discussion, ensure frequent feedback, and encourage a "change to grow" environment.

A career path includes at least three elements in order to be valuable: experiential requirements, education/training requirements (knowledge acquisition), and documentation and tracking mechanisms.

▶*The experiential requirements* detail the types of on-the-job activities that have to be accomplished for each level in the career path. Experiential opportunities need to be coordinated with the appropriate resource manager and the human resource department in the organization. A broad range of experiences are required for future project managers. It is not possible to develop them by restricting their experiences to one function. Thus, rather than climbing the ladder up the functional silo, project managers benefit from being exposed to a number of functions, perhaps moving back to functions they have fulfilled before, but in a more senior role. One writer has labeled this "the spiral staircase" career path.[30]

▶*The education and training requirements* detail the types of knowledge that are required for each rung on the career ladder. At the lower levels, these tend to be basic courses designed to provide exposure and practice to the rudimentary skills required of that level. The upper level positions require more advanced strategic or tactical types of educational experiences. These may include topics that go beyond the realm of project management into business strategy, financial, or leadership opportunities. The educational program should be targeted to the requirements identified in the career path, and be designed in a progressive nature. In other words, the training requirements of team members are prerequisites for project managers and so on.[31]

▶*Documentation mechanisms* include the attainment of certificates, degrees, or other credentials that substantiate the acquisition of the desired set of skills.

The first important criterion for project manager success is the desire to be a manager in general and a project manager in particular. Many organizations force people into the position even if they are not adept at it and do not desire to become one. The step from technical specialist to project manager may be the assumed progression when there is no way to move up a technical ladder. It is better, however, if alternative upward paths exist—one through technical managership and one through project leadership. With such dual promotional ladders, technical managers can stay in their departments and become core team members responsible for the technical portions of projects. Dual ladders also allow progression through project management, but project managers must be able to motivate technical specialists to do their best work.[32]

DISCUSSION QUESTIONS

❶ Based on the discussion of leadership and technical expertise roles in project management in this chapter, map for yourself an ideal career progression. Where do you see the gaps? What strategies can you take to move forward?

❷ How does project manager competency assessment relate to organizational project management capability? In your present project or organization, can you think of ways that assessing competency would be of immediate value?

❸ What are some reasons why people might not want to be assessed for competency? How can project organizations overcome those objections?

REFERENCES

[1] The Standish Group, CHAOS Report, 1999; see also www.standishgroup.com and Johnson, James, Chaos: The dollar drain of IT project failures. *Application Development Trends*, January, 1995. Also, Gartner, Inc. reports that poor project manager competency accounts for 60% of project failures: see [1] M. Light, T. Berg, "The Project Office: Teams, Processes and Tools," *Gartner Strategic Analysis Report*, August 2000, Jeannette Cabanis-Brewin, Interview with Dr. Frank Toney, *Project Management Best Practices Report*, Aug. 2002; and the Robbins-Gioia study on project failure, 1999, posted at www.pmboulevard.com (accessed Sept. 1, 2004).

[2] Jim Pennypacker and Jeannette Cabanis-Brewin, eds. *What Makes A Good Project Manager?* Center for Business Practices, 2003.

[3] Frank Toney. The Superior Project Manager, Center for Business Practices, 2001.

[4] Frame, J.D. *The new project management: Corporate reengineering and other business realities*. San Francisco: Jossey Bass, 1994.

[5] Dennis Comninos and Anton Verwey, Business focused project management, *Management Services*, Jan. 2002; see also R. Graham and R. Englund R., *Creating an Environment for Successful Projects*, Jossey-Bass 1997; and J. Nicholas, *Managing Business & Engineering Projects—Concepts and Implementation*, Prentice Hall, 1990.

[6] Tom Mochal, Is project management all administration? *TechRepublic.com*, posted 29 Nov. 2002. Accessed May 2004.

[7] Christopher Sauer, LI Liu, Kim Johnston, Where project managers are kings, *Project Management Journal*, December, 2001.

[8] David McClelland, *The achieving society,* Van Nostrand-Reinholdt, 1961.

[9] Howard Risher, *Aligning Pay and Results*, Amacom, 1999.

[10] *Project Manager Competency Development Framework,* PMI, 2002.

[11] PM College can be accessed at www.pmcollege.com; Caliper at www.caliperonline.com.

[12] The adoption of any new knowledge areas will be reflected in updates to the testing instruments.

[13] Personal mastery is a concept discussed at length in the works of Stephen Covey, Peter SEnge, and especially Daniel Goleman, Emotional Intelligence, Bantam Books, 1995.

[14] Jimmie West, Building Project Manager Competency, white paper, accessed at http://www.pmsolutions.com/articles/pm_competency.htm, January 15, 2005.10.

[15] Jimmie West and Deborah Bigelow, Competency Assessment Programs, *Chief Learning Officer*, May 2003.

[16] Building Project Manager Competency, White Paper, PM College, June 2004. Accessible at http://www.pmsolutions.com/articles/pm_skills.htm.

[17] J. Kent Crawford, with Jeannette Cabanis-Brewin. *Optimizing Human Capital with a Strategic Project Office.* Aurbach, 2005.

[18] Jeanne Childers, personal interview, August 2003.

[19] Agarwal, Ritu; Ferratt, Thomas W. Enduring practices for managing IT professionals. Communications of the ACM September 1, 2002.

[20] *Jeannette Cabanis-Brewin,* Mentoring: A Core Competency for Project Managers, *People On Projects,* June 2001.

[21] Frank Toney, Ph.D., *The Superior Project Manager,* CBP/Marcel Dekker, 2001.

[22] Larry Hirschhorn, Manage polarities before they manage you, *Research Technology Management,* Sept. / Oct. 2001.

[23] Barry Johnson, Polarity Management: *Identifying and Managing Unsolvable Problems*, HRD Press, Inc., 1992.

[24] Mark Morgan, Career-building strategies: Are your skills helping you the corporate ladder? *Strategic Finance*, June 1, 2002.

[25] Mark Morgan, ibid.

[26] J. Davidson Frame, *Building Project Management Competence*, Jossey-Bass, 1999.

[27] L.P Willcocks, D.E Feeny, & G. Islei (Eds.), *Managing IT as a strategic resource*. McGraw-Hill, 1999; and Christopher Sauer et al, ibid.

[28] Jolyon Hallows, *Information Systems Project Management,* AMACOM, 1998.

[29] Christopher Sauer, LI Liu, Kim Johnston, Where project managers are kings, *Project Management Journal*, December, 2001.

[30] J. Rodney Turner, Anne Keegan, and Lynn Crawford, Learning by experience in the project-based organization, *Proceedings of PMI Research Conference,* PMI, 2000.

[31] Freeman and Gould, The Art of Project Management: A Competency Model For Project Managers, white paper accessed June 2004 at www.BUTrain.com.

[32] Robert J. Graham and Randall L. Englund, *Creating an Environment for Successful Projects*, Jossey-Bass, 1997.

SECTION THREE

ORGANIZATIONAL ISSUES IN PROJECT MANAGEMENT

SECTION THREE

Section Three: Introduction

ORGANIZATIONAL ISSUES IN PROJECT MANAGEMENT

Until the early 1990s, the organizational issues related to project management were largely centered on how a specific project should be organized: Should it be put into a task force mode or somehow be handled from a matrix management standpoint? The concern was based on single-project logic.

Because of the booming number of projects in organizations and the time pressure and cost squeeze associated with them, the organizational concern has moved towards managing multiple projects in a short time frame, with limited resources. This brings focus on more holistic issues in terms of organization. The concerns become of a larger nature than single projects, and thus involve topics such as the following:

▶ *Strategic project management* (using project management to implement strategies and using a strategic approach in each of the projects underway), about which Kam Jugdev offers a contrarian view that asks the reader to consider whether, in fact, project management truly is a strategic resource.

▶ *Enterprise project management* (how to manage all projects across an enterprise), here discussed from both a cultural and tools viewpoint by Chris Vandersluis.

▶ *Project portfolio management* (how to pick and manage the right projects), which is touched on in a number of the chapters in this section, but is described in detail by Gerald I. Kendall.

▶ *Measuring the capability and value of project management processes,* both within projects and across the enterprise, discussed by James S. Pennypacker.

▶ *The project management office* (how to support effectively the multiple projects underway, instill a project management culture, and support project personnel), described by J. Kent Crawford.

▶*Implementing organizational change*—keeping in mind that any project management improvement initiative is a change initiative—is described in a case study by Robert J. Graham.

▶*Multiple-project management,* discussed by Lowell Dye, PMP. Projects, programs, multiple projects, and portfolios—all have organizational or enterprise implications. Dye clarifies the differences and describes accepted multi-project practices.

CHAPTER 20

Project Management: A Strategic Asset?

▶KAM JUGDEV, PHD, PMP,
CENTER FOR INNOVATIVE MANAGEMENT,
ATHABASCA UNIVERSITY

WHAT IS STRATEGY?

"Winning isn't everything, it's the only thing."
—Vince Lombardi (1913-1970)

"Strategy is a quest for profit."[1] Developing and sustaining a competitive advantage is about winning in the marketplace and winning in the marketplace is about improved company performance as measured in financial terms.

In the ever more competitive marketplace, companies must deliver greater value to customers. The struggle to gain and sustain competitive advantage warrants that companies develop certain resource bundles that are fundamental to firm performance. More often than not, these assets are knowledge-based as opposed to physical assets, such as property and technology, or financial resources. The Resource-Based View examines competitive advantage in terms of a company's internal assets. Increasingly, companies are turning to project management as part of their business strategy and project management can be viewed as a bundle of unique knowledge-based assets. Successful projects contribute to business performance, and this can translate into improved chances of firm survival.

Project management has not been extensively studied using the strategy lens, and the dimensions of the meta-capability remain to be understood. This is an important topic because it will help us understand the facets of project management that contribute to a competitive advantage so that companies can invest in the appropriate practices and develop those internal assets relevant to positioning project management strategically.

Background Information: A Look Back at Strategy

Greiner, Bhambri, and Cummings identified seven periods in the history of strategic management.[2]

1. *1940s: Budget extrapolation and financial goals.* In this decade, strategic plans consisted of financial forecasts.

2. *1950s: Long-range planning and formal models.* Detailed, top-down formal strategic plans addressed business strategy.

3. *1960s: Business idea and corporate identity.* The concept of a strengths, weaknesses, opportunities, and threats (SWOT) analysis and corporate identity took center stage as companies pondered what business they should be in.

4. *1970s: Competitive advantage analytics.* Analytic matrices such as scenario planning, experience curves, and growth share matrices emerged as companies focused on strategic management tools and techniques.

5. *1980s: Strategy implementation, capability, and alignment.* Disillusionment with earlier strategic planning practices set in as studies showed that industry factors were not able to fully account for inter-firm profit differentials. Companies turned to the Resource Based View of the firm and examined strategy in the context of the firm's internal assets.

6. *1990s: Strategic leadership and reengineering.* In this era, strategic management was embodied in the Chief Executive Officer as the heroic leader.

7. *2000: Continuous strategic renewal.* Strategic management is about human capital, knowledge management, and organizational learning.

Mintzberg's 1998 book *Strategy Safari: A Guided Tour Through the Wilds of Strategic Management* is an interesting read on the various schools of thought on strategy over the years.[3] In his book, Mintzberg describes these schools of thought about strategy:

▶Design school—strategy is a process of conception.

▶Planning school—strategy formation is a formal process.

▶Positioning school—strategy formation is an analytical process.

▶Entrepreneurial school—strategy formation is a visionary process.

▶Cognitive school—strategy formation is a mental process.

▶Learning school—strategy formation is an emergent process.

▶Power school—strategy formation is a process of negotiation.

▶Cultural school—strategy formation is a collective process.

▶Environmental school—strategy formation is a reactive process.

▶Configurational school—strategy formation is a process of transformation.

Strategy is not just one of the above schools but a blend of them. Greiner, Bhambri, and Cummings offer a good synopsis of strategic management:

- ▶Strategic management is comprehensive and integrative.
- ▶All major business disciplines are relevant to strategy.
- ▶Strategic thinking and behavior are very dynamic.
- ▶Strategy is a constant search for a competitive edge with high returns.
- ▶Every firm is indeed unique in its strategic capabilities.
- ▶The firm's strategy and organizational context must align and reinforce each other.
- ▶Strategic management requires spontaneous thinking and doing.
- ▶Strategic change will happen frequently.

Mintzberg introduced us to the five Ps of strategy whereby strategy is a plan, pattern, position, perspective, and ploy. Whereas Mintzberg favors the concept of "crafting" strategy as an art, others, such as Grant, support a more systematic and analytic approach whereby strategy helps companies make decisions; it is a process for coordination and communication, and it involves a target (vision).[4]

It is clear that strategy is a dynamic and multi-faceted concept. Strategy is not about clear-cut answers. Strategy is more about *understanding* what is happening in the internal and external environment to better grasp the issues and complexities that impact a company. These different perspectives on strategy will help readers refine their understanding of business strategy—the topic of *how* companies compete.

BASIC PREMISE: COMPETITIVE CONVERGENCE AND COMPETITIVE ADVANTAGE

Both formally and informally, companies conduct internal assessments (strengths and weaknesses) and environmental assessments (opportunities and threats) to plan their market positions and strategies. Firms are primarily interested in improving financial returns and shareholder value to avoid situations of competitive convergence or parity (where no one firm has a distinct advantage). Competitive convergence takes place when companies try to do similar activities as their rivals with some variations in practice. Common strategies include operational effectiveness practices, such as quality improvement, empowerment, and outsourcing practices. These practices are a basic requirement of firm survival, but they do not lead to a sustained competitive advantage, though, because after a while, firms look alike and do the same things, and this leads to diminishing returns. In contrast, having a competitive advantage refers to doing different activities from rivals or similar activities differently. A competitive advantage connotes innovation, adaptation, and creativity.

Worldwide, firms are turning to project management as part of business practice. This is evident in the exponential increase of membership in project management associations, such as the Project Management Institute, as well as in the billions of dollars being invested in projects. Prior chapters of this book have examined project management in the context of the *PMBOK® Guide* knowledge areas. Although tangible resources enable a company to execute its business processes, it is the intangible ones—such as project management expertise—that are more likely to be sources of competitive advantage.[5]

However, at present, the project management literature emphasizes tangible and codified practices. In the 1970s and 1980s, the literature focused on various tools and techniques (software, work breakdown structures, Program Evaluation and Review Techniques, design-to-cost, lifecycle costing, risk management, cost and schedule control, and control systems). A review of

3,565 North American project management publications (1987–2001) also confirms the emphasis on operations research, cost engineering, business process reengineering, and infrastructure studies. 19,000 books on project management were published within the 1960–1999 timeframe and focused on normative advice on planning and managing projects from a systems approach, leading to the view that project management is simply a tactical tool.[6]

Industry and Firm-Level Effects on Company Performance

A crucial question in the strategy literature asks, "Why do firms differ and how does it matter?"[7] Examining the external environment to help explain company performance is often called the Industry View in strategy. This approach helps firms look to the marketplace to determine the areas in which they want to compete. Discussions on the external environment entail the economic, social, political, and technological factors in the industry. The SWOT analysis and the five structural forces approach (consisting of threats of new entrants, bargaining power of suppliers, rivalry among existing competitors, bargaining power of buyers, and threats of substitute products or services) are useful techniques, but they are not strategy.[8] The Industry View provides a good description of market conditions and allows firms to identify some of the conditions for making a profit, but this approach does not provide complete information on how to make above normal profits.[9] The Industry View downplays sources of competitive advantage that stem from resource variations between companies.

According to the Resource-Based View, a competitive advantage is rooted in developing key resources that are *different*. In contrast to the Industry View that emphasizes the environment, the Resource-Based View explains firm existence based on internal assets that are valuable, rare, inimitable, and have an organizational focus (VRIO).[10] Resources that meet the VRIO criteria contribute to a firm's competitive advantage. As the Resource-Based View is a complex perspective, this chapter provides a preliminary introduction to the topic.

Most companies have many resources (both tangible and intangible), but few that are strategic in nature. Most strategic assets tend to be knowledge-based (i.e., intangible). Strategic assets involve a mix of explicit and tacit knowledge embedded in a company's unique internal skills, knowledge, and resources.[11] Such strengths are difficult to purchase, let alone copy, so they can contribute to a firm's ability to move beyond competitive convergence toward a competitive advantage. Examples of strategic assets include quality, reputation, brand recognition, patents, culture, technological capability, customer focus, and superior managerial skills.

The Resource-Based View is relevant to project management, because project management is a knowledge-based practice that emphasizes human and organizational assets based on explicit and tacit knowledge, skills, and know-how. In the context of project management, the term meta-resource seems more appropriate to use than strategic asset. The term *meta-resource* is appealing because it connotes the complexities of a set of resources that are an amalgam of tangible and intangible ones.

Research continues on both the individual and firm-level effects on company performance. Perhaps it is not a question of one approach being better at explaining company performance than the other as much as it is a question of the context in which industry and firm-level effects may predominate.[12]

VRIO FRAMEWORK

Next, we look at the four VRIO concepts in more detail and then discuss project management in this context.

Valuable?	Rare?	Difficult to Imitate?	Supported by Organization?	Competitive Implications	Performance
No	-	-		Competitive Disadvantage	Below Normal
Yes	No	-		Competitive Parity	Normal
Yes	Yes	No		Temporary Competitive Advantage	Above Normal
Yes	Yes	Yes		Sustained Competitive Advantage	Above Normal

Adapted from Barney, Jay B., *Gaining and Sustaining Competitive Advantage, Second Edition, 2002.*
Reprinted by permission of Pearson Education, Inc., Upper Saddle River, NJ.

TABLE 20-1. **THE VRIO FRAMEWORK**

▶***Valuable:*** "Do a firm's resources and capabilities enable the firm to respond to environmental threats or opportunities?"[13] Valuable resources contribute to a firm's efficiency and effectiveness. A resource has value when it exploits opportunities and neutralizes threats in the environment. In the Resource-Based View context, valuable resources are defined in economic terms—that is, they generate above-normal returns.

▶***Rare:*** "Is a resource currently controlled by only a small number of competing firms?"[14] Common or generic resources are not sources of competitive advantage. At best, they are a source of competitive convergence or parity. However, rare resources can offer temporary competitive advantages and are sources of strength.[15] Rareness, then, is necessary, but not the only resource characteristic for a competitive advantage.

▶***Inimitable:*** If resources can be easily copied, a firm stands to only achieve competitive parity through value and rareness. The question of inimitability that we should focus on is: "Do firms without a resource face a cost disadvantage in obtaining or developing it?" Inimitability means firms protect their resources so that competitors cannot easily copy them or find substitutes. For example, companies such as Southwest Airlines use extensive selection processes to hire individuals with spirit and spunk to serve and entertain customers.[16] These characteristics are rewarded and encouraged by the company and are not easy for competitors to duplicate.

▶***Organizational Focus:*** Finally, in terms of the fourth question, Barney suggests that we also examine the organization. "Are a firm's other policies and procedures organized to support the exploitation of its valuable, rare, and costly-to-imitate resources?"[17] Organizational focus refers to integrated and aligned managerial practices, routines, and processes. Organizational focus also connotes managerial leadership and decisions that support key assets and how they are developed and sustained.

Within the VRIO framework, if a resource is only valuable, it leads to competitive parity. Both value and rarity are required for a temporary competitive advantage; and value, rarity, and inimitability are required for a sustained competitive advantage. An organizational focus is necessary to both develop a competitive advantage and sustain it. The VRIO concepts are presented in Table 20-1.

Analysis: Project Management as Examined Through the VRIO Lens

Using the VRIO framework, let's examine key project management practices to assess whether they contribute to a competitive advantage. Investments in physical, technological, and financial assets are valuable to a company. Project management involves the use of methodologies, bodies of knowledge, project management offices, and project management maturity models. Some tools and techniques are specific to planning (work breakdown structures) and scheduling (network techniques such as critical path methods, Gantt charts, and Program Evaluation and Review Techniques). Still other tools and techniques are used to address project finances, project monitoring and control, project audits, project termination, and resource allocation. Throughout the project, technology (including hardware and software) is often used as part of the project infrastructure to help improve information and knowledge flow and assist in the decision-making process (e.g., project management information systems, knowledge management systems, and executive decision tools.) The array of physical tools and techniques are readily available on the market so they are not rare. These assets are also readily imitable so they do not meet the VRIO criteria in full, even though they may reflect elements of an organizational focus—i.e., companies appreciate the merits of tools and techniques and invest in them.

An investment in project management methodologies helps companies understand the steps to be followed to achieve project success throughout the project lifecycle. Methodologies also provide guidelines and checklists to ensure that the practices are being followed properly and that the right outcomes are achieved before moving to the next step. Companies develop their own project management methodologies and many are based on the project management bodies of knowledge. Numerous companies, such as project management consulting firms and information technology firms, that use project management practices advertise and sell their own methodologies and related support services to clients. If such methodologies are readily available and imitable, they do not meet the VRIO criteria and are not sources of a sustained competitive advantage.

Worldwide, there are a number of project management associations to support project management (Association for Project Management, Australian Institute of Project Management, Japan Project Management Forum, and Project Management Institute). These associations have developed bodies of knowledge to guide practitioners. The bodies of knowledge are valuable and provide explicit standards on practice in the knowledge areas of time, cost, scope, quality, human resources, risk, communications, procurement, and integration. The guides represent codified knowledge and emphasize the rationalistic view of project management tools and techniques. The bodies of knowledge are important, but not rare. In fact, they are readily imitable as evident by how similar the bodies of knowledge are between countries. An underlying assumption is that these bodies of knowledge are meaningfull regardless of industry or firm-level context.[18] However, knowledge is inseparable from context and involves a tacit and experiential dimension. As the bodies of knowledge do not meet the VRIO criteria, they are not sources of competitive advantage.

These days, more and more companies are establishing project management offices to coordinate the use of tools, techniques, and technology to support projects, ensure consistency of use, and provide training and guidance, particularly on troubled projects. Project management offices may provide the project management methodology to be used, specific project templates, conduct project audits, and even serve as a reporting mechanism.

Some claim that project management offices help reduce project costs, decrease time to market for new products, increase corporate profits, improve practitioner competences, improve quality, and ensure project success.[19] Project management offices reflect a coordinated and structured way of implementing tangible project management assets.

A key function of a project management office is to communicate information, and it could be argued that project management offices are conduits of knowledge. However, since project management offices are touted in the literature as offering tools and techniques, they are a vehicle for coordinating the use of tangible physical assets that helps improve project management processes. Further, efficient factor markets exist for project management offices. The tools, techniques, and practices can be readily purchased and are easily transferred between companies, particularly as people move from one organization to another. According to the Resource-Based View logic then, project management offices do not explain significant variation among companies.

In addition to project management offices, many companies have established program and portfolio management practices as well. Program management practices help companies group projects and manage them by department/division, whereas portfolio management is often described as managing diverse projects across departments/divisions. In some cases, program and portfolio management may also involve a more formal approval process whereby projects are stage-gated through the project lifecycles (e.g., projects are approved and funded, placed on hold, or cancelled). Unfortunately, program and portfolio management practices also do not meet the VRIO criteria. Program and portfolio management practices are valuable and reflect a stronger organizational focus than some of the earlier practices discussed in this section, but they are not unique. These practices are easy to copy and many companies document their program and portfolio practices as well as place them on intranets.

The emphasis on codified and tangible assets in project management is made clear with project management maturity models, which are promoted in the literature as sources of competitive advantage.[20] The project management maturity models are based on the Carnegie-Mellon Software Engineering Institute's Capability Maturity Model for software development.[21] The models consist of five linear stages reflecting software processes and practices that are increasingly more defined and repeatable. The models use a technical, rational, and mechanistic view of organizations because they do not address the social aspects of companies.[22]

Similarly, the project management maturity models address tangible assets but not intangible assets (knowledge assets). Maturity models have value because companies conduct maturity assessments, pay for the consultant fees, software licensing fees, provide staff training on the processes, and implement the processes. Some argue that firms with higher maturity scores perform better and achieve more savings that those with lower maturity scores.[23] However, at this writing, studies on the return on investment from the maturity models are incomplete.[24]

It does not take long for rivals to mimic documented practices or institute project management maturity procedures for staff to follow. Project management maturity models involve codified knowledge that makes them transferable between firms. Tacit knowledge is not expounded on in the maturity model literature. In fact, the ability to imitate them is a feature that vendors highlight when they state that their models were created from best practice databases. The models do not emphasize *organizational* processes and practices. The models typically lack a connection between operations management and strategy. Few project management models have been empirically tested and many are based on anecdotal material, case studies, or espoused best practices. A recent paper analyzed the project management maturity models to assess them against the VRIO framework and found that they did not meet the criteria.[25] In addition, as these models do not draw from the economic or strategy literature on competitive advantage, or meet the VRIO criteria, the arguments put forth towards winning in the marketplace with such models are weak at best.

As companies invest in project management, they primarily invest in components of project management as discussed above. When concrete practices are assessed with the VRIO framework, they do not meet all four criteria whereby the assets are valuable, rare, inimitable, and have an organizational focus. Sometimes, companies may even find themselves investing in processes such as project management that are *not* performing well. Poor performing processes may require increased investments but the quality of the product or service may not improve.[26] In addition, when companies invest in project management, they are not necessarily focusing on quality. An investment in tangible project management assets alone may not enhance the quality of another asset if it is not performing well. However, investments in physical and technological assets, such as methodologies, bodies of knowledge, and project management offices, can be beneficial and potentially lead to complementary assets, which means that they can enhance the development of other more complex assets.[27] These more complex assets could be viewed as intangible assets.

AREAS OF CHALLENGE: THE HIDDEN SOURCES OF COMPETITIVE ADVANTAGE IN PROJECT MANAGEMENT

Because projects are conducted in complex, dynamic environments and involve a strong knowledge-based component, they cannot continue to be assessed as sources of competitive advantage if they are only evaluated on the basis of concrete, codified practices. In order to assess project management's potential as a strategic resource, we should also examine the intangible dimensions of the discipline, such as knowledge-based assets, tacit knowledge, and social capital practices. This section provides a brief introduction to the concept of intangible assets in project management.

Deploying knowledge assets contributes to a firm's competitive advantage. Knowledge is about creating, acquiring, capturing, sharing, and using knowledge. The common thread between knowledge, data, and information is that they all involve a personal dimension. A useful way of looking at knowledge is with the iceberg analogy. The tip of the iceberg represents the explicit or visible body of knowledge, such as the knowledge developed and shared through the tangible project management practices discussed in this paper (e.g., project management office and methodologies). Explicit knowledge is more formal, codified, and transmitted systematically. Explicit knowledge is the "know-what" that can be documented. However, the larger component of the "iceberg" is ignored, submerged, and tacit.

Tacit knowledge is personal, experiential, context-specific, and rooted in action. Nonaka divides tacit knowledge into technical and cognitive dimensions.[28] The technical dimension covers informal personal skills and crafts and could be called "know-how." The cognitive dimension involves beliefs, ideals, values, and mental models. Tacit knowledge involves the ability to innovate, which can also be a source of competitive advantage.

Tacit knowledge has also been likened to the currency of the informal economy, yet little project management research has been done on this topic. Tacit knowledge is shared through socialization. Social capital is an intangible attribute of the relationships among members of a social unit.[29] Project teams share what they know through communities of practice. Communities of practice have social capital underpinnings and social capital is based on making connections with others, promoting durable networks, enabling trust, and fostering cooperation.[30] (See Chapter 29 for further discussion of COPs in project management.)

An extensive literature review did not indicate that project management had been studied using the Resource-Based View lens, and few publications discussed project management in terms of core competencies.[31] Further, few publications have addressed the social capital nature of project management. This is an emerging area of practice development for the discipline.

CONCLUSION

Can project management be a source of competitive advantage, and what is the strategic nature of the practice? Companies face many challenges in the 21st century. Some of these issues include the speed of technological change, international competition, and performance goals. Companies that turn to project management will place the discipline under increasing scrutiny to ensure that the investments are value-adding. These companies will also take with a grain of salt some of the publications that purport to offer "competitive advantages" through project management maturity models, program and portfolio management practices, software, hardware, etc., without providing a clear explanation of how these practices contribute to firm performance.

Project management practitioners should start thinking of project management as more than its tangible components. Companies need to view project management as a set of knowledge-based assets. The intangible elements are very important, albeit currently under-researched. Viewing project management as a source of competitive advantage or as a meta-resource is new to many in the field. However, companies that can begin to assess their project management assets using the frameworks from strategy may be better positioned to understand which aspects of project management they should focus on (e.g., tacit knowledge sharing practices, social capital, and knowledge-based assets.) Over time, we hope to achieve an improved appreciation of how tangible and intangible assets in project management are complementary.

DISCUSSION QUESTIONS

❶ To what extent do you support the view that project management is a source of competitive advantage (versus competitive convergence) for your organization?

❷ Based on your understanding of project management maturity models, present a case that these models meet the VRIO criteria and are a source of competitive advantage.

❸ Discuss the three main topics that you think need to be addressed in the field of project management for the discipline to be recognized as a source of strategic advantage.

REFERENCES

[1] Grant, Robert M. *Contemporary Strategy Analysis: Concepts, Techniques, Applications.* 4th ed. Malden, Massachusetts: Blackwell Publishers Inc., 2002, p. 63.

[2] Greiner, Larry E, Arvind Bhambri, and Thomas G Cummings. "Searching for a Strategy to Teach Strategy." *Academy of Management Learning and Education* 2, no. 4 (2003): 402–420.

[3] Mintzberg, Henry, Bruce Ahlstrand, and Joseph Lampel. Strategy Safari: *A Guided Tour through the Wilds of Strategic Management.* New York, New York: The Free Press, 1998.

[4] Grant, Robert *M. Contemporary Strategy Analysis: Concepts, Techniques, Applications.* 4th ed. Malden, Massachusetts: Blackwell Publishers Inc., 2002.

[5] See Brush, Candida G., Patricia G. Greene, Myra M. Hart, and Harold S. Haller. "From Initial Idea to Unique Advantage: The Entrepreneurial Challenge of Constructing a Resource Base." *The Academy of Management Executive* 15, no. 1 (2001): 64–78; also Ray, Gautam, Jay B Barney, and Waleed A. Muhanna. "Capabilities, Business Processes, and Competitive Advantage: Choosing the Dependent Variable in Empirical Tests of the Resource-Based View." *Strategic Management Journal* 25, no. 1 (2004): 23–37.

[6] Ulri, Bruno, and Didier Ulri. "Project Management in North America: Stability of the Concepts." *Project Management Journal* 31, no. 3 (2000): 33–43. See also Kloppenborg, Tim, and Warren Opfer. "The Current State of Project Management Research: Trends, Interpretations, and Predictions." *Project Management Journal* 33, no. 2 (2002): 5–18.

[7] Nelson, Richard R. "Why Do Firms Differ, and How Does It Matter?" In *Resources, Firms, and Strategies: A Reader in the Resource-Based Perspective,* edited by Nicolai Foss, 257–267. Oxford, United Kingdom: Oxford University Press, 1991, p. 257.

[8] Collis, David J., and Cynthia A. Montgomery. "Competing on Resources: Strategy in the 1990s." *Harvard Business Review* 73, no. 4 (1995): 118–128; see also Porter, M. E. "Towards a Dynamic Theory of Strategy." *Strategic Management Journal* 12, no. 5 (1991): 97–117.

[9] Chakraborty, Kishore. "Sustained Competitive Advantage: A Resource-Based Framework." *Advances in Competitiveness Research* 5, no. 1 (1997): 32–63.

[10] See Barney, Jay B. "Firm Resources and Sustained Competitive Advantage." *Journal of Management* 17, no. 1 (1991): 99–120; Barney (2002, and 1998), ibid, Chakraborty, ibid, Ray, et al., ibid, and Duncan, W. Jack, Peter M. Ginter, and Linda E. Swayne. "Competitive Advantage and Internal Organizational Assessment." *The Academy of Management Executive* 12, no. 3 (1998): 6–16.

[11] Foss, Nicolai J., ed. Resources, Firms, and Strategies: A Reader in the Resource-Based Perspective. Edited by Nicolai Foss, J., first edition, Vol. 1, Resources, Firms and Strategies: A Reader in the Resource-Based Perspective. Oxford, United Kingdom: Oxford University Press, 1997; see also Rumelt, Richard P., Dan E. Schendel, and David J. Teece. "Fundamental Issues in Strategy." In Fundamental Issues in Strategy, edited by R. P. Rumelt, D. E. Schendel and D. J. Teece, 9–47. Cambridge, Massachusetts: Harvard Business School Press, 1994.

[12] Readers interested in further information on these two views and the interrelationshipS are encouraged to read the Summer Special Issue of the *Strategic Management Journal* (1997).

[13] Barney, Jay B. *Gaining and Sustaining Competitive Advantage, Second Edition,* Upper Saddle River, New Jersey: Prentice-Hall, Inc., 2002, p. 160.

[14] Barney (2002), Ibid. 160.

[15] Mata, Francisco J., William L. Fuerst, and Jay B. Barney. "Information Technology and Sustained Competitive Advantage: A Resource-Based Analysis." *MIS Quarterly* 19, no. 4 (1995): 487–507.

[16] Barney (1998), ibid.

[17] Ibid. 160.

[18] Fernie, Scott, Stuart D. Green, Stephanie J. Weller, and Robert Newcombe. "Knowledge Sharing: Context, Confusion, and Controversy." *International Journal of Project Management* 21, no. 3 (2003): 177–187.

[19] Rad, Parviz F., and Ginger Levin. *The Advanced Project Management Office: A Comprehensive Look at Function and Implementation.* 1 ed. 1 vols. Vol. 1. Boca Raton, Florida: CRC Press, 2002.

[20] ESI-International. 2001. In ESI International, http://www.esi-intl.com/. (accessed Nov. 20, 2002). See also Hartman, Francis T., and Greg Skulmoski. "Project Management Maturity." *Project Management* 4, no. 1 (1998): 74–78; Ibbs, William C., and Young Hoon Kwak. "Assessing Project Management Maturity." *Project Management Journal* 31, no. 1 (2000): 32–43; MicroFrame. 2001. Project Management Maturity Model. In, Business Engine: Micro Frame Technologies & Project Management Technologies Inc., http://www.microframe.com/. (accessed November 20, 2002).

[21] Carnegie-Mellon. 2002. Carnegie Mellon Software Engineering Institute: Capability Maturity Models. In, Carnegie Mellon University, http://sei.cmu.edu/cmmi/. (accessed November 20, 2002).

[22] Ngwenyama, Ojelanki, and Peter Axel Nielsen. "Competing Values in Software Process Improvement: An Assumption Analysis of CMM from an Organizational Culture Perspective." *IEEE Transactions on Engineering Management* 50, no. 1 (2003): 100–112.

[23] Ibbs and Kwak, 2000, 1998, ibid.

[24] Ibbs and Kwak, 1998, ibid.

[25] Jugdev, K., and J. Thomas. "Project Management Maturity Models: The Silver Bullets of Competitive Advantage. Student Paper Award." *Project Management Journal* 33, no. 4 (2002): 4–14.

[26] Ray, et al., ibid.

[27] Amit and Schoemaker, ibid; Barney and Zajac, ibid; and Tripsas. "Surviving Radical Technological Change through Dynamic Capability: Evidence from the Typesetter Industry." *Industrial and Corporate Change 6,* no. 2 (1997): 341–377.

[28] Nonaka, Ikujiro, and Noboru Konno. "The Concept of "Ba": Building a Foundation for Knowledge Creation." *California Management Review* 40, no. 3 (1998): 40–54.

[29] Portes, Alejandro. "Social Capital: Its Origins and Applications in Modern Sociology." *Annual Reviews of Sociology* 24, no. 1 (1998): 1–24; Granovetter, Mark. "Economic Action and Social Structure: The Problem of Embeddedness." *American Journal of Sociology* 91, no. 3 (1985): 481–510.

[30] Prusak, Lawrence, and Don Cohen. "How to Invest in Social Capital." *Harvard Business Review: OnPoint,* no. Product number 9381 (2002): 86–9

[31] DeFillippi, Robert J., and Michael B. Arthur. "Paradox in Project-Based Enterprise: The Case of Film Making." *California Management Review* 40, no. 2 (1998): 125–139; Jugdev, Kam. "Developing and Sustaining Project Management as a Strategic Asset: A Multiple Case Study Using the Resource-Based View. Unpublished PhD Thesis." PhD Dissertation, University of Calgary, 2003.

CHAPTER 21

Enterprise Project Management: Elements and Deployment Issues

▶CHRIS VANDERSLUIS, HMS SOFTWARE

Enterprise project management (EPM) is the Holy Grail of project management: The idea that all project management information, reporting, and analysis will be part of an all-encompassing system where virtually every activity, every hour of time, and every dollar spent can be instantly identified.

It's not just senior management that is interested in the subject, although at first glance, they have the most to gain. The Project Management Office (PMO)—or in its absence, whatever level is available of professional project schedulers and project managers—is highly interested in getting access to all levels of data regarding project management. The antithesis of enterprise project management would be an ad-hoc process where everyone does his or her own thing. This is by far the most common scenario we find in organizations today. A PMO can't function without project data and if everyone is doing something different, data isn't easy to come by. For the PMO, getting to see the lowest level of project data is very attractive.

Individual team leaders are interested in seeing the inter-project impact of different project groups, and the ability to resolve resource conflicts between teams is one of the most significant impacts on project performance.

Even team members are interested in the concept. Team members in organizations that manage "by emergency" or continuously in a reactive mode, see tremendous potential benefits in EPM, hoping that an integrated process might bring order to chaos.

What is this phenomenon we refer to as EPM? Like most three-letter acronyms, EPM is bandied about like a complex mysterious topic, but its basis will be familiar to anyone in management. Enterprise project management is essentially the integration into a single system of project and resource data, processes, and analysis for projects in the organization.

For any organization that manages more than one project at a time or that has projects so large they must be broken down into component subprojects, the management of the following two significant elements is critical.

First is the interrelation between projects. If any project is dependent on the completion or delivery of elements from another, the impact of changes in one project can have dramatic effects on the second. For example, one project might be to install a new database on which new software deployments will depend. If the database project is delayed for any reason, all dependent projects will be delayed. Having a process that allows the downstream projects to see potential impact on their projects is a fundamental goal of EPM.

Second is the management of restricted resources. There is virtually no project management environment in the world where resources are standing around, waiting for work to arrive. More likely is that workloads far exceed the availability of key resources to accomplish them. The prioritization of that work and the resolution of conflicts over those resources is a prevalent management concern in organizations around the world.

THE PROJECT MANAGEMENT MATURITY MODEL

There is much talk about a Project Management Maturity model (PMM) that would match the work done in the IT industry of a Capability Maturity Model. While it's not the subject of this section, it's worth taking a moment to see how these two TLAs (Three Letter Acronyms) interrelate. There are several versions of a PMM model that are popular but their root is the same. The notion is that the lowest level of maturity would be one where project management is done on an ad-hoc or casual basis with each project manager managing things their own way. A middle level of maturity would see these processes integrated across the organization and a top level would see a process by which the integrated process itself is self-sustaining through a formal change management and improvement structure.

It's an interesting concept but it takes as its central premise that organizations are more mature if their project management is integrated and this is not necessarily the case. There is an argument to be made that for some organizations, the most effective enterprise standard for project management is to have no standard; to eschew the concepts of enterprise project management altogether and to let individual project managers use whatever systems they wish. It is a tradeoff to be sure but worth taking a moment to think about.

The potential benefits to management of EPM seem obvious but they come at a cost. A centralized structure will serve to implicate several levels of management in project decisions. This may give management better visibility but it will hamper the aggressive "high-flyer" project managers who have fought, connived and scrapped for the internal competitive advantage. Each organization should look at what level on the project management maturity model they should be striving for and there is a case to be made that the right level for your particular organization is any one of the levels displayed. PMM models are discussed in detail on the web in numerous sources, as well as in other chapters of this handbook.

ELEMENTS OF EPM

Let's look at the five basic elements of an EPM environment:

Storage of All Project Data in a Single Location

This is the first thing that must be done in any EPM deployment and, as the first element, is often highly contentious. Lest we confuse this section as having to do only with software, it is certainly possible to create an EPM environment that is completely computerless. In such an environment, the basic requirement of getting all data together is still fundamental. What is most common is that different project data will be stored in different places.

In today's modern organization, many managers equate control of data to power, and there are few managers who will willingly sacrifice what they consider power. Each aspect of project data will likely be jealously guarded by its incumbent owner. The budgets may, for example, be part of Finance. Individual teams of resources may be managed by department managers. Each project manager will have his or her own schedule data that he/she is used to controlling. For an enterprise system to be possible in any way, all project data must be stored in the same place and managed in the same way.

To bring data together, there is some work to be done. Let's start off with naming conventions. For example, if we talk about project resources, let's assume that one group refers to the CEO as "ME," short for Mike Edwards. Another group uses the letters "ME" to refer to the discipline of Mechanical Engineers. Yet another uses "ME" to mean Maintenance Engineers (i.e., Janitors). If we don't first come to some understanding of what coding we will use for resources, when the data is brought together, we will find Janitors, Mechanical Engineers, and the CEO will all be grouped together.

To bring this data together, standards will have to be agreed upon to avoid this type of conflict. The same thing has to be done for project names, task names, department names, and so on.

Now, we've invoked a scary word: "standards." This implies that someone will be the keeper and arbiter of those standards, and that almost certainly means that if you are committed to EPM, there will have to be some kind of central office to be responsible for elements of your EPM, such as naming conventions. Without some kind of PMO, there is little hope that naming conventions will ever be agreed upon, and if they are, they'll never be enforced.

Along with naming conventions, you'll also have to agree on the repository for the data. If you're implementing an EPM software package, then this part of the conversation is quite easy. The new system will have a set method of storing data, usually in a commercial database like Microsoft's SQL Server. Then all you'll have to organize is choosing the single location for that data to reside. Different groups may lobby for why their need for project management is so unique that it's absolutely impossible for them to comply with a single repository of "their" data somewhere else. These various interest groups will have to be dealt with one at a time. Your first mantra for deploying project management has to be "all project data, one location" until there is broad compliance.

Grouping Data by Different Criteria

The ability to group data by multiple criteria is an issue for reporting and analysis, so it is often spoken of last. However, the definition of the data structure makes all those reports and analysis possible, so it really needs to be dealt with first. If there is no coding of data at all, bundling all the project data together essentially will just give you one enormously long list of tasks with no method of subdivision. That's not too useful. Once you are past the mantra of "all data, one location," Project coding is your next challenge.

Coding comes in a variety of flavors, but the easiest way to think about it is grouping by project, by task, and by resource. Coding further should be thought of in two large categories: codes that apply to the entire project data structure to which everyone must comply, and codes that can be personalized project by project.

Some examples of coding might be:

▶A project-level code that identifies the client of this project. This would allow projects to be grouped and sorted by client. This is key for client billing purposes.

▶A resource-level code that identifies the department a particular resource belongs to. This would allow resources to be grouped by department as well as by project.

▶A task-level code that identifies the project phase. This might enable us to create a report of tasks in different categories, such as design, documentation, or deployment.

Coding can be a simple list of values, such as a list of possible locations for a project, or it can be a hierarchical tree of values such as would be used in a Work Breakdown Structure (WBS) or an organigram of resources often referred to as a Resource Breakdown Structure (RBS).[1]

If you are wondering how to decide what coding is appropriate to your organization, here's a simple method of analyzing 90% of all coding requirements:

First, put key personnel into a room with a large white board. At the far right of the board, start listing important decisions that will be made using the resulting analysis or reports from the EPM system. An example decision might be selecting priorities for each project. From each decision, work your way left from right. To the left of the decision, show the final report or reports that would be required in order to make that decision. An example might be a resource conflict report and a project priority report. Draw an arrow from the report(s) to the decision. Left of the report, show a box with the calculations or analysis that would have to be done by the system in order to create that report. An example of an analysis might be a resource leveling calculation of all projects. An arrow goes from the analysis or analyses to the report(s) that require it. To the left of the analysis you can now list the elements of data that the analysis requires. This list defines your key enterprise coding. Using this simple technique and involving a good representation (better yet, everyone) who makes decisions based on the EPM system, you will quickly determine which requirements are critical to the data being able to be grouped together in the manners you'll require.

Resolving Conflicts Such As Use of Resources

For many managers, most of their project-oriented time is spent trying to figure out how to resolve the conflicts inherent in insufficient resources. Not managing at all is not productive. That just makes every project a zero-priority and staff will end up working on whatever task is presented them next, or worse, on whatever interests them in that moment.

Resolving resource conflicts implies several things. First of all, you've got to be able to deal with both resource availability and resource requirements. Next you've got be able to compare them. It is the comparison of availability and requirements that display any potential conflict. This may all seem obvious, but remember that we're referring to *all* the resource availability and *all* the requirements. This means that all project loads, as well as all availability, must be defined in similar ways. Some of the issues you'll need to deal with here include deciding on the resolution of the data. In some organizations, one group will wish to manage resources at a category level (e.g., engineers) and another will wish to work at the individual level. There is no hard and fast rule that says which one is better, but you'll need to decide so that information is consistent across the system.

Next, you've got to make sure that project managers define resource requirements in a consistent manner. Some project managers may, for example, attempt to "pad" their requirements with additional work in order to lock their project team together for an extended period. Other project managers may not, and the result may be an unfair allocation of key resources.

There is a decision to be made as to how productive it is to remove a person from one project and put him or her on another project for a short period of time. His/her workload might show him/her available between tasks on one project, and it is therefore attractive to put on other work, but simple analysis usually doesn't allow for the impact of changing thought processes. To make this point, think about an analysis that would indicate that you would be most productive to the organization if you worked on a task in sixteen separate projects today, each lasting thirty minutes. For most project environments, we'd know this would be impossible. Just the time it takes to change gears from one project team to another and to get the momentum required to do anything productive with that team can often take a lot longer than thirty minutes. There are exceptions of course, but you'll have to decide what kind of resources and what kind of work can pull people from one project to another.

Finally, the notion of prioritizing projects must occur. This can often be a highly contentious issue at the most senior levels of management. Any manager who elects that his or her project carry anything but the highest priority knows that can mean loss of resource allocation. We'll talk about this more in a moment when discussing portfolio management. The idea of prioritizing projects should be part of an empirical analysis. The rules on what makes a project a high priority vs. a low priority are quite easy to get agreement on prior to deployment of your EPM system and just as hard to get afterwards.

Regardless of the system you create for resolving resource priorities, you'll need to set up some kind of referee to arbiter disagreements. This should be someone or a committee that doesn't have a vested interest in the result.

Portfolio Management

For some, portfolio management is all about being able to group projects together for analysis and reporting. For others, it is mostly about the approval of projects from the earliest concept to final completion, such as "stage-gating." Often the notion is combined with financial analysis or other management interests.

Key aspects in portfolio management include the ability to code projects so they can be grouped together for reporting or analysis. This is something you may have dealt with in your coding phase. The ability to organize the projects by priority from whatever perspectives are important to you is also key. Some examples include ranking projects by risk, by return on investment, by alignment to corporate strategy, by cost, by revenue, by manager, or by client.

One of the most interesting aspects of this kind of management is the ability to do forward-looking resource capacity planning. Given that all projects must now be stored in a central location, you may have for the first time the ability to see all resource loads simultaneously. This enables a "what-if?" analysis where the impact of a temporary addition of a proposed project can be assessed instantly. The old system where Marketing invents a delivery date based on a hoped-for schedule can be eliminated in favor of a promise based on actual capacity.

All that's required to deliver this is to create a high-level project plan for the proposed project and then slot it into the existing system with a priority assigned. The impact on all other work when using an EPM system can usually be determined in seconds. Coding must be used to allow proposed work to be distinguished from existing work so that the two aren't mixed up.

The Ability for Project Team Members to Interrelate

Collaboration. This single word has spawned a entire category of project management tools—"collaborative" project management. It's an interesting notion because collaboration is something that can only be *enabled* by technology, not *created* by it.

Enabling collaboration would seem to be a natural aspect of project management. A project manager never works in a vacuum. The fundamental purpose of a project manager requires them to communicate with team members, sponsors, clients, and so on.

Collaboration can play a key role in an EPM deployment. Fundamentally, any function of the EPM system can be considered a collaboration function. These usually include things like instant chatting with team members, the ability to notify team members of events in the EPM system through their regular email, instant messaging, or mobile device. It may also include the ability to create elements such as mini-web sites, online surveys, or online update forms.

This kind of functionality isn't trivial. In the past ten years, the entire project management industry has focused more on having project team members communicate and work together than it has on the algorithmic nature of project scheduling. As interesting as it might be to create the ultimate theoretical schedule, actually managing a project has everything to do with communicating and only a little to do with calculations.

One of the pitfalls in looking at EPM systems, arises in this collaborative area. There is a tendency for some managers to believe that if they purchase and then deploy an EPM system with collaborative functionality, project team members will automatically collaborate. This is not always the case. If this is one of your goals in deploying EPM, it's worthwhile to ask why personnel don't collaborate already.

Here are some questions that you can ask as a litmus test to see if you've got more work to do on the cultural side of deployment than the technical side in order to enable a collaborative environment:

▶If project managers share their true data with the organization, will managers punish them with their own data the next day?

▶Does it concern you that if you share your data with other project managers, they may use it to take unfair advantage?

▶If staff members enter an entire week of work on a single integrated timesheet, will they be concerned that the data will be used to unfairly evaluate them?

If project team members aren't collaborating now, the reasons are almost always culturally oriented rather than technical. You'll need to do some work to evangelize the benefits of collaborating and even make changes in procedure to ensure you remove roadblocks to participation by team members.

EPM SYSTEMS

Given the interest in bringing project data all together, computer systems are ideally suited to showcase this kind of process, and numerous vendors are keen to show what they can do for you.

There's no way in a few pages to show everything there is available on the market, and even if we did, these systems are being updated constantly, with new functionality being released on what sometimes seems to be a daily basis. The trend in the EPM systems industry is in itself interesting. In the late 1970s and early 1980s we saw the first multi-project systems available as commercial packages. Their orientation was very algorithmic; focused on the calculation of the schedule and the calculation of resource requirements. More recently, there has been a major trend away from the algorithmic perspective and towards a more collaborative approach. This makes sense. While the theoretical best schedule is useful information, most project managers spend most of their time working on human issues and on dynamic decision making to resolve issues that arise on the fly.

That said, what functionality should you be looking for in an EPM system? Here are some fundamentals:

Single Repository

The system should provide for storing data from all projects in a single repository. For very large-scale deployments, you'll need to look at functionality for amalgamating data from several large repositories into a single repository for reporting and analysis. Depending on your organization you may have to consider multi-national access, access from slow communications connections, and other communications issues.

Portfolio Management

The system should have an ability to manage at a project level, allowing projects to be added or removed at will and to be grouped by multiple types of coding. A flexible coding structure should allow you to code the projects for use in a stage-gating approval system. Also key is the ability to prioritize projects for resource management purposes.

Multi-User Access

If multiple users can't access data at the same time to view current project data and do project updates, you haven't got an enterprise system. The system has to be user-friendly enough that non-professional users can access it with little training. End users can't have their life become about servicing the EPM system. The system should be there to enable them to do their core work more effectively.

Enterprise Coding

What you're looking for here is first of all a high degree of flexibility. No two organizations are the same and therefore no one can predict how you will need to group and analyze your project data. Ensure that the system you are looking at will be able to adapt to whatever coding you envision now and will have the capacity to extend to the grouping and coding you haven't even imagined yet. Also, critical in this area is the ability to impose some coding as mandatory. Can the system ensure compliance with some critical code elements you have created? This is important when you are linking the EPM system to other corporate systems. For example, in a link with finance systems, you must ensure that work is only coded to accounts which exist and that 100% of the work is coded. Can the system impose this on all tasks?

Collaboration

Look for the simplest elements of collaboration. Does the system enable project management personnel to interrelate? Look for automatic notifications that can be integrated into your standard email or instant messaging systems. The ability to create communications areas such as project websites that are dynamically integrated with the project data can be of great benefit.

Workflow

In larger organizations, the ability to define a sequence of events that must occur in a particular order can be of great interest. Workflow need not be a complicated affair. Can you list a series of steps and then identify when a step has been completed? This type of functionality is important when looking at phased project approvals or when considering any kind of change management, such as a change in project scope.

When looking at project software, the overwhelming number of products that purport to serve EPM requirements can be daunting. Start your analysis by looking around organizations you know already. Most project management associations will sponsor events where multiple software vendors can show their wares. Ask to speak to or even visit existing deployments where you can ask not only what has gone well but also what the most challenging aspects of the deployment were.

A simple search of the Internet will reveal numerous vendors, but don't be fooled by claims or even independent analysis of who is "best." There's really no such thing. Given that each organization will have a different environment, be at a different maturity level, and have different requirements, it is perhaps more appropriate to ask what the most appropriate tool for your particular situation would be.

Don't be too enthralled or concerned over functionality you haven't listed in your list of requirements. Virtually every system will include functionality you can't take advantage of right away. Focus on your key challenges.

One of the best things you can do when evaluating EPM software is to organize yourself as a "solution buyer." There is much talk among software sales organizations to be solutions sellers but solution buyers are more rare. If these systems are the solution, then you should put some time into thinking about what problem they are to solve. Some organizations get caught up too quickly making a list of functions to be responded to. This list usually comes from a pre-supposed list of requirements amassed from existing systems. It's the worst way to look for a new system. Start instead with the business challenges you wish to accomplish, then ask the vendors to respond with how they will enable you to overcome those particular challenges. The response you'll get will not only show you instantly which vendor understands your problem vs. those who do not but will also free up the vendor to respond in a much more imaginative way and to showcase their particular product more completely.

If you've deployed an enterprise resource planning (ERP) system, you are likely to find EPM components either included or available as modules. The orientation of these systems will virtually always be more financial so there is a note of caution to take here. The standard sales mode of an ERP vendor is to focus on the integrated nature of the data and on the dangers of allowing disparate data systems to be supported. However, each management perspective will color how the system should be portrayed. If you have elected to deploy an ERP solution as your EPM product, then make sure it will serve the needs at each level of your organization, not just for finance.

DEPLOYING YOUR EPM SYSTEM

Deployment is where all of this conversation becomes real. There are many challenges in an EPM deployment, but you can avoid most of them by focusing on a few key factors.

By far, the most critical success factor is an appreciation by management of the nature of an EPM deployment. Too often senior management will devolve an EPM deployment to be a technical project and it is mostly not. Thinking of deploying EPM as a change management project is the number one factor for success.

As with all change management projects, the next key element is ensuring you have sufficient management support for the duration of the project. This *has* to come from a senior-enough level to ensure compliance. There may be great interest in EPM from one level or another of the organization, but if it is not shared by an executive who can speak for everyone who would be affected, then the deployment isn't going very far. Whichever executive is sponsoring the project has to commit for the duration. That's longer than the installation of the EPM software. A typical deployment of EPM can take anywhere from several months to a couple of years from the initial concept to final deployment.

If you've overcome these challenges, the most significant decision you have left to make is whether to deploy in a "big bang" where everyone would stop managing in an ad-hoc manner on one day and start managing in an integrated fashion the next, or in a "phased-approach" where the concepts and technology would be rolled out to the organization over a period of time. Start your deployment with a small group who are committed to the success of the deployment. Plan to have these people become part of a core group of users who will assist the deployment effort. They will be able to work on evangelizing the deployment, on training, and on fine-tuning your project management processes.

If you are committed to deploying EPM, follow this advice: Treat your EPM deployment as a project with all the controls and structure you would use with any change management project, and your chances of success increase dramatically.

DISCUSSION QUESTIONS

❶ While there is general expectation that scoring higher on a Project Management Maturity model is better than scoring lower, a case could be made that a particular organization might be most effective at a particular level. Assuming a 5-level model where level 1 is Ad-hoc project management, level 2 is project tracking, level 3 is integrated project management, level 4 is consistent methodology, and level 5 is self-improving process, what might be the most effective level for your organization?

❷ Portfolio management is a top-down approach to looking at groups of projects at one time. Budgeting is often done at the top level and then drilled down to the project level. Integrated project management is a bottom-up approach to looking at multiple projects at once. Both of these aspects are part of enterprise project management. How might you reconcile the two perspectives into one working process?

❸ Once a project is underway, the majority of a project manager's time turns from the analytic viewpoint to the business of managing people. While most modern project tools now include collaborative functionality, many project organizations have not established a collaborative culture. How can you encourage project team members to collaborate when everything they have learned in the organization has taught them not to?

REFERENCES

[1] For more about the Resource Breakdown Structure, consult a project management glossary, such as http:www.maxwideman.com/pmglossary/PMG_R03.htm.

CHAPTER 22

Project Portfolio Management: Principles and Best Practices

▶GERALD I. KENDALL, PMP
TOC INTERNATIONAL

Project Portfolio Management (PPM) is a set of processes to analyze, recommend, authorize, activate, expedite, and monitor projects to meet organization improvement goals (see Figure 22-1). When performed successfully, PPM has yielded the following benefits:

▶20–30 percent improvement in time to market[1]

▶25–300 percent improvement in number of projects completed with the same resources[2]

▶Average project duration cut by 25–50 percent[3]

▶Over 90 percent project success rate, with double the profit margin[4]

▶50 percent improvement in R&D productivity.[5]

These achievements apply to government, not-for-profit, and for-profit entities.

The principles and best practices of PPM presented here are backed up by research, case studies, and many years of experience. To accomplish its primary objective of improved ROI, PPM must ensure that *all three* of the following activities are performed expertly:

▶***Choosing the right project mix***—Choose those projects that will leverage the organization's precious resources to bring large, measurable value to the stakeholders.

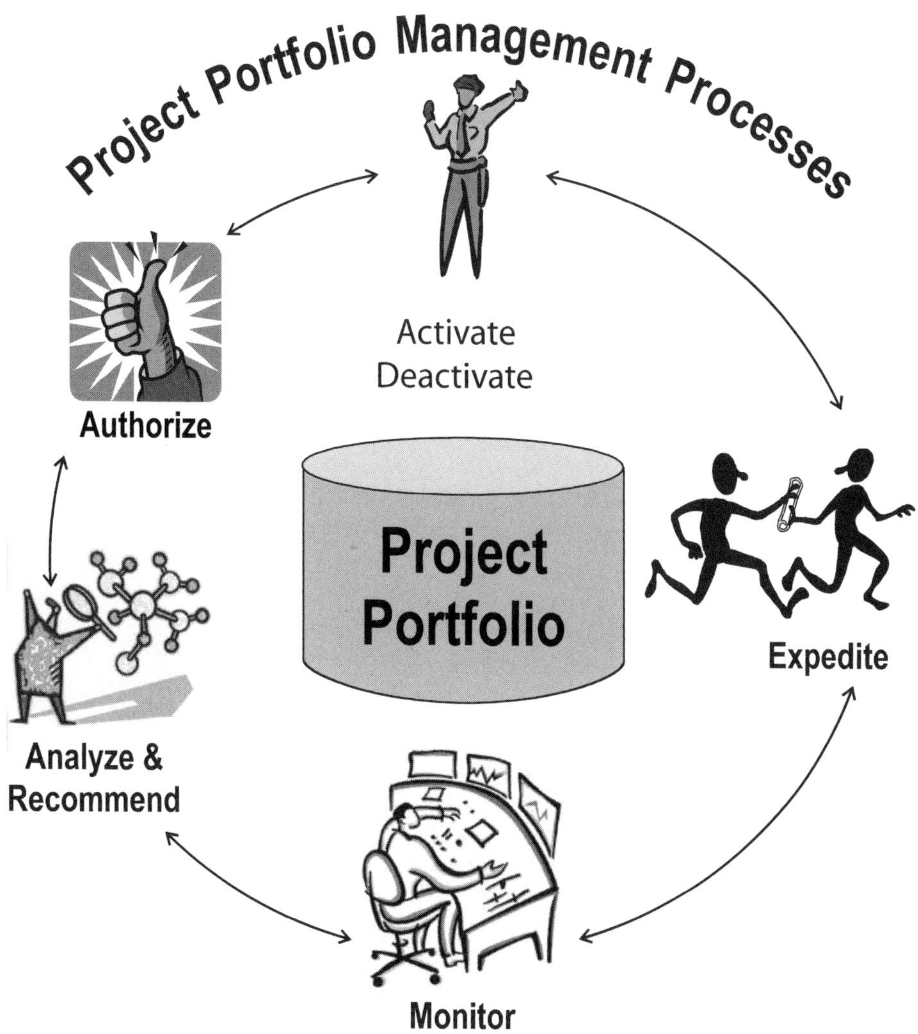

FIGURE 22-1. **PROJECT PORTFOLIO MANAGEMENT PROCESSES**

▶***Ensuring the correct scope***—Align projects and content cross-functionally to ensure that the combined changes will result in measurable improvement in meeting organization goals. Many of today's projects have technical scope relevant to a single, functional area, but lack the organization-wide policy, measurement, and content changes necessary to have a significant impact on organization goals.

▶***Executing quickly, in the correct sequence***—To accomplish this, people performing PPM must understand and convince the organization to adhere to the organization's project capacity. Any organization that is overloaded with too many projects sees a dramatic increase in resource multi-tasking or sharing with a devastating slowdown in project flow. Project durations climb exponentially. Quick execution also demands that PPM effectively monitor project execution to ensure that out-of-control situations are speedily recognized and acted upon.

Executives without effective PPM suffer from cross-functional resource conflicts with continual top management refereeing, poor or anemic organizational performance, and projects where the norm is to deliver late, over budget, or not within scope. Most executives are aware of the need for drastic change in multi-project management practices, but many place the emphasis in the wrong place. Unfortunately, a great deal of such investment is misdirected into multi-year efforts to implement software tools and time sheets *before* dealing with the highest leverage points.

THREE ROLES—GOVERNANCE, MANAGEMENT, AND PROJECT PORTFOLIO MANAGEMENT

To have an effective Project Portfolio Management System, there are three distinct roles that an organization must formally define:

1. *Governance*—This executive role is one of decision making, usually conducted by top management teams. In the most effective implementations that this author has evaluated, this role includes the "C" level executives (CFO, CEO, COO, CIO) who meet monthly to make decisions about:

▶Which projects to approve/reject

▶When to activate projects

▶How many projects to activate and which projects to deactivate

▶Due dates for projects

▶Criteria for project proposals

▶Priorities

▶Resource allocation, including capital expenditure, people, and operating expense budget

▶Project reviews, with approval for a project to proceed to the next stage or to kill the project, or approval/rejection of project improvement plans

▶Investment in project management methodology and tools.

2. *Management*—Relative to PPM, management's job is to ensure that the project management system is "in control." According to the late quality guru W. Edwards Deming, a system is in control when the goals of the system can be predictably met better than 95 percent of the time. Every project has three distinct goals—to be delivered on time, on budget, and within scope, according to original commitments (not the 10th revision to a due date). This role includes providing the project management processes for planning and execution to deliver projects according to their goals. Usually, this is done by a Project Management Office or similar organization. Where such an office does not exist, this role will fall on the project portfolio management person(s).

3. ***Project Portfolio Management***—The person(s) undertaking this role provides information and recommendations to the governance group for improved ROI. They also monitor execution of projects. Usually, there is a close relationship between the person(s) responsible for strategic planning and the project portfolio manager. While strategic planners identify the ideas necessary to meet organization goals, the portfolio manager makes sure that there are corresponding programs and projects sufficient to accomplish those ideas. Furthermore, the portfolio manager maps and tracks the project execution against the strategies and raises the red flag when there is danger of missing a goal. Finally, the portfolio manager also lets strategic planning know when the strategy is not practical relative to project resources available.

CHOOSING THE RIGHT PROJECT MIX

There are three common problems with the way that projects are sanctioned in most organizations.

▶Goals set by the senior executive are *not measurably tied* to projects—i.e., even when a functional VP claims that a project is essential to meet a goal (which is almost always true), the *percentage* of the goal that the project will accomplish is often not identified or committed to. This is vital information for the Portfolio Manager to be able to assess the health of the portfolio.

▶The collection of active projects is *not formally tracked* to see if it is meeting the goals (on time and magnitude of improvement promised). The author's experience is that many projects, even in multibillion-dollar companies, lack formal, valid resource-based project plans. Furthermore, even when the plans exist, they are often sitting on a shelf rather than being used as the performance base to judge the project.

▶Organizations breed *many projects that are not sanctioned* by any executive. In a June 2004 research effort, this was a stated problem with 70 percent of respondents.

A formal portfolio management and governance process will help to overcome these problems. This is a prerequisite foundation for analyzing and improving the project mix.

When considering an organization's project mix, two areas of analysis are very important. The first is whether the projects will provide high leverage on the organization's precious project resources—people and capital—to generate measurable, bottom-line improvements within the coming year. The second area is a question of portfolio balance.

To leverage project resources, a portfolio manager must understand the overall "business" of the organization. Every organization has one major constraint—one area which, more than any other, limits the performance of the organization. In this sense, an organization is like a chain, with one weakest link. Leverage is based on finding and improving the weakest link of the organization. The weakest link can be anywhere in the supply chain—with suppliers who cannot provide enough resource (materials or people) internally, e.g., in production or operations, engineering, IT, in the distribution channels, in retail, or in the market (end customer).

For most for-profit organizations (about 70 percent), their constraint is in the market. This means that the organization has enough internal capacity to handle more business. To have dramatically better results, what they need is more customers who will buy from them. Given this scenario, a healthy project portfolio should have an *imbalance.* The project mix should include a disproportionately larger number of projects to address the market constraint. Many organizations in this situation have a large number of sales campaign projects, but few real market research projects. They must understand the deeper needs of their markets enough to overcome their constraint.

Many project portfolios have significant information technology components. To know that the IT projects in the portfolio are correct, the portfolio manager must be able to answer six questions about these projects.[6] For example, what current technological limitation does the organization or its customers have that the new technology will remove? If the limitation is removed, what impact will that have on the organization's bottom line? When these questions are asked rigorously, it is surprising to find how few of the currently active IT projects really make sense for an organization.

In a June 2004 survey, over 90 percent of organizations recognizing a constrained resource cited a technology resource. Since IT resources are often badly multi-tasked, working on far too many projects, the organization can achieve a much higher return on the IT investment by focusing these resources on those few areas that will address the organization's constraint. In many organizations, the focus on deeper customer needs suggests a different answer in terms of IT projects. For example, many organizations have poor systems in their supply chain (relying on forecasts rather than pull systems, for example), inadequate customer resource management systems, and poor customer service systems.

If an organization does not have the correct balance of projects, with focus on meeting important customer needs, then the project portfolio often contains many projects focused on greater internal efficiencies. Without increased sales and profits, greater internal efficiencies often require layoffs to translate those efficiencies into bottom-line savings. The result, for project management, is that many people become less enthusiastic about working on projects.

Therefore, the second area of analysis of the project mix is vital. The portfolio manager must examine portfolio balance in the following areas:

▶***Focus on market and customer needs vs. focus on internal improvements.*** If the company has cash flow or other serious financial issues, then internal improvements might be the desired "imbalance." However, an organization cannot cost-cut itself to long-term health. It must be able to grow its business. The portfolio manager has the eyes to be able to assess and report an undesirable imbalance in terms of marketing projects.

▶***Short term vs. long term.*** Often, too many projects spend money this fiscal year without bringing benefits until the next fiscal year, or sometime far into the future. This is a huge red flag. Who knows what will happen 1–2 years from now? The portfolio manager should be asking the tough questions, relative to project benefits and why they can't happen sooner.

▶***Research vs. development.*** To have a secure future, every organization must invest some of their project resources into research. Such projects need to focus on market research, experimentation with new methods, tools and processes, training and human development, motivation, and other areas.

▶***Which organization assets are project dollars and human resources focused on?*** Assets are not just bricks and mortar. They include those assets that are strategic to the company's future, such as web site, customers, external sales agents, and distribution channels. The portfolio manager should look at the distribution of project investments to the organization's strategic assets, and determine whether or not the distribution makes sense, relative to the top five assets.

▶***Sponsorship from IT vs. other functional areas.*** In many organizations, the author has witnessed over 70 percent of the projects in the portfolio sponsored by IT. This is a red flag indicating a lack of balanced ownership of project initiatives. It signifies that functional heads are not holding ownership—and therefore ultimate responsibility—for bottom line results.

ENSURING THE CORRECT PROJECT SCOPE

There are two current common practices that are at the heart of project scope problems. One common practice is the dissection of organizations into silos (functional areas) combined with the initiation of projects that try to optimize within a silo. The damage can be illustrated with two real-life examples. In one case, the company had many sales campaign projects that brought customers into their shops and call centers requesting new, advertised products. At the same time, due to poor distribution logistics, the shops were often out of stock of the advertised products. Due to inadequate order entry systems, any customer that wanted two or more products had to wait while the salespeople re-entered all of the same customer information, often infuriating the customer to the point of canceling the transaction.

In another example, a procurement manager claimed to save over a million dollars per year in material costs while, at the same time, production stops due to the new materials were causing lost throughput of $100,000 per week. Every two weeks, the company was losing more than the annual savings from material cost reduction.

The portfolio manager must actively seek to replace this common practice of project scope *within a silo* by looking at the organization *as a whole.* Projects must be connected, cross-functionally, to make sure that the bottom line benefit to the entire organization is increased.

The second common practice that hurts scope is for technology solution providers (internal and external to an organization) to take responsibility solely for the delivery of the technology rather than partnering in responsibility for the business result that the technology is intended for. Technology providers argue that they have no control over the business results. This is correct in the current paradigm. In the future, they must become full collaborators with the functional heads.

In order for this current paradigm to change, one of the following two scenrios much occcur:

▶Technology solution providers must develop a much better understanding of the business requirements to be willing to take a stake in the business results.

▶Business leaders must develop a much better understanding of the technology to better specify their needs, or both.

In either case, the IT resource crisis that we find so common across most organizations could be resolved overnight, simply by significantly reducing the project rework and waste through a strong, collaboration model.

In general, to begin to overcome these two scope issues and create a much more successful project portfolio management outcome, organizations must initiate cross-functional business training to help their top functional leaders, including IT, better understand the cause-effect relationships and conflicts between functions. Further, the organization must be sure that their metrics for each functional area (and the scope for any associated projects) are holistic, not silo-oriented. Finally, IT internal resources and external vendors should be asked to identify the limitation that any new technology is intended to overcome, what rules (policies and procedures) the organization is currently using to cope with those limitations, and how the rules need to change when the new technology is put in place. These actions will go a long way toward overcoming many project scope problems.

EXECUTING QUICKLY: PROJECT FLOW

One of the two keys to managing a project portfolio to execute quickly is to have an anchor mechanism for strictly activating projects according to the organization's capacity. Many organizations make the mistake of trying to balance workload across all project resources. Managing project workload in this manner is far too complex to yield predictable results due to variability of both project task work and operational responsibilities.

The anchor mechanism that works is to recognize and stagger projects according to one strategic resource—that one resource pool, within each collection of projects, which determines how many projects the organization can handle without badly multi-tasking that resource. It is usually the resource which is the most heavily loaded, or the resource that project managers and sponsors fight over the most, or the resource that most delays projects. In many organizations, it is an IT resource, an engineering resource, or an integration group. In smaller organizations, it is often the availability of a project manager that governs how many projects the organization can accomplish.

The governance process, with the portfolio manager's help, must accommodate the de-activation of projects if the strategic resource is overloaded. In organizations such as Alcan Aluminum and TESSCO Technologies,[7] this meant deactivating over 50 percent of the active projects. The portfolio manager must ensure that projects are staggered strictly according to the capacity of the strategic resource. Only then will project flow dramatically improve.

The second key to quick execution is to imbed a relay runner work ethic for people working on the critical path tasks in projects. These two keys—staggering projects according to capacity of the strategic resource and relay runner work ethic—are part of a project management methodology called Critical Chain.[8] (See Chapter 28 for further discussion of Critical Chain project management.)

EIGHT MANDATORY STEPS FOR EFFECTIVE PPM

The following steps can be easily and quickly executed to launch an effective PPM process:

1. ***Collect current project portfolio information.*** If you are new to PPM, focus on basic information. Make a list of the formally recognized projects/programs that the functional heads see as essential to meet the organization's goals. If the list is greater than fifty projects, this is a red flag that the organization is not focused on its key constraint. Collect any project plans associated with those projects, including resources allocated. Determine if there are financial and other justifications. Get a summary status on each active project (red, yellow, green). Document the sponsor.

2. ***Collect goal, asset, and resource portfolio information.*** Determine the official

company goals (increasing revenues, market share, profit growth, etc.). Make a list of the top five organization assets, according to executive perception. For resources, do not go to individual detail. The Resource portfolio should include a list of the 25–35 resource pools (skill sets) used by projects, how many resources exist within each pool, and the approximate percentage utilization of those resource pools.

3. *Measurably link project, goal, asset, and resource portfolios and assess.* In this step, the portfolio manager determines if all projects are connected to organization goals, and to what extent they will meet the goals if executed successfully. Projects are also linked to the Asset portfolio to determine the extent of investment in the company's strategic assets. The link between the project and resource portfolios determines resource loads and to what extent the organization has the capacity to execute successfully, on time.

4. *Determine if the project portfolio is balanced correctly.* See the discussion above regarding balance.

5. *Determine the organization's project capacity.* Every collection of interdependent projects has one resource which, more than any other resource, determines how many projects the organization can complete in a given year, and when the project can get executed. As discussed above, this resource—the strategic resource—has a finite capacity.

6. *Develop and gain consensus on prioritization criteria and perform initial prioritization.* There are dozens of criteria that you can use. However, almost every management team prefers simplicity. Some of the popular criteria that appear in opportunity template rating forms include relationship to organization goals, customer impact, competitive impact, risk, cash flow, level of difficulty to complete the project, and amount of strategic resource needed.

▶***Develop recommendations for the governance board, relative to improving the portfolio ROI.*** Based on the information that you have gathered, make specific recommendations for executive decisions at the next Governance Board meeting.

▶***Prepare for and Facilitate the Governance Meeting.*** Part of the preparation involves gathering information about new project proposals and circulating recommendations among functional heads prior to the meeting.

MONITORING MULTI-PROJECT EXECUTION

When an organization has twenty or more large projects active simultaneously (and this is just a rule of thumb), they usually need a software tool with real-time, online status to help monitor project execution. This is necessary so that the entire community of project and resource managers have a real-time understanding of the impact on their projects and resources—enough to make good decisions on priorities and expediting. It is also necessary for the strategic resource manager to be able to do "what-if" analysis for new projects and stagger the projects correctly so as not to overload the strategic resource.

Executives cannot govern effectively with poor or non-existent data. The data from execution of projects, based on performance against a resource-based project plan, is essential to give executives a meaningful status of any project. Today's common practice is to provide summary reports to executives showing a green, yellow, or red status (green: project is on target, yellow: project has some minor problems, red: project is seriously off-track). However, the summary status often masks or does not have good enough data to help executives really understand the organization-wide resource issues or trend analysis to identify threats early enough to avoid disaster.

With poor data, executives often end up as referees, shifting resources to the major disaster areas. While this often solves one problem in one project, it also creates waves of effects on other projects. The underlying root cause of scheduling beyond the organization's project capacity is not solved permanently, because the anchor mechanism is never identified or accepted in principle. The data does not exist to convince executives of the problem.

Therefore, two essential components of enterprise-wide multi-project management are multi-project software that shows trend analysis for each project and the recognition and acceptance by top management of the strategic resource as the anchor mechanism by which all projects are scheduled. With these pieces implemented, a Governance committee has the tool to identify a negative trend within a project. From that identification, the portfolio manager should be able to state what task, right now, is causing the problem, what action the project manager is taking, and whether or not the portfolio manager believes that action is sufficient to overcome the problem. Then, the Governance Committee has a basis to take action or leave the project alone.

BEST MULTI-PROJECT PRACTICES

The following were cited as the highest value multi-project management processes, from those companies that claimed to achieve 70 percent or better of their projects completed on time and within scope:

▶Visibility of the processes to senior management, with their involvement. This included regular and timely status reporting to senior management and program management, which was used to facilitate multiple business unit and product integration.

▶Stage gate project reviews, especially those conducted by the Governance board with staged funding. This brings "faster kills and better clarity on risks." It also helps to prioritize new projects early on.

▶Prioritization of all projects, based on their value proposition with tangible ROI.

▶Much better resource management and allocation.

▶Consistency of applying best project management practices to all projects.[9]

Exemplary Organizations

I asked several organizations that were achieving much higher-than-average success rates in delivering projects on time, on budget, and within scope: "What do you think is the major reason why your organization has better-than-average success in managing its collection of projects?" Here are a few responses:

> "Part of our success is attributable to the process surrounding the annual budget cycle by which we select our investments for the year. The process drives toward a set of outcomes: to prevent poorly-conceived projects before they start, to select only projects aligned with our organizational goals, and to generate broad support for the resulting portfolio of investments. This helps avoid having a number of executive pet projects, projects to placate a squeaky wheel, or projects that serve only larger departments, with no priorities established among them. We put significant

effort into constructing a decision-making framework that results in a balanced and prioritized investment portfolio that is grounded in our organization's values. The confidence in the selection process at the executive level and the project manager level gives the organization a vested interest in the success of the project. As an initiative encounters difficulty, there is a measure of corporate resolve to right the project and see it through to completion.

Once the best projects are put into the pipeline, the PMO helps keep them flowing by increasing their visibility through regular, standardized status reporting back to the committee that authorized them in the first place. We have structured our status report to convey both milestones and budget in terms of planned (baseline), actual, and forecast, along with a statement of the status of risks and issues affecting the project. Status reporting by itself, however, is insufficient; the value of the status report lies in the ability of the executives to accurately interpret the information presented and from it make informed decisions.

As a further benefit, the visibility into the health of the project creates a powerful dynamic with both the project managers and the project sponsors. Both of these parties want their projects to show well before the executive committee. If project managers are aware of the visibility into their projects' performance they will be more inclined to pursue their projects responsibly and raise red flags earlier than would be the case if their projects did not appear on the radar screen. This is a healthy and productive dynamic to have in place. However, for it to work effectively, it is essential to establish attainable performance standards.

There are many, many other factors to successful project portfolio management, but in Arlington we have found two pieces of the magic that the PMO can work: provide a relevant framework for analysis and decision making and lead the organization toward an on-going dialogue about desired outcomes and the path to reach them."

—Denise Hart, Program Management Officer, Arlington County Government, Virginia

"The BASC PMO credits its strong foundation to the development of a strategic partnership with all operational organizations. This strategic partnership and the continuing efforts in promoting project management with executive sponsorship are the key success factors in meeting customer expectations and overall project success.

The strategic partnership emphasizes a mutual goal of defining and implementing best practices. As part of this effort, the PMO meets regularly with the Executive Director to review the projects within the portfolio. The creation and management of the portfolio includes the PMO conducting interviews with the operational organizations, IT, and finance departments. Several scenarios are then built based on different priorities: ROI, risk, business need, etc. These are then presented to the Executive director and his team for review. The PMO is involved in all stages of managing the portfolio thus creating value for the organization by assisting the operational entities with their resource allocations, requirements, and re-emphasizing the value of project management methodology. This enables the organization to experience first hand the value of the PMO and assists the PMO in assigning the best-suited resource to a project, thereby increasing the probability of a successful project."

—Luke Foster, PMP, with BellSouth Affiliate Services

"The hands-down reason for our early success in project portfolio management has been top-level executive support. Commissioner Andrew S. Eristoff and his Executive Leadership Team understood that instituting a formal, yet flexible structure for managing scarce IT resources was essential to achieving multiple departmental goals. The Executive Team accepted the ownership of the IT portfolio of projects and embraced responsibility for accepting or rejecting new projects, discontinuing existing projects, and adjusting priorities among competing projects on a continuous basis. Our portfolio management process ensures that our scarce IT resources are applied to our most critical projects. The IT Department now has an active and involved partner in the Executive Team for making project decisions."

—Vivian Conboy, Project Management Office Director, NYS Department of Taxation and Finance

"Tinker Federal Credit Union achieves success in managing its projects through their Electronic Services committee, made up primarily of senior managers from all of the organization's operational areas. The committee ranks projects in order of their strategic priority, and only allows one to be activated if adequate resources will be available for its successful completion. By selecting the projects most closely aligned with their strategic plans, the committee guarantees that completed projects will make the most significant impact possible on the organization's future growth and direction.

TFCU's project managers closely monitor each active project's progress and try to spot problems as early as possible so that corrective actions can be taken. Problems that cannot be resolved at the project team level are elevated to the appropriate senior managers on the Electronic Services Committee. This high level of visibility and authority allow resolutions to occur quickly and with minimal disruption to the project's momentum."

—Ben Mannahan, Tinker Federal Credit Union Project Manager

CONCLUSION

Executive understanding, buy-in, and direct involvement at the beginning of any project portfolio management effort are key ingredients for success. While executive understanding can be fostered by education in the form of reading and presentations, do not expect their buy-in to a different approach without giving them some logical data and analysis. The data and analysis are needed to prove that there are too many active projects (well beyond the capacity of the strategic resource to do its work without multitasking). Furthermore, the analysis of the collection of projects, when linked to the goals of the organization, must clearly identify the gaps. Otherwise, executives will perceive the portfolio management recommendations to be illogical and unfounded.

The challenge of the portfolio manager is to perform his/her analysis and recommendations in a way that gets top management to act. If the data presented to senior executives lacks credibility, the portfolio manager will be asked to continually do more research, find more data and be caught in the web of analysis paralysis. Use the eight-step process recommended in this chapter to build a robust portfolio data warehouse that can be continually enhanced.

With the correct understanding of the executives, through the Governance Committee, a project portfolio manager will be able to move his/her entire organization up in portfolio management and project execution maturity level. Communications and collaboration in cross-functional projects will improve dramatically. Most importantly, the organization will move closer to meeting or exceeding its goals, with ever greater predictability on positive project results.

DISCUSSION QUESTIONS

❶ If a project portfolio management process is meeting its objectives, what tangible outcomes would you expect to see in any organization?

❷ How would you bring a top management team to agreement on the choice of projects in a portfolio?

❸ Discuss how the knowledge of an organization's "strategic resource" is helpful in project selection.

REFERENCES

[1] See Performance Measurement Group, LLC, website with several articles about over 1,000 development projects that they have analyzed: www.pmgbenchmarking.com. This data is from an article entitled Better Project Management Practices Drop Time-to-Market 20–30 percent. The article is from the company's publication *Signals of Performance,* Volume 2, Number 1.

[2] See case studies in *Project Management, A Systems Approach, 8th edition,* Dr. Harold Kerzner, John Wiley & Sons, 2002, New York, chapter 22 on Critical Chain.

[3] Ibid—see case studies.

[4] Performance Management Group, LLC, "Pipeline/Portfolio Best Practices Yield Higher Profits," *Signals of Performance,* Vol. 3, Number 1.

[5] *Insight Magazine,* Summer/Fall 2001, "How to Boost R&D Productivity by 50 percent."

[6] See Gerald I. Kendall, *Viable Vision,* J. Ross Publishing, 2004, Boca Raton FL for a full discussion of the I.T. implications of projects and the six questions.

[7] Gerald I. Kendall, J., *Advanced Project Portfolio Management and the PMO,* Ross Publishing, Boca Raton FL, 2003.

[8] Ibid., for a more detailed description and case studies.

[9] Results of research study conducted by the author in June 2004. Quotes from survey participants were also collected during the course of this research.

CHAPTER 23

Measuring the Value Of Project Management

▶JAMES S. PENNYPACKER,
CENTER FOR BUSINESS PRACTICES

More than ever, investment in initiatives designed to improve organizational performance must be justified. Whether it's the implementation of a project management methodology, a project office, project management software, or project management training, these initiatives must deliver positive and tangible results. The good news is that tangible measures of project management value and performance can be established by asking the right questions and developing an appropriate measurement system.

Over the past few years, major companies from a variety of industries—information technology, manufacturing, pharmaceutical, new product development, government, and professional services—have initiated projects to create measurement programs to measure the value that project management provides to their organizations. The goals of these project management measurement programs were to:

▶Provide tangible metrics to senior management, on the value of implementing systematic project management methods in order to reinforce the business case for project management improvement across the organization.

▶Boost customer and project team morale by sharing statistics that show the value their work adds to the organization and the improvement they can achieve.

▶Track on-going project management performance and the business impact of project management to the organization.

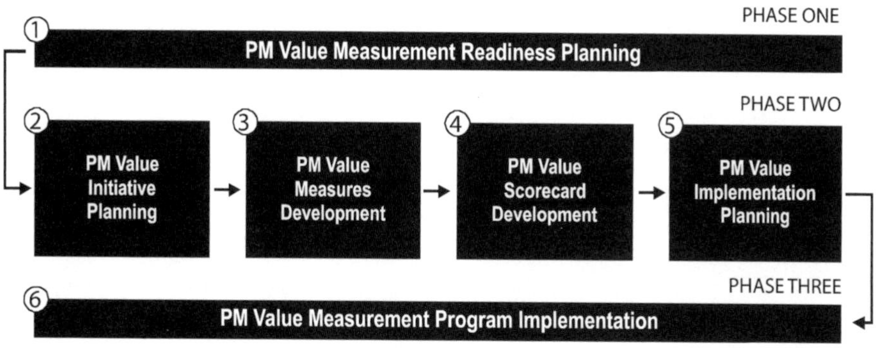

FIGURE 23-1. **THE PM VALUE MEASUREMENT PROGRAM INITIATIVE PROCESS**

- Initiate metric-based efforts to help streamline the project portfolio.

Project management value measurement programs (PM Value Initiatives) consist of three-phase, six-step programs designed to bring a measurement team from an introduction to project management-focused measurements through design, development, and implementation of a project management value measurement program (see Figure 23-1).

PM VALUE INITIATIVE: PHASE ONE

Phase One focuses on educating a measurement team on the PM Value Measurement Program to help them understand and enable them to clearly identify the program's objectives and goals. Organizational constructs that affect the PM Value Measurement Program identified, including stakeholders, organizational mission and strategies, organizational structure, key business processes, project management maturity, prior project management improvement initiatives, current measurement systems, and data availability.

Step 1: Measurement Readiness Planning

Activities in this step ensure that the measurement initiative is clearly understood and aligned to support the organization's strategies—an essential element to support sustained success of the initiative. The primary project management, business unit, and organization goals that influence the development of the measures of project management usually value include:

- ***Organizational Goals and Objectives***
  - Reduced costs
  - Improved quality
  - Improved timing
  - Improved productivity.
- ***Project Management Goals and Objectives***
  - More predictable project performance
  - More repeatable project performance

ACTIVITY	START	FINISH
PM Value Readiness Planning Teleconference	9/2	9/2
PM Value Initiative Workshop	9/18	9/18
PM Value Measures Workshop	9/19	9/19
Draft Scorecard Development	9/19	9/26
Final Report Development	9/19	10/10
PM Value Implementation Workshop	10/3	10/3
Implementation Plan Development	10/3	10/10
PM Value Measurement Program Process Development	10/3	10/10
Final Presentation Development	10/3	10/10

FIGURE 23-2. **HIGH-LEVEL SCHEDULE OF PM VALUE INITIATIVE ACTIVITIES**

- Improved ability to execute projects
- More effective resource management
- Improved internal and external customer satisfaction
- Better alignment of projects to business strategy
- More effective risk management
- Reduced learning curve for new project managers.

▶***PM Value Initiative Goals and Objectives***

- Measure the business impact of project management improvement initiatives
- Compare the costs to benefits of project management improvement initiatives
- Determine if a project management improvement initiative is accomplishing its objectives
- Identify the strengths and weaknesses in project management processes
- Establish a database of key project management measures
- Understand the infrastructure required to support a measurement program
- Gain a sense of whether the project portfolio is as productive as possible
- Spread the acceptance of project management throughout the enterprise
- Help attain project management and organizational goals and objectives.

This step educates the measurement team on the issues of project management value measurement and better prepares them to make key decisions throughout the initiative concerning the program's objectives and measures and the implementation approach.

PM VALUE INITIATIVE: PHASE TWO

Phase Two efforts plan the initiative and engage the team to identify measures, develop a PM Value Scorecard, and plan the implementation of the measurement program. After putting a PM Value Initiative Plan and Schedule in place, subsequent steps in this phase continue to build on the team's understanding of the project management measurement program and engage the team to develop the PM Value Scorecard and PM Value Implementation Plan.

COST MEASURES	QUALITY MEASURES
Project cost	Requirements performance
ROI	Customer satisfaction
Product cost variance to plan	Lessons learned implemented
Start-up costs	Project status communication
Efficiency of delivery	# scope changes/phase
Project profitability	Effectiveness
Product unit cost	AARs
Start-up cost variance to plan	Rework
Resource utilization	Internal customer satisfaction
Market share	Leadership capability
Cost of capital	Staffing conformance to plan
PRODUCTIVITY MEASURES	Project risk management
Project milestone performance	PM training satisfaction
Project success rate	**TIMING MEASURES**
Avg. sales per development FTE	Predictability of delivery
Process improvement	Time to market
Alternatives assessment	Project cycle time
Downtime	Successful phase exits
Capacity/resource planning	Project planning

FIGURE 23-3. **PARTIAL LIST OF PROSPECTIVE MEASURES OF PROJECT MANAGEMENT VALUE**

Step 2: Initiative Planning

In this step the team aligns around the measurement program's objectives, scope, development approach, timeline, deliverables, and implementation strategy. It collaboratively develops a PM Value Initiative Plan and PM Value Initiative Schedule (see Figure 23-2).

Step 3: Measures Development

In the Measures Development step, the team creates and prioritizes the initial list of measures for the Scorecard. It is the initial pass at identifying and prioritizing measures with the primary activity in the step being a collaborative development workshop. A comprehensive list of measures developed keeping in mind that they need to be logically linked to the goals described above. The measures also need to meet the criteria for good measures, which means that the measures selected:

- ▶Provide meaningful information
- ▶Are supported by valid data that is cost effective to capture
- ▶Are acceptable by stakeholders
- ▶Are repeatable
- ▶Are actionable

COST MEASURES	Avg	SDev	QUALITY MEASURES	Avg	SDev
Efficiency of delivery	4.6	0.55	Project status communication	4.6	0.55
Product cost variance to plan	4.4	0.55	Requirements performance	4.4	0.45
Resource utilization	4.2	0.55	Effectiveness	4.4	0.45
Start-up costs	4.2	0.84	Project risk management	4.3	0.71
Start-up cost variance to plan	4.2	1.30	Project leader training	4.3	0.71
Project profitability	4.0	0.71	Customer satisfaction	4.0	1.73
Product unit cost	3.4	0.55	AARs	3.4	0.55
Project cost	3.2	0.84	Rework	3.4	0.89
ROI	2.4	1.14	Internal customer satisfaction	3.2	0.45
Market share	1.8	0.45	# scope changes/phase	3.2	0.84
Cost of capital	1.6	0.89	Lessons learned implemented	2.6	0.55
PRODUCTIVITY MEASURES	**Avg**	**SDev**	Staffing conformance to plan	2.6	1.34
Project milestone performance	4.4	0.45	PM training satisfaction	2.0	0.71
Alternatives assessment	4.3	0.55	**TIMING MEASURES**	**Avg**	**SDev**
Project success rate	3.8	1.14	Project cycle time	4.6	0.55
Process improvement	3.2	0.84	Project planning	4.0	1.00
Avg. sales per development FTE	2.6	0.55	Predictability of delivery	4.0	0.45
Capacity/resource planning	2.6	0.55	Time to market	3.8	0.71
Downtime	2.6	0.89	Successful phase exits	3.8	0.45

FIGURE 23-4. **SAMPLE LIST OF PRIORITIZED MEASURES**

▶Align to organizational objectives.

A sample list of prospective measures developed by the measurement team is shown in Figure 23-3.

The measurement team then prioritizes and selects measures to comprise the PM Value Scorecard. A simple prioritization process can be used: develop criteria for ranking the list of measures in order of importance on a scale of 1–5, and have each of the measurement team members rank the list; calculate average rankings and develop a prioritized list was developed for review in Step 4 (see Figure 23-4).

Step 4: Scorecard Development

In this step the team reviews the prioritized measures information developed to date and develops measure packages (see below) and a cohesive PM Value Scorecard. The team first engages in measures review, prioritization validation, and measure package definition. That information is then used to construct the Scorecard for review and acceptance by the measurement team in preparation for implementation.

MEASURE	OBJECTIVE	METRIC	UNITS	BASE	CURRENT	VALUE
Start-up Cost Variance to Plan	Cost Improvement	(Actual Start-up Cost ÷ Budgeted Start-up Cost) - 100%	Percent Start-up Cost Variance to Plan	64%	29%	123%
Efficiency of Delivery	Cost Improvement	(Total Man-hours Available in Dollars + Actual Labor Cost) ÷ Number of Projects	Average Labor Dollars per Project	263	260	1%
Project Status Communication	Quality Improvement	Projects Using Standard Status Reports ÷ Number of Projects	Percentage of Projects Using Standard Status Reports	20%	30%	50%
Requirements Performance	Quality Improvement	Scope Changes by Phase ÷ Number of Projects	Average Number of Scope Changes by Phase per Project	17.7	15.5	14%
Effectiveness	Cost, Quality, and Timing Improvement	Objectives Met ÷ Objectives	Percentage of Objectives Met	75%	79%	6%
Project Risk Management	Cost and Quality Improvement	Projects Using Risk Management Processes ÷ Number of Projects	Percentage of Projects Using Risk Management Projects	10%	10%	0%
Project Cycle Time	Timing Improvement	Project Cycle Time ÷ Number of Projects	Average Project Cycle Time in Days	270	265	2%
Project Leader Training	Cost, Quality, and Timing Improvement	Project Leaders Trained ÷ Number of Project Leaders	Percentage of Project Leaders Trained	15%	20%	33%
Alternatives Assessment	Cost and Quality Improvement	Projects Using Formal Concept Alternative Selection Process ÷ Number of Projects	Percentage of Projects Using Formal Concept Alternative Processes	10%	30%	200%

FIGURE 23-5. **SAMPLE PM VALUE SCORECARD**

A comprehensive definition of each measure is included in a measure package to support the initial implementation and ongoing collection of data. Each measure package includes the following elements:

▶Measure *(What)*: The data to be collected must be clearly identified.

▶Objective *(Why)*: The measure's objective must be clearly defined. Why is it being collected? How will it be interpreted? What will it tell us? The measurement team must understand the objective of each measure.

▶Data Capture *(How)*: The mechanism for collecting the data must be identified.

▶Timing *(When)*: The timing of data collection must be defined. Data collection must be properly timed to match the type of data and objective. PM value measures are not intended to track individual project progress, so there would most likely not be a need to collect data monthly. Typically a quarterly or longer interval will support the objectives of the initiative.

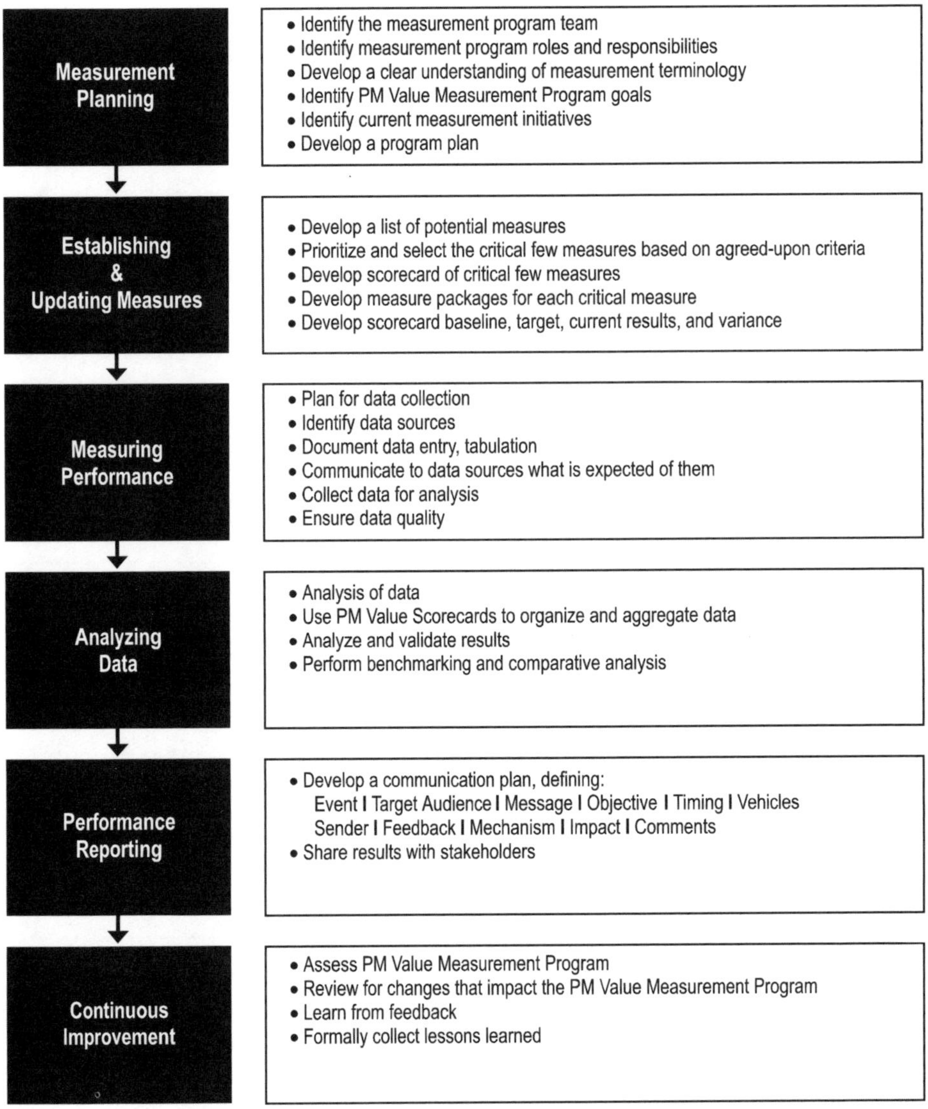

Measurement Planning
• Identify the measurement program team
• Identify measurement program roles and responsibilities
• Develop a clear understanding of measurement terminology
• Identify PM Value Measurement Program goals
• Identify current measurement initiatives
• Develop a program plan
Establishing & Updating Measures
• Develop a list of potential measures
• Prioritize and select the critical few measures based on agreed-upon criteria
• Develop scorecard of critical few measures
• Develop measure packages for each critical measure
• Develop scorecard baseline, target, current results, and variance
Measuring Performance
• Plan for data collection
• Identify data sources
• Document data entry, tabulation
• Communicate to data sources what is expected of them
• Collect data for analysis
• Ensure data quality
Analyzing Data
• Analysis of data
• Use PM Value Scorecards to organize and aggregate data
• Analyze and validate results
• Perform benchmarking and comparative analysis
Performance Reporting
• Develop a communication plan, defining:
Event | Target Audience | Message | Objective | Timing | Vehicles
Sender | Feedback | Mechanism | Impact | Comments
• Share results with stakeholders
Continuous Improvement
• Assess PM Value Measurement Program
• Review for changes that impact the PM Value Measurement Program
• Learn from feedback
• Formally collect lessons learned

FIGURE 23-6. **THE PM VALUE MEASUREMENT PROGRAM PROCESS**

▶Data Location *(Where)*: The location of the data must be identified.

▶Data Contact *(Who)*: The person responsible for maintaining the data must be identified. Who will provide the data? What is the reliability of this source?

Information from the measure packages is used to create a PM Value Scorecard, which is a collection and reporting tool for keeping score and reporting progress (see Figure 23-5).

Step 5: Measurement Program Implementation Planning

The implementation planning efforts in Step 5 define the framework around measurement processes and data collection that will be used to support ongoing measures program implementation. Key activities in this step include development of an implementation strategy and process.

The PM Value Measurement Program process shown below (see 23-6) describes a systematic approach to project management performance improvement through an ongoing process of establishing project management measures, collecting, analyzing, reviewing, and reporting performance data; using that data to drive performance improvement; and using lessons learned to continuously improve the PM Value Measurement Program process.

PM VALUE INITIATIVE: PHASE THREE

Phase Three includes an initial implementation of the program and the transition to ongoing execution of the program.

Step 6: Measurement Program Implementation

The PM Value Measurement Program Implementation is an ongoing effort to execute the program as documented in the Implementation Plan, using the Measures Packages to reinforce the data requirements, collection timing, and data contact responsibilities. Step 6 begins with the preparation for the initial collection-analysis-reporting cycle and continues through transition of ongoing program execution and continuous improvement responsibilities.

LESSONS LEARNED

▶Organizational strategies and objectives set the foundation for effective measurement programs. It's essential to understand how the critical elements of the organization's strategies and objectives are linked to the measures that comprise the PM Value Scorecard.

▶You need to have a very clear idea of the measurement program stakeholders and what their needs and expectations are regarding the program (there are often huge differences in expectation among stakeholders—setting those expectations through clear communication of program goals is a key to success).

▶Clearly identify measurement program goals and objectives. Without this clarity, selecting the right set of critical few measures will be difficult.

▶In most best-in-class organizations, measurement initiatives are introduced and continually championed and promoted by top executives. When measurement initiatives are introduced from the bottom up, getting senior management buy-in is crucial and may take significant effort. Be prepared to make that effort.

▶Develop a clear understanding of measurement terminology, which tends to be confusing and inconsistent, but needs to be understood and agreed upon by the measurement team and program stakeholders.

▶Communication is crucial for establishing and maintaining a successful measurement program. It should be multidirectional, running top-down, bottom-up, and horizontally within and across the organization.

▶The driving force to create a new or improved measurement program is usually a threat to the organization (often a crisis or strong competition). For organizations that are strategically developing measurement programs to enhance their competitive advantage, rather than reacting to their business environment, a sense of urgency must be nurtured and driven by individuals who understand the value of measurement and can evangelize the need for developing a measurement culture. Again, this takes enormous effort and communication.

▶It's critical, and very difficult, to limit the number of measures in the Scorecard. Selecting those critical few measures sharpens the stakeholders' understanding of the issues. Too many measures confuse and complicate (the measurement team can't try to please everyone—selecting too many measures will ultimately kill the program).

▶Pilot the measurement program before full implementation. And implementation should come in phases—implement a critical few high-value measures at first and identify more detailed measures when the organization has developed a measurement culture and is ready to collect and analyze more complex measures.

▶Successful deployment of a measurement program requires a successful system of accountability—that is, all stakeholders need to buy into measurement by assuming responsibility for some part of the measurement process (sponsorship, analysis, data collection and monitoring, evangelism, etc.).

▶Benchmark against industry standards if possible.

▶Identify a central area of responsibility for the measurement program.

▶You need to determine what counts as a project (what exactly will be measured).

▶Reinforce the fact that PM Value measurement is measuring performance change due to project management. Measures, therefore, are process-focused, not project-focused (you are not trying to measure the progress of a particular project).

▶The measures selected are highly influenced by the project management maturity of the organization. Level one organizations generally need to focus on process compliance and simple cost and/or schedule measures. As the organization matures in their project management capability, more sophisticated measures can be used.

▶Analysis is one of the most important steps in PM Value measurement, yet it is often one that is neglected. The insight gained from effective analysis (particularly determining root causes of the results measured) is what makes measurement a valuable business tool.

▶Feedback is one of the best assets for continuous improvement. Seek it and use it.

DISCUSSION QUESTIONS

❶ For an organization with which you are familiar, list the project management initiatives that have been implemented: tools, training, a project office, etc. Did these initiatives solve the problems they were implemented to solve? If not, why not?

❷ Again, for an organization you are familiar with, what metrics are collected about project management performance? How are they used? Can you think of ways to improve metrics collection or development?

❸ What barriers would have to be overcome in your organization in order to set up a value measurement system?

FURTHER READING

Oswald, J., & Pennypacker, J.S. The Value of Project Management: The Business Case for Implementation of Project Management Initiatives. *Proceedings of the Project Management Institute Annual Seminars & Symposium,* 2002.

Pennypacker, J.S. *The Value of Project Management: A Center for Business Practices Research Report.* Havertown, PA: Center for Business Practices, 2001.

Pennypacker, J.S. (Ed.). *Justifying the Value of Project Management.* Havertown, PA: Center for Business Practices, 2003.

CHAPTER 24

The Project Office: Rationale and Implementation

▶J. KENT CRAWFORD, PMP, PROJECT MANAGEMENT SOLUTIONS, INC.

The value of sound project management has never been more in the public consciousness, thanks to studies by the Standish Group, the Gartner Group, and other IT research firms.[1]

But sound project management of individual projects is no longer enough. While there still are some instances in which a company is almost entirely focused on one or two major projects at a time—small software development firms or capital construction firms, for example—in most businesses dozens of projects exist throughout the company in various stages of completion (or, more commonly, of disarray). It wouldn't be at all uncommon for a company to have several new product development projects in process, along with a process reengineering effort, a Six Sigma initiative, a new marketing program, and a fledgling e-business unit. Widen the scope of your thought to take in facilities, logistics, manufacturing, and public relations, and you begin to understand why most companies have no idea how many projects they have going at one time. And, when you consider that technology plays a role in almost all changes to organizations these days and that technology projects have an abysmal record of failure,[2] it becomes apparent: unless all the projects that a company engages in are conceptualized, planned, executed, closed out, and archived in a systematic manner—that is, using the proven methodologies of project management—it will be impossible for an organization to keep track of which activities add value and which drain resources.

And the only way to have a global sense of how a company's projects are doing is to have a project focus point: the Project Office.

No matter what name it carries—Center of Excellence, Project Support Office, Program Management Office, or Project Office—a home base for project managers and project management is a must for organizations to move from doing an adequate job of managing projects on an individual basis, to creating the organizational project management systems that adds value dependably and repeatedly.

WHY IMPLEMENT A PROJECT OFFICE?

Why do companies increasingly find they cannot do projects well enough without a Project Office? Imagine for a moment your organization without a finance department. Without documented procedures or systems, a shared vocabulary, or professional standards. Without systematic data collection or reporting. Without any knowledge transfer or management in the financial practice. Without a CFO or comptroller.

Whereas our imaginary company with no financial processes in place would at least have entry-level employees with four-year degrees in accounting or finance, project managers are often "accidental," with no education in the specialty and no clear training plan for the future in mind. Even if a company has standardized on a project management tool across the enterprise, they may have access to the methodologies inherent in that tool, but it's unlikely that everyone who works on project teams has had adequate training to make the best use of it. This is undoubtedly why the Gartner Group predicted in 2001 that companies that failed to establish a project office would experience twice as many major project delays, overruns, and cancellations as will companies with a Project Office in place.[3]

Project management and, in particular, the project office are critical to the enterprise because most of the value-adding activities that companies do come in the form of projects. Think of operations as interest on capital already amassed; think of projects as the entrepreneurs who create new wealth. New products; new marketing initiatives; new facilities; new organizational processes implemented, mergers, and acquisitions: all of these are projects. Time is money—if a project is late for an amount of time equal to 10 percent of the projected life of the project, it loses about 30 percent of its potential profits.[4]

Ending Project Failure

In the past decade, there has been a trend towards improvement in our ability to pull off projects. Project slippage and failure rates are falling, at least in those application areas that attract research interest, such as software development and pharmaceutical R&D. Cost and time overruns are down. Large companies have made the most dramatic improvement. In 1994, the chance of a Fortune 500 company's project coming in on time and on budget was 9 percent, its average cost \$2.3 million. In 1998, that same project's chances of success had risen to 24 percent, while the average project cost fell to \$1.2 million.[5]

Three factors explain these encouraging results: 1) a trend toward smaller projects which are more successful because they are less complex; 2) better project management; and 3) greater use of "standard infrastructures," such as those instituted through a Project Office. Large companies show up as more successful in the Standish Group study for one simple reason, in our view: large companies lead the pack in the establishment of enterprise-level project offices.[6]

The enterprise-level project office is so powerful because it helps to address the persistent management problems that plague projects:

▶***Poor tool implementation.*** Project managers who lack enterprise-wide multiproject planning, control, and tracking tools often find it impossible to comprehend the system as a whole.[7] Such tools are rarely effectively implemented, trained for, or utilized except under the auspices of a project office. Buying a tool addresses the software issue; the "peopleware" issues must be addressed by a management entity that specializes in projects.

▶***Poor project management/managers.*** Most of the reasons technology projects fail are management-related rather than technical. Many enterprises have no processes in place to ensure that project managers are appropriately trained and evaluated.[8] The average corporate HR department does not possess the knowledge to appropriately hire, train, supervise, and evaluate project management specialists, but an enterprise project office does.

▶***Lack of executive support for/understanding of projects.*** This correlates to project failure.[9] An enterprise project office helps close the chasm between projects and executives. Those companies that have a senior-level executive who oversees the PMO reported greater project success rates (projects completed on time, on budget, and with all the original specifications) than those without.[10]

▶***Antiquated time-tracking processes.*** Accurate project resource tracking is imperative to successful project management. Project-based work requires new processes for reporting work progress and level of effort, but most companies' time-tracking processes are owned by and originate in the HR department, and most HR departments are still using an employment model developed in the early Industrial Age.[11]

▶***Lack of consistent methodology; lack of knowledge management.*** Enterprises that hold post-implementation reviews, harvest best practices and lessons learned, and identify reuse opportunities are laying the necessary groundwork for future successes.[12] A Project Office shines as the repository for best practices in planning, estimating, risk assessment, scope containment, skills tracking, time and project reporting, maintaining and supporting methods and standards, and supporting the project manager.

Adding Corporate Benefits

Project portfolio management. If an enterprise-level project management office does not own the process of project inventory, prioritization, and selection, it cannot be done well. The META Group recommends this strategy, and those companies that have put enterprise-wide PPM in place, such as Cabelas and Northwestern Mutual Life, have relied on it. In fact, while intra-departmental portfolios may perhaps be selected and balanced without involvement of a project management office, it's doubtful that anything on a wider scale can succeed . . . and you can't optimize the system by balancing only parts of it.[13]

You can't manage what you can't measure, the old saying goes, and unless all the projects on the table can be held up to the light and compared to each other, a company has no way of managing them strategically, no way of making intelligent resource allocation decisions, and no way of knowing what to delete and what to add. And the only way to have a global sense of how a company's projects are doing is to have some sort of project focus point.[14]

Problems resolved by project offices. These include projects not supported by senior executives, lack of authority, conflict over project ownership, difficulty of cross functional interface with projects, project prioritization and selection, development of project

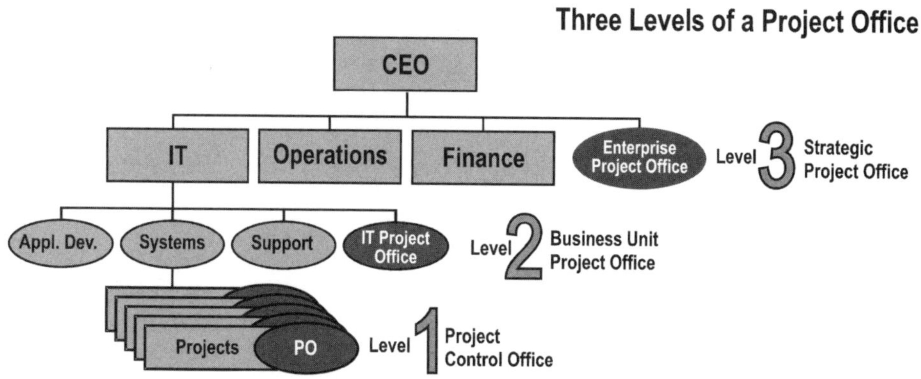

FIGURE 24-1. **THREE LEVELS OF A PROJECT OFFICE**

manager and project team capabilities, and knowledge management issues.[15]

THE CHALLENGES OF IMPLEMENTING A PO

Many hold the misconception that a Project Office is merely a project controls office that focuses on scheduling and reports. At one time, of course, this was true: in the old matrix organization, if a project was lucky to have a "project office," it was usually nothing more than a "war room" with some Gantt charts on the walls and perhaps a scheduler or two. This simple single-project control office is what we'll call a Level 1 Project Office (see Figure 24-1).

Inside the matrix. When project management's early tools—Gantt charts, network diagrams, and PERT—began to be used in private industry, the new project managers faced a hurdle: business was also fashioned on the command-and-control model. Putting together an interdisciplinary team was a process fraught with bureaucratic roadblocks. The earliest uses of project management—in capital construction, civil engineering, and R&D—imposed the idea of the project schedule, project objectives, and project team on an existing organizational structure that was very rigid. Without a departmental home or a functional silo of its own, a project was the organizational stepchild—even though it may have been, in terms of dollars or prestige, the most important thing going on. Thus was born the concept of the "matrix organization"—a stopgap way of defining how projects were supposed to get done within an organizational structure unsuitable to project work. It was a "patch," to use a software development term—not a new version of the organization.

Up the steps to maturity. A Level 2, or "divisional-level," Project Office may still provide support for individual projects, but its primary challenge is to integrate multiple projects of varying sizes within a division from small, short-term initiatives to multi-month or multi-year initiatives that require dozens of resources and complex integration of technologies. With a Level 2 PO, an organization can, for the first time, integrate resources effectively, at least over a set of related projects. We should note that while the Level 2 project office is most often an IT office, organizing around projects is not "an IT thing." Project offices have arisen first in IT because of the competitive pressure to make IT projects work. IT is one of our primary drivers of economic prosperity; America spends over $200 billion annually on software development projects—many of which fail. That IT project offices have been proven to reduce waste, bring projects in on time, and improve morale should be a wake-up call for all areas of the corporation, and in all industries.[16]

For an organization without any repeatable processes in place, which are at the first, or Initial level on a Project Management Maturity Model[17], these levels of Project Office organization are beneficial. At Level 1 or the individual project level, applying the discipline of project management creates significant value to the project because it begins to define basic processes that can later be applied to other projects within the organization. At Level 2 and higher, the project office not only focuses on project success, but also migrates processes to other projects and divisions, thus providing a much higher level of efficiency in managing resources across projects. A Level 2 project office allows an organization to determine when resource shortages exist and to have enough information at their fingertips to make decisions on whether to hire or contract additional resources. And at Level 3, the enterprise project office applies processes, resource management, prioritization, and systems thinking across the entire organization.[18, 19]

Advantages of the Enterprise-Level, or Strategic, Project Office

Although many companies today still struggle to implement even Level 2 project offices, our primary focus is on the Level 3 project office, which we call the Strategic Project Office (SPO). Why? Because that's where organizations can derive the most benefit. Like the matrix organization, lower-level project offices are a waystation: a stage between the old-style organization and the new, project-based enterprise.

At the corporate level, the project office serves as a repository for the standards, processes, and methodologies that improve individual project performance in all divisions. It also serves to mitigate conflicts in the competition for resources, and to identify areas where there may be common resources that could be used across the enterprise. More important, a corporate project office allows the organization to manage its entire collection of projects as one or more interrelated portfolios. Executive management can get the big picture of all project activity across the enterprise from a central source (the Project Office), project priority can be judged according to a standard set of criteria, and projects can at last fulfill their promise as agents of enterprise strategy. The higher the Project Office resides in the organization, the fewer the problems reported. A project office is a communication tool, maintaining a consistent flow of communication to senior executives and report both successes and problem areas.[20]

The Gartner Group has identified several key roles for a Project Office,[21] all of which are most effectively carried out at Level 3:

▶***Developer, documenter, and repository of a standard methodology (a consistent set of tools and processes for projects).*** The SPO provides a common language and set of practices. This methodology boosts productivity and individual capability and takes a great deal of the frustration out of project work. Research by the Center for Business Practices revealed that over 68 percent of companies who implemented basic methodology experienced increased productivity, and 37 percent reported improvement in employee satisfaction.[22]

▶***Center for the collection of data about project human resources.*** Based on experience from previous projects, the SPO can validate business assumptions about projects as to people, costs, and time; it is also a source of information on cross-functional project resource conflicts or synergies.

	Service Offering	Level 1: Project Control Office	Level 2: Business Unit PMO	Level 3: Strategic/ Enterprise PMO	Description of Services
People	Project Planning and Controls Specialists	X		X	Plans all activities for the project; manages the critical path, issues, risk, and budget. Responsible for resource management and schedule/budget status reporting.
	Project and Program Managers	X		X	Coordinates with business sponsors to manage scope of work, business issues, risks, etc. Drives business issues and communicates to project stakeholders and team members.
	Mentoring and Coaching		X	X	Individual coaching for less experienced project managers, to reinforce training and established client methodologies.
	PM Training and Professional Development		X	X	A variety of on-site training courses including certification programs that can be customized for any organization.
	Organizational Change Management		X	X	Assessing current organization's readiness to change, including barriers to change, and developing/executing a plan to successfully implement new project management processes.
Process	PM Organizational Maturity Assessment & Improvement Planning		X	X	Uses PM Solutions' acclaimed Project Management Maturity Model (PMMM) to show how to systematically mature an organizations' project management practices.
	Project Portfolio Management		X	X	Process and software tools to select and manage the optimum set of projects that maximize business value. Provides management visibility through dashboard reporting.
	PM Methodology	X	X	X	Customized methodology—processes, procedures, templates, examples, and guides—delivered through an easy-to-use web-based tool, the PM Community of Practice (PMCOP).
	Functional Methodology		X	X	Customized methodology (SDLC, NPD, Marketing) that integrates into the overall project management methodology.
	PM Value Measurement		X	X	Tangible metrics program established to measure the benefits derived from the PMO.
Technology	PM Software	X	X	X	Proven software tools for planning, managing, and status reporting the full portfolio of project(s).

TABLE 24-1. **CAPABILITIES OF VARIOUS LEVELS OF PROJECT OFFICE**

As a project management consulting center, the SPO provides a seat of governing responsibility for project management and acts as a consultant and mentor to the entire organization, staffing projects with project managers or deploying them as consultants or mentors. As a center for the development of expertise, the SPO makes possible a systematic, integrated professional development path and ties training to real project needs as well as rewarding project teams in ways that reflect and reinforce success on projects. This is quite different from the reward and training systems presently in place in most organizations, which tend to focus on functional areas and ignore project work in evaluation, training, and rewards.

As a knowledge management center for project management, the SPO provides a locus not only for project management knowledge, but for knowledge about the content of the organization's projects. With a "library" of business cases, plans, budgets, schedules, reports, lessons learned, and histories, as well as a formal and informal network of people who have worked on a variety of projects, the SPO is a knowledge management center that maximizes and creates new intellectual capital. Knowledge is best created and transferred in a social network or community, and the SPO provides just that. Through mentoring, both within the SPO among project managers and across the enterprise to people in all specialty areas, knowledge transfer about how to get things done on deadline and within budget is facilitated.[23]

The enterprise-level project office facilitates the management of projects on one level, and improves management of the entire enterprise via project portfolio management and linking projects to corporate strategy on another level. More than establishing an office and creating reports, it infuses cultural change throughout the organization.

Table 24-1 shows the capabilities and features of each level of project office.

▶***A systems-thinking perspective.*** To effectively deploy project management throughout an organization, all the players must be on board. Everyone from the project team member on up to the executive sponsors of projects must understand what is happening with project management. This translates to an organizational setting in which virtually everyone who is touched by a project is impacted by what happens with the project management initiative. Ultimately this impact sweeps across the entire corporation. That's why effective organizations have project offices located at the corporate level, providing data on total corporate funding for projects, the resources utilized across all corporate projects, capital requirements for projects at the corporate level, materials impact, supplies impact, and the procurement chain impacts. A fully mature organization may actually have project offices at each of the levels described in Figure 24-1: a Strategic Project Office at the corporate level to deal with enterprise (cross-divisional) programs/projects, corporate reporting, corporate portfolio management, etc.; and a divisional Project Office to deal with divisional programs/projects, divisional resource management, divisional portfolios, and the division's contribution (technology, labor, etc) to corporate programs/projects. And, there may be one or more Level 1 Project Offices within a divisional PO dealing with major projects.

▶***Knowledge management.*** A whole new set of procedures and standards need to be established along with a common mechanism for storing and sharing that information. Along with this goes the training process and data collection routine that must be established to get information into this database before knowledge transfer can take place.

Project/program managers will make good decisions with good data. Without good data, decisions are going to be very poor. So the organization is faced with a very complex integrated system and process that they have very little knowledge how to deploy. That's why the Gartner Group recommends incorporating a contractor or consultant in the implementation strategy. It's necessary to get folks in who have actually done systems deployment in the past so that the probability of success is going to be much higher.

The Objective: Results, and Fast

All this costs money, so at the end of the day, it is absolutely essential that an organization is able to quantify the value that project management brings.

How can the initiative show results fast enough to avoid top management loss of interest? Dianne Bridges, PMP, writes that there are two ways to demonstrate the immediate value of the Project Office: through short-term initiatives and project mentoring.[24] Short-term initiatives provide solutions to immediate concerns and take care of issues surfaced by key stakeholders. These are items that can be implemented quickly, while at the same time they take care of organizational top-priority concerns. Examples include: support for new projects and projects in need; an inventory of projects (new product development, information technology, business enhancements, etc); summary reports and metrics; informal training lunches; project planning or project control workshops; templates, project audits, and identification of project managers or those who aspire to the role.

In conjunction with the short-term initiatives, project mentoring is an excellent way to provide immediate project management value to projects that are in the initial start-up phase or are in need of support, without waiting for the implementation of formal training programs, or process roll-outs.

The best approach to building organizational and individual maturity is to move forward quickly—show results on specific projects within six months, really begin changing the culture within the first year, and begin showing corporate results within a two-year time frame. But be prepared—this is no quick fix. It will take anywhere up to five years to fully deploy a Strategic Project Office.[25]

What does success look like? How will you know when you have arrived? Research studies allow us to paint a picture of the organization that has demonstrated competence in managing projects, and managing by projects:

- Top management understands project management basics.
- Effective training programs are in place.
- Clear project management systems and processes have been established.
- There is improved coordination of inter-group activities.
- There is an enhanced goal focus on the part of employees.
- Redundant or duplicate functions are eliminated.
- Project expertise is centralized.
- Changes in organizational culture including new information systems, altered communications channels, and new performance measurement strategies.[26, 27]

PMO in Place? Don't Relax Yet

A trend that surfaced in 2002 at the Project Management Benchmarking Forums was of companies that had achieved a mature project management process under the auspices of an enterprise project office, but which were disinvesting in project management in the name of cost-cutting exercises.

Forum participants—representatives of project management practices within some of America's top corporations—described the expressed opinions of their executive leadership as paradoxical: on one hand they claimed to support and value project management; on the other hand they were slashing project management office budgets and cutting training for project managers. In a tight economy, management identified the entire project management exercise as an overhead expense.

Ironically, the most successful and long-standing project management offices may be the most vulnerable to cost cutting because the organization takes good project management for granted. An article in *Computing Canada* by HMS Software president Chris Vandersluis characterized the attitude as: "Can't we just do all of this in Excel like we used to?" and "The projects aren't a problem; why do we spend so much money on managing them?"[28]

Once implemented, good project management becomes invisible and, paradoxically, that can be a problem. The effects of good change management, good planning, resource capacity planning, and variance management mean that projects just seem to run themselves. Management forgets that the costs associated with maintaining a project management structure are outstripped by the potential costs of having no project management structure. Vandersluis describes the PM-free environment as "projects that run late and over budget . . . a mismatch of resources to projects . . . clients [and] suppliers are unhappy . . . shareholders are unhappy . . . ," and boldly states that "losing the efficiency that comes with a corporate-wide project management environment can take a company from barely profitable to completely unprofitable in a short period of time."[29]

Project Office directors and managers often wonder out loud why processes like accounting are accepted as costs of doing business, while the project management process constantly struggles for survival on the organizational edge. The constant effort to make visible to management costs they *didn't* incur saps energy that would be better spent on managing projects. But this vigilance is simply part of the requirements for maintaining your Project Office, once established, as a visible and appreciated part of organizational life.

DISCUSSION QUESTIONS

❶ What types of project office exist in your organization, if any? How closely do they resemble the model project offices described in this chapter?

❷ Imagine that you are the newly appointed director of a start-up project office at the divisional level. For an organization you are familiar with, quickly show results by listing all the projects under way in the division. Don't neglect to list projects in the areas of maintenance, regulatory compliance, and other "must-do" categories. Are there more projects on the list than you expected? Fewer? How many of them overlap in some way?

❸ Again, for a company you are familiar with, consider ways that centralizing project management across the enterprise might streamline decision making. In particular, focus on communication and information sharing between departments and levels of management.

REFERENCES

[1] The Standish Group, 2000 CHAOS Report. See www.standishgroup.com.; M. Light and T. Berg, Gartner Strategic Analysis Report: *The Project Office: Teams, Processes and Tools,* 01 August 2000.

[2] The Standish Group, ibid.

[3] Light and Berg, Ibid.

[4] Preston Smith and Donald Reinertsen, *Developing Products in Half the Time,* Van Nostrand Reinhold, 1991.

[5] Standish Group, ibid.

[6] Value of Project Management Study, Center for Business Practices, 2001.

[7] Lauren Gibbons Paul, "Turning failure into success: Maintain momentum," *Network World,* 22 Nov.1999.

[8] Paul, ibid.

[9] J. Roberts, J. Furlonger, "Successful IS Project Management," *Gartner Group,* 18 April 2000.

[10] Lorraine Cosgrove Ware, By the Numbers, CIO Magazine, July 1, 2003

[11] C. Natale, "IT Project Management: Do Not Lose Track of Time," *Gartner Group,* 9 May 2000.

[12] Bailey, Richard W., II, "Six Steps to Project Recovery," *PM Network,* May 2000.

[13] *Project Portfolio Management: A Benchmark of Current Business Practices,* CBP Research, 2003.

[14] J. Kent Crawford, Portfolio Management: Overview and best practices, *Project Management for Business Professionals,* Joan Knutson, ed., Wiley, 2001.

[15] Comninos and Verwey, ibid.

[16] C.W. Ibbs and Young-Hoon Kwak, *Benchmarking Project Management Organizations,* PM Network, Feb. 1998: 49–53.

[17] A capability maturity model is an organizational assessment tool that helps companies identify process maturity—or lack thereof—by documenting how various processes are actually carried out against a standard of best practice behaviors for that process. While there are several versions of maturity model in circulation for project management, we used one developed by our company as the basis for the assessment described in Table 24-1. This model is described in *Project Management Maturity Model,* by J. Kent Crawford, Marcel Dekker, 2001.

[18] J. Kent Crawford, *Project Management Maturity Model*, Marcel Dekker, 2001.

[19] Software Engineering Institute, "Capability Maturity Model for Software Development," www.cmu.edu/sei.

[20] Ware, ibid.

[21] Light and Berg, ibid.

[22] Jeannette Cabanis-Brewin, The Value of Project Management, *PM Best Practices Report,* Oct. 2000.

[23] J. Kent Crawford, *The Strategic Project Office,* Marcel Dekker, 2001.

[24] Dianne Bridges and Kent Crawford, "How to Start Up and Roll Out a Project Office," *Proceedings of the PMI Annual Seminars and Symposium,* PMI, 2000.

[25] Bridges and Crawford, ibid.

[26]Ibbs and Kwak, ibid.

[27] Dr. J. Davidson Frame, "Understanding the New Project Management," Aug 7 1996 Presentation to Project World, Washington, DC.

[28] Chris Vandersluis, Cutting project office is detrimental to corporate health, *Computing Canada*, Sept. 2002.

[29] Jeannette Cabanis-Brewin, Penny Wise, Pound Foolish: Cost-cutting in the project office, *Best Practices e-Advisor,* Center for Business Practices: accessed at www.cbponline.com/e_advisor, Jun. 2004.

CHAPTER 25

A Process of Organizational Change: From Bureaucracy to Project Management Orientation

▶ROBERT J. GRAHAM, PHD, PMP
R. J. GRAHAM AND ASSOCIATES

This chapter describes a process followed by one organization in an attempt to change from a functional to a project management organization. The organization involved flourished in the bureaucratic mode with limited competition and stable products and services. However, it found itself in the intensive world of deregulated financial services. As more and more projects were developed to respond to the new environment, the company executives discovered that their project management practices were reflections of their bureaucratic past rather than of their project management future.

Attempts to teach managers the basics of project management were not successful. The newly trained people found that the practices necessary for successful project management were not supported by the departments in the organization. From this experience, company executives came to realize that the organization needed to be changed in order to respond effectively to the new business environment. The process they followed in order to achieve that change is outlined here. This process is presented as an example of the steps needed to install sound project management practices into a functional organization.

AN ORGANIZATIONAL CHANGE MODEL

Research on organizational change indicates that most people in organizations will not change their behavior unless they see a clear need for such a change. Some people come to realize the need for change because their culture is not consistent with their business strategy. However, just realizing this does not bring it about. What is needed is a planned and directed organizational change effort that has the support and involvement of senior management.

The components of an organizational change effort are depicted in Figure 25-1. In general, they can be summarized as follows:

▶***Define new behavior.*** The senior managers must lead the move toward new behavior by clearly defining what the new behavior should be and what it should accomplish.

▶***Teach new behavior.*** Once the new behavior is defined, it must be taught. This means that management development programs must be designed and developed to impart the knowledge as well as the feeling of what life will be like in the future organization. Senior managers must be a part of this program so that they understand the new behavior that is being taught. In addition, the program should incorporate feedback from participants to help refine what works in the organization.

▶***Support new behavior.*** Development programs have little effect unless they are supported by senior management. In addition, there often needs to be a change in the reward system to ensure that the new behavior is rewarded and thus supported.

▶***Model new behavior.*** Management development programs are reinforced by a combination of top management support and effective role models. This means that senior managers must exhibit the new behavior that is being taught and thus become effective role models for other organization members.[1]

An organizational culture has been defined as "the environment of beliefs, customs, knowledge, practices, and conventionalized behavior of a particular social group."[2]

So any change effort toward a project management culture must begin with a serious examination of the current beliefs and practices that caused projects to be less than successful. One way to achieve this is to compare successful and unsuccessful projects to determine what practices seemed to be present in the successful projects. This comparison could be augmented by practices that have been proven successful in other organizations. The result of this examination should be a description of the new, desired behavior.

Once this is determined, the new behavioral patterns must be taught. The lessons from the examination above should be put into a case study for use in the training program. At a minimum, the case study of the least successful project could become an indication of the types of assumptions and behavior that are not wanted.

AN ORGANIZATIONAL EXAMPLE

The organization described in this section will be referred to as OE (Organization Example). This organization is used to illustrate the types of problems typically encountered in attempts to change bureaucratic organizations. It is also used to illustrate how the change process described in the previous section can be applied for organizational change.

OE's business began with a series of local offices selling consumer financial services. As the business grew, it became necessary to develop a general procedure manual so that all offices across the country would run according to the same principles and procedures. This manual was developed to such a degree that the placement of everything in the office was defined precisely such that any manager could walk into any office and know exactly where everything was. A highly structured organization grew up to support these procedures, and OE flourished as a result.

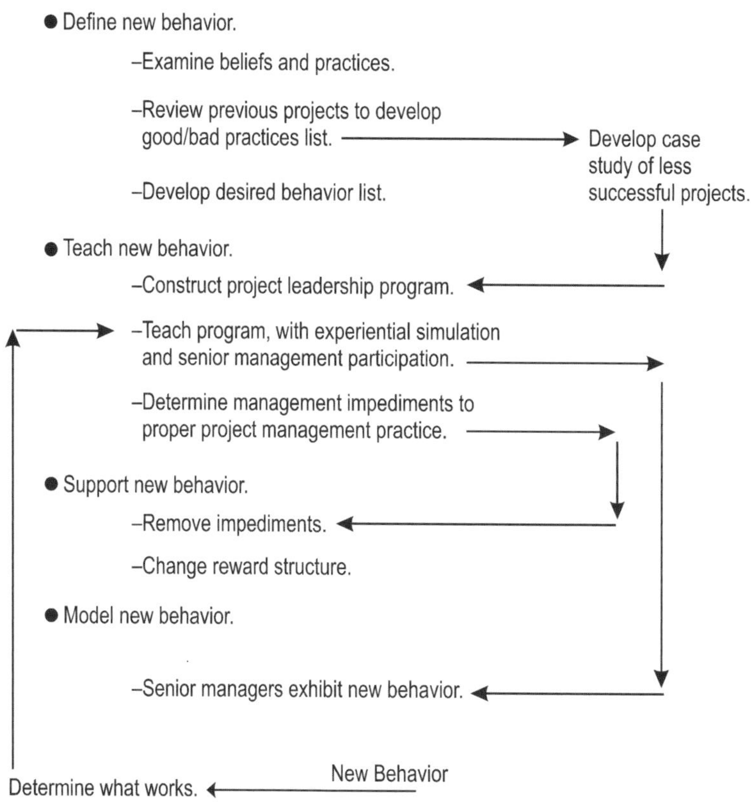
● Define new behavior.
–Examine beliefs and practices.
–Review previous projects to develop good/bad practices list.
Develop case study of less successful projects.
–Develop desired behavior list.
● Teach new behavior.
–Construct project leadership program.
–Teach program, with experiential simulation and senior management participation.
–Determine management impediments to proper project management practice.
● Support new behavior.
–Remove impediments.
–Change reward structure.
● Model new behavior.
–Senior managers exhibit new behavior.
New Behavior
Determine what works.

FIGURE 25-1. **COMPONENTS OF AN ORGANIZATIONAL CHANGE EFFORT**

With such standardized procedures and with everyone going by the same book, it became part of the OE culture that people were interchangeable. That is, it was assumed—and it was true—that any manager could run any office. This assumption of interchangeable parts, such an asset in earlier years, later proved to be quite an obstacle to proper project management. The assumption led to the practice of continually moving people from project to project and changing the composition of the team as the project progressed. As this was common practice in the past, many managers failed to understand that in the project management world, people are not as interchangeable as they were in the past. Some of the general differences between a bureaucratic culture and a project management culture—which OE experienced—are summarized in Figure 25-2.

OE went through a tumultuous change as a result of the deregulation of the financial services market. Suddenly there were more competitors and fewer people on staff. This combination generated a sudden increase in the number of "special projects" in the organization. Most of these new projects involved computer technology, so that projects and project management became associated with the computer department. As there was little history of project management in the organization, it seemed natural that the project managers should come from the computer department. This assumption proved to be another obstacle to proper project management.

Bureaucratic Culture	Project Management Culture
Many standard procedures	Few, new procedures
Repeated processes and products	New process and product
More homogenous teams	More heterogeneous teams
Ongoing	Limited life
High staff level	Low staff level
High structure	Low structure
People more interchangeable	People not interchangeable
Little teamwork	More teamwork and team building
Positional authority	Influence authority
Departmental structure	Matrix structure

FIGURE 25-2. **BUREAUCRATIC CULTURE VS. PROJECT MANAGEMENT CULTURE**

The basic problem was that the person managing the project was not from the department that initiated the request. As such, the project manager had little formal responsibility and accountability other than making the product work technically. He or she had no formal responsibility to make certain that the product performed the way that the initiating department had envisioned.

"Accidental" project managers thus arose from the technical departments, and procedures evolved somewhat haphazardly. Each department involved mostly responded to requests from those project managers and were content to do only as requested. They did not share ownership of the final product. As the project manager was not ultimately responsible for achieving end results or benefits, the role evolved into one of project coordinator. As such, project success depended more on informal contacts, as there was little formal methodology. The role of project manager was highly ambiguous and thus not an envied position.

In addition, there was little concept of a continuing project team. People were often pulled onto a project as needed, and they were just as often pulled off a project in the middle of their work. As the project was identified with the computer department, contributing departments did not feel it necessary to keep people on a project for its duration. Thus, team membership was fluid, and there was often loss of continuity.

Despite all of these problems, there were some OE projects that were decidedly successful. However, there were others that were definitely unsuccessful. After a few of these failures, upper management decided that it was time for a change. This is the normal procedure with any decision about change. Any group will hold onto a set of procedures for as long as the procedures do not cause too many problems. One failure is usually not enough to change people's minds. After a few failures, the need for change becomes clearer.

DEVELOPING THE NEW PROJECT MANAGEMENT CULTURE

Using the organizational change model in Figure 25-1, let's examine the actions of OE executives as an example.

Step 1: Define New Behavior

To begin the change toward better project management, a conference of senior managers was arranged to examine what was right and what was wrong with project management practices at OE. At that conference the managers listed those projects that were deemed to be most—and least—successful. One division president became extremely interested when he realized that most of the failures were from his division. He became the champion for the management development program that was later developed.

From the analysis of the "winners and losers," it became fairly clear what behavior patterns had to be modified. The senior management team then began the task of defining the new behavior, at least in outline form. Some of the changes in behavior defined were as follows:

▶The project manager should be a defined role. The project manager should be designated from the user department and held accountable for the ultimate success of the project. It is up to the user department to define the specifications and see that they are delivered.

▶A core team of people from the involved departments should be defined early on in the existence of major projects. The people on the core team should, if possible, stay on the team from the beginning until the end of the project. The project manager is responsible for developing, motivating, and managing the core team members to reach the ultimate success of the project.

▶A joint project plan should be developed by the project manager and the core team members. This project plan should follow one of the several project-planning methodologies that were in use in the corporation. The specific methodology was not as important as the fact that the planning was indeed done.

▶A tracking system should be employed to help core team members understand deviations from the plan and then help them devise ways to revise that plan. The tracking system should also give good indications of current and future resource utilizations.

A post-implementation audit should be held to determine if the benefits of the project were indeed realized. In addition, the audit should provide a chance to learn lessons about project management so that projects could be better managed in the future.

A case study was developed, based on a project failure, for use in the training program for the new project managers. It highlighted how things had gone wrong in the past and what behavior needed to be changed for the future.

Step 2: Teach New Behavior

Defining new behavior is not difficult; realizing the new behavior is quite a different matter. At this point the people from the management development area began to determine development needs. They began to ask the question of how to teach this new behavior throughout the organization.

In order to implement project management, the role of the project manager had to be redefined. In addition, people throughout the organization had to understand the new role of the project manager. This person was no longer to be just a coordinator, but a leader of a project team. This person had to do more than just worry about technical specifications, but rather, had to see to it that new changes were actually implemented. That is, the project

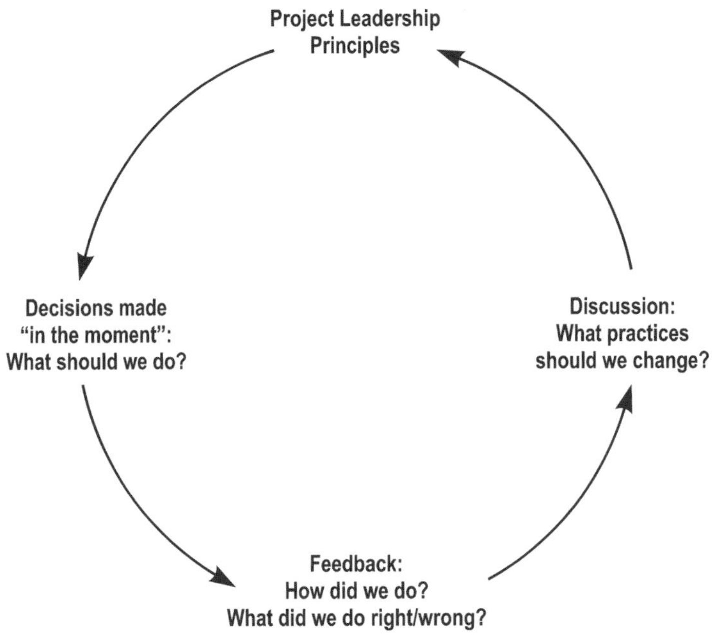
Project Leadership
Principles
Decisions made
"in the moment":
What should we do?
Discussion:
What practices
should we change?
Feedback:
How did we do?
What did we do right/wrong?

FIGURE 25-3. **SIMULATION MODEL TO TEACH NEW BEHAVIOR**

manager had to lead a project team that would develop changes in the way that people in the organization did their business. Thus, the person also had to manage change.

These additional aspects redefined the role from that of project manager to that of project leader. The emphasis was then changed to developing a program on the role of project leadership. The program was aimed not only at the project leader, but also at the other people in the organization who had to appreciate the new role.

In addition to developing an appreciation of the new role, the development program also had to develop an appreciation of the use of influence skills rather than reliance on positional authority. In a bureaucratic culture there is a higher reliance on positional authority, but the increased responsibility of the project leader was not matched with increased authority. This is usually the norm in project management. Sometimes the project is identified with a powerful person so the project manager can reference that person and get referent authority. That is, the project manager can say, "The CEO wants this done," and wield authority based on the CEO's position. But in general, project leadership requires that the person develop his or her own abilities at influence and not depend so much on referent power. Therefore, the development program had to impart this idea in a usable form so the future project leaders would become more self-sufficient and more self-reliant, and would become entrepreneurs rather than simply project coordinators.

The project leadership role can be defined and put on paper, but it is not really meaningful until it is experienced. Thus, it was imperative that the training program be experiential, so that people could have a better idea of what the project leadership role would be like in the future. In addition, it was important that others on the project team, as well as others in the organization, experience what it would be like dealing with the new project leaders. It was thus decided that a simulation experience, involving all layers of management personnel, would be the best management development tool.

Using Simulation to Teach New Behavior

The simulation was a computer-based in-tray exercise where teams of people assume the role of project leader for a new software product. The simulation was used as a part of a learning process to put people "in the moment," making decisions about project leadership. It is easy to teach the principles of leadership and project management, but when managers are "in the moment" of a decision, they often forget these new principles and rely on old patterns of behavior. The idea of the development program was to change those old behavior patterns, so the program was designed to first teach the new behavior and then put people in simulated situations where they learn to apply the new concepts. There is thus a large component of feedback in the simulation, which indicates if the simulation participants used old procedures rather than the new concepts. The simulation model is shown in Figure 25-3.

In the simulation, teams are presented with a variety of situations where they must solve problems that arise during the simulated project. Most of the problems have a behavioral orientation and deal with such areas as team building; obtaining and keeping resources; dealing with requests from clients, top management, and budgeting personnel; and generally living in a matrix organization. Each situation encountered has a limited number of offered solutions, and the team members must agree on one of the possible choices. During the normal play of the simulation, participants are scored on their ability to develop an effective project team and deliver a quality product while satisfying the often conflicting demands of top management, clients, accountants, and other important project stakeholders. The simulation presents situations that emphasize developing skills in the areas of building the project team, motivating the project team, managing diverse personalities on the project team, developing influence to achieve goals, developing a stakeholder strategy, and managing to be on time.

The simulation was used to give people some experience in a different world. It purposely did not simulate their current experience, as the idea was to get them ready for new organizational expectations. The simulation experience thus helped to clarify what the role of the project manager would be in the future and gave people some brief experience in this role. Potential project team members also received benefit as they experienced the problems of project management from the point of view of the project leader. They thus obtained a better understanding of what a project leader does and why they do what they do.

Step 3. Support New Behavior

Many organizational change efforts seem to die from a lack of senior management support. That is, people are trained to practice new behavior, they get excited about the benefits of the new behavior, but then they return to their departments and find that senior management still expects and rewards the old behavior. When this happens, the net effect of the management development program is to cause frustration. Thus, effective change strategies require constant interaction and communication between the training function and senior management to ensure that there is support for the behavior being learned.

The senior management at OE worked to ensure this communication and support. One of the division presidents sponsored the program and was physically present to introduce most courses and discuss why they were being offered. This sent a message to course participants that the move toward a project management culture was serious and supported by senior management.

The development program included a top management review of the perceived impediments to changing behavior in the organization. People in the development program often saw the benefits in changing behavior but sometimes felt that there were impediments in the organization, usually assumptions on the part of upper management that favored old behavior. Each group in the development program thus developed a list of those behaviors that they felt they could change themselves and those where they felt there were organizational impediments. These lists of impediments were then collected from the participants and presented to senior management. The senior management team then worked to remove the impediments and thus helped to support the change.

Step 4. Model New Behavior

Proper project management requires a discipline on the part of project leaders in the areas of planning, scheduling, and controlling the project, as well as dealing with the myriad of other problems that arise during the project execution. One aspect that senior managers may sometimes fail to realize is that it requires a similar discipline on their part. That is, in order effectively to ask subordinates to follow certain procedures, senior managers must be ready to follow those procedures themselves, or subordinates will not take the requested changes seriously. The process of instilling good project management into this organization thus began at the top. In effect, this means that senior managers must be role models for the changes that they want others to implement. This requires a number of behaviors on their part. Some of these are as follows:

▶***Enforce the role of project plans.*** Project management requires planning. However, if senior managers never review the plans, project leaders may not take planning seriously. In addition, project leaders should know how their project fits into the overall strategic plan for the organization. It is thus important that upper management work with the project leaders to review their project plans and show them where the project fits into the overall strategic plan.

▶***Enforce the core team concept.*** Project management requires a core team of people that stays with the project from beginning to end. Most everyone in organizations believes that this is true, but adopting this approach limits senior managers' ability to move people at will. Upper management must thus model the behavior of not moving people off core teams unless there is an extreme emergency. If they do not adopt this posture, the core team concept will fail.

▶***Empower the role of project leader.*** Project management requires that the end-user department take responsibility for the project. The project leader needs to be empowered from that user department. This means that the senior manager from the user department also takes responsibility for all projects in his or her department.

▶***Hold post-implementation audits.*** Project management requires that post-implementation audits be held to determine if the proposed benefits of the project were indeed realized. In addition, audits should be used to help members of the organization to develop better project management practices by reviewing past project experiences. The audit should be seen as a unique chance to learn from experience, and the results of audits should be reviewed by senior management.[3]

How the Process Worked

We began with two programs for Executive Vice Presidents and Senior Vice Presidents. Every program consisted of three days of the simulation. Presenting a program for 25 participants every two months for four years, we had about 500 people exposed to correct project management practice. After the vice presidents were done, we started with the department directors, then on to the project managers themselves. After all of the project managers went through the program we started to train the actual team members.

Most of the programs were done at corporate headquarters. However, many of the problems originated in the credit card processing centers spread across the United States, so the program went on the road to the centers to ensure that they too were up on the new procedures. This had an amazing effect. First, they were learning the procedures just like everyone else. But more importantly, they were surprised that the people at headquarters were actually addressing the problems instead of just complaining about them. This made them eager to adopt the best practices.

At the end of each program, the PIP questionnaire on best practices was developed by Pinto and Slevin,[4] which indicates how well the organization implemented best practices for project management. In every area, the people in this organization consistently scored in the 20th percentile or less. Those scores remained basically static for the first three years of the change process. Toward the end of the third year, we began to see many project team members who, after taking the simulation, would say, "Oh, that's why they told us to do those things." At this point, the scores jumped noticeably. Suddenly, this organization scored in about the 80th percentile on every best practice area. Best practices had finally taken hold in that organization.

LESSONS LEARNED

▶***Think long term.*** It takes a long time to install new procedures in an old organization. This process took about five years to complete in a mid-sized organization.

▶***Start at the top.*** If you truly want the organization to change, you have to start at the top. This is particularly true of a hierarchical organization, like a bank, where all power and direction comes from the top.

▶***Project management is for everyone.*** For project management to really take hold in organization, everyone in that organization must learn the procedures. Merely training the project managers in best procedures is not enough. New procedures must be learned and supported from the top of the organization all the way to the bottom.

▶***Measure your progress.*** Using a normed instrument like the PIP allows you to compare your organization to others, which helps to motivate program participants when they see how far they are behind others, while changes in these scores verify success of the change effort.

▶***Keep the faith.*** Progress does not appear in steady increments. Toward the end of three years, PIP scores remained low and it looked like we had nothing. Then, when we finally got down to the project team members, the scores suddenly jumped and everything jelled. This is a great example of the old parable of comparing change to turning water into ice. When cooling water all the way down to 33°, it looks as if nothing much is happening. Then with one degree cooler to 32°, the water suddenly turns to ice. This certainly happened at OE and would likely be similar in most other organizations.

DISCUSSION QUESTIONS

❶ What are the principal factors that inhibit the implementation of project management practices in organizations you are familiar with?

❷ Critique the process described for successfully implementing project management within a functional organization. Are there any steps that were missing in the process? Could this process be generalized to be used in other types of organizations?

❸ As in any organizational change effort, there were several "chance" occurrences that aided the implementation process. What role did these chance occurrences play in the success of the change effort? What role do you think chance generally plays in successful implementation efforts?

REFERENCES

[1] Graham, Robert J. *Project Management as if People Mattered.* Bala Cynwyd, PA: Primavera Press, 1989.

[2] Cleland, David I. *Project Management: Strategic Design and Implementation.* Blue Ridge Summit, PA: Tab Books, 1990: 352.

[3] Graham, Robert and Randall Englund. *Creating an Environment for Successful Projects: Second Edition.* San Francisco: Jossey-Bass Publishers, 2004. See also Englund, Randall, Robert Graham and Paul Dinsmore. *Creating the Project Office: a Manager's Guide to Leading Organizational Change.* San Francisco: Jossey-Bass Publishers, 2003.

[4] Pinto, Geoffrey, and Dennis Slevin. Project Success; Definition and Measurement Techniques. *Project Management Journal,* 19 (1988).

CHAPTER 26

Managing Multiple Projects: Balancing Time, Resources, and Objectives

▶LOWELL DYE, PMP, TRICON CONSULTING

Corporate downsizing, organizational restructuring, changes in technology, and many other factors have required that most employees become skilled multi-taskers and almost all project managers become multi-project managers. On the surface this may not seem too much of an issue since everyone at some time or another has handled several activities simultaneously. However, because customers, management, and other key stakeholders want immediate response and are typically focused on the short term, there is constant pressure to reduce cycle times and introduce new products and services faster and faster. There is also a natural tendency for achievement-oriented organizations and motivated project managers to want to start more projects than can logically be accomplished given the time and resource constraints often found in today's business environment.

The terms program management, project portfolio management, multi-project management, and multi-tasking are becoming more and more commonplace as projects are continually added, modified, and removed in response to internal and external business activity and changing economic conditions. In fact, a growing part of the project management software industry is around the creation and integration of tools, techniques, methods, systems, etc. for prioritizing and managing the myriad of projects and their associated activities.

Thererfore, project managers must be familiar with several aspects of managing multiple projects:

	Portfolio Management	Multiple Project Management
Purpose	Project Selection and Prioritization	Project Selection and Prioritization
Focus	Strategic	Operational
Planning Focus	Long/Medium Term (Annual/Quarterly)	Long/Medium Term (Annual/Quarterly)
Responsibility	Executive/Senior Management	Project/Resource Managers

Source: James S. Pennypacker and Lowell D. Dye, Project Portfolio Management and Managing Multiple Projects: Two Sides of the Same Coin? *Proceedings of the Annual Project Management Institute Seminars & Symposium, 2000.*

TABLE 26-1. **HIGH-LEVEL COMPARISON OF PROJECT PORTFOLIO MANAGEMENT AND MULTIPLE PROJECT MANAGEMENT**

- ▶What is multiple project management?
- ▶Cultural, political, and organizational elements that affect the management of multiple projects
- ▶Roles and responsibilities in a multiple project environment
- ▶Planning, staffing, and resource allocation considerations
- ▶Project reporting and managerial decision-making
- ▶Achieving success in a multiple project environment.

WHAT IS MULTIPLE PROJECT MANAGEMENT?

In order to be competitive, organizations regularly make hard choices about which projects to start, which to continue or modify, and which projects to terminate. This difficulty is made even worse by the fact that management is often unable or unwilling to label one project more or less important than another project. As a result, there is an unrealistic expectation that the sharing of resources, especially critical resources among "high-priority" projects, can be accomplished with little or no impact to the resources or the organization involved.

It is not uncommon to find program management, project portfolio management, and multi-project management being used synonymously. The management of multiple projects and portfolio management are in fact different. In the purest sense, portfolio management has two major components: a strategic element and an operational element. The strategic element involves project selection and prioritization—making sure the right projects are undertaken that are aligned with organizational goals and objectives. At the other end, managing multiple projects is more concerned with day-to-day operational management and resource allocation of the projects within the portfolio. Table 26-1 illustrates the major differences of multiple project and portfolio management.[1]

Add to the mix programs, strategic projects, and other independent projects and resources become even more stressed. The Project Management Institute defines a program as: "A group of related projects managed in a coordinated way. Programs usually

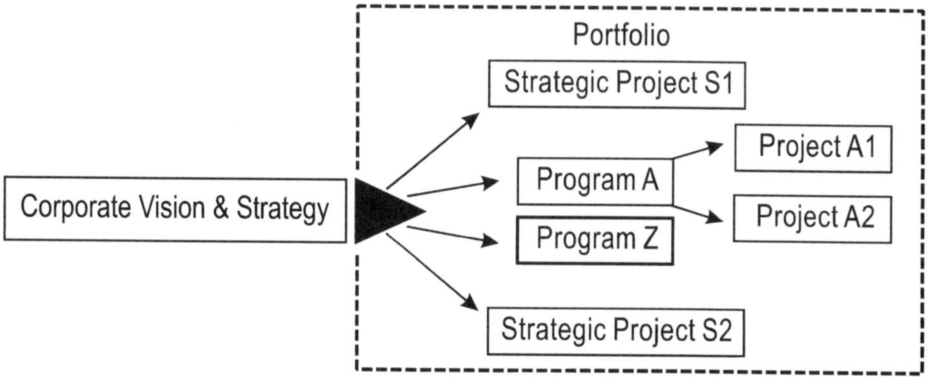

FIGURE 26-1. **PORTFOLIO-PROGRAM-PROJECT RELATIONSHIP**

include an element of ongoing work."[2] Programs have a major deliverable or objective to accomplish that determines which projects are undertaken in order to meet that objective—for example, the building of an aircraft carrier or the overhaul of an IT infrastructure within a large global corporation. In the purest sense, a program is a portfolio of multiple projects with a single focused major goal that requires several separate and unique, but integrated, projects to produce the program elements.

Because programs generally have an overall program manager, a common objective, and defined interfaces, some of the issues faced when managing several independent projects each with its own, and sometimes competing objectives, may not arise or be as obvious, such as the management of project resources.

Strategic projects are typically highly visible corporate undertakings that often become a high priority and pull resources from other projects and programs. An example of a strategic project is the roll out of a corporate-wide project management-training curriculum that has been directed and sponsored by the President or CEO.

It is important to remember that regardless of the initiation source, all of the programs and projects in the portfolio are generally competing for the same resources. The occasional exception being an environment in which resources are dedicated to specific projects. When dealing with multiple project environments, all stakeholders need to clearly understand that resources should go to those projects with the higher priorities as determined by their urgency with respect to time, cost, and ever-changing customer requirements.

Unfortunately priorities are not always established or maintained because of political, cultural, and other organizational factors, as well as a short-term profit-driven focus that almost forces a special emphasis on maximizing resource at 100 percent.

Cultural, Political, and Organizational Elements Affecting the Management of Multiple Projects

How many times have you heard it said, "That sounds fine in theory, but in real life we don't have the option of refusing or even delaying projects," or "Within our company, we don't have the luxury of dedicating any resources to a single project, let alone a project manager." The common view of management is that typical projects are not large enough, complex enough, or economically significant enough to warrant a dedicated project manager or project team.

While resource constraints may be a fact of life in a business environment, many companies fail to realize that committing resources to multiple projects does not speed up delivery, but may actually delay project completion. Without some type of control, projects compete for limited resources, generating much shifting and coordination of resources, thereby causing throughput to go down. Companies often operate under the misconception that a project manager can be given five or more projects, with each project receiving an allocation of twenty to thirty percent or less of the project manager's time. For project team members, the allocation is even worse. Having team members assigned five to ten percent of their time to many projects provides very little actual time for real work. In addition, management often fails to recognize that not only are project resources shared among several projects, each of these members generally have "non-project" related responsibilities as well, such as internal committees, company-sponsored community activities, professional development and training, etc. The additional commitments may be important to the company, but take energy away from assigned projects.

A study on multi-tasking published in 2001 in the *Journal of Experimental Psychology*, discovered that when switching from one task to another, there are "time costs" in terms of productivity, efficiency, concentration, etc. and that these costs increase with task complexity.[3] Another 2001 study of 1,003 workers conducted by the Families and Work Institute revealed that 45 percent of those surveyed felt that they had too many tasks to work on simultaneously and experienced frequent work interruptions, resulting in difficulty focusing on the work to be done.[4] Logic, experience, and common sense show that the more projects that have to be juggled, the less efficient people are at performing any single task; and the longer it takes to return to the interrupted task, the harder it is to reengage in the previous activity.

Obviously, some managers are better at balancing multiple projects and their related tasks than others depending upon their experience and individual abilities—some are not. In such environments, it is important that a flexible process for resource allocation, for setting realistic milestone dates and delivery schedules, and for adding new projects into the existing pipeline be established. It is also important to have a well defined and established project selection and prioritization process and a good mechanism for communicating those priorities. Within the project management industry, there has been much attention to resource allocation with companies spending great financial resources to implement sophisticated resource management software. But, if the organization is allocating resources to the wrong projects, then does it really matter how sophisticated the software?

A key element to managing multiple projects is the culture and support structure established by project sponsors and senior executives—one that emphasizes honesty and clear accountability for decisions and results. Sometimes the greatest bottleneck in a multiple project environment is senior management or the management team. When dissatisfied with project results, one of the first things some companies do is reorganize the project team or replace the project manager, since these are relatively easy solutions. This type of activity is also dangerous if senior managers do not fully understand the many interactions among multiple projects.

The senior and executive management team needs to set the culture, values, and systems that enable the effective management of multiple projects. In most companies there is a certain amount of "gamesmanship" in the creation of project budgets, schedules, and resource requirements. Add to this the sharing of responsibilities between functional managers and project managers—both jockeying for leadership—and things get more complicated. What saves projects in this environment are dedicated and hard working project teams that are willing to go above and beyond the call of duty to ensure that project goals and objectives are satisfied.

Organizational structures, political factors, and cultural influences affect the ability to manage multiple project activities and resources, regardless of the corporate culture, the number of parallel activities, or that there are a number of things that can be done to make the management of multiple projects more manageable. Complete alignment of the management team is essential and one of the best ways is to achieve this is by having clearly defined roles and responsibilities.

ROLES AND RESPONSIBILITIES IN A MULTIPLE PROJECT ENVIRONMENT

It is important that all key stakeholders, especially project managers, sponsors, and functional/resource managers, understand their individual roles and responsibilities and are fully committed to corporate, portfolio, and project objectives. If roles and responsibilities are not aligned, each stakeholder could allow personal agendas to interfere with project decisions and negatively impact project success due to potential infighting and competition for scarce resources.

Project managers must be diligent and proactive in order to identify problems and take appropriate action. Project and functional managers need to work together so that project team members and the project managers themselves are not overloaded. Both have the responsibility to provide skills necessary for project success and, when possible, to put team members in positions that will encourage and enhance professional and personal development. Project managers have the responsibility to coordinate resources among their projects and provide team building for team members. Functional managers have the responsibility to ensure that resources are available when the project manager needs them. With shared responsibility, conflict and confusion can be created for team members if they are unclear about their roles and whose authority to follow and trust. This conflict can be reduced if levels of authority with respect to resource allocation, decision-making, reporting requirement, corrective actions, and baseline management are clearly defined. This is especially true when managing more than one project or in a matrixed organization.

Senior and executive management need to be actively involved with project decisions and the balancing of resources among active and potential projects. However, management involvement should be at an appropriate level and should not be trying to assume the role of the project manager through micro-management. Senior management's role is primarily to ensure that projects are linked to long-term business strategy. This role includes ensuring that projects are properly prioritized, project teams are adequately staffed, obstacles to success are removed, cross-project conflicts are resolved, etc. Senior management also has the responsibility to ensure that methods and tools are available for sharing project information among all the project managers, team members, and other key stakeholders.

As stated earlier, effectively managing more than one project is only possible if project managers and team members can stay focused. The challenge is in how to separate their individual responsibilities for each assigned project, as well as non-project work. In a single project situation, the project manager is often the technical or subject matter expert. In a multiple project environment, it is even more unlikely that the project manager will be a technical expert in all elements of all projects. Since all projects are done for business reasons, it is not necessary for the project manager to be the technical expert, but the project manager does need to understand the technical elements of the project.

Project team members also are assigned to projects because of their knowledge and expertise. Team members may include full-time staff members, part-time employees, or subcontractors. The more specific the skills and knowledge required and the more projects involved, the more important and difficult the allocation process. Because the number of team members is generally limited, there is a tendency to over-commit these resources for the sake of keeping them fully engaged. Team members may have assigned responsibilities that are outside their areas of expertise, creating additional pressure and stress.

Planning, Staffing, and Resource Allocation Considerations Among Multiple Projects

One of the major frustrations for project managers is how to effectively and efficiently plan and schedule project activities in a resource-limited, multi-project environment. Managing multiple projects can create many potential problems for the project manager, stakeholders, and ultimately the customer. If there are too many projects to be handled in a timely manner with the desired quality, several costs could be incurred, such as the following:

▶Costs resulting from late deliveries because of resources working on too many projects are not available to accomplish the scheduled work.

▶Costs resulting from assigned resources being underutilized because of bottlenecks created by overcommitted resources.

▶Costs, both tangible and intangible, resulting from team member burnout, reduced quality due to over-commitment, etc.

The overall process for handling multiple projects is fundamentally the same as that for handling single projects or programs. Project managers and their teams need to develop a detailed management plan for each project using an accepted project management methodology. The establishment of approved technical (scope), schedule, cost, and resource baselines is essential. The integrated planning of each single project should not only look at the internal task dependencies but external dependencies with other projects as well. External relationships also include the influence of functional organizations, vendor and subcontractor activities, and customer interfaces.

This comparison to single project management should not be considered an attempt to oversimplify the handling of multiple projects. While similar, basic planning and control methods and techniques may not be sufficient. Managing multiple projects is a challenge because organizational practices often ignore or underestimate the significance of establishing and adhering to project priorities, defining project standards and acceptance criteria, and integrating project data. The problem increases with the complexity of inter-project links, overlapping schedule and resource requirements, and the fact that project resources cannot be concentrated on multiple projects to the extent they can be dedicated to a single major project or program. There is also a shared misconception among executives and project managers that if someone is skilled at managing one or two projects, they are also skilled at handling many projects.

To optimize time and resource in a multiple project environment, the use of good project management software is beneficial. In many circumstances, software may be required to properly develop a resource-loaded schedule and clearly identify time and resource conflicts. The number of projects and the size of each may determine the level of software sophistication and functionality required. If projects tend to be small, relatively simple, stand-alone projects, then something as simple as a spreadsheet or Gantt chart may be all that is necessary. For programs, large complex projects with many external dependencies, or a large number of small projects with shared resource pools, then an enterprise system that integrates all projects into a master file may be necessary. A word of caution—do not let the use of a software package replace good project planning and decision making.

During the past several years, companies have turned to a myriad of resource planning and optimization techniques with varying degrees of success. Some of the most common include resource planning, scheduling, and optimization techniques such as queuing theory, capacity requirements planning, theory of constraints, resource leveling techniques, and critical chain project management.

One of the best ways to manage resource allocation among multiple projects is to improve the quality of project effort and duration estimates. The value of valid estimates is often overlooked within many organizations. Realistic and supportable estimates can make or break project planning. Estimates, based on a well-defined work breakdown structure, provide the foundation for good time, cost, and resource planning. The importance of good estimation in a multiple project environment is in determining resource task assignments and the creation of each project's critical path. If management clearly understands the requirements of each project and the amount of flexibility available to them, then logical decisions can be made relative to the priorities, value, and contributions of all the projects.

Some of these may be difficult decisions and may go against established norms. For example, if projects are undertaken based on their contribution to the organizations strategic goals and objectives and their benefit to the overall project portfolio, then the highest priority projects should be fully staffed first. The second priority project is fully staffed next, and so on. If sufficient resource capacity is not available, then lower priority projects should not be started. When a project is finished and capacity is again available, the next priority project can be staffed and started.

Many projects are started because of an external customer request or other profit potential. These projects are the most obvious and the ones that get the most attention with respect to resource utilization. But, many projects that compete for limited resources are not as obvious, nor do they get the attention deserved, such as upgrades and enhancements, process improvement and cost reduction projects, internal research and development, infrastructure systems deployment projects, facilities start-up projects, and many more. Sometimes these "non-profit" projects are started in response to a real customer or market need, but often they are initiated by management.

Granted, these projects may be well meaning attempts to strengthen a company's position within the marketplace; however, because organizations typically do not have enough visibility into total capacity requirements, management could operate under the misconception that these projects are simply a means of optimizing resources. But, without defined and integrated portfolio and project management methodologies, resource requirements estimates and the subsequent resource allocation may be determined somewhat arbitrarily.

When handling multiple projects and balancing their associated resource, time and cost constraints, there are several things a management team can do:

1. *Increase capacity relative to demand.* Increase project team members and support staff; add new planning and management tools or enhancing existing tools; reduce non-value added work, such as collateral assignments and meetings that take away from direct project work; provide training to team members, functional managers, and other stakeholders; and cross-train project team members in projects skills outside their area of expertise.

2. *Reduce demand relative to capacity.* Reduce the number of projects during peak demand periods, limit features, and reduce requirements if possible. Demand management is a key principle in project selection and prioritization as part of an overall portfolio management process.

3. *Implement appropriate management and control systems.* As defined in the broadest sense, systems may include a variety of tools, methods, and processes that enable management to establish realistic project/program management plans and enable project and functional manager to react quickly to changes in resource demand or project delivery times.

In addition, having a common set of forms, templates, tools, and approved guidelines that can be re-used and that is shared and communicated throughout the organization will help with the planning and integration of project resources. The forms and templates may include work breakdown structures, common activity lists, schedules, resource pools and skill sets, estimating guidelines, and standardized WBS and resource coding/naming conventions. Shared templates help to expedite the planning process, relieve some of the administrative burdens on the project manager allowing more time to actual project management, and provide confidence on the part of management that the project management process is being consistently applied across all projects and programs.

PROJECT REPORTING AND MANAGERIAL DECISION MAKING IN A MULTIPLE PROJECT ENVIRONMENT

Managers, especially when handling multiple projects, have to make difficult decisions with respect to project priorities, resources, conflicts, etc. To make effective project decisions, project and functional managers need to have a good understanding of individual project resource commitments, how resources are shared among all the projects in the active project portfolio, and where adjustments can be made. This assumes that responsible managers have the authority and experience to shift/reallocate resources from one project to another and, if necessary, adjust activity delivery dates. However, no matter how skilled the manager, if customers and sponsors continually make scope changes or second-guess a project manager's decisions, then it is extremely difficult to efficiently plan activity timelines and resource requirements.

To effectively make logical decisions, it is important that managers be able to quickly analyze the impact of changing, adding, or removing a project and that they be able to respond appropriately. Such analysis requires that project data be accessible, reliable, and timely. There are many reporting tools and techniques of differing levels of sophistication, such as dashboards, scorecards, and variance reports, which provide stakeholders with project status information in an organization's portfolio. The information provided by these tools can be used to make timely decisions, resolve conflict, and respond proactively—not reactively—to the changing conditions.

Project information requirements are essentially the same for all stakeholders, whether communicating information for a single project or multiple projects. However, the amount of detail and the communication mechanism is dependent upon the stakeholder and how the project information will be used. For example, project managers need to see a project performance against the detailed work schedule and budget. If managing more than one project with shared resources, project managers need to make sure that they have current information for each individual project. Functional managers need insight into how resources are being utilized across all projects and programs, and the resource requirements projections are so they can manage their staffing plans and ensure that project managers have the resources when they are needed. Senior managers and executives require much higher-level information that is more strategic, such as portfolio-level data showing how projects and programs in the aggregate are contributing to corporate goals and objectives.

Regardless of the stakeholder, it is important that the recipient have confidence in the reported data and that they be able to see the big picture. Earned value management and variance analysis reporting for programs and major programs have been used to report progress against approved baselines since the 1960s. More recently, organizations have also added Project Dashboard reporting to their toolkit. Dashboards are simply reporting tools that present a consolidated view of the active projects and/or programs in a portfolio. Dashboard reports typically provide project status, baseline and revision status, project budget and schedule information, etc. Dashboards typically use a color-coding structure to graphically report status—Green (on budget, on schedule, no significant issues); Yellow (potential budget or schedule variances, issues need to be addressed); and Red (severe budget or schedule problems, significant issues could impact project success). Management may require that all projects be reported regardless of status, or reporting may be done on an exception basis—only "Yellow" or "Red" projects will be reported. Dashboards or some other type of consolidated reports may be managed by a program manager, a centralized project management/control office, or the responsibility may be shared by the project managers. In either case, data reporting must be consistent. As project management and enterprise software become more sophisticated with respect to features and functions, dashboard generation and data accuracy is becoming much easier.

ACHIEVING SUCCESS IN A MULTIPLE PROJECT ENVIRONMENT

While there are challenges in any environment, the establishment and use of good performance metrics and measurement criteria can lead to effective management of multiple projects and can position the organization to be competitive in a dynamic environment. The creation and implementation of good management practices are important.

In a multiple project environment, it is impossible to please all of the stakeholders all of the time, but it is possible and crucial to be honest and upfront regarding capabilities and capacity. For example, when a customer complains about late deliveries, the first reaction is to push project teams to work harder and faster—to be more productive. The problem is that they are already working on a dozen other projects. In reality, what customers and all stakeholders actually want is a realistic plan and logical deliver dates that can be met. Most customers understand that unexpected events occur and are generally willing to be flexible. Customers and related projects or programs often have activities of their own that must be coordinated with expected activity delivery or project completion dates in order to meet their objectives. If an integrated approach is taken to project planning and control, then managing customer and stakeholder expectations will be much easier.

A best practice in the management of multiple is to avoid the temptation to start more projects than the organization has resources for or can coordinate and manage effectively. This concept challenges common practice for many reasons, many of which were addressed previously.

There is no single "right answer" for how to manage multiple projects, the best software to use, the right organizational structure, or how to properly engage senior managers. What is important is for management to establish a culture that encourages open and honest communication, proactive decision making, accurate documentation, and timely reporting of all project and resource information.

DISCUSSION QUESTIONS

❶ What are the major differences and similarities among project portfolio management, program management, and managing multiple projects?

❷ What are some of the things a management team can do to balance resources, time, and cost constraints in a multiple project environment? What issues and concerns should a project manager consider when trying to balance these constraints?

❸ Reporting project performance can be difficult in a multiple project environment. What make performance reporting so challenging, and how can the project environment support or hinder the reporting process?

REFERENCES

[1] Pennypacker, J. S., and Dye, L. D., Project Portfolio Management and Managing Multiple Projects: Two Sides of the Same Coin? *Proceedings of the Annual Project Management Institute Seminars & Symposium,* 2000.

[2] Project Management Institute. *A Guide to the Project Management Body of Knowledge, Third Edition.* Newtown Square, PA: Project Management Institute, 2004.

[3] Rubenstein, J. S., Meyer, D. E., and Evans, J. E., Executive Control of Cognitive Processes in Task Switching. *Journal of Experimental Psychology: Human Perceptions and Performance,* 27 (2001).

[4] Galinsky, E., Kim, S. S., and Bond, J. T., "Feeling Overworked: When Work Becomes Too Much Executive Summary," retrieved June 25, 2004, from Families and Work Institute, 2001.

FURTHER READING

Brown, Alex. "Of Benchmarks and Scorecards: Reporting on Multiple Projects," in Proceedings of the Annual Project Management Institute Seminars & Symposium, Newtown Square, PA: Project Management Institute, 2002.

Daw, Catherine. "Managing Multiple Projects is Much Like Raising Teenagers . . . Managing Resources Over Multiple Projects," in Proceedings of the Annual Project Management Institute Seminars & Symposium. Newtown Square, PA: Project Management Institute, 1999.

Ireland, Lewis R. "Managing Multiple Projects in the Twenty First Century," in Proceedings of the Annual Project Management Institute Seminars & Symposium, 83–89. Upper Darby, PA: Project Management Institute, 1997.

Levy, Nino, and Globerson, Shlomo. "Improving Multiple Project Management by Using a Queuing Theory Approach." *Project Management Journal,* 1997: 40–46.

Milosevic, Dragan, and Patanakul, Peerasit. "Secrets of Successful Multi-project Managers," in *Proceedings of the Annual Project Management Institute Seminars & Symposium.* Newtown Square, PA: Project Management Institute, 2002.

SECTION FOUR

ISSUES AND IDEAS IN PROJECT MANAGEMENT PRACTICE

SECTION FOUR

Section Four: Introduction

ISSUES AND IDEAS IN PROJECT MANAGEMENT PRACTICE

Project management practice is dynamic: it changes in response to changes in the environment—in response to technological, cultural, and sociological changes. In this section of the book, expert authors highlight some of the areas in project management where new trends or problems are creating new ideas and solutions.

The issues involved in project management are broad and multi-faceted. The topics in this section illustrate some specific approaches to dealing with the management of projects, ranging from political and cultural issues to alternative methodologies that can be applied in unison with project management principles.

Power and politics are always an overriding issue on projects; rather than simply complain about them, Randall L. Englund offers a proactive way to plan for and succeed at organizational politics.

Critical Chain and Six Sigma methodologies are proven approaches that, in certain contexts, can be applied jointly with project management. These methodologies, relatively new to the practice of project management, are described here by Frank Patrick and by Maximiano and Soler.

Communities of practice are a way of organizing project personnel to improve knowledge management and transfer, as well as to provide the satisfaction of social learning and rewarding professional relationships; DeLisle and Rowe are well-versed in both the human and technical aspects of CoPs.

Finally, Dinsmore and Codas provide an overview of the challenges project managers face when working with the increasingly commonmulticultural and/or international project team.

CHAPTER 27

Dealing With Power and Politics in Project Management

▶RANDALL L. ENGLUND, CONSULTANT

Project management is more than techniques to complete projects on time, scope, and budget. Organizations by their very nature are political, so effective project managers need to become politically sensitive. Assessing the environment and developing an effective political plan help to address the power structure in an organization, identify critical stakeholder levels of impact and support, develop a guiding coalition, and determine areas of focus.

Because all projects involve change, project managers and team members find themselves involved in an organizational change process. To be ignorant about leading change can be costly to the organization and the individual. Instead of lamenting about a failed project, program, or initiative, it is possible to learn a proven approach to power, politics, and change that optimizes project success. Let's examine some specific steps that make a difference between success or failure in a political environment.

It takes wisdom and courage to engage in action and change an approach to project work. Instead of facing unknowns, resistance and chaos alone, prepare for a hero's journey. The approach shared below can help turn potential victim scenarios into win-win political victories.

Sooner or later all professionals find a leadership role thrust upon them, a team to lead, or a project to accomplish with others. Greater success comes to those who define, develop, and/or refine a plan to be successful. These people ultimately embrace the journey or process of changing an organization to be more efficient and more profitable by developing an organization-wide project management system, often called enterprise project management. Wise persons choose a proactive path, employing a change management process, replete with requisite political skills, rather than wishing they had done so retrospectively.

The path includes many uncertainties. Luckily, modern project management provides effective strategies to reduce uncertainties throughout the project life cycle. Opportunity comes to those leaders who understand and meld scope management and change management processes with skills in selling, negotiating, and politicking.

A common theme for success or failure of any organizational initiative is building a guiding coalition—a bonding of sponsors and influential people who support the change. This support, or not, represents a powerful force either toward or away from the goal. Gaining support means the difference between pushing on, modifying the approach, or exiting a path toward a new order of business. Moderate success may be achieved without widespread political support, but continuing long-term business impact requires alignment of power factors within the organization. Along the way, adapt effective concepts from nature to make organizations more project-friendly, which in turn leads to greater value-added, economically viable results.

Organizations attempting projects across functions, businesses and geographies increasingly encounter complexities that threaten their success. A common response is to set up control systems that inhibit the very results intended. This happens when we inhibit free flow of information and impose unnecessary constraints.

By contrast, taming the chaos and managing complexity are possible when stakeholders establish a strong sense of purpose, develop shared vision and values, and adopt patterns from nature that promote cooperation across cultural boundaries. These processes represent major change for many organizations.

An organic approach to project management acknowledges that people work best in an environment that supports their innate talents, strengths, and desires to contribute. Many organizational environments thwart rather than support these powerful forces in their drive to complete projects on time, on budget, and according to specifications. Applying lessons from complexity science offers a different approach—one that seeks to tame the chaos rather than implement onerous controls. A key is to look for behavioral patterns and incentives that naturally guide people toward a desired result. Results are similar to those of a successful gardener: combining the right conditions with the right ingredients creates a bountiful harvest. By ensuring that leadership, learning, means, and motivation are all present in appropriate amounts, the right people can employ efficient processes in an effective environment.

Too late, people often learn the power of a non-guiding coalition. This happens when a surprise attack results in a resource getting pulled, a project manager is reassigned, or a project is cancelled. Getting explicit commitments up front, the more public the better, is important to implementing any change. It also takes follow through to maintain the commitment. But if commitment was not obtained initially, it is not possible to maintain throughout. It all starts by investigating attitudes and assessing how things get done.[1]

VIEWS OF POLITICS

Albert Einstein said "*Politics is more difficult than physics.*" Politics will be present anytime an attempt is made to turn a vision for change into reality. It is a fact of life, not a dirty word that should be stamped out. A common view is what happens with negative politics, which is a *win-lose* environment in an under-handed or without-your-knowledge-

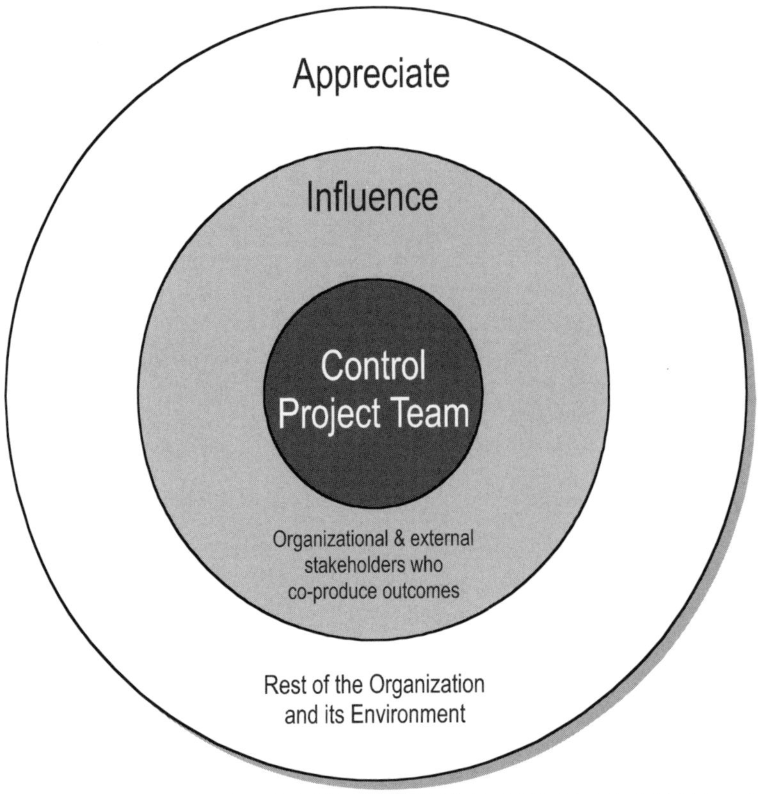

FIGURE 27-1. **TYPES OF STAKEHOLDER POWER**

of-what's-happening approach. People feel manipulated, and the outcome is not desirable from their point of view. Secret discussions are more prevalent than public ones. Reciprocal agreements are made to benefit individuals rather than organizations.

The challenge is to create an environment for positive politics. That is, people operate with a *win-win* attitude. All actions are out in the open. People demonstratively work hard toward the common good. Outcomes are desirable or at least acceptable to all parties concerned. This is the view of power and politics being espoused in this writing.

One's attitude toward political behavior becomes extremely important. Options are to be naive, be a shark that uses aggressive manipulation to reach the top, or to be politically sensible. According to Jeffrey Pinto, "politically sensible individuals enter organizations with few illusions about how many decisions are made." They understand, either intuitively or through their own experience and mistakes, that politics is a facet of behavior that happens in all organizations. Political sensitives neither shun nor embrace predatory politics. "Politically sensible individuals use politics as a way of making contacts, cutting deals, and gaining power and resources for their departments or projects to further corporate, rather than entirely personal, ends.[2]

To make politics work for you, it is important to understand the levels of power in leading a project. As depicted in Figure 27-1:

▶**Control** or authority power is the one most prevalent but not one that project managers can rely on with any degree of certainty in most organizations.

▶**Influence** or status depends upon referent (or appealing to others) powers:

- Willing to challenge the status quo;
- Create and communicate a vision;
- Empower others;
- Model desired behavior;
- Encourage others.

▶**Appreciation** means having awareness of areas of uncertainty outside the realm of control or influence that could nevertheless impact project success. For instance, I cannot know when an upper manager will dictate a change in the project or a system will crash, but I can appreciate that these things happen and provide placeholders with contingencies for them in the project plan.

Politics happen in any and all organizations. Remarkably, power and politics are unpopular topics with many people. That ambivalent attitude hampers their ability to become skilled and effective.

Most organizations do not suffer from too much power; more so people feel there is too little power either being exercised to keep things moving or available to them. They often resort to a victim mode of feeling powerless. One high-level management team almost ceased to function when the general manager could not be present at the last moment for a critical meeting. The facilitator had to help them realize this was their opportunity to build a power base among themselves and to take action that presented a united front.

Lack of demonstrated power is also an opportunity to exercise personal power. Many people shine when they jump in and do something when they first see the opportunity, asking forgiveness later if necessary instead of waiting for permission.

ASSESSING THE POLITICAL ENVIRONMENT

A big pitfall people fall into is not taking the time to fully assess what they are up against—learning how to operate effectively in a political environment.

What is a political environment? A negative reaction to the word "political" could be a barrier to success. Being political is not a bad thing when trying to get good things done for the organization. A political environment is the power structure, formal and informal. It is how things get done within the day-to-day processes as well as in a network of relationships. Power is the capacity each individual possesses to translate intention into reality and sustain it. Organizational politics is the exercise or use of power. The world of physics revolves around power. Because project management is all about getting results, it stands to reason that power is required. Political savvy is a vital ingredient for every project manager's toolkit.

Understand the power structure in the organization. A view from outer space would not show the lines that separate countries, organizations or functional areas, or other political boundaries. The lines are figments that exist in our minds or on paper but not in reality. Clues to a power structure may come from an organizational chart, but how things get done goes far beyond that. Influence exists in people's hearts and minds, where power derives more from legitimacy than from authority. Its presence is shown by the implementation of decisions.

Legitimacy is what people confer on their leaders. Being authentic and acting with integrity are factors a leader decides in relations to others, but legitimacy is the response from others. Position power may command respect, but ultimately how a leader behaves is what gains whole-hearted commitment from followers. Legitimacy is the real prize, for it completes the circle. When people accept and legitimize the power of a leader, greater support gets directed toward the outcome; conversely, less resistance is present.

People have always used organizations to amplify human power. Art Kleiner states a premise that in every organization there is a core group of key people—the "people who really matter"—and the organization continually acts to fulfill the perceived needs and priorities of this group.[3]

There are numerous ways that Kleiner suggests to determine who these powerful people are. People who have power are at the center of the organization's informal network. They are symbolic representatives of the organization's direction. They got this way because of their position, their rank, and their ability to hire and fire others. Maybe they control a key bottleneck or belong to a particular influential subculture. They may have personal charisma or integrity. These people take a visible stand on behalf of the organization's principles and engender a level of mutual respect. They dedicate themselves as leaders to the organization's ultimate best interests and set the organization's direction. As they think or act or convey an attitude, so does the rest of the organization. Their characteristics and principles convey what an organization stands for. These are key people who, when open to change, can influence an organization to move in new directions or, when not open to change, keep it the same.

Another way to recognize key people is to look for decision makers in the mainstream business of the organization. They may be aligned with the headquarters culture, ethnic basis, or gender, speak the native language, or be part of the founding family. Some questions to ask about people in the organization are: Whose interests did we consider in making a decision? Who gets things done? Who could stop something from happening? Who are the "heroes?"

Power is not imposed by boundaries. Power is earned, not demanded. Power can come from position in the organization, what a person knows, a network of relationships, and possibly the situation, meaning a person could be placed in a situation that has a great deal of importance and focus in the organization.

A simple test for where power and influence reside is to observe who people talk to or go to with questions or for advice. Whose desk do people meet at? Who has a long string of voice or e-mail messages? Whose calendar is hard to get into?

One of the most reliable sources of power when working across organizations is the credibility a person builds through a network of relationships. It is necessary to have credibility before a person can attract team members, especially the best people, who are usually busy and have many other things competing for their time. Credibility comes from relationship building in a political environment.

In contrast, credibility gaps occur when previous experience did not fulfill expectations or when perceived abilities to perform are unknown and therefore questionable. Organizational memory has a lingering effect—people long remember what happened before and do not give up these perceptions without due cause. People more easily align with someone who has the power of knowledge credibility, but relationship credibility is something only each individual can build, or lose.

Power and politics also address the priority assigned to project management's triple constraints—outcome, schedule, and cost. If the power in an organization resides in marketing where tradeshows rule new product introductions, meeting market window schedules becomes most important. An R&D driven organization tends to focus on features and new technology, often at the expense of schedule and cost.

POLITICAL PLAN

A quest to optimize results in a convoluted organizational environment requires a political management plan. This is probably a new addition to the project manager's arsenal. Elements of a political plan may have been included in a communications plan. To conduct a systematic approach to power and politics, key element is to prepare a stakeholder analysis. One quickly realizes that it is impossible to satisfy everyone and that the goal might become to keep everyone minimally annoyed and to use a "weighted dissatisfaction" index.[4]

Stakeholder Analysis

Analysis of common success factors indicates that project leaders need to pay attention to the needs of project stakeholders as well as the needs of project team members. Identifying stakeholders early on leads to better stakeholder management throughout the project. Use the diagnostic tools and traits of key powerful people described previously to analyze stakeholders. A stakeholder is anyone who has a "stake in the ground" and cares about the effort—sponsoring the change, supplying, or executing it. Ask, "Who could stop this effort?"

To be thorough, visualize all stakeholders as points on a compass. To the North is the management chain; direct reports are to the South. To the West are customers and end users; other functional areas are to the East. In between are other entities, vendors, or regulatory agencies. Identify all players. Write down names and get to know people in each area. What motivates them, how are they measured, and what are their concerns?

Approach a stakeholder analysis using these steps:

1. Who are the stakeholders?
   - Brainstorm to identify all possible stakeholders.
   - Identify where each stakeholder is located.
   - Identify the relationship the project team has with each stakeholder in terms of power and influence during the project life cycle.
2. What are stakeholder expectations?
   - Identify primary high-level project expectations for each stakeholder.
3. How does the project or products affect stakeholders?
   - Analyze how the products and deliverables affect each stakeholder.
   - Determine what actions the stakeholder could take which would affect the success or failure of the project.
   - Prioritize the stakeholders, based on who has the most positive or negative effect on project success or failure.

- Incorporate information from previous steps into a risk analysis plan to develop mitigation procedures for stakeholders who might negatively impact the project.

Stakeholder Name	Support or Opposition (+5 to -5)	Why? Own Interests?	Relative Power	Management / Communication

FIGURE 27-2. **STAKEHOLDER ANALYSIS TEMPLATE**

4. What information do stakeholders need?

- Identify from the information collected, what information needs to be furnished to each of them, when it should be provided, and how.

The template in Figure 27-2 is one simple means to record information about these people.

Another tool is to complete a spreadsheet scoring levels of power and project support as shown in Figure 27-3.

Prepare an action plan for using the stakeholder "map" to resolve political issues. That plan might include actions such as:

▶Face to face meetings with each middle level manager, explaining the project mission and objectives, and getting them to share their real needs and expectations.

▶Sessions with all middle managers, using "mind-mapping techniques" to brainstorm ideas and get suggestions and real needs from various perspectives, leading up to a more aligned vision for the project.

▶Identifying and avoiding barriers like organizational climate, perceptions, customer pressure, and too many communication links.

Approach stakeholders in each area starting from the position of strength. When, for instance, power is high but agreement about the project is low, start by reinforcing the effective working relationship that exists and how the person may contribute to and benefit from the project. Express desire that this bond will help work through any differences. Only after establishing agreement on these objectives is it then appropriate to

Stakeholder	Power			Level of Concern			Z Axis
	Influence of Others	Control of Resources	Y Axis Score	Technical	Social	X Axis Score	Support / Resistance
TCOM Business Mgr.	5.0	3.0	3.8	3.0	5.0	4.3	1.0
TCOM Delivery Mgr.	4.0	5.0	4.6	3.0	5.0	4.3	5.0
HC Business Mgr.	4.0	3.0	3.4	2.0	3.0	2.7	4.0
BO Manager	5.0	5.0	5.0	5.0	2.0	3.1	3.5
Delivery Mgr.	5.0	5.0	5.0	5.0	2.0	3.1	1.0
FSI Business Mgr.	5.0	3.0	3.8	3.0	2.0	2.4	1.0
Industry Business Mgr.	4.0	3.0	3.4	1.0	1.0	1.0	1.0
GRS Mgr.	4.0	5.0	4.6	1.0	3.0	2.3	2.0
ITS Mgr.	3.0	5.0	4.2	1.5	4.0	3.1	1.0
Country Manager	5.0	5.0	5.0	4.0	3.0	3.4	4.0
PC	3.0	1.0	1.8	5.0	4.0	4.4	2.0
PC	3.0	2.0	2.4	4.0	4.0	4.0	4.5
PC	3.0	2.0	2.4	3.5	3.0	3.2	3.0
PC	3.0	2.0	2.4	4.0	3.0	3.4	1.5
PC	3.0	2.0	2.4	1.0	3.0	2.3	2.0
PC	3.0	2.0	2.4	3.0	4.0	3.7	3.5
NSP SMgr.	4.0	5.0	4.6	4.0	2.0	2.7	2.0
DW SMgr.	2.0	5.0	3.8	1.0	2.0	1.7	3.0
SSMgr.	2.0	5.0	3.8	3.0	4.0	3.7	4.0
SSMgr.	3.0	5.0	4.2	2.0	5.0	4.0	2.5
HR Mgr.	4.0	1.0	2.2	1.0	2.0	1.7	2.5
IT SSMgr.	2.0	1.0	1.4	4.0	5.0	5.0	4.5
FI Mgr.	5.0	5.0	5.0	5.0	3.0	3.7	2.0
ITM SMgr.	3.0	5.0	4.2			0.0	

Weighting:

- Influence of Others 0.4
- Direct Control of Resource 0.6

1

- Technical 0.35
- Social 0.65

1

Notes:

Power and level of concern rated on a 1 to 5 scale, with 5 being the greatest power or level of concern.

Support and Resistance is rated on a scale of 1 to 5, with 5 as most resistant.

Weighting factors for power and level of concern must total to 1 for each category.

FIGURE 27-3. **AN EXAMPLE STAKEHOLDER SPREADSHEET**

address the problem area. People often jump right into the problem. This prompts defensive behavior from the other person. Taking time to reestablish rapport first can prove far more effective to reach a mutually satisfying solution. It is then possible to discover misinformation or negotiate a change in outcome, cost, or schedule that lessens the levels of concern and moves people higher in supporting the project.

To illustrate, the customer says to the project manager, "I'm okay with most of your status report, but I have a big problem with progress on resolving the resourcing issue." Most people only hear the problem and immediately jump into defensive mode. Instead, start with, "I hear that you're satisfied with how we implemented your requests and can continue moving forward. Is that correct? Great! Okay, so now we only have this one issue to work through . . .." The tenor of this approach is positive, the topics on the table for discussion are bounded, and rapport is present, setting the mood for a creative solution.

Positioning

Another element of a political plan is positioning. For instance, where a project office is located in an organization affects its power base. The concept of "centrality" says to locate it in a position central and visible to other corporate members, where it is central to or important for organizational goals.[5] HP's Project Management Initiative started in Corporate Engineering, a good place to be because HP was an engineering company. That put the Initiative into the mainstream instead of in a peripheral organization where its effectiveness and exposure may be more limited. Likewise, a project office for the personal computer division reported through a section manager to the R&D functional manager. This again reflected centrality since R&D at that time drove product development efforts.

Most important decisions in organizations involve the allocation of scarce resources. Position and charter a project office with a key role in decision-making that is bound to the prioritization and distribution of organizational resources. Be there to help, not make decisions. Put managers at ease that they are not losing decision-making power but gaining an ally to facilitate and implement decisions.

An individual contributor, project leader, or *project office of one* needs to consider where he or she is located in an organization when wanting to have a greater impact, make a larger contribution, get promoted, or generally gain more power and influence. Doing service projects in a field office for a manufacturing and sales-oriented company is less likely to attract attention than a product marketing person doing new product introduction projects in the factory. Seek out projects that address critical factors facing the organization. In essence, address in a political plan how important the project is to the organization, where it resides in having access to key decision makers, and the support resources available to it.

Driving Change

Implicit in creating any new order is the notion that change is inevitable. The use of power and politics becomes a mechanism for driving change. Politics is a natural consequence of the interaction between organizational subsystems.

A well-known political tactic that enhances status is to demonstrate legitimacy and expertise. Developing proficiency and constantly employing new best practices around program and project management, combined with some of the above tactics in the political plan, plus communicating and promoting the services and successes achieved, helps a project gain status in the organization. This factor is a recurring theme in many case studies.

Pinto says, "Any action or change effort initiated by members of an organization that has the potential to alter the nature of current power relationships provides a tremendous impetus for political activity."[6]

A business case can be made that changes are often necessary within organizations that set out to conquer new territory through projects and project teams, often guided by a project office. The role of upper managers may need to change in order to support these new efforts. However, it takes concerted effort, often on the part of project managers who are closest to the work, to speak the truth to upper managers who have the authority and power about what needs to happen.[7] The change may be revolutionary and require specific skills and process steps to be effective. Change agents successfully navigate the political minefields by exercising these traits:

- ▶Act from personal strengths, such as expert, visionary, or process owner.
- ▶Develop a clear, convincing, and compelling message and make it visible to others.

▶Use your passion that comes from deep values and beliefs about the work (if these are not present, then find a different program to work on).

▶Be accountable for success of the organization and ask others to do the same.

▶Get explicit commitments from people to support the goals of the program so that they are more likely to follow through.

▶Take action, first to articulate the needs, then help others understand the change, achieve small wins, and get the job done.

▶Tap the energy that comes from the courage of your convictions . . . and from being prepared.

Conflict

Stakeholders' competing interests are inherently in conflict. Upper managers and customers want more features, lower cost, less time, and more changes. Accountants mainly care about lower costs. Team members typically want fewer features to work on, more money, more time, and fewer changes. These voices ring out in cacophony. When people find that telling their problems to the project manager helps them get speedy resolution instead of recrimination, they feel like they have a true friend, one they cannot do without.

Conflict is natural and normal. Too little, however, and there is excessive force—"*Whatever the group wants*." Too much and there is excessive conviction—"*My mind's made up*." These represent the flight or fight extremes of human behavior. The ideal is to create constructive contention where the attitude is: "*Let's work together to figure this out*." This middle ground happens when:

▶A *common objective* is present that all parties can relate to.

▶People understand how they make a *contribution.*

▶The issue under discussion has *significance,* both to the parties involved and to the organization.

▶People are *empowered* to act on the issue, not having to seek resolution elsewhere.

▶Everyone accepts *accountability* for success of the project or organizational venture.

For example, a material engineering manager was in a rage and called the taskforce project manager to ask how the project was proceeding. The project manager asked the other manager to come talk with him in person. Rather than putting up a defensive shield to ward off an upcoming attack, the project manager started the meeting by reviewing the project objectives and eliciting agreement that developing a process with consistent expectations and common terminology was a good thing. He next asked the materials manager about his concern and found out that inserting crosscheck steps early in the process would ensure that inventory overages would not happen when new products were designed with different parts. This represented a major contribution to the project. These individuals were empowered to make this change, which would have significant impact because all projects would be using the checklists generated by this project. Rather than creating a political battle, the two parties resolved the conflict through a simple process, the project achieved an improved outcome, and the two parties *walked off arm in arm in the same direction.*

Recognize that organizations are political. A commitment to positive politics is an essential attitude that creates a healthy, functional organization. Create relationships that are win-win (all parties gain), where actual intentions are out-in-the-open (not hidden or distorted), and trust is the basis for ethical transactions. Determining what is important to others and providing value to recipients are currencies that project leaders can exchange with other people. Increased influence capacity comes from forming clear, convincing, and compelling arguments and communicating them through all appropriate means. Effective program managers embrace the notion that they are salespersons, politicians, and negotiators. Take the time to learn the skills of these professions and apply them daily.

Start any new initiative or change by thinking big but starting small. First implement a prototype and achieve a victory. Plan a strategy of small wins to develop credibility, feasibility, and to demonstrate value. Get increased support to expand based upon this solid foundation.

AUTHENTIC LEADERSHIP IN ACTION

Authenticity means that people believe what they say. Integrity means that they do what they say they will do, and for the reasons they stated to begin with. Authenticity and integrity link the head and the heart, the words and the action; they separate belief from disbelief, and often make the difference between success and failure. Many people in organizations lament how their "leaders" lack authenticity and integrity. When that feeling is prevalent, trust cannot develop, and optimal results are difficult if not impossible to achieve.

Integrity is the melding of ethics and values into action. Individuals who display this quality operate off a core set of beliefs that gain admiration from others. As a leader, integrity is critical for success. It is necessary if leaders wish to obtain wholehearted support from followers.

Integrity is the most difficult—and the most important—value a leader can demonstrate. Integrity is revealed slowly, day-by-day, in word and deed. Actions that compromise a leader's integrity often have swift and profound repercussions. Every leader is in the "spotlight" of those they lead. As a result, shortcomings in integrity are readily apparent.

How do you create an environment that achieves results, trust, and learning instead of undermining them? One can observe many examples of "organizational perversities," most often caused by leaders who are not authentic and who demonstrate lack of integrity. Demonstrating these values in action often makes the difference between success and failure. People generally will work anytime and follow anywhere a person who leads with authenticity and integrity.

It becomes painfully evident when team members sense discord between what they and their leaders believe is important. Energy levels drop, and productive work either ceases or slows down.

These managers display aspects of a common challenge—becoming a victim of the measurement and reward system. The axiom goes: "Show me how people are measured and I'll show you how they behave." People have inner voices that reflect values and beliefs that lead to authenticity and integrity. They also experience external pressures to get results. The test for a true leader is to balance the internal with external pressures and to demonstrate truthfulness so that all concerned come to believe in the direction chosen.

Measurement systems need to reflect authentically on the values and guiding principles of the organization. Forced or misguided metrics do more harm than good.

In order to get people working collaboratively in a political environment, consider ways for them to receive more value from this effort: the project provides means to meet organizational needs; they have more fun; the experience is stimulating; they get more help and assistance when needed; they get constructive feedback; they are excited by the vision; they learn more from this project; their professional needs are met; they travel and meet people; it's good for their careers; together they'll accomplish more than separately; this is neat. . .

Ways to demonstrate authentic leadership in action:

▶Say what you believe.

▶Act on what you say.

▶Avoid "integrity crimes."

▶Involve team members in designing strategic implementation plans.

▶Align values, projects, and organizational goals through asking questions, listening, and using an explicit process to link all actions to strategic goals.

▶Foster an environment in which project teams can succeed by learning together and operating in a trusting, open organization.

▶Develop the skill of "*organizational awareness*"—the ability to read the currents of emotions and political realities in groups. This is a competence vital to the behind-the-scenes networking and coalition building that allows individuals to wield influence, no matter what their professional role. Tap the energy that comes from acting upon the courage of convictions . . . from doing the right thing . . . and from being prepared.

For example, a contractor came to the project manager's desk, made demands about resources on the project, and left. This was out-of-character, for the two people had formed a close relationship. The project manager decided not to act on the critical demands that could have severe negative impact on project relations. Later he sought out the contractor and found him in a different mood. The contractor confessed he was told by his company to make those demands. By correctly reading the emotional state and assessing that something below the surface was going on in that transaction, the project manager was able to work with the other person, keep the issue from escalating, and find a solution.

Leaders who commit "integrity crimes," shift the burden away from a fundamental solution to their personal effectiveness. Trust cannot develop under these conditions. Leaders either get into problems or else tap the energy and loyalty of others to succeed.

In systems thinking terms, this is a classic example of a "shifting the burden" archetype, in which a short-term fix actually undermines a leader's ability to take action at a more fundamental level. The causal loop in Figure 27-4 depicts how many project leaders proceed when under pressure to get results. The quick fix (in balancing loop B1) is to resort to a command and control approach, which on a surface level appears to lessen the pressure. This has an opposite effect on the people they want to influence or persuade (in reinforcing loop R3). These people do not do their best work so more pressure is felt to get results.

A more fundamental solution is to develop skills of persuasion as practiced by a change agent (in balancing loop B2). Help people come to believe in the vision and mission and aid them to figure out why it is in their best interest to put their best work into

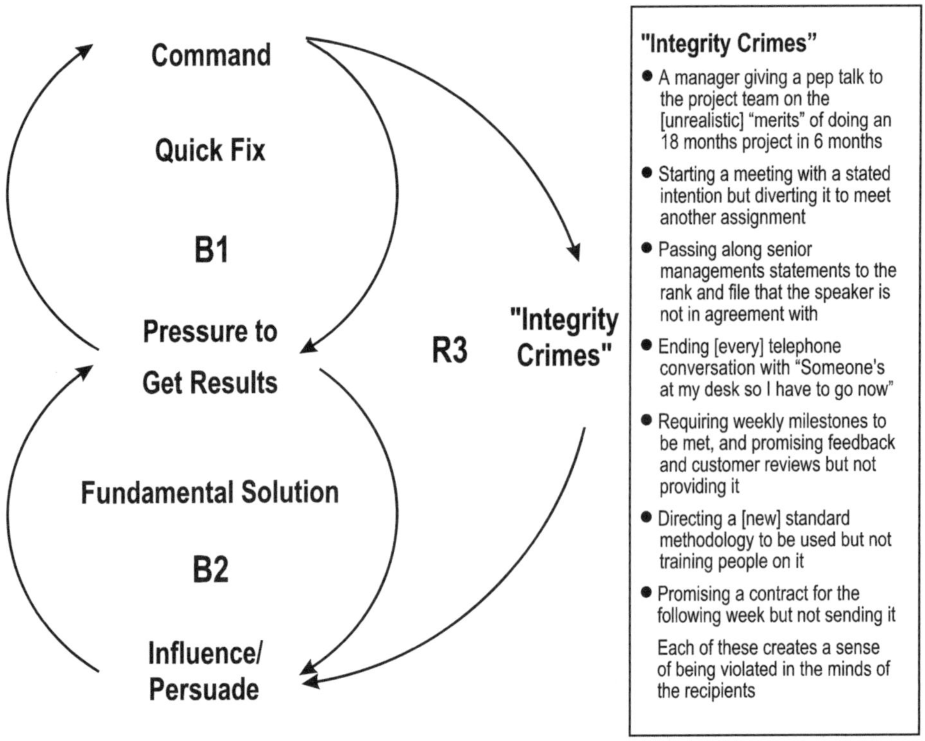

Command
Quick Fix
B1
Pressure to
Get Results
Fundamental Solution
B2
Influence/
Persuade
R3
"Integrity
Crimes"
"Integrity Crimes"
• A manager giving a pep talk to the project team on the [unrealistic] "merits" of doing an 18 months project in 6 months
• Starting a meeting with a stated intention but diverting it to meet another assignment
• Passing along senior managements statements to the rank and file that the speaker is not in agreement with
• Ending [every] telephone conversation with "Someone's at my desk so I have to go now"
• Requiring weekly milestones to be met, and promising feedback and customer reviews but not providing it
• Directing a [new] standard methodology to be used but not training people on it
• Promising a contract for the following week but not sending it
Each of these creates a sense of being violated in the minds of the recipients

FIGURE 27-4. **A "SHIFTING THE BURDEN" CAUSAL LOOP (*S* = SUPPORTING ACTION, AND *O* = OPPOSITE ACTION)**

the project. People usually respond positively to this approach and accomplish the work with less pressure.

Tools of persuasion include:

▶***Reciprocity***. Give an unsolicited gift. People will feel the need to give something back. Perhaps a big contract . . . or maybe just another opportunity to continue building a strong relationship.

▶***Consistency***. Draw people into public commitments, even very small ones. This can be very effective in directing future action.

▶***Social Validation***. Let people know that this approach is considered "the standard" by others. People often determine what they should do by looking at what others are doing.

▶***Liking***. Let people know that we like them and that we are likeable too. People like to do business with people they like. Elements that build "liking" include physical attractiveness, similarity, compliments, and cooperation.

▶***Authority***. Be professional and personable in dress and demeanor. Other factors are experience, expertise, and scientific credentials.

▶***Scarcity***. Remember just how rare good project management practice is, not to mention people who can transform a very culture. This applies to the value both of commodities and information. Not everyone knows what it takes to make a program successful.[8]

A summary of the science and practice of persuasion: *It usually makes great sense to repay favors, behave consistently, follow the lead of similar others, favor the requests of those we like, heed legitimate authorities, and value scare resources.*

To assess effective practices and apply a simple tool for analysis, consider these steps:

1. Identify basic leadership traits and their consequences.
2. Assess and compare leadership approaches in complex situations.
3. Apply a shifting-the-burden structure to create a positive culture.
4. Appreciate the value of authentic leadership and commit to act with integrity.

CONCLUSION

We've covered several techniques for political coalition building. The extent that powerful organizational forces are on board (or not) enables a project to go ahead in a big way, a project to be modified or downscaled, or for people to quit and move on to something easier.

A vision for project management is to become the standard management technique, operating in project-based organizations. Achieving this state requires forming a dream of what it would be like:

Project managers will be like current department managers. Upper managers will be an integral part of the project management process. The organizational building block will be the team. Therefore, upper managers will function as members of upper management teams. Project positions will be based on influence, which is based on trust and interdependence. Any one project will be part of a system of projects, not pitted against each other for resources but rather part of a coordinated plan to achieve organizational goals and strategy. This means project managers will themselves be a team. The upper manager's team will develop the organization structure and lead the project system, or project portfolio. Trust will be supported by open and explicit communication. Upper managers will oversee a project management information system to answer questions and provide information on all projects. There will be less emphasis on rules but a strong emphasis on organizational mission to guide action. There will be clear relationships between individual jobs and the mission. A process for taming project chaos will be based on linking projects to strategy, a focus on values and direction, the free flow of information, and organizing to support project teams.

Between today's situation and this desired state lies a long road of organizational change and the required politicking. Project managers who are skilled at the political arts of communication, persuasion, and negotiation—and who also are authentic and trustworthy—can help their organizations make this transition.

DISCUSSION QUESTIONS

❶ What cultural context or organizational factors influence the development of a political plan? For example: Open, enlightened, closed, exclusive, stimulating, supportive, productive, chaotic, messy, difficult to navigate, etc.?

❷ How can you be more effective in speaking with specific stakeholders?

REFERENCES

[1] Graham, Robert, and Randall Englund. *Creating an Environment for Successful Projects: Second Edition.* San Francisco: Jossey-Bass Publishers, 2004; Lewin, Roger, and Regine, Birute. *The Soul at Work: Listen, Respond, Let Go; Embracing Complexity Science for Business Success.* New York: Simon & Schuster, 2000; and Pinto, Jeffrey K., Peg Thoms, Jeffrey Trailer, Todd Palmer, and Michele Govekar. *Project Leadership.* Newtown Square, Penn.: Project Management Institute, 1998.

[2] Pinto, J.K. *Power and Politics in Project Management.* Upper Darby, Penn.: Project Management Institute, 1996.

[3] Kleiner, Art. *Who Really Matters: the Core Group Theory of Power, Privilege, and Success.* New York: Currency Doubleday, 2003.

[4] Pinto 1996, ibid.

[5] Pinto 1996, ibid.

[6] Pinto 1996, ibid.

[7] See pp. 66–73 in Englund, Randall, Robert Graham, and Paul Dinsmore. *Creating the Project Office: A Manager's Guide to Leading Organizational Change.* San Francisco: Jossey-Bass Publishers, 2003 for a more thorough discussion about *speaking truth to power*).

[8] Cialdini, R. B. *Influence: Science and Practice* (4th ed.). New York: Pearson Allyn & Bacon, 2000.

CHAPTER 28

Multi-Project Constraint Management: The "Critical Chain" Approach

▶FRANK PATRICK, DIGITALGRIT, INC.

Every organization is dependent on projects. From organizational strategy—which could be considered the "meta-project" against which the organization tracks its performance and growth over time—to its portfolios of "improvement projects" and product development projects that keep it effective and competitive, to its day-to-day delivery of unique efforts for which customers or clients pay, an organization relies on projects as the source of its ability to sustain itself over time.

Every organization also has constraints limiting what it can accomplish. With a finite source of time and attention available from the human and other resources that make up the organizational system, it behooves it to assure an appropriate answer to the question, "What should I/we be working on today?" This question, asking about the most *effective* use of limited resources, combined with a similar question, "How should I/we organize and perform the mass of work facing me/us?" which addresses the *efficiency* piece of the equation is the basis for the science and art of project management. These are the critical questions for which project management is meant to provide answers.

Most writings on project management until recently have focused on project management related to the delivery of individual projects. While it's necessary—and nice—to be able to deliver a single project as promised, it's not sufficient to assure the ability of an organization to address its multiple needs.

ORGANIZATIONS ARE MULTI-PROJECT SYSTEMS

Let us assume that the goal of an organization is to sustain itself so that it can profitably deliver products or services not only today, but also in the future.[1] If that's the case, then because its market environment—the demands of its customers and the responses of its competitors—cannot be reasonably expected to remain static, said organization must efficiently deliver today's business and effectively change to address its future circumstances.

Projects as the Business

Drawing a distinction between production-based organizations and project-based organizations, the former is usually dependent on delivering a lot of copies of identical (or at least very similar) units of a product or service, with minimal or easily manageable uncertainty and variation of process. In production environments, the "touch-time" associated with an individual piece of output is usually very small compared to the total duration of building that output, as components tend to spend most of there time in queues awaiting attention or the setup of the machinery that will transform it in some way.

Project environments, on the other hand, are characterized more by uncertainty of expectations, greater variation in the performance against those expectations. Projects also involve larger chunks of "touch time" as a proportion of total project duration. If one's business is based on directly "selling" the outcome of projects developed with a shared pool of resources, as it is in industries such as custom software and IT systems, consulting, construction, maintenance and repair, and engineer-to-build custom manufacturing, projects are "the business." In such arenas, the ability to maximize the throughput of multiple completed projects is directly related to both current and future success.

Projects Supporting the Business

The ability to effectively implement change is clearly related to what most would recognize as projects and project management. Such efforts are typically temporary efforts, with a reasonably finite span of time between launch and completion. In this context, change projects are not only related to tactical, local process improvements or highly visible strategic initiatives, but also to the ability to redefine one's offerings to meet future needs—research and new product/service development and deployment. Regardless of whether the business of the organization is production-or project-based, its future success needs to be supported by effective delivery of change—effective management of multiple projects.

And whether the organization's project portfolio is dominated by today's deliveries to customers or clients supported by future-facing development projects, or primarily limited by the latter development efforts that will deliver its future, these projects will be done largely with a limited source of time and attention of the people and processes that define the organization. Organizations and their resources constitute multi-project systems.

ORGANIZATIONAL EFFECTIVENESS IS RESOURCE EFFECTIVENESS

The old saw defining efficiency largely as doing things right and effectiveness as doing the right things definitely applies to multi-project systems. How individual tasks are defined and delivered are key to the efficient completion of individual projects. And choosing the "right projects" from the portfolio of possibilities is clearly related to the contribution of the efforts to the organization's success. While these single-project and portfolio management concerns are beyond the scope of this chapter, strategies for managing the interaction of various active projects as they vie for the attention of the limited resources are not.

Understanding the importance of getting the right things done at the task level, and behaving accordingly, are significant contributors to efficiency as well and are the basis for multi-project resource (organizational) effectiveness. Unfortunately, too many organizations overlook this and instead emphasize control of costs to the detriment of what they are trying to accomplish.

Maximizing Throughput or Controlling Costs

In the previous section, the dichotomy of managing today's deliveries as well as setting up for the future was discussed. Another pair of necessities for organizational effectiveness is found in the need to maximize throughput of the system and, at the same time, control costs. Many managers look upon these as conflicting requirements, as pressures to keep expenses down have the potential to threaten the ability to deliver more completed projects quickly and with quality.

This sense of conflict comes from confusing organizational effectiveness with efficiency, and even worse, with resource utilization.[2] Assuring that everyone is fully utilized all the time may seem like a reasonable strategy for getting the most out of the individual resources, and, by extrapolation, out of the organization. On the surface, this feels like it makes sense. However, if a system wants to maximize its throughput, keeping resources fully loaded across the board actually hamper that objective for several reasons.

The first reason to avoid striving for full resource utilization is that if everyone is fully loaded, there is no slack to deal with the inevitable run-ins with Murphy's Law. Given the uncertain nature of projects as unique endeavors, any negative deviation from planned expectations will require capacity to recover. If that protective capacity is not available, problems in a project will result in either cascading problems that will threaten the promises of other projects, or burnout of resources, or both. In either case, future throughput is threatened.

Similarly, without protective capacity set aside, there is no ability to capitalize on new opportunities that arise. Potential throughput is lost.

Multi-Tasking Multiplies Time to Complete Projects

Finally, in environments where full utilization of peoples' time is valued, there will usually be timesheets to fill out, or measurement and reward systems—formal or informal—that drive people to keep busy. In addition, in such a situation, projects are usually launched with an eye to making sure that no one is starved for work. As a result, there are usually plenty of choices of things for everyone to work on. With many active projects expecting progress, there is pressure to work on several at one time, splitting one's time and attention across them. Unless an effective multi-project management system provides clear priorities for resource attention, people will strive to make the "measurement" look good by keeping busy and keeping several balls in the air. This is multi-tasking—working on several significant pieces of work simultaneously, switching between them before any one is completed and before its output is handed off to the next task in the project.

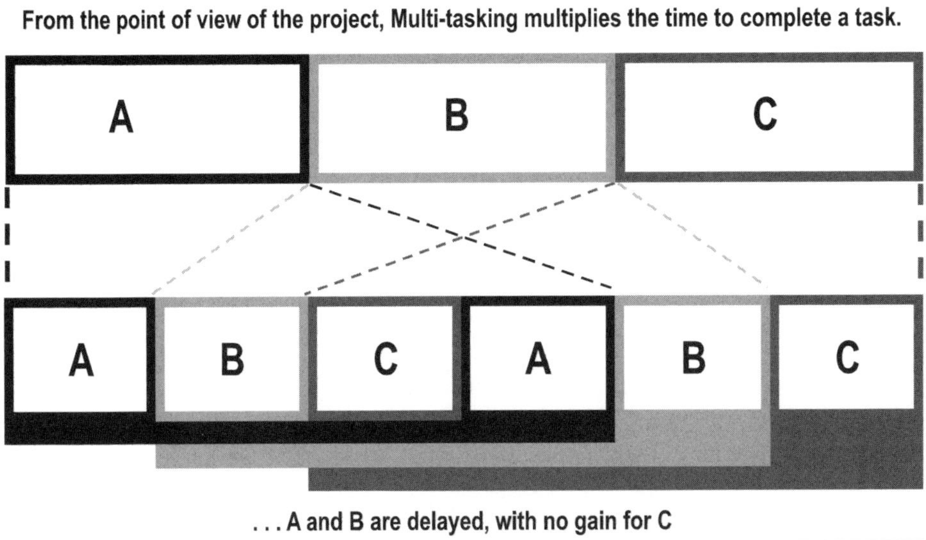
From the point of view of the project, Multi-tasking multiplies the time to complete a task.
A
B
C
A
B
C
A
B
C
. . . A and B are delayed, with no gain for C

FIGURE 28-1. **THE EFFECT OF MULTI-TASKING**

What happens in this situation is that, as a result of trying to make sure that everyone is always fully utilized (a seemingly efficient means of controlling costs), the time it takes to convert a task input into an output that is usable by the next task is expanded by the time it sits while another project gets the attention.[3] In addition, the context switching cost—the time involved in the question, "Where was I?" when returning to a set-aside task—adds to the actual work time, adding further inefficiencies to the project. Throughput associated with these projects is lost as their completions are delayed beyond when they could have been achieved.

Resource Efficiency is Not Organizational Effectiveness

By striving to be "efficient" through high local resource utilization—by striving for cost control through avoiding "wasted" idle resources throughout the organization—the real objective is sub-optimized. Throughput of completed projects and their benefit—paid invoices, improved processes, or new products that will ring new cash registers—associated with those completions is threatened, lost, or delayed.

CONSTRAINT-SAVVY MULTI-PROJECT AND RESOURCE MANAGEMENT

In order for a multi-project system to operate effectively for an organization, it needs to assure that the project pipeline isn't overloaded. Also, when there are decisions to be made between project tasks vying for the attention of a resource, it needs to provide a clear priority that is aligned with maximizing the benefit from the total collection of projects so that the resource in question will pick up and work the "right" task without multi-tasking. The first of these requirements is directly related to understanding and managing the organization through its constraints.

Constraint = Capacity = Throughput

Unless artificially forced otherwise, or unless mismanaged to the point of non-recognition by overload, systems put together for a purpose typically have one or at most very few constraints limiting their ability to deliver that purpose. Like the clichéd "weak link of a chain," a potential bottleneck resource can usually be identified as a limiting factor associated with project throughput.

The capacity of the system is the capacity of this constraining bottleneck. It doesn't pay to try to push more projects into launch mode than this constraint can handle. They'll only back up waiting for it to attend to them and they'll distract and unnecessarily overload all the resources working upstream of the constraint. Rather than trying to tightly balance the load on all resources (and killing throughput in the process), a rational approach to managing such a system is to identify (or design in) a clearly understood constraint and manage that one piece of the system very closely.

Protective Capacity

The current constraining resource in a multi-project system could be located anywhere. By definition, other resources are non-constraints and have more capacity than would be technically needed to support the possible throughput of the system. But to start cutting and slashing this extra capacity indiscriminately would be a mistake. At some point, that would merely shift the constraint from where it is to another, potentially unpredictable part of the system at the same or lower level of capacity, or worse, set up a situation with hard-to-manage interactive constraints.

Instead, the means of managing the constraint for growth of throughput starts with stabilizing the system so that the extra capacity upstream of the constraint assures that the constraint is not starved for work. The only resource that should be kept near high utilization (note "near high" is not "at full") is the constraint, since the output of the system is tied directly to its output. Project launches that are synchronized with the ability of the constraint to deal with them will, if sufficient protective capacity is available upstream, flow smoothly to the closely managed possible bottleneck. Similarly, once through the identified constraint, no downstream resource should be so tight that it delays the conversion of constraint output to a complete accrual of project benefit. Again that implies a necessary level of protective capacity downstream as well.

Once stabilized and ridden of the effects of overload and multi-tasking, the true capacity of the system and of its components is far more easily identified. At this point, the organization can take rational steps to grow its capacity and capabilities by systematic constraint management.

Implications for Project Portfolio Management

Once the constraint of the system is understood, it will have implications beyond just project delivery performance. It will also provide useful input to the project portfolio process. If the organization is limited to taking on projects at the rate that they can pass through the bottleneck, then those projects that have a higher relative benefit value per time required of the bottleneck will be more valuable to the organization than those that require more bottleneck time, all else being equal.[4]

One project may seem to have small face value, but if barely involving the constraint, it will be able to deliver that value while barely displacing some other project

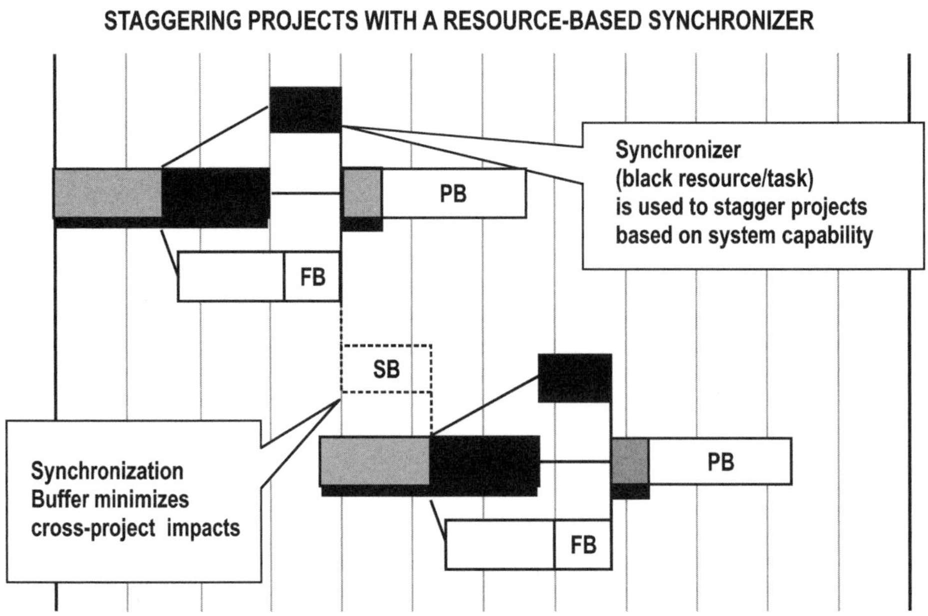

FIGURE 28-2. **STAGGERED PROJECT LAUNCHES**

and its benefit. It's almost a "free" project, taking advantage of the slack in the non-constraint resources. On the other hand, if a project that looks very valuable when complete, but requires so much constraint time that many other projects are denied or delayed, it becomes a serious strategic decision to move forward with it. If, by the nature of a bottleneck or constraint, taking on one project forces us to forego or delay another, then this metric of benefit per constraint usage becomes an important factor in the decision to launch.

MULTI-PROJECT AND RESOURCE MANAGEMENT— MANAGING THE PRESENT AND THE FUTURE

Once an organization understands the constraints associated with its ability to deliver projects, whether for customer-driven deliverables or for internal process improvements, it has the basis to not only avoid overloading its current capacity and capability, but also to smoothly grow the capability to take on more work in the future.

Next Month: "How Much Should We Take On?"—Gating Project Launches

At the border of portfolio management and project management lies pipeline management. Nothing will bog down a project delivery system faster than the premature push of projects into a system that can't really handle them.

Once the portfolio management or sales acceptance process determines the relative ordering of projects, the process for synchronizing project launches to constraint capacity is a simple matter of staggering them at the point of use of the constraint. Once it is known when the constraint can take on a new project, it's a simple matter of placing it there in the calendar, perhaps with a bit of buffer to avoid cross project impacts at the constraint, and examining the resulting schedule to determine where it's appropriate to start the upstream activities.

If project launches are staggered in this manner, then the constraining resource will not be overloaded. And if the constraining resource is not overloaded, then the other non-constraining resources will also, by definition, not be overloaded, thereby reducing pressures to multi-task and simplifying the question of priorities when the occasional need to choose which task to work comes up.

Today: "What Should I Be Working On?"—Clarity of Priority at the Task Level

If projects are not overloading the system, the question of which task to work is simplified by the mere reduction of active tasks in play. In-boxes are less loaded. However, due to the vagaries of project plans, and of variation in task performance, occasionally it might occur that a resource faces the need to choose one task to pick up and finish before addressing another one that is waiting. There are several options to providing such guidance.

Assuming that the individual projects are being actively managed via Critical Path or Critical Chain processes, one consideration is whether any of the waiting tasks are on the critical path or critical chain of the project in question. If so, that task would most likely be the appropriate first choice over a competing "non-critical" task.[5]

If there is a choice of two or more "critical" tasks from different projects, the relative health of the projects in question can be easily assessed based on working one, then the other, and vice versa. The scenario that leaves the best combination of the resulting health of the projects' promises in best condition (or maximizes the benefits associated with both projects) would be preferred. In an environment based on Critical Chain Scheduling and Buffer Management, project buffers provide not only the ability of projects to absorb such decisions, but also make the assessment process straightforward. Critical Path-based projects, usually relying on smaller, if any, schedule reserves, might have to add some additional recovery activities. (Note that this constraint-based approach to multi-project management comes from the same source as Critical Chain Scheduling and Buffer Management; the Theory of Constraints and the two processes work together by design.)

If all queued tasks are "non-critical," it's less of an issue, and while usually a first-come-first-served process will suffice, a consideration of the general health of the project promise, or in the case of a Critical Chain project, buffer consumption, could also provide useful guidance.

Next Year: "How Much Can We Work On?"—Current and Strategic Constraints

In the previous section, the stabilization of the system around the organization's current constraint was described. That current constraint is the result of past actions and staffing levels; it may not be an ideal leverage point for maximum strategic benefit. Once the system is stable, the organization can manage itself proactively by designing a more appropriate system based on what one might call a "strategic constraint."

An appropriate constraining resource would be one that is commonly and heavily used across a range of anticipated projects, but is also hard to augment. If it's easy to get more of it by acquiring more people or improving processes, then it's probably worth doing so to easily grow organizational capacity, assuming the protective capacity around it is also easily grown. If hard to augment, it becomes a matter of offloading and/or improving processes to grow capacity. A constraint that is hard to get more of while commonly and heavily required is a natural candidate for a long-term constraint against which to manage the organization.

Additionally, such hard-to-grow resources are often critical to the organization's competitiveness. For example, a system architect who knows the ins and outs of the firm's software products is far harder to replace, and is inherently more important to its capacity, than some "plain vanilla" developer skill that can be augmented with contractors. If there is some other, easily elevated constraint in place, it behooves the organization to develop plans to grow its capacity along with any others who might be limiting what can be gotten through the expert. Understanding this relationship also highlights and justifies the need to grow that expert skill as well, perhaps through shared work or by determining what it is in the work usually performed by the expert that really needs the expertise.

An interesting offshoot of effective constraint management is that if one considers a limiting factor—a constraint—to be a weakness, then the system's strength—the resource and skill that defines its core competency—should probably be that weakness. After all, you don't want any other aspect of the organizational system to limit the ability to maximize the benefit of that strength.[6]

Developing such a strategy for growth—either growing resources around an appropriate constraint while increasing its capabilities, or providing a clear path to grow the necessary capacities to move the constraint to somewhere more appropriate—provides a smooth transition from one level of performance to the next.

IT'S NOT HOW MUCH YOU START, IT'S HOW MUCH YOU FINISH

Too many organizations act as if by packing the pipeline and keeping everyone heavily loaded with work, a combination of filled queues and busy resources will result in rapid and reliable project completions. Instead, projects bump into one another, adding delays usually unanticipated in individual project promises, and resources burn out jumping between unfinished tasks that then further delay task handoffs and project completions.

▶***Suggested exercise:*** Survey some of your project participants. Ask them how many different tasks they currently have open. How many different project reviews do they attend each week? Ask them how long they expect their current collection of tasks to take to complete. Then ask them if they set aside most tasks and just picked one and finished it as if it was the only thing they had to do, then another, then another, when would the individual tasks and the total collection be complete? How much less time would it take them to complete them all if they focused on one at a time?

Constraint management suggests instead that projects only be launched at a rate that can be handled by the organizational system, and as its surrogate, by the system's constraining resource. This constraint is easily identified as a heavily used resource, skill, or facility common to most projects in the portfolio. Once the pipeline of projects quickly settles down to stability through such an approach, it becomes a matter of systematic constraint management to grow the capacity and capability of the organization to meet strategic needs.

▶***Suggested exercise:*** Consider your organization. Even if it is in a chaotic state in which every resource feels overloaded, ask this question: If you could double the capacity of one and only one resource, skill, or facility, where would it be most beneficial for the organization in terms of helping more projects move to completion quicker? In most organizations, it usually quickly narrows down to a consensus on one or two candidates. Those are your initial candidates for designation as project pipeline constraint.

Every organization needs to consider how it manages the collection of projects it requires to sustain itself. Whether the business is based on delivering project work or process improvements require attention from a limited pool of players, or if the business depends on a steady flow of new product development, maximizing throughput of completed projects is critical to organizational effectiveness.

In summary, it's not about how many projects you launch. It's not about how busy everyone is. It's not about success with one major project that's got everyone's attention anyhow. It's about how many projects you finish in a period of time. It's about finishing many projects rapidly and reliably. It's about maximizing the throughput of your project pipeline, and the key to moving more through a pipeline is not by forcing too much through it, creating turbulence, leaks, and spills. It's about understanding the bottlenecks and constraints, rationally loading them, and systematically growing their capacity.

DISCUSSION QUESTIONS

Consider your organization: How many people are involved in project work? Is this project work revenue enhancing or primarily supporting process improvements? (Don't forget your IT department.) What would be the impact if you could finish most projects in 25 to 50 percent less time than you typically do today by eliminating multi-tasking? More importantly, what would be the impact if you could double or even triple the number of projects completed in a year by synchronizing project launches with your constraint?

REFERENCES

[1] Goldratt, Eliyahu M. *It's Not Luck.* The North River Press, 1994, pp. 270–278.

[2] Goldratt, Eliyahu M. *The Goal, Second Revised Edition.* The North River Press, 1992, pp. 26–33.

[3] Patrick, Francis S. Program Management—Turning Many Projects Into Few Priorities with TOC; http://www.focusedperformance.com/articles/multipm.html, October 1999.

[4] Kendall, Gerald I., and Steven C. Robbins. *Advanced Project Portfolio Management and the PMO.* J. Ross Publishing, 2003, pp. 217–220.

[5] Patrick, Francis S. Program Management—Turning Many Projects Into Few Priorities with TOC; http://www.focusedperformance.com/articles/multipm.html, October 1999.

[6] Patrick, Francis S. Weakness as Strength; http://www.focusedperformance.com/articles/ut06weak.html, January 2001.

CHAPTER 29

Communities of Practice and Project Management

▶CONNIE L. DELISLE, PHD,
CONSULTING AND AUDIT CANADA

▶KIM ROWE, P.ENG,
ROWEBOTS RESEARCH INC.

A great deal of effort has been invested in understanding the value of knowledge and, when applied, its role in shaping society. But few organizations have consistently translated knowledge about the human and technical aspects of successful projects into successful delivery of new projects.

Navigation through a project life cycle often results in project failure, despite application of best-ever tools and technology. Yet the human behavior aspect of project management continues to be the poor cousin to technical solutions. What organizational structures or patterns can optimize human behavior on projects?

OVERVIEW: COMMUNITIES OF PRACTICE

The recent prolification of Communities of Practice (CoPs) in the public, private, and non-profit sectors seems indicative of the need to address this question. Communities of Practice in a business context are characterized as "social networks that individuals use to make sense of the workplace around them and develop a common understanding of the meaning of their roles in projects and to the organization."[1] Arguably, CoPs have resided within organizations and in many different facets of society in the form of non-profit groups and community groups for many years, in both face-to-face and virtual forms. Many people fail to recognize that they are engaged in CoP relationships, they just freely do so, intuitively recognizing the value of the "espirit de corps" and sharing of knowledge and experiences. Community members tend to share a strong desire to enhance, develop and achieve expertise in the area of common interest, understanding the value in pooling efforts even if an immediate or tangible reward is not immediately evident. Community leadership in this context appears as a strategic investment that inadvertently brings the collective membership together to find and maintain an agreed-on direction.

Just as projects are a dynamic environment, CoPs are a dynamic way to make sense of the world. Organizations that use CoPs note improvements in their ability to communicate tacit knowledge[2] and transform it into explicit knowledge, better integration of new practices in projects and organizations, and more creative problem solving across traditional "silos" of practice. From a maturity point of view, CoPs have yet to formally appear in the conventional project management bodies of knowledge in influential organizations such as the Project Management Institute (PMI) or the Association for Project Management (APM). But they are beginning to be talked about, implemented, or planned for in many project settings.

This work is intended to provide the reader with a resource for future inquiry into the role of CoPs in project management. We will investigate four topics related to CoPs:

▶What perspectives dominate knowledge management and learning? How do organizations and their people make sense of the business world? This section discusses Knowledge Management (KM) as a basis for discovering what elements characterize CoPs for project support.

▶How do CoPs influence project management? This section examines how CoPs are related to project management in the context of the *PMBOK® Guide* and the APM guide. CoPs may influence how we initiate, plan, implement, monitor and close projects; this section discusses how they are related to organizational structure and project phases.

▶What tools are needed to make CoPs effective and how are tools best used to build and maintain CoPs?

▶What appear to be best practices of CoPs? The distinction between CoP *tools* and CoP *practices* helps the reader understand practical ways to propagate creative and innovative problem solving, capture and integrate knowledge, and eventually make use of outputs to improve decision making.

KNOWLEDGE MANAGEMENT

To really understand how organizations make sense of the world, we have to look past behaviors to the age-old meta-rules that underlie our attitudes for the picture to come sharply into focus. The dominant Western approach toward management of resources—human included—focuses on adjusting human values, beliefs, and attitudes to make behaviors and outcomes predictable. For example, capturing and maintaining information in policy and operating manuals is a way to control and direct the flow of information, and thus, of action.

In contrast, the thought system identified by Heraclitius (c.540-c.480 BCE) purports that "everything flows." In this world-view, organizations undergo cycles and often-paradoxical processes of innovation.[3]

Practical examination of the way that organizations manage knowledge shows that efforts fall into first- (micro view) and second-generation (macro view) KM. These two views are both important to understanding the development of solutions for a specific project and the preservation of knowledge and understanding between projects.

First Generation Knowledge Management—Micro View

First generation KM mostly focuses on technology to provide answers to organizational woes. The basic premise—valuable knowledge already exists, and all we need to do is capture it—still prevails today in many organizations. To achieve better performance, organizations tend to focus on at least five areas:[4]

1. ***Customer Focus***. The project management priority triangle (time, cost, quality/scope) plus client or customer satisfaction, suffice as the main predictors of successful projects. Lessons learned serve as a way to justify this approach; if the customers were not satisfied, then new business is not available from the customer.

2. ***Project Focus.*** Individuals charged with solving project problems rely on resources at hand to deal with the issues (i.e., personal experience, lessons learned, best practices). Projects are units of effort that can be reasonably controlled, and thus, the same is believed for behavior and outcomes.

3. ***Driving Decisions Down***. By driving decisions down the organization to the lowest possible level, better quality decisions are made because the people closest to the problems are making them. Often this is an optimal solution in a project environment.

4. ***Trust and Sharing***. Without trust, knowledge sharing and collaboration do not occur. For this reason, many organizations have tried to increase trust within and outside organizational boundaries in order to increase knowledge sharing and the organization's ability to work as a team.

5. ***Leadership***. Here the focus is on the leader's role in meeting goals by coordinating the efforts of organizations, groups, and individuals who will complete specific tasks. Excessive dependence on heroic leadership may mean that not everyone understands his or her role within the project and organization so that common vision evolves and increases motivation.

The heavy emphasis on technology in first-generation KM does not address inadequate knowledge sharing, limited trust, and lack of vision and poor motivation. Anticipated improvement to managing projects and resulting organizational performance cannot be realized by simply capturing, coding, and distributing existing knowledge. In response, many organizations began to focus heavily on creating conditions for accelerating use of new knowledge across the organization or rate of innovation. This course of action did not often translate into tangible value, making the idea of KM itself a tough sell.[5]

Second-Generation Knowledge Management—Macro View

Second-generation KM takes the position that knowledge is produced through social systems. The individual learner and collective group members both have critical roles to play in project knowledge acquisition and development. To achieve this end, organizations tend to be aware of and seek to improve collective group performance in five ways:[6]

1. *Gap Orientation*. People learn about whatever they need to help the organization by filling gaps in their knowledge. They consult colleagues to fill these gaps and develop new knowledge.

2. *Self-organization*. This occurs naturally in organizations as like-minded individuals group together for the purpose of solving problems. The group will jointly evaluate and refine their understanding for everyone's benefit. This work will result in new knowledge claims that can be further evaluated and used by the organization.

3. *Mental Models*. Information about the collective organizational effort may serve as the basis for employees developing mental models as a guide to problem solving. For example, development of a "networked view" of people interacting in organizations is a mental model that might be contrasted with a standard "organizational hierarchy" view.

4. *Dissemination and Diffusion*. New knowledge and new mental models are diffused throughout the organization using a variety of methods. By improving diffusion, organizations may increase their rates of innovation. A key missing part in first generation KM is that a large component of information is tacit and cannot be codified and transferred. Communities of practice solve this by providing a forum for tacit knowledge sharing.

5. *Non-Linear Feedback System*. Because people are in the loop, they often willingly provide experiential feedback, and the rate and type of knowledge production varies in a non-linear fashion. Thus, it is not often possible to predict how knowledge will form with any kind of accuracy.

In summary, organizations benefit from first generation KM through testing and experimenting with technology to better manage knowledge and to determine how individual contributions strengthen or weaken the knowledge base of the organization. Second-generation KM uses the process of sharing knowledge across projects, both inside and outside an organization to achieve creative and effective solutions. Naturally, these solutions assume a project-based organizational culture that is amenable to a collaborative approach. If an organization is strictly "command and control," implementation of a community approach might not be possible. In this case, very informal use of communities can assist in managing projects, but little dependence can be put on the communities to solve problems of a business or systemic nature.

Practical Uses of CoPs for Project Knowledge Management and Transfer

The majority of organizations still subscribe to first-generation KM. In organizations adopting second-generation KM principles, informal CoPs appear as a way to consult with colleagues and for problem solving. Individual learning tends to remain as the central focus. For example, an individual generates a solution for the task in question so that the project may be completed. Group evaluation of information sharing approaches, and dissemination to a broader set of individuals outside the immediate project rarely occurs. As well, organizations tend to focus on the capture and storage of "know how" (i.e., knowledge in the form of lessons learned) as a source of competitive advantage, but often this repository is tied to a functional department or individual without resources dedicated to its maintenance.

Second-generation KM has sparked a more broad application of CoPs. Whether project-specific or not, CoPs tend to cut horizontally across organizations, allowing participants outside a project to provide expertise and solve problems creatively. The project manager becomes a participant, not a leader, and thus does not dictate when or how participants provide solutions. More mature CoPs tend to go through cycles of knowledge creation, evaluation, learning, and sharing across projects. For example, a problem in one project may serve as a partial solution in another project. In this way, KM has evolved through CoPs in a way that puts the act of creating knowledge, and the people who do so—rather than technology—at the heart of project management.

COPS AND PROJECT MANAGEMENT

If CoPs are deemed useful by project managers and their teams, why do they remain a tough sell to senior management in terms of support for the time necessary to participate and resources to fund web-based technology?

One reason may be the lack of shared understanding of what CoPs actually do. Factors such as the membership, medium (i.e., mix of face-to-face and/or web-based discussion), the sector maturity (i.e., understanding of CoPs within the industry), and purpose of the CoP vary greatly. This makes nailing down a definition and documentation of activities difficult, and perhaps not seen by participants as necessarily desirable.

One reason that CoPs have not become part of senior executive decision-making is simply that they are an emerging practice. Turning research ideas into common business tools (the mobilization of knowledge for consumption) often takes ten or more years. Although CoPs are a well-known phenomenon, they have not really been studied as a research concept until the past five years. Therefore, we may expect a few more years to go by before widespread adoption of CoPs occurs.

Part of the task of researchers investigating CoPs is to show the impacts CoPs have on initiating, planning, implementing, monitoring and closing projects. The *PMBOK® Guide* is a useful starting point to begin to examine how CoPs may someday impact knowledge about managing projects.

Project Organizational Design

The *PMBOK® Guide* presents several organizational types: from functional organizations at one extreme to project-based organizations at the other. In practice, it appears that many, if not most, organizations use a combination of types and can be characterized as "hybrids." One of the hallmarks of hybrids is that professionals and groups within them function independently, relying on informal communication channels to exchange information and create knowledge. CoPs appear to be a natural fit into this environment and some organizations use them as a way to preserve knowledge that can be more readily shared across projects and develop faster and better solutions.

CoPs fit into functional organizations just like projects do: in the background, providing a means for professionals to engage in discussions outside the narrow bounds of their own professional discipline. CoPs fit into project environments in a similar way. They provide a unifying force behind the scene to allow specialists to share and develop expertise relevant to their field while still providing this expertise to the projects. In a hybrid environment, CoPs support both functional and project organizations. Often they have executive level sponsors, making support easier to secure.

How may a CoP promote project-related learning and create value within program or project offices?

Project Life Cycle (Phases)

The typical project life cycle—initiating, implementing, and closing—has critical decision points where the project may continue, be changed, or be abandoned. There are many points within the project life cycle where CoPs may provide support and guidance. For example, initiating the project involves such activities as identifying the project team members, defining the scope and business objectives of the project, and identifying key stakeholders.

CoPs can provide a source of information about who within the organization has the required skills set, who has worked on similar projects, what scope issues they have dealt within in a particular type of project, and which stakeholders to consider. During the planning, a careful analysis should be done to ensure that the communities that could be of use (if more than one exists) are identified and information within these communities is passed on to the correct team members. As well, if critical types of communities need to be created, and the project is large, there may be sufficient justification for including a community's development effort as part of the project. One practical internal application that is less time consuming is to create a CoP as part of learning support for project management courses. This is understood quite easily in terms of providing a venue for those new to managing projects to turn learning into practice.

Monitoring and controlling the project may involve the communities, too. Community reevaluation of time, cost estimates, and work in progress; and evaluation of quality and community feedback on scope changes and change control is very useful in bringing the correctly scoped project in on time, on budget, and with the desired level of quality. Monitoring of stakeholder views in the CoP environment is also a very useful addition to the project and can ensure that everyone's expectations are dealt with appropriately.

Finally, during project close, reassignment and intelligent preservation of resources, knowledge products (i.e., deliverables), and sharing lessons learned are facilitated by a CoP.

These are just some of the areas in which a community-based support system can help project managers and their teams navigate successfully through a project lifecycle. This may spark the reader to think about how community based assistance can augment all of the nine knowledge areas in the *PMBOK® Guide*. To date, project management bodies of knowledge have not considered the role and benefits of CoPs as they relate to managing projects either internally, or within the context of improved service delivery within a consulting environment.

Project Processes

Within project processes, there are two groups: project management processes (how the work is described, organized, and completed) and product-oriented processes (how the product is specified and created). CoPs within manufacturing sectors or those within federal government task forces, for example, are more product-oriented. CoPs within the consulting sector tend to be more focused on discussing how to do the work most efficiently. Within each group, CoPs have a great deal to offer in terms of being a sounding board for decisions about the management of the project, as well as the type of deliverables to create.

A historical example of a CoP that focused on specific project problem solving during all phases is that of the "Turbodudes" at Shell Oil. They meet regularly to share knowledge and help each other with their specific problems. These solutions are vetted within the group before being used on specific projects. It's a tried and proven CoP that has saved substantial amounts of time and money in producing innovative solutions.[7]

In terms of the process groups (project initiating, planning, executing, controlling, and closing), results are linked. That is, the outputs for one process can become the inputs for others. The connections are iterative and require a complete understanding of interactions. To the novice project manager, a CoP may be an excellent test-bed for proof of concept prior to moving to the next phase of a project. Members within a CoP make sense of the complexity of a project by testing, challenging, discussing, and either validating or rejecting premises so that conclusions or steps forward are strengthened by this process of "sense making." Since the process group interactions cross phases, this process of "peer review" provides the organization with a level of comfort in assuring for less rework or misalignment of the project and the client expectations.

CoPs and PMOs

The Project Management Office (PMO) sets project standards and oversees the organization's portfolio of projects. This allows the organization to evaluate the use of resources across all projects and resolve conflicts that affect project timelines. The PMO is also a very good place to examine how communities are linked across projects. Using the communities as the linkage point for knowledge transfer is far more efficient for several reasons:

▶In communities, the evaluation of knowledge is generally done by a broader range of people, ensuring that the ideas are more completely vetted.

▶Communities generally exist outside the project framework and trust is already established. They can be used as opposed to setting up more formal structures and methods to get the required information transferred to the project.

▶In communities, knowledge is transferred from expert to recipient. This includes tacit knowledge transfer as well as explicit knowledge transfer. This is a much more efficient transfer mechanism than is normally used. Generally, documents would be transferred from project to project with minimal expert knowledge available to add value.

▶Community transfer shares the knowledge broadly, strengthening the entire organization for future projects.

Every indication is that there are many benefits of CoPs for projects in general and that PMOs can play a significant role. However, PMOs are not necessary overarching structures to enable CoPs. Often PMOs are rules-bound, whereas CoPs are emergent. Trying to control the membership and activities of a CoP through standardization runs a risk to its effectiveness. However, by evaluating the various community and project linkages, the PMO can tell the organization how critical information can be shared between projects via the CoP structure.

SPECIFIC COP DESIGN AND MANAGEMENT TOOLS

Technology is an enabler of CoPs, not its core function. Arguably, CoPs have been around for decades, in one form or another, given shared interest around topics. Thus, CoPs do exist and may start to form from discussion around water coolers, in

• Learning management systems • E-learning content management • Portals • Project, portfolio and program management tools • Task management • Workflow • Version control • Document lock up • Calendar • Calendar coordination • Brainstorming • Group decision making tools • White boards (electronic and otherwise) • Video-based visualization • Application sharing • Video/audio broadcast • Simulation • E-learning synchronous classrooms	• E-learning testing • Document management • Content management • Data mining • Read indicators • Presence • Wiki • Blogging • Subscription • Turn taking management • Chat • Teleconference • VoIP • Phone • Discussion boards • Blog comment features • Q&A • Profiles • Rating • Social networking • Social networking analysis	• Member directory • Recognition • Access and security • Subgroups • SMS polling • Voting/polling • Participation statistics • Behavioral parameters • Reflection (360° feedback) • Photo/image sharing • File sharing • Taxonomy • Collaborative filtering • Search • Landing page • Email • RSS • Email lists • Visit management • Instant messaging (IM).

TABLE 29-1. **KEY COP DESIGN AND MANAGEMENT TOOLS**

lunchrooms, and so forth. Thus, the suggestion to formalize a CoP by setting up a complex technology platform or a project management office may not be desirable to its members. Overcoming their resistance is a topic beyond the scope of this chapter. The tools that are used to build and maintain CoPs are also a large subject area in their own right. It includes a broad set of technologies including, but not limited to, those listed in Table 29-1. The reader should also realize that a community or communities could be formed using a variety of different technologies, and the tool choice will not necessarily reflect the quality of the domain, community or practice. Today the trend is towards greater integration of subsets these above tools into integrated collaboration and community environments.

A key area here is the link between the project tools that are now being fielded and the community tools that are being used. Communities may undertake projects that will involve the use of project tools, so communities are end users of project tools. In addition, projects have a need for communities to support their efforts.

The ability of a project to use a shared repository and have the repository directly linked to the project plan to monitor progress is an example of the strong links being developed between project tools and community tools. From these strong links, greater integration in the monitoring and control area of projects may be developed. In the future, integration with workflow tools and communities will see a broad set of other new features to automate rework, estimation, and scope control.

Best Practices

Best practices refer to the processes, practices, and systems that perform exceptionally well, and are widely recognized as improving an organization's performance and efficiency in specific areas.[8] In the context of CoPs, best practices are actually "best processes"—those that have been proven to work within many organizations for various projects. The key distinction is that practices tend to be recorded and in doing so, become obsolete quite quickly. Processes are more amenable to change and are understood to evolve as organizations become better at managing projects.[9] The topic of best practices is extensive, reaching beyond the scope of this chapter, but a few key best practices are presented.

Seed CoPs

The use of existing CoPs is the most obvious best practice. That is, determine who (or which groups) within the organization is acting as an informal source of information and knowledge exchange. The cost in terms of time and effort to establish a new community is substantial and reuse of appropriate communities that exist within and outside an organization should be considered first. Community reuse requires a clear confidentiality understanding—essential with communities that span multiple organizations or even multiple groups.

Smooth Transition to CoPs

To allow those unfamiliar with community participation to make the transition to a community-based project environment more easily, create psychological safety through use of the following best-practice mechanisms:[10]

1. State and reiterate a compelling positive vision for being a member of a community and an active participant.
2. Offer formal training for the use of tools, and participation in the community should be included. Ensure that trust building is a key component of the CoP development.
3. Involve the learner in hands-on components during training so they may put concepts of knowledge sharing into practice.
4. Train informal groups or teams together in CoP functioning.
5. A practice field, coaches, and feedback are essential parts of helping the community and individuals to achieve effectiveness quickly.
6. Use positive role models.
7. Make support groups available for both management and technical aspects of a CoP.
8. Put consistent systems and structures in place to ensure that the user is not hunting for information on how to join and participate in the CoP to get rewarded for participation.

Free Flow of Membership

Project managers and Cop managers may consider not limiting membership or assign people to take on roles because it may stall or derail a CoP. The core of a CoP is difficult to "pin down" because the very culture promotes the movement of people and ideas.

Unlike a list-server, web community, or online community, CoP life cycles are open-ended and needs based. If a particular issue or problem is solved, a CoP may cease to exist, or be reshaped into a new community with some returning and some new members. Participation (under or over) is also not a reliable indicator or usefulness because experience shows that people often "lurk" but still find value.

Although projects have a need to solve specific problems, CoPs are best when self-governing. The means of self-governance should be agreed upon by the community members. This was a clear need at Clarica, where individuals needed specific problems solved for their individual projects, and needed to feel that the environment was safe and supporting.[11] Above all, a community leader is often the single largest factors in ensuring this community success. For example, the West Coast CoP, a federal government service delivery community, found this to be true.

Clarica Insurance developed an external agent CoP to provide support for individual agents as they developed various projects in the field. These agents were independent of Clarica and yet needed support from the parent company during implementation of various complex proposals. The trust of others in the community and the trust placed in Clarica was an essential ingredient of success. Without this trust, agents would have been unwilling to use the community. The community became a significant strategic asset of Clarica and the lifeblood of many agents.

Directory of CoPs

Projects can be managed more effectively when everyone knows where to find information if they need it. This makes the inclusion of CoPs an integral part of the Communication Plan under the area of Organizational Process Assets, for example. CoPs facilitate the transfer of knowledge to project members, saving valuable time, although with some risk of compromise from external members. Providing a directory of CoPs and their members who are relevant to different tasks is a means to direct people to the right places to solve problems and discuss issues. The directory may be broken down by task and by domain so that users can quickly find the relevant community.

Tacit vs. Explicit Knowledge

Knowledge may be roughly divided into that which is known, knowable (just missing some pieces), complex (could be known), and chaotic (not yet knowable). Accessing the domains of "complexity" and "chaos" is perhaps the most undervalued aspect of a CoP but very useful for project-related communities. CoPs contain tacit knowledge, which is in the heads of experienced professionals, and explicit knowledge, which is coded or written down in formal ways. Dialoguing among a community members taps into complexity and chaos domains by creating new possibilities, including challenging common beliefs, norms, and drawing together multiple ways to approach a risky situation. The decision model is to create probes that have the potential to result in identification of links between existing patterns and even new patterns of knowledge. This knowledge is often movable across to the ordered domains where it can lead to reshaping of current practices and approaches.[12]

The most unordered domain, that of chaos, seems to be connected closely to the practice of managing in crises mode. The decision model is to act quickly, reduce turbulence, and sense the immediate reaction. CoPs are well versed as a collective membership to create new ways to address chaotic events in a time frame that is not possible in the ordered domains. For example, response to a fictional safety threat turned real may not be contained in any manual. This is an ideal backstop for most projects.

As project managers and organizations embrace communities of practice (CoPs), improvements in all areas of project management are expected.

DISCUSSION QUESTIONS

❶ Discuss situations you are familiar with in which informal groups of people—not official teams—have contributed positively to the meeting of project objectives.

❷ If you were to initiate a Community of Practice for project management within your workplace, how would you go about it? (Sponsors, technology, mentoring, events...) Use project management methods to come up with a plan.

❸ From the materials in this chapter, and your own experience, describe how you think CoPs might change project management practice in the future.

REFERENCES

[1] In this paper, we define communities of practice in the same terms as in the work of Dawson, "Developing Knowledge Based Client Relationships." Butterworth Heinemann, 2000.

[2] Explicit knowledge is what we can express to others, while tacit knowledge comprises the rest of our knowledge—that which we cannot communicate in words or symbols. For more on tacit knowledge, see Dawson, ibid.

[3] Vasilou, I. "Paramenides and Zeno of Elea." *A Companion to the Philosophers* (R. L. Arrington, Ed). Malden, MA: Blackwell Publishing Inc., 1999, pp. 299-301.

[4] McElory, Mark. *The New Knowledge Management. Complexity, Learning and Sustainable Innovation.* Knowledge Management Consortium International Press: USA, 2003.

[5] McElroy, ibid.

[6] McElroy, ibid.

[7] Wenger, Etienne, et al. *Cultivating Communities of Practice.* Harvard Business School Press, 2000.

[8] The literature confuses the role of benchmarking and best practices because the terms are often used interchangeably. The relationship between benchmarking and reviewing best practices is most clearly made by Margaret Matters in *The Nuts and Bolts of Benchmarking*, Alpha Publications Pty Ltd., 1995. She states that organizations use internal best practice reviews to make some immediate business improvements in selected areas, and this base-level knowledge may be later used in other parts of an organization. Finally, this knowledge may later serve (depending on the organizational context) as a baseline for future measurement that involves benchmarking with external partners.

[9] General Accounting Office. "Best Practices Methodology: A New Approach for Improving Government Operations"; http://www.dtic.dla.mil/c3i/bprcd/3209.html, 1995. See also Pinto, Jeffery, and Dennis Slevin. Balancing Strategy and Tactics in Project Implementation. Sloan Management Review, 33, 1987, Fall and into, Jeffery K., and Dennis P. Slevin. Critical Factors in Successful Project Implementation. IEEE Transactions on Engineering Management, Vol. EM-34 (1). pp. 22-27, 1987, Feb.

[10] Schein. *The Corporate Culture Survival Guide,* San Francisco: Jossey-Bass, 1999.

[11] Sainte-Onge, Wallace. Leveraging Communities of Practice. Butterworth Heinemann, 2003 and Wenger, Etienne. Communities of practice: Learning, meaning, and identity. Cambridge: University Press, 1999.

[12] Snowden, Kurtz, C. F., and D. J. Snowden. "The New Dynamics of Strategy: Sense-Making in a Complex and Complicated World." *IBM Systems Journal,* 42 (3), 2003.

CHAPTER 30

A Project Management Strategy for Six Sigma Projects

▶ANTONIO CESAR AMARU MAXIMIANO,
UNIVERSIDADE DE SÃO PAULO, BRAZIL

▶ALONSO MAZINI SOLER,
UNIVERSIDADE DE SÃO PAULO, BRAZIL

This methodological combination of the Six Sigma business strategy and the project management approach is aimed at:

▶Better understanding and effective selection of Six Sigma projects and their objectives (problems and/or businesses opportunities to be attacked).

▶Clear definition of business cases and chartering of Six Sigma projects.

▶Increasing the rate of success of Six Sigma project goals through the use of a comprehensive standard methodology for project management.

▶Completion of Six Sigma project in accordance with expected time, costs, and quality requirements, achieving their planned business targets.

▶Improving customer satisfaction by means of exceeding their expectations.

SIX SIGMA BUSINESS STRATEGY AND PROJECT MANAGEMENT BASIC CONCEPTS

Let's briefly outline the conceptual aspects of the Six Sigma

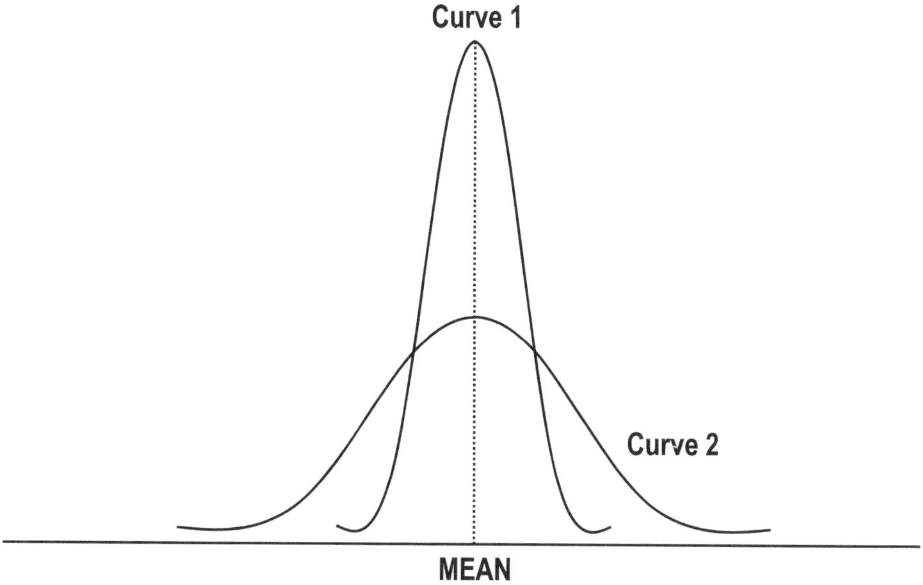

FIGURE 30-1. **THE NORMAL CURVE AND THE REPRESENTATION OF DISPERSION THROUGH THE STANDARD DEVIATION**

business strategy, the project management conceptual framework, and the potential benefits from the combination of these two approaches.

Six Sigma Basics

In the early '80s Motorola pioneered the Six Sigma management approach to eliminate defects and waste from manufacturing processes. This strategy was based on understanding the customers' needs and expectations, knowledge of engineering, use of statistical data, and systems analysis tools. The Six Sigma concept has since left the manufacturing benches to reach the operational and administrative applications. Early adopters and followers as well as a large number of Fortune 500 companies, including General Electric, Seagate, Honeywell, JP Morgan, and Raytheon, became Six Sigma enthusiasts as a business strategy to improve financial businesses performance and increase customer loyalty.

The Six Sigma concept comes from the standard deviation parameter of the probabilistic Gaussian normal curve, and it is related to the amount of variability observed in a process response. Figure 30-1 illustrates the bell shape characteristic and the location (mean) and dispersion (standard deviation) parameters representation of the normal curves. In this figure, Curve 1 represents smaller dispersion from the mean than Curve 2.

According to Walter Shewart, Edward Deming, and Genichi Taguchi, among other quality gurus, the closer to the defined nominal target a process response operates, the better the quality (of conformance) of the product, and the better performance results can be expected from the business. On the other hand, the more dispersion the process response demonstrates, in comparison with the defined nominal target, the worse the expected results. This maxim has been accepted as the basis of the search for quality and efficiency since the beginning of the last century. It was then that the Statistical Process Control idea and the Control Charts tools were introduced.

By the early 1900s Walter Shewhart developed a conceptual threshold area, limited between a lower and an upper Control Limits, based on the same probabilistic normal distribution. Within this area, the process responses are highly expected to vary (approximately 99.7 percent, considering the ±3 sigma limits), independently, through time. By the other hand, an individual process response laid out of these control limits indicates that something is affecting the natural behavior of the process and it would be better and preventive to investigate the special causes provoking it. That's the principle of Statistical Process Control using Control Charts as a tool.

In other contexts, there was established the process response Specification Limits based on customers' expectations and product design and engineering. Any individual process response outside of the specification limits was considered a defect and represented a real problem that should be analyzed. Both of the thresholds, the control and the specification ones, represent different and dissociated concepts. While the control limits represent the natural variable behavior of the process response, the specification limits represent its acceptance criteria.

The conceptual connection between both of the thresholds is called Process Capability Analysis and it is measured by two defined indexes, the Process Capability Index (Cp) and the Process Capability Index Corrected due to non-centrality (Cpk). The Process Capability Index (Cp) expresses the quotient relationship between the maximum variability allowed to the process response (the length of the specification limits, or upper minus lower specification limits), and the natural process variability (the length of the control limits under natural conditions, or upper minus lower control limits).

$$CP = \frac{\text{Upper Spec Limit} - \text{Lower Spec Limit}}{\text{Upper Control Limit} - \text{Lower Control Limit}} = \frac{USL - LSL}{6\sigma}$$

$$CPk = \text{minimum}\left(\frac{USL - \text{Target Nominal Value}}{3\sigma} \; ; \; \frac{\text{Target Nominal Value} - LSL}{3\sigma}\right)$$

The Six Sigma goal, therefore, represents a process capability performance defined by the efficiency of Cp = 2.0 and, at least, Cpk = 1.5. This means that the natural process variability represents no more than 50 percent of the target required process variability, while both of the nominal centers do not differ by more than 1.5 standard deviations. This Six Sigma performance represents, theoretically, no more than 3.4 defects per million opportunities (DPMO), which means an extraordinary process performance level and virtually zero defects. This is the reason for today's enthusiastic adoption of the Six Sigma approach for most process improvement initiatives. Figure 30-2 illustrates the statistical background of Six Sigma capability measurement.

The DMAIC Model

To implement the Six Sigma approach as a strategy of efficiency and quality improvement, a life cycle process model called DMAIC (Define, Measure, Analyze, Improve, and Control) was developed. Starting with a fuzzy problem/opportunity on process quality,

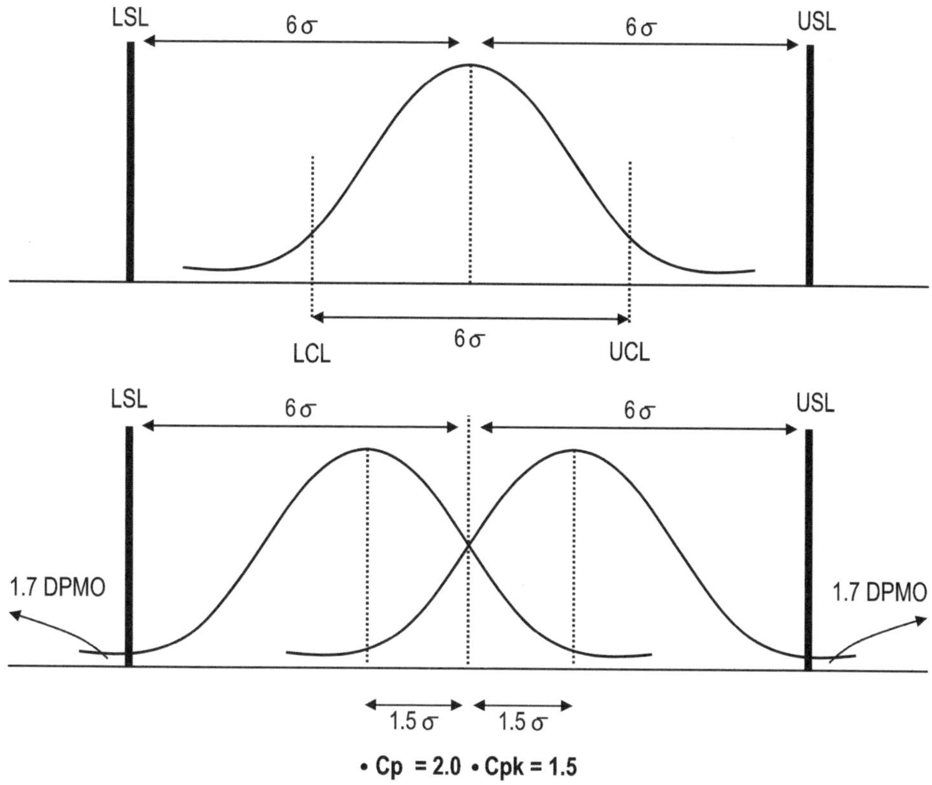

FIGURE 30-2. **STATISTICAL BACKGROUND OF SIX SIGMA PROCESS CAPABILITY**

DMAIC provides orientation and tools to be executed, aiming to plan, implement, and standardize highly significant process improvements (Six Sigma), which are almost always associated with financial and/or customer's loyalty gains. DMAIC consolidates the using of formal logic reasoning: it is based on experimental data collection and analysis, as well as specific and proven statistical and process-oriented tools. Ultimately, DMAIC represents the transition from statistical concept goals (the Six Sigma fundamentals) to a practical step-by-step method, focused on process improvements and business results.

Six Sigma (implemented through DMAIC) is, therefore, not another quality or training program or a quick-fix approach with some statistical complexity. It is rather an added-value strategy able to impact positively the company's financials, eliminate defects/problems to ensure products and services align to the customer's expectations, and sustain improvements and gains over time, based on factual data and a defendable experimental reasoning.

The main deliverables for each phase of DMAIC, as illustrated in Figure 30-3, include:

▶***Define.*** The problem/opportunity to be attacked in a given business process is chosen under a top-down decision process. The objectives and scope of the project are defined and the financial impact is roughly estimated, and the project benefits and goals are defined. Relevant information about the process and customer is collected.

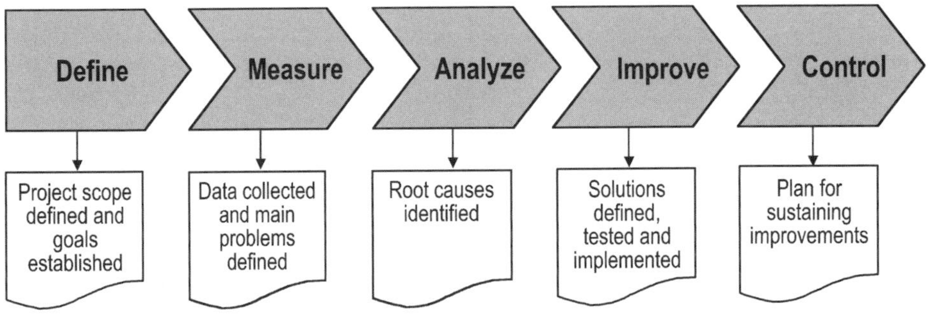

FIGURE 30-3. **DMAIC PHASES AND MAIN DELIVERABLES**

▶***Measure.*** Reliable metrics and a data collection system are established to monitor the process measurements (Key Performance Indicators), and to define the starting point in the search for a solution. Current data are mined and the main problems become explicit. Their contributions for the achievement of the project goals are determined.

▶***Analyze.*** Additional data are collected and the root causes for the main problems are analyzed and defined.

▶***Improve.*** The solutions for each of the main problems identified are searched, tested, and implemented. The planned project benefits and goal achievements are evaluated.

▶***Control.*** The improved processes are standardized and a plan to ensure the sustainability of the achievements is established. The possibilities of deploying the solutions among other areas and company branches are evaluated.

Several attempts to facilitate the process of managing this efficient tool have been reported recently. The emergence of PMI's *A Guide to the Project Management Body of Knowledge (PMBOK® Guide)* offered a significant contribution for this purpose, since implementation of Six Sigma efforts is essentially a project management problem.

The Project Management Processes

The emerging discipline of modern project management has systematically extended its domains. It is a common practice in these days to consider the company value as the consolidated value of the individual projects in the company portfolio. New challenges in the business environment, such as pressures for cost reduction and for increasing value to the customer, as well as aggressive competition and compression of time to market, turned project management into a strategic driver for many companies. Effectiveness in the achievement of expected results and predictability of changes are considered the main advantages in this discipline.

The *PMBOK® Guide* is the reference for modern project management. In this guide, project management processes are organized in five overlapping and interactive process groups—Initiating Processes, Planning Processes, Executing Processes, Controlling Processes, and Closing Processes—which represent a logical sequence of reasoning, to be followed along the life cycle of any project.

DMAIC and *PMBOK® Guide* Joint Potential Benefits

Understanding both the DMAIC model and the project management processes framework, it's inevitable to perceive a strong relationship and a potential interaction between them, favorable to the achievement of the company's strategic objectives.

First of all, Six Sigma projects are, in fact, a project in the same sense defined by the *PMBOK® Guide*, undertaken to create an unique product or service (a processes change) and restricted by resources, costs, and/or time. Six Sigma projects should thus be managed appropriately in order to ensure performance, completion of the project in accordance with the committed time, cost and technical performance, achievement of better customer satisfaction, loyalty, and financial gains to the company.

On the other hand, the *PMBOK® Guide* offers a processes framework to describe, organize, and complete the work of the project. This means that it's reasonable to realize a consistent added value Six Sigma Strategy for the company that adopts the *PMBOK® Guide* as its guide to project management, aiming to increase efficiency and predictability, eliminate defects/problems in processes, and ensure the achievement of the company's strategic objectives.

SIX SIGMA AND PROJECT MANAGEMENT DUAL AND COLLABORATIVE APPROACHES

Considering the DMAIC model and the *PMBOK® Guide* processes framework, one can summarize that, while the DMAIC model is most focused on finding solutions for problems/opportunities through factual and data-based decision-making, the *PMBOK® Guide* offers a well known path to implement these solutions. As a matter of fact, it's reasonable to define two approaches to connect Six Sigma DMAIC and the *PMBOK® Guide* processes:

▶Six Sigma strategy could be implemented (through DMAIC) in a company in which the *PMBOK® Guide* is adopted, aiming to improve processes performance, potential strategic gains, and customer loyalty;

▶The *PMBOK® Guide* could be integrated within the DMAIC Model—complementing its road map, tasks, and tools—in a methodological approach, aiming to ensure better results for the solutions implementation.

Improving Project Management Processes Through Six Sigma Business Strategy

It has been common to read about project failures and problems. In 1994, the Standish Group reported survey results indicating that 46 percent of IT projects were over budget and overdue, while 28 percent failed altogether. In 1999, a Robbins-Gioia Inc. survey of project managers found that 44 percent of them have had cost overruns of 10 to 40 percent, and only 16 percent consistently met schedule due dates. In 1999, the Standish Group updated its report results and showed improvements in project failure rates, although the percentage was still considered very high and profit-consuming.

No matter how projects fail, it always means losses in terms of a company's financials and customer loyalty. For this reason, failures in project management should be treated as strategic challenges.

Someone charged with company results, facing project failures and profit challenges, would be tempted to adopt generic evaluations and prescriptions that could be quickly implemented, without a deep understanding of the company- and environment-specific characteristics. What companies really need is to understand their own project management maturity—represented by their project management approach associated with their business environment—in order to surgically implement effective actions to improve their project management processes.

Here rests the justification for the adoption of a Six Sigma strategy for a project-driven company. A Black Belt certified professional, using DMAIC, could evaluate and find the real problem(s) and root causes within the project management processes and suggest customized solutions. Like an experimenter at his or her lab bench, the Black Belt could precisely respond to questions like: In which corner of the magic triangle (scope, time, and cost) lies the major problem? What are the project management processes to focus on? What are the causes for the problems? Which engine associates each of the causes to each of the problems? What are the best solutions to attack these causes? What are the impacts of these solutions on project results? On company-wide results?

A Six Sigma approach to this situation means: No generic solution is acceptable, but rather a fact-based specific process-improvement solution that fits the company maturity phase and its business environment is what's necessary.

Improving Six Sigma Projects Results Through Project Management Processes

Whenever there are process changes and improvements to be made, they have to be managed as projects, undertaken to create a new different situation. A Six Sigma project is commonly associated with a business case based on some measurable and representative need for improvement in a process. Any deviation from the achievement of the expected results of this business case implies an unsuccessful Six Sigma project. The success criteria for any Six Sigma project is to achieve the committed goals—in a sustainable way—under a planned schedule, budget, and technical performance.

The DMAIC model stresses the use of statistics and analytic tools that are applied to define the best customized solution to the company's problem, based on facts and current data, rather than on management intuition alone. DMAIC, however, is almost negligent in the solutions implementation planning, execution, and controlling orientation. These processes are superficially mentioned and loosely integrated into the process improvement context. The DMAIC model jumps from the solution-finding to the maintenance of sustainable results. This lack of project management planning, execution, and controlling processes represents a strong weakness in the DMAIC model and is, effectively, the strength of the *PMBOK® Guide*.

Almost all of the work advocated by the DMAIC model (in fact, the work activities associated with the "D," "M," "A," and most of "I") is dedicated to finding and defining the effective solution(s) for a problem. The DMAIC model dedicates only the last effort of the "I(mprove)" phase to planning and implementing this solution, while the "C(ontrol)" stage is dedicated to consolidating and monitoring this implementation. One who is used to working with the *PMBOK® Guide* can rephrase this, saying that most of the DMAIC work is dedicated to defining the scope statement and the "product" definition of the project solution. Very little orientation is devoted to plan, execute, control, and close the solution implementation. Figure 30-4 illustrates a suggested correspondence between DMAIC phases and the *PMBOK® Guide* groups of processes. It shows the differences in focus between both of the frameworks—while DMAIC dedicates most

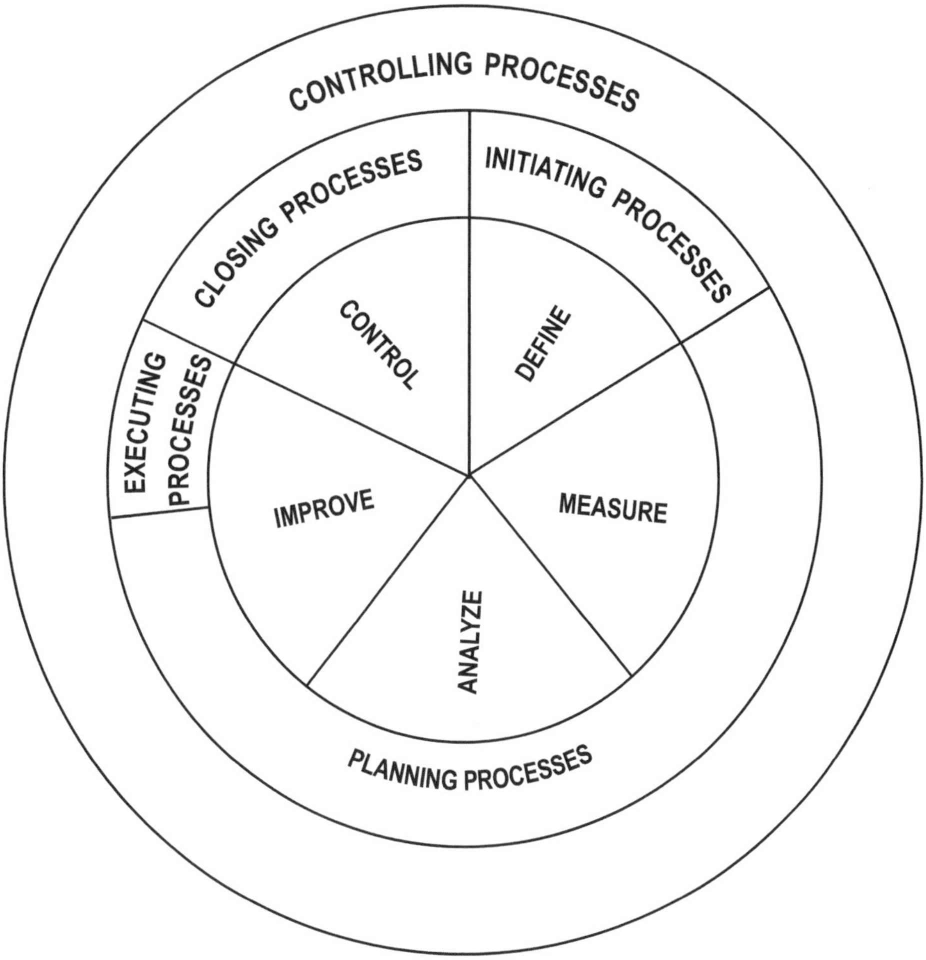

FIGURE 30-4. **CORRESPONDENCE BETWEEN DMAIC PHASES AND *PMBOK® GUIDE* GROUPS OF PROCESSES**

of its efforts to define clearly the problem's solution, the *PMBOK® Guide* drives its major efforts to the planning and implementation of the solution.

Both models add significant value for the achievement of company strategies and can be viewed in a complementary way. Some companies like GE and NCR have indeed customized the DMAIC model as a proprietary structured methodology, adding project management processes to the Six Sigma project life cycle phases.

PROJECT MANAGEMENT METHODOLOGY FOR SIX SIGMA STRATEGY

The definition, adoption, and deployment of a standard project management methodology is a well-known fundamental responsibility of any Project Office. Beyond the dictionary meaning of methodology, it extends to the sequence of the project work as a processes framework, and includes the description of the practices and the definition of standard tools and templates. All of these are aligned with the company's strategy, maturity characteristics, and business environment, and generally adopted as a standard rule for the individual conduction of any project. It is well accepted that the adoption of a project management methodology makes the project results more predictable and repeatable, and results in the more efficient use of the company's resources.

Considering the DMAIC model and its phase activities as Six Sigma project guidance, it should be effective to complement its framework with knowledge from the project management environment, in order to consolidate a Six Sigma project management methodology.

The Phase Review Model Concept

Six Sigma projects start with the perception that the company has a problem or opportunity for improvement, followed by a rough estimate of the potential financial benefits associated with the problem solving. In the beginning of the Six Sigma project, the information supporting the business case does not allow for precision of the figures. Precision comes later, as the project work advances. A company striving to execute a Six Sigma project should monitor closely project progress, along the DMAIC life cycle, in order to constantly evaluate the project benefits and cost deviations from the plan. This is to help them decide if they should continue or interrupt the project execution. Uncertainties, mostly in the beginning, are always characteristic of Six Sigma projects. A company must keep theses uncertainties under close control in order to avoid wasted time and money and, at the same time, capitalize on benefits from the project.

For instance, a reduction in the energy consumption was defined as an opportunity for a company's cost reduction efforts. It was assumed that a reduction of 20 percent in this line item was feasible, considering a known benchmark. A Black Belt was designated to analyze the problem situation. After some months of work and hundreds of working hours dedicated to finding a solution, the Black Belt concluded the best solution to be applied to the case. The solution proposed the replacement of wiring and light bulbs, among other strategies. The cost of the solution was estimated as a huge sum that was considered not feasible at that time, and the project was canceled. One who was out of the decision chain, might ask: "Why did it take so long to cancel the project? Why didn't the company's executives review the potential solution much earlier and save money by canceling the project? How should they deal with the Black Belt and the Six Sigma project team dissatisfaction at this time, considering their full dedication and motivation for the project?"

The phase review model is a conceptual strategy that breaks the project work down into a set of "stages" of prescribed activities, and defines some project performance reviews, called "gates," during the project execution. At each of theses "gates" the project sponsors are able to review the project progress and performance, determining the achievement (or lack of) of the criteria, in order to: 1) move the project on to the next "stage"—approving the required resources (go decision)—or to 2) ask for more information (recycle decision), and/or stop definitely or freeze the project ("no-go" decision).

Considering the nature of uncertainty that characterizes most Six Sigma projects, it's easy to see the value added by the phase review strategy in building a Six Sigma project management methodology.

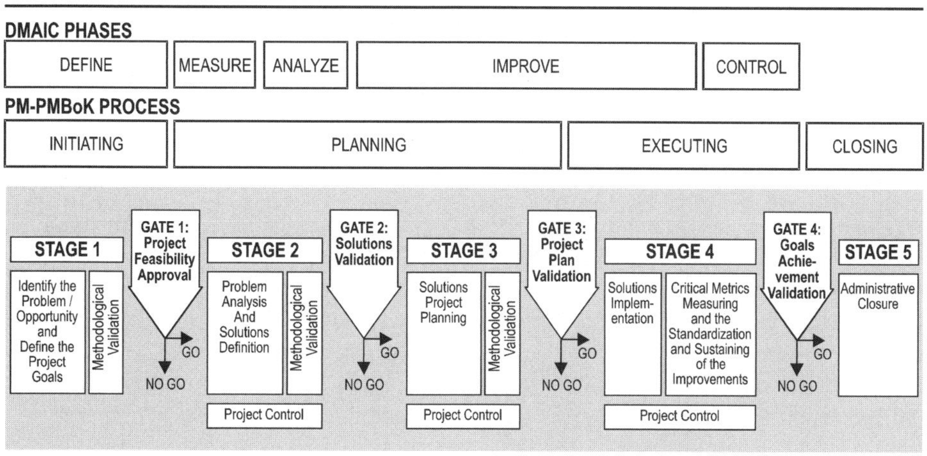

FIGURE 30-5. **PHASE REVIEW FOR SIX SIGMA PROJECTS**

The Phase Review Methodology Framework for Six Sigma Projects

Figure 30-5 illustrates a suggested generic methodology framework for managing Six Sigma according to modern project management processes. It's made up of five "stages" and four "gates," representing the reasoning and the totality of work that consolidates the mixed approach between DMAIC and the *PMBOK® Guide*.

▶Stage 1 work is dedicated to a deep understanding of the problem or opportunity, formalizing the estimation of the expected project benefits, detailing the financial information contained in the business case and corroborating them (or not), and establishing the Key Performance Indices (KPIs) and their goals into the project charter.

▶Gate 1 is a criteria for revising the project charter figures by the project sponsors, after an analysis of the proposed KPIs and their goals, and deciding about the project feasibility and the continuity of the project to the next stage. If the project benefits are considered insufficient or if the uncertainties are considered too risky, the project's sponsors could decide to cancel it immediately, saving time and money (although nobody will ever know whether a decision in favor of continuing the project would be the best decision).

▶Stage 2 work is characterized by the majority of the phases included into the DMAIC model. It includes analysis of the project's problem/opportunity, root causes definition, and the proposed solutions development—all based on factual data collection, analysis, and experimental logical reasoning.

▶Gate 2 is a formal review on the proposed solutions for the project's problem/opportunity, validating them (or not), and deciding for or against continuing the project to the next stage. If the solutions (or part of them) are considered unfeasible or don't meet the current strategic drives of the company, they are immediately discontinued. In this case, the next forward stage is allowed for just the set of solutions approved. If none of the proposed solutions was validated, some rework can be required, or the project can be canceled or frozen.

▶Stage 3 is the planning phase for each of the project's problem/opportunity solutions approved. In this stage, we find the planning processes described in the *PMBOK® Guide*. At the end of this stage, a project plan made up of a well-defined scope statement, quality requirements, time and costs baselines, risk responses, project team structures and populations, and communication and acquisition requirements is submitted for the project sponsors' validation.

▶Gate 3 is a formal review the detailed project plan, validating it (or not), and deciding whether to continue the project to the next stage. If the project plan is considered unfeasible, some rework can be required, or simply, the project can be canceled or frozen. It's interesting to observe that only after the project plan and the project budget are concluded can the company review the project's benefit/costs figures and decide about its gains. It isn't uncommon for most of the companies implementing Six Sigma strategy to arrive in this project phase and decide for project cancellation, absorbing the sunk costs and impacts.

▶Stage 4 is the execution phase of the project plan. While monitoring KPI performance trends toward the achievement of the project goals, process changes are consolidated, and planning for sustainability of the achieved project results carried out.

▶Gate 4 is a formal review of the project results, validating the achievement (or not) of the project goals, and the continuity of the project to the next stage. In this review, the project can be recommended to be closed in various ways: (a) Considered a success due to the achievement of all the project goals within the time planned, (b) Considered partially successful due to the achievement of some project goals within the time planned, and (c) Considered closed "in the state" due to the impossibility of the achievement of the project goals within a reasonable time expectation.

▶Stage 5 refers to the administrative closure of the project, including registering all the project documentation and the deployment of the lessons learned within the company.

Figure 30-5 still shows a correspondence between the DMAIC phases, the *PMBOK® Guide* group of processes, and the suggested phase review methodology framework for Six Sigma projects.

Core Processes of the Methodology Framework for Six Sigma Projects

Figure 30-6 illustrates the breakdown of the suggested methodology framework for Six Sigma projects into its core processes. Three kinds of different and complementary processes are considered in this figure:

1. The specific working activities processes, represented by the majority of the boxes, refer to the sequential working activities established for each of the "stages." One who is used to working with the DMAIC model and the *PMBOK® Guide* can easily identify these activities.

2. The controlling processes, represented by the vertical boxes in the figure, refer to the controlling activities conducted by the periodical interaction between the Black Belt Project Manager and the PMO representative. These formal controlling "ongoing" activities are made up of some performance and progress communication figures, situational analysis, and the decision for planning and execution of conditional corrective actions. These processes aim to assure the achievement of the expected progress of the project, in terms of time, costs, and resource demands.

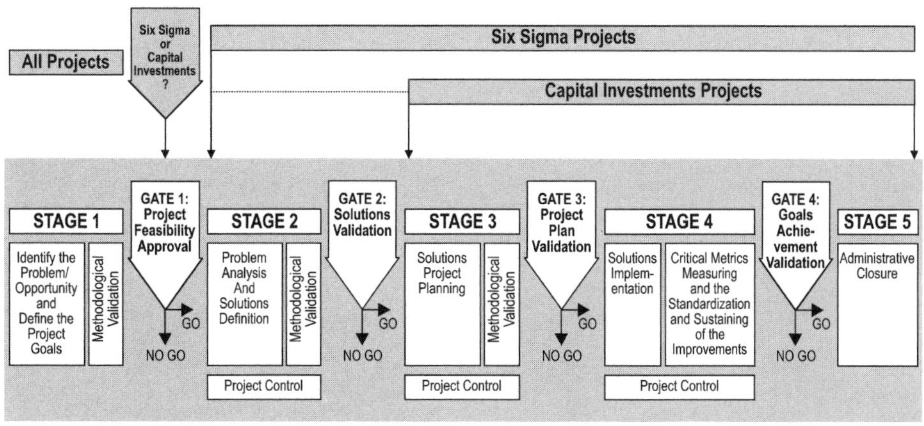

FIGURE 30-6. **SIX SIGMA AND CAPITAL INVESTMENTS PROJECTS WORKFLOW**

3. The methodological revision and validation processes, represented by the boxes just before each of the "gates," refer to the methodological acceptance of the work done during the "stages," before the appointment of the "gates" review meetings. These processes are conducted on behalf of the PMO by expert professionals, like Master Black Belts and/or Certified Project Management Professionals, and aim to assure the consistency of the information that will be submitted to the project sponsors during the gates.

FURTHER CONSIDERATIONS

Two other points subject to consideration here, emerged from the authors' practical consultancy experience. First of all, it's interesting to raise questions on the nature of the responsibilities between the professionals, the Black Belt and the Project Manager. Who will be in charge of Six Sigma project management? Secondly, it's considered fundamental to discuss the responsibilities of the Project Management Offices within the company environment of the Six Sigma strategy adoption.

Belts or Project Manager Professionals?

The Black Belt is a role dedicated to the professional who successfully completed training in methods, practices, and tools of Six Sigma DMAIC, and has already experienced Six Sigma complex projects. Theoretically, he/she is a full time professional working on selected projects, fixing the problems, and finding the "hidden money." Black belts are the most representative and strongest role in the Six Sigma projects responsibilities chain—that's the reason we are using them to represent the professionals who have the Six Sigma knowledge.

The project manager is a role occupied by the person who is in charge of any project, responsible, generically, for its planning, execution, and closing, and accountable for its results. The skill development of the project manager is based primarily on the best practices advocated by the *PMBOK® Guide*, plus practical experience in the management of businesses, projects, and people.

Black Belt and Project Manager are just names of roles, expressing specific training and experience that easily can be shared. What really matters here is the demonstration of

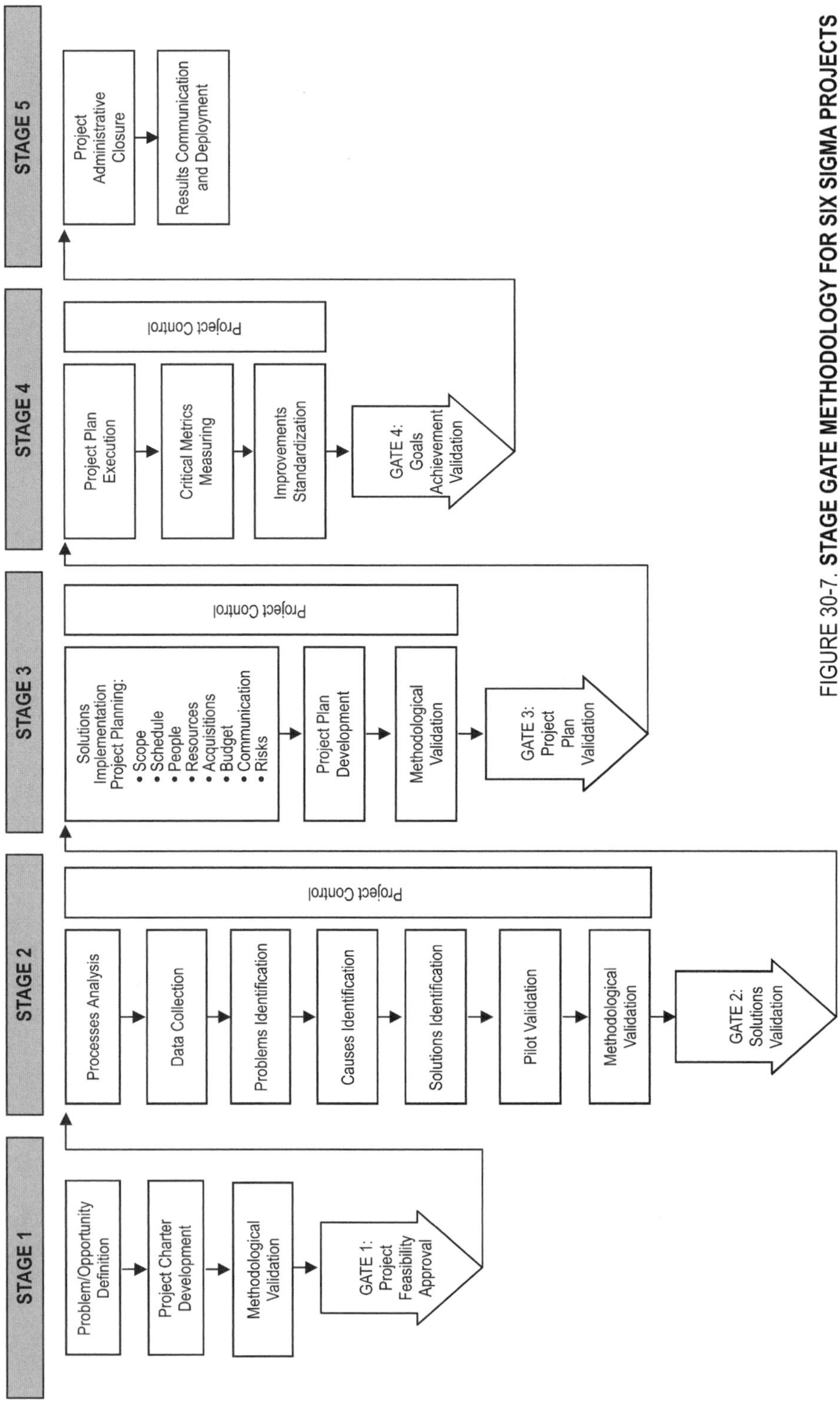

FIGURE 30-7. **STAGE GATE METHODOLOGY FOR SIX SIGMA PROJECTS**

knowledge and ability, and the commitment and motivation to conduct the project through its challenges towards the expected results. The preference should go to that professional who demonstrates better capacity to conduct that specific project, through the Six Sigma project management methodology, to the achievement of its expected goals.

Considering the methodology introduced in this chapter, we might suggest that the Black Belt with no skills in project management can better manage the specific processes during "stages" 1 and 2; while a project manager with no skills in DMAIC can easily run the specific processes during "stages" 3, 4, and 5. Therefore, why not implement a change in the Belts training contents, including some detailed project management training?

The Six Sigma Project Management Office (PMO)

The PMO has become one of the most popular concepts within the project management environment. It refers to the most common infrastructure to support management by projects—a system that integrates all the project activities with the organization-wide strategies, priorities, and resources.

We can envision PMO support in at least three specific cases of the Six Sigma strategy within the company:

1. The PMO supports problems/opportunities selection, establishing criteria and managing the Six Sigma Project Portfolio, aligned with the company's strategies and the resources availability.

2. The PMO supports the Black Belts' project management demands and the controlling of time, costs, and resources restrictions during the project execution.

3. The PMO supports monitoring project results, as well as the deployment of project knowledge and the replication of some successful projects among the company branches.

DISCUSSION QUESTIONS

❶ How can project management principles be integrated into the daily routine of Six Sigma project managers?

❷ What are the major advantages of Black Belts employing project management in Six Sigma projects?

❸ What makes more sense, Black Belts becoming Project Managers, or Project Managers certifying as Black Belts?

FURTHER READING

Anbari, Frank T., PMI. *Proceedings of Project Management Institute Annual Seminars & Symposium,* Six Sigma Method and Its Applications in Project Management, 2002.

Brue, G. *Six Sigma for Managers.* New York: McGraw-Hill, 2002, p. 189.

Crawford, J.K. *The Strategic Project Office. A Guide to Improving Organizational Performance.* New York: Marcel Dekker Inc., 2002, p. 367.

Dinsmore, Paul Campbell. Transformando Estratégicas Empresariais em Resultados através da Gerência por Projetos. RJ: Quality Mark, 1999.
Johnson, J. "Turning CHAOS into SUCCESS." *Software*, Dec. 1999.
Kerzner, Harold. Gestão de Projetos—As Melhores Práticas. PO; 2002; Artmed Ed.
Maximiano, A.C.A. Administração de Projetos. Como Transformar Idéias em Resultados. Atlas, São Paulo, 2002, pp. 281.
Renslow, D.W. "Six Sigma at NCR." The Critical Path Newsletter of the Dayton/Miami Valley Chapter of PMI, Volume 5, Issue 3, June/July 2002.
Simpson, Randy. The pursuit of Program Management Excellence. Proceedings of the Project Management Institute Global Congress North America. September 18–25, 2003. Baltimore, Maryland USA.
Verzuh, E. *The Portable MBA in Project Management.* New Jersey: John Wiley & Sons, Inc., 2003, p. 436.

CHAPTER 31

Cultural Challenges in Managing International Projects

▶PAUL C. DINSMORE, PMP,
DINSMORE ASSOCIATES

▶MANUEL M. BENITEZ CODAS,
CONSULTANT

A backhanded "V for victory" sign is an uncomplimentary gesture in Australia. In Brazil, the American "A-OK" sign is also offensive. These are lessons that some presidents, diplomats, and businesspeople have learned the hard way. Awareness of such cross-cultural subtleties can spell success or failure in international dealings, whether in diplomatic relations, general business, or the project arena.

Projects conducted in international settings share these sometimes embarrassing communications pitfalls and others as well. They are subject to cultural, bureaucratic, and logistical challenges just like conventional domestic projects are. In fact, project management approaches to international ventures include the same items common to domestic projects. Under both circumstances, successful project management calls for performing the basics of planning, organizing, and controlling. This also implies carrying out the classic functions outlined in the Project Management Institute's *Project Management Body of Knowledge (PMBOK®)* of managing scope, schedule, cost, quality, communications, human resources, contracting and supply, and risk, as well as the integration of these areas across the project life cycle.

Understanding culture is the starting point for planning for the challenges that face international projects. *The American*

Heritage Dictionary defines culture as, "The totality of socially transmitted behavior patterns, arts, beliefs, institutions, and all other products of human work and thought characteristic of a community or population." For an organization, culture may be more simplistically perceived as the guiding beliefs that determine the "way we do things around here." The challenge in international project settings revolves around the fact that projects are usually made up of multiple organizations, thus involving multiple organizational cultures in settings that involve several ethnic or country-based cultures. An example is an Anglo-American joint venture working in Saudi Arabia, with Japanese and Indian subcontractors. So the issues are actually cross-cultural in nature and involve multiple issues.

The primary factors in cross-cultural settings that call for special attention and an "international approach" are: functional redundancy, political factors, the expatriate way of life, language and culture, additional risk factors, supply difficulties, and local laws and legislation. Of the items pinpointed, some offer particular challenges from the viewpoint of the *PMBOK*®. Some comments on these critical topics follow. These are the subjects that require special care to ensure that the internationally set project meets its targeted goals.

▶***Functional redundancy*** means the duplication or overlap of certain functions or activities. This may be necessary because of contractual agreements involving technology transfer requiring "national counterparts." Language or organizational complexity of the project may also be responsible for creating functional redundancy. Special attention is called for, therefore, in managing the project functions of human resources and communications.

▶***Political factors*** in international projects are a strong influence and are plagued with countless unknowns. Aside from fluctuations in international politics, project professionals are faced with the subtleties of local politics, which often place major roadblocks in the pathway of attaining project success. In terms of classic project management, this means reinforcing the communications function in order to ensure that all strategic and politically related interactions are appropriately transmitted and deciphered.

▶***The expatriate way of life*** refers to the habits and expectations of those parties who are transferred to a host country. This includes the way of thinking and the physical and psychological needs of those people temporarily living in a strange land with different customs and ways of life. When the differences are substantial, this means making special provision for a group of people who would otherwise refuse to relocate to the site, or, if transferred on a temporary basis, remain highly unmotivated during their stay. The basic project management factors related to the expatriate way of life include communications, human resources, and supply. Personal safety issues may affect the coming and going of expatriates and family members.

▶***Language and culture*** include the system of spoken, written, and other social forms of communication. Included in language and culture are the systems of codification and decodification of thoughts, beliefs, and values common to a given people. Here all the subtleties of communications become of special importance.

▶***Additional risk factors*** may include personal risks such as kidnapping, local epidemics, and faulty medical care. Terrorism and local insurgencies are also critical risk factors in some settings. Rapid swings in political and economic situations, or peculiar local weather or geology, are also potential uncertainties. These different risk factors

	Internationally Sensitive Factors						
***PMBOK®* Areas**	**Functional Redundancy**	**Political Factors**	**Expatriate Way of Life**	**Language and Culture**	**Additional Risk Factors**	**Supply Difficulties**	**Local Laws and Legislation**
Scope							
Schedule							
Cost							
Quality							
Communications	X	X	X	X			X
Human Resources	X		X				
Contracting and Supply			X			X	X
Risk					X		

FIGURE 31-1. **RELATIONSHIP OF INTERNATIONALLY SENSITIVE FACTORS TO THE BASIC CONCEPTS OF THE *PMBOK® GUIDE***

require analysis and subsequent management to keep them from adversely affecting the project. The obvious basic project management tenet in this case is risk management.

▶***Supply difficulties*** encompass all the contracting, procurement, and logistical challenges that must be faced on the project. For instance, some railroad projects must use the new railway itself as the primary form of transportation for supplies. In other situations, waterways may be the only access. Customs presents major problems in many project settings. A new concept in logistics may need to be pioneered for a given project. Contracting and supply on international projects normally calls for an "overkill" effort, since ordinary domestic approaches are normally inadequate. This usually requires highly qualified personnel and some partially redundant management systems heavily laced with follow-up procedures. Heavy emphasis is needed in the areas of contracting and supply.

▶***Local laws and legislation*** affect the way much of business is done on international projects. They may even affect personal habits (such as abstaining from drinking alcoholic beverages in Muslim countries). Here the key is awareness and education so that each person is familiar with whatever laws are applicable to his or her area. In this case, the project management tenets that require special attention are communications and supply.

It is apparent from Figure 31-1 that in terms of classic project management, special emphasis is required on international projects in the areas of communications, contracting and supply, human resources, and risk. Since all of the project management areas—including the basic areas of managing scope, schedule, cost, and quality—are interconnected (a communications breakdown affects quality, for instance), extra diligence is called for in managing communications, contracting and supply, human resources, and risk. It must be assumed that a conventional approach to managing these areas will be inadequate for international projects.

A MODEL OF INTERCULTURAL TEAM BUILDING

The challenge in international team building boils down to creating a convergence of people's differing personal inputs toward a set of common final outputs. This means developing a process that facilitates communication and understanding between people of different national cultures. Making this process happen signifies the difference between success and failure on international projects.

People's inputs are things like personal and cultural values, beliefs, and assumptions. They also include patterns of thinking, feeling, and behaving. Expectations, needs, and motivations are also part of people's inputs into any given system. The outputs are the results or benefits produced by a given system. They may be perceived as a combination of achievements benefiting the individuals, the team, the organization, and the outside environment. The outputs are the object of the efforts generated by the inputs.

The secret is to transform the way people do things at the beginning of the project into more effective behavior as the project moves along. This transformation initially involves identifying the intercultural differences among the parties. Once this is done, a program of intercultural team building is called for in order to make the transformation take place. The result of the team-building process is to influence the behavior of the group toward meeting the project's goals. Intercultural team building thus calls for developing and conducting a program that will help transform the participants' inputs into project outputs.

SOME GLOBAL CONSIDERATIONS

Globalization affects all areas of endeavor, including how projects are managed. It affects the internationally sensitive factors mentioned earlier in this chapter and reinforces the need to create teams that are capable of dealing with the dynamics of globalization.

The groundswell toward globalization stems from a number of factors, from advances in transportation and communications technologies through international trade agreements. New international standards, replacing national standards that impeded the movement of goods and services, also open doors toward a more globalized economy.

While the trends toward globalization of project management and related technologies such as the construction industry are apparent, there still remain basic differences in the way business is performed from one land to the next. A contrast between the United States and Japan appears, for instance, when examining the relationship between general contractor and architects. This relationship is traditionally adversarial in the United States, as is reflected by the habitual finger-pointing that goes on at the end of contracts, sometimes resulting in litigation. In contrast, in Japan these relationships are much more cooperative in nature; there is a certain congeniality between design and construction. Also in contrast, mutual risk-taking between contractors and clients is a more common practice in Japan than in the United States. It is a common practice in Europe as well. Meanwhile, partnering—one form of mutual risk-taking—is growing in the United States, but it is almost routine procedure in Japan and Europe.

Information technology projects are becoming increasingly globalized, largely due to massive outsourcing of services to parts of the world where the expertise exists and cost is less than in highly developed countries. Some manufacturing projects are highly globalized, both in terms of development as well as fabrication. Such is the case in aircraft manufacturing, where components are developed and manufactured in sundry parts of the world and then consolidated at a central location.

The way technical information is developed and transferred also affects how business is performed, and consequently, how projects are managed and implemented. Various systems or models are in place for generating and transferring knowledge in different parts of the world. Here are some of the models applicable to the construction industry. In general terms, the basic models may be called the European, the North American, and the Japanese. (These terms are used only to identify trends, as all three models can be found in most countries.) The characteristics of the models are as follows:

The European Model

In Europe, there are highly structured, formal, and centralized national systems for generating and disseminating technical knowledge. Responsibilities are clearly defined, with specific national organizations charged with generating research, while other organizations take care of transferring the result to industry. The Swedish system is a typical example, with the National Swedish Institute for Building Research responsible for knowledge generation, and the Swedish Institute for Building Documentation responsible for dissemination. National systems in Europe are often jointly financed by government and industry.

The North American Model

The system in North America is less formal than in Europe. There is, in fact, little coordination in the construction research effort in North America. In contrast to the European model, advanced construction knowledge is mainly generated at the university level. The dissemination to industry is largely performed by broad-based engineering or trade associations, such as the American Society of Civil Engineers and the Construction Industry Institute. The technical work is carried out in these associations partially by committees made up of volunteers.

The Japanese Model

In the Japanese model, research is concentrated in a handful of integrated companies that dominate Japanese construction, where technology development is considered a significant competitive tool. Therefore, as much as $100 million is invested annually by those companies, which is considered proprietary and subject to commercial confidentiality. Companies invest in research to attain competitive advantage.

In spite of these differences in philosophy and style, globalization is evident at every level of the construction industry—from material, through manufactured goods, to services. The general trend in international industrial research and development is toward strategic alliances and joint ventures to reduce the risk factor and share the spiraling costs.

Governments are now changing previous policies aimed at achieving regional goals in favor of sponsoring research and development at the multinational level. Examples are projects such as Airbus and jointly funded R&D programs underwritten by the European Community. While there is sharing going on, which points to increased globalization, the fight for the competitive edge is always under way.

Another factor that influences managing projects internationally is the increasingly active role being taken by the owner organizations in the management of their projects. In the case of developing countries, this often reflects a national policy aimed at attaining greater managerial and technical capability so as to be less dependent on the developed world. Owners in such countries have a need for contracting services toward getting their project completed as well as transferring experience to their own organizations.

The globalization of project management information and know-how takes place through independently published literature and through two major internationally recognized organizations that are dedicated exclusively to the field of project management—PMI (the Project Management Institute) and IPMA (International Association of Project Management)—both of which are affiliated with numerous other organizations with related interests. Another association with significant published literature in project management is the AACE (the American Association of Cost Engineers).

INTEGRATING TWO CULTURES

While globalization is an ongoing influence on the management of international projects, success depends primarily on giving the proper emphasis to those factors that are particularly vulnerable in cross-cultural settings and on building a team capable of dealing with the challenges presented.

This discussion is drawn from the experience of co-author Codas in the management of "binational projects" in South America that involved the merging of cultures of projects jointly owned by the governments of two countries bordering rivers of staggering hydroelectric potential.

It is common practice in binational projects to have formal authority shared by two people, one from each country. This shared authority ranges from an integrated partnership of managers to a lead-manager/backup-manager situation.

Binational projects are products of hard political processes that involve long and difficult negotiations. In most cases each side has a different perception about the adopted solution, and during the project phase each side may try to "win back" some of the points initially "lost" at the negotiating table. The final diplomatic agreements are lengthy texts that are usually rich in political rhetoric and poor in operational and technical considerations. This sets the stage for conflict during the implementation phase of the project. The need for strong communications management becomes immediately evident in such a setting. An additional complicating factor is the fact that diplomatic documents contain writing "between the lines" and are consequently not easily decipherable by project managers and engineers.

Most binational agreements for developing projects state a philosophy of equity regarding the division of the work to be executed by each side. The unclear definition of what "equal parts" means is the prime source of inbred interest-based conflicts, which also affect the culture of the project.

THE DEVELOPMENT OF A PROJECT CULTURE

Experience in managing binational projects indicates that, for cultural convergence to take place, managers of both sides need to understand the culture of the other side, analyzing the different patterns that make up that culture. This means learning the other country's history, geography, economy, religion, traditions, and politics. Both sides, therefore, need to become fully aware of basic differences involving educational level,

	Country 1					Country 2				
	Values					Values				
	Minimum				Maximum	Minimum				Maximum
Characteristic	1	2	3	4	5	1	2	3	4	5
Gregariousness			X					X		
Technically Oriented		X							X	
Formal Behavior		X					X			
Consensus-Oriented					X					X
Internal Project Experience	X					X				
Rational Behavior	X									X
Non-nationalistic Posture		X							X	
TOTAL	16					24				

FIGURE 31-2. **EVALUATION OF CULTURAL PATTERNS OF TWO COUNTRIES INVOLVED IN A JOINT VENTURE**

professional experience, experience on this kind of project, knowledge of the language, and host country way of life.

Aside from this information, which can be readily obtained and assimilated, other perceptions must be taken into consideration, such as beliefs, feelings, informal actions and interactions, group norms, and values. These factors strongly affect behavior patterns. A simple way of tabulating the different factors that affect cultural behavior is shown in Figure 31-2. Although the judgment criteria are basically subjective, the chart pinpoints some of the basic differences in culture that tend to affect managerial behavior. In the binational situation used as a basis for this discussion, both sides filled out the charts and jointly evaluated the results.

Based on the analysis of the cultural differences, behavioral standards need to be developed. The objective is to define a desirable behavior or a "project culture" most suitable to the project objectives and the group's culture. In other words, cross-cultural team building must take place so that the individuals' inputs can be effectively channeled to meet the project goals. Forming a project culture is a project in itself; therefore, it must have an objective, a schedule, resources, and a development plan. Its execution becomes the responsibility of the management team. The objective of building a project culture is to attain a cooperative spirit, to supplant the our-side-versus-your-side feeling with a strong "our project" view. The project culture is developed around the commonalities of both groups, identified in the analysis shown in Figure 31-2. As other desirable traits are identified, they must be developed through a training program designed to stimulate those traits.

THE PROJECT CULTURE OVER THE LIFE CYCLE OF THE PROJECT

Culture on international projects begins to establish itself during the early stages of the project. The participative process in the development of the work breakdown structure and the project activities network can stimulate the "our project" spirit. It is also then that the first problems arise. Problems at this stage are relatively easy to solve, because enthusiasm on the part of the team members is generally high. The cultural model to be established at this stage is that of strong cooperation of all parties where and when necessary, in the spirit of "all for one, one for all."

If some individuals at this stage don't demonstrate efforts toward integration or show uncooperative attitudes, project managers should seriously consider taking them off the project, because if they create problems in blue-sky conditions, they may be impossible to work with when stormy weather appears. On the other hand, emerging team leaders need to be identified and motivated early on in the project.

During the maturing stages of international projects, when the organization is well defined and each unit or department is supposed to take care of its own tasks, the culture tends to become competitive as project groups try to show efficiency in relation to the other groups. Problems mainly arise at this stage because of unbalanced workloads. Some groups may claim to be overworked, while others have little work to do. Strong coordination and regular follow-up meetings are required during these intermediate project stages.

The final stage of the project is particularly difficult in terms of cultural integration. There is less work to do, and people are leaving to go on to other new international projects, often earning more than on "this old and uninteresting project." At this point, project managers are hard-strapped to maintain the spirit of the remaining group. This is the moment for the managers to show their leadership capabilities to make sure that the final activities of the project are performed with the same efficiency as the previous ones.

DISCUSSION QUESTIONS

❶ From the following list of cross-cultural factors, choose the three factors that you deem most critical in an international setting: *functional redundancy, political factors, the expatriate way of life, language and culture, additional risk factors, supply difficulties, and local laws and legislation.* Discuss with your study group.

❷ What are the main differences between project management models as practiced in Europe, North America, and Japan?

❸ In international project settings, what steps need to be taken to ensure the generation of a healthy "project culture"?

FURTHER READING

Casse, Pierre. *Training for the Multicultural Manager.* Washington, D.C.: SIETAR, 1982.
Halpin, Daniel W. "The International Challenge in Design and Construction." *Construction Business Review Magazine* (January–February 1992).
Seaden, George. "The International Transfer of Building." *Construction Business Review Magazine* (January–February 1992).
Hofstede, G. *Cultures and Organizations.* McGraw Hill, 1997.
Scott C., and D. Jaffe. "How to Link Personal Values with Team Values." *Training and Development*, March 1998.
Youker, Robert. "What is Culture in Organizations?" *Project Management World Today*, March–April 2004.

SECTION FIVE

INDUSTRY APPLICATIONS OF PROJECT MANAGEMENT PRACTICE

Section Five: Introduction

INDUSTRY APPLICATIONS OF PROJECT MANAGEMENT PRACTICE

Some professionals argue that a project is a project and therefore, the principles of project management are generically applicable. Others proclaim that an IT project is totally different from building a house or launching a new product. There is truth in both positions, of course. Principles of navigation are generically applicable, but putting them to proper use in the Antarctic continent or in the middle of the Pacific Ocean requires different experiences and knowledge.

The project management principles are indeed generically applicable, yet to use them intelligently, knowledge of the specific type of project is required. In this section, some of the peculiarities of project management practice across different industries are explored.

In Chapter 32, Christopher Sauer of Oxford University explores how the mature practices of project management in the engineering and construction field may have applicability to the IT industry.

In Chapter 33, Dennis Smith, of CompanySmith, lays out a process for adhering to project management principles within the time-to-market constraints of new product development.

Chapter 34 features a discussion of IT project management practice and pitfalls by Karen R.J. White, PMP, of Project Management Solutions, Inc.

Two chapters from our first edition have been held over in recognition of the timeless content they offer:

Author and consultant Lois Zells' updated Chapter 35 on software development practices brings order to the sometimes chaotic environment of software development.

Lee Lambert, PMP, of Lambert and Associates covers research and development projects in his updated Chapter 36.

Looking to the future, the ecosystem restoration industry applies the proven practices of project management to a work environment characterized by evolving science. The challenges of this application are discussed in Chapter 37 by Stan Veraart, PMP, and Donald Ross, CEO of EarthBalance.

While these chapters represent a sample of the many industries where project management is making a difference, the list is of course not exhaustive. Health care, transportation, energy, and retail are all sectors in which project management has gained a foothold and is now expanding rapidly. The chapters in this section may give the reader an idea how the discipline might be applied in the particular environment of his or her own workplace.

CHAPTER 32

Building Organizational Project Management Capability: Learning from Engineering and Construction

▶CHRISTOPHER SAUER, TEMPLETON COLLEGE, OXFORD UNIVERSITY

Construction is the industry that is widely accepted to have the most mature project management processes. IT project managers envy the accuracy with which their construction colleagues can estimate and predict progress on a building. They borrow their tools and techniques but struggle to emulate their results. They fall back on the conviction that "it's different in our industry." Thus, they resign themselves to continuing levels of underperformance.

This is a strange response when even IT project managers would agree that there is a core of project management knowledge that is common to all projects—who would doubt the wisdom of scope control in any project circumstance? Failure to leverage the learning of one industry into another is therefore normally explained by appeal to the need for domain knowledge. For example, the rate of change of technology, the volatility of requirements, and the invisibility of software are all supposed to make IT project management radically different. Fortunately, we do not need to resolve the debate about the importance of domain knowledge in order to improve learning.

The central point of this chapter is that industries can improve their own capabilities by adopting a model of project management capability development from the construction and engineering sector. Domain specifics may apply to projects but they do not apply to the structures and processes by which project management itself is managed within an organization—

mentoring can be effective in both construction and IT even though the learning may be different in certain respects. The domain independence of the model can be seen from its application to high-tech product development.[1] Research has shown that the construction industry has improved its performance over the last 20 years.[2] Despite embarrassing blips from time to time, it has managed down its performance variance. Many high profile mega-projects are today successfully delivered against demanding specifications and stretch targets. These range from Hong Kong's International Airport, which met its multibillion-dollar budget, to the Sydney Olympic Stadium that was in service 12 months before the start of the Games, to the first half of the $8bn Channel Tunnel Rail Link project installing a high-speed rail infrastructure and service from the Channel Tunnel to London. During the 1980s and 1990s and into this century, new ways of managing project management at the enterprise level have been adopted. This has had the effect of creating enhanced capability through support for performance and learning.[3] Transfer of the new ways to other industries will allow them to learn from their own experience so that any uniqueness of domain will be irrelevant. The benchmark for improvement will not be comparability with projects in other industries but improvement against your own organization's past performance and that of your industry peers today.

A model of the organizational and management system by which construction and engineering companies manage project management is presented in this chapter. By this we mean such practices as recruitment and development of talent, employment policies, role design, reporting processes, performance management and organizational learning.

Transferability of the practices common to construction and engineering is an important issue covered below. Engineering and construction are project-centric industries—that is, businesses that earn their revenues through projects. There are two targets for transfer—companies in other project-centric industries, such as management consultancies and systems integrators; and companies in industries where projects are only a part of their total activity, such as new product development by an automotive manufacturer or policy development by an industry regulator.

Finally, we assess developments that indicate progress towards adoption of the capability development model, and examine new challenges for project-centric and non-project-centric organizations as the performance demands on project managers grow.

GOOD PRACTICE IN BUILDING PROJECT MANAGEMENT CAPABILITY—THE CONSTRUCTION AND ENGINEERING EXAMPLE

Project management capability operates at three levels:

1. Project level
2. Individual level
3. Organizational level.

The project is both the start point and the end point. It is the focus for the application of individual and organizational capability. It is the source of experience on which learning is based.

The individual project manager is the linchpin, the essential ingredient. No project of any size or complexity can hope to be successful without an appropriately competent project manager. Equally, without project managers contributing their ideas and experience to the common pool of knowledge, organizations cannot expect to improve from project to project.

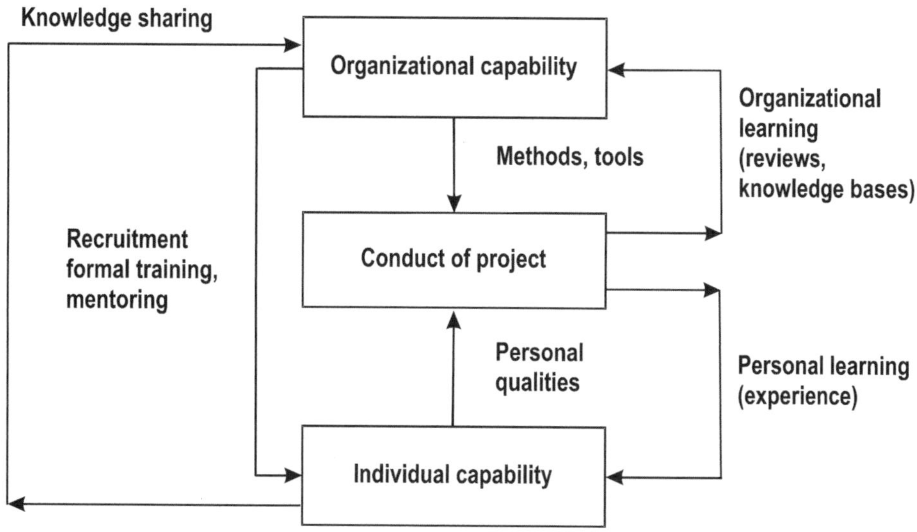

FIGURE 32-1. **MODEL OF PROJECT MANAGEMENT CAPABILITY DEVELOPMENT**

Organizational capability contributes to improving project performance by providing supports for the manager working on a project. It also assists the individual to learn, and grows the organization's communal knowledge of projects.

Figure 32-1 summarizes our model of project management capability development with examples of how the three levels interact.

Organizational capability consists of a number of elements. These were identified in an earlier research study in which we intensively interviewed project managers and directors of a number of top-level Australian construction companies.[1] None of the companies fully employed all the elements described but together they amount to a coherent set of practices that support both performance improvement and the development of lasting project management capability. These capability elements have been subject to continued verification subsequently and include:

- Organizational structure
- Role design
- Knowledgeable superiors
- Values
- Human resource management
- Methods and procedures
- Individuals' personal characteristics
- Conduct of the project.

We see these elements of capability working in a number of ways:

1. Making the job easier
2. Facilitating the application of knowledge
3. Ensuring a supply of capable project managers
4. Developing individual knowledge
5. Developing organizational knowledge
6. Motivating learning.

Organizational Structure

Business units in construction and engineering companies typically have flat structures that serve two main purposes. They place project managers and their projects close to the locus of power and decision-making in their organization, which gives them high visibility and access to resources and decisions as needed. They de-emphasize other functions, such as finance, design and estimation, so that by contrast with non-project-centric organizations, these are clearly support functions, not internal competitors for resources and attention. By placing projects at the center of the structure, these companies eliminate a lot of possible organizational noise, and thereby make the job of project management easier.

Role Design

The crucial element of role design involves balancing responsibility with accountability, resourcing, and authority. This equation is crucial to making the job easier and facilitating the application of knowledge. Plainly, having resources and authority are necessary to making a project doable. Without them it is hard to hold the project manager to account. To penalize a project manager who has not been given the wherewithal to succeed sends a message to others that the organization does not understand the challenge of project management and that it is not an organization in which projects represent a realistic career. Learning is likely to be retained by the individual rather than shared.

Knowledgeable Superiors

Project managers' superiors in construction have three important characteristics. Because of the flat structure, they are likely to be people with authority and access to resources that can help solve unexpected problems. They can thus make the project easier. Second, they are also typically highly knowledgeable having graduated from many years in the project manager role themselves. This means that they understand progress reporting and have a nose for potential problems. They are thus able to prevent problems from getting out of hand and are equipped to guide their project managers through difficulties thus enabling knowledge to be successfully applied. Third, project managers' superiors usually are involved in the client relationship from the start. They will have sold the project to the client and will have helped shape its initial stages. Because they accept responsibility for the project and will themselves be held accountable by their executives, they are highly motivated to share their knowledge with the project manager and do everything they can to help make the project successful.

Values

Three values underpin project capability in construction companies—focus on performance, relationships, and knowledge. The focus on performance is evident in the reputational advantages that accrue with success—"X built the tallest high rise in Western Europe," or "Y installed the first horizontally suspended bridge." Conversely, it is also apparent in the careful weeding out of non-performing project managers. This performance management has become more sophisticated over recent years in recognizing the value of mistakes. While repetition of the same mistake will not be tolerated, the recognition that errors represent an opportunity for learning and that admission of mistakes will not necessarily be punished encourages individual and organizational learning through openness and sharing of lessons.

Focus on relationships relates to customers, partners, and subcontractors. Greater awareness that customers usually represent opportunities for future business and that retaining an existing customer is easier than winning a new one has led to contractors trying to establish contracts and relationships that encourage win-win. In some cases this has been extended to their supply chain. The result is that project managers see value in investing in understanding the customer, and partners and subcontractors see value in sharing their ideas and knowledge. So, not only is useful knowledge shared, the job is made easier for the project manager because of a less adversarial environment. And, as several companies have noted, because of less litigation, there is a further benefit in being able to close out projects sooner.

Focus on knowledge is apparent in the explicit recognition of project managers as an asset. In the recession of the early 1990s, a number of the companies with deep pockets kept their better managers on the payroll despite a lack of revenue-earning projects. Symbolically, this sent a strong message that the retained managers were valued, leading them to see it as worth their while to develop new and better ways of working. At the same time, these project managers had more opportunity than they had ever previously had to reflect and share their ideas. Once initiated, the practice of continual improvement has remained. So both individual and organizational learning have been encouraged.

Human Resource Management

Construction and engineering companies do not always have substantial HR departments, but they typically do have significant HR practices designed to create and sustain a talent pool of project managers. These practices include recruitment, development, career management, and performance management. Recruitment focuses on identifying appropriate talent, often at graduate level or before. Development involves a managed progress through different project roles to a junior project management position. From there, subject to performance management, the project manager moves into progressively more difficult challenges. Mentoring is built into the reporting relationship because the manager's superior has a shared accountability that encourages knowledge and experience sharing. So, individual capability development is strongly supported by HR practices. The availability of a career path that sees project managers in their fifties and sixties valued and rewarded for performance also encourages individuals to take the long view and to invest in building and sharing knowledge.

Few, if any, companies offer the kind of highly incentivized financial package so common among bankers and software salespeople. Project managers are paid a decent salary and may receive some bonus although it is usually paid annually and not on the basis of performance on any single project. In fact, by selecting "project people," companies typically populate their project manager roles with individuals whose biggest motivation is to take on ever-greater challenges. Thus continual learning by the individual is built in.

Methods and Procedures

Companies typically have their own set of methods and procedures for project management. These are internalized and used with discretion rather than slavishly followed. Their principal role is to provide structure and commonality of practice so that reporting can be reliably monitored. They also provide a shared language with which to talk about projects that facilitates sharing of experience and the development of new methods.

Individuals' Characteristics

Many of the elements of organizational project management capability we have described encourage the acquisition and development of individuals with the right skills and competencies. These include the classic competencies in planning, monitoring, controlling, forming and leading teams, communicating, managing stakeholders, negotiating problem solving, and leading. These are necessary to the effective conduct of projects. But they are not sufficient. Three personal characteristics stand out as driving personal performance—a thirst for experience, personal commitment to delivering projects, and the desire to enhance their reputations through association with a successful outcome. One project manager encapsulated the project manager mind-set:

"In the construction industry, you'll find that for a lot of project managers it's a heart-and-soul type thing. It's a lifestyle. You live, sleep, and eat project. You're here six days a week. Sometimes you're working the night shift. Sometimes you're in here seven days a week. So it's a lifestyle and it's a total commitment."

All three personal characteristics are powerful motivators of individual learning.

Conduct of the Project

In describing organizational and individual capability above, we have shown how both provide essential inputs to the conduct of projects through the individual competencies of the project manager applied to the project, and through oversight, support, and intervention by knowledgeable superiors. However, projects are also the source of much learning and some companies act to capture that through encouraging informal interaction among project managers on a regular basis. Others conduct reviews and maintain more formal databases of experience that can be uniformly shared across the business and that can be used to inform future projects even when the original project manager has moved on.

The following case study shows how one leading international construction company exemplifies the model.

CASE STUDY: MULTIPLEX—THE WELL-BUILT AUSTRALIAN

Multiplex is a diversified property business, employing over 1,500 people across four divisions: construction, property development, facilities management, and investment management. Based in Australia, it has a presence in Southeast Asia and Europe. Its core construction business involves managing the design and construction of urban developments, such as office buildings, shopping centers, apartment buildings, hotels, hospitals, and sporting complexes. Landmark projects have included the $430 million Sydney Olympic Stadium. It is currently re-building the UK's iconic sporting venue—Wembley National Stadium.

Multiplex is highly regarded for its ability to compete on cost, but it does so without damage to client satisfaction and as a result seeks to secure repeat business. It operates a flat structure. The board of directors is usually fully aware of what is happening at the construction project "coalface." Head office functional managers support projects in specialist disciplines including design, contract administration, estimation, employee relations, finance, and legal affairs.

Multiplex's project managers are highly experienced in construction and project management. The company sets high performance standards, requiring its managers to deliver the building or facility to the client and continue responsibility for any subsequent modification once in service. The company gives project managers control over resources and, within broad limits, the authority to take whatever decisions are necessary to complete the project—they "can make a large number of decisions related to the project with complete autonomy."

Because performance matters, so too accountability is important. But accountability is exercised in a rounded manner. Reasonable mistakes are understood and recognized as a learning opportunity. While management does focus on project outcomes, overall performance is assessed relative to the challenge. Thus retrieving a potentially damaging situation may be valued more than the final outcome against targets. Small financial bonuses are paid against annual performance rather than specific projects. But the company recognizes that for most of its managers association with a success and the challenge of something new are the key motivators.

Control against project schedule, cost, and quality is tight. The Board receives reports monthly. Formal reporting to the project director is weekly, informal reporting daily. Senior managers actively follow progress also through site visits.

The project directors and construction managers to whom project managers report are highly knowledgeable about project management. Their involvement in business development ensures that their projects can be successfully achieved with commercial returns. The company's recognition of the challenges of projects means that project managers feel comfortable sharing difficulties with their superiors. As a result, problems are rapidly dealt with before they accumulate long-term consequences.

Recruitment and development of aspiring project managers is based on an "apprenticeship" model to build long-term commitment to the company and to demonstrate its own commitment to project managers. Consequently, retention is high and turnover is low. Development includes on-the-job-training, mentoring, and formal management development courses. The company's commitment to its project managers and hence its ability to build organizational capability is reinforced by its preference for internal promotion.

Each of the capability elements described makes sense on its own. However, much of the power of this model to make a difference derives from the interlocking reinforcement among its elements. For example, greater tolerance of mistakes encourages openness that permits knowledgeable superiors to assist at an early stage so performance is sustained while learning is enabled. At the same time, this tolerance reflects a fairer form of performance management that in turn supports retention of individuals and retention of their knowledge.

Another way of putting this is to say that by managing the talent pool and making the job easier, the right people are given time in which to learn. By motivating learning, they are encouraged to develop individual and organizational knowledge. Through the application of knowledge, that learning is internalized. Through organizational processes, the learning is externalized and so made available throughout the company.

TRANSFER AND ADOPTION

Our model for developing project management capability has been synthesized from practice in the engineering and construction sector. For those in other sectors, the question remains—how transferable is the model? And how readily can it be adopted?

There are no in-principle barriers to transferring substantial elements of the model to other industries because it focuses on learning and support for performance within an individual company. So while a biotech company developing new drugs and an IT systems integrator implementing enterprise software systems may face radically different challenges in terms of the technologies they employ, the regulatory regime they confront, the demands of trials and testing, and so forth, each can develop its own learning, including whatever knowledge is sector- or company-specific. As we shall see in the next section, a number of IT companies have started to transfer the model to their own situation.

The one area of the model that can be problematic is transfer of those elements that are more dependent on the project-centric nature of the organization. For non-project-centric organizations, such as retail banks, supermarkets, logistics companies, and similar, it will not be thought desirable to emulate structural characteristics which we have seen create visibility, enable executive attention, and deliver necessary resources, at the expense of focus on day-to-day operations.

Our model was derived from the practices of large companies. This raises the concern that size may be a barrier to transfer. Obviously, large companies are to some extent better positioned—for example, for a company undertaking one hundred projects per year, the return to scale of investing in project management capability development is greater than for a company undertaking just ten each year. But the investment need not be a fixed cost regardless of size. As we noted earlier, none of the engineering and construction companies we studied exhibited all the characteristics described in the model. Learning can be seeded and performance improved even in small companies by such simple and cheap devices as organizing Friday evening drinks for project managers once a month. Celebrating their successes can be as potent a reward as financial bonuses. So, while larger companies may have the resources to dedicate to developing formal supports for project management capability, smaller companies can still gain benefit from the model.

How then should companies set about adopting the model or elements of it? Identifying an organizational lead and focal point is the first priority. For a larger company this may involve the creation of a corporate project/program office. For a smaller company, it may be nomination of an individual, either a senior project manager or an executive responsible for project managers. In either case, an individual should be tasked with developing organizational project management capability and evaluated accordingly. The task itself should include providing processes to support existing projects, a common set of tools and knowledge bases, structures and processes to permit learning, motivation and support for the sharing and capture of learning, and support for the development of a set of performance management and HR practices to grow the talent pool of project managers.

Even with organizational commitment and resources behind the organizational lead, it takes years to design, introduce, and embed all the relevant practices. This is not a quick fix. That said, once achieved, it need not be a continuing direct cost. Some organizations we researched, such as Multiplex, had no corporate project office but had embedded the relevant practices in their everyday organizational processes.

EMERGING DEVELOPMENTS

This chapter has implicitly assumed a traditional model of project management focused on build or design-and-build projects conducted by a prime contractor supported by subcontractors. However, the project environment is dynamic and it is worth reviewing a number of new developments that are now with us or just around the corner. These are extending the scope and challenge of traditional project management, extending the need for capability development to more complex organizational forms, and extending the focus of development beyond the project manager.

First, though, we can report that diffusion of the capability development model is occurring. The IT sector's reputation for project performance is poor and its track record in developing project management capability is equally poor.[4] But the pressure for action is growing. A UK government department recently asked one of its international IT suppliers what it was doing to improve its project performance. The company's inability to answer the question galvanized it into action.

In the last two or three years, we have seen several large IT companies, as well as hardware, software, and systems integrators, adopting some form of capability development initiative. For example, in 2004 the UK arm of one major European IT company identified a project management champion as lead for capability development. She has instituted a project management career structure, assessed its project manager pool, undertaken appraisal and mentoring, defined development paths for individuals, implemented a recruitment and selection process, and agreed a code of practice for the conduct of projects as well as training them in a standard methodology. And confirming that the champion role need not be an ongoing cost, she explained, "It's my aim to work myself out of a job." This kind of example suggests that much of the model is transferable.

But even while the model is diffused more widely, the environment is changing and placing new and greater demands on many project managers. We find that customers are increasingly demanding not merely a delivered project but the tangible benefits for which the project investment was made. In construction, BOOT (build-own-operate-transfer) contracts require the successful operation of a building or infrastructure that implies responsibility for operational services, such as heating and elevators, and for continuing maintenance. In defense, governments require not merely the delivery of aircraft but the ability to destroy enemy targets that implies responsibility for maintenance, spare parts logistics, and munitions. In IT, customers demand not just delivery of a system but also the achievement of cost or revenue benefits that implies responsibility for business process change. Many companies see that, as a result, they must involve the project manager more closely in the development and selling of the business so as to ensure that the end result is deliverable. Thus, project managers are being called upon to extend their skills both at the front-end and back-end of projects.

Two implications are worth drawing out. First, as the scope of the role extends, so our model needs to reflect the new competences required. This in turn may require adjustments to performance management systems, to career structures, to tool sets, and so forth. Second, members of the current pool of project managers may no longer be suitable for the new role. There may therefore need to be an exit strategy for them or a re-conceptualization of the role so that their skills can be exploited within the framework of the extended project.

A further dimension of added complexity for capability development is the consequence of joint venturing. Joint ventures are usually established for a quite limited duration among companies that in other circumstances may be thought of as competitors. Thus, not only may there be no long-term pay-off from learning, sharing of knowledge may be seen as counter-productive. However, win-win contracting can counter these tendencies. In the UK, the Channel Tunnel Rail Link project is widely seen as exemplary. A complex joint venture to deliver the railway in two sections, it has created a common culture such that there are no external signs of which member company any individual works for. Identification with this enormous project is strong. Although more than ten years in duration, it was necessary to have as much knowledge as possible available at the start. Learning was brought in through a policy of recruiting people with experience of two major rail projects of recent years—the Channel Tunnel itself and London Underground's Jubilee Line. Within the project, a thriving lessons-learned program has generated a mass of knowledge. When the project for the second section was launched, kick-off days were organized to ensure no learning from the first section was lost. Thus where a joint venture has a long enough life and where there are commercial advantages, capability development may still be a worthwhile investment.

Finally, in thinking about the future developments, two are worth watching for. First, project contractors are increasingly focusing on their clients as a point of leverage for improvement. They argue that the client gets the projects it deserves. Poor contracting by clients engenders counter-productive behaviors from contractors. A better-educated client will make for better projects. The plausibility of this argument was borne out recently by an IT project manager who invested in teaching her client how to estimate a project. Subsequently, she found re-negotiation of the contract much easier because she could hold a more informed conversation with the client. So, it is likely that we will start to see capability development efforts extending beyond the boundaries of the contracting organization.

Second, non-project-centric businesses are becoming more dependent on projects. Recently, an insurance company conducted a work audit and discovered that its managers spent more than 50 percent of their time on projects. With large-scale operational businesses of this kind finding themselves continually pressed to change and improve, they are obliged to undertake more and more projects. Over time, it is possible that the financial markets will increasingly value these companies according to their project portfolio and their capability to execute successfully. Organizing in a more project-centric way may then become common among supermarkets, banks, and insurance companies, as well as those in construction, engineering and IT. In the meantime, there is no reason why non-project-centric businesses which nevertheless conduct projects as a continuing aspect of business improvement should not adapt and adopt elements of our model. While internal organizational structures may impede role design that balances authority and resourcing with responsibility thereby limiting accountability, HR processes that focus on recruitment and development, mentoring, and the creation of knowledge bases can all be implemented. What is typically lacking is the organizational will to invest in project management because it is seen as non-core, but as we have just suggested, even this attitude may be about to change.

The model of project management capability development presented here therefore represents a solid foundation on which any organization in any industry can base its own initiative. None of the emerging developments we have described undermines the model. Rather they amplify the need for organizations to pay explicit attention to project management capability. But they do also remind us that, because the demands of projects are changing, it will be necessary over time to adapt the basic model.

DISCUSSION QUESTIONS

❶ Thinking about companies that you know, how well do they manage the continuing development of their project management capabilities? What more could they do?

❷ What issues would you envisage in the acquisition and maintenance of adequate project management capability in a multi-year, multi-project joint venture? How might you tackle these issues?

❸ In what ways do extensions of the project manager's role into activities, such as business case development and post-implementation benefit delivery, require capability development? What management initiatives would you take to ensure that they are adequately included in a company's capability development practices?

REFERENCES

[1] Sauer, C., Liu, L., and K. Johnston. "Where Project Managers are Kings." *Project Management Journal,* December, 2001.

[2] Graham, R. J., and R. L. Englund. "Creating an Environment for Successful Projects: The Quest to Manage Project Management." San Francisco: Jossey-Bass, 1997.

[3] Vlasic, A., and P. Yetton. "Delivering Successful Projects: The Evolution of Practice at Lend Lease (Australia)." 16th International Project Management Association World Congress, Berlin, 2002: pp. 4–6. Also Walker, D. H. T., and A. C. Sidwell. "Improved Construction Time Performance in Australia." *Australian Institute of Quantity Surveyors Refereed Journal,* AIQS, Canberra, 2 (1), 1998, pp. 23–33.

[4] Sauer, C., Liu, L., and K. Johnston. "Where Project Managers are Kings." *Project Management Journal,* 32 (4), 2001, pp. 39–50.

[5] Sauer, C. and Cuthbertson, C. "The State of Project Management in the UK"; http://www.computerweeklyms.com/pmsurveyresults/surveyresults.pdf, published September 2003, cited 28 July 2004.

CHAPTER 33

New Product Development: Issues for Project Management

DENNIS M. SMITH, COMPANYSMITH

Product development is a specialized case of the project methods described in the *PMBOK® Guide.* By adding product-specific focus, the product development leader can increase the probability of success over what otherwise would be attained by implementing a process that might be applicable to other types of projects, such as IT, construction, or public works.

Focus areas include understanding and factoring customers' requirements, ensuring distribution channels, cost and price goals, and building competitive differentiators.

If one of these were to be singled out as the most important, it is clear that the majority of product development projects that fail do so because of defects in requirements. New product development failure rates are reported to be as high as 85 percent to 95 percent.[1]

Failures due to problems with requirements account for 50 percent to 60 percent of those total failures. Too often enthusiasm predates facts, and that enthusiasm—while a necessary ingredient—if not surrounded by practices that make sense, can be the downfall of a project.

A second reason commonly cited for failure of product development projects is failure of distribution. Especially in engineering or technology driven companies, not having sales, marketing, physical distribution, and appropriate access to customers in place when the product is ready leads to loss of competitive advantage due to a slow rollout or canceling of a great product idea due to inadequate access to customers.

Unclear or unrealistic goals for product factory cost (cost) and net sales price to the customer (price) are also leading causes for failure. Too often in the excitement of a product development project, the financial goals are unclear, ignored, or the project goes forward without ever agreeing as to whether the product costs meet the needs of market reality.

And last of the top four issues is having a clear and realistic understanding of the product's or businesses' competitive differentiators. There are many strategies or competencies for building, and whichever of those is selected, they must be built into the team's culture. Lowest price sounds like a simple strategy; however, there are few markets where that strategy can work and few companies who can deliver that strategy. Products based on a competency of best service are also well founded, but the strategy must meet the customers' needs. Selling an exquisitely supported product into a market where price is "king" is at best a fleeting strategy, for once buyers know the product works, and the differentiation value of services fades to insignificance.

These themes will be woven through this chapter as basic tenets of product development projects. Much of what is required for product development beyond the *PMBOK® Guide* practices ties back to these four concepts. A wealth of additional information is available through the Product Development and Management Association.[2]

STARTING THE PRODUCT DEVELOPMENT

Most product development projects start without requirements. The ideas come from a customer's need to solve a particular problem, a marketing need to counter a competitive product, a new technology that might disrupt the marketplace, a cost reduction of a current product, or a whim of a great idea. All of these are legitimate, and most do not have enough detail to start a *project*, but this is where *product development* starts—it starts when the idea is born or when the challenge is presented, both long before the project team is assembled.

The first challenge is to assemble the core team. This is usually made up of two to four part-time people who will build enough clarity around the product idea to gain project approval and justify startup of the project team. Critical to this step is that it is a small number of dedicated people who are committed to move forward—too many people at this time and the project will probably stall.

If a product champion is not apparent when this team starts, they will emerge early in the process. The champion is not the formal organizational leader, but is the first-among-peers who wants to live the challenge of insuring that the project moves forward both now in the formative stages and later when the project is formalized.[3]

If there is not an apparent champion, then the sponsors should question the project. There are many people who need to be influenced and many customers to be listened to and persuaded. If there is no active, leading, assertive, believing champion, it is unlikely that the product development will succeed. The best champions are self-proclaimed; appointing one rarely works other than for the least-contentious product developments.

REQUIREMENTS

Clarification of requirements starts at the source of the idea for the product. The idea can come from any source, and that source needs to be involved in the first expansion of the idea into requirements. The first descriptions of the idea should be expanded into six to ten use-cases.[4] Use-cases are brief written cases or scenarios that clarify the actual use of the product from the point of view of the user. For a car, one use-case might be from the time the person reaches for the door handle until they are driving down the road. For a vacuum cleaner, it might be from the time it is noticed that the bag is full until vacuuming has resumed with a clean bag. For a software application it might adding a new user to a system.

Scenarios capture many requirements but also provide a framework for capturing the details of the product. The goal of scenarios is to write in prose-like flowcharts. PowerPoint should not be used for use-cases, as its organization is not conducive to writing good cases.

It is important at this stage to focus on completing a high level of requirements prior to moving to details. There is a tendency to write the most about the things that one knows best, but the objective is to write completely at the highest levels first, and then move through two or three additional levels of detail toward a complete definition of the product.

For best overall quality and schedule predictability, the people who will be responsible for qualification testing, manufacturing, and field support should be on the team as the requirements are written. Writing requirements and project plans with the needs of these teams in hand will reduce confusion and improve schedule predictability as the project nears completion.

As the first scenarios and product descriptions are completed, the first customer reviews should take place. Customer interaction should start here and run through project completion.

Now is the time for the first round of competitive analysis,[5] long before the development project starts. Analysis must include costs, price features, functions, and benefits. With customers, the emphasis is on benefits, but to your business the emphasis is on competitive differentiators. The differentiators must be compelling to both the sponsors and to your customers. If differentiators are marginally competitive, boring, or lack sizzle, the product should be reconsidered. If you don't see a way to achieve the product cost requirements, proceed with skepticism and plan to revisit the cost estimates at short intervals with the intention of showing that the cost requirements can be met or stopping the project.

At this time it will also become apparent that there is probably more work to do than is allowed by the project end-date and budget. Start now to prioritize the features and benefits, with those priorities set at the macro level of features, well above the details of the product.

Now with a top-level description in place, several use scenarios that describe the product in operation—with leadership of a motivated champion and the support of excited potential customers—and it's time to start thinking about building a project.

These steps are summarized in Table 33-1.

PROJECT APPROACHES

Unstructured Projects

Most organizations that develop products use a structured approach. The costs of project failure and the high likelihood of failure in the best of projects support the need for structured approaches, yet most businesses do not build project plans or build only token plans that are not useful in managing the project.

Before we dive into structured approaches, I want to emphasize that for teams of eight to twelve people, with experienced participants, great teamwork, great communications, and

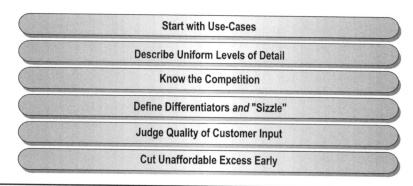

Start with Use-Cases
Describe Uniform Levels of Detail
Know the Competition
Define Differentiators *and* "Sizzle"
Judge Quality of Customer Input
Cut Unaffordable Excess Early

TABLE 33-1. **REQUIREMENTS FOR REQUIREMENTS**

strong focus on the customers, an unstructured process may lead to higher productivity, shorter time to market, and build a superior product.[6] These groups can be driven by leaders, product champions, or even by the soul of the team. This approach has been proven time and again by small startups that rock the market. What you read about are the well-publicized exceptions that succeed—most projects run in this fashion disappoint or fail.

The conditions for the success of non-structured product development are hard to achieve. Too often small teams believe they meet the criteria for an unstructured project, only to learn in failure that they were shortsighted in their understanding of their customers, skills, focus, commitment, or chemistry; or to learn that they simply overlooked some area that was critical to their success.

For the other 95+ percent of product development projects, structure approaches are best. Structure fed by enthusiasm and competency builds great products.

Buying Outside

Many companies build their new products but just as many choose a development partner or outright buy their products from other businesses. These alternate sources are especially favored by companies that have unique opportunities, are anxious to enter markets, or are too bureaucratic to tolerate the risks and uncertainties of product development.

Outside procurement of a product should be carefully considered when your team is not experienced with the product's technology, time is more important than investment, an external source has the product in deliverable form, and you have adequate expertise and resources to manage an external project or to complete due diligence on a potential acquisition. Due diligence on acquiring a product from an outside source must include testing the product to its specifications.

The most common cause of disappointment with outside sourced products is caused by failure to adequately project-manage or exercise continuous due diligence with the outside partner.

Iterative or Waterfall

Waterfall methodology is based on defining the entirety of the product in advance of starting the project and then proceeding step by step to completion—kind of like fitting yourself into a barrel and then falling over the edge of the waterfall . . . movement to completion with no reassessment or change in scope.

There are many types of projects where the waterfall methodology makes sense such as repetitive construction, but it is rarely used in development of innovative products.

Iterative or spiral methodologies are based on the idea that you need to change features and implementation during the course of the project as the team and the customer-partners get smarter about the product and how it meets the needs of the customers. In practice this is usually accomplished via an evolving prototype. While this process will likely produce better results, it is less predictable in terms of total investment and end date.

Most product development projects are started without all of the details known and without all of the features defined. This means that even if the leaders want a fixed project cost and time, in fact the project will invent some of the features and design during the life of the project. In its simplest form, if a great idea emerges part way through the project, the iterative methodology will capitalize on it. Most waterfall projects will probably make the change either through an approved change process or in a manner hidden from the project managers. Mature iterative processes are better able to take changes and improvements in stride.

For product development, building project and sponsor teams that can deal with the ambiguities of iterative methodologies is a superior approach to the control-from-the-top mentality that is often part of waterfall methods.

STAGES AND PROGRESS

Work in product development projects proceeds in chunks. Whether these chunks are called stages, phases, periods, quartiles, or steps, they are basically a coherent chunk of work followed by a review or checkpoint that ensures that the previous work was completed and that the team is justified in proceeding with the next chunk of work.

Since 40 to 50 percent of product development runtime is spent before the project team starts, when working to reducing time-to-market, give half of your attention to pre-project time.

For products, the chunks should be related to the evolution of the product, not to arbitrary process milestones. While there are many standard processes, potential milestones can include things such as: completion of scenarios, first budget estimate, first completion estimate, demonstration of major subsystems, completion of design, start of qualification testing, engineering complete, all features available, and quality verification milestones. While a team could use a set of company-wide milestones, using milestones that make sense to the project team will ensure both their buy-in to the deliverables and the applicability of the milestones.

At the reviews between the chunks of work, the tone must be set by the leadership that creates an open and honest discussion of the state of the product and project. The objective is neither to fail the review nor to pass the review. The objective is to openly share the project information from all perspectives and to reach agreement between the reviewers that it's time to proceed to the next chunk of work. The norm should be developed that it is any attendee's responsibility to speak up with their concern; it is not just their right.

The most important thing that this group can do at the review is to kill a bad product or bad project. When all energy is focused on success, it's the hard job to proclaim that the product should be stopped. Open and honest communications and dialog in full view of the facts is the fuel for the best decision.

Two other processes that should be in place as the work chunks and reviews move forward are a *change board* and a *risk management process.* The change board is a group of three or four people who have final say if a change to the product is accepted for inclusion in the current release of the product. At a minimum the product champion, the product development leader, and the testing leader should be on this board.

Risk management is a difficult process. At best it is exposing your worst fears about the product to your executives and sponsors. Talking about the risks and letting everyone on the team suggest mitigations is always better than hiding them under the table. Building norms around openness, shared responsibility, and rational behavior are necessary to make this practice work. If those norms are not in place, open risk management planning will fall to the wayside as it becomes too uncomfortable for any of the participants.

CUSTOMER INVOLVEMENT

Involving customers as early and often as possible to talk about your product is the best step you can take to ensure your product's success.

While signed non-disclosure agreements with the individuals are almost universally required, the ethics of the individual should be taken as the first defense of your product secrets.

Customer involvement comes in several levels. First and easiest are customers that your sales department has concluded might be influenced for current purchases or for early sales of the new product. These casual reviewers should be avoided until your project team has demonstrated that they are near completion, generally when beta testing is in progress. Presenting new products to customers can increase company viability, but also can severely stress the team and compromise product development progress.

The second level of customer participation is critical reviewers. These are people who listen to your preliminary presentation on the product and give you their immediate feedback based on what they have seen. These opinions can be valuable, but care must be taken to ensure that the background of the reviewers is known and understood. Their feedback should be considered and factored into the product development, but only after it is viewed through the lens of their knowledge, biases, affiliations, and predispositions.

The third level of customer participation in an ongoing relationship between the customer and the product development team. These customer-partners see the progress of the team and arrive at review meetings or participate in calls with deep background and knowledge of both the product and the motivations for the product. Their role must be carefully defined, their company agreeable to the relationship, and their integrity and openness unquestionable. While bringing partners into this role from the beginning of the project is challenging, it is well worth the effort. Not only do you get great insight from a credible and unbiased source, the relationship can easily develop into a field trial arrangement and ongoing sponsorship of the product.

While focus groups are a standard means of gathering customer opinion, at best they present casual reviewers. Anyone venturing into the one-time or paid relationships of focus groups must exercise great caution both in the validity of the opinions presented and in carefully asking questions so that the questions do not bias the answers. It is essential that the leaders of the focus group manage participation to ensure that a few vocal participants don't block participation by others.

The practice of paying customers to participate in reviewing your product is questionable. If possible, do not compensate or pay expenses for customer partners. If their interest in genuine, the most you should consider is covering their travel and living expenses for the reviews.

A common error on the part of product managers or product champions is that in their quest for achieving total customer satisfaction, they fail to recognize and account for questionable or biased opinions. Customers have biases towards products they have purchased or supported and technologies that they believe are desirable—those biases can negatively impact your product features unless the needs and motivations have been adequately vetted.

In all cases of customer participation, the critical skill for the product team is to be able to separate the fact-based, sincere, well-thought opinions from the seat-of-the-pants or otherwise biased opinions that some customers bring. In most cases, a customer's opinion can be found to support any position and any product feature. It is a required skill for product managers and product champions to sort the important opinions from the unimportant and the team must understand and trust that opinion.

PRODUCT JUSTIFICATION

The best justification for a project is a customer-savvy person with a clear understanding of the potential product, its customer benefits, and how to get customers to say "this is a great idea." Many of the most important products of the past decade came to market with that level of justification and that kind of a vision.

The worst way to justify products is by careful calculation of Return on Investment (ROI) with a pass/fail decision made on that exact calculation. A large number of the most influential products of the past decade would never have been started, continued, or finished if straight ROI were the guiding principle. Businesses using straight ROI run the risk of killing the very projects that might make them great.[7] ROI is necessary but not sufficient as a tool to judge product opportunities. While neither of these justification processes is sufficient, completing both is necessary to justify a project.

If you can't find an excited person—a potential champion for the project, someone who can tie the customer need to the product and can envision how to get the product into a distribution system that will sell and deliver it to potential customers—then the idea is not ready to move forward. Let the pre-project team further develop the idea or kill it.

ROI is an important exercise, but it is more important for the rigor of developing all of the product cost, project costs, and sales estimates that comprise it than it is important for the final numeric result. Look for the final numeric result to be reasonable and little else.

ROI is also not a useful concept for comparing product ideas that are in competition for funding. It is too easy to misjudge estimates of costs or sales for any product in pre-development. It is also too easy for a less than reputable or overly enthusiastic champion to consciously or subconsciously raise or lower estimates in a way that might bias the resultant number.

Cash flow is probably the most important element of the financial analysis. There is no point in starting a project that you can't afford to finish, although with a great product idea, cash sometimes appears.

A cost overrun on a product development project is financially insignificant compared to the financial gains of a successful product. Build a successful product and the financial sins of the project are quickly forgotten—build an unsuccessful product on plan and on budget and no one will care.

Timing is one of the most critical factors in any financial analysis. In the 1980s it was likely that a new concept, an innovative product, might enjoy two years in the market before competitors responded in kind. For Internet-based products, that competitive-timing advantage is now likely measured in days or weeks. For some technology products, such as notebook computers, the product life can be shorter than the product development time.

So a product having a great "gut feel" is best. If a team shares that feeling, all the better. If the ROI is credibly interesting, all the better. The challenge of a large business is to be able to spend the leaders' time to invest in the understanding of the product success factors in order to make an informed judgment that goes beyond a rote review of numbers.

This process requires time and non-adversarial authentic dialog—two things that are often in short supply and that might take years to develop in a small to mid-sized organization and may be unattainable in the largest of organizations. Successful large organizations generally answer this need by delegating those decisions to the lowest organizational level possible in an attempt to streamline the process.

MANUFACTURING AND FIELD SUPPORT

For physical products, manufacturing and field support must be a part of the product development process from the beginning. Manufacturing must own the cost estimates and they must certify the manufacturability by developing the manufacturing processes during the product development project.

The field support team needs to provide requirements to the project to ensure that the product is supportable once in the field. Support requirements, along with manufacturability requirements, should be considered a priority equal to those expressed by the customers.

This can be a challenge to a product development team, as their work is strategic, while the priorities of manufacturing and field support are usually driven by hourly or daily priorities. The process can be further complicated by a common if not traditional rivalry that exists between product development, manufacturing engineering, and field support over designs, support, customer ethics, and many more issues.

The product team must assure the participation of the manufacturing and field service teams before the formal product development project is designed and committed. If rivalry exists, structured team building should be an explicit part of the project plan.

PREPARING FOR SALES

The first step in preparing for sales is to have a clear set of terms describing the level of commitment of the organization to the dates that are shown on the project plans. I recommend these:

▶ ***Target***. The team has thought about the project and is working to the target date, but there are not yet supporting plans and resources in place.

▶ ***Estimate***. The team has built a project plan and is in the process of executing against that plan, but there are sufficient risks or unknowns that make the team not yet ready to commit to the dates.

▶ ***Commitment***. The team is committed to the product delivery dates.

Sales often feels that every date is a commitment and every product is available for sale. Any information presented to sales or to customers needs to be explicit about the meaning of dates with clear expectations set about how the sales force may use the dates outside of the company. Releasing a product for sale is an informed business decision with the current state of the project being just one of many considerations leading up to that decision.

CONCLUSION

Product development is a specialized case of project management. If the team pays careful attention to customers, differentiators, product costs, sales channels and support, the platform for product development provided by project management will drive the team to success.

DISCUSSION QUESTIONS

❶ How can a product team balance the importance of responding to specific customer requests with the need for proprietary innovation that exceeds competitive capability?

❷ Do product teams favor projects that they "like" with low estimates? Do vendors provide low estimates when they bid competitively? How can someone letting a contract for product development ensure realistic estimates?

❸ Why do many product teams exclude the costs and planning for transitioning the product into the sales channel? Should it be the product team's responsibility to ensure that the sales channel is ready to accept their product?

❹ When is it more important to be on schedule and on budget rather than having the right product? When is it appropriate to provide a low-quality product to a customer?

REFERENCES

[1] Primary data on these failure rates is not current in that it does not include the affects of distributed and offshore development teams and rapid advances in tools. The fallacy of most data of this type is the ambiguity of the point in time where failure is determined. For example, whether or not the project is determined a failure after one month (perhaps due to unattainable cost goals) or after two years of low sales strongly biases the insights that might come from the data.

[2] See the PDMA website at www.pdma.org.

[3] For more descriptive material on product champions see: http://www.companysmith.com/News/workofchampions percent2015jan02.htm.

[4] Kurt Bittner and Ian Spence, *Use Case Modeling,* Addison-Wesley, 2002.

[5] *Competitive Strategy: Techniques for Analyzing Industries and Competitors* by Michael E. Porter. Free Press; 1998.

[6] Tom DeMarco and S. Lister, *Peopleware: Productive Projects and Team,* Dorset House, 1987, pp. 24–29.

[7] Rebecca Henderson of the MIT Sloan School, quoted from a presentation to the New England Chapter of PDMA held at Northeastern University, November 20, 2002.

CHAPTER 34

Why IT Matters: Project Management for Information Technology

▶KAREN R.J. WHITE, PMP,
PROJECT MANAGEMENT SOLUTIONS

Information technology plays an ever-increasing role in the delivery of the services that we rely on in our everyday lives. Information technology surrounds us, from the technology with which we manage our households, to the technology that is used in our schools and workplaces, to the technology we use to interact with one another. Information technology is no longer confined to the business community. Management of the projects by which that technology is delivered to us is of ever increasing importance.

VISIBILITY OF IT PROJECT FAILURES

It should come as no surprise that failures of information technology (IT) projects often have a negative impact on the business organization sponsoring the project. There have been numerous reported cases where the failure of IT to deliver much needed capabilities impacted a company's financial standing, market shares, or even worse. A list of some of the more visible IT project failures was published by *Computerworld* in September 2002. Some of the projects cited in that article include ERP implementations and large-scale custom development efforts.[1] In 2003, *CIO* magazine discussed some of the challenges facing the IRS Modernization Project, an $8 billion project involving infrastructure upgrades and modifications or replacement of over 100 separate applications, and the issues confronted in AT&T's Wireless recent upgrade.[2] While the various lessons cited in these references were certainly of interest,

	Functional IT Manager	IT Project Manager	Business Sponsor
Responsibility	Continued operations	Completion of project objectives	Completion of project objectives
Authorization	Position in organization	Project Charter	Position in organization
Assignment	Permanent	Temporary	Temporary

TABLE 34-1. **TYPICAL ROLES AND RESPONSIBILITIES**

what is even more important a lesson to learn is the potential impact these failures had on the corporations, their markets, their customers and their employees. IT matters in a technology-enabled world, and IT project management matters as well.

IT PROJECT MANAGEMENT MATTERS

As information technology becomes more pervasive in our lives (programmable dishwashers, cell phones, GPS systems, home networks, medical diagnostic and drug-delivery techniques, etc.), the need to treat the development of the products and software embedded in them as true engineering activities has increased. These products could have as much safety implications as building a bridge or constructing a house. That level of engineering requires formal project management discipline.

In addition, many corporations are feeling pressure from participation in a global economy. The need to develop products and services faster and more economically translates into a requirement for a more disciplined approach to managing their development.

What does all this mean?

For companies, it means recognizing formal project management as a discipline within their information technology departments, a discipline as crucial as database management or network security management. For the project manager, it means recognizing the need to acquire and apply additional knowledge and skills, perhaps in a more formal manner than traditionally. And, for the project team (which includes business participants), it means understanding—and appreciating—the contributions formal project management makes to the overall project success.

FORMAL IT PROJECT MANAGEMENT

A project, by definition, has a specific beginning date and a specific end date. Thus, operations and maintenance of an IT system is not a project, although there might be maintenance projects undertaken in the fulfillment of that objective. Establishing user access and monitoring network security is also not a project, although introduction of a new security capability would be a project. It is important to realize that formal IT project management does not mean mounds and mounds of more paper, nor does it mean lots of additional project staff. What it means is recognizing there are some formal project management roles to be fulfilled and formal project management disciplines to be applied within an IT project.

FORMAL IT PROJECT MANAGEMENT ROLES

Formal IT project management begins with a clear understanding of the roles and responsibilities of the IT project manager, versus the roles and responsibilities of the project's business sponsor, versus the roles and responsibilities of the functional IT manager. These roles and responsibilities are briefly summarized in Table 34-1.

Let's start with an exploration of the IT Functional Manager role. Many IT organizations are structured around business areas supported, which often translates into oversight of specific applications or product lines or specific operational activity. Titles used for the individuals who manage these operational activities are Application Manager, Product Line Manager, and Data Center Manager. Their responsibilities often include an operational or maintenance type of function, the "Lights On" role within IT. While their daily activities are quite varied, their overall contribution to the business is the same: keep operations running, ensure the various IT capabilities are available to the business units relying on them. IT Functional Managers are often key stakeholders in IT projects, most often as providers of knowledgeable, experienced project staff, as quality control participants and as the recipients of the project's deliverables.

Compare these responsibilities with those of the IT project manager. An IT project manager's responsibilities are established when the project is initially conceived and are concluded when the project's deliverables are completed, when the end state is achieved. The typical responsibilities associated with the project manager role include identifying the work to be performed, determining and obtaining the corporate resources (budget, people, facilities) required to achieve the project's objectives, and then managing those resources as they are used to perform the project's identified work. It is the project manager's responsibility to ensure that any changes in the definition of the project's end state are reflected in the project's governing documents, that the Business Sponsor agrees to impacts to budgets or schedules. The project manager is also responsible of the communication of the project status to the Business Sponsor and other project stakeholders, which often include the functional IT managers.

There are organizations where an IT Functional Manager will assume the role of IT project manager on occasion, managing the enhancement of an existing application or the introduction of a new capability into the IT portfolio. It is important for the person fulfilling these two roles to be aware of the distinctions and to not allow operational considerations, such as staff availability, impede success of the project. As the project manager, the IT Functional Manager needs to ensure that the staff time required to work on the project is made available and that operations "hot items" do not prevent project progress.

The Business Sponsor role is akin to that of the homeowner in a construction project. The Sponsor is the ultimate owner of the project, representing the business users for whom the IT product or service is being provided. The Business Sponsor is responsible for making decisions regarding scope, schedule, and budget trade-offs, after listening to advice and recommendations from the experienced IT project manager.

FORMAL IT PROJECT MANAGEMENT METHODOLOGY

Before discussing methodologies and application of them within IT projects, it is necessary to define some common terms often used interchangeably. A *methodology* is defined as a body of methods and rules followed in a science or discipline. Christensen and Thayer cite IEEE Standard 12207.0-1996 as defining a *life cycle model* as "a framework

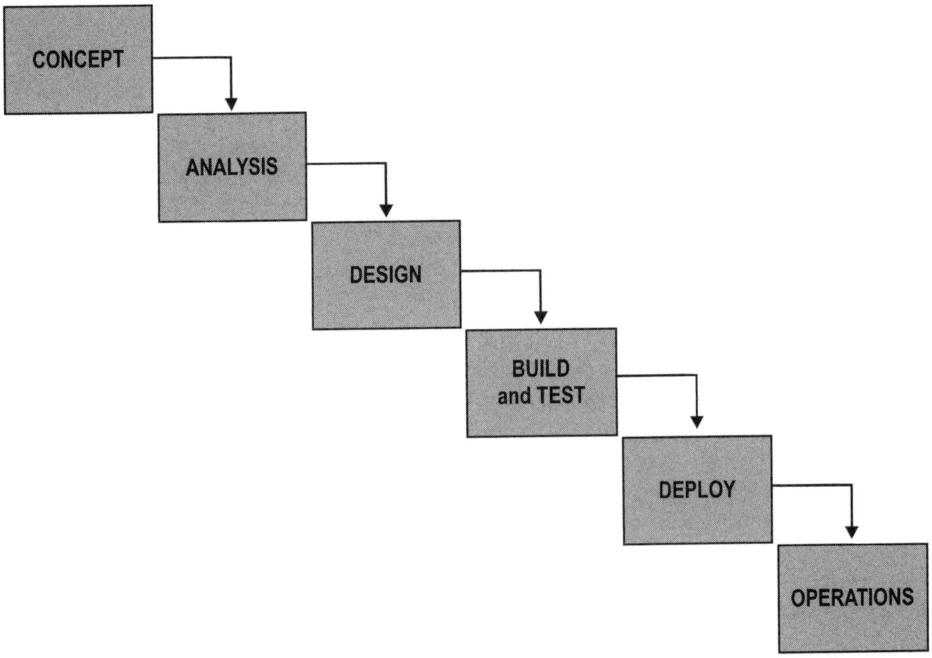

FIGURE 34-1. **TYPICAL WATERFALL LIFE CYCLE METHODOLOGY**

containing the processes, activities, and tasks involved in the development, operation, and maintenance of a software product, spanning the life of the system from the definition of its requirements to the termination of its use."[3] *A project life cycle* is a collection of generally sequential project phases, the names and number of which are determined by the control needs of the organization or organizations involved in the project. Finally, a *body of knowledge* can be defined as the sum of knowledge within a profession. Bodies of knowledge are often used as best-practice standards.

There are a number of bodies of knowledge with which the IT project manager should be familiar. Of particular interest is the project management body of knowledge, as described in the Project Management Institute's standards document.[4] The *PMBOK® Guide* identified the primary practices involved in managing any project. Available since 1996, the *Guide* is a mature and evolving representation of the project management body of knowledge.

Another guide to a body of knowledge is IEEE's *Guide to the Software Engineering Body of Knowledge* (SWEBOK).[5] At this writing, still in the early stages of industry awareness, the SWEBOK Guide provides knowledge and insight into software engineering practices such as requirements definition and management, software quality control, and software design.

One other often cited collection of best practices with which the IT project manager should have some familiarity is the Software Engineering Institute's Capability Maturity Model (Integrated), commonly called CMMI.[6] The CMMI identifies best practices an IT organization (which could be defined as an IT project organization!) should deploy in support of successful systems development. Grouped around nine key practice areas, the CMMI associates objectives and goals with specific activities.

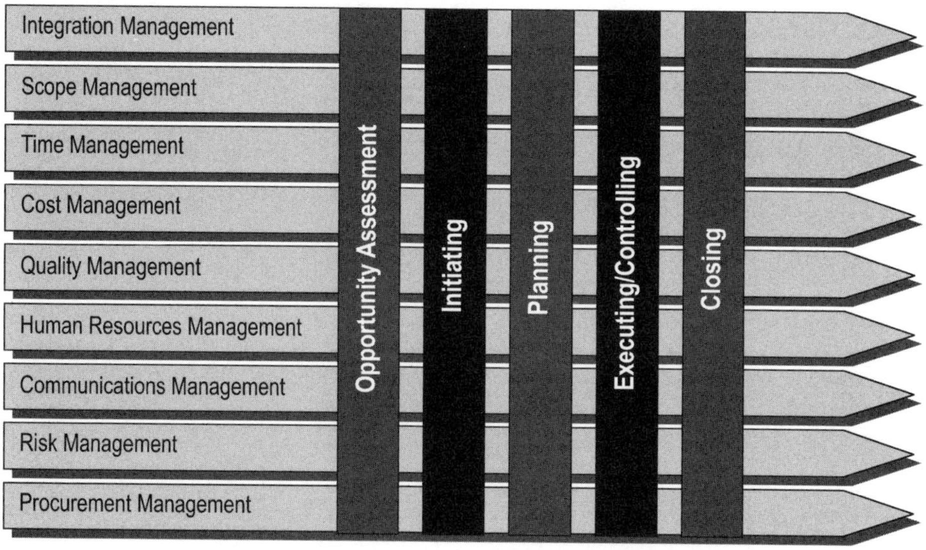

FIGURE 34-2. **TYPICAL PROJECT MANAGEMENT METHODOLOGY**

Many organizations have well-established systems development methodologies (SDLCs), addressing the activities required to conduct the technical work of the project. Figure 34-1 depicts a typical Waterfall Life Cycle Model. Note that the work to be performed is discussed in system development terms.

A formal IT project management methodology would describe the activities and steps associated with each of five project phases: Initiate, Plan, Execute, Control, and Close. For instance, the methodology would prescribe how to develop the project charter, the content of the project charter, and who should participate in its development, review, and signoff. The methodology would contain a sample of a project charter, as well as a template for the project manager to use. Figure 34-2 depicts the processes one would typically find in a project management methodology.

BEST PRACTICES

As the formal practice of project management within information technology organizations has matured over the last decade, several practices have become generally recognized as "best practices" that, when applied, can assist project teams in meeting deliverable expectations.

Establish a Formal Project Life Cycle Model

Within formal IT Project Management, one of the initial activities the IT project manager undertakes is developing his project's specific life cycle model, drawing from both a project management methodology and a systems development methodology.

It is often observed that formal methodologies impose additional work on project teams. A well-developed methodology does not impose additional work unnecessarily. Rather, the methodology provides the IT project manager and the project team a guide

PM Methodology	Waterfall Development Methodology
INITIATING PHASE	**CONCEPT DEVELOPMENT**
Perform Project Management	**Feasibility Assessment**
Project Administration	Review and Document known requirements
Change Control	Assess system architectures ability to support needs
Team Meetings	Identify probable risk areas
Quality Assurance	
Cost Control	**Scope Definition**
Schedule Control	Document In and Out of scope conditions
Risk Control	Create first level functional prioritization matrix
Status Reporting	Document critical success factors
Establish System Request	**Scope Review**
Enter System Request	Develop Presentation
Develop Project Charter	Schedule Review
Develop Goals and Objectives	Present Findings
Develop Business Case	**Business Case Development**
Develop Cost Benefit	Apply ROM estimates to functional priorities
Secure Sign-off	Determine risk weighting factors
Establish Project Planning Schedule	Develop probable cost model
Develop Project Planning Schedule	
Select Project Team	
Perform skills analysis	
Select team members	
Communicate Project Charter	
Goals and Objectives	
Business Case	
Obtain Project Approval	
Approval	
PLANNING PHASE	**REQUIREMENTS ANALYSIS**
Establish Project Plan	**Hold Team Kickoff Session**
Develop Project Plan	
Develop Scope Statement	**Requirements Gathering**
Develop Team Assignments	Gather documentation
Develop Communication Plan	Perform necessary interviews
Develop Change Control Plan	Establish requirements prioritization matrix
Prepare Project Plan Document	
	Requirements sessions
	Review Critical Success Factors
	Review Risk Factors
	Validate Requirements Matrix
Establish Project Schedule	Prioritize Requirements
Develop WBS	Validate Cost estimates per functionality
Develop Estimates	Develop Use Case Scenarios
Develop Critical Path	Develop performance requirements
Produce Project Schedule	
Resource Schedule by Role/Skill set	**Package Evaluation**
Resource Schedule by Name	Perform industry search
	Validate package functionality against requirements
Schedule & Resource Validation	Perform Gap Analysis & costing
Validate Resources (per increment if necessary)	Develop trade-off matrix
Validate Schedule (per increment if necessary)	Vendor recommendation

PM Methodology	Waterfall Development Methodology
Obtain Vendor Information	**Visual Specification Development**
Develop RFI	Develop story board
Issue RFI	Design screen mock-ups
Acquire Vendor(s)	Review content against requirements
Develop RFP	Develop functional flow
Develop Contract and SOW	Finalize graphical presentation
Negotiation	Perform team review and validation
	Requirements Review
	Develop Presentation
	Schedule Review
	Present Findings
	Make team recommendation

FIGURE 34-3. **SAMPLE PARTIAL PROJECT LIFE CYCLE MODEL**

by which they can conduct project activities. The project team should use the IT Project Management methodology and the System Development methodology as resources from which they can develop their project's life cycle model, applying the concepts of "tailoring" and "just enough process" to ensure the project's life cycle model meets their needs.

Let me explain further. When the IT project manager surveys the PM Methodology and the SDLC to be applied within his project life cycle model, he should consider the risk profile of the project. For instance, if the PM is working with a close-knit, co-located project team, he might find formal weekly status reporting to the project team is not necessary, but if the project team is working together for the first time or is geographically dispersed, it might be advantageous to have a formal time each week for the team to interact with each other. Formal change control processes are indicated if the work is being performed under a fixed price contract with a business unit or external customer. The risk profile of the project will indicate how much formality is needed in the project and which system development life cycle should be followed. A risky project should consider an iterative development approach, with formal scope statements and frequent schedule/budget updates, and a more rigorous approach to identifying and managing risks. A project that is viewed less risky, perhaps a repetitive maintenance project to an existing application, might not require as much rigor.

When the project team has developed their project's life cycle model, identifying the approach and processes they will use to manage the project's activities, it is recommended that the Business Sponsor and any internal oversight body, such as a Quality Assurance organization, review and approve the tailoring. The project manager should be able to defend the decisions made as to the degree of formal methodology compliance he will follow on the project.

Figure 34-3 shows a possible partial project life cycle model developed using a waterfall systems development methodology, in addition to a project management methodology, and expressed in terms of an activity list.

Leveraging Project Sponsors and Business Community

It is important to realize that most projects are not IT projects, but business projects being completed by the IT organization. The resourceful IT project manager will view his business sponsor as an equal partner in the project. Even those projects that are mostly technology in nature (for instance, an operating system upgrade) have a business sponsor, perhaps one of the IT Functional Managers.

Involving the Business Sponsor and user representatives in the planning of a project might seem risky and politically unsafe to the IT project manager. However, the more participatory and open the planning activities are, the fewer surprises there will be for the Business Sponsor when the project schedule or budget is presented. It has been my personal experience that often times the Business Sponsor does not appreciate the details associated with developing software or implementing a new package. Involving that Sponsor in the development of the project's work breakdown structure, or in the Risk Identification workshop, or in the development of the project's communications plan, provides the IT project manager with an opportunity to educate the Sponsor and to get the Sponsor's buy-in on the project management deliverables. The Sponsor will understand why these additional activities are actually to his benefit.

Representatives from the user community should also be viewed as resources to be assigned to an IT project. They are the experts when it comes to defining the project's business requirements. They are also the experts as to how those business requirements should be validated as implemented. User representatives should be assigned as project team resources to participate in the definition and creation of test cases, and then in the execution of those test cases. Because they defined the requirements, they will best know when the requirement is implemented correctly.

When status reports are to be delivered, or important project decisions are to be made, the Business Sponsor should be actively involved. In fact, one could argue the Sponsor is the *only* member of the project team empowered to make decisions regarding scope, budget, and schedule. The project manager 's role is to make sure the Sponsor makes an *informed* decision.

Internal Contracts

When managing internal IT projects for one of my former employers, I often negotiated contracts with my internal customers. What did this mean? It meant the project charter and associated project plan (including schedule, budget, deliverable definitions, and responsibility matrix) was a document that we both agreed to and signed. This then became a contract upon which our performances would be evaluated. I committed to delivering on schedule and within the prescribed budget; the customer agreed to actively participate in requirements management and testing activities, and to managing scope. Any change to the content of the project plan was treated as a contractual change, resulting in a new contract.

IT Project Management Office

The use of an IT Project Management Office has become an industry best practice.[7] The IT Project Management Office is often implemented in one of two models: A "Center of Excellence" or a "Shared Services."

In a "Center of Excellence" model, the IT Project Management Office serves as the keeper of the methodologies and all related activities, including methodology training and mentoring, as the quality assurance mechanism, and as the ultimate source on all matters related to IT Project Management best practices. Note that in this model, the IT PMO also oversees all IT methodologies and standards, not just those pertaining to project management. The PMO staff would oversee the systems development methodologies, the configuration management and quality control standards and the use of any supporting tools such as scheduling and estimating tools. In this model, project managers do not report to the PMO.

In a "Shared Services" model, the IT PMO provides the above activities in addition to being the functional provider of project managers to projects within the IT organization.

A third function often played by an IT PMO is that of "project portfolio manager." Staff within the IT PMO obtains project status data from project managers and administers periodic project reviews. They facilitate reviews of the IT Project Portfolio, assisting in determining which projects require additional management attention and which projects should be initiated or cancelled.

Power of Internet Collaboration

One of the side benefits from the emergence of technology into our everyday lives is the availability as a tool for other IT projects to leverage. The power of the Internet and online collaboration tools and web-based repositories means that project teams (including user representatives) no longer need to sit in the same conference room to review a presentation. They can participate in a virtual project room, where they all have access to the project documentation being reviewed. Certain technologies support real-time editing of the documents. Other products support team brainstorming and decision-making. This ability to function as a team while physically dispersed means an IT project manager potentially has a greater resource pool upon which to draw.

CHALLENGES FOR THE IT PROJECT MANAGER

What challenges exist today and in the near future for the IT project manager?

Staying Abreast with Technology

One of the most obvious challenges is the ability to stay abreast with the technology. The onslaught of wireless technologies, in addition to the legacy mainframe and client server technologies, is changing the way we think of information technology. The effective use of information technology is indeed a strategic market differentiator for many businesses. A prime example is the rollout of RFID within the Wal-Mart business community. [8]

The management of the projects associated with this particular endeavor can mean tremendous profits to some companies. So while the affected project managers do not need to personally be RFID experts, they do need to be sure they are comfortable with the plans and schedules they are operating under, and that any risks of schedule slippage are communicated in a timely manner to their business sponsors.

Increased Emphasis on Security and Privacy

Another emerging technology issue is the increased emphasis on security and information privacy. In particular industries, notably healthcare and financial services, this issue is of real concern to the IT project manager. There are legal requirements that limit how one uses "live data" to create "test data" and how much data can be displayed to a particular user. The IT project manager needs to be aware of these requirements in order to ensure that the product he delivers to his user community is in compliance, just as the general contractor in a construction project needs to ensure compliance to building and safety codes.

Should the IT project manager be involved in a project introducing wireless technologies into an organization, he needs to be sure that the activities associated with protecting the data being transmitted over that technology have been considered and are suitably addressed.

Outsourcing

One other trend that continues to haunt the IT project manager is outsourcing. This business trend can result in the IT project manager being the manager of a services contract, with associated service level agreements, where the actual information technology development work is performed by a third-party. This means that an IT project manager needs to be up to speed on reading and interpreting contracts and enforcing their terms, as opposed to managing a project team. Many IT project managers will lack the business law training required to feel totally comfortable in this role. If you are a "technology-focused" project manager, with a degree in Computer Sciences, enroll in a Contractual Law course to obtain a basic understanding of contract management.

OUTLOOK FOR THE FUTURE

By now, you will have an appreciation of the pervasiveness of information technology and the need for increased discipline in the management of those technology projects. The future will indeed include further personal accountability for the IT project manager. Just as society holds the General Contractor accountable for safety and code compliance in his construction projects, so will society hold the IT project manager accountable for safety and information privacy. There will be an increased emphasis on licensure, oversight boards, and specialized certifications in order to manage certain types of projects.

That said, the field of IT Project Management will indeed become a profession, through the efforts of organizations such as Project Management Institute (PMI), Association for Computing Machines (ACM), Software Engineering Institute (SEI) at Carnegie-Mellon University, and IEEE's Computer Society, to name just a few. The forward-thinking IT project manager will stay abreast with the developments within these organizations in order to be better positioned as a "professional IT project manager."

DISCUSSION QUESTIONS

❶ How is formal IT project management practiced in the organizations with which you are familiar? Consider the various roles and responsibilities and discuss how they are fulfilled.

❷ Think of a project with which you have been involved, and discuss the project's life cycle model: What activities were included? Which ones were not? How would a different project life cycle model have affected the project's completion?

❸ What challenges are the IT Project Managers in your organization facing in the near future? How are they, and the organization, preparing for the challenges?

REFERENCES

[1] The Best and the Worst, *Computerworld*, September 30, 2003.

[2] Elana Veron, For the IRS, "There is No EZ Fix," CIO, April 1, 2004; Christopher Koch, "Five Lessons from AT&T's Wireless Project Failure," CIO, April 15, 2004.

[3] *The Project Manager's Guide to Software Engineering's Best Practices*, Mark J. Christensen and Richard H. Thayer, IEEE Computer Society, Los Alamitos, CA, 2001

[4] Project Management Institute, *A Guide to Project Management Body of Knowledge, Third Edition,* PMI: Newtown Square, PA: 2004.

[5] IEEE Computer Society, Guide to the Software Engineering Body of Knowledge, IEEE Computer Society, Los Alamitos, CA, 2001. 10. Further information on the SWEBOK and the associated certification program can be found at www.swebok.org.

[6] Further information on the CMMI model can be found at www.sei.cmu.edu/cmmi/cmmi.html.

[7] Richard Pastore and Lorraine Cosgrove Ware, The Best Best Practices, *CIO*, May 1, 2004.

[8] Carol Sliwa and Bob Brewin, RFID Tests Wal-Mart Suppliers, *Computerworld*, April 5, 2004.

CHAPTER 35

Project Management for Software Engineering

▶LOIS ZELLS,
LOIS ZELLS & ASSOCIATES, INC.

Software engineering is the term applied to all aspects of information processing systems development and maintenance. The term *engineering* is used to indicate that the procedures used in software projects are comparable to the scientific method rather than to artistic endeavors.

The study of software engineering management is broken into people issues and process issues. Although the people issues are very important, they are not within the domain of this chapter. On the other hand, the process issues will be covered in depth. The procedural side of software engineering management is further divided into work that is done to build the system, and work that is done to manage the project. When practitioners do work to build the system, their efforts result in software specifications—and subsequently: code. When they do work to manage the project, their efforts result in estimates and plans. Even in a construction project, these two separate types of work occur, usually simultaneously. For example, the cement subcontractors may be pouring the foundation (building work), while the project manager is planning the tasks for construction of the walls (project management work).

Furthermore, the best project management skills alone do little to overcome deficiencies in the software engineering management process—without an equivalent level of mastery in building the system. If the project is on time and within budget and it solves the wrong problem, it is not likely to be of much use to anyone. Furthermore, until planners understand the deliverables that are produced while building the system, they will be hard-pressed to develop a thorough and all-inclusive plan. Identifying what deliverables are to be produced, then, requires a complete understanding of the phases of development.

TRADITIONAL DEVELOPMENT PHASES

In any kind of a project—even a project to build a simple birdhouse—there are at least four phases:

1. *Analysis:* The builders must first determine what is to be constructed.
2. *Design:* The builders must then create a blueprint for the construction.
3. *Construction:* The product must actually be built.
4. *Installation:* The product must be qualified and put into use.

Distilled down to their most fundamental components, software projects also must complete the analysis, design, construction, and installation phases.

1. *Analysis:* The software engineers must first define the business problem the software will ultimately solve.
2. *Design:* The software engineers must then create a blueprint for the software solution.
3. *Construction:* The software engineers must write the code.
4. *Installation:* The code must be tested and accepted.

Actually, before *any* phases are initiated, it is necessary to evaluate the justification for software systems services. A quick assessment is made to determine the justification of the request. Many projects, perhaps even 50 percent, do not survive this initial screening.

The Analysis Phase

During the first phase, the developers must determine what business problem is to be solved through the installation of the software. This is called business requirements analysis. This analysis effort is driven from the business perspective of the customer (sometimes called user, client, etc.). Answering the question, "What would be the problem if this were 1901 and there were no computers?" helps to identify the correct business requirements. During this process there may also be some limited technical aspects that need to be taken into consideration. Thus, it would be useful to think of analysis as 90 percent business-driven and 10 percent technically driven.

Preanalysis

The early part of the analysis phase of most software projects is typically somewhat chaotic. Project participants may not know one another and may be unsure of themselves, customers may have a hard time conveying what they want, meetings may go astray, and the whole project may seem ungovernable. Furthermore, one of the most serious difficulties that continues to plague software systems developers is getting a clear understanding and agreement of who's in, who's out of the project effort; and what's in, what's out of the product effort. This definition is called the *domain of study*. Furthermore, it is essential to develop a concise declaration of what's important to the product and the project. In other words, the agree-upon priorities must drive the project.

To crystallize these requirements, today's more enlightened software organizations have added an introductory phase to the project development process, called the preanalysis phase. Preanalysis is an orientation and screening phase that helps to: (1) identify and resolve problems before the analysis and design stages; then to (2) identify the operational features and procedures necessary to complete the work successfully; and finally to (3) diffuse any issues that will become obstacles.

Many of the current software specification techniques are weak from the perspective of not being able to capture and address the questions of who the customer really is, what's most important to the customer, and which customers should have the highest priority. Lack of a clear definition of these elements is a significant contributor to the creeping commitment that often destroys any success potential a project may have.

During this preanalysis phase, customers are identified; their high-level wants, needs, and tastes are captured and prioritized; and the customers themselves are prioritized with respect to who should drive feature and functionality decisions. Customer requirements are prioritized by customer area. A very important aspect of this process is the resolution of conflicts in customer priorities.

Partitioning Analysis

Most software engineering authorities now agree that analysis, as a single phase in all but the smallest software systems projects, is simply too big. Therefore, expert practitioners often take a spiral approach, dividing analysis into more than one go-round. This technique employs the concept of *controlled iteration:* for example, a high-level analysis, an intermediate-level analysis, and a detailed analysis. Some or all of the specification development is executed concurrently—with each successive iteration becoming more and more detailed—until all of the requirements have been accurately and completely captured.

The high-level analysis is an orientation and screening effort that, most importantly, confirms the domain of study. It also provides a cursory evaluation of the business requirements, confirms the priorities, and describes the value of each required feature.

During the intermediate-level analysis, the high-level specification is expanded, a project management agreement is written, and the team drives to get a handle on how big the project really is. If the group is able to ascertain that the risk is too high to try the project as it is currently defined, its members may reduce the domain of study and the proposed system scope before proceeding any further. (The true definition of scope is the part of the system, in a software engineering project, that will be committed to automation.)

The third analysis iteration is the time to dissect the business problem completely. It is during this effort that the real job of analysis is completed. The most significant deliverable of this effort is the verified requirements definition, which establishes the specifications for building the system. It describes in thorough detail *what* the system must do in order to be deemed a success. Most failures to deliver the correct system can be traced to the fact that even by this stage there was still no unambiguous agreement between the developers and the customers about the system's requirements. Emphasis, then, must be on the document's completeness and accuracy.

Postanalysis

At the conclusion of the business analysis, it is necessary to designate which features (or parts of features) will be automated and which will remain as manual operations.

Additionally, the parts elected for automation should be mapped into hardware and software requirements. Decisions are made regarding batch processing, on-line processing, distributed processing, database requirements, or any other technical approach.[1] These decisions serve as input to the selection of one or more purchased package solutions and/or to the design of the automated portion of a new system.

Although the domain of study must be specified at the beginning of the project, it is not until the process of carving out the boundaries for automation has been completed that the final decisions regarding scope are made. Therefore, the scope is not truly defined until the end of this postanalysis phase. Subsequent changes to the scope of the system are subject to the change management procedures described later in the chapter.

The Design Phase

This phase provides the transition from the selection of a solution to the ability to construct a reliable, high-quality product. The objective is achieved through systematic software design methods and techniques that are applied to the chosen automated solution from the prior phase in order to obtain a computer system that can be implemented. The design phase is partitioned into three types of work: (1) the design of the technical architecture of the system, (2) the external design, and (3) the internal design.

Design of the Technical Architecture of the System

The system is partitioned into pieces that will ultimately become groupings of source code instructions. These groupings, usually called subsystems or programs, are in turn divided into modules, routines, subroutines, etc. How these groupings interface with one another is called the technical architecture of the system. It is analogous to the blueprint for a construction project and, as such, may be graphically represented in one of the many acknowledged design-diagramming techniques that are used by software engineers. The technical architecture declares the basis system design, the control subsystems, and the data structure control interfaces for intermodule communication.

External Design

External design—so-called because it considers design from the outside of the system (that is, the customer perspective) without regard to the internals of the modules, programs, etc—addresses such issues as design of input screens and forms, hierarchy of screen menus, and design of output reports. In a prototyping environment, some of the external design may have been done much earlier in the project. If so, the external design (to the extent that it was not completed in the earlier phases) is finished now. Many of the deliverables in this subphase will be direct input to customer procedure guides and manuals. Therefore, since external design is so closely related to the documentation factors, these tasks must be closely coordinated with the individual(s) responsible for customer documentation.

Internal Design

The internal design provides the detailed directions for module design, program design, database design, and so on. These internal specs will be used during the coding phase to create source codes in one or more compiled programming languages. Team members are assigned the responsibility for designing each module (generally less than or equal to

100 source code instructions) or program (group of modules, routines, or subroutines). The specifications include the name, purpose, language, calling parameters, calling sequence, error routines, algorithms, module logic, and restart and recovery procedures. The database design—complete with names, descriptions, values, size and format of fields, data usage statistics, the distinction between stored and derived data, keys, access relationships and methods, and backup and retention criteria—is also finalized.

The Construction Phase (Coding)

It is during this phase that the code is actually written from the design specifications that were developed for the program modules and databases. Programming considerations are influenced by the type of language (e.g., third or fourth generation), the choice of the language itself (e.g., COBOL, C), and the installation of productivity aids (e.g., code optimizers, application generators). The units coded during this phase are also tested.

The Installation Phase

During the installation phase, all of the activities carried out during the project finally come to a climax. Characterized by the integration of software development, hardware installation, documentation, testing, training, and conversion, this last phase of the project life cycle marks the ultimate joining of all of the deliverables from each of these efforts. During systems testing and acceptance testing, the successful integration of these outputs and the smooth operation of the system are verified, and the final decisions regarding implementation are made.

ITERATIVE DEVELOPMENT

It is sometimes the case that software engineers assume that all of the analysis must be completed before any design can start, that all of the design must be completed before any coding can start, and so on. To complete one phase completely before embarking on the next phase is referred to as the conventional "waterfall" approach to systems development. This is the most systematic technique, one that enables the lowest risk, and is best in environments where:

- ▶The system is large and complex.
- ▶There is not an abundance of business expertise.
- ▶The technology is *very* leading edge.
- ▶There is not a lot of software engineering development and/or project management expertise.

On the other hand, the danger of this sequential approach is that developers may spend so long in their attempt to complete one phase that (1) the business requirements may change by the time they are finished, (2) an important feature may be overlooked, (3) the technology may evolve to yet another level, or (4) valuable resources may be spent on the wrong effort.

To compensate, there are several innovative approaches to development—variously called iterative phasing, incremental implementation, prototyping, staged delivery, design to tools delivery, and rapid application development—that may be used individually or in concert in an attempt to shorten project duration.

However, the use of these approaches has long been misunderstood and abused. Many people have interpreted the use of these techniques as a license for sloppy analysis and design—or to skip them altogether. This is an absolute fallacy.

In the software engineering environment, the concepts of prototyping and iterative development have become invaluable aids—when the developer is able to work side-by-side with the customer to build increasingly feature-rich versions of the end product. The key to success in this strategy is that *both the customer and the developer* develop the iterations *together*. They do this in cycles: re-developing working models until a final product is developed that satisfies the customers' needs.

Iterative Development works best when: (1) Requirements are well established and stable, (2) requirements are unambiguous; and (3) there are no contradictions in the way people work. Furthermore, upfront preliminary work is always required as part of the Preanalysis and Analysis Phases, and requirements specifications must always be created for the system internals.

What is always true, however, is that iterative development is *never* intended to be an excuse for "hacking." It is *never* intended to be an excuse for not doing requirements or design specifications. It is *never* intended to be an excuse for not using "proven methodologies."

Some important benefits of iterative development include the following:

▶There is a lot to be learned by experimentation.

▶Many changes can be made quickly and easily using inexpensive throwaway models.

▶It allows users and developers to get early feedback on the system's idiosyncrasies.

▶Together, the developers and users can build a series of successively more enhanced versions—incorporating user experience into each enlarged subset of the product—until the whole problem has been solved.

As a result of the joint developer/user iterative building effort, major misunderstandings, errors, omissions, ambiguities, and inconsistencies are easily discovered—and then eliminated during subsequent refinements.

Iterative Development is not without its challenges and risks:

▶In iterative development, the requirements and design specifications are, by the very nature of iterative development, often co-mingled.

▶Because systems development is not a familiar environment for users, the co-mingling of business and technical requirements often makes it very difficult for them to verify and validate either specification. Developers, then, have the obligation to work with the users to, one at a time, validate first the business aspects of each iteration and then, and only then, its technical aspects.

▶Scope management is hard to understand: it may be confusing to some to differentiate between the normal process of refinement (that is the expected purpose of the iterations) and actual changes to scope.

▶It is impossible to predict the number of iterations that will be required before reaching the customer's approval.

▶Unrealistic time, people, and dollar schedules are continuously unrealistic.

▶In the absence of formal reviews and inspections, there is a good risk of poor design and an architecturally unsound system.

▶All of the "ilities" may be seriously affected: performability, reliability, maintainability, testability, and usability.

▶Developers often fall in love with the process, and then they miss their target dates.

Before project teams embark on iterative development, it is advisable that they master an understanding of the objectives of each phase in the development process, the completion criteria, and the cost of doing the right work at the wrong time and its associated rework. Then, depending on the learning curves involved and the risks that can be borne, the group can choose a strategy that integrates some (or all) of the innovative techniques with the traditional approaches.

For example, in iterative development, it is perfectly acceptable to overlap analysis, design, and coding—that is, the major phases; but not the unique tasks within the phases.

However, if the developers do choose to overlap the phases, the group must always first complete what is called the major interface model: the technical architectural definition of how all the components of the system will work together and communicate. Maintaining the integrity of this model during the development of the iterations is essential. Only after the interface model has been completed and approved can the group then select subsets of features to deliver in separate releases.

If the developer management wants then to mitigate the risk, the next step is crucial. If the risk is to be totally mitigated, analysis, design, coding, and unit testing are never overlapped for an individual feature or function, or technical grouping. Once the customers have selected the features or functions that are to be delivered in a release, all of the analysis of a specific feature must be completed before embarking on the design of the technical grouping. Then, all of the technical grouping design must be completed before coding is initiated, and so on.

METHODOLOGY MODIFICATION

In summary, (1) the major interface model is developed and maintained; (2) individual features or functions are developed sequentially by completing all of the analysis, then the design of the technical grouping, then coding, and finally unit testing; and (3 the other features or functions within their technical groups can be done in parallel in the same manner as just described. Even though they often include such innovative approaches as those just described, many methodologies may sometimes need some level of adaptation to the unique needs of the developers.

When the methodology is not appropriate for their project, the developer is obliged to tell the customer. In addition, the developer must inform the customer of the risks of changing the methodology.

If they decide that the departure from the methodology and its associated risk are worth it, they must work out and document an agreement that describes where the departures from the methodology will be made and how they will share the risk.

For example, coding before the specifications are completed may, for some reason, be determined to be a necessary strategy.

However, the developer must first ensure that the customer understands and accepts that there is a high risk of required rework later, and that such rework may delay the project and/or increase the costs.

There must therefore be a clear and documented understanding of who absorbs the schedule and cost overruns

There must also be a firm plan in place defining when the developers will actually finish the requirements.

Finally, rigorous procedures must be in place for keeping the impacts of the rework synchronized with all of the other work that is going on. There must be a mechanism for handling a change when it occurs:

Keeping track of the change; keeping the specifications current to reflect the change; and keeping the name of (and notifying) every person, every requirement, and every program that is affected by the change.

THE RUSH TO CODE

Unfortunately, sometimes a team may, on their own, elect to start early coding because they are tempted into believing that this is an acceptable strategy (1) to meet a target date; or (2) when they see that their project progress has seriously slipped. If they are not aware of the software engineering principles described earlier, it is often the case that only too late do they discover that the project actually takes much longer than doing it right in the first place. Wise organizations know better than to proceed without a risk management strategy such as the one described above.

While a team can surely be faulted for early coding before all of the requirements are in, it is severe mismanagement to do so without explaining the risks to the customer and first getting the customer's written approval. If the team embarks on early coding before getting approval, they do it at their own peril and at their own risk.

DOING THINGS RIGHT

There is a saying in the software engineering community that quality is *built* in and really cannot be *tested* into a system. Yet it is alarming how many software managers still cling to the mistaken belief that more testing as well as improving testing skills will bring quality to their systems.

If practitioners have the skills to develop a complete and comprehensive set of test cases, and if they can then measure the time and effort involved in executing those test cases one time, those onetime measurements represent the true cost of testing. Almost every minute spent after the first execution of those test cases is *not* being spent on testing! Instead, time is being spent on work that *should* have been completed in the earlier phases. Examples of work being done at the wrong time are specification reexamination and correction, redesign, recoding, and retesting.

Since the fastest, cheapest, highest-quality way to build software is never to make any mistakes during development and never to do any job more than once, it is a good idea to learn how to do the right things right—the first time! Thus, good systems development techniques are the essential requirements for improved quality and faster project completion times, and they may not be ignored.

Furthermore, to the surprise and chagrin of those who look for their productivity solutions in the latest silver bullets, they are looking in the wrong place. Experts in software engineering management now acknowledge that 40 to 65 percent of the errors in delivered software systems arise from poor analysis and design. Proper analysis and design, then, are crucial to effective testing of the system and the ultimate delivery of a good product. Not fully appreciating this, participants in traditional project development rushed through the early phases in order to ensure that they would have enough time for testing. At a maximum, they spent 25 to 40 percent of the software development effort on analysis and design. Consequently, programmers spent the majority of their time fixing errors that were carried over from the early phases. Of course, what they were really doing was the analysis and design that ought to have been done earlier in the project. This is a very poor approach, because requirements errors discovered during testing cost fifteen to seventy-five times more to fix than those that are discovered during analysis. Sooner or later, analysis and design will be done! It's not a question of whether they *will* be done, but a question of *when* they will be done and *how much* the organization is willing to pay for them.

MANAGING CHANGES TO THE DOMAIN OF STUDY AND THE SYSTEM SCOPE

It is also in the early stages that unknown requirements start to emerge, both the domain of study and the scope start to enlarge, target dates begin to slip, groups begin to make compromises, and the project often starts to fall apart.

The organization must have a way to respond to changes in the domain of study and/or the scope of the system. Many people try to freeze the specifications, but that often only leads to: (1) the discovery that people change their minds anyway; (2) animosity when the system users feel they didn't understand what they were signing off to; or (3) an "on-time" system that doesn't fulfill the customer requirements.

It is not possible to control change, but it is possible to manage it. Changes are initiated through a change request that is assigned a number and entered into a change management log that keeps track of the current status of the request. An analyst assesses the costs, the benefits, and the impact in terms of time, money, and people. The change is then scheduled for consideration by a group of change management decision makers. The change management decision makers consider the impact and prioritize the request: accepted, rejected, or postponed until the next release. The necessary parties are notified of the decision and its impact on the time, money, and resources of the project(s).

THE DIFFICULTY OF MANAGING BY PHASES ALONE

Early project management concepts introduced the idea of gaining control by partitioning the project into phases. Because it was moving in the right direction, this was a good step, but it didn't solve the total problem. As practitioners have come to recognize, using the disciplines, methodologies, and development techniques did not automatically guarantee project success. Those early project developers found that the phases could be very long and that they still couldn't determine if they were on schedule. So they tried breaking the phases into major milestones, with each milestone representing a significant project event.

Again, the use of milestones was a move in the right direction, but it was still not the total answer. The significant events were hard to identify, and progress was hard to monitor. Milestones were very far apart, and estimators had a difficult time sizing up the effort it took for completion. Long periods elapsed before the project manager could evaluate status; consequently, valuable time would be wasted before the problems were recognized and corrective action could be taken. There was no really effective way to evaluate progress, so status was reported as a function of percentage against hours used (e.g., if a job was estimated at forty hours and the worker had spent twenty hours on it, the job was reported as 50 percent completed). This is one of the ways projects got to be 90 percent complete so quickly, while the last 10 percent took another 90 percent of the time.

A better approach is to partition each milestone into smaller pieces. Commonly referred to as *inch-pebbles*, these bits and pieces afford better control of the unknowns and easier monitoring of progress. The sum of many small estimates is more reliable than one large estimate and is also harder to shave down during scheduling negotiations.

To begin, inch-pebble jobs can be assigned to one person, making status easier to determine. Similarly, status is easier to report when the state of a job can only be binary: The job is either 100 percent complete or 0 percent complete; no other status is meaningful. This approach diffuses the impact of the subjective reporting of fractional percentages of completion, which are often expressed simply as a function of how much of the original effort has been consumed. Using smaller estimates and reporting binary status also reduces the possibility of the last 10 percent of the project taking another 90 percent of the time.

With smaller jobs, status is reported more frequently. If progress is poor, the manager knows it right away. Corrective action may be taken sooner, thus helping to avoid the wide differential between expected progress and actual progress. And finally, the smaller the estimate, the smaller the interval between the extremes. The smaller the confidence interval (the range between the longest and shortest estimates), the higher the level of statistical accuracy in the estimate.

Thus, the secret to successful project management is to partition the project into pieces of pieces of pieces until a statistically reliable level is reached. For example, the project can be divided by phase deliverables. The phase deliverables, in turn, are separated into their significant milestone deliverables. The milestone deliverables are then partitioned into major deliverables, and the major deliverables are broken into individual deliverables. Inch-pebbles are statistically reliable and are usually found at the individual deliverables level. It takes the completion of a significant number of inch-pebbles to produce a major deliverable. A fair number of major deliverables contribute to the completion of a milestone. And, of course, every phase has a certain number of milestones.

Implementation of Inch-Pebbles

How small is small? What is the size of an inch-pebble? Each of the inch-pebbles must be small enough so that:

- A reasonable estimate may be figured for its completion.
- The estimate reflects reality.
- The confidence interval will be small.
- The organization may be comfortable about the level of "accuracy."
- It will be hard to intimidate the estimator into reducing the estimate.
- The 100 percent completion level can be reached rather quickly.
- Managers know they're in trouble before disaster descends upon them.
- When the job is done, there is a meaningful and verifiable deliverable.

An inch-pebble thus represents a work unit that cannot be meaningfully subdivided and is best completed without interruption. In addition, to afford effective partitioning, estimating, scheduling, and status reporting, a unit of work (an inch-pebble) produces a meaningful and tangible deliverable that can be verified, is commonly assignable to one and only one person, and is usually completed in four to forty hours.

Identification of meaningful deliverables is an area that causes lots of confusion when trying to partition the development of specifications. For example, if an analysis specification is to be produced across the span of several phases, it may be prepared at a high level in a Phase 1, an intermediate level in a Phase 2, and a detailed level in a Phase 3. One could then say that it will not be completed until the end of Phase 3. However, this would make status reporting and management of each phase very difficult. A better approach would be to partition the development of each specification into a job that can be worked on as an inch-pebble and later designated as 100 percent completed when it is finished. For example, an administrative system deliverable could be (1) the high-level specification of payment processing, (2) the intermediate-level specification of payment types, or (3) the detailed specification of backdated payment processing.

The implementation of the inch-pebble concept allows organizations to achieve many of the goals they are attempting to satisfy. It also helps them recall that many small estimates added together have less margin for error than a single large estimate; therefore, they may more quickly realize their ambition for "accurate" estimates. Additionally, "one job-one person" combined with the status of "done-not done" dramatically simplifies status reporting and thus the management of the project. (Remember: "one job-one person" is a rule of thumb and, as such, there are always exceptions. For example, meetings and reviews are inch-pebbles that, obviously, are assigned to more than one person.)

Setting a forty-hour maximum on inch-pebbles creates an environment in which a number of jobs are being completed every week. As a result, crises are frequently identified soon enough to avert disaster. Not every inch-pebble, however, is exactly forty hours long. Many are less than that and some may even be greater. Therefore, not every job starts on Monday morning and finishes on Friday evening.

Lastly, because most organizations have few to no experts in estimating, the discipline of getting down to the confidence intervals of four to forty hours goes far to diffuse the novice effect.

You will encoubter resistance from many groups. To identify inch-pebbles of four to forty hours is not a trivial task. Although they are never faced at the same time, there may ultimately be as many as 2,000 inch-pebbles in a medium-size project. Frequently, people balk at what appears to be just so much overhead.

It is important to determine what makes sense in the organization, what information is needed, how often it is required, and how reliable it must be. Organizations should decide:

▶How much estimating expertise is on the team—and its effect on the accuracy of the total plan.

▶If the range that is selected is small enough to support a high degree of confidence in the accuracy of the estimate.

▶If the range that is selected gives the status data soon enough (that is, how long the group members can comfortably wait before knowing if they're in trouble).

▶How much risk can be borne.

This approach has been implemented in many enlightened companies. Those that accept this concept buy into certain givens. It is agreed that the project team members will be allowed the time to plan, in the first place. Furthermore, since it is impossible to identify all of the inch-pebbles for the entire project at one sitting, only those inch-pebbles in the short term will be included in the plan. Then, after completion of a preselected and limited number of inch-pebbles, it is agreed that the team members will be allowed to use their newly acquired knowledge (and be given the time) to plan the next short-term effort. It is also agreed that this process may be repeated more than once for each milestone, phase, or project, depending on its size and complexity.

THE IMPLICATIONS OF REPLANNING

Furthermore, it is also accepted that during each replanning exercise, the new knowledge that is gained may necessitate the implementation of one or more of the following project management strategies:

1. Extending the finish date
2. Adding more resources
3. Eliminating features
4. Risking (sacrificing) some degree of quality and/or reliability and/or performance
5. Finding a low-risk method of improving productivity[2]
6. Canceling the project.

These appear to be the only six choices. For example, the date may be locked in and the project must not be cancelled (because of a valid business requirement); but then, some combination of the second through fifth choices must be selected.

Realize that there's no free lunch! There is often a disconnect between making the target date of the current project and the costs of maintaining the system after it's put into production. Of course, no one advocates risking quality (and so on), but sometimes, it is the default decision. If—in order to save time during the project—quality, reliability, and/or performance are unintentionally (or consciously) sacrificed in order to make a critical target date, then operational costs are likely to be increased later during maintenance. Many organizations are either not aware of this obvious state of affairs or they just refuse to acknowledge it. The result is that, unwittingly, they often choose unrealistic strategies that, by default, simply lead to the ultimate sacrifice of quality. There are enough sorry practitioners around (who remember burning the midnight oil while trying to maintain a poor-grade system) who can attest to the results of such choices.

On the other hand, sometimes projects must be managed with a fixed date to completion (for example, because of regulatory requirements and strategic product development). When groups do not have the luxury of moving the date, they simply integrate the other management strategies of adding more resources, descoping, introducing productivity measures, or canceling the project. If canceling the project is not an alternative, then teams are obviously left with the first three choices. If the regulatory requirements or strategic product development absolutely drive the date, then sacrificing quality may be the only choice. But that choice is made while consciously acknowledging the trade-offs.

ESTIMATING

Some people would insist that accurate estimates in the software industry are impossible. It even seems contradictory to put these two words together. To the contrary, in some organizations there are groups that consistently give good estimates. Yet the skill does not seem readily transferable, and sadly, many people do give very poor estimates.

Careful investigation, however, has surprisingly shown that it isn't the estimate that has been so wrong. The problem often stems from the fact that the bulk of the effort required to complete the job is simply overlooked during the estimating process. In other words, it's what is left *out* of the estimate that usually gets the estimators into trouble. Thus, the first challenge lies in finding an estimating method to ensure that everything that needs to be included in the estimate is recognized. As a group, though, the software engineering community has been unable to agree upon one commonly accepted estimating technique. Because this discipline is still so new, no models have yet emerged as the standard.

ESTIMATING IN UNCERTAINTY

In software projects, unless they are repeating the exact same projects over and over, team members are, in truth, usually trying to estimate in uncertainty. In estimating in uncertainty, it may be possible to derive acceptable results by using just one estimate. But if there are unknowns that may influence the estimate, it is advisable to provide a range of estimates instead of one predictor. This is because it is preferable to compensate for the uncertainty or lack of knowledge. By providing estimates for: (1) the best case (optimistic), (2) the worst case (pessimistic), and (3) the most likely, we may come up with a statistical formula to compute the effort:

[(1 times the optimistic) + (4 times the most likely) + (1 times the pessimistic)] / 6

In analyzing these three estimates, it is expected that the pessimistic and optimistic would occur least often. The weighted average gives more importance to the estimate about which the estimator is most certain (the most likely). It assumes that the most likely will occur four times more often that either of the other two estimates. At the same time, it biases the results so that the expected effort will be skewed towards the side of greatest uncertainty (either the optimistic or the pessimistic). Thus, it also allows for some compensation due to that uncertainty.[3]

STATISTICS FOR PROJECT MANAGEMENT

The use of statistical theory can provide a foundation for: (1) providing estimates earlier in the project life cycle than many of the traditional lines of code and function point techniques, (2) overcoming the uncertainty experienced in estimating software projects in general, and (3) addressing the noncode-related aspects of project management. The science of probability allows managers to substitute numbers in place of their hunches or conjectures.

The Navy Special Projects Office, Lockheed Aircraft, and Booz-Allen and Hamilton employed statistical theory in estimating and managing the Polaris missile submarine project way back in 1958. Specifically, they applied the concept of uncertainty, the beta distribution, and a formula for expected effort. They called their process the Program Evaluation and Review Technique (PERT). This PERT estimating method was quickly adapted in many commercial sectors, such as the construction industry. Similarly, use of PERT estimating concepts for assessing lines of code was employed as early as 1976. Unfortunately, because of our tireless search for the silver estimating bullet, the concept was usurped by other lines of code formulas and such. To our chagrin, there is still no such thing as mindless estimating.

DISCUSSION QUESTIONS

❶ How is formal IT project management practiced in the organizations with which you are familiar? Consider the various roles and responsibilities and discuss how they are fulfilled.

❷ Think of a project with which you have been involved, and discuss the project's life cycle model: What activities were included? Which ones were not? How would a different project life cycle model have affected the project's completion?

❸ What challenges are the IT Project Managers in your organization facing in the near future? How are they, and the organization, preparing for the challenges?

NOTES

[1] Note, the use of terms pertaining to client server, multiple tiers, web-based, internet, intranet, and so on have intentionally been ignored—because the concepts remain the same regardless of platforms.

[2] There are efficiencies to be gained in both the project management process and in the development techniques. The introduction of new methodologies and/or technologies may, in the long term, improve productivity. However, in the short term, the associated learning curve may actually appear to reduce productivity and will certainly extend the dates. On the other hand, this learning curve may be offset by "buying the expertise"—either by reassigning in-house experts or by hiring outside consultants.

[3] Portions of this chapter have been excerpted from Lois Zells, *Managing Software Projects: Selecting and Using PC-Based Project Management Systems* (Wellesley, Mass.: QED Information Sciences, 1990). Used with permission of the publisher. © Lois Zells, 1991; all rights reserved.

CHAPTER 36

R&D Project Management: Adapting to Technological Risk and Uncertainty

▶LEE R. LAMBERT, PMP
LAMBERT CONSULTING GROUP, INC.

Achieving a sensible, beneficial, and cost-effective application of project management in the research and development environment can be as difficult and challenging as the technical problems the researcher is attempting to solve.

Senior management, with a focus clearly on the business aspects of the task at hand, looks to the project management process for assistance in "controlling" the research and, along with it, the cost and schedule associated with the project deliverables. Unfortunately, especially for these business-driven managers, the use of a project management process does not provide the panacea for the problems that historically rear their heads when dealing in the volatile environment of uncertainty and risk. Any work effort given the distinction of being classified as an R&D project is, by definition, riddled with uncertainty and all of the accompanying risks. This condition is a given. Otherwise, it wouldn't be called an R&D project.

In assessing the applicability of using the project management process and in determining the degree to which the process is implemented, the amount of uncertainty and risk associated with the specific project must be thoroughly understood. Project management can't be applied in the same way to all R&D projects. The greater the level or degree of uncertainty, the more carefully the utilization of project management techniques must be evaluated. Once this applicability assessment is complete, the project management tools and techniques selected must then be conscientiously implemented and

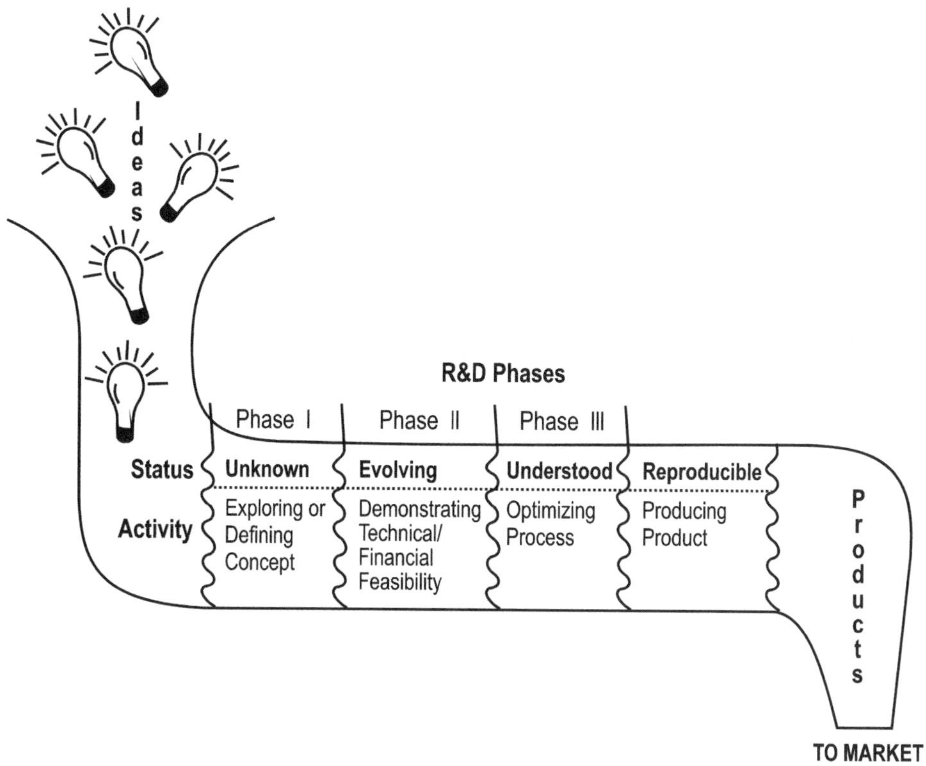

FIGURE 36-1. **PRODUCT DEVELOPMENT FLOW CYCLE**

monitored to assure that the maximum benefit-to-cost ratio derived from using project management is realized and maintained throughout the life of the project.

Selecting the most appropriate project management tools for R&D is no easy chore. It is clearly a misnomer to view R&D as a single component process. Realizing the maximum benefit of project management requires the user to recognize the subtle, but critical differences between the *R* and the *D*. The life cycle of an R&D project can realistically be divided into three distinct phases, two of which are research and one of which is of development. The Phase I research (R1) phase is exploring, or "basic." The Phase II research (R2) phase is feasibility, or "applications." Phase III development (D) can best be described as refinement, or "optimization."

As further clarification, when considering the many variations of R&D project management applications, the potential user must understand that there are considerable differences in the technical scope and management needs depending on the type of project being undertaken. There are two major types. Type 1 involves product-oriented R&D projects, which are conducted in support of the development of a new product or to facilitate the improved performance of an existing product. Type 2 involves information R&D projects, which are initiated to gather, manipulate, and analyze data; support conclusions; and eventually produce a formal report for publication as information for private organizations or government agencies.

Although the Type 2 example does clearly produce a product—a report—the output itself rarely passes beyond Phase I of the process. However, the contents of this R&D-generated report may well serve as a catalyst for additional R&D targeted at product development or product improvement.

Type 2 projects realize benefits from selective application of project management techniques. Caution must be exercised to avoid over-application. Any extensive or rigid use of project management techniques, beyond that which will be discussed for Type 1-Phase I activity, most likely will prove counterproductive and could actually impede Type 2 progress, rather than expedite it.

The consideration and selection of appropriate project management tools and techniques for application on Type 1 R&D projects and the associated phases are the primary focus of this chapter.

APPLICATION CONSIDERATIONS

The world of research and development is a stimulating and exciting place to spend a career. Brilliant minds produce a constant flow of bright ideas—ideas that promise products that improve the environment in which we live and at the same time generate huge profits for corporations. The flow of ideas seems to be endless. Unfortunately, only a few of the seemingly great ideas are able to survive the challenge of moving through the product development flow cycle. As depicted in Figure 36-1, idea input is relatively unrestricted: Any good idea is usually accepted into the cycle. The role of an R&D project is to bring realism to the process and to substantiate which ideas are truly feasible and will, in fact, have significant social and financial impact on the marketplace.

Because it is critical not to stifle creativity by limiting the number of ideas that are allowed to enter the process, it is imperative that the evolution of each idea is carefully managed to assure proper balance of resource utilization and timely decisions regarding the idea's advancement to the next phase of the project. Using the project management process improves a manager's chances of "turning off" the idea faucet at the appropriate time, therefore maintaining focus on those few ideas that present the highest return-on-investment (ROI) opportunities.

As the traditional life cycle of an R&D project progresses from an idea to an actual new or improved product, it passes through the three distinct phases cited earlier. The benefits realized from utilizing project management techniques increase rapidly as a function of, and in direct proportion to, the reduction of uncertainty. (See Figure 36-2.) It should be recognized that the project management process is founded on the concept of fundamental structure and discipline—two words that literally send chills up the spine of most research professionals. Experience shows that when the use of project management concepts is suggested to a researcher, likely responses are "Project management doesn't really apply. My project is unique," or "Project management is too constraining. It stifles creativity."

Those comments often are made with limited understanding and appreciation of the powerful potential benefits of properly used project management tools. But for those researchers spending the majority of their time investigating ideas in Phase I or even pre-Phase I, these or similar project management application disclaimers may have merit and should be properly considered. However, it has been demonstrated that even the most basic research effort, with its associated high levels of uncertainty, can realize important benefits from selective and common sense-based use of some of the

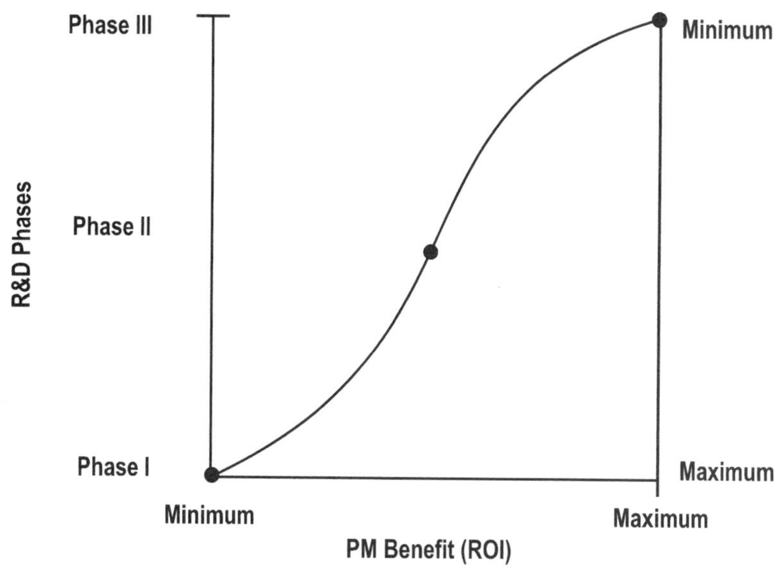

FIGURE 36-2. **BENEFITS OF UTILIZING PROJECT MANAGEMENT TECHNIQUES**

elementary project management tools and techniques—specifically, work breakdown structures (WBS, of vertical or hierarchical work scope relationships) developed to the third level and network logic flow diagrams (horizontal or work flow relationships) without critical path considerations, but with third-level WBS efforts' dependent work output-input relationships established.

Phase II and Phase III both realize substantial returns from the use of a project management approach. Clearly, Phase III (development) stands to realize the highest returns as the level of uncertainty typically reaches its lowest point in this later phase. Applications in Phase III have proved that the effort devoted to developing project structure and using management discipline begins to pay big dividends.

The type and sophistication of the application of project management on any R&D project is often dictated by the project organization structure (POS) being employed by the organization undertaking the project. Many POS variations exist, but two specific approaches seem to be most popular and suitable for the R&D environment. The first approach is the multi-disciplinary/functional project team with a strong marketing representative serving as project manager. This approach can be defined as market-driven or product-focused.

The second organizational approach frequently used is again a multi-disciplinary/functional team, but with the most critical or challenging technical area representative filling the role of project manager. This approach is best described as functionally driven or technology-focused.

Both of these organizational options have proven effective, although recent experience has shown that the balance has begun to shift to the market-driven approach. Because the basic content of the project substructure is the same for both approaches—that is, the same technical areas of R&D are involved and the technical contributors face the same challenges—the responsibility for achieving a smoothly operating and productive project team falls squarely on the shoulders of the assigned project manager.

In either configuration, the project manager must possess excellent communications, negotiation, and influencing skills. In most cases the project is conducted under the restrictions that come with operating in a matrix environment. The project and its contributors often fall victim to the dreaded "two-boss" syndrome, where perceived or actual higher priority technical challenges or "pet" projects threaten to impact the original project's resource commitments. History indicates that most technical researchers assigned to support a specific project continue to respond to their "home" functional organization manager's request for contribution. Oftentimes, this "back home" support is provided at the expense of the project to which the researcher is assigned. Project managers must be aware of this condition and take steps to minimize its impact on the project. These steps include holding regularly scheduled meetings with the team member's functional boss to discuss performance and contribution, as well as perceived personal and professional development needs; obtaining agreement for formal input into the assigned professional's performance review and suggested salary adjustment; and obtaining agreement to discuss any planned or actual change in commitment level as early as possible.

A third project organizational configuration—although used much less frequently on R&D projects because of the significantly higher cost associated with this approach—is that of a stand-alone, dedicated, multi-disciplined project team or, as it is often called, task force. In this case the theories of product-and technology-driven projects become one. The project manager for this task force approach may be drawn from any part of the parent organization, with the selection criteria emphasis being on project management experience and/or hierarchical position. The project manager on a task force effort must have the organizational clout or reputation to facilitate productive cooperation from the various factions of the parent organization.

Regardless of the project organization employed, the types of project management tools or techniques selected, or the sophistication of the project management implementation, ultimately two factors hold the key to how big a contribution project management makes to the R&D project: (1) clarity and understanding of the project's goals and objectives, and (2) the commitment to and understanding of the project management process by people—the users of the process.

Perhaps more than any other type of project manager, those charged with the duty of managing R&D projects walk a precarious tightrope, constantly adjusting to maintain the delicate balance between technical, time, and cost considerations, in hopes of avoiding a potentially fatal fall. The importance of establishing well-defined technical objectives early in the R&D project can't be overemphasized. The number of failures resulting from poorly defined goals and objectives is second only to the number caused by inability to solve critical technical problems. The early objectives for the R&D project are oftentimes generated by the marketing organization and have a heavy "business" focus. It is imperative that before these early objectives (including performance criteria and physical characteristics) are finalized, the appropriated technical experts have ample input opportunity as well as an opportunity to thoroughly review and concur in these objectives before finalization. Agreement or buy-in by the technical staff that will be held responsible for delivering the final results must be gained very early in the process. Failure to obtain this buy-in results in a condition of catch-up from almost the first day of the R&D project.

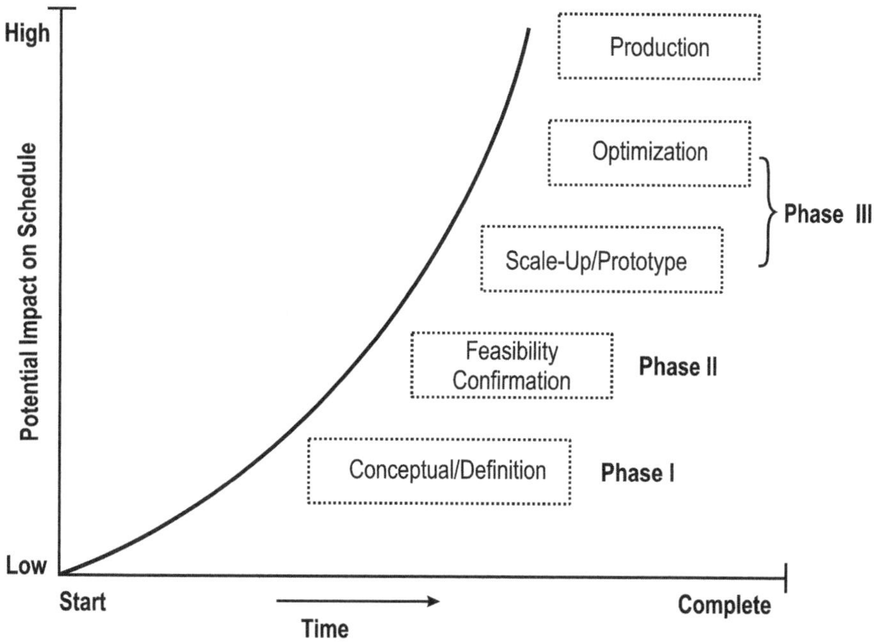

FIGURE 36-3. **ASSESSING THE IMPACT OF SCOPE CHANGES**

Everyone recognizes how important it is to freeze project scope. In R&D projects this is extremely difficult to accomplish. As research is undertaken and results analyzed, the scope of the project requires adjustment to accommodate the findings. Project management *does not* eliminate this condition. However, the project management process does allow the project manager to recognize the need for scope change and provides the ability to assess the potential impact of any potential scope change much sooner than would have previously been possible. In R&D projects, as illustrated in Figure 36-3, the sooner the better when it comes to modifying the project scope!

Once the project's objectives, target time, and cost constraints have been clearly defined and understood by the appropriate team members, the project management process should provide the mechanism or conduit for moving forward. As stated earlier, the role of project management in Phase I is limited. However, as the project enters the late stages of Phase I and prepares to move into Phase II, the project management process begins to play a more significant role.

The effort to assure that maximum benefit is realized from using the project management process on R&D projects focuses on six key areas.

1. *Refinement and expansion of the Phase I WBS.* All required work packages must be identified and the appropriate responsibility assigned. This expansion effort includes a clearly defined scope of work for each detailed WBS element (approximately five to seven levels) and the time and resources required to complete the scope of work assigned at those lowest WBS levels.

2. *Refinement and expansion of the Phase I integrated work flow diagram.* The detailed work packages identified in the expanded WBS must be incorporated, and there must be development and incorporation of time estimates for each working level WBS element. This supports the development of an integrated critical path schedule for the project. Where possible, the work package flow should be optimized through the use of overlap or lead/lag dependent relationships, but on R&D projects, utilization of the overlap or lead/lag scheduling technique should be very carefully applied. While the approach can result in notable projected timesavings, it often significantly increases the risk associated with starting one work package before another work package is completely finished. In R&D projects the uncertainty factor can have a major impact on the actual value or contribution of this technique.

3. *Identification of all organization/technology interface dependencies where any form of output-input relationship exists.* Any critical decision points that may have significant impact on the smooth flow of work on the project must also be isolated. The integrated network diagram is the most effective project management tool for accomplishing this important activity. These interface points and key decisions must be closely managed throughout the life of the R&D project. The result of technical breakthroughs, technical problems, and the accompanying actions taken should be analyzed in regard to these interface and decision points.

4. *Development of fallback or contingency plans and approaches in those areas where the initial planning process indicates that a high level of uncertainty exists or a great deal of technical risk is obvious.* These contingency plans should be developed *now*—not when the problem actually presents itself. Too often in R&D projects there is no attention given to anticipating problems and making allowances for dealing with the little problems early so they don't become big problems later. This contingency planning method may actually result in some redundancy in the project. Parallel research efforts should be considered when the project can't afford the loss of time associated with investigating research options in a linear mode. If two or more promising solutions to the same technical problem exist and none clearly has a better chance of success, simultaneous research may be warranted with the potential outcomes of each option carefully considered in the planning and analysis of the total R&D project.

5. *Establishment of a comprehensive material and equipment needs list in the first few weeks of the project.* The ordering and obtaining of special materials are two of the most important activities supporting a successful R&D project. Wherever possible, obtain backup materials with similar technical characteristics. To the extent financial resources allow, procure spare material and equipment as reserve in the event some material is out of specification, equipment failure occurs, or the need to repeat research investigations is required. The lead times for achieving this material and equipment procurement must be factored into the planning process. Overlooking or ignoring the potential impact of not having the required material or equipment are common shortcomings of R&D project managers and have resulted in numerous project failures.

6. *Preparation of a schedule for the various technical reviews that are necessary during the life of the project, once the WBS has been expanded and the logic network diagram has been completed, including the identification of a critical path.* In addition to the normal technical reviews that occur on an R&D project, internal and occasional external or

third-party peer reviews should be incorporated into the plan. The pride of ownership or closeness to the research being conducted often results in tunnel vision on the part of the researcher. These independent reviews and the comments that result serve as a sanity check for those deeply involved in the research process. Effective use of this peer review approach facilitates the early warning mechanism that is so critical to achieving quality R&D output within the most reasonable time and cost considerations.

The world of business is understandably cost-driven. However, in R&D the overemphasis on planning and managing costs can lead to less-than-quality R&D output. Granted, the reality of organizations precludes what was once known as the blank check mentality, where research essentially said, "Tell me what you want and when I'm done, I'll tell what you get." Money was not a major factor. Those days are gone forever. But R&D project managers (and business managers) must remember that you can't control innovation and creativity. You can put some boundaries around R&D, but you can't—with any confidence or semblance of reality—provide precise estimates of time, resource, and budget needs.

With this fact in mind, the R&D project manager should consider range estimating whenever possible. This technique suits the R&D environment very well. This range estimating approach is effectively used for planning project cost or time requirements. The normal range estimates depend on the specific Phase of the project. Typical ranges are +75% and –25%; +25% and –10%; and +10% and –5%. The range selected is dependent on the state of the "unknowns." As the degree of uncertainty or technical difficulty increases, the range expands to account for these unknowns.

Business managers within organizations performing R&D projects should recognize the value of allowing this range-estimating approach. Essentially, range estimating provides an opportunity to incorporate reserve into the R&D project plan. If this reserve consideration is not addressed and clearly stated, experienced R&D project managers simply bury it in the estimates that are provided for business management use—a practice colloquially known as "padding." This lack of visibility prevents realistic management of the range and results in less than effective utilization of money and time. Additionally, the ability to recognize problems and take early corrective action is seriously compromised.

TECHNOLOGY-BASED EARNED VALUE

The concept of Earned Value (EV) has become extremely popular in the project management environment. The EV approach comes from the Earned Value Management System and is typically applied to large, well-defined projects, where management can use "dollars" as the common denominator for planning, statusing, analyzing, and forecasting the work packages required to accomplish project objectives.

Projects with substantial R&D content have often found the use of the traditional dollar- or cost-based EV techniques too cumbersome, too restrictive, and considerably less than effective. Despite the relatively bad experience with EV on R&D projects, there is a modified EV approach that has demonstrated the capability to provide realistic, accurate, and timely technology-based information for R&D project managers and task managers without relying on dollars as a data element.

The technology-driven EV approach relies on developing and combining three independent "point value" data elements to generate the project's technical performance measurement baseline (PMB), as outlined in Table 36-1. The three critical components of the R&D EV methodology are: (1) the position of each task on the project's integrated critical

FI. Position on the Critical Path Schedule	
On critical path	30 points
10 days or less off critical path	25 points
11–49 days off critical path	15 points
50 or more days off critical path	10 points
FII. Technical Difficulty	
Phase I: Exploring	The high level of uncertainty associated with Phase I research severely limits the benefit of using an EV approach here.
Phase II: Applications	3–5 points
Phase III: Optimization	2–4 points
Production (if included)	1–3 points
FIII. Project Risk	
All project work packages	0–5 points

TABLE 36-1. **THE TECHNOLOGY-DRIVEN EARNED VALUE APPROACH**

path network schedule; (2) the technical difficulty of each research work package, as assessed by the individual responsible for achieving the specific technical objectives; and (3) the work packages' relative risk to the successful and timely completion of the project, as assessed by the managers of the respective technical expertise areas involved.

The assignment of total EV point values for each task is determined based on the following factors:

To determine any work packages' EV point value, the formula is very simple: FI(FII + FIII) = EV points. Using this formula, the maximum value for any single work package is 300 EV points, and the minimum for any single work package is 10 EV points.

When the proper values have been determined for each work package, the point values are assigned to the calendar month in which the work package is scheduled to be completed. It should be noted that since EV is awarded only when work packages are completed, the shorter the individual work package duration, the less distortion of the plan-to-actual comparison database. Subjectively determined EV "progress points" can be awarded as work proceeds, but before actual completion. Although possible, this approach is not highly recommended unless the use of intermediate progress measurement milestones (objective indicators) is incorporated into the plan. Once all work package point values have been properly assigned to a planned completion month, a project PMB curve (similar to a cost plan curve) is generated as shown in Figure 36-4.

As technical work packages are completed, point values are earned. The total EV for the individual or current month, or the total for the cumulative-to-date period, can be determined and then compared to the expected achievement point value represented by the PMB.

These EV plan-to-actual comparisons can be generated and analyses conducted for the project total or any subdivision of the total R&D project, i.e., by individual work package, by technology or functional group, by product component, or even by individual responsible research investigator.

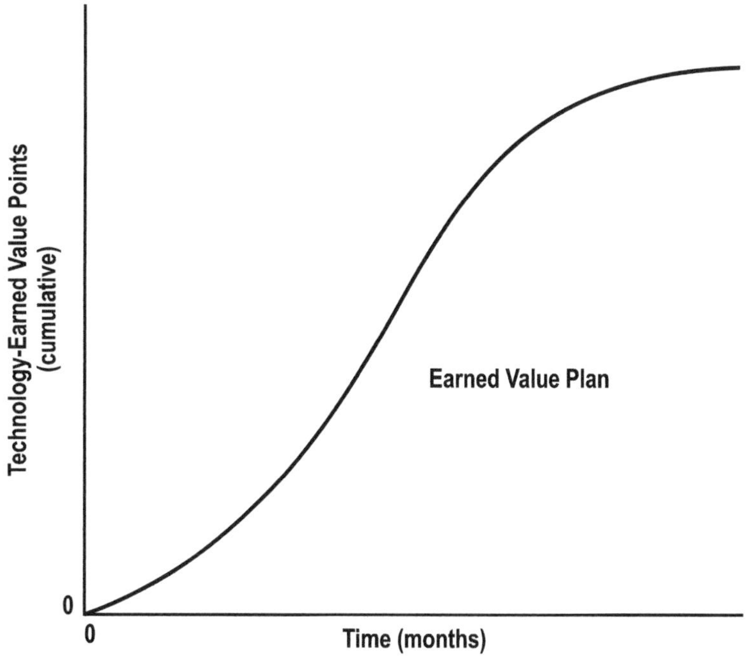

FIGURE 36-4. **PERFORMANCE MEASUREMENT BASELINE**

This unique application of EV to R&D projects provides management information that is, by its very derivation, clearly consistent with planned technical work, and that work that has been accomplished. Obviously, the EV integration of planned effort and actual accomplishment relies heavily on input from the project research professional. The R&D project manager serves as the catalyst for the development of the EV data and as a coordinator and/or integrator of the EV data at the various project summary levels. To realize the full range of benefits from this EV approach, it is imperative that the WBS is properly structured and carefully numbered to facilitate the many different "information sorts" requested for management use.

Two years of experimental use of this technology-based earned value concept was conducted on a sophisticated R&D new product introduction project. This trial application During the two years of use, the EV data generated was extremely accurate in illustrating the true status of the project and reflecting the impact of problems and facilitated corrective action being taken.

DISCUSSION QUESTIONS

❶ What challenges would need to be overcome in order to implement an Earned Value approach in the R&D environment?

❷ How would you create an R&D Performance Measurement Baseline that would provide realistic and meaningful status information during the product execution stage?

❸ During the planning stage, what would constitute a meaningful milestone completion criteria for determining realistic status on R&D project work packages?

CHAPTER 37

Applying Project Management Tools and Techniques in the Ecosystem Restoration Industry

▶STAN VERAART, PMP,
ENVIRONMENTAL CONSULTANT

▶DONALD ROSS, EARTHBALANCE

The ecosystem restoration industry is a rapidly emerging industry that is firmly rooted in science. Increasing threats to and destruction of our ecosystems make us realize that restoring the building blocks of our biological life support systems—our planet's ecosystems—is becoming a necessity. This industry therefore is of importance now and in the future.

Implementing ecosystem restoration projects can be a challenge. The management methodology currently applied in this industry is Adaptive Management, which is explained below. Project implementation has to proceed concurrently with finding the path that will lead you to the desired results. Before we take a look at applying project management tools and techniques in the ecosystem restoration industry, let's have a quick look at what this industry does.

THE NATURE OF THE ECOSYSTEM RESTORATION INDUSTRY

An ecosystem is the complex community of organisms and their environment functioning as an ecological unit. Restoration is defined as the return of an ecosystem to a close approximation of its condition prior to disturbance. In restoration, ecological damage to the resource is repaired. Both the structure and the functions of the ecosystem are recreated. The goal is to

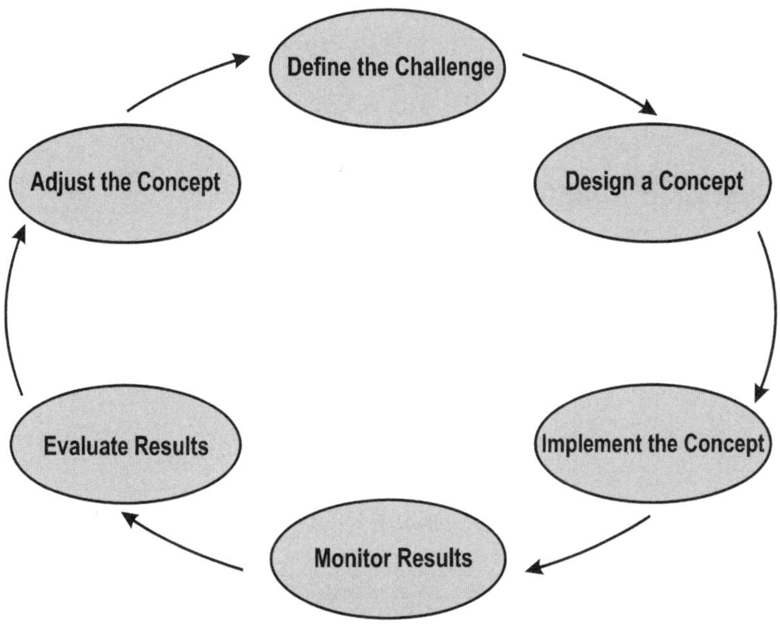

FIGURE 37-1. **STANDARD ADAPTIVE MANAGEMENT LIFE CYCLE**

emulate a natural, functioning, self-regulating system that is integrated with the ecological landscape in which it occurs.

While the world's economic systems have enjoyed unprecedented expansion, ecological systems have been degraded and diminished. We live in a critical time in human history. The air, land, water, and wildlife resources of the planet are being decimated with astonishing speed. The science of restoration ecology is young and rapidly evolving. Looking ahead toward the future, we need to develop, test, and refine the science and technology of restoration ecology further, so it is capable of meeting the challenge of global repair tomorrow. Ecosystem restoration is a growing industry because the relationship between human society and natural systems are in balance between economic growth and maintaining or integrating healthy ecosystems. Humanity must find long-term solutions to losses of biodiversity, and solutions that will support the highest levels of human fulfillment with the minimal stress on natural ecosystems. How can this be done?

SIX STEPS: THE ADAPTIVE MANAGEMENT LIFE CYCLE

Ecosystems are complex and dynamic. As a result, our understanding of them and our ability to predict how they will respond to management actions is limited. Ecosystem restoration projects are currently being implemented by making use of a formalized management process called Adaptive Management, which can be defined as an iterative approach in which the methods of achieving the desired objectives are unknown or uncertain—learning while doing, so to speak. Adaptive management was developed in the 1970s by C.S. Holling and co-workers at the University of British Columbia and by the International Institute for Applied Systems Analysis. Since we are literally dealing with a "living base line" of a project (the ecosystem) and are facing the challenges of constant changing factors

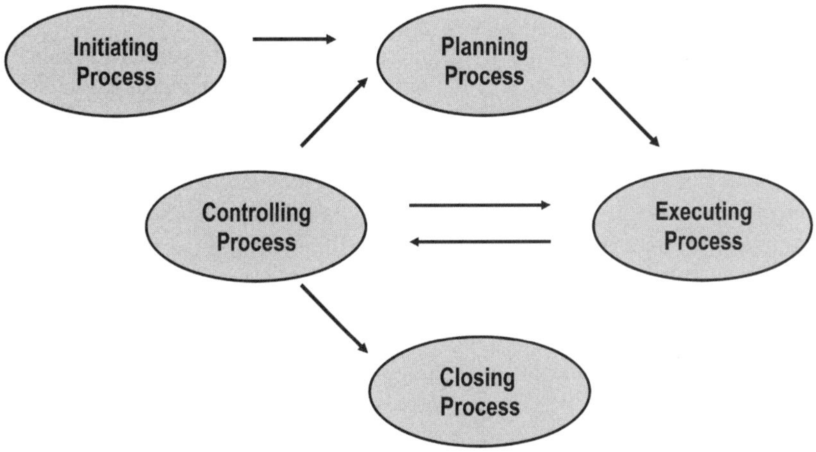

FIGURE 37-2. **STANDARD PROJECT MANAGEMENT LIFE CYCLE**

and changing understanding of the processes that take place in an ecosystem, this alternative technique is used in an attempt to increase overall project success. The typical Adaptive Management life cycle shown in Figure 37-1 illustrates the six steps of the process:

▶Step 1—**Define the Challenge:** Acknowledgement of uncertainty about what policy or practice is best for the particular management issue.

▶Step 2—**Design a Concept:** Thoughtful selection of the policies or practices to be applied (the assessment and design stage of the cycle).

▶Step 3—**Implement the Concept:** Careful implementation of a plan of action designed to reveal the critical knowledge that is currently lacking.

▶Step 4—**Monitor Results:** Monitoring of key response indicators.

▶Step 5—**Evaluate Results:** Analysis of the management outcomes in consideration of the original objectives.

▶Step 6—**Adjust the Concept:** Incorporation of the results into future decisions.[1]

This lifecycle formed by these six steps is intended to encourage a thoughtful, disciplined approach to management, without constraining the creativity that is vital to dealing effectively with uncertainty and change. How the steps are applied depends on the complexity of the problem and on the imagination of participants.

This iterative process appears to be very similar to the project management life cycle (Figure 37-2). However, the project management life cycle provides a consistent structured roadmap of how to reach the desired project results, whereas Adaptive Management provides a framework to *discover* what the best road to take is in reaching the desired project results. In project management we strive to meet or exceed our clients' expectations by trying to describe those expectations to the finest detail as early on in the project as possible. This allows us to create the scope statement, the work breakdown structure, the network diagram, critical path calculations, and the risk response plan, to name just a few. In ecosystem restoration, the final objectives and expectations are known and clear from the beginning—it is the path to get there that is unknown and uncertain. This path has to be discovered by making use of the Adaptive Management approach.

The ecosystem restoration industry is among one of the last industries converting to the project management language. It is necessary that the ecosystem restoration industry be involved in new projects that deal with finding a balance between economic growth and keeping or restoring our ecosystems as early on in the project process as possible. Using the tools and techniques offered by the Project Management Institute is of critical importance, enabling this industry to communicate clearly and precisely across other industries.

Fortunately the iterative process of the project life cycle offers enough flexibility to apply the tools and techniques in this industry without too many adjustments. Project management is based on the principle of implementing controlled change. The life cycle is constructed in such a way that if deviation of the projects baseline occurs, action (re-planning followed by implementation) can be taken. After each projects phase, a "phase exit" or "stage gate" provides the opportunity to re-assess the projects' health. It is during these phase exits that a project manager in cooperation with the senior manager and/or client can decide to kill (end) a project for various reasons. Some common reasons are that the deviation of the baseline is too high, that the product of the project changed, or that the original project expectations changed and are not in alignment with the project scope any longer. In the ecosystem restoration industry, it is not very often that the project objectives change; however, the path to reach the project objectives often changes. Remember that the goal of ecosystem restoration is to emulate a natural, functioning, self-regulating system that is integrated with the ecological landscape in which it occurs. If the road of how to reach this goal changes, it carries large consequences for the project setup. In order to compensate for this industry-specific characteristic, an easy adjustment to the project life cycle can be made during the controlling process. By adding a Scope Discovery Process in the controlling process of the project life cycle, extra attention is given to not only the project's own baseline by studying the project status reports, but also to the results of the Adaptive Management process—the re-evaluation of the living baseline of the ecosystem so to speak.

It is important that during the Scope Discovery Process the project managers, the client, and possibly other stakeholders investigate both baselines. The Scope Discovery Process can either be done through a meeting or through clearly written status reports. Specific attention should be given to the living baseline. Information about this baseline can be found in the Adaptive Management process. It is especially important that the living baseline investigation is done while being in the evaluation stage of the Adaptive Management cycle. In case the road that has to be traveled in order to reach the project objectives needs to be changed, the project has to be re-planned as indicated in the project life cycle. After re-planning your project, implementing the plan, and controlling your project according to your new project baseline, it again is time for implementing the Scope Discovery Process. In this way, you allow controlled scope drift, letting your project grow and evolve, which is a necessary process in order to find the best possible solution for ecosystem restoration while staying on good communication and management terms with other industries.

By adding this extra iterative step to the project management life cycle, it is possible to apply the project management tools and techniques to the ecosystem restoration industry. Fortunately, there are currently ecosystem restoration companies applying project management to their field of expertise, raising the industry management standards by developing a more professional and more widely recognized level of management.

An additional benefit is that the project management profession is very keen on documenting lessons learned from implemented projects. By letting our latest scientific discoveries and new technologies assist us in ecosystem restoration and documenting the lessons we learn from this process, it will be possible to find the lowest possible price for the maximum amount of desired results.

If we adapt ourselves to the extra step in taking two different baselines in consideration by implementing the Scope Discovery Process during the controlling process in the project life cycle, we can create a working symbiosis between Adaptive Management, used extensively in the ecosystem restoration field, and project management—a technique new to this industry but promising great potential. It is this symbiotic process that allows implementation of the ecosystem restoration projects, carrying, expending, and changing scope due to the living baseline, while maintaining control over the management process. This reduces the risk and improves cross-industry communications by standardizing on project management tools, techniques, and methodologies.

CASE STUDY: MITIGATING THE ENVIRONMENTAL IMPACTS OF RESERVOIR EXPANSION

The Boran Ranch Mitigation Bank in DeSoto County, Florida, provides proven, advance wetland mitigation for public and private projects within the Peace River basin. In general, mitigation banks are awarded "credits" as they reach milestones of improvement to wetlands they permanently protect, and these credits are later transferred to other projects as compensation for wetland losses. At Boran Ranch, land managers earn mitigation credits by restoring natural hydrology to wetlands that have been historically drained for cattle pasturing, and by establishing natural plant communities to replace the non-native pasture grasses.

This case study involves a 40-acre wetland at the Boran Ranch Mitigation Bank, informally called "the bowl" because of its obvious concavity on an otherwise flat landscape. The wetland had been drained in the 1950's and planted in pasture grasses, the most dominant of which was *Hemarthria altissima.* By studying persistent natural indicators of historic seasonal flooding, land managers had established the height and shape of the water control structure needed to reverse the drainage effects of the ditching. Before installing the structure, however, they faced decisions about the nature and intensity of measures they would take to eradicate *Hemarthria* and the other exotic pasture grasses.

Research on *Hemarthria* revealed that it was intolerant of prolonged inundation and favorably competed with other plants in a nutrient-rich environment. Since installation of the water control structures and cessation of cattle grazing would cause prolonged inundation and a gradual depletion of nutrients, land managers had to decide whether these measures alone would eradicate *Hemarthria,* or would they need to eradicate the pasture grasses before installing the water control structure. Effective, safe herbicides (such as Glyphosate) were available, but various costs were an issue. Aside from the inherent cost of herbicide application, land managers faced a regulatory requirement that success milestones (and credit release) could only be achieved after a year without herbicide treatment. Since wetland mitigation banks have highly negative cash flows in their permit approval and establishment years, land managers were reluctant to extend the establishment period by another year as a price for using herbicide. They decided to "drown" the *Hemarthria* and installed the water control structure without first eradicating the pasture grasses with herbicide.

Fortunately, other situations on the project received a slightly different management prescription where either the duration of flooding was not as great as it was in the "the bowl" or the delay of the success milestones was not as critical. Glyphosate was successfully used to eradicate *Hemarthria* and condition the site for establishment of native vegetation. This success provided the information and experience needed to adapt the management plan for "the bowl."

As with many outcomes in ecosystem restoration, "the bowl" was both a huge success and a disappointment. Hydrology is the dominant factor in any wetland, and restoring a more natural period of inundation had immediate and profound beneficial effects on "the bowl." Wetland plants sprung up from the soil seed bank in response to the "just add water" prescription, but *Hemarthria* proved to be a tenacious survivor. With its roots established in the old pasture soils, it responded to inundation by sending a stem up through the water column and sprouting leaves on the water's surface. While it was less persistent in the deeper areas of "the bowl," it was prevalent for three years in the shallow perimeter, which was the greater land area. As its persistence became the major obstacle to reaching the success milestone, land managers decided to revisit the decision not to use herbicide.

Armed with specific experience about the use of Glyphosate to eradicate *Hemarthria* and condition other sites for native vegetation, land managers were prepared to change course. Their previous experience with Glyphosate provided a basis for discussions with the regulatory authorities, who not only approved of its use, but waived the one-year waiting period. The problem then became how to effectively apply the herbicide in an area with prolonged inundation.

Sometimes the vagaries of nature work in favor of the land manager. In this case, the entire state of Florida was in the second of two back-to-back years of drought, and water tables were at historic lows. Land managers waited until late in the normal annual dry cycle and were able to apply the herbicide to the shallow perimeter areas using standard land application equipment. Glyphosate is a systemic herbicide that kills roots as well as the aboveground portion of the plant. It does not, however, affect seed. Following the Glyphosate treatment, the dead material was burned to complete the eradication of any plant material that may have eluded herbicide application in the heavy biomass. With the resumption of wet season rains later in the year, native wetland plants sprouted from the soil seed bank, but *Hemarthria* was absent.

The replanning of the project based on new scientific information represents an example of using adaptive management, while still applying project management tools to issues of communications, procurement, and integration.

DISCUSSION QUESTIONS

❶ How would you go about handling and simplifying the complexity of this project, while being able to stay in control of the desired outcome?

❷ Did land managers fully appreciate the risk of not eradicating *Hemarthria* before they flooded "the bowl"?

❸ For a project with which you are familiar, how might the Scope Discovery step be of benefit?

REFERENCES

[1] Halbert, C.L. 1993. *How Adaptive is Adaptive Management? Implementing Adaptive Management in Washington State and British Columbia.* Reviews in *Fisheries Science* 1:261-283. See also the explanation of the Adaptive Management model archived on the British Columbia Ministry of Forests and Range website at http://www.for.gov.bc.ca/hfp/amhome/Amdefs.htm (accessed November 2004).

ABOUT THE CONTRIBUTORS

▶**Muhamed Abdomerovic, Dipl. Eng., PMP,** is a Civil Engineer specializing in project management. He has over thirty years of experience in the application of project management system knowledge to projects in the information technology, construction, process industry, and energy sectors. Currently Master Scheduler in FKI Logistex's Integration Division, he was previously a Program Manager with Luckett & Farley. Prior to this, he worked with Energoinvest and had various responsibilities related to project management. He has conducted consultations and courses for executives, managers, and project management professionals. An active participant in the development of the project management profession, Mr. Abdomerovic has published more than thirty professional journal articles on project scope, time, and cost management, along with articles in six proceedings of Project Management World Congresses and two books. He is a member of the International Project Management Association, the Project Management Institute, and several of PMI's specific interest groups. Mr. Abdomerovic graduated from the University of Sarajevo with the Diploma of Civil Engineer, and is certified as a Project Management Professional.

▶**Theodore R. Boccuzzi, PMP,** has over 20 years of capital, manufacturing, and product development project experience serving as Program Manager, Project Manager, Engineering Manager, Construction Manager, and Mechanical Design Leader supporting worldwide programs. He is the holder of three patents for work associated with web conveyance. Mr. Bocuzzi provides consulting on all phases of project management to businesses in the U.S. Specializing in areas such as project planning, project change control, earned value analysis, risk management, project management best practices, establishment of project management offices, and facilitate value engineering sessions. He has helped organizations implement project management methodologies and best practices that meet their specific organizational needs. Mr. Bocuzzi is a graduate of the Rochester Institute of Technology and a member of the

Project Management Institute, serving as President of the Rochester Chapter (2002-2003) and a contributor to *A Guide to the Project Management Body of Knowledge, Third Edition,* and *The PMBOK® Guide, Third Edition: An Overview of the Changes.*

▶**Manuel Benitez Codas** is a consultant in project management and strategic planning with M.M. Benitez Codas in Brazil. Prior to staring his own consulting company in 1990, he worked for more than twenty years in large Brazilian and Paraguayan engineering organizations, involved with large hydroelectric and mass transport projects. Mr. Codas also developed intensive training activities related to project management for several companies in Brazil. He has published articles in the *International Journal of Project Management* and *RAE-Business Administration Magazine.* Mr. Codas is the founder and former president of the Sao Paulo Project Management Association and a member of the Project Management Institute and the Association of Project Managers.

▶**J. Kent Crawford, PMP,** is founder and Chief Executive Officer of Project Management Solutions, Inc., a management consulting, training, and research firm headquartered in Havertown, Pa. For more than 20 years, Mr. Crawford has been responsible for the development and implementation of project management improvement initiatives for top companies, including AstraZeneca, FedEx, General Motors, Monsanto, NCR, Procter & Gamble, SAP, and The New York Times Company. Prior to establishing PM Solutions, Mr. Crawford served as a President and Chairman of the Project Management Institute during a period of innovation that saw 40 percent membership growth for the Institute. Mr. Crawford is the 2003 recipient of the PMI Fellow Award and the award-winning author of *The Strategic Project Office: A Guide to Improving Organizational Performance* (for which he won the 2002 David I. Cleland Project Management Literature Award from PMI), and of *Project Management Maturity Model: Providing a Proven Path to Project Management Excellence.* Mr. Crawford's latest book is *Optimizing Human Capital with a Strategic Project Office,* with Jeannette Cabanis-Brewin (Auerbach, 2005).

▶**Connie Delisle, Ph.D.,** is a Principal Consultant with the Environmental Management and Sustainable Development Practice of Consulting and Audit Canada (CAC), where she manages complex projects and programs in the areas of environment, sustainable development, executive education, knowledge management, and project evaluation. Prior to joining CAC, Dr. Delisle studied Kinesiology at the University of Victoria while working for the regional government (Victoria, BC) in the mid 1980s. She completed a second Bachelor degree at University of Victoria with a double major in psychology and environmental studies. She then brought her education and experience to bear in several positions within Calgary`s energy sector in the early-mid 1990s, while concurrently pursuing a Masters of Science in Environmental Management. Connie's approach was to bridge the gap between community and companies by building knowledge capacity within organizations.

▶**Lowell D. Dye, PMP,** is President of TriCon Consulting, Inc., a project management training, mentoring and consulting firm. He has extensive experience in project management training, consulting, and implementation with commercial companies, public organizations, and government agencies. He has worked with large and small organizations in a variety of industries, including Information Technology, Utilities, Insurance, Pharmaceuticals and Health Care, and Manufacturing. He has also been on the adjunct faculty of several colleges and universities. He is the co-editor of *Project Portfolio Management: Selecting and Prioritizing Projects for Competitive Advantage* and *Managing Multiple Projects: Scheduling and Resource Allocation for Competitive Advantage.* An active member of the Project Management Institute (PMI) at the local and international levels since 1991, he has authored several project management articles and is a frequent speaker and presenter at PMI's annual Congress and Seminars World. Mr. Dye holds a B.S. from Excelsior College, an M.S. in Operations Management from the University of Arkansas, and is a PMI-certified Project Management Professional.

▶**Judith Edwards, Ph.D., PMP, IEEE, SM,** works in the Program Management Office (PMO) at Diebold, Inc in the self-services systems organization. Her current activities include process improvement initiatives involving SEI CMMI® and ISO 9000. She supports Supply Chain Management (SCM) automation efforts. Earlier responsibilities at Diebold involved leading the creation and training for her department process assets for ISO 9000 and updates for standard changes. In previous employments, she was Director of Software Engineering at Loral Defense Systems in Akron responsible for the initiative for engineering organization to reach SEI CMM level 2 and 3. This was attained within three years. Prior to that position, she held both software project and line management positions at General Dynamics in avionics, support software systems, integrity management, and special applied research projects. She represented the company in government-industry standardization efforts. She has taught both mathematics and computer science at the university level. Ms. Edwards has a BS in mathematics education, MA in mathematics, and Ph.D. in Computer Science. She has served as reviewer for *A Guide to the Project Management Body of Knowledge, Third Edition* and several IEEE computer standards efforts. Her professional memberships include the Project Management Institute, the Association for Computer Machinery, and IEEE.

▶**Ralph D. Ellis, Jr.,** is a professor of Construction Engineering and Engineering Management in the Department of Civil Engineering at the University of Florida. Dr. Ellis has had more than fifteen years of experience as a manager of his own company providing construction services on both domestic and overseas projects. Principal clients have included the US Army Corps of Engineers, the US Dept. of the navy, and the Panama Canal Commission. Dr. Ellis is a registered Professional Engineer and a member of the American Society of Civil Engineers, the American Society of Cost Engineers, the American Society for Engineering Education, and the Project Management Institute. He is also a member of the Construction Industry Research Council and serves on several national professional committees.

▶**Randall L. Englund** is an executive consultant, author, and speaker, who is a frequent contributor to PM Network magazine and project management seminars. For many years he was a senior project manager and a member of Hewlett-Packard's Project Management Initiative, a project office that led the continuous improvement of project management across the company. Together with cultural anthropologist Dr. Robert J. Graham, he co-authored *Creating an Environment for Successful Projects* and *Creating the Project Office: A Manager's Guide to Leading Organizational Change.* In his work and presentations, Randy uniquely blends metaphors, multimedia, examples, and insights to motivate others and attain desired results.

▶**Irving M. Fogel, P.E.,** is founder and president of Fogel & Associates Inc., a New York City-based consulting engineering and project management firm. Fogel & Associates has served as project management, scheduling, and claims consultant to builders, developers, contractors, engineers, architects, manufacturers, and government agencies. Mr. Fogel is a registered professional engineer in twenty states and the state of Israel. He has worked on projects worldwide.

▶**Robert J. Graham, Ph.D., PMP,** is an independent management consultant in the areas of project management and organizational change. Previously he was a senior staff member of The Management and Behavioral Sciences Center at The Wharton School, University of Pennsylvania. While at Wharton he taught in the MBA and Ph.D. programs and was also a part of the Wharton Effective Executive program teaching Project Management to practicing executives. Bob has held Visiting Professor positions at the University of Bath, in England, and the University of the German Armed Forces in Munich, Germany. He continues as Adjunct Professor at the University of Pennsylvania and as a part of the Project Management Unit at Henley Management College in Henley, England. His first book is entitled *Project Management as if People Mattered,* his second book, co-authored with Randall Englund, is *Creating an Environment for Successful Projects.* His third book, co-authored with Dennis Cohen, is *The Project Manager's MBA,* and his most recent book, co-authored with Randy Englund and Paul Dinsmore, is *Creating the Project Office.* Dr. Graham has a B.S. in Systems Analysis from Miami University, as well as an MBA and Ph.D. in Operations Research from the University of Cincinnati. He was also a Post-Doctoral Fellow at The Wharton School. In addition, he has an M.S. in Cultural Anthropology from the University of Pennsylvania. He has also earned the Project Management Professional certification from the Project Management Institute.

▶**Valis Houston, PMP,** is an IT Project Management Consultant with Acacia PM Consulting. He possesses a broad range of international experience in the software development arena (dotcom, telecomm, and defense sectors) with specific know-how in Project Management and Software Process Improvement. He received his BS in Computer Engineering Technology from Prairie View A&M University, his MS in Management Information Systems from Bowie State University, and his MS in Software Engineering from Southern Methodist University. He is certified as a Project Management Professional as well as a Certified Software Quality Engineer (CSQE). He currently sits on the Executive Board of the Dallas/Ft. Worth Chapter of the Software Engineering Institute's (SEI) Software Process Improvement Network (SPIN). He can be contacted at valis@acacia-software.com.

▶**Michael Howell, ASQC,** is a Manager with the BearingPoint Global Solutions Group. Prior to his current role, he served as Director of Six Sigma, Six Sigma Master Black Belt and Black Belt, and Quality Manager in several Sears, Roebuck, and Co. business units and functions. He has extensive experience in the design, implementation, and management of business process management, continuous improvement, TQM, ISO-9000, and six sigma initiatives within multiple industry settings. Prior to joining Sears, Mike spent seven years in the defense contract industry in a variety of technical and quality positions. His involvement in continuous improvement began in 1985 during his service in the US Army, and has been his full time focus since 1990. Mike established two quality programs while with Lockheed-Martin. He wrote the quality plans and served as a Quality

Engineer and as a Quality Program Manager at the Joint National Test Facility. He then moved on to the role of Senior Quality Specialist with the US Postal Service, responsible for implementing a Malcolm Baldrige framework and business process management within the Great Lakes Area. Mike has a Bachelor's Degree in Electrical Engineering, is a Member of the American Society for Quality, and is an ASQ Certified Quality Manager.

▶**David Hillson, Ph.D., PMP, FAPM, FIRM,** is an international risk management consultant and Director of Risk Doctor & Partners (www.risk-doctor.com). He is a popular conference speaker and award-winning author on risk. He is recognized internationally as a leading thinker and practitioner in the risk field, and has made several innovative contributions to improving risk management. He is well known for promoting the inclusion of proactive opportunity management within the risk process. Dr. Hillson has been active for many years in the Project Management Institute, and was a Founder Member of the PMI Risk SIG. In 2002 he was honored with the PMI Distinguished Contribution Award for his sustained contribution to advancing the field of risk management. Dr. Hillson was part of the core team responsible for updating the risk chapter of PMI's *A Guide to the Project Management Body of Knowledge, Third Edition.* He is a certified Project Management Professional, a Fellow of the UK Association for Project Management (APM), a Fellow of the UK Institute of Risk Management (IRM), and a member of the International Council On Systems Engineering (INCOSE) Risk Management Working Group. He can be contacted at david@risk-doctor.com.

▶**Kam Jugdev, Ph.D., PMP,** (kamj@athabascau.ca), Assistant Professor of Project Management and Strategy in the MBA program at Athabasca University in Alberta, has university teaching experience in online and traditional formats, and over twelve years of experience as a senior project manager in public and private sector organizations. She has led the development of many online courses relating to her research interests in project management and strategy. Dr. Jugdev's current areas of research include project management as a source of competitive advantage. Her research is funded by Athabasca University. Dr. Jugdev holds a Ph.D. in Project Management from the University of Calgary, a Master of Engineering in Project Management (Civil Engineering, Calgary), a Master of Health Services Administration (Alberta), and two undergraduate science degrees. She has published in *PM Network,* the *Project Management Journal,* and the *International Journal of Project Management,* where she has also served as a reviewer. As a member of the Project Management Institute, Academy of Management, Strategic Management Society, Administrative Sciences Association of Canada, and the Western Academy of Management, Dr. Jugdev actively contributes to the advancement of academic and professional communities of management practice across Canada and throughout the world.

▶**Gerald I. Kendall, PMP,** Principal, TOC International, is an expert in strategic planning and project management. As a management consultant, public speaker, and facilitator, he has served clients worldwide. Mr. Kendall began his career with IBM as a systems engineer. After becoming an I.T. director, he broadened his experience in strategic planning, marketing, sales, supply chain, and operations. He has worked with small and large multi-national firms, as well as government and not-for-profit organizations, to better manage large-scale organizational change issues. Recent clients include Telstra, British American Tobacco, Raytheon, Babcock & Wilcox, Alcan Aluminum, Covad Communications, Lockheed Martin, and many others. He is certified by the TOC International Certification Organization (www.tocico.org) in all six disciplines of Theory of Constraints, and is a graduate and silver medal winner of McGill University. He is a member of the Project Management Institute. Gerald is the author of *Viable Vision, Advanced Project Portfolio Management and the PMO,* and *Securing the Future: Strategies for Exponential Growth Using the Theory of Constraints.* He is also the author *of the chapter on Critical Chain in Dr. Harold Kerzner's book, Project Management, A System's Approach, Eighth edition.* You may email him at gerryikendall@cs.com.

▶**Joan Knutson,** principal of PM Guru Unlimited, enjoys an international reputation as a project management thought-leader. Her experience includes founding and managing for more than 25 years of Project Mentors, a successful, multi-million dollar project management training and consulting firm. In 1999 Joan led her company through a merger/acquisition by a prestigious training conglomerate, staying on for three more years as President. Ms. Knutson then established PM Guru Unlimited. She developed and teaches the Drug Information Association's (DIA) benchmark Project Management Training course as well as other project management related courses as a member of the Continuing Education Faculty at Villanova University. A long-time and active member of the Project Management Institute, Ms. Knutson is a former member of the PMI Board of Directors. She was a Contributing Editor to *PM Network* magazine for more than a decade, writing the Executive Notebook column. Some of her other project management activities include sitting on Project World's Advisory Council and on the Center for Business Practices' Knowledge Board. Joan writes the "Dear PM Guru" column for PMI's largest specific interest group, the Information Systems SIG. She is the author of several highly regarded books on project management; including *Succeeding in Project-Driven Organizations,* published by John Wiley & Sons.

▶**Lee R. Lambert, PMP,** principal of Lambert Consulting during a career that began in 1966, has held key executive level positions, developed enterprise project management processes, and managed multi-million dollar new product development projects. Since founding Lambert Consulting Group in 1984, his focus turned to education. He has shared his knowledge with over 25,000 students in twenty-one countries. Mr. Lambert has a Masters Certificate in Project Management from George Washington University. He is a Founder of the Project Management Institute's PMP Certification program and was named a Distinguished Contributor to the profession by PMI in 1995. Lambert is an accomplished author with three books and dozens of articles published, as well as a popular speaker for private organizations and professional associations.

▶**Antonio C. A. Maximiano** is professor of management theory at the University of Sao Paulo in Brazil. He is also a management development consultant and instructor. Maximiano has conducted several project management seminars for leading government agencies and multinational corporations in Brazil and Latin America. His professional interests include research and teaching in the areas of project management and management of technology.

▶**Thomas Mengel, Ph.D., PMP,** (Fredericton, NB, Canada) is an associate professor of leadership at Renaissance College, University of New Brunswick. He also works as management and leadership consultant in cross-cultural settings with various organizations. He has developed the model of Values-Oriented-Leadership and helped many leaders to implement business and project ethics processes, and to create a meaningful work and project environment. Previously to teaching at the University of New Brunswick, he also served as a faculty member of the following institutions: Athabasca University, Center for Innovative Management, MBA in Project Management Program; Trinity Western University, Master of Arts in Leadership Program; Royal Roads University, Executive MBA Program; University of Victoria, School of Public Administration; Selkirk College, Business Administration Program. In addition to his graduate studies and degrees in computer science, business administration, and adult education, Thomas has a Ph.D. in theology and an MA in history, which drive his research interest in the historical development and philosophical underpinnings of leadership and management practice. He is particularly interested in how learning from psychology, complexity theory, information technology, and human spirituality are likely to intersect to influence the development of managers and leaders. His current writing covers leadership education and values and ethics in leadership and project management.

▶**Alan Mendelssohn** is a Senior Manager of Organizational Performance at OfficeMax. He has extensive experience in the design, implementation, and management of process management, continuous improvement, and Six Sigma initiatives within diverse industry settings. Prior to joining OfficeMax, Alan spent 20 years in the electric utility industry in a variety of cost engineering, project management, and continuous improvement positions. His involvement in continuous improvement initiatives began in 1983 while at Florida Power and Light Company and has been his full time focus since 1991. He served as Director of Quality for Budget Rent a Car and as Director of Continuous Improvement with AAR CORP, responsible for all aspects of continuous process improvement in both organizations. More recently, he was a Master Black Belt and a Business Process Consultant at Sears, Roebuck, and Co. Alan has a Master's Degree in Nuclear Engineering, is a Senior Member of the American Society for Quality, and is an ASQ Certified Six Sigma Black Belt. He has authored a number of papers and articles on quality management and project management and has served a number of years as a member of the Board of Examiners for the Malcolm Baldrige National Quality Award.

▶**Peter W. G. Morris** is Professor of Construction and Project Management at University College, London, and Visiting Professor of Engineering Project Management at The University of Manchester. He is also Executive Director of INDECO Ltd., an international management consultancy. He is a past Chairman and Vice President of the UK Association for Project Management and past Deputy Chairman of the International Project Management Association. He has written over 100 papers on project management, as well as the books *The Anatomy of Major Projects* (Wiley, 1988), *The Management of Projects* (Thomas Telford, 1997), with Ashley Jamieson, *Translating Corporate Strategy into Project Strategy* (PMI, 2004) and, with Jeff Pinto, *The Wiley Guide to Managing Projects* (Wiley, 2004). He is a Fellow and Honorary Fellow of The Association of Project Management, a Fellow of the Institution of Civil Engineers, a Fellow of the Chartered Institute of Building, and a Fellow of the Royal Society of Arts.

▶**Francis S. "Frank" Patrick** is Director of Project and Process Management at DigitalGrit, Inc., an Internet services and technology development firm. Before joining DigitalGrit in 2004, from 1996, he was founder and principal consultant of Focused Performance, a management consultancy focusing on the application of the Theory of Constraints (TOC) to help organizations achieve more of their goals. Prior to Focused Performance, Mr. Patrick had over 25 years of industrial experience with Revlon, Johnson & Johnson, Nabisco, and AT&T/Bell Labs. It was at Bell Labs that he came across TOC and its potential for providing guidance on how to rationally manage organizations as whole systems, and for identifying and implementing necessary changes for significant bottom line improvements. Industries impacted by his guidance in strategic project management include telecommunications equipment, precision machining and manufacturing, semiconductor manufacturing, medical equipment, and financial services, and now, Web development. Mr. Patrick has also authored numerous papers and presented both nationally and locally on TOC topics for such professional associations as the Institute of Industrial Engineers, APICS, ASQ, and the Project Management Institute. More of his thoughts on organizational effectiveness can be found at www.focusedperformance.com.

▶**David L. Pells** is the president of iWorld Projects & Systems, Inc., a public business development company based in Dallas, Texas and focused on investments in the project management marketplace. With over 25 years experience in various project and executive positions, Mr. Pells has project management related experience in the construction, defense, energy, science, technology, and transportation industries. He has been responsible for developing program and project management plans for multi-billion dollar environmental, energy, and transportation programs funded by the US government. A former member of the PMI board of directors, Mr. Pells has been the president of several PMI chapters and chair of PMI's first specific interest group. He was awarded PMI's person-of-the-year award in 1998 and Fellow award in 1999.

▶**James S. Pennypacker** is Director of the Center for Business Practices, the research arm of Project Management Solutions, Inc. He has directed numerous research projects on a variety of project management issues, including the value of project management, project management maturity, project portfolio management, implementing project management systems, and project control functions. He is an editor of several books, including *Project Portfolio Management, Managing Multiple Projects,* and *Justifying the Value of Project Management.* He is facilitator of the Project Management Benchmarking Forum and regularly presents papers at professional conferences, including Project World, Project Leadership Conference, and Project Management Institute Global Congress. He formerly served the project management profession as the Project Management Institute's Publisher/Editor-in-Chief and Manager of the James R. Snyder Center for Project Management Knowledge and Wisdom.

▶**Renee Mepyans Robinson** teaches project management and leadership training at Nashville State Community College. She formerly taught the Boston University Project Management curriculum to major corporations in Tennessee. As a Consulting Project Manager in Informational Technology, Healthcare, Financial, Government, and Educational Industries, Ms. Robinson has been able to provide working solutions to requirements and successfully implemented planning processes throughout the life cycle of the project. She has also demonstrated leadership skills through her involvement with the local PMI Nashville Chapter as Founding President in 1996 and continues to serve on their Board of Directors in various capacities. On a regional level, she was the Southeast Region 14 Mentor for five years, assisted Chapter Presidents, and conducted regional meetings to increase knowledge on specific areas. She was selected by PMI Headquarters to deliver a presentation, "How PMI Regional Efforts Benefit Components" at a leadership meeting in Vancouver, Canada. She is a graduate of the PMI Leadership Institute and a Program Manager on the PMI Education Enrichment Program, which was created to expose elementary, middle, high school, and university age students to the concepts of project management as well as to actually teach them the processes and knowledge in a classroom setting.

▶**Donald Ross** is president and CEO of EarthBalance®. He has been at the forefront of environmental regulatory policy for more than two decades and understands the challenges of blending environmental protection into the economics of successful community development. With a commitment to environmental stewardship, Mr. Ross is a tireless advocate for the preservation and restoration of our natural environment, in conjunction with economic development. Mr. Ross holds an M.S. degree in Ecology and a B.S. degree in Forestry from the University of Tennessee. In April 2004, Mr. Ross was appointed by Governor Bush to the Environmental Regulation Commission for a three-year term. He has also served four years as a local elected official (Charlotte County Commission, 1990 -1994), was a member of the Southwest Florida Regional Planning Council and a member of the Charlotte Harbor National Estuary Program Policy Committee, was appointed to the Peace River Basin Board by Governor Bush, and has participated in the establishment of indicators and grant review for the Florida Coastal Management Program. He has been active on numerous statewide environmental policy advisory panels ranging in scope from technical to budgetary and has been appointed to numerous policy committees, including the Vegetation Index Review Committee, which developed the current wetland jurisdiction plant list. His private non-profit interests have led him to serve on the boards of 1000 Friends of Florida, Leadership Florida, the Myakka Conservancy, and the Council for Sustainable Florida, where he recently completed two years as president.

▶**Kim Rowe, P. Eng,** is Vice President of Engineering at Agile Systems in Waterloo, Canada. He brings over 25 years of experience in business management and systems engineering to the company and holds both an MBA and MEng. He has been instrumental in the startup of several companies and several business units in the computer systems and services areas. He has extensive international experience, having taken a broad set of software and hardware products to market in over 20 countries. Mr. Rowe's primary interests at present are the match of organization culture, processes, and systems (both business and software) to the organization's needs. Using the latest ideas from the collaboration technology area in conjunction with the latest business management ideas, he helps companies analyze, design, and implement business models, organizational culture, and underlying systems that make good organizations great. He also has a strong personal interest in real-time and embedded systems, software engineering, and signal processing. He has published approximately 30 papers and articles in various journals and magazines.

▶**Christopher Sauer** is Fellow in Information Management at Oxford University's Templeton College and Co-Director of the Oxford Advanced Management Programme. In his early career he designed, built, and managed IT systems projects. As an academic, he has worked in Australia and the UK. His research has focused on the challenges of IT projects. In addition to four books, his work has been published in the Project Management Journal, Sloan Management Review, IEEE Transactions of Software Engineering, and the European Management Journal, among others. His current research focuses on understanding the drivers of IT project performance and charting the changing role of IT project and program managers. He is an active member of the Major Projects Association, and is currently Joint-Editor-in-Chief of the Journal of Information Technology.

▶**Dennis M. Smith** is the founder and CEO of CompanySmith Inc. He has more than 30 years of project leadership experience in software, electrical, and mechanical technologies. He has served in many technical and leadership positions including project manager, marketing director, engineering vice president, and general manager at leading companies—large and small—including Honeywell Industrial Automation and Phoenix Controls. Mr. Smith is the creator of Team/Project Acculiticssm, a breakthrough data-driven process that uncovers hidden team practices to greatly improve the predictability of technical and non-technical projects. Team/Project Acculitics uses proprietary methods that determine a project's requirements for teamwork and compare them to measurements of actual project teamwork. With his focus on project leadership, predictability, and risk mitigation, Mr. Smith's insights have helped over a dozen project start-ups and turnarounds become successful. Active in TEC Associates and the Project Management Institute, Mr. Smith is the author of over 60 articles in the popular "Ideas for Project Leaders" series. In addition, he has published over 30 articles on project management and product development including his monthly column as a contributing editor to *People on Projects: Skills for the Superior Project Manager,* a publication of the Center for Business Practices.

▶**Alonso Mazini Soler** is a Senior Partner of the J2DA Consulting and Training Co., managing the Project and Quality Management practice. He is also professor for the MBA Program of the Institute of Administration Foundation. Alonso holds a doctoral degree in Production Engineering and an MBA in Corporate Finance, and is a regular and active member of the Project Management Institute in Brazil. For the last 15 years, Alonso has been working as a consulting and education business executive for Hewlett Packard and IBM Brazil, where he pioneered the deployment of the Six Sigma concepts. Alan M. Stretton is an Adjunct Professor of Project Management in the Faculty of Design, Architecture, and Building at the University of Technology, Sydney (UTS), Australia, where he designed and delivered a Master of Project Management program from 1988. Prior to joining UTS, Mr Stretton worked in the building and construction industries in Australia, New Zealand, and the USA for some 38 years, which included the project management of construction, R&D, introduction of information and control systems, internal management education programs, and organizational change projects. Mr. Stretton was Chairman of the Standards (*PMBOK®*) Committee of the Project Management Institute from late 1989 to early 1991. He held a similar position with the Australian Institute of Project Management and was a member of the Core Working Group in the development of the Australian National Competency Standards for Project Management. He has published over 60 professional articles.

▶**Geree Streun, PMP, CSQE,** is a Test Manager with Advanced Neuromodulation Systems, Inc. She received her Master's degree in Computer Science from Southern Methodist University and her Bachelor's in Computer Science from Kansas State University. She is a Senior Member of IEEE, a PMI-certified Project Management Professional, and an ASQ Certified Software Quality Engineer. She has a wide range of experience in both Process Improvement and Project Management to drive an organization to FDA compliance for companies developing medical devices and for medical process companies, such as Abbott Labs and Olympus. Ms. Streun was a Team Leader for developing two chapters for the *PMBOK® Guide, Third Edition.* Since 1996, she has written questions for future ASQ certification exams and has worked to validate future certification exams. She served as President of the Austin SPIN group for four years. She has presented papers at the Project Management Institute's Software Special Interest Group and at International Test Conferences. She has published several papers on transitioning an organization from structured techniques to Object Oriented (OO) Techniques, while evolving project management maturity within the organization. Additionally, she has been a Course Designer and Instructor for four years for the Project Management Certificate Program at the Software Quality Institute at the University of Texas in Austin.

▶**Janice Thomas, Ph.D.,** is an associate professor of project management and Program Director for the Executive MBA in Project Management at the Center for Innovative Management (CIM) at Athabasca University. She is also an adjunct professor in the University of Calgary joint Engineering and Management, Project Management Specialization, and a visiting professor with the University of Technology, Sydney, where she supervises Master and Ph.D. research students. Prior to becoming an academic, Dr. Thomas spent 10 years as a project manager in the fields of Information Technology and Organizational Change. Janice is now an active researcher presenting and publishing her research to academic and practitioner audiences around the world with research interests in organizational change, project management, teambuilding and leadership, complexity theory in relation to organizations and the professionalization of knowledge workers. Recent research projects have explored the following: the Path to Professionalization for Project Management; the Role of the Personality of the Project Manager in Project Management Competency; the Impact of Differing Sensemaking Approaches on Project Communication; the Nature of the Assumptions underlying Project Management Methodologies; the Relationship between Certification and Professional Attitudes; and How to Sell Project Management to Senior Executives. She is currently preparing to lead a major research initiative aimed at Defining and Measuring the Value Project Management Contributes to Organizations.

▶**Karen R.J. White, PMP,** is the Director for Consulting Services for PM Solutions, where her responsibilities include oversight of the company's consulting engagements and management of its consulting staff. She also serves as a "thought leader" in the company's software engineering process services. Before assuming this executive position, Karen provided consulting services to numerous Fortune 500 companies, with a focus on information systems project management. Prior to PM Solutions, Ms. White was a senior manager for a national systems integration firm, where she managed multi-million dollar systems engineering projects. An active member of the Project Management Institute, she currently chairs the Ethics Review Committee and serves on the Ethics Standards Development Committee. She previously served on PMI's Board of Directors and several member advisory groups, and co-chaired the PMI'96 Annual Seminar/Symposia. Ms. White is active in IEEE Computer Society's Technical Council on Software Engineering, where she was a member of the Executive Advisory Board. Ms. White has contributed to various bodies of knowledge and books, including *Project Management Maturity Model* (Marcel Dekker, 2001) and *Data Reverse Engineering* (Aiken, Peter; McGraw-Hill, 1996). A recipient of the US Army Commendation Medal for demonstrated leadership within the US Army Reserves, she holds an MS in Information Systems from Northeastern University's Graduate School of Engineering.

▶**Stan Veraart, PMP,** is an independent international consultant who assists in applying project management tools and techniques to various environmental companies. He provides project management training and certification, and assists in the establishment and maintenance of a Project Management Office tailored to the environmental industry. Mr. Veraart holds a M.S. degree in Project Management and a B.S. in International Agriculture. He has worked for the Dutch government, private companies, institutions, and, NGO's in nine countries on six continents, and thus has firsthand experience in combining work ethics of different cultures as well as finding workable solutions for integrating different industrial sectors. Mr. Veraart believes that the project management profession can greatly contribute to the challenge of blending environmental protection and environmental enhancements into the sustainable economy of the future, and hopes to contribute to this transition through his work. He can be reached at stan_global@yahoo.com.

▶**Hans Thamhain, Ph.D., PMP,** (hthamhain@bentley.edu) specializes in team leadership for complex project environments. He is a Professor of Management and Director of MOT and Project Management Programs at Bentley College, Boston. His industrial experience includes 20 years of management positions with high-technology companies, like GTE/Verizon, General Electric, and ITT. Dr. Thamhain has written over 70 research papers and five professional reference books in project and technology management. He is the recipient of the Distinguished Contribution Award from the Project Management Institute in 1998 and the IEEE Engineering Manager of the Year 2000 Award. He is widely published in the project management field, and in addition to Project Management Professional certification, is certified in New Product Development (NPDP).

▶**Lee Towe, PMP,** is President of Innovators International, Inc., a Project Management Institute Global Charter Registered Education Provider. Their PMLeader.com division specializes in project management training and consulting. Mr. Towe has been managing projects for more than twenty years and delivering training workshops for sixteen years. He served on the project leadership team of nine people that updated PMI's *PMBOK® Guide* in 2004, as team lead for the Human Resources chapter. He earned his Masters of Business Administration (MBA) degree from Drake University. Mr. Towe is a frequent trainer and speaker, including PMI's SeminarsWorld workshops and Global Congresses. One industry conference had such regard for his speaking that they placed Lee's general session presentation between television personalities George Will and Bryant Gumbel. Lee is the author of two books: *Why Didn't I Think of That?,* which demonstrates ways to increase creative thinking at work; and *Strategic Planning Handbook,* a basic foundation for conducting organizational strategic planning.

▶**John Tuman, Jr., P.ENG,** is senior vice-president with Management Technologies Group, Inc., a consulting firm in Morgantown, Pa., that provides consulting, training, and implementation services in organizational development, project management, change management, and information technology. Mr. Tuman's career spans thirty years of diverse engineering and project management experience. He was a project manager and a program manager on several major military and commercial aerospace programs for General Electric and the AVCO Corporation. He also held various management positions with Gilbert/Commonwealth, where he was responsible for developing computer-based management systems, as well as providing consulting services and training. Mr.

Tuman has given numerous presentations and seminars in the United States and abroad. He has written extensively on management methods, systems, and trends. He is a registered professional engineer.

▶**Chris Vandersluis, PMP,** is the president and founder of HMS Software based in Montreal, Canada. He has an economics degree from Montreal's McGill University and over 20 years experience in the automation of project control systems. He is a long standing member of both the Project Management Institute (PMI) and the American Association of Cost Engineers (AACE) and is the current president of The Microsoft Project Users Group (MPUG) in Montreal. Mr. Vandersluis has been published in numerous publications including *Fortune Magazine, Heavy Construction News,* and *PMNetwork,* and is a regular columnist for *Computing Canada* magazine. He teaches Advanced Project Management at McGill University's Executive Institute and often speaks at project management association functions across North America and around the world. HMS Software is the publisher of TimeControl—a project-oriented timekeeping system—and has specialized in the implementation of enterprise project management systems since 1984. Mr Vandersluis can be contacted by email at chrisv@hmssoftware.ca.

▶**Francis M. Webster, Jr.,** is a retired professor emeritus of management at the School of Business, Western Carolina University, in Cullowhee, N.C., where he specialized in teaching project management courses and concepts. For many years, he served as editor-in-chief for the Project Management Institute, responsible for the editorial content and publication of the *Project Management Journal* and *PM NETwork.* Dr. Webster has had extensive experience in the design and application of project management software and in the management of project work. He was manager of Operations Research at Chrysler Corporation and served on the DOD/NASA PERT/COST Coordinating Council during the early days of the development of modern project management concepts and practices. He has published widely and contributed in a variety of ways to defining the profession of project management through his activities at PMI.

▶**Lois Zells** is an international author, lecturer, and business consultant, specializing in software engineering consulting. As Co-founder and Past Executive Advisory Chair for the Information Systems Specific Interest Group of the Project Management Institute, she was honored as a PMI Woman of the Year in 1993; and is co-honoree of the PMI Wilson/Zells Scholarship Fund. Because of her acknowledged expertise in software engineering and project management, Ms. Zells frequently serves as an expert witness in multi-million dollar software litigations. She served as an examiner for the Arizona Statewide Baldridge Award and on the review committee for the revision of ISO 9000-3 (International Standard ISO/IEC 12207.) Highly specialized in Structured Analysis, Structured Design, and Structured Programming, she taught these subjects for five years at Phoenix College as well as for three and a half years with Yourdon, Inc., where she also developed their project management curriculum, the Project Planning and Control Workshop. Ms. Zells graduated Summa Cum Laude in Data Processing Management from the University of Baltimore and did her master's studies in Computer Sciences at Johns Hopkins University and Arizona State University. Her most recent efforts include the Total Quality Management seminar series Excellence Through Performance and Excellence Through Total Quality Management. She authored *Managing Software Projects: Selecting and Using PC?Based Project Management Systems* (QED

Information Sciences), and contributed chapters to *Total Quality Management for Software* (Van Nostrand Reinhold) and *The Program and Project Handbook* (AMACOM). She has contributed to and published many articles in industry publications such as *Investor's Business Daily, National Computer Society Proceedings, PM Network, The Federal Systems Journal, and Application Development Trends,* where she is a former contributing editor.

▶**Bill Zwerman,** in the Sociology Department in the University of Calgary, Bill worked in the area of organizations and occupations for 30 years, focusing on new occupations that have been developing in association with new, computer-based technologies. Over the last six years, he focused his research on software developers and project managers. Mr. Zwerman had extensive experience in the area of applied research, and functioned as a consultant in the private and public sectors. He presented his research at practitioner and academic conferences around the world, as well as in corporate training venues. Sadly, Mr. Zwerman passed away shortly before this edition went to press.

INDEX